The Matrix

Computer Networks
and Conferencing Systems
Worldwide

The Matrix

Computer Networks
and Conferencing Systems
Worldwide

John S. Quarterman
Texas Internet Consulting

d|i|g|i|t|a|l ™
Digital Press

9 8 7 6 5 4 3 2

Order number EY-C176E-DP.

Printed in the United States of America.

A list of trademarks and registered trademarks mentioned in this book appear as Credits and Trademarks at the end of this book.

The following figures are printed with permission from the authors referenced in the appropriate figure legends:

Figures: 7.1; 7.2; 10.1; 10.2; 10.3; 11.1; 11.2; 11.3; 11.4; 11.5; 11.6; 11.7; 11.8; 11.9; 11.10; 11.11; 11.12; 11.13; 11.14; 11.15; 11.16; 11.17; 11.18; 11.19; 11.20; 11.21; 12.1; 12.2; 12.3; 12.4; 12.5; 12.6; 12.7; 12.8; 12.9; 13.1; 13.2; 13.4; 14.1; 15.1; 15.2; 18.1

Copyediting: Barbara Jatkola
Index: Gordon Brumm
Typesetting: Jaap Akkerhuis
Production: Editorial Inc.

Library of Congress Cataloging-in-Publication Data

Quarterman, John S., 1954 –
     The matrix: computer networks and conferencing systems worldwide
               John S. Quarterman.
          p. cm.
     Includes index.
     ISBN 1-55558-033-5
     1. Computer networks. 2. Telecommunication. I. Title.
     TK5105.5.Q37 1990
     621.382--dc20   89-1392
                                                   CIP

à la femme blanche

"Freedom of expression is the matrix,
the indispensable condition of nearly every other form of freedom."
Benjamin Nathan Cardozo
Palko *v.* Connecticut, 302 U.S. 319, 327

Contents

II   *The Matrix*

Appendixes

Forewords

In your hands you hold a window to the world. This is *The Matrix*, John Quarterman's thorough guide to networks and conferencing systems. This is a travelogue for anyone, whether you're a free-spirited network pioneer whose login sessions include trips around the world, a novice computer user who is just embarking on a new journey, or a researcher who collaborates with colleagues.

With *The Matrix*, you'll save the most precious of travel commodities—time. Fewer hours are wasted trying to figure out the right network to reach your destination. It explains how your mail can cross borders, make layovers, and change gateways. It covers limits, regulations and rules, languages and protocols. It will help you explore new vistas: from accessing databases and archives on a wealth of subjects to participating in discussions, from sending and receiving mail anywhere to making friends around the world and visiting new lands. *The Matrix* spans geographical boundaries, foreign cultures, and areas of interest.

Departure is at any time from any place and you can return whenever you want. You set the time; you set the pace. You have the freedom to explore and discover as you please. The only limit is your imagination.

Tracy L. LaQuey
Editor, *Users' Directory of Computer Networks*
February 1989

The Matrix is a successor to the author's earlier and extremely well received article "Notable Computer Networks" published in the *Communications of the Association for Computing Machinery* in October 1986. In the last 20 years, packet switched computer networking has become a major support and infrastructure technology, but by far the most interesting aspect of computer networking has been its impact on personal interactions in the research community.

As Mr. Quarterman's book reveals, the phenomenon knows no international boundaries. As the technology penetrates beyond the computer science and engineering communities into regular use in other disciplines and in government and industry, many of the phenomena experienced by the research community will be rediscovered. Readers of this book will be glimpsing the twenty-first century norm. The details may differ, but the general thrust of computer mediated communication suggests, and Mr. Quarterman's book documents, the growing use and dependence on computers and communications for everyday commerce.

Vinton G. Cerf
Chairman, ACM SIGCOMM
January 1989

John Quarterman's book, *The Matrix*, is a practical road map through the mind-numbing detail and countless idiosyncracies of the world's networks and protocols. Those who use wide area networks, and many who do not, will find this book opens doors for them—doors previously shut, doors whose existence was not even dreamed of. The networks described here, and particularly the interconnections among them, have begun to have a revolutionary effect: electronic mail can reach any part of the world in hours or minutes, where postal mail would take weeks; data, programs, and documents of all sorts can be shared among collaborators in diverse nations; standards organizations are forced to come to grips with basic issues of international communication—languages, alphabets, and protocols at all levels. Through these networks, individuals are gaining an unprecedented freedom to communicate, sometimes in spite of organizational or national policies. *The Matrix* is a comprehensive reference on today's corporate and academic regional, national, and international networks. A thorough index provides quick access to any desired piece of information; numerous maps and tables furnish at-a-glance summaries; and sections on the history, funding, standards, and services of each network provide valuable insights to designers and administrators, as well as to users. This is a highly recommended, invaluable, one-of-a-kind book.

Frank da Cruz
Author, *Kermit: A File Transfer Protocol*
March 1989

Preface

The *Matrix* is a worldwide metanetwork of connected computer networks and conferencing systems that provides unique services that are like, yet unlike, those of telephones, post offices, and libraries.

It is a major tool in academic and industrial research in computer technology, physics, and astronomy, and increasingly in biological, social, and other sciences. When a small but useful biological discussion forum was recently slated to be cancelled, responses came in a few days from Australia, Finland, the United States, Canada, and the United Kingdom; dozens were received in the first 24 hours, many with carefully reasoned and presented positions.

The *Matrix* affects the personal and social lives of millions of users. Marriages and divorces have been made because of it. Research and subjective evidence indicate that those who use it tend to interact with many more people, not only by the new technology but also by telephone, paper mail, and physical travel.

Users of this technology include political action groups such as the U.S. space lobby, public interest groups such as Amnesty International, religious organizations, and political parties of all kinds. This technology even influences national and international politics. The 1988 French Presidential election was discussed online by a sizable percentage of the French population. Documents affecting funding decisions by the U.S. Congress about foreign insurgency movements have been prepared in time only by use of the networks.

The most striking use of the *Matrix* occurred too late to be described elsewhere in this book. When the Chinese government cleared Tianamen

Square on the morning of 4 June 1989, reports of eyewitnesses were sent out by Chinese students by telephone and facsimile within hours of the actual events, typed in by Chinese students abroad, and immediately broadcast throughout the world on dozens of networks and mailing lists. These reports were of an immediacy, detail, length, and diversity not achieved by the print, radio, or television media. The same medium was used simultaneously by Chinese students abroad to organize protest meetings, collection of funds, lists of missing students, itineraries of exiled activists, and political appeals to host governments as well as their own. The Chinese government noticed some of this activity and attempted to cut off the telephone and facsimile transmissions that were the link to the outside world. They even set up telephone numbers to call for their side of the story, but these were flooded by calls from overseas, largely organized by overseas students, partly through the networks. For the moment, the Chinese students have the upper hand in the *Matrix*, and it will be interesting to see what effects the isolation of the mainland from this technology will have on its economy, even as the rest of the world becomes more dependent on it. But the technology itself is neutral, and its later effects on this and other events cannot easily be predicted.

The full extent and composition of this *Matrix* of society and technology is unknown even to its users. This book contains detailed descriptions of many of these systems and their interconnections, overviews of the technology and standards that underlie them, and sketches of the history of the *Matrix* and the communities it supports.

The first half of the book contains background material that introduces some important topics for readers who are not familiar with them. References are provided for those who want more complete treatments. Chapters 1 and 2 introduce basic terminology and services so that Chapter 3 can discuss networked communities and the effects of this technology and its applications on them and on the larger world. The basic underlying networking protocols are outlined in Chapter 4. Management protocols and issues such as naming, addressing, routing, and interconnection of networks are treated in Chapter 5. Chapter 6 considers building actual networks from the technology, including network names, numerical size and speeds, geographical extent, administration, and funding. Chapter 7 sketches the 20 year history of the *Matrix*, the intrinsic limitations that affect it, its user communities, and constructed and de facto standards for protocols; some speculations on the future are also included. Interoperability requires standards and committees to produce them; these are discussed in Chapter 8.

Descriptions of specific systems occupy the second half of the book. They are organized geographically to facilitate discussions of regional history and approaches, and each is characterized according to the background material developed in the first half of the book. Maps are included when available. Syntaxes and gateways are provided for sending mail from one system to others. Access information is given for those wishing to join or research a system, and the extensive references found at the end of each chapter will be useful for further investigation.

Most descriptions are of wide area networks of at least national extent or of conferencing systems with national or international clienteles, but there are some selected examples of campus, metropolitan, provincial, and regional networks. Appendix A gives essential information on public data networks worldwide, while Appendix B deals with legal issues. Trademarks are listed after the appendixes.

This is a random access book. Few readers are likely to read it in page order from one end to the other. Most will dip into it for information about topics of interest. For this reason, there is an extensive index of terms, organizations, and acronyms; programs, protocols, and standards; networks, conferencing systems, gateways, and countries; and personal names. Many companies and programs are mentioned and indexed, although such mention does not imply endorsement.

For those who have wondered what computer networks and conferencing systems are used for, how they are constructed, or how they are interconnected, this book is the single most comprehensive source.

Users may discover here more than they knew about their own systems and will be able to see what other systems are available, as well as ways to reach some of them. The book should also be useful as a secondary textbook in a course on network protocols, illustrating how protocols have actually been used to build networks.

Internal documentation on networks is often scanty, seldom describing interconnections with other networks. Network administrators will find such information here. A single question asked of the administrations of several systems often produces many answers to different questions. This book is an attempt to view such material from a common perspective: a set of vanishing points and grid lines to use in comparing systems. This is not necessarily the correct perspective (whatever that might be), but it is more uniform than that usually found elsewhere.

Companies and universities designing internal networks will be able to see what kinds of networks others have already installed and interconnected with wide area networks. Those actively involved in advancing the science and technology of networking will see here the applications of their efforts. Those planning new wide area networks will find the current state of computer networks in the world.

Acknowledgments

This book draws on hundreds of articles and books, electronic and paper correspondence, and telephone calls with sources around the world, as well as a number of personal visits with administrators, developers, and other interested parties. Where possible, each section on a system has been reviewed by at least one person associated with that system. Numerous people have contributed ideas and draft text for both parts of the book.

For these reasons, those who have provided information and context for this book are far too numerous to name here. Many of them are cited in the references. In addition, I would like to thank the administrators or developers of most of the systems listed in the second half of the book, both for permission to list their systems, and for information provided. Special thanks are due to some people whose assistance has gone far beyond the call of duty and their own systems: Rick Adams, Piet Beertema, Jon Boede, Linda Branagan, Hans-Werner Braun, Russ Briggs, Paul Bryant, John B. Chambers, Vinton G. Cerf, Peter Collinson, Gordon Cook, Sue Couch, Frank da Cruz, John Demco, Yves Devillers, Robert Elz, Anil Garg, Michel Gien, Anke Goos, Mark Graham, Trevor Hales, Linda Harasim, Susan Hares, Fernando Herrera, Mark Horton, Christian Huitema, James Hutton, Dennis Jennings, William P. Jones, Mic Kaczmarczik, Daniel Karrenberg, Peter Kaufmann, Brian W. Kernighan, Steve Kille, Carol Kroll, Larry Landweber, José Mañas, Marilyn Martin, Fletcher Mattox, Duncan McEwan, Marshall Kirk McKusick, Michael E. Meehan, Jun Murai, Henry Nussbacher, Rory O'Brien, Jacob Palme, Craig Partridge, Philip Prindeville, David Leon Quarterman, Mr. and Mrs. D. S. Quarterman, Dr. Elsie Quarterman, Graham Rees, Brian Reid, Jeffrey Shapard, Barry Shein, Keld Jørn Simonsen, Gunnar Stefansson, Hans Strack-Zimmermann, Gligor Tashkovitch, Klaus Ullmann, Mario Vachon, Rüdiger Volk, Ben Yalow, Professor Karl Zander, and doubtless others whom I have inadvertently neglected to mention.

Thanks to William Gibson, whose science fiction novel *Neuromancer* was the source for the title of this book, to Smoot Carl-Mitchell, for persistent patience, and to Tracy LaQuey, for most varied contributions. More indirect inspirations include *The Times Atlas of the World* and the *Whole Earth Catalog*.

It was not always possible to have material reviewed, whether because of distance, time, or other logistical reasons. In the process of condensation and interpolation, it is conceivable that errors have occasionally crept in. Any misrepresentations, inaccuracies, or other mistakes in this book are the sole responsibility of the author.

Despite more than two years of research, not every network has been covered in detail. During the months this book was in production at the publisher, the network world has already changed visibly. Additions, corrections, and comments are solicited for future printings and editions, and may be sent to the addresses given below.

Access
matrix@tic.com
The Matrix
P.O. Box 14621
Austin, TX 78761
U.S.A.

Paper is not the most natural medium for discussions of electronic media. If you would be interested in subscribing to a continuously updated online database of material similar to that in this book, please contact the author at the above address. Suggestions for database access methods, user interfaces, and material to include are welcome, in conjunction with a project already in progress.

John Sinclair Quarterman
Austin, Longway Farm, and Santa Clara Valley
October 1986 – July 1989

I   Background

1   *Introduction*

Isolated computers are useful. Connected computers are more useful and in new ways. The *metanetwork* of connected computer networks described in this book is the prototype of a new communications infrastructure that will be as pervasive as the international telephone network. This *Matrix* of technology and society promises to have effects as important and far-reaching as those of the postal service, the telephone system, or television.

1.1   *Organization*

The heart of this book is the second part, which describes specific networks and conferencing systems and their interconnections. Copious references and access information are provided for those who want to join a system or investigate it further.

A number of topics must be introduced before systems can be described, and the first part of the book is devoted to that purpose. For each of those introductory chapters, there is a subsection below in this chapter. Each subsection gives a brief overview of the chapter with the same number.

This book is *not* intended to be an independent textbook on any of the subjects in these introductory chapters. Rather, this material is presented to provide enough of an overview for the casual reader to be able to understand the network descriptions in the second part of the book. References are provided at the end of each chapter for readers who want to examine any of these topics in more detail.

1.2   *Services*

Most users are interested in the services a system can provide.

1.2.1   Resource Sharing

A *computer network* may allow a user of one computer to use resources of another computer, such as storage space, central processing unit (CPU) speed, databases, programs, or printers. Hardware and users can be distributed among various locations. Costs can be shared, and incremental expansion and redundancy are made easier. This *resource sharing* was the original objective of distributed computer networks. Common resource sharing services include *remote login, file transfer, remote procedure call, remote job entry*, and *batch file transfer*.

1.2.2   Computer Mediated Communication

Computers can also allow users to communicate with each other: this is *computer mediated communication (CMC)*. There are many systems that are implemented primarily for supporting CMC. Their primary CMC service is usually *computer conferencing*—that is, many-to-many discussion groups. Such systems are often called *conferencing systems* after this service. Many conferencing systems are implemented on a single machine and are thus not networks in the sense that term is used in this book, although they may have users in many geographical locations. This kind of service is also supported on some of the largest distributed networks in the world.

Computer *bulletin boards* on small systems such as IBM PCs are rudimentary but ubiquitous current examples. There are subtle but important differences between bulletin boards and *true conferencing systems* mostly having to do with the degree of interaction of participants.

The one service implemented on almost every network is *electronic mail*, or just *mail*, which is another CMC service. In this type of service, messages are addressed to *mailbox*es for specific users. Mail is the glue that binds the *Matrix*. It is like the telephone but without the repeated connection attempts of *telephone tag*; like paper mail but faster. Inexperienced users often confuse it with one or both of those other two services, but it is neither, as it has rules, capabilities, and drawbacks of its own.

1.2.3   Networks and Conferencing Systems

Both *computer networks* and *computer conferencing systems* are described in this book because they have similar services and are used for similar purposes. In addition, many of them are connected so that at least mail can be exchanged. A generic term is needed to include both, and it is convenient for it to be short. In this book the word *system* is used for this purpose.

1.3   *Uses*

Communities of people form around particular networks and topics of discussion supported by networks. Face-to-face conventions have been held and marriages and divorces have been made because of CMC. Preexisting communities use these systems to further their goals.

Some tasks could not be completed in time to be useful without computer networks. Large computer software projects coordinate large numbers of programmers through computer networks. Astronomers transfer data to coordinate observations around the world. Medical researchers exchange information about cases. Social scientists collect information on political situations and use networks to collaborate on writing the information up. Books (including this one) are researched and reviewed using networks. Scholarly reports composed using computer networks have affected decisions of war and peace and superpower relations. In all these cases, the alternative would be transferring data on tapes or disks, coordinated by telephone calls or paper post. The time lost in using these other means would cause such projects to take longer and, in many cases, not to be practicable at all.

The appropriate service to use for a given purpose is not always obvious. Knowing how to use a service is not the same as using it well: *etiquette* and *ethics* are needed for that.

Few people appear the same to other people across a network as they would through a telephone or in person. The location, gender, and character of a network user may bear little relation to the user's mundane *identity*. A user may even create several online identities, perhaps simultaneously. Such identities may be used for improved communication. For instance, personal traits that might be distracting to a listener can be left out, or an argument can be furthered by constructing a personality to match. Network identities can also be used for shadier purposes, including espionage and international piracy. Thus, this new means of privacy is at the same time a threat to privacy.

1.4   *Layers and Protocols*

Many network users do not understand the underlying technology, but many distinctions between networks and much of the organization of individual networks are due to the technology used to construct them. New technology will lead to new or more widespread services.

Some basic terminology can be given here. A *computer network* is a set of *computers* communicating by common conventions called *protocols* over *communication media*. Computers in a network are called *network nodes*, and those that people use directly are called *hosts*. Computer network protocols usually involve the exchange of discrete units of information called *messages* over some form of physical *medium*, such as coaxial cable, microwaves, or a twisted pair of copper wires. There is a field of technology and research sometimes known as *networking* that deals with technical aspects of the software and hardware involved in building networks, such as the *fragmentation* of messages into *packets* because of size limitations of certain media or protocols, *routing* of packets among nodes of a network, and their *reassembly* into messages. Packets may be routed individually as *datagrams*, or paths called *virtual circuits* may be set up for them to travel between fixed endpoints. This distinction has political as well as technical connotations.

1.5   *Management Protocols*

There may be networks of networks in layers, each layer having a topological form; mappings are required among all the entities involved. There may be special computers whose purpose is to serve as *packet switches* in a *communications subnet* that transfers packets around the network. Two or more networks may be interconnected by a special host called a *gateway*, *router*, *bridge*, or *repeater*. Most people do not realize the extent of the specialized protocols that may be required to manage large networks. Routes between machines must be kept up-to-date, time must be synchronized, and reliability must be ensured.

1.6   *Administration*

Real networks have to have people to run them, money to fund them, and information available about them. Their size can be measured, perhaps in number of hosts or users. They have names and access information.

It is useful to distinguish several common terms as used in this book:

A *machine* is a computer of any size.

A *system* is a computer system of any size. This term is usually used synonymously with machine. In this book, we also use *system* to mean a *computer network* or a *computer conferencing system* when it is not appropriate to specify one or the other.

A *node* is any vertex of a graph representing a network — that is, any machine on a network.

A *host* is a network node that has resources of its own (such as disks, user mailboxes, or user accounts). A host is not a node (such as an X.25 PAD or an *ARPANET* TAC) used only to connect across the network to other nodes. Nor is a gateway a host, although a single machine may serve both as a host and as a gateway.

A *site* is a place (such as a building, company, or campus) where a group of network nodes is located. Although *site* is used as a synonym for *host* on some networks, that usage is avoided in this book in an attempt to prevent confusion.

1.7   *History and Future*

Bits and pieces of the history of computer networks have been treated in other publications. Some of that information is brought together in this book to outline the general history of the *Matrix*. There are also some speculations on the future.

1.8   *Standards*

Much of the political history of networking has involved standards for protocols and the committees that produce them. Chapter 8 also contains notes on organizations, conferences, and publications.

1.9   *Part II*

The networks and conferencing systems described in this book encompass continents, hundreds of thousands of machines, and millions of users. The entire second part of the book, which begins with Chapter 9, is about specific systems, their interconnections, and their uses. Details of the organization of Part II may be found in Chapter 9, which serves as its introduction.

1.10   *Appendixes*

Appendix A deals with public data networks, and Appendix B with legal issues. Trademarks are listed after the Appendixes.

1.11   *Index*

The index is the place to find references to programs, protocols, and protocol suites; discussions of networks, gateways, countries, and people; definitions of terms; mentions of companies and organizations; and expansions of acronyms.

1.12   *Typographic Conventions*

This book is written in American English. Technical terms and proper names in other kinds of English are preserved in their original spelling— e.g., Coloured Book. Where possible, names or terms in other languages are given in both the original language and in an English translation. If there is a corresponding index entry, it is usually for the term in the original language. Terms or names from languages that are not ordinarily written in alphabets derived from Latin are transliterated. However, names of countries and cities are always given in English.

Short network names are always printed in italics in this book. This is to indicate that such a name is a network name and that there is probably a section describing it. All network names appear in the index, and the boldface page number or range for a network is for its defining section. Top level domains are treated similarly. Italics are also used for the introduction or definition of terms, which also appear in the index. In general, italics (except where obviously used for *emphasis*) indicate something that can be found in the index.

Acronyms are spelled out where introduced (perhaps several times). These appear in the index.

Programs (including operating systems) and computer programming languages are always printed in boldface and are indexed.

Protocols, protocol suites, personal names, and names of countries are not distinguished typographically, although many of them appear in the index.

Written references are cited in the text by author and date, with the full bibliographic references appearing at the end of each chapter. They may include papers in refereed journals, articles in popular publications, or unpublished material such as user's manuals, tutorials, or white papers. Some articles from public electronic mailing lists or conferences are cited with the mailing list or conference name as the periodical name. Information acquired by verbal conversations (in person or by telephone), personal computer mediated communications, or paper mail is usually cited as Personal communications.

2 _User Services_

There are two basic kinds of services: _computer mediated communication (CMC)_ services, which allow people to exchange messages, and _resource sharing_ services, which allow users to access computing resources (such as files, databases, and CPU power). Although CMC services are often used to coordinate sharing of non-computing resources, such as money, information, or food, the term _resource sharing_ refers to computing resources.

Either type of service may also be either _batch_ or _interactive_. A message may be delivered and read immediately in an interactive service or after a delay in a batch service. Batch systems are necessarily asynchronous (though many implementations attempt to impose at least the illusion of ordered synchronous discussion), while interactive systems tend to be more synchronous.

CMC services may be primarily either one-to-one (mail), one-to-many (distribution lists or bulletin boards), or many-to-many (news or true conferencing systems). Some types of services are sketched in Figure 2.1.

This chapter discusses services without going into detail about the underlying protocols, software, and other technology. That material is left to Chapter 4 and Chapter 5.

2.1   _Computer Mediated Communication_

The most widely used services are for CMC, and electronic mail is the most common of these. A casual user may not know whether a conferencing service is implemented on a single machine or across a network.

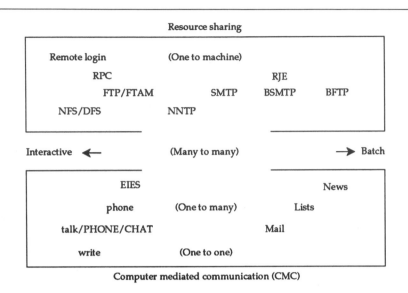

Figure 2.1. *Types of services*

2.1.1   Batch CMC

Batch CMC does not require immediate action on the part of participating users or supporting programs and protocols. Thus, neither dedicated connections between machines nor simultaneous communication by users are required. This makes such services easy to implement and easy to use.

Their asynchronous nature also has a built-in problem: if one user sends two messages, there is no inherent guarantee that a recipient will read or even receive the second message before replying to the first one. Ordering of messages can only be approximate, and the more users, hosts, and time delays are involved, the more pronounced is the effect. Many user interfaces attempt to minimize this phenomenon by ordering messages according to time of posting and by reducing communication delays. But nothing can be done about delays introduced by the readers themselves (by going on vacation, for example), and so the problem cannot be completely eliminated. In practice, experienced users do not find this to be a big problem. The simplest way to deal with it is to read all of the messages in a discussion that have already been received before replying to any of them.

Novice users sometimes find the inherent delays of these asynchronous services to be annoying, preferring immediate response instead. But experienced users often find that such delays provide much-needed pauses for thinking and time to cool down before firing off a reply. The most obvious advantage of batch services is that the recipients of a message do not have to be actively participating when the message is sent. There is no *telephone tag* of repeated attempts by each party to find the other.

2.1.1.1   *One-to-One (Mail)*

Electronic mail allows an individual user to post a message to another user. The message is delivered to a *mailbox* where the target user will find it later (perhaps after immediate notification). Usually it is possible to indicate more than one *addressee* when sending or *posting* mail. This service is sometimes called *e-mail*, but in this book it is referred to either as *electronic mail* or just as *mail*. Users often refer to traditional paper postal services as *paper post* or even *snail mail* and occasionally contrast it with *real mail*, meaning, of course, electronic mail.

The traditional and electronic postal services are similar in some respects:

- They deliver written messages.
- They deliver the messages to specific addresses.
- They involve a delay before receipt.
- They sometimes provide a method of verifying receipt.

There are also differences that become more obvious the more the electronic service is used:

- Original composition and reuse of material in electronic mail messages is far easier because previous text is already in machine readable form.
- Delivery of electronic mail is almost always faster.
- Delivery of electronic mail is usually less expensive.
- Reliability of electronic mail varies considerably, especially when network boundaries are crossed.

Mail is the most common service, since almost every network and conferencing system supports it. Most networks allow any user to send mail to any other user on the network and often to users on other networks as well.

2.1.1.2   *One-to-Many (Mailing Lists)*

Networks that support mail by individuals to individuals often extend the same mechanisms to support *mailing lists*—that is, long-lasting *distribution lists* involving people who want to hold extended discussions on the same subjects. Often these are supported with the same software as for one-to-one mail. Because new people want to join, old subscribers want to drop out, and people move and change mail addresses, such lists usually require someone to maintain them and to make sure their addresses are correct. Some networks, such as *BITNET*, have mechanisms that allow people to *subscribe* or *unsubscribe* without human intervention.

Mailing lists allow a specificity that many conferencing systems cannot match. They go only to certain people, and newcomers have to ask to get in. They are also directly integrated into the same user interfaces that are used for ordinary mail, so a user does not have to do anything special to read messages in a mailing list. Each user must, however, keep a set of back messages for each list or be able to retrieve an *archive* from a central location in order to refer to past discussions. This is inconvenient for the user and an inefficient use of computing resources. The user also has to sort messages in one mailing list from those in another and from ordinary mail messages. This can be a real problem for verbose lists.

2.1.1.3   *Many-to-Many (Computer Conferencing)*

Many networks or conferencing systems allow large groups of people to post messages to all members of the group. These computer conferencing services differ from mailing lists in scale, both in the numbers of people that can be readily supported in a group and in the numbers of groups. Usually one copy of a message is kept per host rather than one per user as for mail. Automatic separation of messages into categories by topic is usually supported. Sophisticated user interfaces are often provided. These can display lists of categories and lists of subjects of messages per category, and the user can select messages (either to display or to avoid) by subject, sender, and logical combinations of these and other attributes. A service with all these features is a *true conferencing system*. (Some would say that an ability to see who has read a message is another necessary attribute, but this is often not possible on very large distributed systems.)

People not familiar with this type of service usually think of personal computer *bulletin board systems*. These are rudimentary single machine conferencing systems, but they usually tend to have a small number of topics available and not very sophisticated user interfaces. More importantly, they are frequently *used* as bulletin boards — that is, users post messages as if on a physical pegboard and with no real idea of who will read them or reply to them. True conferencing systems are used for detailed threads of discussions within continuous topics, and the participants are usually known to each other.

Many IBM PC or similar **MS-DOS** systems are connected in a network called *FidoNet*. Perhaps the largest conferencing network is *USENET*.

It supports a conferencing system known as *news*, which is an appropriate name because it indicates the global distribution of the service. The *Internet* component network *WIDEBAND* is frequently used for multimedia conferences involving voice, data, and video images [Partridge 1988].

There are intermediate systems: **TOPS-20** and other hosts on the *Internet* have long supported local one-to-many *BBOARD* conferences and exchanged them using distribution lists, producing something almost like a general distributed conferencing system. The basic distinction is that each BBOARD will usually have an associated mailing list (or even a list of hosts for some sort of ad hoc file transfer method), perhaps each supported from a different machine, and each must be updated to add a new host to the system. A true news system is closer to broadcasting in that a new host just picks up the transmission from a neighbor, as in *USENET*. Many people have taken to having their personal computers dial up commercial systems such as *CompuServe* in the middle of the night (when telephone rates are low) and download many articles for later perusal. This is a step in the *USENET* direction. A further step may be seen in *DASnet*. See also the discussion of *porting* in Chapter 3.

A problem that may occur with any kind of large-scale conferencing system is finding storage space for records of conferences, which tend to accumulate very quickly. Some systems, such as that of *Tandem*, alleviate the problem by making references to old messages be merely pointers rather than copies, but that does not solve the problem of an influx of new messages.

2.1.2   Interactive CMC

Interactive CMC services are not as common as batch services on networks. Many networks are based on intermittent dialup connections, and many that are based on dedicated connections are fast enough to make do with mailing lists. Interactive CMC services are common on single machine conferencing systems, though their use may require careful planning to make sure all desired participants know when to participate.

2.1.2.1   *One-to-One*

Many single machine conferencing systems provide a way for two people to communicate interactively. This is the conferencing service most like a telephone call, being interactive and immediate. Often no transcripts are kept, making it more like oral communication than most of these written media.

2.1.2.2   *One-to-Many*

A simple elaboration of one-to-one conferencing is the extension to small groups. This kind of service is much like a telephone conference call. It has an advantage in that input from each participant can be displayed in a different area of the screen so that everyone can simultaneously see what everyone else is adding to the discussion. Who gets everyone's attention is another problem, but with small groups, it is usually not a serious one.

2.1.2.3   *Many-to-Many*

Even larger groups can be accommodated simultaneously on conferencing systems. Numbers of people that would be impractical over telephones can be involved. This is because computer mediated systems can arrange that only one participant can hold the floor at a time. This can be done by various means, including having each "speaker" pass a token to the next or by having a facilitator determine who will speak next. The latter is much like having a chair for an in-person committee and can be made to work better in a computer mediated medium than over telephones. This kind of conference allows an immediacy and clarity that could otherwise be achieved only by face-to-face meetings (if at all), and the cost is so much less that conferences can be held much more frequently.

2.2   *Resource Sharing*

The earliest purpose of early research networks such as the *ARPANET* or *CYCLADES* was *resource sharing*—that is, the use of distant computing resources by means of the network. Such services are specific to networks and do not occur on non-networked conferencing systems, since they must involve multiple host computers.

2.2.1   Interactive Resource Sharing

Interactive resource sharing is the easiest kind to understand and to implement.

2.2.1.1   *Remote Login*

The most basic kind of resource sharing is *remote login*, which is the use of a network to access a remote machine as if one were logged in on it from a local terminal. Most interactive networks support this.

2.2.1.2   *File Transfer*

The ability to get a file from a remote host and put it back (and possibly to delete it, create or delete a directory, change directories, etc.) is called *file transfer*. This is probably the second most common interactive resource sharing service. It is sometimes referred to as *FTP* or *FTAM* from the names of two widely used file transfer services.

Since data formats vary widely among operating systems and machine types, there are usually several file transfer formats supported. The most generally usable one is plain text in 7 bit USASCII, although the line delimiter may still vary. The user initiating a transfer must have read access on the source file and write or create access on the destination file or directory. However, there is a special case called *anonymous FTP* in which specific files are put where anyone can transfer them by using widely known access permissions.

2.2.1.3   *Remote Procedure Call*

The ability to call programming language level functions on a remote host without logging in is called *remote procedure call*. This is often used to support distributed file systems, remote file locking, or device access. This is commonly supported only on small and fast networks, but use on wide area networks is increasing, even over satellite networks such as *SATNET* [Partridge 1988].

2.2.1.4   *Distributed File System*

Fast networks sometimes support access of remote files as if they were part of a local file system. This is called a *distributed file system* or a *network file system*, depending on the degree of integration of the remote part into the local part. Such services are sometimes built from remote procedure call services.

2.2.1.5   *Remote File Locking*

This service is sometimes provided as part of a distributed file system, sometimes separately. It allows locking files so that no other process may change them simultaneously. It is important in building many other services, such as mail or access to databases or devices.

2.2.1.6   *Remote Device Access*

This service provides a way to use devices such as printers or tape drives on other systems as if they were on the local system. Printers are also commonly attached to networks as independent hosts so that they can provide their own locking facilities.

2.2.1.7   *Window Management*

Especially on a local area network (LAN), it is common for most hosts to be diskless workstations using disks on one or more server machines and having high-resolution bit-mapped displays. Such displays are usually divided into windows, and each window may show activities on a different machine, perhaps including sophisticated graphics. There must be a *window management* protocol to coordinate transmission of information in windows and often to transfer concise descriptions of graphics data efficiently over limited bandwidth.

2.2.1.8   *Videotex*

The integrated display and interchange of text and images is known as *videotex*. This is widely supported by the French government telephone system with three million specialized *Minitel* terminals in private homes. Conferencing services are supported, as are advertising, shopping for consumer goods, and sophisticated directory services. That network is probably the most direct application of CMC technology to the needs of the general public of any nation.

2.2.1.9   *Shared Memory*

One of the most complete elaborations of the resource sharing idea is *shared memory*, where resources on a remote system look like resources on a local system.

2.2.1.10   *Distributed Operating System*

The logical extreme of resource sharing is a *distributed operating system* in which the distinction between local and remote systems is completely obliterated. This has been done already in some wide area networks, such as *Tandem*. This distribution requires a certain sacrifice, though, as all systems in the network must present exactly the same interface. That is, a true distributed operating system can only be done as a *closed system*. Most wide area networks (at least outside of individual companies) are *open systems* that allow many different vendors' systems to be interconnected. Systems that are closed to other vendors may still run on a wide variety of software and hardware from a single vendor, as in DNA, NCA, or SAA, which are described in Chapter 4. Some comments on future services such as these may be found in Section 7.8.

2.2.2   Batch Resource Sharing

Some resource sharing services just do not make sense as batch services. What would batch remote login mean (maybe remote job entry)? Others involve submitting a request and waiting for completion. These can be done almost as readily in batch.

2.2.2.1   *Remote Job Entry*

The submission of a *job*, or set of instructions for various programs to run to completion, is a time-honored batch service from the days of punch cards before time-sharing. When this is done across a network, it is called *remote job entry* or sometimes *remote command execution*. One might look at it as large-scale remote procedure call in a batch context. There are security problems with this service on interactive networks. Protection mechanisms may differ between hosts. One may do the equivalent of a login when submitting the job, but this often involves having a supposedly secret password available in a file.

2.2.2.2   *Batch File Transfer*

Batch file transfer makes as much sense as the interactive kind, perhaps more, but many interactive networks do not support it, probably for security reasons similar to those for *remote job entry*. However, it is frequently supported on top of *mail* for specific databases or libraries of information that are intended to be publicly accessible. This is similar to *anonymous FTP*. And users often send files as mail to other users, although some are perhaps not aware that most mail systems are not at all secure.

2.3   *Bibliographic Notes*

The basic reference for computer conferencing is Hiltz and Turoff 1978. Recent comments on how to make conferencing services usable may be found in Hiltz and Turoff 1985. Of interest for some current conferencing software is Cook 1987.

Since this book is about current and widely used systems, this chapter has concentrated on widely used services. For a readable introduction to more esoteric but not necessarily far distant applications, such as *multimedia mail*, *broadcatch*, or *video conferencing*, see Brand 1987. A few comments on plausible future services appear in Chapter 7 of this book.

2.4 *References*

Brand 1987. Brand, Stewart, *The Media Lab: Inventing the Future at MIT*, Viking, New York, 1987.

Cook 1987. Cook, Gordon, "A Survey of Computer Mediated Communications: Computer Conferencing Comes of Age," Gartner Group, Inc., Stamford, CT, 9 November 1987. This paper was published in a series available only to subscribers who paid a substantial fee.

Hiltz and Turoff 1978. Hiltz, Starr Roxanne, and Turoff, Murray, *The Network Nation: Human Communication via Computer*, Addison-Wesley, Reading, MA, 1978.

Hiltz and Turoff 1985. Hiltz, Starr Roxanne, and Turoff, Murray, "Structuring Computer-Mediated Communication Systems to Avoid Information Overload," *Communications of the ACM*, vol. 28, no. 7, pp. 680–689, July 1985.

Partridge 1988. Partridge, Craig, Personal communications, August–November 1988.

3   *Uses*

Network users group together in a variety of ways related to the underlying technology or to mutual interest. The networks and conferencing systems themselves produce communities of convenience of people with access to the same services and interfaces. More specialized communities form on the basis of interest and accessibility, whether on a single system or across several.

This chapter is *not* intended to completely describe any network or conferencing system; that is the task of the second part of the book. The purpose of this chapter is to bring together some topics that might be lost to the reader if they were only scattered through the system descriptions in Part II. If you see a system mentioned in this section and want to know more about it, you can look it up in the index and turn to the section about it in Part II.

3.1   *Communities*

Networks may be not only communities of convenience, but also communities of interest. Many of them form around people who are involved in the same sorts of activities. Here are some examples of communities of researchers, of communities formed around certain kinds of facilities or around the use of certain software, and of political communities.

3.1.1   Network Researchers

Users of *ARPANET*, *CYCLADES*, and *HMI-NET* were originally almost solely researchers in networking technology. This was true of most of the early computer networks. Some current networks, such as *ARISTOTE*, retain that characteristic.

3.1.2   Scientific Researchers

Some networks are so specific to a particular use that they take their name from it. These include *MFEnet* for Magnetic Fusion Energy, *HEPnet* for High Energy Physics, and *Starlink* for astronomers.

3.1.3   Computer Centers

Most *BITNET* users tend to be users of large IBM mainframes at large computer centers, usually at universities. (There may be more non-IBM *machines* on *BITNET* than IBM machines now, but IBM mainframes support so many users that the typical *user* is still as described.) This is also true of *REUNIR* and to some extent of *JANET*.

3.1.4   Operating Systems

As mentioned, the *BITNET* community is mostly a community of users of IBM mainframes. The *UUCP* network is just as largely a community of users of the **UNIX** operating system. Many DECNET-based networks, such as *MFEnet*, *HEPnet*, and *SPAN*, consist almost solely of Digital machines running **VMS**; many large conferencing systems or commercial systems such as *TWICS* or *CompuServe* are **VMS**-based. And many machines on *FidoNet* run **MS-DOS**.

3.1.5   Small Facilities

USENET was formed as a sort of poor man's *ARPANET*. Although it now reaches into facilities that were formerly the exclusive domain of networks such as *ARPANET* or *BITNET*, it also connects many small facilities in universities but outside of their large computation centers, and small companies that may not be connected to *CSNET*. This tendency to connect small, independent facilities is also visible in *UUCP* and *EUnet*. Similarly, one of the original reasons for *FidoNet* was a desire for something like *USENET* for personal computers.

3.1.6   **Political Communities**

CARINET is a political and economically oriented system that is primarily concerned with the Third World. *PeaceNet* was formed to allow kinds of political organizing that would be hard to do on other networks. Its parent organization has since branched out to form the related systems *EcoNet* and *GreenNet*. The latter is based in London, and there is an hourly UUCP link between it and the *PeaceNet* machine, so the two form a true network, albeit a small one.

3.2   *Conferences*

Most computer conferencing systems organize messages into *conferences* according to subject matter. Other terms for these organized topics are Special Interest Group (SIG) or *newsgroup* (the *USENET* term).

Many conferences are overseen by a person who may be referred to as one of the following :

- *Editor*: a term derived from print media
- *Moderator*: from broadcast media and commonly used on the *Internet*, *EIES*, and *USENET*
- *Facilitator*: a term popular with political groups in reference to face-to-face meetings
- *Monitor*: the term used on *EMISARI*, which is usually considered to be the first conferencing system
- *Coordinator*: the term used on the Swedish *QZCOM* system
- *Sysop*: for system operator; the term used on most commercial and personal systems

The term usually used in this book is *moderator*. The moderator filters out duplicate submissions and may in some cases reject objectional submissions or remove them after they are posted. Reasons for rejection vary widely with the network, conference, and people involved. Sometimes actual editing is done. The roles of moderators as perceived by themselves, network administrators, submitters, or readers can vary widely. For example, moderators are often accused of censorship, but few moderators believe such accusations are justified.

Another important task of the moderator is to reply directly to simple queries so that the general readership does not have to see them (and so the moderator does not have to filter out numerous similar responses later, and the network does not have to carry them). For mailing lists, the moderator often is responsible for adding or deleting people's addresses from the list. In some cases of groups related to software, such as *Info-Kermit@CUNIXC.CC.COLUMBIA.EDU*, the moderator also announces new releases of software [da Cruz 1988].

Certain newsgroups, mailing lists, bulletin boards, conferences, and SIGs have reliable followings that form social groups. These range from groups interacting strictly in pursuit of technical goals to others interacting for the sake of interaction, to still others for whom the networked interaction is an aspect of or leads to outside interaction.

Many systems keep lists of conferences that can be used to discover what conferences exist. Methods of finding such lists of lists are discussed under individual networks, in Part II of this book. For example, for *Internet* mailing lists, look in the section for that network, and for *USENET* newsgroups, look under *USENET*. The location of the section on a network may be found in the index.

3.2.1   Technical Groups

UNIX-WIZARDS@BRL.MIL: this *Internet* mailing list* dates back to around 1977 on the *ARPANET* and is currently gatewayed bidirectionally and automatically with the *USENET* newsgroup *comp.unix.wizards*. It is possible that most working **UNIX** software developers and system administrators read this list up to a few years ago, but many have since unsubscribed because of the time required to sort through the much larger volume of submissions.

There have been several attempts to reduce the traffic and to keep it more technical. The *comp.unix.questions* newsgroup, which is gatewayed with the *INFO-UNIX@BRL.ARPA* mailing list, was created to provide access for novices to knowledgeable people while keeping elementary questions out of *UNIX-WIZARDS*. There is also a moderated newsgroup, *comp.unix*. It has little traffic, apparently because people do not want to have to justify the value of their submissions. *UNIX-WIZARDS* still has a recognizable group of technical contributors and readers who use it in their work. Many of them can also be found attending USENIX conferences for the same reasons. Many of the ones who no longer follow *UNIX-WIZARDS* use other newsgroups or mailing lists or private mail for the same purpose.

---

* The standard procedure for subscribing to an *Internet* mailing list is to send a request by mail to *list-REQUEST@domain*, not list@domain. So if you want to get on the HUMAN-NETS list, mail a request to *HUMAN-NETS-REQUEST@RED.RUTGERS.EDU*. Only actual submissions should go to *HUMAN-NETS@RED.RUTGERS.EDU*.

Info-Kermit@CUNIXC.CC.COLUMBIA.EDU or *comp.protocols.kermit* or *I-KERMIT*: this list, moderated by Christine Gianone of Columbia University (Columbia), is about the **Kermit** software, which allows interchange of data among 300 different kinds of host machines. The software is mostly written by volunteers coordinated from Columbia. The list is a major mechanism for announcing new releases and for discussing bugs, features, and design features. It is a very large list, with 500 direct entries but many more readers. It illustrates a common feature of very large lists: many of the entries on the master list (as many as half in this case) are themselves aliases for further lists, which may themselves have such aliases. Thus, the real distribution paths are tree structured and are not completely controlled from one place; the moderator has no way of knowing who subscribes, or even how many. The organization of the tree is usually good enough that messages reach many parts of the world within a short time (usually hours) of posting. This is because administrators of large systems will ask for entries in the top level list, and smaller systems will then feed from them.

Any of the lists in the tree may have addresses for several kinds of networks. This is a major factor in being able to have such a wide distribution, but it also means that multiple address formats and mailer protocols are used, resulting in peculiar error notifications from all over the world, many of them for sublists that the principal moderator has no control over [da Cruz 1988]. Subscription requests from the *Internet*, *CSNET*, *UUCP*, or *EASYnet* should be mailed to

Info-Kermit-Request@CUNIXC.CC.COLUMBIA.EDU

From *BITNET*, *NetNorth*, or *EARN*, a SUBSCRIBE message for *I-KERMIT* should be sent to

LISTSERV@CUVMA

On *USENET* the equivalent is the newsgroup *comp.protocols.kermit*.

AILIST@SRI-AI.ARPA or *comp.ai*: this is a general technical discussion list or newsgroup for Artificial Intelligence (AI) researchers. It is moderated and digestified. The volume is high, and topics range from press treatment of AI to esoteric points of logic to implementation details. Submitters range from the most eminent practitioners to novices, with the moderator selecting more of the former. It is not clear that this list accurately reflects the working AI community, but it certainly has its own following.

TCP-IP@SRI-NIC.ARPA or *comp.protocols.tcp-ip*: this is an *Internet* mailing list whose subject is the TCP/IP protocol suite. It is used both for dissemination of information to people not familiar with the protocols and for working technical discussions among their implementers, most of whom appear to follow the list. There are similar lists on more specific networking topics.

news.groups: this is a *USENET* newsgroup that is used to discuss the creation and deletion of newsgroups. It has occasionally been one of the highest volume newsgroups on the network. There are other newsgroups that discuss *USENET* itself.

INFO-NETS@THINK.COM: this is a mailing list about networks. Postings have ranged from requests for paths to specific hosts on certain networks to position statements by people involved with *NSFNET*. Some information in this book was obtained in response to requests on this list.

HUMAN-NETS@RED.RUTGERS.EDU or *soc.human-nets*: HUMAN-NETS is perhaps the prototypical technical list about social issues. It is for discussions of the social effects of computers and specifically of computer networks. A discussion in this list led in 1984 to the writing of a ten-page paper that was the predecessor of an article in *Communications of the ACM* [Quarterman and Hoskins 1986] and of the present book. Unfortunately, this list appears to have subsequently died out.

RISKS@KL.SRI.COM or *comp.risks*: this group is about the risks involved in the use of computers. It tackles many of the issues that were formerly discussed in HUMAN-NETS.

OMNET: this is a discussion group for oceanography users on *Telemail* [Cerf 1988].

NANET: numerical analysts use this distribution list on the *Internet*. Its server creates virtual mailboxes that make it look as if each member is on a single machine although actual mailboxes are elsewhere [Cerf 1988].

There are technical mailing lists for such things as workstations, local area networks, and many different lists for many different manufacturers' computers. Not all technical lists or newsgroups are computer related. There are newsgroups about astronomy and biology, for instance. However, researchers in other fields use newsgroups in their fields for actual work less than researchers in computer fields do, probably because researchers in other fields are less familiar with unusual uses of computers. But this is changing; astronomers, in particular, have found that computer networks are extremely convenient media for coordinating observations at observatories in places as far apart as Chile, Australia, and South Africa.

soc.roots or *ROOTS-L@NDSUVM1.BITNET*: this is a *USENET* newsgroup that is gatewayed with a *BITNET* mailing list, and there is apparently a link with a *FidoNet* BBS in San Francisco. The topic is genealogy, and the postings range from requests for information on lists of names to reviews of sources. This is a somewhat unusual group because the topic is not directly related to computers and because it is carried by three major worldwide networks.

3.2.2   Social Groups

CompuServe SF SIG: *CompuServe* has a very popular though not very old SIG on science fiction. The instigators had great difficulty convincing the network management that a conference on that topic would be viable, but it has turned out to be one of the fastest growing SIGs. Similar groups exist on some other systems; one dates back to at least 1978. There is a *UUCP* mailing list for writers of science fiction.

There are many newsgroups or mailing lists that exist only for social purposes. An example famous among afficionados was a mailing list started in 1985 by a student who had lost his girlfriend and wanted to commiserate with all his friends, most of whom he knew through the various networks. This list used considerable portions of the bandwidth of several networks over many months and led to a number of parties in several parts of North America where the participants met each other directly. Needless to say, this list was never sanctioned by the administrators of any network. It no longer exists, but descendant lists involving its former participants continue to spring up.

3.2.3   Public Interest Groups

Political reporters following the 1988 U.S. presidential election pooled their reports on a bulletin board system that was used by reporters and editors throughout the country, giving small-town editors access to essentially the same information as was available to reporters from major metropolitan newspapers. The precise effects of this are not clear. Some say increased homogeneity of news reports was caused; others say the reverse.

Amnesty International (A.I.) makes increasing use of computer systems (such as *PeaceNet* [Miller 1987]) for general communication among members and in its Urgent Action Project. This project encourages members to write letters to government officials when people are abducted by governments. Participants are informed of what happened and whom to contact. Electronic alerts are posted on the Amnesty International Urgent Action Network (AIUAN) over many academic and personal computer networks, as well as inside large corporations such as Lotus and Apple.

A typical urgent action runs for six weeks, but the first two to three weeks are critical. If a prisoner is not released within that short initial period, release is unlikely. Electronic communications offer an increase in speed over postal alerts. Alerts can reach participants within a day, possibly leading to responses on the same day. Problems found with initial manual forwarding included occasional editing and postings left visible after their alert stop dates. This could cause alert messages to circulate beyond their intended life span, irritating not only the people for whom they were intended, but also the target government officials, who may have already released the prisoner in question and do not appreciate being inundated with now irrelevant complaints. Automatic forwarding and designated redistributors inside closed communities have minimized these problems [Axelson 1989].

AIUAN currently has about 300 people in the United States specifically working on action alerts. AIUAN also distributes into the United Kingdom, but into no other countries. For comparison, there are about 3,860 local A.I. groups in more than 60 countries, plus individual members, supporters, and letter writers in more than 150 countries and territories, for an estimated membership (in 1985) of more than 500,000. A.I. is probably the leader in the use of electronic media for these purposes, but other organizations may want to do the same.

3.3   *Effects*

Networks have effects on their users beyond their immediate practical uses [Hiltz and Turoff 1985; Zuboff 1988].

3.3.1   Basic Effects

The primary effect of CMC (at least with heavy use) is increased human interaction, which can lead to better technical productivity through the exchange of ideas and references (both to documents and to people) [Hiltz 1980]. Not only work-related communications and contacts increase, but informal communications of all kinds usually increase by an order of magnitude. Murray Turoff and Starr Roxanne Hiltz named this phenomenon *superconnectivity* [Turoff 1985, 361; Hiltz and Turoff 1985, 688].

Increased connectivity quickly leads to *information overload* [Hiltz and Turoff 1985], which is the receipt of too much unwanted information, and was encountered early in the history of CMC [Hiltz and Turoff 1981]. This phenomenon has been compared to living in a crowded dormitory, and similar solutions may be appropriate [Hiltz and Turoff 1985]. The system can provide ways to avoid the contributing factor of *information entropy* — that is, lack of organization or labeling of pieces of information [Hiltz and Turoff 1985, 682]. Likely ordering primitives include indexes of available articles, subjects, and keywords in each article [Hiltz and Turoff 1985, 686] and automatic detection of articles cross-posted to several conferences. But the user has to be selective in what is read according to sender or topic, and what is sent according to expected response. This becomes more a matter of *etiquette* than technology. It is usually counterproductive to ignore messages from anyone but a fixed set of people, because useful information will be missed [Hiltz and Turoff 1985, 684]. Instead, one must learn how to avoid unproductive conferences, how to scan items rapidly for interest, and how to politely and effectively stop junk messages. Most users learn to manage this with practice.

Apparently about 25 percent of the salaries of office workers is used in time spent in communications by managers and professionals, compared to about 5 percent for word processing [Turoff 1980, 237]. If appropriate CMC services are widely used, one can expect some widespread effects to come of them, especially considering that any means of communication strongly affects the actual communications and thus the organization of any group using it [Turoff 1980, 252, 256]. But design or choice of appropriate services can be a difficult task, especially considering that people cannot say what they need before they use a service or even after only short test uses [Hiltz and Turoff 1981, 750]. They may think they can, but experience has almost universally proven otherwise. Modeling services on existing behavior, especially on specific behavior such as how a secretary types a memorandum [Hiltz and Turoff 1981, 750], has proven to be inadequate to the task.

3.3.2 Appropriate CMC Services

Chapter 2 briefly described various services, including CMC, but did not say much about when to use them, because that is mostly a matter of their effects.

For detailed but not pressing discussions, mail or batch conferencing may be the best service to use. They usually tend to be used together, as conferencing generates need for private mail messages on specific topics to specific people, and mail messages may be reworked later and posted to conferences [KOMunity 1987]. Conferencing is usually not successful below a critical mass, which varies but is often about ten people [Hiltz 1978], although a moderator may manage to attract enough interest among an even smaller group, and previous interest of the participants in the subject is also a strong factor. As the number of participants, their geographical separation, their schedule differences, or the urgency of the situation increases, a true conferencing system becomes more useful. People who have successfully used a system tend to get interested in it and spread its use [Turoff 1980].

If the participants in a conference differ greatly or violently among themselves, a moderator may be needed. If the level of interaction of the discussion increases too much (e.g., by smaller messages, shorter time limits, or more alternative paths) users may resort to interactive conferencing, or eventually to voice telephones. For high-level decisions that are driven more by opinion than fact, or for scanning large amounts of data in a brief time, images may be necessary. Most long-term users of CMC find situations where the only really appropriate electronic medium is none: face-to-face meetings can provide a level of context that nothing else can.

CMC should be used in conjunction with other media, not necessarily to replace any other one [Featheringham 1977]. In fact, it is not uncommon to see an *increase* in the use of telephones and paper mail along with an increasing use of CMC, as the user comes in contact with many more people, including ones not geographically local [Hiltz 1980]. Also, paper mail is more appropriate for bulk mail such as book drafts, and use of CMC may increase the number of people who want or need to receive such drafts.

The dynamics of face-to-face meetings have often been studied as a parallel to conferencing systems. But conferencing systems do not require participants to be in the same place (or the same time). This can be a great advantage if users are distributed over widely separated time zones or countries [Featheringham 1977] or if there are many users (with many schedules).

In a physical meeting only one person can speak at once, but in a computer mediated conference any number of participants may type in comments simultaneously [Hiltz 1977]. There is no waiting for *airtime* [Price 1975] and no danger of being shouted down, although, conversely, readers may choose to ignore anything they feel is inappropriate [Hiltz 1977] (see *flaming* in Section 3.3.5). For these reasons, conferencing can readily support much larger groups than would be practical in face-to-face meetings [KOMunity 1987], and meetings of any size take less time of each participant in CMC than in person [Palme 1984].

Speed of response, or inverse latency of verbal response (LVR), is often a major factor in dominating a face-to-face meeting but is much less of a factor when using a conferencing system. Many more people can converse intelligibly using an asynchronous online service than in a personal meeting. Because several people can provide input at the same time, there is less need for a single leader to control the floor and more likelihood of several leaders developing in different areas [Hiltz 1977]. But anyone who has participated in a very large conference can attest that the CMC equivalent of low LVR does exist. Some people apparently spend their lives glued to keyboards, and can thus always have more and faster responses than others.

CMC is so flexible that people can even be involved in many conferences at the same time. But this flexibility can make it harder to reach a conclusion online than in person, although any eventual conclusion may be of higher quality [Hiltz 1980] and will probably be reached with as few as a quarter as many words [Turoff 1985, 361].

Another common comparison is with telephone conference calls. These have many of the same problems as physical meetings, such as requiring all users to be present at the same time, permitting only one simultaneous speaker, and speed of response. An even more obvious, but often overlooked, advantage of CMC is that there is a written record [Advertel 1988].

An advantage of either mail or conferencing over voice communications is that people with different native languages can often communicate better with each other in writing [Palme 1984; KOMunity 1987].

Both CMC and telephone conferences share a counterintuitive advantage over physical meetings: because there are no physical cues other than the voice or the text, it is easier to concentrate on the topic rather than the person [Hiltz 1977]. A rather extreme example of this is rank in military situations [U.S. Army Forum 1984]. Some even say it is easier to detect when someone is lying, because lying is usually reinforced with nonverbal signals [Turoff 1980].

Some formerly anticipated technologies, such as the *picturephone*, failed after only field trials [Hiltz 1978]. One reason for this may have been that the technology *did* carry nonverbal and nontextual cues. Combined with no strong limitations on the timing of picturephone calls, this could get messy: if someone did not allow their picture to be seen, did it mean they were still asleep, not dressed, just being rude, or didn't have a picturephone?

CMC can have an obscure advantage that neither personal meetings nor telephones can manage as well: *anonymity*, that is, the lack of almost *all* personal cues. Although the medium itself seems to produce greater candor in its participants, including more willingness to criticize bad ideas [Hiltz 1977], hiding the identity of a participant may be useful or necessary in some situations [Featheringham 1977], such as when low-ranking people are communicating with high-ranking people or in public conferences when personal experiences are being discussed.

3.3.3   Identity

There are few more obvious subjects for science fiction than CMC, and there is a long tradition of stories about it. One of the most famous (and pessimistic) early treatments was "The Machine Stops," by E. M. Forster

[Forster 1956]. That story was mostly about dependence on machine mediated communication to the extent that most people had no identity apart from it.

In 1980, a science fiction writer noticed an interesting property of computer aided interaction and wrote a story about it called "True Names" [Vinge 1987]. He noticed that computer users can sometimes masquerade under false identities and defeat attempts to determine who they are: this was well known to system administrators, but Vernor Vinge was apparently the first to turn it into fiction. This is an attractive fictional conceit, involving as it does the possibility of creating whatever *identity* the perpetrator finds useful, appropriate, or amusing. It has spawned a whole subgenre in recent years, most obviously represented by *Neuromancer* by William Gibson [Gibson 1984], and had predecessors as well [Brunner 1975]. Networks are involved more often than single computers, as distance and heterogeneity make detection more difficult. Much of this literature is devoted to the use of invented identities to defeat security mechanisms. Real-life examples of such uses have been part of the computer industry and culture since the beginning [Levy 1984] and show no signs of not continuing indefinitely (see Section 3.3.7).

But most of the best of fiction concerning computer networks (including Gibson, Sterling [Sterling 1985], and Williams [Williams 1986]) is also concerned with other aspects of *identity*. One of the clearest explorations of the *political* use of *personae* created by means of computer networks is *Ender's Game* by Orson Scott Card [Card 1985]. It involves invented characters who expound on political theory in order to influence public opinion and elections. This idea has been ridiculed by some writers, but there are contemporary parallels. I was twice elected to the board of directors of a technical association largely, as near as I can determine, on the basis of exposure on *USENET*.

Newspaper columnists and television commentators routinely assume didactic personae in order to put forth their views and, they hope, influence public opinion and political elections. It is a common and easily documented assertion that television exposure is a major determinant of political elections in the United States and other countries. Computer networks are just another medium, which is not accessible to the general public in most places as yet but is becoming more so all the time. In France, a large fraction of the total population uses the *Minitel* system provided by the government telephone bureau. It was widely used by all parties in the 1988 French presidential election.

Science fiction also deals with other aspects of CMC, such as *information overload*, as in William Gibson's idea of the *scroll* of information impinging on everyone from many sources [Gibson 1984].

3.3.4   Telecommuting

Increased use of this technology will lead to more telecommuting, and thus less physical commuting, as predicted as long ago as 1975 [Price 1975]. Research organizations such as XEROX PARC and Bell Labs have existed because there was a need to collect highly educated and talented people in one place so that they could communicate. Many towns exist because workers had to be gathered near workplaces. Neither of these things is as likely to be as necessary as it used to be [Brilliant 1985]. This may be good in the sense that pressures on cities and road systems may be relieved. But affluent telecommuters leaving cities could leave them to people who can not afford the technology [Hiltz 1977], and the population may spread into rural areas [Clarke 1953] better used for farmland or left as wilderness [Price 1975].

There are already more people working from their homes because of this technology [Brand 1987]. This may in some cases cause problems of isolation having to do with the lack of work-related social contacts [Hiltz 1977], management difficulties, etc. But there may also be increased confidence from feelings of independence, and use of the technology often causes the development of better communication skills [Mills 1984]. It also often leads to a greater number of acquaintances, coworkers, and friends, who may in turn, paradoxically, lead to more long-distance travel [Hiltz 1980].

Effects on families are also a concern. Some people find working at home very useful in multiplexing domestic and work requirements [Hiltz 1977]. But quite a bit of self-control on the part of the worker and cooperation from the family may be necessary to make sure that both (or either) kinds of tasks get done. Many are the spouses who have lost a partner to a home terminal, and many are the companies that have lost a good employee to a spouse.

Some predict that CMC will be used to destroy individual initiative and to repeat the errors of the Industrial Revolution that destroyed cottage industry and produced the assembly line [Mills 1984]. But the opposite is just as plausible: because of the increased independence that the technology offers, more small groups and individuals may become productive in a greater variety of ways. This is already happening. Publishing information used to mean printing it on paper and distributing it physically. This is usually economical only in bulk. With electronic media, the opposite is true, and thus production of information by individuals is encouraged [Turoff and Chinai 1985, 81].

3.3.5   Etiquette and Ethics

Learning how to use a computer system properly takes much longer than simply learning the mechanics of making it do things [Turoff 1980]. Learning to use a system without offending other users and to maximum benefit involves *etiquette*. Learning to use a system without causing harm to others involves *ethics*. These are not completely separable subjects, and the former tends to blend into the latter as the seriousness of the situation increases.

This section draws on several documents on these subjects, including an early Rand report on ethics and etiquette for electronic mail [Shapiro and Anderson 1985], guidelines posted monthly on *USENET* for several years [Von Rospach and Spafford 1988; Spafford and Horton 1988], other guidelines developed from the experience of a more exclusive small group [Umpleby 1986], and some resolutions on ethics adopted by *BITNET* and *CSNET* [BITNET/CSNET 1988] and *NSFNET* [DNCRI-DAP 1988] after a recent (November 1988) and very publicized problem on the *Internet*. The guidelines presented here are common to several of these documents and were chosen based on personal experience.

3.3.5.1   *Etiquette*

Problems of misunderstanding and rudeness are matters of *etiquette*. One of the most obvious effects of networks is a tendency of users to *flame* — that is, to produce many words on an uninteresting topic or in an abusive or ridiculous manner; *raving* is almost a synonym for *flaming*. The usual supposition for why computer networks tend to aggravate flaming is that the flamer is isolated from the readers and has no immediate negative feedback to reduce this behavior. Flamers do, however, tend to get many mail replies (this kind of attention may actually be what some of them want).

Here are a few guidelines and epigrams for etiquette.

CMC services are not like other media. The most basic guideline for using CMC media is that they are not like other media, no matter how many superficial similarities there may be. Treating a CMC service just like the telephone, paper mail, or any other medium will lead to misunderstandings and mistakes. Even if you are using CMC to communicate with people you know well, you will not see them the same way with CMC services.

Emulate experienced users. The best way to learn is by emulating others who have already learned how to make the best use of a system — with etiquette and ethically.

It's not just a machine. All that is in front of you may be a piece of hardware, but there are people on the other end of CMC services, and there are people responsible for maintaining and developing resource sharing services.

Be brief. Using many words is more likely to cause misunderstandings than using a few well-chosen words. People are also less likely to read long messages. More than a page or two is probably too much. When responding to a message and including part of it for context, include as little as possible while maintaining clarity and precision.

Label your message. Choose a title that fits the subject and stick to it. If you need to bring in another subject, consider posting an additional message. Supply keywords if the system supports them.

Remember your audience. When sending a message, remember who will be reading it and tailor it to them. Use language, references, and subjects that will be comprehensible. Do not use buzzwords or other terms the audience will not know unless you define them in your text. Be aware that certain topics are objectionable to some people.

Choose an appropriate medium and forum. Use a conference or mailing list on a topic related to that of your message. Do not cross-post to many different fora without thinking about the ones you choose. Use a style appropriate to the topic, the medium, and the forum (e.g., a chatty conversational style may be appropriate for a social conference but not for a serious technical discussion group). Sometimes personal mail is most appropriate for clarifications or criticisms. Other services may also be appropriate, as has been discussed at length in previous sections. Be aware that some systems prohibit certain types of messages, such as commercial advertising. Do not try to duplicate traditional news media. Assume everyone will have heard of a natural disaster or political assassination and that you do not have to tell them the basic outline.

Identify yourself. Sign your message with some appropriate information such as your name and your affiliation. If you have several affiliations (work, hobby, professional association), pick one appropriate to the subject. Sometimes anonymity is appropriate. In general, choose and make plain an appropriate *identity*. But do not use lengthy signatures with long quotations or large graphics; they waste resources and annoy people.

Observe technical restrictions. Much computer software and display equipment cannot handle lines longer than 80 characters. Escape sequences that cause one effect on one device may do something entirely different on another. Do not use them unless you are sure they are standard. Control characters in general may have varying effects, and are often not passed through intervening links: avoid them (even tab characters) when possible.

Avoid formatting problems. Adjusted right margins are hard to read without proportional fonts. Lots of vertical white space just takes up space. Paragraph breaks are very useful.

Post new ideas. If you have something to say and no one else has said it, do so. But try not to repeat what has already been said, except in brief confirmation.

Respond to the topic, not the person. Avoid ad hominem attacks and try to understand what the person is saying. If you can't tell from what they wrote, ask. If you must criticize someone, attempt to give them a chance to respond. If you comment on the style of a message, respond to the content as well.

Read other messages before responding. Don't dash off a message making an obvious response; somebody else has probably already made the same response. Read all the relevant messages first to see if you're the first to make that response.

Don't respond in anger. Wait a few minutes or hours, or even until the next day. Anger feeds on anger, especially in CMC media, where body language and tone of voice are not present. Read any later messages. Consider asking for clarification. If you are still angry when you respond, say so.

Give the benefit of the doubt. Mistakes, misunderstandings, and ignorance are far more common than maliciousness. Don't take offense without evidence.

Be careful with humor and sarcasm. Many people have trouble recognizing these things even in person. With CMC, it's best to label them somehow or to avoid them altogether. Some networks have developed typographic conventions to get around the difficulties of expressing subtleties of expression through ASCII characters. One of the more universal is that UPPERCASE means shouting (much to the chagrin of those with microcomputers that only have uppercase). Some *surround phrases with asterisks* to indicate emphasis, while others s p a c e the characters out. People will mark sarcasm <sarcasm> or irony <irony> with stage instructions in angle brackets. Facial expressions often get similarly spelled out<*grin*>. There are many ways to indicate the start of a flame, such as *FLAME ON!*. On *USENET* there are shorter ways to indicate lack of serious intent, such as :−) (look at it sideways and it will be obvious why it's called a *smiley face*). As users become more sophisticated, some eschew these lexical aids in favor of more evocative writing.

Do be encouraging and polite. New users (and often old ones as well) tend to be hesitant. Encourage them when they do well. The most effective encouragement is often a simple response acknowledging a posting.

Discourage when necessary. But do it privately and politely when possible. Use personal mail if you can and public conferences only when necessary. Don't discourage at all unless you're sure it's needed and that you are an appropriate one to do it.

Assume permanence and ubiquity. Anything you post to any CMC medium or release through any resource sharing service may be saved permanently, with or without your knowledge, and may be read by anyone, at any time, anywhere. Readers may include anyone from national security agencies, to your boss, to your employees, to your family, to the print or broadcast media. Many conferencing systems support privacy features, but they probably keep backups, too.

3.3.5.2 Ethics

Destruction of data or property, disruption of facilities depended upon by others, loss of time, physical harm, and loss of life are problems of *ethics*. Some simple examples of ethical problems are viruses and worms.

A *virus* is a program that infects a computer system by inserting itself into another program, replicates itself, and manages to infect other computers by being carried along with the infected program. Viruses in personal computer programs have been a serious problem for several years.

A *worm* is a program that uses network communication facilities to transport itself from one computer on a network to another, and then to repeat the process. Unlike a virus, a worm does not usually insert itself into other programs, nor is it usually passed along by being carried inside another program. There was a very well-publicized worm in the *Internet* in November 1988. It replicated itself so quickly that it overloaded many of the machines it reached, apparently having escaped from its creator before it was finished.

Both worms and viruses are often constructed as games or to make political points by people who mean no harm, and many of them do not actually cause any direct damage. But even an apparently harmless virus or worm can take large amounts of time on the parts of many people in order to determine that it is harmless.

Ethical guidelines are more difficult to construct than ones for etiquette, but a few plausible ones are given here.

Observe copyrights. Don't quote text verbatim if it is copyrighted or covered by a restrictive license. Unless you have a philosophical objection to intellectual property, remember that breaking a copyright or license probably takes income away from the owner.

Cite sources. When presenting an idea that originated with someone else, give proper credit, either by naming the source or by citing a formal bibliographic reference.

Be careful with private correspondence. Do not redistribute private correspondence without permission. Don't read other people's mail without permission. If you receive a message by accident, return it to the sender or forward it to the intended recipient.

Be honest. Don't distribute false information, and don't pretend to be someone you aren't in order to take unfair advantage of someone else.

Someone is paying the bills. Even if you are paying for access and by the message, other people are also having to pay to read what you post, and that costs them money and time. If you are not paying, somebody is, whether it is the system operators, the message recipients, or the taxpayers. Try to stick to useful information distributed to appropriate people.

Don't post harmful instructions or information. Posting credit card numbers will probably cost someone else. Posting recipes for bombs may result in physical harm.

Resource sharing services are not like anything else. A computer network is neither like a home computer system nor like any other single computer system. The damage that can be caused by mistakes or malevolence increases with the power and extent of the system.

People depend on networks and conferencing systems. Damaging such a system damages people.

Don't leave a security hole unfixed. A system administrator who installs a system with a well-known user and password combination or who fails to fix a network service security problem to which the solution is well known invites abuse. Vendors who distribute systems with such problems contribute to the problem and increase the likelihood of widespread abuse of such holes, as in networks. Users who choose obvious passwords should know they are increasing the likelihood of damage not only to their own files but also to those of others.

Don't use security holes to cause damage. Regardless of the origin or notoriety of a security hole, using it to cause damage is wrong.

3.3.6   Security and Privacy

To control what is posted on a network one must control access to the network. Most existing networks are not strong on security. The safest policy in using networks is to assume that any network can be broken, that any transmission can be recorded, and that most can be forged. (There was a famous hoax on April Fool's Day, 1984, when moskvax!kremvax!chernenko joined *USENET* and many people believed it.) Encryption techniques exist that can provide a rather high degree of security, but few people are willing to pay the price in CPU time, and few networks incorporate them.

The popular impression of the meaning of the word *hacker*, due to the popular press and movies such as *Wargames*, is someone who breaks into computer systems, particularly networks, for financial or other gain. Some of us remember the original meaning of that term [Levy 1984] and prefer to use *cracker* for break-in artists. But they do exist. A recent case involving international espionage, a major national U.S. laboratory, and military secrets is well documented [Stoll 1988; Markoff 1988], but apparently no military secrets were actually obtained. This was a famous and somewhat unusual incident, but there were earlier ones [Reid 1987].

3.3.7   Legal Issues

The specific liabilities that arise when computers communicate with other computers over public airways or through the telephone system can be difficult to recognize. Different standards of responsibility exist depending on the activities involved and the extent to which the content of messages is controlled.

There are legal precedents covering the liabilities of more traditional communications media such as newspapers, radio and television broadcasting, and cable television. The two major legal classifications are *broadcasters* and *common carriers*. Although computer networks do not neatly fit either of them, these classifications are likely to provide the legal precedents that will apply to computer communications [Shulman 1984]. The alternative is to define a special classification for computer communications. The classification is important because common carriers are not held to as high a standard as broadcasters. Some liabilities of network administrators are related to defamatory material, obscenity, content of transmission, and faulty transmission. Individual users might also be liable for defamatory material and obscenity, as well as for copyright infringement and invasion of privacy. However, publishers of printed journals and books face similar liabilities and still function: that is what insurance is for.

An existing legal category might be appropriate for some kinds of networks: *enhanced service provider*. In the United States, the Federal Communications Commission (FCC) retains jurisdiction over such entities but declines to regulate them. Because the FCC retains jurisdiction, most other federal and state agencies and laws do not apply. Even copyright infringement cannot be prosecuted. Other bodies cannot impose tariffs or other financial regulation, but because the FCC declines to regulate enhanced service providers, the FCC does not impose tariffs, either. Although no system appears to have received specific acknowledgment that it fits this class, several appear to do so and thus may have quite convenient legal status.

This is not to say that problems cannot exist. There was a recent case of someone using a commercial conferencing system with *USENET* access to post an article worldwide and to numerous newsgroups asking for each reader to send one dollar to a post office box. If the poster was not who he said he was (and there is no way to tell) or did not use all the money collected for the stated purpose, this could have been mail fraud, which the

U.S. government takes rather seriously. The administrators of the posting machine took the problem seriously: they quickly removed the user's account.

The ease of use of conferencing systems can be a problem, especially for libel. There has apparently been at least one case of a lawsuit produced by a user posting a defamatory message about a computer manufacturer to a technical list related to that manufacturer's products.

There have been attempts in the U.S. Congress to require registration of bulletin board systems. None of these have as yet succeeded, and it is not clear what effect such a law would have on larger systems or networks. See Appendix B.

3.4   *Boundaries and Access*

The use of conferencing systems and networks is expanding, but boundaries often get in the way.

3.4.1   Bypassing Hierarchies

One reason for the popularity of CMC is that it can be used to reach people directly without going through established bureaucratic hierarchies. This is a source of concern to some people. Some well-known computer scientists do not have electronic mail addresses because they do not want junk mail. Business executives don't want hierarchies bypassed in their companies because they like the way they are set up. Executives worry that electronic mail systems will be used for nonbusiness purposes or to reach people who would not otherwise be available. In fact, most business computer systems are used for business, just as most business telephones are. Executives who worry about frivolous use of computer communication systems probably don't understand their potential value in company morale.

Eventually, most CMC may be controlled by governments, just as telephones are in most countries of the world today. Whether that would mean less anarchistic access by computer remains to be seen.

3.4.2   Political Boundaries

Few Western networks connect to any of the Soviet bloc countries. For different political reasons, few of the major international networks (other than public data networks) connect to South Africa.

3.4.3   Boundary Bashing

There are many apparent boundaries to electronic communication. The process of transcending them is sometimes known as *boundary bashing*.*
Technical boundaries include the following:

- Differing protocols: this is common even within countries.
- Scale: as the size and number of systems connected increase, information overload becomes a problem.
- Restrictions on exportation of hardware or software, as from the United States to Eastern Europe and sometimes even Western Europe or Japan.
- Lack of infrastructure: this is the infamous *last mile* problem that makes connections in the Third World so difficult. Getting to the capital by satellite may be easy, but getting ten miles down the road may be impossible.

Financial boundaries include the following:

- Tariff rates that differ more than an order of magnitude between countries.
- Lack of local funds; very common in the Third World.

Some conferencing systems with international clienteles charge less or nothing for connections from overseas in order to encourage foreign users.
Ignorance and fear can be large problems:

- Ignorance of how to set up systems or links is prevalent. Patient education is the only solution.
- Fear of the technology is very common. Exposure is about the only remedy.

Cultural boundaries can be overt or subtle:

- Language problems are among the most obvious.
- Differing social customs can be among the most subtle: does "maybe" mean yes, no, or maybe?

* The title of this subsection and much of its content are taken from a session of the same name facilitated by Jeffrey Shapard of *TWICS* in Tokyo and Gerri Sinclair of Simon Fraser University (Simon Fraser) Burnaby, BC, Canada, at the Fourth Electronic Networking Association (ENA) Conference in Philadelphia, 12–15 May 1988. None of Shapard, Sinclair, ENA, or the session participants are responsible for the interpretations found herein of that material.

- North/south antagonisms can be particularly difficult for people from the industrialized countries to even see.

Information boundaries—how to get it, and how to cope with it—include the following:

- Censorship is a major problem in many countries. Persistence, publicity, and patience are needed, and a change of government often doesn't hurt.
- Once a user has access to the worldwide *Matrix* of interconnected systems, how do they sort through the never-ending *scroll* of information? This problem of *information overload* exists everywhere, and better user interface software is still needed. Familiarity also helps and can be gained only by experience.

Bureaucracy is unavoidable, especially since communication systems in most countries are run by the government:

- First, one must find out whom to contact; this often involves coping with an initial runaround. Contacts with others with experience at attempting to make network connections can be very helpful.
- Bureaucracy exists not only in governments, but also in network administrations. The most useful tactic here is to demonstrate that you can supply useful information, not just take it.

Finally, the most subtle boundary is the illusion of boundaries: many of them do not actually exist.

3.5   *References*

Advertel 1988.   Advertel, "An Introduction to Confer II," Advertel Communication Systems, Inc., Ann Arbor, MI, 1988.

Axelson 1989.   Axelson, Kevin, Personal communications, May 1989.

BITNET/CSNET 1988.   BITNET/CSNET, "Joint Ethics Committee," BITNET and CSNET, New York and Cambridge, MA, 25 November 1988.

Brand 1987.   Brand, Stewart, *The Media Lab: Inventing the Future at MIT*, Viking, New York, 1987.

Brilliant 1985.   Brilliant, Lawrence B., "Computer Conferencing: The Global Connection," *BYTE*, vol. 10, no. 13, pp. 174–175, December 1985.

Brunner 1975.   Brunner, John, *Shockwave Rider*, Ballantine Books, New York, 1975.

Card 1985.   Card, Orson Scott, *Ender's Game*, Tom Doherty Associates, New York, 1985.

Cerf 1988.   Cerf, Vinton G., Personal communications, August 1988.

Clarke 1953.   Clarke, Arthur C., *Childhood's End*, Ballantine Books, New York, 1953.

da Cruz 1988.   da Cruz, Frank, Personal communications, October–November 1988.

DNCRI-DAP 1988.   DNCRI-DAP, "Ethical Network Use Statement," Division Advisory Panel, Division of Networking and Communications Research and Infrastructure, National Science Foundation, Washington, DC, 25 November 1988.

Featheringham 1977.   Featheringham, Tom, "Teleconferences: the Message is the Meeting," *Data Communications*, vol. 6, no. 7, pp. 37–41, July 1977.

Forster 1956.   Forster, E. M., "The Machine Stops," in *The Eternal Moment*, Harcourt Brace Jovanovich, Inc., New York, 1956. "The Machine Stops" was originally published in 1928.

Gibson 1984.   Gibson, William, *Neuromancer*, Ace, New York, 1984.

Hiltz 1977.   Hiltz, Starr Roxanne, "Communications Medium," *Technological Forecasting and Social Change*, vol. 10, no. 3, pp. 225–238, 1977.

Hiltz 1978.   Hiltz, Starr Roxanne, "The Human Element in Computerized Conferencing Systems," *Computer Networks*, vol. 2, no. 6, pp. 421–428, December 1978.

Hiltz 1980.   Hiltz, Starr Roxanne, "Experiments and Experiences with Computerized Conferencing," in *Emerging Office Systems*, ed. Robert M. Landau, James H. Bair, Jean H. Siegman, pp. 187–204, Ablex Publishing Corporation, Norwood, NJ, 1980. Based on Proceedings of the Stanford University International Symposium on Office Automation.

Hiltz and Turoff 1981.   Hiltz, Starr Roxanne, and Turoff, Murray, "The Evolution of User Behavior in a Computerized Conferencing System," *Communications of the ACM*, vol. 24, no. 11, pp. 739–751, November 1981.

Hiltz and Turoff 1985.   Hiltz, Starr Roxanne, and Turoff, Murray, "Structuring Computer-Mediated Communication Systems to Avoid Information Overload," *Communications of the ACM*, vol. 28, no. 7, pp. 680–689, July 1985.

KOMunity 1987.   KOMunity, "PortaCOM Computer Conferencing System," Komunity Software AB, Stockholm, Sweden, 1987.

Levy 1984.   Levy, Stephen, *Hackers: Heroes of the Computer Revolution*, Anchor Press/Doubleday, Garden City, NY, 1984.

Markoff 1988.   Markoff, John, "Breach Reported in US Computers," *New York Times*, p. 1, 18 April 1988.

Miller 1987.   Miller, Debbie, "Save a Life: The Urgent Action Network," *NetNews*, vol. 1, no. 5, p. 4, IGC, San Francisco, Winter 1987.

Mills 1984.   Mills, Miriam K., "SMR Forum: Teleconferencing — Managing the 'Invisible Worker'," *Sloan Management Review*, vol. 25, no. 4, pp. 63–67, Summer 1984.

Palme 1984.   Palme, Jacob, "The COM and PortaCOM Computer Conference Systems," Stockholm University Computing Centre — QZ, Stockholm, Sweden, 1 August 1984.

Price 1975.   Price, Charlton R., "Conferencing via Computer: Cost Effective Communication for the Era of Forced Choice," in *The Delphi Method*, ed. Murray Turoff, Addison-Wesley, Reading, MA, 1975.

Quarterman and Hoskins 1986.   Quarterman, John S., and Hoskins, Josiah C., "Notable Computer Networks," *Communications of the ACM*, vol. 29, no. 10, pp. 932–971, October 1986.

Reid 1987.   Reid, Brian, "Reflections on Some Recent Widespread Computer Break-ins," *Communications of the ACM*, vol. 30, no. 2, pp. 103–105, February 1987.

Shapiro and Anderson 1985.   Shapiro, Norman Z., and Anderson, Robert H., "Toward an Ethics and Etiquette for Electronic Mail," Rand Corporation, Santa Monica, CA, 1985.

Shulman 1984.   Shulman, Gail H., "Legal Research on USENET Liability Issues," *;login:*, vol. 9, no. 6, pp. 11–17, USENIX Association, Berkeley, CA, December 1984.

Spafford and Horton 1988.   Spafford, Gene, and Horton, Mark, "Rules for posting to Usenet," *news.announce.newusers*, USENET, 17 August 1988.

Sterling 1985.   Sterling, Bruce, *Schismatrix*, Arbor House, New York, 1985.

Stoll 1988.   Stoll, Clifford, "Stalking the Wiley Hacker," *Communications of the ACM*, vol. 13, no. 5, pp. 484–497, May 1988.

Turoff 1980.   Turoff, Murray, "Management Issues in Human Communication Via Computer," in *Emerging Office Systems*, ed. Robert M. Landau, James H. Bair, Jean H. Siegman, pp. 233–257, Ablex Publishing Corporation, Norwood, NJ, 1980. Based on Proceedings of the Stanford University International Symposium on Office Automation.

Turoff 1985.   Turoff, Murray, "Information, Value, and the Internal Marketplace," *Technological Forecasting and Social Change*, vol. 27, no. 4, pp. 357–373, July 1985.

Turoff and Chinai 1985.   Turoff, Murray, and Chinai, Sanjit, "An Electronic Information Marketplace," *Computer Networks and ISDN Systems*, vol. 9, pp. 79–90, 1985.

Umpleby 1986.   Umpleby, Stuart, "General Systems Theorists' Online Group Process Guidelines," *ENA NETWEAVER*, vol. 2, no. 9, p. 6, September 1986.

U.S. Army Forum 1984.   U.S. Army Forum, "U.S. Army Forum: A Way to Tap Experience and Wisdom Off-line," *Government Executive*, vol. 16, no. 6, pp. 55–57, June 1984.

Vinge 1987.   Vinge, Vernor, "True Names," in *True Names and Other Dangers*, Baen Books (Simon & Schuster), New York, 1987. Originally published in 1981, Dell Binary Star #5.

Von Rospach and Spafford 1988.   Von Rospach, Chuq, and Spafford, Gene, "A Primer on How to Work With the USENET Community," *news.announce.newusers*, USENET, 11 September 1988.

Williams 1986.   Williams, Walter Jon, *Hardwired*, TOR, New York, 1986.

Zuboff 1988.   Zuboff, Shoshana, *In the Age of the Smart Machine: The Future of Work and Power*, Basic Books, New York, 1988.

4 *Layers and Protocols*

Network protocols are many and various. Some work together, others do not. Textbooks on them exist, but tend to emphasize certain protocols and neglect the majority. The reader of this book needs brief descriptions in one place. There is no attempt to describe every known networking protocol here; rather, this chapter is intended to mention some of the most widely used or influential ones. More specifically, it is intended to mention those protocols that are referred to in the second part of the book.

This chapter begins with a discussion of the layering models that make networking protocols implementable and conceptually understandable. This is followed by descriptions of some of the major protocol suites (sets of protocols), both for dedicated links and for dialup networks.

The bulk of the chapter consists of descriptions and citations of references for specific protocols. These are arranged in sections starting with the lower layers and moving to the higher ones. The seven ISO-OSI layers each have a major section, and there is also a section for internet protocols following that for network protocols. There are actually five sections for application protocols.

Not all protocols were designed to fit the ISO-OSI layering model. Names for protocols often come from the documents that specify them, and some of those documents specify protocols for more than one layer. The layer to which a protocol is assigned also depends to some extent on what other protocols it is used with. For these reasons, some of the assignments of protocols to layers found in this chapter may differ from what some readers expect.

4.1   *Layering Models*

Computer network protocols can be quite complex. To keep complexity manageable, protocols are designed in *layers* or *levels*, building up from those near the hardware to those near the users [Tanenbaum 1988, 9–12]. In each layer there may be one or more protocols that *peer entities* on that layer may use to communicate with one another. The interfaces between adjacent layers are defined, and protocol designers usually assume that nonadjacent layers do not communicate directly [Denning 1985].

4.1.1   ISO Reference Model

The International Organization for Standardization (ISO) has proposed a standard reference model, the ISO Reference Model (ISORM), for what they call Open Systems Interconnection (OSI) [ISO 1981]. This model has seven basic layers: physical, data link, network, transport, session, presentation, and application. The network layer is often assumed to be X.25, a protocol in a series promulgated by CCITT, an international group of telecommunications companies. The transport protocols, TP0 through TP4, provide different classes of service ranging from simple datagrams to reliable connections. The higher layers are nearing design completion, and many of them are already implemented. The whole set of protocols that fit the model and are intended to be used together is sometimes referred to as the ISO-OSI protocol suite.

4.1.2   Internet Reference Model

Much of the ISO work is based on the work of those who designed and continue to do research on the *ARPANET* and the *Internet* [Cerf and Cain 1983], as well as on related early network efforts such as *CYCLADES* [Pouzin 1982]. The *ARPANET* originally had three basic layers—network, transport, and process/applications—as expressed in the ARPANET Reference Model (ARM) [Padlipsky 1985]. The *Internet* adds a fourth, internet layer, for which the Internet Protocol (IP) is used [Cerf and Cain 1983]. There is also a physical layer, and some descriptions distinguish a link layer plus a utility layer, which is similar to a combination of the ISO presentation and session layers. ISO has also recently adopted an internet sublayer of the network layer; that sublayer strongly resembles IP. The two most commonly used transport protocols in the *Internet* are the Transmission Control Protocol (TCP) (reliable connections) and the User Datagram Protocol (UDP) (unreliable datagrams). The whole set of protocols is usually called TCP/IP.

4.1.3   Model Comparisons

In this chapter and this book, all seven ISORM layers, plus an internet layer, are used to characterize protocols. This is not due to any particular belief on the part of the author in any specific number or set of layers as optimal, but merely because these layers are widely known and are thus convenient for categorizing protocol descriptions. Figure 4.1 shows some of the differences in layering in the two models, as well as the layers used in a networking implementation in the **4.3BSD** version [Leffler et al. 1989; Quarterman et al. 1985] of the **UNIX** operating system [Ritchie and Thompson 1978].

4.2   *Protocol Suites*

In addition to layering models, there are actual protocols that fit the models. These are usually grouped into sets corresponding to specific layering models, and those sets are called *protocol suites*. Major protocol suites intended for networks of dedicated connections are described here.

4.2.1   TCP/IP

The TCP/IP protocol suite, also known as the Department of Defense (DoD) protocol suite or the *Internet* protocol suite, was largely developed between 1973 and 1981, partly under the sponsorship of the U.S. Advanced Research Projects Agency (ARPA), now called the Defense Advanced Research Projects Agency (DARPA). The idea of TCP was proposed in 1974 [Cerf and Kahn 1974] by Robert Kahn and Vint Cerf, then both of DARPA, from which positions they guided the development of the TCP/IP protocol suite until TCP and IP became DoD standards. Architectural responsibility for the protocol suite was taken over by Dave Clark of MIT in 1981; he now chairs the Internet Activities Board (IAB), which is one of several committees concerned with further development [Clark 1988, 114].

By the mid-1980s the protocol suite had become very popular in the business community, and it is believed to be the most widely implemented of the vendor independent protocol suites in the United States, available on computers ranging in size and expense from supercomputers to personal computers. Although most of the TCP/IP protocol suite is well defined, research and development continues to be done to improve and enhance the protocol suite. This is done by people in commercial companies and government agencies, academia and vendors, administrators and users. Input is limited neither to the U.S. government nor to the United States. Recent areas of work include network management and improved routing

ISO Reference Model	ARPA Internet layers	4.3BSD implementation layers	Examples of uses of layers in 4.3BSD	
Application		User programs and libraries	TELNET, FTP, SMTP, SUPDUP, rlogin or rcp	NTP, TFTP, rwho, or talk
Presentation	Process / Applications			
Session		Sockets	SOCK_STREAM	SOCK_DGRAM
Transport	Transport	Protocols	TCP	UDP
(Internet)	Internet		IP	
Network	Network	Network interfaces	Ethernet driver	
Data Link				
Physical	Physical	Network hardware	Interlan controller	

Figure 4.1. *Network reference models and layering*

protocols. The main protocols and their specifications are indicated in Table 4.1 and Table 4.2.

A good general reference on the protocol suite is Comer 1988, which also contains practical comments on the implementation and interface of **4.3BSD**. For details of the design and implementation of the latter, see Leffler et al. 1989. Also for the TCP/IP protocols, see Stallings et al. 1988 and Comer 1987. The latter is a continuation of Comer 1984 and relates the protocols to their implementation in **XINU**, a public domain variant of **UNIX**. For an introduction to the protocol suite, try Davidson 1988.

The primary goals of this protocol suite were to develop a communications architecture that was robust in the face of damage to the network or faulty network components and that could accommodate multiple types of communications services over a wide variety of networks [Clark 1988]. The resulting protocol suite uses an unreliable datagram protocol, the Internet Protocol (IP), as the network layer protocol. A variety of reliable and unreliable transport protocols are used on top of IP, the best known and most used of which is the Transmission Control Protocol (TCP), a reliable stream protocol.

There are two sets of specifications for many of the TCP/IP protocols. One is a set of Requests for Comments (RFC), which are somewhat informal working documents produced by the *Internet* community of researchers and by other network researchers around the world. All the protocols are indexed in RFC1010, "Assigned Numbers" [Postel 1987], RFC1011, "Official ARPA-Internet Protocols," and RFC1012, "Bibliography of Request for Comments 1 through 999"; there is also a current index online. A catalog of the first 1,000 RFCs may be found in Comer 1988.

Table 4.1. *TCP/IP lower layer protocols*

Protocol	RFC	MIL-STD	Description
	1011		Official Internet Protocols
Network layer			
BBN 1822L	878		ARPANET Host Access Protocol
X.25	877		IP transmission over PDNs
IEEE 802.3			CSMA/CD
IEEE 802	1042		IP transmission over IEEE 802
ARP	826		Ethernet Address Resolution Protocol
subnets	950, 1027		IP subnetworks
Internet layer			
IP	791, 963	1777	Internet Protocol
ICMP	792		Internet Control Message Protocol
RIP	1058		Routing Information Protocol
GGP	823		Gateway to Gateway Protocol
EGP	888, 904, 911, 975		External Gateway Protocol
Transport layer			
UDP	768		User Datagram Protocol
TCP	793, 964	1778	Transmission Control Protocol
ISODE	1006		ISO Transport on top of TCP
TP4	1007		ISO Transport Military Supplement
TP4	1008		ISO Transport Implementation Guide
NETBIOS	1001, 1002		NETBIOS over TCP or UDP

The other specifications are Military Standards (MIL-STDs), which are used by U.S. military agencies in ordering equipment. The MIL-STDs are in some sense more authoritative, but the RFCs are often more accurate in depicting the intent of the developers and the details of the implementations. See Table 4.1 and Table 4.2 for the RFCs and MIL-STDs specifying some of the major protocols. Many relevant RFCs and MIL-STD documents have been collected in a single volume [SRI-NIC 1985]. There is a implementations and vendors of TCP/IP, as well as many of ISO-OSI and X.25: about 300 products are included [Oakley et al. 1985].

Access

RFCs:
DDN Network Information Center
SRI International
Room EJ291
333 Ravenswood Avenue
Menlo Park, CA 94025
U.S.A.

Table 4.2. *TCP/IP higher layer protocols*

Protocol	RFC	MIL-STD	Description
Presentation layer			
ASN.1	X.208, X.209	DIS 8824, DIS 8825	Abstract Syntax Notation One
XDR	1014		Sun External Data Representation
RPC	1057		Sun Remote Procedure Call Protocol
Applications			
TELNET	854, 930, 1041, 1043	1782	Remote login
FTP	959	1780	File Transfer Protocol
NTP	1059		Network Time Protocol
SMTP	821, 974	1781	Simple Mail Transfer Protocol
Mail	822		Basic mail format
DNS	1034, 1035, 1032, 1033, 974		Domain Name System
X.400	987, 1026		X.400/RFC822 address conversion
Network management			
SNMP	1067, 1065, 1066		Simple Network Management Protocol

MIL-STDs:
Naval Publications and Forms Center
Code 3015
5801 Tabor Avenue
Philadelphia, PA 19120
U.S.A.

4.2.2   ISO-OSI

The ISO-OSI model was first codified in 1980 in a document by Hubert Zimmermann [Zimmermann 1980]. The main ISO-OSI protocols and their specifications are indicated in Table 4.3 and Table 4.4. ISO, unlike CCITT and most other standards organizations, carefully distinguishes between a service and the protocol that supports it; thus ISO specifications tend to come in pairs. Good references for the model and the protocols are Knightson et al. 1988; Stallings 1987a; and Tanenbaum 1988.

There is a software package, the ISO Development Environment (**ISODE**) [Rose and Cass 1987; Rose 1987a; Rose 1987b; Rose 1988a; Rose 1988b], that allows use of ISO-OSI services on top of TCP/IP. This is useful for development of implementations of protocols in the higher ISO-OSI layers on top of existing TCP/IP networks.

Table 4.3. *ISO-OSI lower layer protocols*

Protocol	CCITT (IEEE, RFC)	ISO (ANSI)	Description
ISORM	X.200	ISO 7498	ISO-OSI Reference Model
1. Physical layer			
	X.21		Circuit switching
2. Data Link layer			
	X.25		Packet switching
	IEEE 802.3	ISO8802/3	CSMA/CD (Ethernet)
	IEEE 802.2	ISO8802/2	Logical link control
3. Network layer			
ISDN	I.440, I.441		Integrated Service Digital Network
	X.25	ISO8208	Packet switching
CONS		ISO8878	Connection Oriented
(X.25)			Network Service
	X.121		Address formats for X.25
	X.75		PSDN call control procedures
			(X.25 network interconnection)
		DIS 8348	Network Service Definition
CLNS	RFC994	DIS 8473	Connection-less mode
(ISO-IP)			Network Service
ES-IS	RFC995	ANSIx353.3	End System to Intermediate
			System Routing Exchange
			Protocol for ISO8473
4. Transport layer			
	X.214	ISO8072	Connection-oriented
	X.224	ISO8073	Transport
		8072/DAD 1	TP4 over CLNS
		8073/DAD 2	TP4 over CLNS
TP4	RFC905	DP 8073	Reliable transport
TP0		DIS 8602	Connection-less transport

Sources: [Tanenbaum 1988; Stallings 1987a, Appendix B]
Note: Pairs of ISO specifications are shown with service specification first and protocol specification second.

Access

See the sections on ISO, OMNICOM, and ANSI in Chapter 8.

4.2.3 Coloured Book

Development of the Coloured Book protocols started in 1979, mostly on the network *SERCnet*. They are sometimes called the Rainbow Book protocols and are listed in Table 4.5. These protocols are primarily used in the United Kingdom in *JANET* [Spratt 1986], but they are also used in *HEANET* in Ireland and in *SPEARNET* in Australia and New Zealand.

Table 4.4. *ISO-OSI higher layer protocols*

Protocol	CCITT (IEEE, RFC)	ISO (ANSI)	Description
5. Session layer			
	X.215, X.225	ISO8326, 8327	Connection-oriented
6. Presentation layer			
ASN.1	X.208, X.209	ISO8824, 8825	Abstract Syntax Notation One
		DIS 8822, 8823	Connection-oriented
	X.409		MHS Presentation
7. Application layer			
VTP		ISO9040, 9041	Virtual Terminal Protocol
FTAM		ISO8571, 8572	File Transfer, Access and Manipulation
JTM		ISO8831, 8832	Job Transfer and Manipulation
MHS	X.400		Message Handling System
MOTIS	X.400		Message-Oriented Text Interchange System
	X.500		Directory service for X.400
Network management			
CMIP		DP 9595/2, 9596/2	Common Management Information Protocol

Sources: [Tanenbaum 1988; Stallings 1987a; Partridge and Rose 1988]
Note: Pairs of ISO specifications are shown with service specification first and protocol specification second.

Table 4.5. *Coloured Book protocols*

Protocol	Coloured Book	Description
Network layer		
CR82	Orange Book	Cambridge Ring 82
Ethernet	Pink Book	CSMA/CD Implementation Details
Transport layer		
NITS	Yellow Book	Network Independent Transport Service
Applications		
NIFTP	Blue Book	Network Independent File Transfer Protocol
Triple-X	Green Book	Character Terminal Protocols on *PSS*
JTMP	Red Book	Job Transfer and Manipulation Protocol
Mail	Grey Book	JNT Mail Protocol
SSMP	Fawn Book	Simple Screen Management Protocol

Access

The Coloured Books are available from the Joint Network Team (JNT). See the section on *JANET* in Chapter 13.

4.2.4   MAP/TOP

The MAP/TOP protocol suites are closely related to the ISO-OSI protocol suites. Both Manufacturing Automation Protocol (MAP) and Technical and Office Protocols (TOP) use ISO-OSI protocols in the higher (network and up) layers, and both use IEEE 802 in the lower layers. MAP uses IEEE 802.4 (token bus); TOP uses IEEE 802.3 (CSMA/CD, or Ethernet) and IEEE 802.5 (token ring). General Motors (GM) was the primary developer of MAP and coordinated development of TOP with Boeing Corporation (Boeing), its originator [Tanenbaum 1988, 36–39].

4.2.5   XEROX Network Services (XNS)

The XEROX Network Services (XNS) protocol suite is used within the *XEROX Internet* and in numerous local area networks. XEROX has also been extremely influential in its work on remote procedure calls [Birrell and Nelson 1984], external data formats [XEROX 1981a], and naming [Schroeder et al. 1984].

4.2.6   Digital Network Architecture (DNA)

The Digital Network Architecture (DNA) [Lauck et al. 1986] and the DECNET protocols are developed and used within Digital Equipment Corporation (Digital) and are employed in Digital's *EASYnet*, as well as in many outside networks, such as *SPAN*, *HEPnet*, *SURFnet*, and *THEnet*. It is also influential in research, in part because Digital has attracted a number of prominent researchers to work in its labs. There has been especially notable work on congestion control [Jain 1986; Jain et al. 1987]. The current version is called Phase IV. DECNET Phase V is expected to be interoperable with ISO-OSI [Carpenter et al. 1987].

4.2.7   Apollo Network Computing Architecture (NCA)

Apollo Computer, Inc. (Apollo) has specified an "object-oriented framework for developing distributed applications" called the Network Computing Architecture (NCA) [Dineen et al. 1987]. There is a portable implementation of NCA called the Network Computing System (NCS) that runs under implementations of the **UNIX** operating system, such as Apollo's

DOMAIN/IX. The purpose of NCA is to promote resource sharing on a large scale, including parallel use of resources on different computers. Unlike some similar frameworks promulgated by specific vendors, NCA is intended for a heterogeneous environment of systems from different vendors. See also OSF in Chapter 8.

4.2.8   IBM System Network Architecture (SNA)

The System Network Architecture (SNA) was developed and used within International Business Machines (IBM). It is influential elsewhere, both in its layering and in specific protocols, such as SDLC (its data link protocol), which have influenced CCITT and ISO.

4.2.9   IBM Systems Application Architecture (SAA)

The IBM Systems Application Architecture (SAA) is a coordinated framework for application development intended to allow applications to run consistently on IBM computers. It has a large networking component and is intended to foster the development of *enterprise information system*s that integrate the computing facilities (from workstations to mainframes, and with dissimilar operating systems) of an entire *enterprise* (large corporation, government agency, etc.) into a single large distributed system with distributed services [Wheeler and Ganek 1988, as well as that entire issue of *IBM Systems Journal*]. Although SAA is explicitly about IBM equipment and software, such as **OS/2**, **System/36**, **System/38**, and **OS/400**, the basic idea behind it is quite similar to that behind vendor independent protocol suites such as ISO-OSI, TCP/IP, and Coloured Book.

4.2.10   Others

There are quite a few special purpose or early protocol suites that were developed for certain networks and are not widely used elsewhere. These are described in the sections on their originating networks and include at least NCP of *ARPANET*, CYCLADES and CIGALE of *CYCLADES*, PUP of the *XEROX Internet*, DSIR of *DSIRnet*, Uninett of *UNINETT*, HEP of *HEPnet*, and NSP of *MFEnet*. See the index for the appropriate sections.

4.2.11   Local Area Networks

There is a large amount of literature on local area networks (LANs), including McNamara 1985 and Stallings 1987b. Descriptions of some real campus networks and the decisions that were made in their construction may be found in Arms 1988. There is an *Internet* interest list on campus networks, and some of the references in this chapter were found through it [Spurgeon 1988].

4.3   *Dialup Protocols*

The protocol suites discussed in the previous section were designed with the assumption of dedicated links between nodes of networks. There are other sets of protocols that were designed for use with intermittent connections. They tend to differ in that they primarily support batch services, and they usually depend on virtual circuits. They do not usually have many or clearly defined layers.

The SUN-III protocols are exceptions: they were originally designed for dedicated connections [Dick-Lauder et al. 1984]; they are clearly layered; and they support protocols other than remote job entry. For that matter, UUCP was originally used over dedicated links, and still can be, but its most widespread use is over dialup connections. And IBM's Network Job Entry (NJE) is usually used over dedicated links.

Some of the protocols listed at the end of this section, such as Kermit, are not ordinarily used to build networks; rather, they are used in manually dialed connections. But they are referred to in network sections later in the book and need to be defined somewhere. Kermit and Xmodem are somewhat similar in function, but Kermit was originally implemented for large machines and later extended to smaller ones, while Xmodem was originally implemented for **CP/M** on micros and has since been implemented for larger machines. UUCP gained its initial popularity from being distributed with **UNIX** and NJE from being distributed with **VM**.

Some protocols originally intended for dedicated connections have been adapted for dialup use, as in Dialup SLIP.

Some asynchronous serial point to point data transfer protocols, most of them proprietary, that are not discussed below include Microcom Networking Protocol (MNP), X.PC, Poly-Xfr, DX, CompuServe-B FAST, and DART [da Cruz and Gianone 1987].

4.3.1   **UNIX to UNIX CoPy (UUCP)**

The UNIX to UNIX CoPy (UUCP) protocol is used in such systems as *UUCP, USENET, EUnet, UUNET, JUNET, SDN, AUSEAnet*, and *PACNET*. The normal transmission protocol, the g protocol [Chesson 1988], fragments data into packets, uses checksums to detect errors, and retransmits when necessary. The f protocol is used over X.25 and leaves most of the work to the latter protocol. Similarly, the t protocol is sometimes used over TCP/IP. All of these protocols are half duplex.

4.3.2   Sydney UNIX Network (SUN-III)

The current Sydney UNIX Network (SUN) protocols, SUN-III, are used not only in *ACSnet* in Australia, but also in other networks, such as *TCSnet* in Thailand.

The current version is a complete redesign and reimplemention done in 1983 and is called SUN-III [Kummerfeld and Dick-Lauder 1981]. It is layered in the traditional networking manner and provides a message delivery service with implicit (system) routing and domains in order to support higher level protocols, including file transfer, electronic mail, news, remote printing, simple directory service, and a number of experimental services. It can transfer messages in both directions simultaneously over full-duplex links. The transport protocol can make use of any form of virtual circuit between hosts. It supports multicasting, which is useful with *USENET* news and also with mail addressed to users on multiple hosts.

SUN-IV was being finalized in late 1988 and will include better domain handling and some accommodations to eventual migration to X.400.

4.3.3   Network Job Entry (NJE)

The IBM Network Job Entry (NJE) protocols are the basis of *VNET*, as well as of *BITNET*, *NetNorth*, *EARN*, *ILAN*, *GulfNet*, and others. It is often used over BSC, but can be used over IP, as in *BITNET II*.

NJE is implemented on the following systems:

- **VM** as **RSCS** (Remote Spooling Communications Subsystem)
- **MVS** as **JES/NJE**
- **UNIX** as **Urep**, developed at Pennsylvania State University (PSU)
- **VMS** as **JNET**, also developed at PSU and sold to Joiner Associates
- **Primos** by an implementation done by Prime [Nussbacher 1987]
- **NOS** by an implementation done by Control Data Corporation (CDC) [Nussbacher 1988]

4.3.4   Fido

The Fido protocols were invented for *FidoNet* (see Chapter 10).

4.3.5   **Kermit**

Kermit is an error correcting file transfer protocol originally intended for use on direct or dialup RS-232-C asynchronous serial connections and also adapted for use on Ethernet, token rings, and other kinds of infrastructure. Kermit was developed at the Columbia University Center for Computing Activities in 1981 and is modeled on the *Internet* FTP and TELNET file transfer and remote login services. There are text and binary file transfer modes for similar and heterogeneous hosts, and most implementations also provide terminal emulation [da Cruz 1987a].

The Kermit protocols have distinct layers. There are framing, transparency, and error detection data link mechanisms. At the data link layer, Kermit provides mechanisms for framing (frames start with ASCII SOH — i.e., Control A — and end with a carriage return), transparency (frames are otherwise printable ASCII text, with encoding mechanisms for data of other types), and error detection (a checksum is appended to the frame). The protocol is half duplex [da Cruz and Gianone 1987]. There is no network or routing layer, because Kermit is used strictly between pairs of points. Transport mechanisms include sequencing and error recovery by retransmission and discarding of duplicates [da Cruz and Gianone 1987]. Sliding windows of up to 32 unacknowledged packets and selective retransmission are supported [da Cruz and Gianone 1987].

Features and parameters are negotiated within a session. Many implementations allow one of the pair of participants in a session to be negotiated into a server mode in which it obeys commands given it by the other, client participant, including directory listing, file deletion, etc. Various rudimentary presentation formats, such as ASCII and EBCDIC, records and streams, etc., are supported, and text files are handled with a common intermediate format similar to that developed for TELNET. Files may be sent either singly or in sets. Each file has a header with a filename prepended and a trailer to mark the end of file. Kermit is sometimes used for automated mail transfer or print spooling [da Cruz and Gianone 1987].

This software is far more widely used than many people realize, often in conjunction with well known networks. At universities with a collection of odd computers, network mail is often transported to the leaf nodes using percent sign source routing and Kermit, because that is the only error correcting protocol supported on many machines [da Cruz 1988]. **Kermit** is also used to cross boundaries not ordinarily crossed by networks, connecting agricultural research stations in India [Lindsey 1987], allowing for scientific exchanges between the Soviet Union and Western Europe [de Broeck 1987], and making possible satellite communication between the United States and Antarctica [da Cruz 1987b].

Kermit programs are normally copyrighted so that they can remain sharable and noncommercial, but they are distributed free of charge. The original implementations (done at Columbia) were for **CP/M**, **TOPS-20**, **VM/CMS**, **MS-DOS**, and **UNIX**. Others have been contributed by other organizations, and there are now more than 300 implementations. These have been written mostly by volunteers, coordinated by Christine Gianone of Columbia. There are even firmware implementations in modems by Telebit and AST [da Cruz and Gianone 1987].

The **Kermit** source code and documentation, which together take up about 60Mbytes, are available over *BITNET* through the **KERMSRV** software on *CUMVA.BITNET* at Columbia and on *UOFT02* at the University of Toledo; over the *Internet* via *anonymous FTP* from *CUNIXC.CC.COLUMBIA.EDU* and *uunet.uu.net*; by UUCP dialup from *UUNET* or Oklahoma State University (OSU). OSU also allows dialup retrieval using **Kermit** itself. Additional repositories are being set up in other locations, including Japan and Europe. *CUMVA.BITNET* and *CUNIXC.CC.COLUMBIA.EDU* are at the Columbia University Center for Computing Activities, which also accepts mail orders for a variety of magnetic media with a moderate distribution fee. Redistribution is permitted and encouraged. See also *Info-Kermit@CUNIXC.CC.COLUMBIA.EDU* in Chapter 3.

Access
Kermit Distribution
Columbia University Center for Computing Activities
612 West 115th Street
New York, NY 10025
U.S.A.

4.3.6   Xmodem

Xmodem and Ymodem are the most widely used of the set of protocols that also includes Umodem and Zmodem [Forsberg 1988]. Although Xmodem is the most primitive of these protocols, it is found in hundreds of public domain programs and in hundreds more commercial communication packages [da Cruz 1987a; da Cruz 1988].

Xmodem detects and corrects errors and ensures packet order with checksums, retransmissions, and discard of duplicates. The protocol is half duplex. It uses 8 bit bytes without conversion of control characters; thus XON/XOFF flow control cannot be used, because the Control S and Control Q characters can occur in packet control fields. Acknowledgments are sent as raw control characters with no error checking. Filenames are not transmitted, and there is no distinction between text and binary files. There is no provision for option negotiation, nor for a server mode of operation [da Cruz and Gianone 1987].

Like those of Kermit, Xmodem sources and protocol specifications are publicly available. There are commercial implementations of Xmodem, such as that in **Crosstalk** [da Cruz and Gianone 1987], coordinated by Jeff Garbers [Forsberg 1988].

The proper name for the Xmodem protocol is the Christensen protocol, after its designer, Ward Christensen, who invented it in 1977 for use between machines running **CP/M** and made his original **MODEM** program public domain. Keith Petersen coined the name Xmodem for his adaptation of **MODEM** for **RCPM (Remote CP/M)** systems; this program is also called **MODEM** or **MODEM2** [Forsberg 1988]. Other adaptations include Ymodem by Chuck Forsberg [Forsberg 1988] and MODEM7 (both Ymodem and MODEM7 can transfer multiple files), Zmodem (with checkpoint and restart), Xmodem-CRC (which uses a 16 bit cyclic redundancy check instead of the Xmodem 8 bit checksum), Wmodem (with sliding windows that work if there are no errors [da Cruz and Gianone 1987]), and Umodem, which is basically a **UNIX** implementation of Xmodem.

4.3.7   Blocked Asynchronous Transmission (BLAST)

The Blocked Asynchronous Transmission (BLAST) protocol is a full-duplex commercial point to point asynchronous data transfer protocol [da Cruz and Gianone 1987].

4.4   *Physical Layer Protocols*

The *physical layer* transmits and receives sequences of bits. At its lower interface, it is concerned with pins, connectors, cables, waveforms, and other physical characteristics of actual hardware media, and conversion of digital data into an analog form used by the underlying medium is often required. A hardware device for this purpose may be called a *modem (modulator and demodulator)*.

The physical layer hides most of the complexities of such conversions from upper layers and presents a digital interface to the data link layer. But the data link layer may have to convert fixed length data objects into bit streams for an *asynchronous* interface, or it may have to provide bits at a regular rate for a *synchronous* interface. Important terms associated with a pair of communicating physical interfaces are *data communications equipment (DCE)* and *data terminating equipment (DTE)*. A DTE is usually a modem, while a DCE is a terminal [Bertsekas and Gallager 1987, 17–20]. The actual usage may be confusing because the terms were intended to designate a terminal (the DTE) and a communication carrier's equipment (the DCE), but they are also applied to situations involving communications between computers (DTE) and modems or communication carriers (DCE) [Tanenbaum 1988, 82] and even between pairs of computers.

4.4.1   Asynchronous Physical Layer Protocols

4.4.1.1   *RS-232-C*

RS-232-C is the common serial line protocol used in connecting terminals to computers; it is also used in many dialup networks and protocols, such as in *ACSnet* and SUN-III, and in *UUCP* and UUCP, and it is the common infrastructure used with Kermit and Xmodem. RS-232-C was developed in 1969 by the Electrical Industry Association (EIA) in cooperation with the then Bell System, independent modem manufacturers, and computer manufacturers [EIA 1969; McNamara 1988, 17].

4.4.1.2   *EIA-232-D*

EIA, now known as the Electronic Industries Association, has revised RS-232-C as EIA-232-D, which is the first modification of RS-232-C since 1969 [da Cruz 1988; McNamara 1988, 17 – 36, 80 – 93]. The differences are minor.

4.4.1.3   *EIA-422-A and EIA-423-A*

EIA has also promulgated EIA-422-A and EIA-423-A, which have different numbers of pins and distance limits from each other and from EIA-232-D and RS-232-C [McNamara 1988, 17 – 36, 80 – 93].

4.4.1.4   *X.21*

CCITT X.21 provides the physical layer interface for X.25 in the ISO-OSI protocol suite. Its calling procedures are specified in X.96 [Tanenbaum 1988, 82 – 84].

4.5   *Data Link Protocols*

The *data link layer* handles point to point communications between peer entities, each of which communicates directly with the physical layer. The primary concern of this layer is error detection, and this is usually done by encapsulating data submitted from the network layer in a *frame* with a header and possibly a trailer, one of which may contain a checksum or other consistency code. This layer is sometimes called the Data Link Control (DLC) layer. A lower sublayer of it is sometimes distinguished and called Media Access Control (MAC). The purpose of the MAC layer is to multiplex access to a common medium. This may involve detecting when there are no data on the medium before sending a frame, or when a frame seen on the medium is directed to the listening node. Another header with an address for the node may be included for this purpose. If there is a MAC sublayer, DLC is considered an upper sublayer of the data link layer [Bertsekas and Gallager 1987; Tanenbaum 1988, 188–190].

4.5.1 Synchronous Data Link Protocol

4.5.1.1 *BSC*

The Bi-Synchronous Communication (BSC) protocol is used in *VNET* and *BITNET*.

4.5.2 Asynchronous Data Link Protocols

4.5.2.1 *SDLC*

The SNA data link protocol is called Synchronous Data Link Control (SDLC). ANSI modified it to make Advanced Data Communication Control Procedure (ADCCP). ISO modified that to make High-level Data Link Control (HDLC). CCITT modified that to make Link Access Procedure (LAP) for use with X.25. These are all bit-oriented protocols with bit stuffing and cyclic redundancy checks [Tanenbaum 1988, 254].

4.5.2.2 *X.25*

As mentioned in the previous section, the data link part of X.25 is called LAP [Tanenbaum 1988, 254].

4.5.2.3 *DDCMP*

The Digital Data Communications Message Protocol (DDCMP) is the DNA data link layer protocol for use over synchronous or asynchronous links, perhaps arranged in a star [Lauck et al. 1986].

4.5.2.4 *SLIP*

Serial Line IP (SLIP) can be used over an RS-232-C link to support IP [Romkey 1988]. This has been adapted as *Dialup SLIP* for use with intermittent connections. *CSNET* uses this [Lanzillo and Partridge 1989], and various organizations such as the Ballistics Research Laboratory (BRL) have versions of it. The former will establish a connection when a datagram arrives and needs to be gatewayed; the latter requires manual setup [Partridge 1988a]. The Dialup SLIP implementation used in *JUNET* may be the earliest one [Murai and Kato 1988].

4.5.3   CSMA/CD Protocols

Carrier Sense Multiple Access/Carrier Detect (CSMA/CD) protocols have become popular since XEROX pioneered them in the early 1970s with 3Mbps Experimental Ethernet.

4.5.3.1   *Ethernet*

The original 10Mbps Ethernet specifications are in XEROX 1980. Ethernet Version 2 is specified in Digital-Intel-XEROX 1982. Some comments on Ethernet and IEEE 802.3 hardware logistics can be found in HP 1986. An early paper on the predecessor, 3Mbps Experimental Ethernet, is still useful as a lucid discussion of the basic principles [Metcalfe and Boggs 1976].

A popular misconception about Ethernet is that its effective throughput is substantially lower than its nominal throughput of 10Mbps. In fact, recent experiments have shown this is not true: an Ethernet can be driven at 10Mbps [Boggs et al. 1988].

4.5.3.2   *IEEE 802.3*

The IEEE standard related to Ethernet is IEEE 1985, with updates (such as thin and broadband CSMA/CD) in IEEE 1988. There is a reference that explains the 802.3 standard and details its differences from Ethernet [Stallings 1987b].

4.5.3.3   *Pink Book*

The *JANET* recommendations for use of CSMA/CD protocols (Ethernet) are given in the Pink Book [JNT 1985a].

4.5.3.4   *HYPERchannel*

HYPERchannel is a fast (50Mbps) channel protocol designed and implemented by Network Systems Corporation (NSC) and commonly used with supercomputers. It is CSMA/CD. Packet sizes can vary from relatively small to quite large (more than 64Kbytes). This protocol and hardware have seen a variety of uses, ranging from simple bulk data transfer links to connecting terminals through a front end (as on Cray 2s) to more sophisticated networks, ranging from special purpose user space networks to general TCP/IP internets [Yamasaki 1988].

4.5.4   Token Ring Protocols

Many people consider CSMA/CD too unreliable because of its stochastic properties and the presumption that it cannot perform well under heavy load. Token ring technology allows predictable performance by passing a virtual token among all participating machines in a circular manner, giving each machine a chance to transmit when it has the token.

4.5.4.1   *Cambridge Ring*

The Cambridge Ring 82 slotted ring local area network protocol specifications come in two Orange Books, one specifying the interface [Sharpe and Cash 1982] and the other the protocol proper [Larmouth 1982].

4.5.4.2   *IEEE 802.5*

802.5 is the IEEE specification of IBM token ring.

4.5.4.3   *FDDI*

Fiber Distributed Data Interface (FDDI) is a 100Mbps token ring protocol that is designed to be implemented in an offboard processor [Chesson 1987]; preliminary implementations were available in early 1989 [Stallings 1987b].

4.6   *Network Protocols*

The *network layer* handles routing and flow control among nodes on a network. Several data link layer connections may be multiplexed by the network layer. Another header and another address may be added for this purpose, and the result is usually called a *packet*, which is encapsulated by the data link layer into a *frame*. There are often both data packets, using data submitted by the transport layer, and control packets, which are generated by the network layer [Bertsekas and Gallager 1987, 22 – 24].

4.6.1   ISO-OSI Network Protocols

4.6.1.1   *X.25*

X.25 is used as the main ISO-OSI network layer protocol and is very widely supported in public data network (PDN) and some research network implementations. The network layer part of X.25 is sometimes called Packet Layer Protocol (PLP) to distinguish it from the lower layer parts. In addition to the terms DCE and DTE, defined above for the data link layer, there is another term, Data Switching Exchange (DSE), that refers to nodes within a network that communicate with each other [Tanenbaum 1988, 350]. X.25 is often used to supply the ISO-OSI Connection Oriented Network Service (CONS), which is specified in ISO8878 [Tanenbaum 1988, 358].

There are several versions of X.25, the most important ones being the following [Tanenbaum 1988, 356 – 358]:

X.25 (1976)   This is the original standard.

X.25 (1980)   In 1980, CCITT added negotiation of packet length and window size, a diagnostic packet (allowing the network to inform the user of errors), and the *D bit* (specifying end to end acknowledgment). Two kinds of datagram facilities were also added, one proposed by Japan and one proposed by the United States.

X.25 (1984)   Since no one had implemented the datagram facilities added in 1980, CCITT removed them in 1984. Instead, a *fast select* feature was added to handle applications such as electronic funds transfer (EFT) that need to send single short bursts of data. This feature piggybacks data on a call request packet.

X.25 (1988)   This is the current version.

There is a worldwide X.25 address space organized according to X.121.

4.6.2   Packet Radio Network Protocols

Packet radio has been important from early times, when it was used in the *Aloha* network in Hawaii [Abramson 1970; Abramson and Kui 1975]. Early development of TCP/IP was partly motivated [Clark 1988] by a desire to interconnect the *ARPANET* with a packet radio network [Kahn 1975], *PRNET*. *AMPRNET* is a current packet radio network that uses the TCP/IP protocols [Karn 1988].

4.6.3   Other Network Protocols

4.6.3.1   *BBN 1822*

BBN 1822 is the name of the *ARPANET* communications subnet to host interface protocol and is specified in a report of that number [Malis 1983]. X.25 is also used now.

4.6.3.2   *NSP*

DNA distinguishes a *routing layer* corresponding to the routing functions of the ISO-OSI network layer. The corresponding protocol is Network Service Protocol (NSP) [Lauck et al. 1986]. Some comments on DNA routing appear in Chapter 5.

4.7   *Internet Protocols*

The purposes of the *internet layer* include those of the network layer — routing and flow control — but an Internet Protocol (IP) is also usable over multiple network protocols so that it may support a virtual network over several different kinds of physical media. Another header with an address, and possibly a checksum, may be added for this purpose; the result is still called a *packet*. The internet layer is often considered to be the upper sub-layer of the network layer. But the internet layer is sometimes considered to *be* the network layer, and any protocol used underneath it is then considered to be a data link layer protocol.

4.7.1   DoD

4.7.1.1   *DoD IP*

The Internet Protocol (IP) is the most basic protocol in the TCP/IP suite. IP is quite useful without TCP, but TCP is never used without IP. IP provides addresses, basic packet fragmentation and reassembly, various options, and a rudimentary checksum.

4.7.1.2   *ICMP*

The Internet Control Message Protocol (ICMP) is required to be implemented with IP, and provides routing and management functions, including host and network redirects in response to packets originally routed to the wrong place and fast acknowledgments useful in timekeeping.

4.7.2   ISO

4.7.2.1   *ISO-IP*

The ISO-OSI internet protocol provides the Connection-less mode Network Service (CLNS) and is sometimes known as ISO-IP. It is largely based on DoD's IP and is specified in DIS 8473, plus commentary in RFC994 [ISO 1987a]. It is used in MAP and TOP.

4.7.2.2   *ES-IS*

The End System to Intermediate System Routing Exchange Protocol (ES-IS) for ISO8473 is specified in ANSIx353.3, also available as RFC995, and provides services somewhat similar to those of ICMP.

4.8   *Transport Protocols*

The *transport layer* is concerned with communications between processes on nodes rather than just communications among nodes, as in the network layer. The basic unit of data is the *message*, submitted from higher layers (and perhaps preserving boundaries set by the final end user process), which may have its own header, perhaps including a checksum or other information. Messages must be encapsulated in network layer *packets*, and since messages may be long and packets are often of limited size, this may involve *fragmentation* on transmission and *reassembly* on receipt. (The network layer sometimes does this to packets in fitting them into frames.) Either the transport layer or the network layer must multiplex packets among the processes using the network. For this purpose, there is an additional identifier, the *port*, which is used in addition to the network layer address of the host in identifying a process.

There are many kinds of possible transport services, and thus many kinds of possible transport protocols, depending on their degree of reliability, ordering, preservation of record boundaries, and connection orientation [Bertsekas and Gallager 1987, 24–25].

4.8.1   TCP/IP Transport Protocols

4.8.1.1   *TCP*

The Transmission Control Protocol (TCP) is one of the main protocols commonly used over IP. TCP provides reliable, ordered, end to end delivery of byte streams. It is used by applications such as TELNET, FTP, and SMTP.

4.8.1.2   *UDP*

The User Datagram Protocol (UDP) is a minimal transport protocol designed for use over IP. UDP essentially provides applications with direct access to the datagram service of the IP layer, which attempts to deliver datagrams but does not guarantee order or success of delivery, although a minimal checksum is applied. UDP is typically used by applications that do not need the reliable delivery service of more powerful transport protocols such as TCP, or that need access to specialized services such as multicast or broadcast delivery, which reliable transport protocols do not offer.

A surprising number of applications have been built over this very simple service. Examples include NFS, SNMP, and many *Internet* routing protocols.

4.8.1.3   *RDP*

The Reliable Data Protocol (RDP) is a reliable, connection-oriented transport protocol similar to TP4. While it is not widely implemented [Partridge 1987], its specification in RFC908 [Velten et al. 1984] contains a number of innovative features such as selective acknowledgments, some of which have been incorporated into TCP; see RFC1072 [Jacobson and Braden 1988].

4.8.1.4   *NETBLT*

NETBLT is a protocol designed for high-throughput bulk data transmission applications, even over unreliable long-delay data paths [Clark et al. 1987a]. There are implementations at least for **UNIX** on Sun workstations, for **MS-DOS** on IBM PC/ATs, and for the Symbolics **LISP** machine. This protocol is the current holder of the long-delay/high-bandwidth pipe speed record, achieving transmissions using 92 percent and more of the 1Mbps bandwidth of the very long and high variance delay satellite network *WIDEBAND* [Clark et al. 1987b, 311].

4.8.2   ISO-OSI Transport Protocols

4.8.2.1   *TP0*

TP0 is the preferred transport protocol in much of Europe for use directly over X.25 and under X.400 and other application protocols.

4.8.2.2   *TP2*

TP2 is designed especially for use over X.25, although Europeans mostly prefer to use TP0, in the belief that their X.25 services are sufficiently robust not to need assistance in reliability. See the section on RARE in Chapter 8.

4.8.2.3   *TP4*

TP4 provides reliable end to end data connections and is largely based on TCP, partly as a result of the efforts of the National Bureau of Standards (NBS), now known as the National Institute of Standards and Technology (NIST), which was convinced that the functionality of TCP was needed in TP4. In Europe, TP4 and ISO-IP are mostly not used, in favor of X.400 and similar protocols directly on top of X.25.

Differences between TP4 and TCP include the following [McKenzie 1985]:

- Use of structures and naming conventions common to the other four ISO transport protocols
- A prohibition against sending into a closed window and a way of announcing that a window is now open (otherwise, a sender would have to continue sending into a closed window until it opened, and this is expensive on networks that charge per message)
- Preservation of fragmentation buffer sizes as transmission units for performance
- No graceful close [Partridge 1988a].

There is a portable implementation called **OSIAM_C**, marketed by MARBEN Informatique in Europe and by OMNICOM in the United States [Carpenter et al. 1987].

4.8.3   Other Transport Protocols

4.8.3.1   *Yellow Book*

The *JANET* Network Independent Transport Service (NITS) is specified in the Yellow Book [SG3 1980], which has two related books, one about the use of the protocol over asynchronous lines [TSIG 1983] and the other about a common programming interface [JNT 1985b].

4.8.3.2   *Digital Transport*

DNA distinguishes an *end communications layer*, corresponding roughly to the ISO-OSI transport layer. The DECNET protocol in this layer is the Network Service Protocol (NSP), which provides a reliable, sequenced, connection-oriented service, including multiplexing of data links and isolation from transient lower layer errors [Lauck et al. 1986].

4.9   *Session Protocols*

The *session layer* is used in setting up a *session* — that is, a sequence of related communications. This may involve mapping different kinds of addresses or checking access rights [Bertsekas and Gallager 1987, 26]. The session layer is primarily an ISO (and IBM SNA) invention, but one can stretch the definition and include the UCB **4.3BSD** socket mechanism and AT&T TLI, as is done here. DNA distinguishes a session layer and usually has recognizable software modules to implement it [Lauck et al. 1986]. There are also some session features of the TCP/IP TELNET protocol. Other TCP/IP application protocols, such as FTP and SMTP, also tend to have session features; see the comments and references later in this chapter. This phenomenon is also common in other protocol suites because of the late development of the session layer.

4.9.1   ISO Session Protocols

4.9.1.1   *X.215, X.225, ISO8326, ISO8327*

For some comments on the ISO-OSI session layer, which is specified in X.215, X.225, ISO8326, and ISO8327, see Caneschi 1986.

4.9.2   Other Session Protocols

4.9.2.1   *UCB Sockets*

When the Computer Systems Research Group (CSRG) of the University of California at Berkeley (UCB) was charged by DARPA with producing a DoD standard research version of UNIX, including networking facilities compatible with those then in use on the *ARPANET* and with those forthcoming on the *Internet* (i.e., TCP/IP), they produced the socket interface [Leffler et al. 1989].

4.9.2.2   *AT&T TLI*

The AT&T Transport Layer Interface (TLI) is an elaboration of the UCB socket mechanism, with the intent of generalizing from the TCP/IP orientation of the socket interface, particularly in order to accommodate AT&T Remote File System (RFS) and ISO ISO-OSI protocols.

4.10   *Presentation Protocols*

The *presentation layer* is concerned with encoding and decoding data, perhaps involving conversion with dissimilar host operating system encodings, and perhaps with compression or encryption [Bertsekas and Gallager 1987, 26–27]. This level may include presentation formats such as the ASCII and EBCDIC character codes, or sophisticated encoding schemes for complex data. It is not as well defined as some others, such as transport, even though the idea is quite old, having been considered in the early days of the *ARPANET* [Anderson 1971]. Many application protocols such as FTP and TELNET include presentation features. A useful and lucid survey of some major well-defined presentation protocols may be found in Partridge and Rose 1988. Possibly the most widely used nontrivial presentation format is the RFC822 TCP/IP mail format, which is the basis for mail systems on many networks.

4.10.1   Character Codes

4.10.1.1   *ASCII*

The American Standard Code for the Interchange of Information (ASCII), produced by ANSI, encodes the basic Latin alphabet as used in English with both uppercase and lowercase characters, plus digits, punctuation, and control characters. This is a 7 bit code that is normally transmitted in 8 bits, with the eighth bit sometimes used for parity. There are many variants that use the eighth bit to allow encoding more characters in order to handle other European languages or that redefine some of the punctuation characters for the same purpose. Since all of these are sometimes collectively referred to as ASCII, in this book the term USASCII is sometimes used when emphasis on the original encoding is important.

4.10.1.2   *EBCDIC*

IBM produced the Extended Binary Coded Decimal Interchange Code (EBCDIC) at about the same time as the development of ASCII and for the same purposes. EBCDIC differs somewhat in having only one case for letters. There are also many variants of it, and this can affect networking, as *BITNET* has discovered in practice.

4.10.1.3   *ISO8859*

ISO has defined an 8 bit character set as a superset of ASCII in order to accommodate most European national character sets. This is ISO8859/1, or ISO Latin Alphabet 1. This character set was produced by ANSI X3L2 and adopted by ISO, with the assistance of the European Computer Manufacturers Association (ECMA). ISO8859/2 and ISO8859/3 are available for characters not included in ISO8859/1, such as those used in Cyrillic, Welsh, and Basque. ISO6937 handles all these characters in one standard by composing letters of 2 bytes.

4.10.1.4   *Japanese Encodings*

Several encodings of Japanese characters are discussed in Section 14.3.1. These include JIS X 0208, ISO2022, JIS X 0202, JIS X 0201, Digital Kanji, and Shift-JIS.

4.10.2   **ISO-OSI Presentation Protocols**

The most influential current presentation protocol is probably the ISO-OSI ASN.1 protocol.

4.10.2.1   *ASN.1*

Abstract Syntax Notation One (ASN.1) is the standard promulgated by ISO for describing and encoding data structures. It is specified in two parts, one on data types [ISO 1987b; CCITT 1988a] and one on binary representation [ISO 1987c; CCITT 1988b]. These are derived from the X.400 encoding scheme given in CCITT X.409. ASN.1 uses tagged types—that is, some type information is prefixed to each data element. It allows construction of composite types from primitive types, as well as nesting of types within the data part of other types, and data elements of variable length. The specification language is quite abstract, and several different implementation techniques have been used, as in **ISODE**, HEMS, and SNMP. This is possibly the most general of the current presentation syntaxes and is perhaps too general to be readily and efficiently implemented [Partridge and Rose 1988].

4.10.3 Other Presentation Protocols

4.10.3.1 *XEROX Courier*

The most influential of the early presentation development efforts was Courier, developed by XEROX [XEROX 1981a; XEROX 1981b]. It strongly influenced most of the later presentation specifications mentioned below.

4.10.3.2 *Sun XDR*

A very popular presentation method, because it is used in Sun Microsystem's Network File System (NFS), is their External Data Representation (XDR) language [Sun 1987], which is usually used with their Remote Procedure Call (RPC). Unlike ASN.1, XDR does not use tag or length fields except where there is no choice. Constructed types are allowed, but the basic type set is not as flexible as that of ASN.1 (although anything that can be encoded in ASN.1 can apparently be encoded in XDR). Efficiency is catered to by padding fields to 4 byte boundaries to simplify alignment and byte ordering problems. The specification of the language looks much like the C programming language [Ritchie et al. 1978; Kernighan and Ritchie 1978], making it easy for programmers to understand and easy for XDR to be defined as an extension of it. Most implementations follow that of Sun in being stub compilers [Partridge and Rose 1988].

4.10.3.3 *Apollo NDR*

As part of their NCA, Apollo Computer has specified a Network Data Representation (NDR) language [Dineen et al. 1987]. NDR is the data encoding specification; it is used with Apollo's Network Interface Definition Language (NIDL), which specifies the types to be encoded. There are few data type tags, but there is a format label that precedes a data stream and whose purpose is to specify the machine type, which in turn implies many data type characteristics. Data are actually sent in the format natural to the sending machine. If a foreign machine is of a different type, it converts data formats on reception; if the foreign machine is of the same type as the sender, no conversion is necessary. Like Sun's XDR, NDR is intended to be closely related to standard procedural programming languages, although it is not specifically tied to a particular language. This method is intended to be, and usually is, compiled. Also like XDR, NDR is efficient (at least with a small number of machine types), but does not allow specification of as rich a set of types as ASN.1. The especially distinguishing feature of NDR is the multiple machine formats used in data transferred over the network. Each machine must recognize numerous types, and there is no obvious mechanism for adding new types globally to existing implementations. Thus, it is not clear whether this technique scales well [Partridge and Rose 1988].

4.10.4   TCP/IP Presentation Protocols

The earliest presentation protocols may have been the *ARPANET* ones for remote login, file transfer, and mail format. Although the early versions of these were used over NCP, the current ones are usually used with TCP/IP.

4.10.4.1   *TELNET*

The TCP/IP remote login protocol, TELNET, has certain presentation features that are used in other TCP/IP protocols, such as FTP and SMTP. The most basic is the idea of a Network Virtual Terminal (NVT) — that is, a uniform format for transmission of data over the network. Local data streams are converted into that format for transmission and back out at receipt; this avoids having every implementation interpret the data formats of every known host type. Since its development on the early *ARPANET*, this idea has been widely used in later protocols, such as X.29, and in later networks, such as *CYCLADES, Telenet, EIN, Datapac,* and *EPSS* [Davidson et al. 1977]. This format uses USASCII 7 bit characters, with the two character sequence of carriage return and line feed as the line terminator, and this much of the format is common to FTP and SMTP.

4.10.4.2   *FTP*

The TCP/IP File Transfer Protocol (FTP) uses (in addition to the basic presentation features derived from TELNET and mentioned in the previous section) several data formats that are intended to be abstract enough to be implemented on most host operating systems, as well as a few that are specific to certain host types.

4.10.4.3   *RFC822*

The format of mail used in the *Internet* is given by RFC822 [Crocker 1982]. This document specifies a format for messages but does not specify delivery mechanisms. The format is quite simple and is encoded entirely in 7 bit USASCII as lines of text. This is its main strength, as it can be implemented on almost any system, and users can even make up their own headers. It is also its major weakness: languages that require other character sets are hard to support, and there is no structure provided for either the headers or the body of the message, making multimedia mail hard. Because this format is widely used in many networks, including ones that use no other DoD or TCP/IP protocols or formats, it is described in some detail here.

The basic format involves a set of *headers* and the *body* of the message. No *envelope* of delivery information is specified, although the document acknowledges that such an envelope may appear as additional header fields. The headers come first and are terminated by a blank line. The rest of the message is the body and has no format imposed on it; the body is not even required to be present.

The basic header format is a line with a *field-name* and a *field-body*. The *field-name* is terminated by a colon followed by a space, cannot contain white space, and can contain only printable ASCII characters; the *field-body* can contain any ASCII characters (except carriage return or newline, and many systems do strange things with control characters, regardless of what RFC822 says). A header line may be folded onto several ASCII lines by replacing any white space in the field-body with a newline followed by at least one white space character. For example,

        To: jsq, jbc, joe

and

        To: jsq,
          jbc, joe

are equivalent.

The newline marker is the two character ASCII carriage return and line feed sequence, as in TELNET NVT. This specific sequence is only required for interchange of messages between machines, just as all of RFC822 is intended to constrain only intermachine transfer of messages. Local mail systems may (and do) use some other newline indicator in storage and interpretation of RFC822 messages.

Uppercase and lowercase are equivalent in field-names—e.g., these are all equivalent:

        From:
        FROM:
        from:
        fRoM:

A field-body may require case folding in whole or in part according to its field-name. In general, mailbox addresses of the form *user@domain* require the domain part (to the right of the at sign) to be folded, while case must be preserved in the local part (to the left of the at sign). An exception is the local part *postmaster*, which must be recognized in any mixture of cases; this is the only local part required by RFC822 and should cause mail to be delivered to someone responsible for the mail system on the host named by the domain part of the address.

Some headers are required by SMTP, and others are optional. Some have very specific formats imposed for their field-bodies, and others do not. Table 4.6 lists all of the headers mentioned in RFC822 (and a few others). For details of header formats, see RFC822 [Crocker 1982]. Many user interfaces deliberately do not display all headers of a message.

Received: lines are the headers most commonly ignored by user interfaces because they accumulate as a message travels.

Message-ID: is also often ignored for display because it means little to the user. Its field-body is usually composed using the source domain name and a sequence number, but it should be interpreted as an unstructured text string. This field is very important for detecting loops in mailing lists.

Reply-To: is often used by mailing list moderators to direct replies back to the moderator while leaving in the original *From:* field found in a submitter's message when posting it to the list. It can also be used to send mail by proxy for someone who does not actually have a mailbox — i.e., to use with a fake *From:* address.

From: specifies the logical sender of the message and may be supplied by the user; otherwise it must be added by the mail delivery software. This field must refer to a mailbox of a specific user (or several such mailboxes) and not to a redistribution list. *Reply-To:* can refer to a list.

Sender: is added by the mail delivery system if *From:* was supplied by the user and does not match the real sender. This feature appears to have been designed to allow secretaries to send mail for their bosses or for a single person to send mail on behalf of a group. The *Sender:* header itself, like the *From:* header, can only contain addresses of personal mailboxes.

To: specifies the mailbox of the intended recipient of the message. *Cc:* specifies additional recipients, and *Bcc:* specifies recipients which other recipients will not be informed about. Either *To:* or *Cc:* is required, and either one, if present, must have at least one address.

Addresses used in *Reply-To:, From:, Sender:, To:, Cc:, Bcc:,* or other headers that require addresses in the field-body should *always* be fully qualified domain addresses — i.e., not just Jane or some other abbreviation such as Jane@VAX, but Jane@VAX.CS.BIGU.EDU, which is a complete address. The mail delivery software on every host should expand abbreviations to full domain addresses when sending any mail to another machine. This is often overlooked by implementers but is very important, as anyone who has tried to reply to messages containing such addresses can attest.

Table 4.6. *RFC822 headers*

Field-name	Type	Description
Tracing		
Date:	Date[†]	Specific date format; by source machine
Message-ID:	Msg-id[†]	Unique per message; by source machine
Received:	[†]	By each machine on route
Return-Path:	Source route	By final recipient machine
Source addresses		
Reply-To:	Mailbox	User-specified reply address
From:	Mailbox[†]	Added by mailer if not present; for error messages if no *Sender:* field
Sender:	Mailbox	Required if *From:* not real sender; for error messages if present
Target addresses: *To:* or *Cc:* is required		
To:	Mailbox[†]	Primary addressee(s)
Cc:	Mailbox	Secondary addressee(s) (carbon copies)
Bcc:	Mailbox	Addressee(s) invisible to others (blind carbon copies)
Context		
Subject:	Text	Topic description
In-Reply-To:	Text/msg-id	Refers to a previous message
References:	Text/msg-id	Refers to other previous messages
Keywords:	Text	Keywords or phrases, separated by commas
Comments:	Text	Comments message without disturbing body
Encrypted:	Two words	Software type and decryption key; headers may not be encrypted
Forwarding: all optional, types as for corresponding headers above		
Resent-Date:		
Resent-Message-ID:		
Resent-From:		
Resent-Reply-To:		
Resent-To:		
Resent-cc:		
Resent-bcc:		
Extension fields		
*:	Varies	Specified in an extension to RFC822
X-*:	Text	Excluded from RFC822 extensions
User defined fields		
Errors-To:	Address	For **sendmail** error delivery
*:	Text	Anything not otherwise specified

[†] Required headers.

Subject: is used to supply a brief description of the topic of the message. By convention (not specified by RFC822), replies to a message have *Re:* prepended to the field-body of the original *Subject:* header so that chains of messages on the same topic can be readily identified. This header and this reply convention are optional but very useful. The original *Subject:* header, before any replies, is ordinarily supplied by the user.

Resent-*: headers, such as *Resent-To:*, are intended for use when mail is forwarded and the original headers are to be preserved. Attributes of the forwarder are recorded in the *Resent-*:* headers.

There is no requirement for order of headers, except that they must all come before the message body. It is permitted, but not encouraged, to have multiple address fields of the same type in the same message, such as several *To:* fields.

4.11   *Application Protocols*

The *application layer* provides services to end users, which may be people or other protocols or programs, or people. The order of presentation here is the same as in Chapter 2 — that is, batch CMC, interactive CMC, interactive resource sharing, and batch resource sharing. The order of service types within the categories is also the same as in Chapter 2.

To save space, not every *Internet* RFC or ISO document specifying a protocol is referenced when referred to in this book. The appropriate specifications may be found in Tables 4.2 through 4.5 and ordered according to the information already given.

4.12   *Batch CMC*

4.12.1   **Mail**

In addition to mail formats and protocols used on specific networks and those that are used on many different networks, mail is also used across networks that have different underlying mail protocols and formats. More details are given in Section 5.6.3, as well as in Chapter 9.

4.12.1.1   *SMTP*

The mail transfer protocol used in the *Internet*, Simple Mail Transfer Protocol (SMTP), is specified in RFC821 [Postel 1982], as augmented by RFC974 [Partridge 1986]. SMTP defines an envelope to be used in delivering messages that are in RFC822 format, as well as commands and conventions for performing the delivery. Many other networks use RFC822 format without SMTP. There is an associated Domain Name Scheme (DNS) (see Chapter 5).

The most notorious implementation of SMTP and RFC822 is probably **sendmail**, which also handles converting mail formats and addressing structures of various other types, particularly that of UUCP, and is extensible to do almost anything because it is a Post machine. This is the **4.2BSD** and **4.3BSD UNIX** mail system [Allman 1983; Allman and Amos 1985]. **MMDF** is an implementation of SMTP that was developed for *CSNET*. There is a **Pascal** version called **PMDF** [Szurkowski 1980; Crocker et al. 1979; Crocker et al. 1983; Long 1987].

4.12.1.2   *BSMTP*

BSMTP format as used in *BITNET* is shown in Table 4.7. The name of the sending host appears three times, in the *HELO, MAIL FROM:*, and *From:* headers. The sending user's user name appears twice, in the *MAIL FROM:* and *From:* headers. The number in the *TICK* header is a sequence number used to distinguish messages from the same sender; some user interfaces supply it. There can be up to ten *RCPT TO:* lines, and their contents should match entries in the *To:* BSMTP fields. Everything between *DATA* and *QUIT* is in RFC822 message format. The *Date:, From:, To:*, and *Subject:* headers correspond to RFC822 and RFC974; other RFC822 headers could also be used for target networks that recognize RFC822. The period on the line before *QUIT* is the SMTP terminator and is required, as is the blank line before the SMTP headers. Addresses must be in SMTP format — i e , with an at sign. To send mail that requires some other syntax, such as *UUCP* source routing, it is necessary to specify indirection through the gateway host, as in

> To: h1!h2!*host*!*user*@PSUVAX1

Finally, all lines must be limited to 80 characters. Even this doesn't suffice for lines that start with periods (as is common with input source for some text formatters). A leading period is doubled by SMTP in order to avoid its inadvertent interpretation. If the line was already 80 characters long, the last character on the line will be lost (this actually happens) [da Cruz 1988].

4.12.1.3   *Grey Book*

The JNT mail format and protocol is specified in the Grey Book [Kille 1984], and is related to RFC821 and RFC822. It has an associated Name Registration Scheme (NRS) (see Chapter 5).

Table 4.7. *BSMTP in BITNET*

HELO *host*.BITNET
VERB ON
TICK nnnn
MAIL FROM:*user@host*.BITNET
RCPT TO:*user@domain*
DATA
Date: whenever
From: *user@host*.BITNET
To: *user@domain*
Subject: <optional>
<blank line>
<arbitrary number of lines of text>
.
QUIT

4.12.1.4   *XEROX Grapevine*

The *XEROX Internet* includes the implementation of Grapevine, one of the earliest distributed electronic message handling systems that supports services such as a hierarchical name system, authentication, resource location, and device access [Schroeder et al. 1984].

4.12.1.5   *X.400*

X.400 is the ISO-OSI Message Handling System (MHS) specification. Message-Oriented Text Interchange System (MOTIS) is a related term. X.400 is used in academic and research networks such as *Ean*, *DFN*, and *ARISTOTE*, as well as in a growing number of commercial networks. It is basically different from RFC822, SMTP, and Grey Book in several ways:

- Structure is provided for both the headers and the body of the message, with the intent of being able to support multimedia mail.
- Address and other header information is recorded in binary form, and there is no single canonical textual representation.
- Addresses are expressed in the form of attributes, by use of enough of which sufficient information is given to specify a target.

Some details of X.400 attributes may be found in the description of mail gateways in Chapter 5. A complete description of this protocol, comprising as it does many sub-specifications in many documents, is beyond the scope of this book, despite the importance of this standard.

4.12.1.6   *MMM*

DARPA has sponsored a long series of multimedia mail experiments [Reynolds et al. 1985]. An implementation at Stanford Research Institute (SRI), **MMM**, proves that the concepts are implementable and usable [Postel et al. 1986].

4.12.1.7   *Diamond*

The Diamond multimedia message system allows the integration of text, graphics, images, voice, and other forms of information in a document that can be transmitted over a network [Thomas et al. 1985]. Diamond is also known as Slate [Long 1988] and was developed at BBN.

4.12.1.8   *EXPRES*

EXPRES is a multimedia mail project sponsored by the National Science Foundation (NSF) and partly based on work done at the University of Michigan (Michigan).

4.12.2   Lists

4.12.2.1   *Digests*

The *Internet* de facto standard for mailing list digests is RFC934 [Rose and Stefferud 1985]. It specifies the separators to use between messages within a *digest* so that user interface software can read them; this is known as *encapsulation* of messages during *forwarding*. It includes guidelines for *bursting* digests into individual messages so that normal mail software mechanisms may be used for replies or redistribution. The format is based on RFC822, using lines in the body starting with dash characters to separate forwarded messages. The special case of a dash followed by a space is prepended to actual text lines that start with a dash. Each forwarded message within a pair of such separators must have *From:* and *Date:* header fields, but it is not required to have a *To:*, *Cc:*, or *Bcc:* field. RFC934 also makes a case for handling *Bcc:* copies of messages by forwarding the original message to the *Bcc:* recipients.

4.12.2.2   *LISTSERV*

LISTSERV is the *EARN* (and *BITNET* and *NetNorth*) mailing list management software, written by Eric Thomas, then of the Ecole Centrale in Paris, about July 1986. Users can add and remove themselves from a list by sending a message with SUBSCRIBE or UNSUBSCRIBE in the message body (any *Subject:* headers are ignored, since NJE does not require the use of RFC822 or other formats that include such a header). It is not necessary to send such a message to the distribution machine for the list of interest. The message can be sent to any host that supports LISTSERV and will be forwarded automatically to the correct machine [Thomas 1988].

A list breaks itself up into pieces automatically, in a way that minimizes routing hops and duplication for individual messages [da Cruz 1988]. The algorithm is called *DIST2*. For a complete list of **LISTSERV** lists, send the command

LIST Global

to any **LISTSERV**. The information returned is automatically maintained by the software. For a brief description of most lists, send the command

GET LISTSERV GROUPS

to LISTSERV@BITNIC: this list is maintained manually. Any of these commands can be sent either in mail or as an NJE interactive message [Thomas 1988].

Any number of commands can be put in a single message. Other commands allow searching archives of lists and some other databases, including the list of lists and the *EARN* node database. This permits retrieving only selected pieces, thus reducing the network load. There are plans to provide a new User Directory Database (UDD) to replace the User Directory Service (UDS) currently provided by **NETSERV**. The new UDD is intended to allow keywords to be associated with both users and lists, which in turn will allow users to more easily determine which lists are of interest [Thomas 1988].

4.12.3   Conferencing

There are few standards for conferencing, and no ISO-OSI ones [Karrenberg 1988]. But there are many techniques, implementations, and services used in actual networks.

A basic technical difference distinguishing conferencing systems from mail systems is that the former need multicast or broadcast transport mechanisms to support them, while the latter can get along with unicast mechanisms. This and other technical issues related to the extent and method of distribution of the message database (such as compression on transmission and storage of one copy of a message per machine rather than per user) are not highly visible to the users of conferencing systems. They are nonetheless useful in understanding conferencing systems.

4.12.3.1   *Structure Within Conferences*

A useful classification of conferencing software is by the structure it imposes on conferences. Most such software supports a set of conferences on general topics that exist for a long time. There are three common kinds of structure imposed on messages *within* conferences [Cook 1987] — that is, on *conversation* [Palme 1988]:

Line structure was found in early systems such as *EMISARI* and *EIES*, which simply stored and displayed messages in linear chronological order. Early *USENET* news software worked like this. This is probably still the most common kind of system.

Tree (branching) software allows users to form branches from the basic line at any point and to branch the branches by the same mechanisms. Examples of such software include **COM**, **Participate**, *PLATO*, **VAXnotes**, and **notesfiles**. The *USENET* news interface **rn** gives the user the impression of such a structure by taking identical *Subject:* headers to indicate branches. Different software allows different actions on trees and branches. **PortaCOM** allows scanning a conversation but not skipping part of it. **COM** allows skipping messages that have already arrived when the command to skip is given but does not allow skipping future messages. **Participate** allows skipping a whole conversation but not a single branch. **Super-COM** allows skipping any tree or branch, for any messages, whether they are already present or forthcoming. The **rn** program already handles all these possibilities.

Star (item and response) structure is a compromise produced because many users find tree-structured conferences hard to follow. Some software, such as **Confer** and, more recently, **Caucus**, takes a middle ground of permitting branches from the basic linear conference stream, but not branches from branches. That is, when someone posts a message that raises a new topic, it is called an *item*, and a message posted in response to such an item is called a *response*. The software often presents the user with new responses to items that the user has previously read before presenting new items. This produces a star-structured conference.

There are other possibilities of organization or presentation, such as allowing the user to attach keywords to each message, and allowing the user to choose messages by combinations of keywords or by searches of the full text for words of interest, perhaps in logical combinations. *EIES* (keywords), Participate (full text searches), and **rn** (both) support some such possibilities. Most of these systems and software allow closed conferences that are limited to a list of participants fixed by the moderator; *USENET* news is an exception.

4.12.3.2   *Structure Among Conferences*

In addition to structure and presentation of messages within individual conferences, conferences themselves may be grouped in a tree structure by topic in order to make finding the appropriate conference easier. Confer, CoSy, and Caucus allow at least two levels of such grouping. *USENET* software handles an arbitrary number of levels, and some *newsgroup* classifications go four or five levels deep. COM and PortaCOM do not allow this kind of nesting, but SuperCOM will allow any number of levels [Palme 1988].

Some systems allow messages that appear in more than one place to be seen only once by the reader. *USENET* does this for articles in newsgroups, and COM, PortaCOM, and SuperCOM do it for messages in both conferences and personal mailboxes. *Tandem* does this for messages in personal mailboxes.

There has to be a means for creating a new conference. On single machine systems, this is usually done by the system operator. In *USENET*, any administrator of any news system can create a new newsgroup, although getting political consensus to do so may take a long time. **SuperCOM** will allow a moderator to split one conference into several, to carry information from the original into the new ones, and to do this across a distributed system [Palme 1988].

4.12.3.3   *Logistics of Conferencing*

The following subsections give brief notes on some of the more widely distributed conferencing software and protocols. The order of presentation is roughly according to the number of machines the software runs on, most first. Some other conferencing software is described in sections on specific systems, particularly those on *EMISARI, EIES, QZCOM,* and *PLATO*. See Chapter 7 for a guide to the historical interrelations of this software and these systems.

A few factors appear to be strongly related to the success of conferencing software, measured as the number of machines it runs on or the number of people who use it. In order of importance, these factors seem to be as follows:

Price: the most widely used conferencing software in the world is **B news 2.11** and **echomail**, both of which are free. Inexpensive and well-marketed software such as **Caucus** also has a distinct advantage.

Portability and distributability: software that runs on only one machine type is limited to the users of that machine type (some early software was further limited to a single machine). Portability permits not only vendor independence, but also the use of machines of widely varying sizes.

Software written in a portable language, such as **C**, or on a portable operating system, such as **UNIX**, is more easily portable than other software. **Caucus, PortaCOM, SuperCOM, B news 2.11, echomail, CoSy,** and others are all portable. Distributing the information databases of conferences across multiple machines allows supporting more and more geographically dispersed users, as in **VAXnotes, B news 2.11, echomail,** and eventually **SuperCOM.**

User interface: simple, and perhaps menu-driven, user interfaces are needed to make systems accessible to new users, but fast user interfaces are needed for experienced users.

Structure of information: there are advantages to star or tree structure for messages within a conference, but a linear system with all the other advantages listed previously will still have an edge over a well-structured system lacking any of those advantages.

4.12.3.4   *News*

B news 2.11, written by Rick Adams, with suggestions and code from many people, is the current version of **B news**, the most widely used variety of the *USENET* news software. Details about it (and about **C news, A news,** and **notesfiles**) are given in the *USENET* section in Chapter 10. There are also full implementations for **VMS** and for IBM **VM** [Spafford 1988]. A news *message* is usually called an *article*, and the basic format, which is modeled after RFC822, is given in RFC1036 [Horton and Adams 1987].

4.12.3.5   *NNTP*

The Network News Transfer Protocol (NNTP) [Kantor and Lapsley 1986] is the common method of transferring *USENET* news over TCP/IP networks. It was produced by Brian Kantor of the University of California at San Diego (UCSD) and Phil Lapsley and Erik Fair of the University of California at Berkeley (UCB), with later help from Steven Grady, Mike Meyer, and others at Berkeley. There are news reading client NNTP implementations available for Digital's **VMS** and **TOPS-20** operating systems, as well as full implementations of NNTP for **UNIX**.

4.12.3.6   *notesfiles*

The **UNIX notesfiles** implementation was done by Ray Essick and Rob Kolstad and is related to the *PLATO* **NOTES** system. This **notesfiles** software is also closely related to **VAXnotes**, by their common parent, **NOTES**. The **rn** program, used with **B news**, has much of the functionality of the **notesfiles** user interface. The **notesfiles** software is described under *USENET*.

4.12.3.7   *echomail*

For **echomail**, see *FidoNet* in Chapter 10.

4.12.3.8   *VAXnotes*

VAXnotes is a Digital conferencing system that is now available as a product, even though it was originally developed in 1980 as a private project of a member of the **VMS** development group. It is modeled largely after the *PLATO* **NOTES** conferencing software. In 1984 it was rewritten to be distributed and to separate the user interface software from the database server software. It became an officially sanctioned project as it was being finished in 1985. It was released to customers in March 1986. VAXnotes is widely used in *EASYnet* [Cook 1987] and in *Starlink*.

4.12.3.9   *Participate*

Participate, or PARTI for short, was developed by C. H. "Harry" Stevens, original president of Participation Systems Incorporated, and George Reinhardt. This software was influenced by EIES 1. There was a predecessor system called TOPICS that ran on *EIES*. It was written by Peter Johnson-Lanz and Trudy Johnson-Lanz (inventors of the term *groupware*) with Harry Stevens and had a sort of rudimentary branching structure [Cook 1988]. Participate was apparently the first to introduce branching tree-structured conferences in order to facilitate what Stevens calls *inquiry networking*. This new software was first made available to the general public on *The Source* [Meeks 1985]. The implementation for Participate was done in 1981 for **Primos** on Prime computers and has since been ported to Digital **VMS** and IBM operating systems. The software is also used on *Dialcom* and inside numerous large corporations [Cook 1987]. Stevens is now with a new company, EVentures, which distributes **Participate**.

4.12.3.10   *CoSy*

The CoSy (Conferencing System) conferencing software was developed by Alastair J. W. Mayer at the University of Guelph (Guelph) in Ontario [Meeks 1985]. CoSy is similar to both EIES 1 and Participate but is not directly descended from either; it may be related to COM. The software is written for **UNIX** and is thus portable to many base systems (there is apparently also a **VMS** version). There are various other explanations for the acronym, including Collaboration System, Conversational Syncretism, and Conduité à Synérgie. This software is used on the system at Guelph that originally produced it (among other places) and is described in the *CoSy* section of Chapter 12.

4.12.3.11   *GENIE*

GENIE was developed by Stephen Heitmann and has sophisticated database locking techniques that allow group editing of documents. It is intended for scientific and engineering users [Meeks 1985].

4.12.3.12   *Caucus*

Caucus is a descendant of Confer and is distributed by Metasystems Design Group (MDG); see *THE META NETWORK* in Chapter 21. It was created by Charles Roth of Ann Arbor, Michigan, and Camber-Roth, a division of Aule-Tek, Inc., of Troy, New York [Burns 1988]. The software runs on **VMS; UNIX (XENIX, Ultrix, 4.3BSD, System V**, and other versions); **MS-DOS** on IBM PCs; **VM** on mainframes; **Primos** of Prime and Novell NetWare. It is also used by *Dialcom* [Cook 1987]. All system produced user interface text displayed by the software is taken from an ASCII text dictionary file. System managers may edit this file for different classes of end users — e.g., for different levels of experience or different native languages. There may be several such dictionaries on line, and the user can choose among them [Cook 1988].

4.12.3.13   *Confer*

Confer was developed by Robert Parnes in 1975 on a mainframe at Wayne State University (Wayne State). It is also used by administrators at Hewlett-Packard (HP) and by some other government and commercial organizations, including *Army Forum* of the U.S. Army. Confer was apparently the first system to introduce star-structured conferences [Meeks 1985]. Its user interface can be customized to some extent [Morabito 1986] and is based on commands rather than menus, for speed. The current version of the software is called **Confer II** [Advertel 1988]. Most of the features of Confer have been incorporated in Caucus. See *Confer* in Chapter 7 and *Army Forum* in Chapter 12.

4.12.3.14   *COM*

See *QZCOM* for COM, a very influential conferencing system, KOM, the Swedish language version of COM, PortaCOM, a recent portable reimplementation of both, and SuperCOM, a reimplementation with many new features and related software packages.

4.12.3.15   *EIES*

See the section on the *EIES* conferencing system for EIES software.

4.13   *Interactive CMC*

4.13.1   One-to-One

One-to-one interactive CMC is widely implemented on time-sharing systems as **talk** on **4.3BSD UNIX** systems, **PHONE** on **VMS**, and **TALK** on **TOPS-20**. The *EIES* equivalent is **LINK**.

4.13.2   One-to-Many

There is a public domain program called **phone** that does this on **UNIX** systems.

4.13.3   Many-to-Many

International conferences of this type are common on systems such as *EIES*.

4.14   *Interactive Resource Sharing*

4.14.1   Remote Login

Remote login, the most basic interactive resource sharing service, is implemented on most networks of dedicated links.

4.14.1.1   *TELNET*

TELNET is the standard TCP/IP remote login protocol. *ARPANET* and *MILNET* support special hosts called Terminal Access Controllers (TACs) that allow dialup use of TELNET to reach hosts on the *Internet*.

4.14.1.2   *rlogin*

The rlogin protocol was invented by UCB CSRG for **4.2BSD** and provides remote login service in a convenient manner between **UNIX** machines, handling details such as terminal type automatically [Comer 1988, 236 – 237].

4.14.1.3   *Triple-X (XXX)*

Remote login is often handled over X.25 networks by use of the so-called Triple-X, or XXX, set of protocols, which consists of the following:

> X.3, the Packet Assembler Disassembler (PAD), maps between the X.25 interface and what a dumb terminal can handle.
> X.28 defines the interface between the PAD and the terminal.
> X.29 specifies the interface between the PAD and the network.

4.14.1.4   *VT*

ISO is developing a Virtual Terminal (VT) specification that will have more facilities than Triple-X.

4.14.1.5   *Green Book*

The preferred method of using terminals on *JANET* over *PSS* is specified in the Green Book [SG3 1981], which gives recommendations for the use of Triple-X.

4.14.2   File Transfer

4.14.2.1   *FTP*

The TCP/IP file transfer protocol is called File Transfer Protocol (FTP). The convention for *anonymous FTP*, whereby a user may retrieve files from a host without having an individual login account on that host, is to connect with FTP, log in as user *anonymous* (or, on **4.3BSD** systems, as *ftp*), and use any password. The files that can be transferred are normally limited to a small subset of all those on the host, and transfers *to* the host are often prohibited entirely.

4.14.2.2   *rcp*

The rcp protocol was invented by UCB CSRG for **4.2BSD** to provide a file transfer service modeled closely on the **UNIX cp** program.

4.14.2.3   *FTAM*

The ISO-OSI File Transfer, Access and Manipulation (FTAM) protocol is specified in ISO8571 and ISO8572.

4.14.2.4   *Blue Book*

The *JANET* Network Independent File Transfer Protocol (NIFTP) is specified in the Blue Book [FTPIG 1981].

4.14.2.5   *DAP*

The Data Access Protocol (DAP) is the DNA file transfer and access protocol [Lauck et al. 1986].

4.14.3   Remote Procedure Call (RPC)

The purpose of Remote Procedure Call (RPC) is to make accessing a remote resource from a program appear the same as calling a local subroutine. This idea grew from the development of tightly integrated distributed operating systems. It turns out that RPC is a more general tool, and it has become the most common building block for new distributed applications [Partridge 1988a].

4.14.3.1   *ECMA ROS*

The European Computer Manufacturers Association (ECMA) and ISO have developed a Remote Operations Service (ROS), or remote procedure call facility [ECMA 1985; ISO 1988a; ISO 1988b]. There is also an associated Remote EXecution Service (REX), which is a transport protocol. ROS uses ASN.1 as a presentation layer. The design of all of these has been influenced by the Advanced Network Systems Architecture (ANSA) research group, with the goal of providing a system where code for client/server model interactions may be generated automatically (RPC type work), but other types of interaction are also allowed for.

4.14.3.2   *XEROX Courier*

XEROX Courier encompasses both remote procedure call and presentation layer mechanisms and is described later in this chapter as a presentation layer protocol.

4.14.3.3   *Sun RPC*

Sun's Remote Procedure Call (RPC) [Sun 1988] is widely used because of the widespread use of NFS. RPC is largely based on XEROX Courier.

4.14.3.4   *Apollo NCA/RPC*

Apollo Computer has developed a remote procedure call facility, NCA/RPC [Dineen et al. 1987] as part of its NCA to be used with its NDR.

4.14.4   Distributed File Systems (DFS)

Network and distributed file systems have become increasingly popular in the past several years due to the wide availability of fast LAN technology. The idea is not new, however, having been implemented at least as early as 1981 [Popek et al. 1981].

4.14.4.1   *Sun NFS*

Sun Microsystems, Inc. (Sun) produced a Network File System (NFS) about 1984 that has since become very widely used on campus and local area networks [Walsh et al. 1985; Sandberg et al. 1985]. This is called a network, rather than a distributed, file system to emphasize that it is not intended to be a distributed implementation of the **UNIX** file system; rather, it is intended to be a virtual file system that can be implemented on various operating systems. Implementations exist for at least **UNIX**, **VMS**, and

MS-DOS. The protocol is stateless because its designers believed that to be important for robustness, allowing systems and networks to fail and recover without losing context (since there is none to lose). Remote device access and file locking were deliberately left out (though separate protocols were provided later) because they require state. NFS is based on Sun's RPC and XDR and is usually used over UDP and IP.

4.14.4.2   *Apollo Domain*

The Apollo Domain distributed file system is one of the older ones intended for a workstation environment and was designed to scale well into networks of very large numbers of nodes.

4.14.4.3   *AT&T RFS*

The Remote File System (RFS) that is distributed with AT&T's **System V Release 3** version of the **UNIX** operating system is an attempt to extend the **UNIX** file system semantics over a network. Unlike Sun's NFS, it makes no attempt to handle other kinds of operating systems, and it is a stateful protocol. RFS is loosely based on the network file system implemented by Peter Weinberger for **Eighth Edition UNIX**, the version of **UNIX** maintained and used by the original developers of the system at AT&T Bell Laboratories (Bell Labs) [Weinberger 1984; Weinberger 1986]. RFS is strongly based on the **STREAMS** mechanism for implementing network protocols, which, in the form distributed in **System V Release 3**, is based on the **streams** mechanism developed at Bell Labs by Dennis Ritchie and others [Presotto 1986; Presotto and Ritchie 1985; Ritchie 1984].

4.14.5   **Remote File Locking**

See NFS earlier in this chapter.

4.14.6   **Remote Device Access**

See NFS earlier in this chapter.

4.14.7   **Window Management**

4.14.7.1   *Fawn Book*

The Fawn Book specifies a Simple Screen Management Protocol (SSMP) for management of screens of constant pitch and height characters in rectangular matrices [JNT 1985c]. The characters transmitted and displayed are those of ISO646 [ISO 1983], which is identical to USASCII. SSMP is intended to be used with the Green Book interpretation of Triple-X.

4.14.7.2   *X Windows*

X Windows is perhaps the most widely used window system [Scheifler et al. 1988].

4.14.8   Shared Memory

This is used in *Tandem,* and there has also been recent theoretical work on it, such as *Memnet* [Delp et al. 1988].

4.14.9   Distributed Operating Systems

A number of research or commercial operating systems are designed to be distributed. Some of them are mentioned briefly here, with references; these are not all of them. In this book, see also *Tandem* in Chapter 10.

4.14.9.1   *V System*

The **V System** of Stanford is one of the more influential research distributed operating systems [Cheriton 1988].

4.14.9.2   *Mach*

Mach is a reimplementation of the **UNIX** kernel on an object-oriented and distributed basis, starting with the **4.3BSD** kernel and gradually replacing it. **Mach** is done at Carnegie-Mellon University (CMU) and is supported by DARPA through the DSAB [Young et al. 1987; Accetta et al. 1986].

4.14.9.3   *Chorus*

Chorus is a distributed operating system based on **UNIX**. It is object oriented and emphasizes portability, modularity, and scalability [Rozier and Legatheaux-Martins 1987; Rozier et al. 1988; Armand et al. 1986; Armand et al. 1988]. The current kernel, **Chorus-V3**, is a complete reimplementation of **UNIX**, mostly in **C++**, with some parts in **C**. The user level programs are **System V**. Applications may use only **UNIX** facilities, or they may access the **Chorus** IPC mechanisms. **Chorus** draws on early experiences of researchers at the French national research institute INRIA regarding their **Sol** reimplementation of **UNIX** in **Pascal**. Early work on **Chorus** was done at INRIA [Zimmermann et al. 1981; Guillemont 1982; Zimmermann et al. 1984; Banino et al. 1985], where it was instigated by Hubert Zimmermann. He and other researchers formed Chorus systèmes of Montigny-le-Brettoneux, near Paris, which currently develops and markets **Chorus**.

4.14.9.4   *Cronus*

Cronus is an object-oriented system being developed at BBN. It is designed to be independent of underlying hardware, programming languages, and networking technologies and to be interoperable with existing applications and operating systems such as **UNIX, VMS,** and **Genera.** It is also designed to be a complete application development and delivery environment for large-scale distributed heterogeneous applications. **Cronus** is layered, with object-oriented application design and implementation tools abstracting lower level IPC mechanisms and providing both object-oriented and RPC style programming views [Berets 1988; Dean et al. 1987; Schantz et al. 1986; Gurwitz et al. 1986; Berets et al. 1985].

4.14.9.5   *FREEDOMNET*

FREEDOMNET provides remote execution, device access, and file access for otherwise normal **UNIX** systems. It is developed and marketed by Research Triangle Institute (RTI), a participating institution of the Microelectronics Center of North Carolina (MCNC), Research Triangle, North Carolina. It is used to connect seven universities and research institutions across the state [Truscott et al. 1986].

4.14.9.6   *Locus*

Locus is an early distributed operating system that is also a product, marketed by the corporation of the same name. It is based on **UNIX** [Popek et al. 1981].

4.15   *Batch Resource Sharing*

4.15.1   **Remote Job Entry (RJE)**

This is often supported on interactive networks such as the *Internet*, but it is more basic to dialup networks such as *UUCP, USENET,* and *EUnet.*

4.15.1.1   *Red Book*

The *JANET* Job Transfer and Manipulation Protocol (JTMP) is specified in the Red Book [JTPWP 1981].

4.15.1.2   *rsh*

The rsh protocol was invented by UCB CSRG for **4.2BSD** and provides remote job entry by invoking a **UNIX** shell on the remote machine [Comer 1988, 236 – 237].

4.15.2   Batch File Transfer (BFTP)

The Batch File Transfer Protocol (BFTP) defined in RFC1068 [DeSchon and Braden 1988] is built on top of FTP.

4.16   *Bibliographic Notes*

There are several good books on the theory of computer network protocols, including the original standard, recently revised [Tanenbaum 1988], one somewhat more oriented toward IBM protocols [Schwartz 1987], and a set covering a wide range of specific protocols [Stallings 1985]. Another is more analytical, without eschewing description entirely [Bertsekas and Gallager 1987]. All of these contain some information on the lower layers, but the standard reference for those layers is McNamara 1988.

For a brief (but somewhat dated) introduction, see Tanenbaum 1981 or papers in IEEE 1982 or Cerf and Kirstein 1978. A perspective on historical and recent developments in protocol design and implementation may be found in Padlipsky 1985. A very useful retrospective anthology of major papers in the field is Partridge 1988b, which was a gold mine of information on protocols. It and the assistance of Craig Partridge were invaluable in compiling the material in this chapter. Very useful guidance on the material about conferencing systems was received from Gordon Cook [Cook 1988], who runs one at JVNC.

Any of the above references should be supplemented by recent publications on the various protocols, protocol suites, and software. See the specific references throughout this and other chapters.

4.17   *References*

Abramson 1970.   Abramson, N., "The Aloha System," *AFIPS Conference Proceedings*, pp. 281–285, AFIPS Press, Montvale, NJ, 1970.

Abramson and Kui 1975.   Abramson, N., and Kui, F. F., *Computer-Communication Networks*, Prentice-Hall, Englewood Cliffs, NJ, 1975.

Accetta et al. 1986.   Accetta, Mike, Baron, Robert, Bolosky, William, Golub, David, Rashid, Richard, Tevanian, Avadis, and Young, Michael, "Mach: A New Kernel Foundation for UNIX Development," *Proceedings of the 1986 Summer USENIX Conference (Atlanta, 9–13 June 1986)*, pp. 93–112, USENIX Association, Berkeley, CA, 1986.

Advertel 1988.   Advertel, "An Introduction to Confer II," Advertel Communication Systems, Inc., Ann Arbor, MI, 1988.

Allman 1983.   Allman, Eric, "Sendmail, An Internetwork Mail Router," in *UNIX Programmer's Manual, 4.2 Berkeley Software Distribution*, USENIX Association, Berkeley, CA, 1983.

Allman and Amos 1985. Allman, Eric, and Amos, Miriam, "Sendmail Revisited," *Proceedings of the Summer 1985 USENIX Conference (Portland, Oregon, 11–14 June 1985)*, pp. 547–555, USENIX Association, Berkeley, CA, 1985. Also in Partridge, *Innovations in Internetworking*, 1988.

Anderson 1971. Anderson, R., "Status Report on Proposed Data Reconfiguration Service; RFC138," *ARPANET Working Group Requests for Comments*, 28 April 1971.

Armand et al. 1986. Armand, François, Gien, Michel, Guillemont, Marc, and Léonard, Pierre, "Towards a Distributed UNIX System, the Chorus Approach," *EUUG Conference Proceedings (Manchester, U.K., 22–24 September 1986)*, pp. 413–431, European UNIX systems User Group, Buntingford, Herts., England, 1986.

Armand et al. 1988. Armand, François, Herrmann, Frédéric, Gien, Michel, and Rozier, Marc, "Chorus, A new Technology for Building UNIX Systems," *EUUG Conference Proceedings (Cascais, Portugal, 3–7 October 1988)*, pp. 1–18, European UNIX systems User Group, Buntingford, Herts., England, 1988.

Arms 1988. Arms, Caroline, *Campus Networking Strategies*, Digital Press, Bedford, MA, 1988.

Banino et al. 1985. Banino, Jean-Serge, Fabre, Jean-Charles, Guillemont, Marc, Morisset, Gérard, and Rozier, Marc, "Some Fault-Tolerant Aspects of the Chorus Distributed System," *IEEE 5th International Conference on Distributed Computing Systems Proceedings (Denver, 13–17 May 1985)*, pp. 430–437, IEEE, New York, 1985.

Berets 1988. Berets, James C., Personal communications, November 1988.

Berets et al. 1985. Berets, James C., Mucci, Ronald A., and Schantz, Richard E., "Cronus: A Testbed for Developing Distributed Systems," *1985 IEEE Military Communications Conference Proceedings (Boston, October 1985)*, pp. 409–417, IEEE, New York, 1985.

Bertsekas and Gallager 1987. Bertsekas, Dimitri, and Gallager, Robert, *Data Networks*, Prentice-Hall, Englewood Cliffs, NJ, 1987.

Birrell and Nelson 1984. Birrell, A., and Nelson, B., "Implementing Remote Procedure Calls," *ACM Transactions on Computer Systems*, vol. 2, no. 1, pp. 39–59, February 1984. Also in Partridge, *Innovations in Internetworking*, 1988.

Boggs et al. 1988. Boggs, David R., Mogul, Jeffery C., and Kent, Christopher A., "Measured Capacity of an Ethernet: Myths and Reality," *Proceedings of the ACM SIGCOMM '88 Workshop (Stanford, 16–19 August 1988)*, pp. 222–234, ACM SIGCOMM, New York, 1988.

Burns 1988. Burns, Frank, "How We Use Caucus in Developing and Managing Our Business," Metasystems Design Group, Inc., Arlington, VA, 23 August 1988.

Caneschi 1986. Caneschi, F., "Hints for the Interpretation of the ISO Session Layer," *ACM Computer Communications Review*, vol. 16, no. 4, pp. 34–72, July/August 1986.

Carpenter et al. 1987. Carpenter, B. E., Fluckiger, F., Gerard, J. M., Lord, D., and Segal, B., "Two Years of Real Progress in European HEP Networking: A CERN Perspective," *Computer Physics Communications*, vol. 45, pp. 83–92, August 1987.

CCITT 1988a. CCITT, "Specification of Abstract Syntax Notation One; CCITT X.208," *CCITT Recommendations*, no. X.208 (data types), CCITT, Geneva, 1988.

CCITT 1988b. CCITT, "Specification of Basic Encoding Rules for Abstract Syntax Notation One; CCITT X.209," *CCITT Recommendations*, no. X.209 (binary encoding), CCITT, Geneva, 1988.

Cerf and Cain 1983. Cerf, Vinton G., and Cain, Edward, "The DoD Internet Architecture Model," *Computer Networks*, vol. 7, no. 5, pp. 307–318, October 1983.

Cerf and Kahn 1974.   Cerf, Vinton G., and Kahn, Robert, "A Protocol for Packet Network Interconnection," *IEEE Transactions on Communications*, vol. COM-22, no. 5, pp. 637–648, May 1974. Also in Partridge, *Innovations in Internetworking*, 1988.

Cerf and Kirstein 1978.   Cerf, Vinton G., and Kirstein, Peter, "Issues in Packet Network Interconnection," *Proceedings of the IEEE*, vol. 66, no. 11, pp. 1386–1408, November 1978. Also in Partridge, *Innovations in Internetworking*, 1988.

Cheriton 1988.   Cheriton, D. R., "The V Distributed System," *Communications of the ACM*, vol. 31, no. 3, pp. 314–333, March 1988. Also in Partridge, *Innovations in Internetworking*, 1988.

Chesson 1987.   Chesson, Greg, "Protocol Engine Design," *Proceedings of the Summer 1987 USENIX Conference (Phoenix, Arizona, 8–12 June 1987)*, pp. 209–215, USENIX Association, Berkeley, CA, 1987. Also in Partridge, *Innovations in Internetworking*, 1988.

Chesson 1988.   Chesson, Greg, "Packet Driver Protocol," *comp.std.unix*, vol. 14, no. 13, USENET, 5 May 1988.

Clark 1988.   Clark, Dave, "The Design Philosophy of the DARPA Internet Protocols," *Proceedings of the ACM SIGCOMM '88 Workshop (Stanford, 16–19 August 1988)*, pp. 106–114, ACM SIGCOMM, New York, 1988.

Clark et al. 1987a.   Clark, David D., Lambert, Mark L., and Zhang, Lixia, "NETBLT: A Bulk Data Transfer Protocol; RFC998," *ARPANET Working Group Requests for Comments*, March 1987.

Clark et al. 1987b.   Clark, D. D., Zhang, L., and Lambert, M., "NETBLT: A High Throughput Transport Protocol," *Proceedings of the ACM SIGCOMM '87 Workshop (Stowe, Vermont, 11–13 August 1987)*, pp. 353–359, ACM SIGCOMM, New York, 1987. Also in Partridge, *Innovations in Internetworking*, 1988.

Comer 1984.   Comer, Douglas, *The Xinu Approach*, vol. 1 of *Operating System Design*, Prentice-Hall, Englewood Cliffs, NJ, 1984.

Comer 1987.   Comer, Douglas, *Internetworking with Xinu*, vol. 2 of *Operating System Design*, Prentice-Hall, Englewood Cliffs, NJ, 1987.

Comer 1988.   Comer, Douglas, *Internetworking with TCP/IP Principles, Protocols, and Architecture*, Prentice-Hall, Englewood Cliffs, NJ, 1988.

Cook 1987.   Cook, Gordon, "A Survey of Computer Mediated Communications: Computer Conferencing Comes of Age," Gartner Group, Inc., Stamford, CT, 9 November 1987. This paper was published in a series available only to subscribers who paid a substantial fee.

Cook 1988.   Cook, Gordon, Personal communications, November 1988.

Crocker 1982.   Crocker, David H., "Standard for the Format of ARPA Internet Text Messages; RFC822," *ARPANET Working Group Requests for Comments*, 13 August 1982.

Crocker et al. 1983.   Crocker, D. H., Reilly, G. B., and Farber, D. J., "MMDF—An Inter-Network Memo Distribution Facility," *Digest of Papers from the IEEE Computer Society International Conference (26th COMPCON, March 1983)*, pp. 314–315, IEEE Computer Society Press, New York, 1983.

Crocker et al. 1979.   Crocker, D. H., Szurkowski, E. S., and Farber, D. J., "An Internetwork Memo Distribution Capability—MMDF," *Proceedings of the Sixth Data Communications Symposium (November 1979)*, IEEE, New York, 1979.

da Cruz 1987a.   da Cruz, Frank, *Kermit, A File Transfer Protocol*, Digital Press, Bedford, MA, 1987.

da Cruz 1987b.   da Cruz, Frank, "Kermit in Antarctica," *Kermit News*, vol. 2, no. 1, p. 6, November 1987.

da Cruz 1988.   da Cruz, Frank, Personal communications, October–November 1988.

da Cruz and Gianone 1987. da Cruz, Frank, and Gianone, Christine, "Shopping for Software That Lets PCs Chat with Mainframes," *Data Communications*, vol. 16, no. 12, pp. 155–170, December 1987.

Davidson 1988. Davidson, John, *An Introduction to TCP/IP*, Springer-Verlag, Berlin, 1988.

Davidson et al. 1977. Davidson, J., Hathaway, W., Postel, J., Mimno, N., Thomas, R., and Walden, D., "The ARPAnet Telnet Protocol: Its Purpose, Principles of Implementation, and Impact on Host Operating System Design," *Proceedings Fifth Data Communications Symposium (Snowbird, Utah, September 1977)*, IEEE, New York, 1977. Also in Partridge, *Innovations in Internetworking*, 1988.

Dean et al. 1987. Dean, Michael A., Sands, Richard M., and Schantz, Richard E., "Canonical Data Representation in the Cronus Distributed Operating System," *1987 IEEE Communications and Computer Societies INFOCOM Conference Proceedings (San Francisco, March 1987)*, pp. 814–819, 1987.

de Broeck 1987. de Broeck, Paul, "Kermit Aids in Giotto Project," *Kermit News*, vol. 2, no. 1, p. 5, November 1987.

Delp et al. 1988. Delp, Gary S., Sethi, Adarshpal S., and Farber, David J., "An Analysis of Memnet: An Experiment in High-Speed Shared-Memory Local Networking," *Proceedings of the ACM SIGCOMM '88 Workshop (Stanford, 16–19 August 1988)*, pp. 165–174, ACM SIGCOMM, New York, 1988.

Denning 1985. Denning, Peter J., "The Science of Computing: Computer Networks," *American Scientist*, vol. 73, no. 2, pp. 127–129, March/April 1985.

DeSchon and Braden 1988. DeSchon, A., and Braden, B., "Background File Transfer Program (BFTP); RFC1068," *ARPANET Working Group Requests for Comments*, August 1988.

Dick-Lauder et al. 1984. Dick-Lauder, Piers, Kummerfeld, R. J., and Elz, Robert, "ACSNET—The Australian Alternative to UUCP," *Proceedings of the Summer 1983 USENIX Conference (Salt Lake City, Utah, 12–15 June 1984)*, pp. 11–17, USENIX Association, Berkeley, CA, 1984.

Digital-Intel-XEROX 1982. Digital-Intel-XEROX, *Ethernet Local Area Network Specification Version 2.0*, Digital Equipment Corporation, Marlboro, MA, November 1982.

Dineen et al. 1987. Dineen, Terence H., Leach, Paul J., Mishkin, Nathaniel W., Pato, Joseph N., and Wyant, Geoffrey L., "The Network Computer Architecture and System: An Environment for Developing Distributed Applications," *Proceedings of the Summer 1987 USENIX Conference (Phoenix, Arizona, 8–12 June 1987)*, pp. 385–398, USENIX Association, Berkeley, CA, 1987.

ECMA 1985. ECMA, "Remote Operations: Concepts, Notation and Connection-Oriented Mappings," ECMA, Geneva, December 1985.

EIA 1969. EIA, "Interface Between Data Terminal Equipment and Data Circuit-Terminating Equipment Employing Serial Binary Data Interchange (RS-232-C)," Electrical Industry Association, Washington, DC, 1969.

Forsberg 1988. Forsberg, Chuck, "Xmodem/Ymodem Protocol Reference," Omen Technology, Inc., Portland, OR, 1988. A compendium of documents describing the Xmodem and Ymodem File Transfer Protocols.

FTPIG 1981. FTPIG, *Network Independent File Transfer Protocol (Blue Book)*, originally prepared by the High Level Protocol Group., revised by FTPIG, NPL, Teddington, Middlesex, England, 5 February 1981.

Guillemont 1982. Guillemont, Marc, "The Chorus Distributed Operating System: Design and Implementation," *ACM International Symposium on Local Computer Networks Proceedings (Florence, Italy, April 1982)*, ACM, New York, 1982.

Gurwitz et al. 1986. Gurwitz, R., Dean, M., and Schantz, R., "Programming Support in the Cronus Distributed Operating System," *Sixth International Conference on Distributed Computing Systems Proceedings (Cambridge, MA, May 1986)*, pp. 486–493, IEEE Computer Society, 1986.

Horton and Adams 1987. Horton, Mark R., and Adams, Rick, "Standard for Interchange of USENET Messages; RFC1036," *ARPANET Working Group Requests for Comments*, December 1987.

HP 1986. HP, *LAN Cable and Accessories Installation Manual*, Hewlett-Packard, Cupertino, CA, January 1986.

IEEE 1982. IEEE, *Proceedings of the IEEE Computer Society International Conference (25th COMPCON, September 1982)*, Society Press, Los Angeles, 1982.

IEEE 1985. IEEE, *Carrier Sense Multiple Access with Collision Detection*, IEEE, Piscataway, NJ, 1985. ANSI/IEEE Std 802.3; ISO DIS8802/3.

IEEE 1988. IEEE, *Supplements to Carrier Sense Multiple Access with Collision Detection*, IEEE, Piscataway, NJ, 1988. Includes thin Ethernet standard 10BASE2 and broadbase standard 10BROAD36.

ISO 1981. ISO, "ISO Open Systems Interconnection—Basic Reference Model," *ISO/TC 97/SC*, vol. 16, no. 719, August 1981.

ISO 1983. ISO, "Information Processing—ISO 7-Bit Coded Character Set; ISO646," ISO, Geneva, 1983.

ISO 1987a. ISO, "Final Text of DIS 8473, Protocol for Providing the Connectionless Mode Network Service; RFC994," *ARPANET Working Group Requests for Comments*, January 1987.

ISO 1987b. ISO, "Specification of Abstract Syntax Notation One; IS8824 (data types)," *Information Processing Systems; Open Systems Interconnection*, ISO, Geneva, May 1987.

ISO 1987c. ISO, "Specification of Basic Encoding Rules for Abstract Syntax Notation One; IS8825 (binary encoding)," *Information Processing Systems; Open Systems Interconnection*, ISO, Geneva, May 1987.

ISO 1988a. ISO, "Information Processing Systems—Text Communication—Remote Operations Part 1: Model, Notation and Service Definition; WDIS9072-1," ISO, Geneva, March 1988.

ISO 1988b. ISO, "Information Processing Systems—Text Communication—Remote Operations Part 2: Protocol Specification; WDIS9072-2," ISO, Geneva, March 1988.

Jacobson and Braden 1988. Jacobson, Van, and Braden, Bob, "TCP Extensions for Long-Delay Paths; RFC1072," *ARPANET Working Group Requests for Comments*, October 1988.

Jain 1986. Jain, R., "A Timeout-Based Congestion Control Scheme for Window Flow-Controlled Networks," *IEEE Journal on Selected Areas of Communications*, vol. SAC-4, no. 7, pp. 1162–1167, October 1986. Also in Partridge, *Innovations in Internetworking*, 1988.

Jain et al. 1987. Jain, R., Ramkrishnan, K.K., and Chiu, D.M., "Congestion Avoidance in Computer Networks with a Connectionless Network Layer," Digital Equipment Corporation, Bedford, MA, 1987.

JNT 1985a. JNT, *Implementation Details for Protocols on CSMA/CD LANs (Pink Book)*, Joint Network Team, Rutherford Appleton Laboratory, Chilton, Didcot, Oxfordshire, England, August 1985.

JNT 1985b. JNT, *A Common Procedural Interface to Yellow Book Transport Service*, Joint Network Team, Rutherford Appleton Laboratory, Chilton, Didcot, Oxfordshire, England, January 1985.

JNT 1985c. JNT, *Simple Screen Management Protocol (Fawn Book)*, Joint Network Team, Rutherford Appleton Laboratory, Chilton, Didcot, Oxfordshire, England, July 1985.

JTPWP 1981. JTPWP, *A Network Independent Job Transfer and Manipulation Protocol (Red Book)*, JTP Working Party of the Data Communication Protocols Unit, London, September 1981.

Kahn 1975.   Kahn, R. E., "The Organization of Computer Resources in a Packet Radio Network," *Proceedings of the National Computer Conference (May 1975)*, pp. 177–186, AFIPS Press, Montvale, NJ, 1975.

Kantor and Lapsley 1986.   Kantor, Brian, and Lapsley, Phil, "Network News Transfer Protocol; RFC977," *ARPANET Working Group Requests for Comments*, February 1986.

Karn 1988.   Karn, Phil, "Amateur Packet Radio and TCP/IP," *ConneXions — The Interoperability Report*, vol. 2, no. 9, pp. 8–15, Advanced Computing Environments, Mountain View, CA, September 1988.

Karrenberg 1988.   Karrenberg, Daniel, "EUnet and ISO Transition Plans," *EUUG Conference Proceedings (Cascais, Portugal, 3–7 October 1988)*, pp. 107–113, European UNIX systems User Group, Buntingford, Herts., England, 1988.

Kernighan and Ritchie 1978.   Kernighan, Brian W., and Ritchie, Dennis M., *The C Programming Language*, Prentice-Hall, Englewood Cliffs, NJ, 1978.

Kille 1984.   Kille, S. E., *The JNT Mail Protocol (Grey Book)*, Joint Network Team, Rutherford Appleton Laboratory, Chilton, Didcot, Oxfordshire, England, March 1984.

Knightson et al. 1988.   Knightson, Keith G., Knowles, Terry, and Larmouth, John, *Standards for Open Systems Interconnection*, McGraw-Hill, New York, 1988.

Kummerfeld and Dick-Lauder 1981.   Kummerfeld, R. J., and Dick-Lauder, P. R., "The Sydney Unix Network," *Australian Computer Journal*, vol. 13, no. 2, pp. 52–57, May 1981.

Lanzillo and Partridge 1989.   Lanzillo, Leo, and Partridge, Craig, "Implementation of Dial-up IP for UNIX Systems," *USENIX 1989 Winter Conference Proceedings (San Diego, 30 January–3 February 1989)*, USENIX Association, Berkeley, CA, 1989.

Larmouth 1982.   Larmouth, J, *Cambridge Ring 82 Protocol Specifications (Orange Book)*, Joint Network Team, Rutherford Appleton Laboratory, Chilton, Didcot, Oxfordshire, England, November 1982.

Lauck et al. 1986.   Lauck, Anthony G., Oran, David R., and Perlman, Radia J., "Digital Network Architecture Overview," *Digital Technical Journal*, no. 3, pp. 10–24, September 1986.

Leffler et al. 1989.   Leffler, Samuel J., McKusick, Marshall Kirk, Karels, Michael J., and Quarterman, John S., *The Design and Implementation of the 4.3BSD UNIX Operating System*, Addison-Wesley, Reading, MA, 1989.

Lindsey 1987.   Lindsey, Georg, "The Green Revolution," *Kermit News*, vol. 2, no. 1, pp. 4–5, November 1987.

Long 1987.   Long, Daniel, "CMDF Version 1.2," *CSNET-FORUM Digest*, vol. 3, no. 7, 14 December 1987.

Long 1988.   Long, Daniel, Personal communications, November 1988.

Malis 1983.   Malis, Andrew G., "The ARPANET 1822L Host Access Protocol; RFC878," *ARPANET Working Group Requests for Comments*, December 1983.

McKenzie 1985.   McKenzie, Alex, "Re Comments on NRC Report," *TCP-IP@SRI-NIC.ARPA*, Internet, 20 March 1985.

McNamara 1985.   McNamara, John E., *Local Area Networks*, Digital Press, Bedford, MA, 1985.

McNamara 1988.   McNamara, John E., *Technical Aspects of Data Communication*, 3d ed., Digital Press, Bedford, MA, 1988.

Meeks 1985.   Meeks, Brock N., "An Overview of Conferencing Systems," *BYTE*, vol. 10, no. 13, pp. 169–184, December 1985.

Metcalfe and Boggs 1976.   Metcalfe, R. M., and Boggs, D. R., "Ethernet: Distributed Packet Switching for Local Computer Networks," *Communications of the ACM*, vol. 19, no. 7, pp. 395–404, July 1976. Also in Partridge, *Innovations in Internetworking*, 1988.

Morabito 1986.   Morabito, Margaret, "Confer: An Electronic Roundtable," *Link-Up*, vol. 3, no. 7, pp. 8–9, Learned Information, Inc., Medford, NJ, July/August 1986.

Murai and Kato 1988.   Murai, J., and Kato, A., "Current Status of JUNET," *Future Generations Computer Systems*, vol. 4, no. 3, pp. 205–215, North-Holland, Amsterdam, October 1988.

Nussbacher 1987.   Nussbacher, Henry, "Conversion Plans from RSCS to Tcp/Ip for Israel Academic Network," *TCP-IP@SRI-NIC.ARPA*, Israeli University Telecommunications Subcommittee, Tel Aviv, 7 July 1987.

Nussbacher 1988.   Nussbacher, Henry, Personal communications, 8 August 1988.

Oakley et al. 1985.   Oakley, Daniel J., Perillo, Francine, Dorio, Nancy, and Ward, Carol, "DDN Protocol Implementations and Vendors Guide," DDN Network Information Center, SRI International, Menlo Park, CA, CA, December 1985. Available by anonymous FTP as NETINFO:VENDORS-GUIDE.DOC; paper copies $30 domestic, $35 overseas.

Padlipsky 1985.   Padlipsky, M. A., *The Elements of Networking Style*, Prentice-Hall, Englewood Cliffs, NJ, 1985.

Palme 1988.   Palme, Jacob, Personal communications, October–December 1988.

Partridge 1986.   Partridge, Craig, "Mail Routing and the Domain System; RFC974," *ARPANET Working Group Requests for Comments*, January 1986. Describes how mailers use MXs.

Partridge 1987.   Partridge, Craig, "Implementing the Reliable Data Protocol," *Proceedings of the Summer 1987 USENIX Conference (Phoenix, Arizona, 8–12 June 1987)*, pp. 367–379, USENIX Association, Berkeley, CA, 1987.

Partridge 1988a.   Partridge, Craig, Personal communications, August–November 1988.

Partridge 1988b.   Partridge, Craig, *Innovations in Internetworking*, ARTECH House, Norwood, MA, October 1988.

Partridge and Rose 1988.   Partridge, Craig, and Rose, Marshall T., "A Comparison of External Data Formats," *Proceedings of the IFIP WG 6.5 Conference (Irvine, California, 10–12 October 1988)*, Elsevier, Amsterdam, 1988. Also in Partridge, *Innovations in Internetworking*, 1988.

Popek et al. 1981.   Popek, B., Walker, B., Chow, J., Edwards, D., Kline, C., Rudisin, G., and Thiel, G., "Locus: A Network Transparent, High Reliability Distributed System," *Proceedings of the Eighth Symposium on Operating Systems Principles (Pacific Grove, California, December 1981)*, pp. 169–177, ACM, New York, 1981.

Postel 1982.   Postel, Jonathan B., "Simple Mail Transfer Protocol; RFC821," *ARPANET Working Group Requests for Comments*, August 1982.

Postel 1987.   Postel, Jonathan B., "Assigned Numbers; RFC1010," *ARPANET Working Group Requests for Comments*, June 1987.

Postel et al. 1986.   Postel, Jonathan B., Finn, Gregory G., Katz, Alan R., and Reynolds, Joyce K., "The ISI Experimental Multimedia Mail System," *ISI Research Reports*, no. ISI/RR-86-173, Information Sciences Institute, Marina del Rey, CA, September 1986.

Pouzin 1982.   Pouzin, Louis, *The CYCLADES Computer Network — Towards Layered Network Architectures*, vol. 2 of Monograph Series of the ICCC, Elsevier, New York, 1982.

Presotto 1986.   Presotto, David L., "The Eighth Edition UNIX Connection Service," *EUUG Spring '86 Conference Proceedings (Florence, Italy, 21–24 April 1986)*, p. 10, European UNIX systems User Group, Buntingford, Herts., England, 1986.

Presotto and Ritchie 1985.   Presotto, D. L., and Ritchie, D. M., "Interprocess Communication in the Eighth Edition Unix System," *Proceedings of the Summer*

1985 USENIX Conference (Portland, Oregon, 11−14 June 1985), pp. 309−316, USENIX Association, Berkeley, CA, 1985.

Quarterman et al. 1985.   Quarterman, John S., Silberschatz, Abraham, and Peterson, James L., "4.2BSD and 4.3BSD as Examples of the UNIX System," *ACM Computing Surveys*, vol. 17, no. 4, pp. 379−418, December 1985.

Reynolds et al. 1985.   Reynolds, Joyce K., Postel, Jonathan B., Katz, Alan R., Finn, Greg G., and DeSchon, Annette L., "The DARPA Experimental Multimedia Mail System," *IEEE Computer*, October 1985. Available from ISI as ISI/RS-85-164.

Ritchie 1984.   Ritchie, D. M., "A Stream Input-Output System," *AT&T Bell Laboratories Technical Journal*, vol. 63, no. 8, October 1984.

Ritchie et al. 1978.   Ritchie, D. M., Johnson, S. C., Lesk, M. E., and Kernighan, B. W., "The C Programming Language," *Bell System Technical Journal*, vol. 57, no. 6, part 2, pp. 1991−2019, July/August 1978.

Ritchie and Thompson 1978.   Ritchie, D. M., and Thompson, K., "The UNIX Time-Sharing System," *Bell System Technical Journal*, vol. 57, no. 6, part 2, pp. 1905−1929, July/August 1978. This version describes Seventh Edition UNIX.

Romkey 1988.   Romkey, J., "A Nonstandard for Transmission of IP Datagrams over Serial Lines: SLIP; RFC1055," *ARPANET Working Group Requests for Comments*, June 1988.

Rose 1987a.   Rose, Marshall T., "ISO Transport Services on Top of the TCP Version 3; RFC1006," *ARPANET Working Group Requests for Comments*, May 1987.

Rose 1987b.   Rose, M. T., "ISODE: Horizontal Integration in Networking," *ConneXions — The Interoperability Report*, vol. 1, no. 1, pp. 8−12, Advanced Computing Environments, Mountain View, CA, May 1987.

Rose 1988a.   Rose, M. T., "ISO Presentation Services on Top of TCP/IP-Based Internets; IDEA #17," *Internet Working Group IDEAs*, Internet Engineering Task Force, March 1988.

Rose 1988b.   Rose, M. T., "Building Distributed Applications in an OSI Framework," *ConneXions — The Interoperability Report*, vol. 2, no. 3, pp. 2−7, Advanced Computing Environments, Mountain View, CA, March 1988.

Rose and Cass 1987.   Rose, Marshall T., and Cass, Dwight E., "OSI Transport Services on Top of the TCP," *Computer Networks and ISDN Systems*, vol. 12, 1987.

Rose and Stefferud 1985.   Rose, Marshall T., and Stefferud, Einar A., "Proposed Standard for Message Encapsulation; RFC934," *ARPANET Working Group Requests for Comments*, January 1985.

Rozier et al. 1988.   Rozier, M., Abrossimov, V., Armand, F., Boule, I., Gien, M., Guillemont, M., Herrmann, F., Kaiser, C., Langlois, S., Léonard, P., and Neuhauser, W., "Chorus Distributed Operating Systems," *Computing Systems*, vol. 1, no. 4, pp. 305−372, USENIX Association, Berkeley, CA, Fall 1988.

Rozier and Legatheaux-Martins 1987.   Rozier, Marc, and Legatheaux-Martins, José, "The Chorus Distributed Operating System: Some Design Issues," in *Distributed Operating Systems, Theory and Practice*, ed. Yakup Paker, Jean-Pierre Banâtre, and Muslim Bozyigit, pp. 261−287, Springer-Verlag, Berlin, 1987.

Sandberg et al. 1985.   Sandberg, R., Goldberg, D., Kleiman, S., Walsh, D., and Lyons, B., "Design and Implementation of the Sun Network File System," *Proceedings of the Summer 1985 USENIX Conference (Portland, Oregon, 11−14 June 1985)*, pp. 119−130, USENIX Association, Berkeley, CA, 1985. Also in Partridge, *Innovations in Internetworking*, 1988.

Schantz et al. 1986.   Schantz, R., Thomas, R., and Bono, G., "The Architecture of the Cronus Distributed Operating System," *Sixth International Conference on Distributed Computing Systems Proceedings (Cambridge, MA, May 1986)*, pp. 250−259, IEEE Computer Society, New York, 1986.

Scheifler et al. 1988.   Scheifler, Robert, Gettys, James, and Newman, Ron, *X Window System: C Library and Protocol Reference*, Digital Press, Bedford, MA, 1988.

Schroeder et al. 1984.   Schroeder, M. D., Birrell, A. D., and Needham, R. M., "Experience with Grapevine: The Growth of a Distributed System," *ACM Transactions on Computer Systems*, vol. 2, no. 1, pp. 3–23, February 1984. Also in Partridge, *Innovations in Internetworking*, 1988.

Schwartz 1987.   Schwartz, Mischa, *Telecommunication Networks*, Addison-Wesley, Reading, MA, 1987.

SG3 1980.   SG3, *A Network Independent Transport Service (Yellow Book)*, Study Group Three of The Post Office PSS User Forum, Cambridge, England, February 1980. SG3/CP(80)2.

SG3 1981.   SG3, *Character Terminal Protocols on PSS: A Recommendation on the Use of X3, X28, and X29 (Green Book)*, Study Group 3 of the British Telecom PSS User Forum, Cambridge, England, 17 February 1981. SG3/CP(81)/6.

Sharpe and Cash 1982.   Sharpe, W. P., and Cash, A. R., *Cambridge Ring 82 Interface Specifications (Orange Book)*, Science and Engineering Research Council and Joint Network Team, Chilton, Didcot, Oxfordshire, England, September 1982.

Spafford 1988.   Spafford, Gene, "USENET Software: History and Sources (Updated: 2 April 1988)," *news.admin, news.announce.newusers*, USENET, 3 April 1988.

Spratt 1986.   Spratt, E. Brian, "Networking Developments in the U.K. Academic Community," *Proceedings of the International Conference on Information Network and Data Communication (Ronneby Brunn, Sweden, 11–14 May 1986)*, IFIP TC.6, Elsevier, Amsterdam, 1986.

Spurgeon 1988.   Spurgeon, Charles, "List of Recommended Books, TCP/IP and Ethernet," *BIG-LAN@suvm.acs.syr.edu (Campus-Size LAN Discussion Group)*, Internet, 7 June 1988.

SRI-NIC 1985.   SRI-NIC, *1985 DDN Protocol Handbook*, DDN Network Information Center, SRI International, Menlo Park, CA, 1985.

Stallings 1985.   Stallings, Richard, *Data and Computer Communications*, Macmillan, New York, 1985.

Stallings 1987a.   Stallings, William, *The Open System Interconnection (OSI) Model and OSI-Related Standards*, vol. 1 of *Handbook of Computer Communications Standards*, Howard W. Sams, Indianapolis, 1987.

Stallings 1987b.   Stallings, William, *Local Network Standards*, vol. 2 of *Handbook of Computer Communications Standards*, Macmillan, New York, 1987.

Stallings et al. 1988.   Stallings, William, Mockapetris, Paul, McLeod, Sue, and Michel, Tony, *Department of Defense (DOD) Protocol Standards*, vol. 3 of *Handbook of Computer Communications Standards*, Macmillan, New York, 1988.

Sun 1987.   Sun, "XDR: External Data Representation Standard; RFC1014," *ARPANET Working Group Requests for Comments*, June 1987.

Sun 1988.   Sun, "RPC: Remote Procedure Call Protocol Specification; RFC1050," *ARPANET Working Group Requests for Comments*, April 1988.

Szurkowski 1980.   Szurkowski, Edward S., "MMDF Dial-Up Link Protocol," *CSNET Design Notes*, no. DN-4, April 1980.

Tanenbaum 1981.   Tanenbaum, Andrew S., "Network Protocols," *ACM Computing Surveys*, vol. 13, no. 4, pp. 453–89, 1981.

Tanenbaum 1988.   Tanenbaum, Andrew S., *Computer Networks*, 2d ed., Prentice-Hall, Englewood Cliffs, NJ, 1988.

Thomas 1988.   Thomas, Eric, Personal communications, 9 December 1988.

Thomas et al. 1985.   Thomas, R. H., Forsdick, H. C., Crowley, T. R., Schaaf, R. W., Tomlinson, R. S., Travers, V. M., and Robertson, G. G., "Diamond: A Multimedia Message System Built on a Distributed Architecture," *IEEE Computer*, pp. 65–78, December 1985.

Truscott et al. 1986. Truscott, Tom, Warren, Bob, and Most, Kent, "A State-wide UNIX Distributed Computing System," *Proceedings of the 1986 Summer USENIX Conference (Atlanta, 9 – 13 June 1986)*, pp. 499 – 513, USENIX Association, Berkeley, CA, 1986.

TSIG 1983. TSIG, *Networking Over Asynchronous Lines: A Realization of the Yellow Book Network Service*, Transport Service Implementors Group of the British Telecom New Networks Technical Forum, TE/SES 7.2.3, London, England, 4 February 1983. CP(82)/12 is the long form; CP(82)/11 is the short form.

Velten et al. 1984. Velten, David, Hinden, Robert, and Sax, Jack, "Reliable Data Protocol; RFC908," *ARPANET Working Group Requests for Comments*, July 1984.

Walsh et al. 1985. Walsh, Dan, Lyon, Bob, and Sager, Gary, "Overview of the Sun Network File System," *Proceedings of the Winter 1985 USENIX Conference (Dallas, Texas, 23 – 25 January 1985)*, pp. 117 – 124, USENIX Association, Berkeley, CA, 1985.

Weinberger 1984. Weinberger, Peter J., "The Version 8 Network File System," *Proceedings of the Summer 1983 USENIX Conference (Salt Lake City, Utah, 12 – 15 June 1984)*, p. 86, USENIX Association, Berkeley, CA, 1984.

Weinberger 1986. Weinberger, Peter J., "The Eighth Edition Remote File System," *EUUG Spring '86 Conference Proceedings (Florence, Italy, 21 – 24 April 1986)*, p. 1, European UNIX systems User Group, Buntingford, Herts., England, 1986.

Wheeler and Ganek 1988. Wheeler, E. F., and Ganek, A. G., "Introduction to Systems Application Architecture," *IBM Systems Journal*, vol. 27, no. 3, pp. 250 – 263, 1988.

XEROX 1980. XEROX, *The Ethernet, A Local Area Network: Data Link Layer and Physical Layer Specification*, Xerox Corporation, Stamford, CT, October 1980.

XEROX 1981a. XEROX, "Courier: The Remote Procedure Call Protocol," in *Xerox System Integration Standard*, Xerox Corporation, Stamford, CT, December 1981.

XEROX 1981b. XEROX, "XEROX System Integration Bulletin," Xerox Corporation, Stamford, CT, 1981.

Yamasaki 1988. Yamasaki, Michael J., "Special Purpose User-Space Network Protocols," *Proceedings of the Winter 1988 USENIX Conference (Dallas, Texas, 9 – 12 February 1988)*, pp. 63 – 69, USENIX Association, Berkeley, CA, 1988.

Young et al. 1987. Young, M., Tevanian, A., Rashid, R., Golub, D., Eppinger, J., Chew, J., Bolosky, W., Black, D., and Baron, R., "The Duality of Memory and Communication in the Implementation of a Multiprocessor Operating System," *Proceedings of the Eleventh Symposium on Operating System Principles (Austin, Texas, November 1987)*, pp. 63 – 76, ACM, New York, 1987.

Zimmermann 1980. Zimmermann, Hubert, "OSI Reference Model — The ISO Model of Architecture for Open Systems Interconnection," *IEEE Transactions on Communications*, vol. COM-28, no. 4, pp. 425 – 432, April 1980. Also in Partridge, *Innovations in Internetworking*, 1988.

Zimmermann et al. 1981. Zimmermann, Hubert, Banino, Jean-Serge, Caristan, Alain, Guillemont, Marc, and Morisset, Gérard, "Basic Concepts for the Support of Distributed Systems: the Chorus Approach," *IEEE 2nd International Conference on Distributed Computing Systems Proceedings (Versailles, April 1981)*, pp. 60 – 66, IEEE, New York, 1981.

Zimmermann et al. 1984. Zimmermann, Hubert, Guillemont, Marc, Morisset, Gérard, and Banino, Jean-Serge, "Chorus: A Communication and Processing Architecture for Distributed Systems," INRIA, Rocquencourt, France, September 1984.

5 *Management Protocols*

Networks may be arranged in several kinds of layers and may take various topological forms. There must be names for nodes at each layer and mappings between them.

5.1 *Connectivity*

Any set of hosts that are connected in such a way that any host can exchange messages of some kind with each other host can be called a network. Different types of networks can be distinguished according to the highest level at which the same protocol and address space are used throughout.

5.1.1 Network

A *simple network* (or just *network*) uses the same network layer protocol and network layer address space throughout.

5.1.2 Internetwork

An *internetwork* or *internet* may use several different network layer protocols in different parts, but all of its constituent networks use the same internet layer protocol and the same internet layer address space.

5.1.3   Subnetwork

Some protocol suites, such as TCP/IP, allow the address space of a simple network to be further partitioned at the network layer in order to distinguish a *subnetwork* or *subnet* of hosts that are administratively or technologically related, such as by being on the same physical cable. A subnet bears the same hierarchical relation to a simple network as a simple network does to an internet. Subnets are often used to hide local administrative details, such as the topology of a campus network, from the outside world.

The term *subnet* is sometimes used to refer to any administratively related subset of hosts on a network, regardless of address space issues.

5.1.4   Metanetwork

A *metanetwork* or *metanet* may use several different network, internet, or transport layer protocols. A metanet is usually connected only at the application layer, and the usual common protocol is mail. Even that may not be the same throughout a metanetwork, as conversion from one format to another may be performed within the metanet.

5.2   *Configuration*

In a given protocol layer, network nodes may be organized in various topological configurations [Harary 1969].

5.2.1   Star

Some networks are constrained by their technology to have a *star* shape — i.e., one central node and leaf nodes that communicate only through the central node. The canonical example of this is the *Aloha* network of the University of Hawaii (UH), which used packet radio to communicate with remote campuses. Other networks adopt this configuration to limit redundant transmissions and thus cost; *EUnet* shows some of this structure. Still others choose this configuration to concentrate maintenance problems in one place.

5.2.2   Tree

Avoidance of routing problems may lead to a network structured as a *tree*; NJE forces this structure on *BITNET*. The main problem with a tree structure is its lack of redundancy: the loss of one link partitions the network.

5.2.3   Clique

Some protocols were designed with the intention of having every node talk directly to every other node, forming a *clique*. The UUCP protocols were originally intended to be used in a network where every machine dialed up every other machine. This kind of organization does not scale well and is found in no very large network.

5.2.4   Graph

A network may tend to look more like a general *graph*, perhaps with small segments that form stars or cliques. Some networks, such as *ARPANET* or *MILNET*, deliberately avoid trees and stars even in subsets of their nodes, because redundant links are important to them for robustness. Others, such as *USENET*, use a central clique that is small in number but large in geographical distribution so that data can be distributed quickly, yet arrange local connections in trees for reduced costs.

5.2.5   Other

A common configuration is a communication subnet with hosts attached to its nodes in a tree structure, as in *ARPANET*. Configurations common on a small (local area to campus) scale, but rare in wide area networks, are buses and rings.

5.3   *Naming, Addressing, and Routing*

Each layer of a protocol suite may have its own way of referring to hosts, process, or users. Mappings of these addresses between layers must be supported. Mappings must also be supported between hosts or other endpoints and routes through the network.

5.3.1   Mappings

There are three important, related, and often confused terms [Kluger and Shoch 1986; Shoch 1978]. The *name* of a host, mailbox, or other resource is what a user uses to indicate the resource desired. Its *address* specifies the location of the resource to the network software. A *route* is used by the network software to determine how to get there. In the public switched telephone network (PSTN), a name is a personal name, such as Jane Doe, an address is a telephone number, and a route is a sequence of telephone lines and exchanges that are used to reach Jane's number from the caller's telephone.

Consider hosts on the *Internet*. A host might be named ucbvax.berkeley.edu and have an *Internet* address of 10.0.0.78. The address would be discovered by the software on the user's machine (either by old-style static host table lookup or by new-style domain nameserver protocols). The IP protocol would then use the address to route the packet to the appropriate network. The network named by the address 10.0.0.78 is network 10, the *ARPANET*. The *ARPANET* has a communications subnet of computers. Each host is attached to a Packet Switch Node (PSN). A host's PSN extracts an *ARPANET* BBN 1822 address (host 0 on PSN 78) from the IP address and uses it to determine a route to the destination PSN and thence to the destination host. Names and addresses are relative to network protocols. The IP address is treated as a name when the *ARPANET* address is extracted from it. Routing is done first on the IP address and then on the *ARPANET* address.

5.3.2   Hierarchies

Naming, addressing, and routing can be hierarchical. As an example, ucbvax.berkeley.edu is an *Internet* DNS domain name, where *EDU* is a top level domain, berkeley.edu a subdomain of *EDU*, and ucbvax.berkeley.edu a further subdomain (in this case, ucbvax.berkeley.edu is a host machine). The user interface software on machines in the berkeley.edu domain may allow users to abbreviate ucbvax.berkeley.edu as VAX (or whatever other name they're used to using). However, there could be another host named vax.css.gov, in which case the abbreviation VAX on hosts in the domain css.gov would not refer to the same host as in berkeley.edu.

The address 10.0.0.78 is actually a two-level *Internet* IP address. The prefix 10 is the network number of the *ARPANET*, and the rest (the local part) is a host number on the *ARPANET*. The local part may be mapped to a network address by different methods for different networks. In this particular case, the network address is actually contained in the *Internet* address, and there is a further hierarchy in the host address. The final 78 is the PSN number and the rest is the host-on-PSN number.

Routing in the *Internet* is also hierarchical. First a route is found to the appropriate network through gateways by the Gateway to Gateway Protocol (GGP) [Hinden and Sheltzer 1982] and the Exterior Gateway Protocol (EGP) [Seamonson and Rosen 1984; Mills 1984]. Then a route is found to the appropriate host on the network by protocols appropriate to the network. In the *ARPANET*, the latter problem reduces to finding the host's PSN, the number of which is encoded in the address. For an address on an

Ethernet—e.g., 128.83.138.11—finding the appropriate host is usually simpler since Ethernets are broadcast networks.

A resource may have more than one name, address, or route. In the *Internet*, berkeley.edu might have two addresses, 10.0.0.78 and 128.32.130.1, if it were connected to two networks. Although hosts in the *Internet* have only one primary name, they may be known by other names on non-*Internet* networks. For instance, berkeley.edu might be known as ucbvax on the *UUCP* network. It would be better if every host had one name for all networks, but that is not yet possible. Both IP and the *ARPANET* BBN 1822 network protocol are datagram based, and different datagrams can pass through different routes to reach the same destination, even when the source is the same.

5.3.3   Source or System Routing

There are two kinds of routing: *source routing*, where the user supplies the route to the desired resource, and *system routing*, where the network software determines a route. Most networks and internets provide system routing [Ginsberg 1986]. There are a few exceptions, most prominently *UUCP*. The metanetwork of differing networks and internets frequently requires source routing to reach the appropriate network because there is as yet no universally accepted network addressing convention. Source routes such as alpha!beta%gamma@delta are thus unfortunately still common. This situation is partly due to lack of distinction among naming, addressing, and routing on networks such as *UUCP*.

5.3.4   Relative Addressing

Names and addresses can be either *absolute addresses* or *relative addresses*. In the *Internet*, both IP addresses and fully qualified domain names are absolute (within the *Internet* DNS), but user mailbox names are relative to domain names. Most other networks have absolute names and addresses (again, *UUCP* is an exception).

Relative names are a problem because they make mapping into addresses ambiguous. This is why short names such as VAX are considered to be only abbreviations for a single primary name such as vax.berkeley.edu; it is the responsibility of the local user interface to produce the primary name when communicating with any other host.

Relative addresses are a problem because a host may have a different address depending on where it is being addressed from. Both relative names and relative addresses lead to the possibility that two hosts might have the same address, making proper routing impossible. Nonetheless, maintaining absolute names is difficult, since absolute really means relative to some standard, and there is no universal standard. X.400 is one attempt to handle this problem.

The *UUCP* network has not had absolute host names or addresses. A single name (e.g., bilbo) may be assigned by several different companies to several different machines. This may happen because a company was not connected to the general *UUCP* network at the time and thus was unaware of the conflict, because a host was not originally expected to communicate with the world at large, because the first bilbo was not listed in the *UUCP* map, or for other reasons.

One method for disambiguating such conflicts is to refer to each bilbo by a route from a well-known neighbor (e.g., princeton!bilbo or ihnp4!bilbo). These partial routes are rather like *attribute lists* in the X.400 sense. Of course, if someone names another host princeton, or if princeton leaves the network, a longer or different partial route must be given for that bilbo. This problem occurs with all attribute list schemes: names and addresses are not absolute.

Another possible solution is to give each *UUCP* host an *Internet* DNS domain name, such as bilbo.princeton.edu. (This solution is also being pursued in *BITNET* to some extent.) The former *UUCP* name would still be used as a kind of network address. Routing would be done from domain to domain, so networkwide tables would only be needed for routes to domain gateway hosts, and complete connectivity information would only be kept on hosts within a subdomain by those same hosts (similar methods are already used in *EUnet*). The *UUCP* network would thus be integrated into the *Internet* DNS. This plan is opposed by some people who actually like *UUCP* source routing. For an interesting discussion of related issues by a prominent party on each side, see Allman 1986.

Source routing, attribute lists, and domain names all can be and are used simultaneously on the *UUCP* network. Use of one does not exclude use of either of the others.

5.4   *Address Spaces*

It is not enough to know the general meaning of the bits of a network address. In a functioning network, addresses must be unique, which means that there must be methods for assigning them to organizations and hosts. This requires a detailed address format and often an assigning authority.

5.4.1   X.121

The format of X.25 addresses is given in CCITT X.121. There are two parts [Brunell et al. 1988; Cerf and Kirstein 1978]:

1. The Data Network Identification Code (DNIC) has four digits and is used for international routing. It is subdivided into a Data Country Code (DCC) in the first three digits and a Network Digit (ND) in the fourth digit.
2. The Network Terminal Number (NTN) is of variable length, with a maximum of ten digits, and is used for national routing. The last two to four digits are normally reserved for local routing within an organization.

5.4.2   IP

IP addresses consist of 4 bytes, often expressed in *dotted decimal format* — i.e., one decimal digit for each byte, separated by dots, as in

192.32.13.1

Such addresses are logically divided into network and local parts. This division is done in five ways:

Class A	One byte network, 3 bytes local (n.l.l.l); this is only used for very widespread long-haul networks or for campus networks with extremely numerous hosts.
Class B	Two bytes network, 2 bytes local (n.n.l.l); this is usually used for campus networks and for some wide area networks. Such campus networks are usually subnetted.
Class C	Three bytes network, 1 byte local (n.n.n.l); this is often used for LANs such as Ethernets.
Class D	All 4 bytes are used for *Internet*-wide multicast addresses [Waitzman et al. 1988; Deering 1988].
Class E	This is reserved for experimental use.

Only Classes A, B, and C are commonly used.

The current *Internet* subnet specification uses a bitmask to take any number of bits from the local part of an IP address for use as a subnet number [Mogul and Postel 1985]. This may be done on any of the three classes of IP addresses, including Class C, the one with the least number of local part bits. Although some implementations set the subnet mask per interface [Leffler et al. 1989], ordinarily all subnets of the same IP network have the same subnet mask.

The largest IP address space is that of the *Internet*.

5.4.3   DECNET

HEPnet and *SPAN* have developed a scheme for managing the 64 DECNET Phase IV area codes in a way that allows each country to get one. The numbers 1 – 46 are reserved for an international DECNET, and each country devotes one machine to handling a connection to it, using an area for its country. Each such machine sets the DECNET parameter *MAXIMUM AREA* to 46. Networks within the country may use the numbers 47 – 63 as they wish, overlapping with such use in other countries. International connections are then done using Poor Man's Routing (PMR), which allows mail and file transfer through the gateway machines. Each backbone machine uses the *MAXIMUM AREA* parameter to distinguish national and international areas. Remote login has to be done by logging in on each of the two backbone machines in the countries involved, as well as on the target machine [Brunell et al. 1988]. Digital uses the terms *Level I routing* and *Level II routing* to refer to routing within areas and between areas, respectively — i.e., what are referred to above as national and international areas [Lauck et al. 1986].

5.5   *Domain Naming Systems*

Although there are domain naming systems specific to certain vendors' networking technology, such as XEROX's Grapevine [Schroeder et al. 1984], space permits the examination here of only a few non-vendor-specific systems.

5.5.1   Internet DNS

The *Internet* Domain Name System (DNS) is an attempt to decentralize administration of the mapping of host names to host addresses by the use of nameservers, each of which controls part of the name space [Mockapetris 1984; Mockapetris et al. 1984; Postel 1984; Postel and Reynolds 1984]. This became necessary partly because the static host table formerly used for that purpose had become unwieldy with the growth of the *Internet* and partly because most of the hosts in the *Internet* are on networks local to particular organizations and it is desirable to allow the local administration to control that mapping. The DNS also implements a hierarchical naming scheme and provides protocols for communication with the nameservers [Mockapetris 1983a; Mockapetris 1983b; Mockapetris 1986]. It even provides a method, *MX records*, of transparently connecting hosts on networks with different underlying protocols into the DNS [Partridge 1986a; Partridge 1986b] (the latter paper contains some surprisingly accurate indications of how the DNS was supposed to be used). The current authoritative DNS specifications are RFC1034 [Mockapetris 1987a] and RFC1035 [Mockapetris 1987b].

A set of top level domains are administered by the *Internet* and are defined in the basic DNS specifications; some of these domains are listed in Table 5.1. The old top level domain *ARPA* is still used for many hosts on *MILNET*, a component network of the *Internet*, but it is transitional and will eventually vanish completely. Although a previous attempt at a domain name system, that of RFC733 [Crocker et al. 1977], tied domain names to networks, domains in the current DNS are explicitly not one-to-one with networks, and the other top level domains reflect this. Several networks may be in the same domain (as at large universities), and a single network may have hosts in several domains (as does *CSNET*). There are also domains for countries, such as *UK* for the United Kingdom and *AU* for Australia. There are many people outside the United States (and some within) who claim that *COM, EDU, GOV*, etc., should be under the top level domain *US*. There is such a domain, but it is used for geographical organization of smaller companies that do not fit under the other top level domains. The purpose of the top level domain *NET* is often misunderstood: it is not intended to be used for every host on a network (domains are not tied to networks), but rather to be used for administrative hosts or gateways of networks, as in *relay.cs.net* of *CSNET*. This distinction is not always observed, however, and some exceptions can be seen in the way *DASnet* and *UUNET* handle some of their subscribers.

At a recent meeting, North American representatives of the *Internet, CSNET, BITNET*, and *UUCP* decided to adopt the *Internet* DNS syntax and domains as a common naming syntax [Partridge 1986b; Partridge 1986c]. The adoption is voluntary on a per-host basis on *UUCP* and *BITNET*. *EUnet* in Europe is moving in the same direction and has already registered several top level national domains. *JUNET* in Japan already has a similar domain system. *NSFNET* has also standardized on TCP/IP and related protocols.

5.5.2   **X.400 Attribute Lists**

The ISO-OSI X.400 mail standard also has a domain system, which uses *attribute lists*. A resource is defined by a name and several attributes. Name conflicts can be resolved by specifying sufficient attributes. There is a similar mechanism at the network level in X.175.

The *Ean* networks use a simplified version of the X.400 system because there is as yet no registry for X.400 domains.

Table 5.1. *Internet Domain Name System (DNS) top level*

Domain	Explanation
COM	Commercial organizations
EDU	Educational organizations
GOV	Civilian government organizations
MIL	Department of Defense
NET	Administrative organizations for networks such as *CSNET, UUCP*, and *BITNET*
ORG	Other organizations
US	United States geographically

Source: [Lederman et al. 1988]
Note: There were 37 top level domains as of 22 November 1988.

The user interface may vary among systems on the same network, as in the examples in Table 5.2, which all address the same person. User Interface Presentation (UIP) refers to the representation of an address to the user. The first three examples are for networks whose internal naming formats use ASCII text and are the same as the UIP. The next five examples represent the same binary X.400 encoding, and the last two represent the same *Ean* address. The binary encoding of X.400 addresses allows all networks that use it to communicate, but there is no single standard human readable text UIP.

5.5.3   JANET Grey Book

The British network *JANET* has a Name Registration Scheme (NRS), which is defined in the Grey Book [Kille 1984]. This is similar to the *Internet* DNS, but the domains are in the opposite order; the root is on the left rather than on the right.

5.5.4   ACSnet SUN-III

The Australian network *ACSnet* also has a DNS-like domain name system [Kummerfeld and Dick-Lauder 1985] associated with its SUN-III protocols [Kummerfeld and Dick-Lauder 1981].

5.6   *Interconnection*

Otherwise unrelated networks may be connected so that some services are exchanged.

Table 5.2. *X.400 encodings*

Type	Example address
{DNS}	steve@cs.ucl.ac.uk
UUCP	...!ucl-cs!steve
{NRS}	steve@uk.ac.ucl.cs
X.400 UIPs	
GIPSI (of INRIA)	gb/bt/des/steve(ucl/cs)
RFC987	/C=GB/ADMD=BT/PRMD=DES/O=UCL/
	OU=CS/S=Kille/
Another	<C=gb;A=bt;P=des;O=ucl;S=steve;OU=cs>
DFN	steve!ucl!cs&des%bt&gb
EARN/X.400 gateway	steve!ucl!cs#de s&bt.gb
Ean, RFC822 UIP,	
and domain order	steve@cs.ucl.des.bt.gb
Ean, X.400,	
RFC987 UIP	/C=/ADMD=/PRMD=UK/DD.=cs.ucl.ac/DD.=steve/

Source: Courtesy Christian Huitema and Steve Kille.

5.6.1   Gateways

Several related and somewhat controversial terms refer to machines that interconnect networks. Such a machine may be called a *repeater*, a *bridge*, or a *router*, corresponding to interconnection at the physical, data link, or network layers, respectively [Tanenbaum 1988, 39–40]. Sometimes the term *IP router* is used to refer to a router that interconnects at the internetwork layer. Since these operate below the upper layers of protocols, they are largely transparent to the user.

    The term *gateway* is somewhat more generic and has sometimes been used to refer to the same thing as any or all of the above terms. Here we are concerned with gateways between networks with dissimilar internet layers (or network layer, if there is no internet layer)—that is, the kind of gateways that form a *metanetwork*. They usually work less well than gateways at lower layers, are often less transparent, and usually have to be considered by the user when sending mail across such network boundaries. Mail is often the only service that can be used. The *Internet* has devised a method of making mail gatewaying even to networks with dissimilar underlying protocols transparent to its users [Partridge 1986a; Partridge 1986b], but most networks are not so fortunate. In some cases, such gateways may not be known. In others, it may not be possible to reveal them because of political or economic considerations.

Addresses using a percent sign (%) to indicate indirection through a relay host (a kind of source routing) are a kludge that most people hope will be temporary. For example, a specification, RFC987 [Kille 1986; Kille 1987], has recently been formulated for translation between *Internet* DNS domain addresses and X.400 attribute addresses. Software now exists to do that translation and also to translate between X.400 and *Ean* addresses. When such software is in general use, percent sign source routing should no longer be necessary between those kinds of networks.

Mapping between DNS or NRS domains and X.400 attribute lists is possible because they both record similar kinds of information. There tend to be common subtrees in the two naming tree structures, as shown in Figure 5.1. For example, it is possible to map,

huitema@mirsa.inria.fr

into

/C:Fr/A:PTT/P:aristote/o=INRIA/a=mirsa/s=huitema/

The top level domain *FR* is mapped into

/C:Fr/A:PTT/P:aristote/

The PTT service indication (/P:aristote/) is required because the PTT uses it for routing. The rest of the domain address is an organizational subtree of the naming tree and maps directly into the X.400 subtree:

/o=INRIA/a=mirsa/s=huitema/

This kind of naming is used for X.400 MHS, FTAM, and other services [Huitema 1987].

5.6.2 Protocol Conversion

The basic business of at least one system, *DASnet*, is mail format and protocol conversion. Lower level protocols are also sometimes converted, as in projects by *DFN* and RARE.

At the spring 1987 Hannover Fair (and again in 1988), there were many European TCP/IP vendors with mostly local area networks. There were also many European ISO-OSI vendors with mostly wide area networks, and little overlap. This means conversion between ISO-OSI and TCP/IP protocols for the foreseeable future (see *DFN* in Chapter 13).

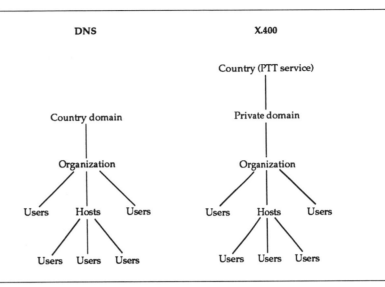

Figure 5.1. *Naming trees*

5.6.3 Mail Distribution

Mail is often used to distribute software and text across disparate networks, often ones that do not even have the same mail format. Some notable systems include the following:

- **MOSIS** is a server supporting the design and fabrication of computer chips by distribution of information through electronic mail [MOSIS Project 1984].
- **Netlib** is a program that supports the retrieval of mathematical software through electronic mail [Dongarra and Grosse 1987].
- The *CSNET* **Info-Server** is a general purpose program for information retrieval, patterned after **MOSIS** [Partridge 1987].
- The *SUNET* and *UNINETT* **QZCOM** or **QZKOM** information service [Palme 1987] is complemented by a portable version called **PortaCOM** that has recently been made compatible with RFC822 and is expected to be converted to X.400 as well [Palme 1988].
- The *EARN* **NETSERV** facility (also used on *BITNET* and *NetNorth*) handles general file retrieval, including documents. It is somewhat similar in function to *anonymous FTP* on the *Internet*, but commands received by NJE messages are handled asynchronously, and requests can be received by mail as well. In addition, it is possible to subscribe

to new versions of a file and to receive either the file itself or a notification when a new version is available. *EARN* **LISTSERV** can also do all of these things, and, unlike **NETSERV**, it also handles mailing lists. **NETSERV** is used in *EARN* to store information about sites, hosts, routes, and users, the latter in a User Directory Service (UDS) [Thomas 1988].

Although the reference for **Netlib** claims that that was the first such system, that is not the case [Oberst and Partridge 1987].

5.7   *Adaptation*

Static configurations cannot be assumed at any level of naming, addressing, or routing hierarchies, and therefore methods of supporting services over dynamically changing networks have been developed.

5.7.1   Distributed Nameservice

In a large network, a centralized single table to map host names to addresses is not adequate. Many organizations have large numbers of internal hosts and wish to assign such mappings themselves. There are often departments of other subdivisions within organizations that want to handle their own mappings as well. It is thus useful for such mappings to be distributed among organizations that are closely associated with groups of hosts. This has been done in the *Internet* [Mockapetris and Dunlap 1988].

5.7.2   Adaptive Network Routing

Adaptive network routing is commonly done within many networks, such as *ARPANET*. The ISO-OSI method for interconnecting X.25 networks involves X.75, which uses virtual circuits between peer networks that are presumed to run at similar data rates, obviating the need for gateways [Kahn 1987]. Many of the issues involved in deciding how to interconnect networks (particularly whether to do it at the network layer or whether to introduce an internet layer, and whether the network or transport layers should be reliable or unreliable) are discussed in Cerf and Kirstein 1978.

5.7.3   Adaptive Internetwork Routing

Gateways (routers) need to communicate with one another in order to know where to route traffic.

5.7.3.1   *TCP/IP Internet Routing*

The earliest TCP/IP internetwork routing protocol was the Gateway to Gateway Protocol (GGP). Later, distribution of routing authority was desired, and the Exterior Gateway Protocol (EGP) was developed [Mills 1984; Seamonson and Rosen 1984]. Possibly the most influential implementation of EGP was that for **4.2BSD UNIX** by Paul Kirton of ISI (Information Sciences Institute). This may be the basis for the implementations of vendors such as cisco and Proteon. Another implementation was done by Merit for *NSFNET*, with assistance from Cornell University (Cornell) partly funded by a grant from NSF [Braun 1988]. Extensions for non-spanning-tree internets were made [Mills 1986], as were revisions for protection of the core and better communication among autonomous systems [Gardner and Karels 1988].

5.7.4   Adaptive Subnetwork Routing

Gateways have to handle not only routing for hosts and other networks, but also routing among themselves within a set of related networks. Such a set of networks is called an *autonomous system* in the *Internet*. A protocol used by the gateways within such a system to communicate among themselves may be called an Internal Gateway Protocol (IGP). This same kind of protocol may be needed by gateways between subnetworks. Common examples include HELLO, RIP, and **gated** [Comer 1988, 181–192].

5.7.4.1   *RIP*

The Routing Information Protocol (RIP) was invented by XEROX PARC for XNS and extended by UCB CSRG for **4.2BSD** in the **routed** program for use on the *Internet*. It is widely used both for routing among subnetworks and for routing among wide area networks [Comer 1988, 182–186].

5.7.4.2   *HELLO*

The HELLO protocol allows clock synchronization and path delay computation [Comer 1988, 187–188].

5.7.4.3   *gated*

A routing daemon that understands many of these protocols simultaneously is **gated** [Fedor 1988; Comer 1988, 188–189], which was developed by Cornell with help from the *NSFNET* community. The gated HELLO component had roots at the University of Maryland (Maryland) and possibly before that at Linkabit. Its EGP implementation is largely derived from that of Paul Kirton.

5.7.4.4   *Proxy ARP*

It is possible to have subnet routers use ARP [Plummer 1982] to answer for hosts that do not understand subnets, and thus to have subnetted IP networks even when not all the hosts understand subnets; this is called Proxy ARP [Carl-Mitchell and Quarterman 1987].

5.7.5   Time Synchronization

The larger and more diverse the network or internet, the more difficult it is to synchronize the time of day as kept on its hosts. Yet this is important for performance measurement and analysis, as well as for distributed applications. It is not sufficient to simply synchronize to a radio clock, since interference can cause signals to be lost or altered. Synchronization to any one clock is not adequate, since it can go down or become incorrect. A sufficient algorithm must use several clocks and be able to detect incorrect ones. It is also useful to take into account factors such as round trip delay. Calendar artifacts such as leap days and leap seconds should be accounted for. A rather sophisticated time synchronization mechanism has been developed in the *Internet*: the Network Time Protocol (NTP) [Mills 1988]. There are also time synchronization protocols designed for local area networks, such as TEMPO [Gusella and Zatti 1984], the Time Synchronization Protocol (TSP) for **4.3BSD** [Gusella and Zatti 1986].

A typical situation might involve the use of NTP to synchronize one or more hosts on a LAN according to reliable distant time sources, and to use TSP to synchronize the clocks of other hosts on a local area or campus network. These protocols can provide synchronization within a few milliseconds locally and within a few hundred milliseconds over long distances.

5.7.6   Security

There are various methods of attempting to ensure the security of a network, including access limits such as passwords and physical protection of networking hardware, as well as several forms of encryption of data in order to make it unusable even if it is intercepted. This topic, although interesting, has mostly been excluded from this book due to lack of space.

5.8   *Internetwork Management*

In addition to specific protocols that handle specific network management problems, there need to be protocols and programs devoted to monitoring and adjusting a network. This need for network management protocols becomes particularly acute in a large internetwork. The IAB and IETF have pursued extensive work on network management in the *Internet* and other TCP/IP networks [Cerf 1988].

The basic network management architectures used by ISO-OSI and TCP/IP are very similar. This similarity is not a coincidence: their development efforts have mutually influenced each other. Both architectures manage networks through the use of a Management Information Base (MIB) that contains data in forms defined by a Structure of Management Information (SMI). However, the MIB and SMI are quite different in the two protocol suites, and different protocols are used to manage the MIB: SNMP in TCP/IP and CMIP in ISO-OSI [McCloghrie et al. 1989]. SNMP and CMIP are described in subsections below.

The basic ideas of MIB and SMI may also be appropriate for operating system administration in a networked environment.

5.8.1   HEMS

The High-Level Entity Management System (HEMS) was a proposal for remote node management on TCP/IP networks [Partridge 1988a]. Although HEMS is technically interesting (and many of its ideas have already appeared in other protocols), its authors withdrew it from consideration for the *Internet* standard protocol to help avoid lengthy debates about which management protocol to prefer (and thus lengthy delays in the deployment of a standard management protocol) [Partridge 1988b].

5.8.2   SGMP

The Simple Gateway Monitoring Protocol (SGMP) was imagined as early as April 1984 but not specified until 1987 [Davin et al. 1987]. Its purpose was to monitor the fast-growing *Internet* and *NSFNET* TCP/IP internetwork. It was superseded by SNMP [NYSERNet 1988].

5.8.3   SNMP

The Simple Network Management Protocol (SNMP) evolved from SGMP as additional needs were identified, such as the following [NYSERNet 1988]:

- A need to actually manage an internetwork, not just monitor one
- A need to monitor entities other than networks and gateways (such as hosts and terminal servers)
- A need to ease the eventual ISO-OSI transition

SNMP was specified in its initial form in June 1988 and in its final form in August 1988 [Case et al. 1988]. NYSERNet converted a former implementation of SGMP to SNMP Network Management Station (NMS) in the same year [Schoffstall and Yeong 1988; Fedor et al. 1988].

There are also detailed specifications of the Structure of Management Information (SMI) [Rose and McCloghrie 1988] and of the Management Information Base (MIB) [McCloghrie and Rose 1988], and these are both designed to be usable by a future ISO-OSI network management standard; for example, they use the ASN.1 presentation syntax. SMI and MIB are in fact shared between SNMP, the current *Internet* network management standard, and CMIP over TCP/IP (CMOT), the intended replacement standard. Thus, the information managed can be kept in the same form through the ISO-OSI transition.

This work was all coordinated by IAB task forces and has been approved by IAB as the basis of network management in the *Internet* [Cerf 1988]; see IAB in Chapter 8.

5.8.4   CMOT

CMIP over TCP/IP (CMOT) is a project to experiment with the ISO-OSI management protocol, CMIP, in the TCP/IP environment, with the goal of ensuring that CMIP works on large, complex internets and that it will be suitable for use as the eventual TCP/IP management protocol.

5.8.5   CMIP

The Common Management Information Protocol (CMIP) is the ISO-OSI protocol for MIB management. CMIP has reached the Draft International Standard level as DP9595/2, the Common Management Information Service (CMIS), and DP9596/2, CMIP. It should become an ISO standard by about 1990. Other ISO-OSI management architecture pieces are less complete. A detailed description of the SMI is now circulating in draft proposal form. The MIB is only beginning to be defined.

5.8.6   Netview and Netview-PC

Another well-regarded network management system is IBM's Netview. Unlike the other network management protocols mentioned here, all of which focus on designing a general suite of protocols that can be used by any management application, **Netview** is a program, and the protocols developed with it were designed to be convenient for **Netview** rather than for other applications. The apparent success of this approach largely reflects IBM's experience with managing SNA networks. **Netview-PC** allows systems that have not been designed to work with Netview to communicate with the **Netview** program through an IBM PC by converting information from the systems into the format required by **Netview**. This sort of network management scheme is now often referred to as *management by proxy* [Kanyuh 1988].

5.9 *Bibliographic Notes*

Most of the references for Chapter 4 are relevant for this chapter as well, and Partridge 1988c is of particular interest.

5.10 *References*

Allman 1986. Allman, Eric, "Interview with Peter Honeyman," *UNIX REVIEW*, vol. 4, no. 1, p. 64, January 1986.

Braun 1988. Braun, Hans-Werner, Personal communications, September 1988.

Brunell et al. 1988. Brunell, Mats, Lunds, Jan Engvald, Salminen, Harri, Soerensen, Jan P., and Torbergsen, Roald, "X.EARN," NORDUNET, 23 March 1988.

Carl-Mitchell and Quarterman 1987. Carl-Mitchell, F. Smoot, and Quarterman, John S., "Using ARP to Implement Transparent Subnet Gateways; RFC1027," *ARPANET Working Group Requests for Comments*, October 1987.

Case et al. 1988. Case, J., Fedor, M., Schoffstall, M., and Davin, J., "A Simple Network Management Protocol; RFC1067," *ARPANET Working Group Requests for Comments*, August 1988.

Cerf 1988. Cerf, Vinton G., "IAB Recommendations for the Development of Internet Network Management Standards; RFC1052," *ARPANET Working Group Requests for Comments*, April 1988.

Cerf and Kirstein 1978. Cerf, Vinton G., and Kirstein, Peter, "Issues in Packet Network Interconnection," *Proceedings of the IEEE*, vol. 66, no. 11, pp. 1386–1408, November 1978. Also in Partridge, *Innovations in Internetworking*, 1988.

Comer 1988. Comer, Douglas, *Internetworking with TCP/IP Principles, Protocols, and Architecture*, Prentice-Hall, Englewood Cliffs, NJ, 1988.

Crocker et al. 1977. Crocker, David H., Vittal, John J., Pogran, Kenneth T., and Henderson, D. Austin Jr., "Standard for the Format of ARPA Network Text Messages; RFC733," *ARPANET Working Group Requests for Comments*, 21 November 1977.

Davin et al. 1987. Davin, J., Case, J., Fedor, M., and Schoffstall, M., "A Simple Gateway Monitoring Protocol; RFC1028," *ARPANET Working Group Requests for Comments*, November 1987.

Deering 1988. Deering, S. E., "Multicast Routing in Internetworks and Extended LANs," *Proceedings of the ACM SIGCOMM '88 Workshop (Stanford, 16–19 August 1988)*, pp. 55–64, ACM SIGCOMM, New York, 1988.

Dongarra and Grosse 1987. Dongarra, Jack J., and Grosse, Eric, "Distribution of Mathematical Software via Electronic Mail," *Communications of the ACM*, vol. 30, no. 6, pp. 403–407, May 1987.

Fedor 1988. Fedor, Mark S., "Gated: A Multi-Routing Protocol Daemon for UNIX," *USENIX 1988 Summer Conference Proceedings (San Francisco, 20 – 24 June 1988)*, pp. 365 – 376, USENIX Association, Berkeley, CA, 1988.

Fedor et al. 1988. Fedor, Mark S., Schoffstall, Martin Lee, and Yeong, Wengyik, *SNMP: Network Management Station (NMS) and Agent/Server Implementation; Version 3.0*, NYSERNet, Inc., Troy, NY, 1988.

Gardner and Karels 1988. Gardner, Marianne L., and Karels, Mike, "Exterior Gateway Protocol, Version 3, Revisions and Extensions; IDEA009," *Internet Working Group IDEAs*, February 1988.

Ginsberg 1986. Ginsberg, Kylo, "Getting from Here to There," *UNIX REVIEW*, vol. 4, no. 1, p. 45, January 1986.

Gusella and Zatti 1984. Gusella, Riccardo, and Zatti, Stefano, "TEMPO: A Network Time Controller for a Distributed Berkeley UNIX System," *Proceedings of the Summer 1983 USENIX Conference (Salt Lake City, Utah, 12 – 15 June 1984)*, pp. 78 – 85, USENIX Association, Berkeley, CA, 1984.

Gusella and Zatti 1986. Gusella, R., and Zatti, S., "TSP: Time Synchronization Protocol for UNIX 4.3BSD," University of California at Berkeley EECS, Berkeley, CA, 1986.

Harary 1969. Harary, Frank, *Graph Theory*, Addison-Wesley, Reading, MA, 1969.

Hinden and Sheltzer 1982. Hinden, Robert, and Sheltzer, Alan, "The DARPA Internet Gateway; RFC823," *ARPANET Working Group Requests for Comments*, September 1982.

Huitema 1987. Huitema, Christian, Personal communications, 29 September 1987.

Kahn 1987. Kahn, Robert E., "Networks for Advanced Computing," *Trends In Computing*, pp. 34 – 41, October 1987.

Kanyuh 1988. Kanyuh, D., "An Integrated Network Management Product," *IBM Systems Journal*, vol. 27, no. 1, pp. 45 – 59, 1988. Also in Partridge, *Innovations in Internetworking*, 1988.

Kille 1984. Kille, S. E., *The JNT Mail Protocol (Grey Book)*, Joint Network Team, Rutherford Appleton Laboratory, Chilton, Didcot, Oxfordshire, England, March 1984.

Kille 1986. Kille, S. E., "Mapping between X.400 and RFC822; RFC987," *ARPANET Working Group Requests for Comments*, June 1986.

Kille 1987. Kille, S. E., "Addendum to RFC 987 (Mapping between X.400 and RFC-822); RFC1026," *ARPANET Working Group Requests for Comments*, September 1987.

Kluger and Shoch 1986. Kluger, Larry, and Shoch, John, "Names, Addresses, and Routes," *UNIX REVIEW*, vol. 4, no. 1, p. 30, January 1986.

Kummerfeld and Dick-Lauder 1981. Kummerfeld, R. J., and Dick-Lauder, P. R., "The Sydney Unix Network," *Australian Computer Journal*, vol. 13, no. 2, pp. 52 – 57, May 1981.

Kummerfeld and Dick-Lauder 1985. Kummerfeld, R. J., and Dick-Lauder, P. R., "Domain Addressing in SUN III," *Proceedings of the EUUG Paris 1985 Conference (Paris, 1985)*, European UNIX systems User Group, Buntingford, Herts., England, 1985.

Lauck et al. 1986. Lauck, Anthony G., Oran, David R., and Perlman, Radia J., "Digital Network Architecture Overview," *Digital Technical Journal*, no. 3, pp. 10 – 24, September 1986.

Lederman et al. 1988. Lederman, Sol, Harrenstien, Ken, and Stahl, Mary, Personal communications, 22 November 1988.

Leffler et al. 1989. Leffler, Samuel J., McKusick, Marshall Kirk, Karels, Michael J., and Quarterman, John S., *The Design and Implementation of the 4.3BSD UNIX Operating System*, Addison-Wesley, Reading, MA, 1989.

McCloghrie and Rose 1988. McCloghrie, K., and Rose, M., "Management Information Base for Network Management of TCP/IP-Based internets; RFC1066," *ARPANET Working Group Requests for Comments*, August 1988.

McCloghrie et al. 1989. McCloghrie, Keith, Rose, Marshall T., and Partridge, Craig, "Defining a Protocol-independent Management Information Base," *Proceedings First International Symposium on Integrated Network Management (Boston, May 1989)*, Boston, 1989.

Mills 1984. Mills, Dave, "Exterior Gateway Protocol Formal Specification; RFC904," *ARPANET Working Group Requests for Comments*, April 1984.

Mills 1986. Mills, Dave, "Autonomous Confederations; RFC975," *ARPANET Working Group Requests for Comments*, February 1986.

Mills 1988. Mills, Dave, "Network Time Protocol (Version 1) Specification and Implementation; RFC1059," *ARPANET Working Group Requests for Comments*, July 1988.

Mockapetris 1983a. Mockapetris, Paul, "Domain Names — Concepts and Facilities; RFC882," *ARPANET Working Group Requests for Comments*, November 1983.

Mockapetris 1983b. Mockapetris, Paul, "Domain Names — Implementation and Specification; RFC883," *ARPANET Working Group Requests for Comments*, November 1983.

Mockapetris 1984. Mockapetris, Paul, "The Domain Name System," *Proceedings of the IFIP 6.5 Working Conference on Computer Message Services (Nottingham, England, May 1984)*, 1984. Also as ISI/RS-84-133, June 1984.

Mockapetris 1986. Mockapetris, Paul, "Domain System Changes and Observations; RFC973," *ARPANET Working Group Requests for Comments*, January 1986.

Mockapetris 1987a. Mockapetris, Paul, "Domain Names — Concepts and Facilities; RFC1034," *ARPANET Working Group Requests for Comments*, November 1987.

Mockapetris 1987b. Mockapetris, Paul, "Domain Names — Implementations and Specifications; RFC1035," *ARPANET Working Group Requests for Comments*, November 1987.

Mockapetris and Dunlap 1988. Mockapetris, Paul, and Dunlap, Kevin J., "Development of the Domain Name System," *Proceedings of the ACM SIGCOMM '88 Workshop (Stanford, 16–19 August 1988)*, pp. 123–133, ACM SIGCOMM, New York, 1988. Also in Partridge, *Innovations in Internetworking*, 1988.

Mockapetris et al. 1984. Mockapetris, Paul, Postel, Jon, and Kirton, Paul, "Name Server Design for Distributed Systems," *Proceedings of the Seventh International Conference on Computer Communication (Sydney, Australia, October 1984)*, 1984. Also as ISI/RS-84-132, June 1984.

Mogul and Postel 1985. Mogul, J., and Postel, J., "Internet Standard Subnetting Procedure; RFC950," *ARPANET Working Group Requests for Comments*, August 1985.

MOSIS Project 1984. MOSIS Project, "The MOSIS System (What It Is and How to Use It)," USC/Information Sciences Institute, Marina Del Rey, CA, March 1984.

NYSERNet 1988. NYSERNet, "Internet Network Management: Simple Network Management Protocol," NYSERNet, Inc., New York, 1988.

Oberst and Partridge 1987. Oberst, Dan, and Partridge, Craig, "Letter to ACM Forum," *Communications of the ACM*, vol. 30, no. 8, p. 659, August 1987.

Palme 1987. Palme, Jacob, "QZCOM AMIGO Directory Service," Stockholm University Computer Centre — QZ, Stockholm, Sweden, 12 September 1987.

Palme 1988. Palme, Jacob, Personal communications, October–December 1988.

Partridge 1986a. Partridge, Craig, "Mail Routing and the Domain System; RFC974," *ARPANET Working Group Requests for Comments*, January 1986. Describes how mailers use MXs.

Partridge 1986b.   Partridge, Craig, "Mail Routing Using Domain Names: An Informal Tour," *Proceedings of the 1986 Summer USENIX Conference (Atlanta, 9–13 June 1986)*, pp. 366–376, USENIX Association, Berkeley, CA, 1986. A general discussion of the motivation behind domain names and how mailers in different networks were expected to use them.

Partridge 1986c.   Partridge, Craig, "Report From the Internet NIC on Domains," *CSNET-FORUM Digest*, vol. 2, no. 2, 19 February 1986.

Partridge 1987.   Partridge, Craig, "The CSNET Information Server: Automatic Document Distribution Using Electronic Mail," *Computer Communication Review*, vol. 17, no. 4, pp. 3–10, October/November 1987.

Partridge 1988a.   Partridge, Craig, "A UNIX Implementation of HEMS," *Proceedings of the Winter 1988 USENIX Conference (Dallas, Texas, 9–12 February 1988)*, pp. 89–96, USENIX Association, Berkeley, CA, 1988.

Partridge 1988b.   Partridge, Craig, Personal communications, August–November 1988.

Partridge 1988c.   Partridge, Craig, *Innovations in Internetworking*, ARTECH House, Norwood, MA, October 1988.

Plummer 1982.   Plummer, David C., "An Ethernet Address Resolution Protocol; RFC826," *ARPANET Working Group Requests for Comments*, November 1982.

Postel 1984.   Postel, Jonathon B., "Domain Name System Implementation Schedule — Revised; RFC921," *ARPANET Working Group Requests for Comments*, October 1984.

Postel and Reynolds 1984.   Postel, Jonathon B., and Reynolds, Joyce, "Domain Requirements; RFC920," *ARPANET Working Group Requests for Comments*, October 1984.

Rose and McCloghrie 1988.   Rose, M., and McCloghrie, K., "Structure and Identification of Management Information for TCP/IP-Based Internets; RFC1065," *ARPANET Working Group Requests for Comments*, August 1988.

Schoffstall and Yeong 1988.   Schoffstall, Martin L., and Yeong, W., "SGMP/SNMP Implementation," NYSERNet, Inc., New York, 1988.

Schroeder et al. 1984.   Schroeder, M. D., Birrell, A. D., and Needham, R. M., "Experience with Grapevine: The Growth of a Distributed System," *ACM Transactions on Computer Systems*, vol. 2, no. 1, pp. 3–23, February 1984. Also in Partridge, *Innovations in Internetworking*, 1988.

Seamonson and Rosen 1984.   Seamonson, Linda J., and Rosen, Eric C., " 'Stub' Exterior Gateway Protocol; RFC888," *ARPANET Working Group Requests for Comments*, January 1984.

Shoch 1978.   Shoch, J. F., "Internetwork Naming, Addressing, and Routing," *Proceedings of the IEEE Computer Society International Conference (17th COMPCON, September 1978)*, pp. 430–437, IEEE, New York, 1978.

Tanenbaum 1988.   Tanenbaum, Andrew S., *Computer Networks*, 2d ed., Prentice-Hall, Englewood Cliffs, NJ, 1988.

Thomas 1988.   Thomas, Eric, Personal communications, 9 December 1988.

Waitzman et al. 1988.   Waitzman, D., Partridge, C., and Deering, S., "Distance Vector Multicast Routing Protocol; RFC1075," *ARPANET Working Group Requests for Comments*, November 1988.

6 *Administration*

In addition to characteristics already discussed in previous chapters, such as services and protocols, real networks have purposes, names, administrations, funding, sizes, extents, and speeds. There is some way to contact their administrators and to get information about them. All of these characteristics are given (when known) in the descriptions of systems in Chapter 7 and Part II of this book.

6.1   *Purpose*

Networks may be classified according to their purposes. Two strong groupings are readily visible in the real world: noncommercial and commercial. Most noncommercial networks are closely interconnected into a metanetwork that allows electronic mail to pass between almost any pair of them. This metanetwork is sometimes called *Worldnet*. The commercial systems do not have a collective name, perhaps because most of them were not interconnected until recently. All of the networks and conferencing systems that are interconnected for mail transfer form a worldwide metanetwork, the *Matrix*, which is the subject of this book.

6.1.1   Noncommercial Systems

Noncommercial systems either do not charge for their services (at least not to the end user) or are nonprofit. They can be further categorized into several types, such as research, military, academic, company, and cooperative. Most of these are true networks—i.e., they are made up of many communicating computers. Most of them support mail, but many of them do not support computer conferencing. Most of the ones that use dedicated links support remote login, but most of the dialup networks do not. File transfer support varies widely. Noncommercial does not necessarily mean free; many of the international gateways charge for their services, *CSNET* and *UUNET* charge for all traffic, and even the *Internet* is moving toward cost recovery. But they are all nonprofit.

6.1.1.1   *Research Networks*

Research networks have research into networking technology as their primary purpose. Examples include *ARPANET* and *MFEnet* in the United States, *CYCLADES* and *ARISTOTE* in France, *SERCnet* and *JANET* in the United Kingdom, and *HMI-NET*, *BERNET*, and *DFN* in Germany.

6.1.1.2   *Military Networks*

Military networks are used in support of military operations. (Some research networks are supported by military funds but are not used for operations.) Examples of military networks include *MILNET*, *AUTODIN*, *WIN*, *DISNET*, *SCINET*, *WINCS*, and *WWMCCS* in the United States and *DREnet* in Canada. There are also military conferencing systems, such as *Army Forum*. Most military systems are *not* described in this book. Many do not communicate with each other, much less with nonmilitary networks.

6.1.1.3   *Academic Networks*

Many universities support campus networks that are not intended as testbeds for research in networking but may be used in support of research, perhaps in other fields. There are wide area networks of this kind as well, such as *REUNIR* in France, *EARN* in Europe, *BITNET* in the United States, and *NetNorth* in Canada.

6.1.1.4   *Company Networks*

Many large companies maintain internal networks for their own uses. These include *VNET* of IBM, *Easynet* of Digital, *HP Internet* of Hewlett-Packard (HP), *XEROX Internet* of XEROX, and *Tandem* of the company of the same name. When such a network is used to support all the operations of a single corporation, it is called an *enterprise information system*.

6.1.1.5   *Cooperative Networks*

A cooperative network is decentralized in administration and funding. That is, it is not primarily paid for or run by a single corporation or agency. Examples include *JUNET*, *ACSnet*, *UUCP*, *USENET*, and *FidoNet*.

6.1.2   Commercial Systems

Commercial systems charge for their services in order to make a profit. Systems such as *CompuServe*, *The Source*, *GEnie*, *EIES*, the *WELL*, *MCI Mail*, and *AT&T Mail* each usually pretend to be a single machine, and usually that is actually true: they are generally not true networks. Most of them do support true conferencing systems, although there is a class of networks, such as *MCI Mail* and *AT&T Mail*, that support only electronic mail. There are few points of interconnection among these systems, and even fewer between them and the noncommercial metanetwork, although *DASnet* is an exception on both counts. Although they all charge for their services, some of them, such as *TWICS*, act remarkably like nonprofit services in their attitudes toward interconnections and attracting users.

6.1.3   Summary of Groupings

Some of the distinctions between the two primary groupings of systems are shown in Table 6.1. Some of these differences are diminishing. Many of the noncommercial systems are moving toward charging for cost recovery, and others already do this. Interconnections among commercial services and with noncommercial services are increasing, as some noncommercial systems are adding conferencing services. But the user communities of the two groups are still largely and strongly distinct: a user of a system in one group usually will not even have heard of major systems of the other group. People on the oldest *(EIES)* and the largest *(USENET* or France's *Minitel)* computer conferencing systems in the world may never have heard of the other system.

6.2   *Names*

One of the more obvious characteristics of an actual network is its name. Most networks have a short name for everyday use, such as *ARPANET*, *DFN*, *JUNET*, or *CYCLADES*. Uppercase and lowercase are often significant, as in *EUnet*, *USENET*, *Easynet*, or *RangKoM*. A few networks do not have short names, e.g., *HP Internet*. Some names have meanings in languages other than English — for example, *REUNIR* means "to reunite" in French; these are translated in the network descriptions.

The short name for a network is always printed in italics in this book. This is to indicate that such a name is a network name and that there is probably a section describing it. All network names appear in the index, and the first page number given for a network is that of its defining section.

Table 6.1. *Noncommercial versus commercial systems*

	Noncommercial	Commercial
Profit	Nonprofit	Usually for-profit
Charging	Sometimes	Always
True network	Always	Seldom
Mail	Mostly	Mostly
True conferencing	Sometimes	Mostly
Interconnection	Close	Loose

Most networks have a longer name. Examples include Deutsches Forschungsnetz (*DFN*), Japan UNIX Network (*JUNET*), or Rangkaian Komputer Malaysia (*RangKoM*). These are translated into English where appropriate and possible, as in German Research Network (*DFN*) or Malaysian Computer Network (*RangKoM*). Some networks do not have a longer name, e.g., *CYCLADES*.

Occasionally there are connotations to either the short name or the long name that are not obvious. For example, the Cyclades are a group of islands. This is well known in France but may not be elsewhere.

6.3   *Administration and Funding*

Networks and conferencing systems need income to support them and administrators to run them. Such administration and funding affect the above classifications and are also important in themselves. Several related terms are used in this book.

6.3.1   Administration

The most general term is *administration*, including all of the others below. This may not be the usage some people expect, but a general term is needed, and this one is used.

6.3.2   Policy

High-level decisions about classes of acceptable users and organizations, kinds of interconnections to other systems, protocol suites, planned growth rates, and future sources of funds involve *policy*. Those who fund the network, whether a government agency, a private company, or end users, usually have a strong say in this. All the other kinds of administrators listed below implement policy.

6.3.3 Management

Managers are primarily concerned with the technology of the system, not with users or outsiders. Management can be further classed into two groups: *development* and *operations*.

6.3.3.1 *Development*

Developers do tasks such as analysis of performance or implementation of protocols.

6.3.3.2 *Operations*

Operations groups perform practical technical functions, such as installation of hardware or software. This term is sometimes used as a synonym for *management*.

6.3.4 Support

Although *support* is sometimes used as a synonym for *operations*, it usually refers to interactions with end users, such as informing them about policies, making specific decisions about access, collecting fees, and taking orders for new links. Actual installation of links may be done by operations.

6.3.5 Public Relations

Informing potential funding agencies or users about the system can be very important to its future viability. Informing the general public can ward off misunderstandings and helps others building similar systems. In general, *public relations* helps avoid misunderstandings.

6.3.6 Administrative Organizations

Smaller systems may have all these roles handled by a single person. Large ones may distinguish any or all of these categories, and each category may be handled by a different organization. Some common terms for organizations concerned with aspects of network administration are NOC and NIC.

6.3.6.1 *NOC*

A Network Operations Center (NOC) usually handles *operations*.

6.3.6.2 *NIC*

A Network Information Center (NIC) usually handles both end user *support* and *public relations*.

6.3.6.3   *Management Organizations*

Some networks have both a NIC and a NOC and make them both responsible to a separate management organization, which usually has a name specific to the network. The management organization may also take on public relations functions. Many large networks with such elaborate administrative structures have policy set by an outside funding agency.

6.4   *Connectivity and Configuration*

As discussed in Chapter 5, the *connectivity* of networks may vary according to whether more than one network is involved and at what protocol layer connections are made. That is, a network may be a *simple network* (or just *network*), it may include *subnets*, or it may be an *internet* or *metanet*. The *configuration* of the links of a network often has a recognizable form, such as a *star*, *tree*, *clique*, or *graph*.

6.5   *Extent*

One of the most readily comprehensible characteristics of a network is the geographical area it covers. There are recognizable categories of extent that are distinguished largely by the technology used to support the network and the services provided, but also by political divisions such as international borders.

6.5.1   Local Area Networks

Several popular kinds of local area network (LAN) technologies, such as Ethernet, token bus, and token ring, are commonly used for connecting hosts inside single buildings or other small areas. These are usually simple networks, not internets or metanets.

6.5.2   Campus Networks

Campus networks are like LANs, but they connect hosts on an entire academic or company campus. These are what long-haul networks often connect, and they have some interesting aspects (multiple protocols, centralized security, and controlled economics) that are not found as frequently on larger networks. Many campus networks are themselves internetworks or even metanetworks of LANs.

6.5.3   Metropolitan Area Networks

Metropolitan area networks connect hosts in an area of the scale of a city or county. They are frequently internetworks. Examples include *BERNET* in Berlin and *BARRNet* in the San Francisco Bay Area.

6.5.4   State or Provincial Networks

The next scale up is an entire state or province. Examples of this type of network are *THEnet* and *Sesquinet* in Texas, *MRNet* in Minnesota, *Onet* in Ontario, and *BCnet* in British Columbia. One of the oldest statewide networks is in North Carolina.

6.5.5   Regional Networks

A regional network can have any scale larger than campus and smaller than national, including metropolitan and state or provincial. Regional networks often act as backbones interconnecting smaller networks. There are numerous examples, including *MIDnet*, *SURAnet*, *NYSERNet*, *CRIM*, and other *NSFNET* and *NRCnet* regional networks.

6.5.6   National Networks

Almost every industrialized country has at least one national research network, and usually several, each specializing in a different protocol suite, academic discipline, funding source, etc. Examples include *JANET*, *Starlink*, and *UKnet* in the United Kingdom, *DFN* and *Dnet* in Germany, *FNET*, *ARISTOTE*, and *REUNIR* in France, *CDNnet* in Canada, *JUNET* in Japan, and *SDN* in Korea. Sometimes national networks are not used much for research, such as *Minitel* in France. National networks are often built by interconnecting regional networks with a wide area backbone network.

6.5.7   International Networks

Any network that has large numbers of hosts on different sides of a national boundary is an international network. There are quite a few of these, such as *NORDUnet* in the Nordic countries, *AUSEAnet* in Australasia and Southeast Asia, *SPEARNET* in the South Pacific, and *PACNET* for the Pacific Basin.

6.5.8   Worldwide

The largest international networks are worldwide, which in this book is taken to mean having large numbers of hosts on more than two continents. Examples include *BITNET*, *HEPnet*, and *UUCP*.

6.5.9   Clusters

Most of the networks described in this book have wide geographical extent, but the distribution of their hosts and users is not uniform. Many of the internets consist of many LANs connected by a few long-haul networks. Thus, the hosts cluster on the LANs, which themselves tend to cluster. Most continental networks in North America have concentrations of hosts in Silicon Valley near San Francisco, Route 128 around Boston, and the Toronto area, because many North American computing related companies and academic institutions have offices in those places. Networks such as *CSNET* that are primarily academic are widely dispersed, with nodes mostly at academic institutions. *USENET* and *UUCP* have concentrations in New Jersey because of AT&T.

6.6   *Size*

It is difficult to find a single metric for size that is meaningful on all systems.

6.6.1   Hosts, Sites, Users, and Mailboxes

The traditional unit for networks is number of hosts. This is useful for networks such as *ARPANET* and *CSNET* where most nodes are medium size time-sharing systems and the exact number of users on each is hard to determine. Some networks consist primarily of workstations (*XEROX Internet*) or personal computers (*FidoNet*) where there is usually one user per host (though many *FidoNet* nodes are bulletin boards that may have many users). Others, such as *BITNET* and its relatives, consist mostly of large IBM and Digital mainframes that are hosts in the *ARPANET* sense but have many more users per host. Also, the number of users who have access to a network is not usually the same as the number who actually use the network. Thus, the number of active mailboxes, for instance, may be interesting but is usually hard to determine. Sometimes it is possible to get a breakdown of hosts by operating system type, such as 60 percent **UNIX**, 30 percent **VMS**, and 10 percent other. Users may occasionally be categorized in groups such as 40 percent computer science, 10 percent administration, and 50 percent students.

This book does not list all of the sites, hosts, or users of any system. There are others that do that [LaQuey 1989; Karrenberg and Goos 1988].

6.6.2   Growth

Several large networks have moved from static host tables to distributed nameservice due to growth. This happened successively to the *Internet* (about 1984 – 1985), *EUnet* (1986 – 1988), *UUCP* (1986 – 1989), *BITNET* (probably 1989), and *FidoNet* (possibly 1990). Each network changed at a different size according to obvious measurements such as numbers of hosts, sites, users, or mailboxes. The deciding factors seem to have been a critical size (thousands of hosts) and a high rate of growth (perhaps 15 percent per year). Growth rates are recorded in this book when information is available.

6.6.3   Other

Sometimes other measures are obtainable, such as network diameter; throughput (messages, packets, or bytes) over a reasonable time period such as per hour, day, or week; or physical distances between hosts (linear or traveled by data). An especially interesting measure of increasing interest with the spread of campus networks is network diameter in *fiefdoms*: a single Ethernet can span half a dozen academic departments and the personal empires of countless professors. Many of the other measures do not apply to conferencing systems, but *fiefdoms* do.

6.7   *Speed*

There is no single commonly accepted measure for the throughput or responsiveness of a network. This book uses a few simple metrics that may serve as rules of thumb.

6.7.1   Common Link Speed

A useful comparative speed metric is that of the most common long-haul links between widely separated hosts. This is not the speed of the fastest link, unless most traffic travels over it. It should be the speed of the links most commonly used in ordinary traffic (not necessarily the speed of the most common link). A network with 9600bps telephone links and one T1 microwave link should have the speed of the T1 link listed here if it carries most of the traffic. For single machine conferencing systems, speeds of common access methods, such as dialup modems or X.25 PDN, are used. Examples of speeds include 300bps, 1200bps, 2400bps, 4800bps, 9600bps, 19.2Kbps, 32Kbps, 56Kbps, 64Kbps, 68Kbps, 448Kbps, 1.544Mbps (North American T1), 2.048Mbps (European T1), 10Mbps (Ethernet), 45Mbps (DS3), 100Mbps (FDDI), and 1Gbps.

6.7.2   Mail Delivery Time

The average time for delivery of mail is of interest to users, but it varies so much even within networks that only three values are usually cited:

Minutes	Delivery takes less than an hour.
Hours	Delivery takes at least an hour, but less than a day.
Days	Delivery usually takes at least a day.

6.8   *Services*

Users want to know what services a network offers, and these are usually listed, although sometimes they are obvious from the protocols a network uses and are not explicitly discussed.

6.9   *Uses and Effects*

Some uses and effects of a system may be described.

6.10   *Protocols*

The protocols used in a network are listed where known and are sometimes discussed. Short descriptions of unfamiliar protocols can usually be found in Chapter 4 or Chapter 5 by looking for them by name in the index. Actual uses of protocols in networks may vary from the simple layering models presented in Chapter 4.

6.11   *Naming, Addressing, and Routing*

Sometimes management protocols such as those described in Chapter 5 are discussed separately. The most common kind to be treated this way are protocols for naming, addressing, or routing or for interconnections.

6.12   *Interconnections*

Actual connections from the network to other networks are often listed, with syntaxes to use for sending mail and names of necessary user visible gateways.

6.13   *Standards*

Standards promulgated by bodies such as those discussed in Chapter 8 may be very relevant to some networks and are discussed wherever appropriate in a section on a network.

6.14   *History*

Most networks have histories, even if only of a few months. Some network descriptions include notes on interesting developments.

6.15   *Plans*

Many networks have plans for future developments. Growth and protocol conversion are the two most common topics in such plans.

6.16   *Access*

Most network descriptions in this book include a few words at the end about access. Kinds of information that may be given include those listed in the following subsections.

6.16.1   **People**

Contact people who can handle requests to join the system, questions about sending mail to the system, or provide other information might be provided. The information may be the same for any two or three of these purposes, and if the system has a NIC, it is probably listed for all of them. A paper mail address and an electronic address are included where possible, and a telephone number where convenient.

6.16.1.1   *Electronic Addresses*

Electronic addresses are in whatever form could be obtained, but where possible an *Internet* DNS domain address is given because that is the most common address form I have used in communicating with sources for this book and conversions from it to other formats are usually straightforward. DNS and *UUCP* addresses are given without type indication, e.g.:

>   matrix@longway.tic.com
>   uunet!longway!matrix

DNS addresses are recognizable by the at sign, the dots, and the top level domain. *UUCP* addresses are recognizable by the exclamation points and are usually given starting at some well-known host such as *uunet* or *mcvax*. Other kinds of electronic addresses are often given with a type indicator prepended, which usually is the name of the network and a colon, e.g.:

>   SPAN: ABCDEFG::HOST
>   Telex: 012-34567

For addresses in DECNET format, however, the type prefix may be omitted when it is obvious from the context what network is being referred to (the DECNET address form itself is recognizable by the double colon).

6.16.1.2   *Telephone Numbers*

Telephone numbers are in international format, beginning with a plus sign and a country code (e.g., +44 for the United Kingdom, +49 for West Germany, +33 for France, +81 for Japan, +82 for Korea, +61 for Australia, +64 for New Zealand, +1 for the United States or Canada, and +52 for Mexico). Thus,

>   +33 1 2233 4455

might be a French telephone number. When dialing this number from another country, it is necessary to dial a sequence of digits to get an international line, followed by the country code and the entire number. The prepended sequence may vary depending on where the dialing is done, and it may be necessary to have operator assistance instead. A common international dialing prefix in the United States is 011, so to call this French number from the United States, one might actually dial

>   011 33 1 2233 4455

It may or may not be necessary to wait for a secondary dial tone after the 011, depending on where the call is dialed. In France, it is not necessary to use the country code. To dial this number from Paris, one would also omit the 1 after the 33, because the 1 is the area code for Paris.

The North American country code, +1, sometimes confuses people in the States, who think it is the American long-distance prefix, 1. But in a number like

    +1-512-555-1212

the +1 is the country code. Although it is necessary to dial 1 before the area code 512 when calling this number from another area code within the United States, it is not necessary to prepend 011. When dialing the number from another country, a locally defined international dialing prefix should be prepended.

In this book, European telephone numbers are usually given with spaces as separators, and all others generally appear with hyphens as separators.

6.16.1.3   *Postal Addresses*

Although it is conventional in many countries to put the postal code on the same line as the country name, this practice leads to confusion if used in the United States, where such a line is often mistaken for a state address, causing insufficient postage to be applied. Postal addresses in this book include the postal code but have the country name last, on a line by itself.

6.16.2   Programs

Many networks support automatic facilities to return answers to queries on selected topics, either interactively or by mail. Other networks have large libraries of materials that are accessible by file transfer.

6.16.3   Publications

Some network administrations publish newsletters, magazines, or bibliographies.

6.17   *Reference Sections*

Finally, written references were often used in compiling the information about a system. They are given in the format specified at the end of Chapter 1.

6.18 *References*

Karrenberg and Goos 1988.   Karrenberg, Daniel, and Goos, Anke, *European R&D E-mail Directory*, European UNIX systems User Group, Buntingford, Herts., England, December 1988.

LaQuey 1989.   LaQuey, Tracy Lynn, *Users' Directory of Computer Networks*, Digital Press, Bedford, MA, 1989.

7   *History and Future*

Computer networks have spread to larger and smaller machines, different lower layer technologies, different protocols, and many nations. Although their diversity continues to increase, most noncommercial networks are connected at least for mail exchange, and thus already constitute a world-wide metanetwork, first predicted years ago and called *Worldnet*.

7.1   *Time-Sharing Services*

One of the first ways computing facilities became available to the public was through time-sharing services, in the 1960s [Kahn 1987]. Since computers were big and expensive, it was desirable to have remote users. This required remote terminal communications, which was a motivator for the development of networks. Some early pioneers in this area were General Electric (GE) and Tymshare, Inc. (Tymshare). Public data networks (PDNs) such as *TYMNET* and *Telenet* were later developed to meet this need [Schwartz 1987, 3–4].

7.2   *Corporations*

Some companies developed their own networking technologies, usually starting with local area networks. Long-haul networks came to be used not only for communication among directly connected hosts, but also to tie LANs into internets.

7.2.1   XEROX

XEROX was a pioneer in network research, and in fact Robert Metcalfe and David Boggs of XEROX invented Ethernet [XEROX 1980; Tanenbaum 1988, 36]. The PARC Universal Packet (PUP) protocol [Boggs et al. 1980] and XEROX Network Services (XNS) protocol suites also came from XEROX. The first version of PUP and the *XEROX Internet* was working around 1975, just before or concurrent with the first TCP implementations at BBN, Stanford, and University College London (UCL) [Cerf 1988].

7.2.2   General Motors

General Motors (GM) was influential in early networking standards efforts aimed at automating factory floors and most of the rest of the company. They preferred a token bus instead of CSMA/CD. GM was instrumental in the later development of the MAP/TOP protocols, which are related to the ISO-OSI protocol suite. The Manufacturing Automation Protocol (MAP) is widely used in manufacturing. The Technical and Office Protocols (TOP) were originally designed by Boeing but were developed in cooperation with GM [Tanenbaum 1988, 36 – 40].

7.2.3   IBM

International Business Machines (IBM) built an early prototype token ring network at its Zurich laboratories and pressed for that as a standard: this is the ancestor of IEEE 802.5 [Tanenbaum 1988, 37]. IBM is perhaps even better known for its System Network Architecture (SNA). SNA was very influential in the development of the ISO-OSI model and protocol suite [Tanenbaum 1988, 43 – 47]. The NJE protocols used in *BITNET* also originated inside IBM, although apparently not originally as a sanctioned project. NJE was used to build the internal network *VNET*.

7.2.4   Digital Equipment Corporation

DECNET Phase I was announced by Digital Equipment Corporation (Digital) in 1975 and delivered in 1976 to connect PDP-11s running **RSX-11**. Phase II was announced in 1977 and delivered in 1978; Phase III was both announced and delivered in 1980; and Phase IV, the current one, was announced in 1982 and delivered in 1984 [Lauck et al. 1986]. Phase V was expected in 1989 and was expected to be compatible with ISO-OSI protocols. Digital was taking orders for an X.400 implementation in 1988.

7.2.5　AT&T

The best known protocol from American Telephone & Telegraph Company (AT&T) is probably UUCP, which is used in the *UUCP* mail network and the *USENET* news network. The *UUCP* network itself had its beginnings at AT&T Bell Laboratories (Bell Labs). *USENET* began elsewhere, but both networks became quite popular within AT&T. There are also many other internal AT&T networks.

7.2.6　Burroughs

Another early pioneer in this area was Burroughs, with the Burroughs Network Architecture (BNA) [Schwartz 1987, 4].

7.3　*Researchers*

As soon as it became economically feasible to use computers to determine the use of communications bandwidth, packet switching technology and networks were developed [Roberts 1974]. It is hard to say which was the first packet switching network, but there are few contenders. Although early British experiments may have taken place before the deployment of the *ARPANET* in 1969, Britain's National Physical Laboratories (NPL) experimented with a single node, and the *ARPANET* was actually built in 1968, though not delivered until the following year. There was an experimental packet switching network at the Société International de Télécommunications Aéronautiques (SITA) [Schwartz 1987, 7–11] from 1968 to 1970 [Cerf 1988].

With the planned demise of the *ARPANET*, none of the early research networks will continue to exist under its original name. Some have successor networks, such as *JANET* for *SERCnet*, *Internet* and *DRI* for *ARPANET*, *DFN* for *HMI-NET* and *BERNET*, and *ARISTOTE* for *CYCLADES*. But they have had greater influence in producing networking protocols, standards, and communities of researchers experienced with both theory and practice.

7.3.1　United Kingdom

7.3.1.1　*NPL*

The first packet switching network was implemented at the National Physical Laboratories (NPL) in the United Kingdom about 1968. An international connection was established to *CYCLADES* in France in August 1974 [Pouzin 1982]. It is not clear whether there was any direct descent in technology or administration to *SERCnet*, and thus to *JANET*, but there was influence nonetheless.

7.3.1.2   *SERCnet*

In 1966, a report [Flowers 1966] was published in the United Kingdom that led to the formation of the Computer Board for Universities and Research Councils (CB), funded by the Department of Education and Science (DES). CB was to plan university computing on a long-term basis. It chose to have regional computing centers that would be connected to universities by star networks based on PTT leased lines. This pattern can still be seen in academic networking in the United Kingdom today, although current services are mostly quite a bit different from remote batch, which was the main service of early networks [Spratt 1986].

There were some intersite connections among universities by 1976, which was also the year in which CCITT approved the first version of X.25. The British Post Office Experimental Packet Switching Service (EPSS) encouraged the development of general networking protocols in this community during the 1970s and set up a network, *EPSS*. This network predated the CCITT X.25 recommendations and used similar but incompatible protocols. Although much useful development and research was done, the network was finally closed in 1980 when X.25 services became established. The Science Research Council (SRC), which later became the Science and Engineering Research Council (SERC), set up a network based on the EPSS protocols but later moved to X.25 for network support in 1977. The high-level protocols providing job entry and interactive services were preserved in the transition and were finally phased out when the Coloured Book protocols became established in the early 1980s [Bryant 1988].

This early network became *SERCnet* in 1977. There were switching centers at Rutherford Appleton Laboratory (RAL), Daresbury Laboratory, and the Universities of London, Cambridge, and Edinburgh. Many universities and polytechnic sites had connections. The Coloured Book protocols were developed on this network.

Meanwhile, CB set up several Working Parties to examine the possibility of a national backbone network, and in 1976 it set up a Network Unit (NU) to further the use of standards for academic network communication. Among other activities, CB sponsored a series of Networkshops and investigated the needs of the academic community. CB and SERC considered NU plans for networking based on open systems and, on 1 April 1979, reformed NU into the Joint Network Team (JNT) to implement those plans and to emphasize the cooperation of the two parent agencies.

The choice between leased lines or British Telecom (BT) Packet Switchstream Service (PSS) was controversial (like a similar discussion currently in progress between *EARN* and RARE, as described in those sections in Chapter 13 and Chapter 8). Leased lines were eventually chosen because *PSS* would have required volume charges. The already existing *SERCnet* was to be used, in combination with other existing links, as the core of a new network, which would, in turn, be the backbone of an internet connecting to LANs on the various sites. The new network was to be called *JANET*, for Joint Academic Network. Its Network Executive was formed in 1982, and *SERCnet* was integrated into *JANET* on 1 April 1984 [Spratt 1986]; the network *SERCnet* no longer exists.

The Natural Environment Research Council (NERC) was closely associated with *SERCnet* and operated switches at Swinton and Bidston; these were also incorporated into *JANET*. Other organizations funding wide area networks at the time included the Agricultural and Food Research Council (AFRC), the University Grants Committee (UGC), and CB. Each of these, together with NERC and SERC, are in turn funded by DES. This single ultimate source of funding made the merger of all these projects acceptable to the telecommunications licensing authority. Some direct funding was provided at the outset by NERC and SERC. Although funding is mainly from DES, this is funneled through the budgets of the CB and the Research Council (RC). Some funding comes from the many polytechnics now connected that are supported by local authorities [Bryant 1988].

Combining all of these networking efforts led not only to increased connectivity, but also to reduced overall cost. Some redundant links were merged, and some switches were removed. Consolidation was not the only goal, however. Improved and new services, connections to new sites, and interconnections with other networks were also of interest [Wells 1984].

7.3.2   United States

7.3.2.1   *ARPANET*

The *ARPANET* began in 1968 as a small research experiment [DARPA 1983; McQuillan and Walden 1977; McQuillan et al. 1972] and was delivered to the Advanced Research Projects Agency (ARPA) in 1969. This network demonstrated the viability of long-haul packet switched computer networks. It eventually grew into a national U.S. backbone network, leading to the current *Internet*, including *NSFNET* and others that are interconnected using TCP/IP.

In the beginning, ARPA, an arm of the U.S. Department of Defense (DoD), noticed that its contractors were tending to request the same resources (such as databases, powerful CPUs, and graphics facilities) and decided to develop a network among the contractors that would allow sharing such resources [Roberts 1974]. In addition to the original goals of networking research and resource sharing, researchers almost immediately began using the network for collaboration through electronic mail and other services. The network worked so well that it had developed into a research utility, run by the Defense Communications Agency (DCA), by the end of 1975 [Cerf 1988]. In 1983, it was split into *MILNET*, a production military network, and *ARPANET*, which reverted to research. ARPA had meanwhile changed its name to the Defense Advanced Research Projects Agency (DARPA). There were plans to phase out the *ARPANET* in 1988 and 1989 because its long-haul links have been overtaken by newer technology, but the internet that has grown around it, the *Internet*, continues, with *NSFNET* and *CSNET* as major parts. The successor of *ARPANET* for research will be *DRI* [Lederman et al. 1988].

Administration and Funding

Policy is set by DARPA and executed by the Defense Data Network Program Management Office (DDN/PMO), which also manages *MILNET* [Dennett et al. 1985]. *ARPANET* is funded by DARPA and other government agencies. The main contractor for the communications subnet was Bolt Beranek and Newman (BBN) of Cambridge, Massachusetts [Roberts 1974]. Access to the *ARPANET* is officially limited to organizations doing research funded by federal money [Dennett et al. 1985].

Protocols

ARPANET uses a communications subnet, each of whose nodes is called an Interface Message Processor (IMP). These IMPs were originally Honeywell 516s and then Honeywell 316s, followed by BBN C-30s and C-300s. They communicate with hosts using the BBN 1822 protocol, which is named after the report that describes it. The original host – host protocol was called Network Control Protocol (NCP), of which there were several versions.

It became clear by 1976 that local area network protocols and technology such as Ethernet [XEROX 1980] would lead to a proliferation of LANs that would need to be interconnected. This led to the development of the TCP/IP protocols. Since 1983, the fourth version of TCP has been current. Details have been improved since then, and implementations continue to improve [Jacobson 1988; Karn 1988].

IMPs were renamed Packet Switch Nodes (PSNs) about 1984. Most of the links between them were 56Kbps leased lines [McQuillan et al. 1972]. These were originally state of the art and more than adequate, but increasing load led to increasing congestion, and by 1988 DARPA decided to retire the transcontinental links and nodes in favor of satellite and *NSFNET* links, and to break the network into several pieces on the coasts. There were about 150 *ARPANET* hosts at that time, as shown in Figure 7.1. The research capability of *ARPANET* is to be taken over by *DRI*.

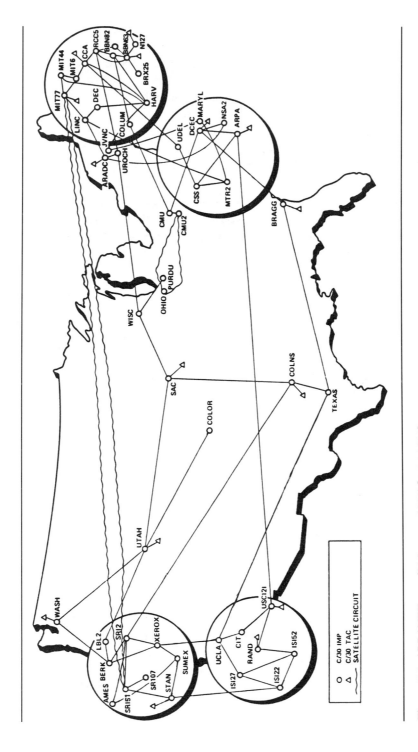

Figure 7.1. *ARPANET map (31 January 1988)* [DCA 1988]

Address Space

The original NCP address space was 8 bits, as this was thought to be larger than would ever conceivably be used. This was changed in 1977 to 16 bits. The address space for the newly invented IP protocol was made to be 4 bytes, or 32 bits, as, once again, this was thought to be larger than would ever be used. By 1983 it had become clear that clever allocation of these bits would be necessary. Originally, the first byte designated a network (e.g., 10 for *ARPANET*), while the other three designated a host on that network. There were clearly going to be more than 256 networks in the newly emerging *Internet*, so the address space was bit encoded to allow 1, 2, or 3 bytes to be used as the network designator. Eventually, a third level of hierarchy, subnets, was introduced between the network and host levels. Details on these addressing schemes can be found in Chapter 5.

7.3.2.2   *Aloha*

The *Aloha* network at the University of Hawaii (UH) uses packet radio to connect nodes scattered among seven campuses on four islands to the main campus in Honolulu [Abramson 1970; Abramson and Kui 1975]. The transmission speed is 9600bps, and the network is apparently still operational and connected to *ARPANET* and *PACNET*.

The *Aloha* network was developed by Norman Abramson and colleagues and was first operational in 1971 [Tanenbaum 1988, 121–126, 177–182, 182–183]. The protocols developed (with the same name) [Abramson 1985] have been highly influential in the development of network channel allocation schemes.

7.3.2.3   *MAILNET*

MAILNET originated as a joint project of the Massachusetts Institute of Technology (MIT), EDUCOM, and fifteen pioneer sites, with some initial funding from the Carnegie Foundation. Unfortunately, the network vanished by the end of 1986 due to a lack of funds. *MAILNET* was an inexpensive mail network connecting heterogeneous computer systems at academic institutions. It was run by EDUCOM and was a star network around a Multics machine at MIT, *MIT-MULTICS*. That machine ceased operation on 2 January 1988. Institutions with *MAILNET* hosts were charged an installation fee ($2,100) and a monthly service fee ($190), plus usage charges based on the number and length of messages sent each month. Eighty percent of all *MAILNET* messages cost less than 20 cents. Monthly traffic averaged just over 12,000 messages from 1,800 users. There were about 30 hosts in the United States, Canada, and Europe.

Most mail transfers were done by telephone dialup from the central mail relay machine, though *Telenet* or *TYMNET* could also be used. An early version of *CSNET*'s **MMDF** software was used to coordinate the calls, and the *ARPANET* SMTP protocol was used for addressing and transferring messages in RFC822 format. The only hardware required was a modem. Speed depended on the underlying transfer mechanism, but hosts were polled at least twice a day. Reliability was high.

Interconnections

The old-style *ARPANET* syntax (e.g., *user@host*) was used. Gateways existed to the *Internet*, *BITNET*, *CSNET*, and *JANET*. But since *MAILNET* doesn't exist anymore, there's no way to get to or from it.

7.3.3   Germany

7.3.3.1   *HMI-NET*

The early experimental network at the Hahn-Meitner Institut (HMI) in Berlin was called *HMI-NET*. There were two distinct stages, *HMI-NET 1*, from 1974 to 1976, and *HMI-NET 2*, from 1976 to 1979. This research contributed directly to the development of *BERNET* and *DFN* [Zander 1987]. Many of the researchers involved are still active today. The main person behind *HMI-NET*, Professor Karl Zander, was one of the first proponents of what became COSINE; he is now proposing a continent-wide fiber-optic network, *TUBKOM*, of 100Mbps or faster speeds. Thus, *HMI-NET* is similar to *CYCLADES* or *ARPANET* in its development of a community of experienced people and its effects on widely used standards and networks.

7.3.3.2   *BERNET*

BERNET links all notable academic and research institutions in West Berlin, such as Technische Universität Berlin (TUB) and Free University of Berlin (FUB), both of which have CDC Cyber 180s; the Konrad-Zuse-Zentrum für Informationstechnik Berlin (ZIB) which has a Cray X-MP/24; and the Bundesanstalt für Materialprüfung (BAM), which runs some Digital VAXes [Elsner 1988].

BERNET has developed in several discrete stages from the work done on *HMI-NET*. It is currently the Berlin regional part of *DFN*. In between, there was *BERNET 1*, from 1976 to 1978, and *BERNET 2*, from 1979 to 1982 [Zander 1987]. The current *BERNET* uses protocol implementations from *DFN* on X.25 [Volk 1989].

7.3.4   France

7.3.4.1   *CYCLADES*

The *CYCLADES* network was developed between 1972 and 1975 in France as a prototype network for experimentation in network protocols and uses of networks, such as database access and cooperative research. That is, it was intended for both resource sharing and conferencing, and it was both an object of research and a platform for other research [Pouzin 1982]. Similarities to the early *ARPANET* were explicitly acknowledged. For example, *CYCLADES* minimized changes to host computers by the use of an independent packet switching communications subnet, *CIGALE*. (A *cigale* is a cicada or grasshopper, an insect known for making loud, short noises in concert. The Cyclades are an archipelago in the Aegean Sea that were named for their circular configuration.) *CYCLADES* went farther in some of the directions also taken by *ARPANET* researchers, as in multiple routing of packets that could be delivered out of sequence. But in addition to portable specification of protocols, *CYCLADES* also emphasized careful layering of software and the development of layering models. Several of the researchers involved in *CYCLADES* were later principals in the early development of the International Organization for Standardization (ISO) Open Systems Interconnection (ISO-OSI) layering model.

The project was instigated under the auspices of the Delegation à l'Informatique (DaI) of the government of France. Coordination was done by a team at the Institut de Recherche d'Informatique et d'Automatique (IRIA), which was the predecessor of the Institut National de Recherche en Informatique et Automatique (INRIA), or the National Research Institute for Computer Science and Automation. Although IRIA maintained nominal control of the whole project throughout, much of the work was done in a distributed fashion among the various regional participating organizations or with mixed teams from various places. There was even a designated "gossip carrier" whose function was to travel among the participating sites and communicate. The manufacturer of most of the host hardware, Compagnie Internationale pour l'Informatique (CII), which later merged with Honeywell-Bull (Bull), was also closely involved, due to the need for the development of access methods in the operating system. Meetings of all participants were held no more often than quarterly. A more structured operational organization did evolve in later years (1978–1980) due to a desire to support a larger number of users who were not directly involved in research on *CYCLADES* itself.

The first public demonstrations of a working network were in November 1973. It had three hosts and one packet switch and did file transfer, remote job entry, and some sort of communication between users.

A demonstration of *CIGALE* with four hosts and three packet switches was done in February 1974. There were seven packet switches by June 1974, and four terminal concentrators were installed by July 1974. The date acknowledged by its developers for initial operation of *CYCLADES* proper is last quarter 1974, and emphasis shifted by January 1975 from development of the infrastructure and the CYCLADES protocols to making the network readily usable.

Budget constraints in 1975 caused the loss in February of all but three packet switches, but several terminal concentrators were converted to have host interfaces (this was made easier by both concentrators and switches being the same MITRA-15 computers). Thus, no hosts were lost. In fact, the total number of available host interfaces increased. Some hosts were multihomed, allowing experiments in the delivery of packets by multiple routes to improve reliability.

By July 1975, the services available were remote login for time-sharing, remote batch job entry, and file transfer, although only three of the hosts provided all of these services. The most notably *missing* service was electronic mail. The communications subnet, *CIGALE*, was actually operational only intermittently until early 1976, after which it was available continuously. Several of the protocols, particularly Transport and Virtual Terminal, were designed and implemented twice. This accounts for some of the problems with keeping the network up. These redesigns were necessary because, as in the *ARPANET*, it was not possible to anticipate the right solutions in new technological areas. *CYCLADES* provided a valuable opportunity to redo things when necessary, which was a major reason for its technical success [Gien 1988]. The transport protocol was replaced without modification of lower layers. The ability to change a protocol in one layer without affecting any protocols in other layers is usually considered to be one of the major advantages of a layered protocol architecture, but it is seldom exploited [Pouzin 1988].

The network eventually grew to 20 hosts, of which six offered the above services regularly. The rest mostly acted as clients, though they would occasionally act as servers for experiments. There were about a hundred terminals attached to the network. *CIGALE* was arranged as a closely connected graph, with all the nodes around Paris and Grenoble, and with hosts and terminal concentrators in Paris, Rennes, Nancy, Lyon, Toulouse, Nice, and Saint-Etienne, as can be seen in Figure 7.2. The initial *CIGALE* link speeds were from 4.8Kbps to 48Kbps through leased lines provided by the PTT. For some short-distance connections, 19.2Kbps base band modems were used over telephone lines [Pouzin 1982, 89].

International connections were established to the National Physical Laboratories (NPL) in London in August 1974, to the European Space

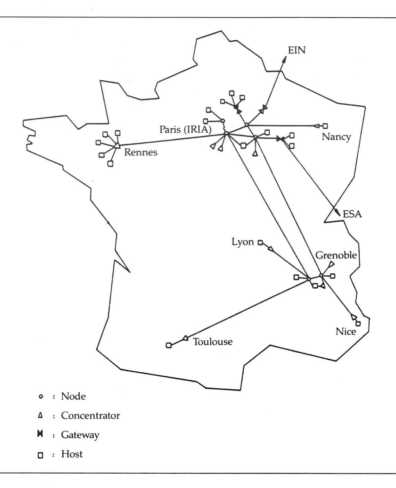

Paris (IRIA)

Rennes

EIN

Nancy

ESA

Lyon

Grenoble

Nice

Toulouse

o : Node

Δ : Concentrator

Ж : Gateway

□ : Host

Figure 7.2. *CYCLADES map (1978) [Pouzin 1982, 258]*

Agency (ESA) in Rome in October 1975, and to the newly established European Informatics Network (EIN) in June 1976.

The CIGALE protocol had a number of interesting features, such as a hierarchical addressing structure of three levels (network, region, and local destination) that was designed for internetworking with other networks and protocols. Adaptive routing was implemented to cope with potential component failure. There was even a distributed time synchronization service. Congestion and traffic management were major topics of research, leading to the conclusion that bandwidth, not buffers, was the critical resource and therefore that multiple routing was a better solution than the use of virtual circuits. This was a pure datagram network, with no hidden virtual circuits such as could be found in the *ARPANET*.

CYCLADES was eventually phased out by 1981, due to the development of more sophisticated facilities and to the shift in emphasis in France from packet switching to circuit switching, particularly as seen in the wide availability of such services from the government PTT. But this was a very influential network, having resulted before its demise in the development of statistical multiplexers, terminal concentrators, host adapters for PDNs, and packet switching networks for a military organization and a railroad company. In addition to the principals behind the origination of the network, Louis Pouzin, Hubert Zimmermann, and Gérard LeLann, *CYCLADES* produced a national community of experts of international reputation, and many of them are still active today. This community interacted with researchers in other countries, such as the Computer Communications Networks Group (CCNG) of the University of Waterloo (Waterloo), Ontario, Canada, which worked on many of the early experiments in routing, flow control, and congestion control. *CYCLADES* also influenced the developers of the TCP/IP protocols in topics such as the size of the unit to be retransmitted on packet loss, and Vint Cerf derived the early TCP window scheme from discussions with Louis Pouzin and Gérard LeLann, the latter of whom was a visiting scholar in Cerf's Stanford research lab in 1973 [Cerf 1988]. The greatest influence of the network internationally, however, may have been on the development of the ISO-OSI model.

7.3.4.2   *RPC*

RPC, or Reseau Communication par Paquet, was an early network sponsored by the French PTT and founded partly by Remy DesPres, who also played a major role in the evolution of X.25, along with Larry Roberts, Barry Wessler, and personnel at the British PTT [Cerf 1988].

7.3.4.3   *COSAC*

COSAC (COmmunications SAns Connections) was a French research network that was operational beginning in 1984 [Quarterman and Hoskins 1986]. The research taking place on *COSAC* was completed about 1987, and most of its former hosts are now connected to *SMARTIX, ARISTOTE,* or *FNET* [Devillers 1988a].

The Centre National d'Etudes des Télécommunications (CNET) administered the network and also funded it through the organizations CNET, Institut National de Recherche en Informatique et Automatique (INRIA), Centre National de la Recherche Scientifique (CNRS), or National Center for Scientific Research, and Honeywell-Bull (Bull). The last three organizations also conducted some of the *COSAC* studies [Devillers 1988b]. *COSAC* had 27 hosts in France as of September 1986, of which about a dozen each were **Multics** and **UNIX** machines, a couple each were IBMs and DEC-20s, and there was one **VMS** VAX. Most were in the environs of Paris or in the provincial capitals, although the two DEC-20s were in Dublin, Ireland.

COSAC used the CCITT X.400 protocols over X.25. Local links used 64Kbps X.25 links, and long-distance ones used *TRANSPAC*, the French PDN. There was a gateway with *FNET* (the French UUCP network; part of *EUnet*). It was possible to get to *CSNET* and through it to *Internet* and *BITNET* from *COSAC*. The gateway between *CSNET* and *COSAC* was the French *CSNET* host *france.csnet*.

Development of the protocols and software for *COSAC* started in 1981 at CNET. Version 3 was operational in 1984, when CCITT was finishing its first specification of X.400, which encoded only the envelope, in a format resembling the current X.409; the body was not encoded. **COSAC** Version 3 was written in **Pascal**. It was sold to industry as a prototype from which they could make a commercial product [Devillers 1988b]. This version is no longer used. Version 5, developed in 1986, was a full X.400 implementation [Quarterman and Hoskins 1986], was operational by the end of 1987, and is used in *SMARTIX*. Version 5 was eventually licensed as a commercial product by CNET [Devillers 1988b].

Access
Claude Kintzig
kintzig@Timdrim2.Paris.CNET.Fr
Projet SMARTIX
CNET (PAA/TIM)
38 – 40 Rue Général Leclerc
F-92131 Issy-les-Moulineaux
France

7.3.5 Europe

7.3.5.1 *EIN*

EIN, the European Informatics Network, was an early attempt (1974 – 1978) at a continental research network in Europe [Barber 1976]. It had connections to *CYCLADES* and *NPL* [Deparis et al. 1976].

7.4 *Commercial Networks*

Datapac in Canada began in 1976 and was the first PDN in the world [Schwartz 1987, 6]. *ARPANET* technology was used by Bolt Beranek and Newman (BBN) to build the commercial network *Telenet* (later sold to GTE and reimplemented) by 1976. Other commercial X.25-based networks followed. In Europe, the PTTs controlled (and still control) the PDNs in each country (one per country) and have universally settled on X.25 as their network layer protocol. (A few countries, such as the United Kingdom, allow alternative service providers.) The PTTs favor circuit switching rather than packet switching, so most of the CCITT protocols such as X.25 and X.400 are oriented toward virtual circuits.

There is no actual legal monopoly on data carrying within most European countries (although there are restrictions on carrying data for third parties and restrictions on what types of equipment can be used), but there are very few leased lines in use (some are in London, Manchester, and other big cities). Electronic data communication was largely deregulated in 1986, so some changes may be seen eventually.

7.5   *Conferencing Systems*

It is useful to categorize the history of conferencing systems into four periods, plus a future period.

7.5.1   **Prehistory, 1945–1969**

From the first imaginings of conferencing services, perhaps in 1945 with an article by Vannevar Bush [Bush 1945], until the first systems were actually established in 1970, the prehistory of conferencing systems was dominated by one theme: lack of adequate hardware. Techniques were developed during this period for making the most out of meetings conducted by mail or where the participants were physically all present. The most influential of these techniques was the *Delphi* method [Linstone and Turoff 1975], which influenced many conferencing systems, such as *EMISARI* and *EIES*.

7.5.2   **Early, 1970–1979**

The first computer conference, a computerized *Delphi* conference, took place in 1970 [Hiltz 1977]. The first software and hardware specifically dedicated to conferencing, *EMISARI*, was operational in 1971. Early conferencing systems were dominated by two themes: (1) expensive and slow hardware that limited access, and (2) attempts to model existing structures (or to fit in the gaps left by inadequacies in existing mechanisms) [Price 1975]. Both of these themes tended to lead to conferences with set time periods or tasks to perform, with an emphasis on formal proceedings and final reports [Featheringham 1977]. Ongoing conferences unlimited in time were not much mentioned until late in the literature of this period [Featheringham 1977; Hiltz 1977].

This period also saw the split between researchers concerned with distributed networks such as *ARPANET* and those primarily concerned with conferencing on a single machine, such as *EIES*. As late as 1973, an Institute for the Future (IFF) project to study the effects of conferencing (see *PLANET* in this chapter) was directly influenced by *Delphi*, conducted partly on *ARPANET*, and written up in the literature next to *EMISARI* [Price 1975]. However, toward the end of this period, people began to notice that conferencing didn't have to be deadly serious research but could actually be fun [Hiltz 1978]. Informal mailing lists on the *ARPANET* concerning topics such as science fiction led to the development of digests to group articles in those lists together for reading, separately from ordinary personal mail, and to reduce network load by reducing the number of messages sent. Such digests presaged later conferencing user interface features, as well as the batch distribution mechanisms of *USENET*.

7.5.3   Middle, 1980 – 1984

The middle period began with existing experience in conferencing and with new systems and software, such as **NOTEPAD**, *QZCOM*, *PLATO*, and **Confer**, that offered new services. Cost of equipment was still a major factor but had decreased sufficiently that some portable conferencing software was written. Speed began to figure more prominently, as, for example, 1200bps modems replaced 300bps ones. Many experiments in the organization of the information in software were carried out, particularly in the **Confer**, **Participate**, **notesfiles**, and **VAXnotes** systems. As the previous emphasis on modeling existing structures receded, a prediction [Price 1975] came true that conferencing would lead to people meeting who would not otherwise have encountered one another.

Some systems ran on more than one machine and in at least one case (*USENET*), formed a distributed network. Starting in 1979, *USENET* was apparently the first conferencing system put together entirely by users with no academic purposes and heralded the second major split in conferencing: the cooperative distributed networks instigated by users, later to include *BITNET*, *FidoNet*, and others. These are almost never considered in academic papers on computer mediated communication (CMC) and have different membership restrictions than the distributed research networks.

7.5.4   Current, 1985 – 1989

The current period has seen a great emphasis on speed, at least in distributed systems such as *USENET*. Hardware cost has receded so much as a factor that a network based on personal microcomputers, *FidoNet*, has spread a conferencing service, **echomail**, worldwide. Although internal software-imposed organization of information has continued to be developed in software such as **Caucus, GEnie, Dialcom, eForum, B news 2.11, PortaCOM**, and **SuperCOM**, the emphasis has shifted strongly toward the user interface. This is largely because of *information overload* produced by the decreased cost and increased speed of hardware and the greatly increased number of people participating in conferencing systems. Some software attempts to deal with the problem by simplifying the user interface or by attempting to model the user interface on that of some existing non-computer-mediated services.

This period saw a partial healing of the former splits. *USENET*, *FidoNet*, and *BITNET* all communicated among themselves, and with government-sponsored networks such as *ARPANET* and the *Internet*, toward the beginning of this period. Systems specifically concerned with interconnecting what used to be separate have sprung up. These include *UUNET* and *DASnet*. *DASnet* connects many previously isolated single machine and large commercial systems, not only to themselves but also to noncommercial systems.

A few particularly historically significant conferencing systems are described in subsections below.

7.5.5   Mature, 1990 – 1995

Many people are beginning to emphasize that CMC is not like previous forms of communication and that modeling the internal organization of information or the external user interface of a conferencing system on a previous service is counterproductive [Turoff 1980; Turoff 1985]. Instead, the emphasis should be more on providing mechanisms with which the *user* can organize information to avoid *information overload* [Hiltz and Turoff 1981; Hiltz and Turoff 1985]. This is not the same as providing *user-friendly* interfaces, which often merely look like previous media the user was used to. A successful system must cater to the expert user [Hiltz and Turoff 1985, 682] — i.e., it must be *expert-friendly* — while still providing convenient access to the new user [Turoff 1982], as in Caucus or perhaps eventually in EIES 2.

Cost and speed of hardware are no longer limiting considerations in software design. Most conferencing software will be written to be portable to multiple underlying operating systems and hardware configurations. Most conferencing systems will communicate with most other conferencing systems and mail systems.

There also seems to be increasing emphasis on *groupware* — i.e., software meant to help group interaction [Tazelaar 1988; Engelbart and

Lehtman 1988a]. This is a rather general term and is used to refer to anything from electronic mail to distributed databases that facilitates groups working together [Grudin 1988]. In other words, it includes both CMC and resource sharing. Perhaps this is a sign of eventual better communication between the conferencing and networking communities.

7.5.6   Augment

One of the main places where the early problem of lack of adequate hardware was addressed was the Augmented Knowledge Workshop (AKW) at Stanford Research Institute (SRI), which, under the direction of Douglas Englebart, worked on such now ubiquitous gadgets as the cathode ray tube (CRT) display, text editing, graphics [Price 1975], windows, the mouse, and consistent user interfaces across facilities. They also produced the On-Line System (*NLS*) about 1978 [Engelbart and Lehtman 1988a] using ideas partly derived from Vannevar Bush [Bush 1945], such as associative indexing, windowing, and database trails. *NLS* is much like an early *hypertext* implementation.

Original development of *NLS* began in 1963 and continued until 1976. In addition to the facilities already mentioned that have since become widespread, *NLS* includes some other unusual hardware interface features, such as a one-handed (chording) keyboard [Engelbart and Lehtman 1988b]. This system was adopted for marketing by Tymshare in 1978 as *Augment* [Meeks 1985].

The most distinctive feature of this research organization is probably that its goal was always *augmentation*, not *automation* [Engelbart and Lehtman 1988a]. Tools and conventions for group authorship—what is now called *groupware*—were an early development at this facility [Engelbart and Lehtman 1988b].

7.5.7   EMISARI

In 1970, President Richard Nixon imposed a wage and price freeze on the American economy. A means was needed to handle much information about this freeze quickly and accurately and to disseminate it among people widely separated geographically and with greatly varying schedules. The Office of Economic Preparedness (OEP) had Murray Turoff, then of Language Systems Development Corporation (LSDC), produce what OEP thought of as a computerized version of a telephone conference call. This was the Emergency Management Information System and Reference Index, or *EMISARI*, which is usually considered to be the first computerized conferencing system [Meeks 1985]. It was used by OEP during the 90-day wage–price freeze in 1971. Various other agencies participated, including the Internal Revenue Service (IRS), which used it for field enforcement. There were about 30 terminals at the beginning and about 70 at the end; more than one person used each terminal. There were other later uses, and the **EMISARI** software was made available at nominal cost in August 1973 from the National Technical Information Service (NTIS) [Price 1975].

A related program, **PARTY LINE**, was an interactive synchronous system that was closely modeled on telephone conferencing, although a transcript of each session was recorded. Apparently this program preceded **EMISARI** and was originally intended primarily for use in automating *Delphi* sessions [Price 1975].

EMISARI itself could also include tables and computations and apparently operated asynchronously. Each conference could have a *monitor*, who would guide the discussion [Price 1975] and could also determine who could alter specific items in a database [Turoff 1980].

There was a rather elaborate division of participants into the following categories:

- *Process specialists*, including the *monitor*, who are more concerned with the process of collaboration and the general context of information
- *Stakeholders*, who have an interest in, or responsibility for, making decisions
- *Experts*, who have knowledge particularly relevant to the topic under discussion

These roles are apparently derived from similar ones observed in face-to-face situations, and the system in fact attempted to enforce such distinctions. There was explicit acknowledgment of the influence of the *Delphi* method [Price 1975]. These last two points illustrate how this early conferencing system tended to model existing mechanisms and situations.

EMISARI had an immediate descendant, *Discussion*, and eventually led to *EIES*, the most studied of all conferencing systems, and still later to the **Participate** software [Meeks 1985].

7.5.8   PLANET

PLANET was a conferencing system developed and run by the Institute for the Future (IFF) of Menlo Park, California, which originally included Robert Johansen, Richard Miller, Hubert Lipinski, and Jacques Vallee. This system was used for experimental work in conferencing, a large part of which had to do with categorizing styles of interaction, of which five basic kinds were distinguished: *notepad, questionnaire, seminar, assembly,* and *encounter* [Hiltz and Turoff 1978, 65–67], all of which can still be observed today.

There was an earlier IFF system called *FORUM* (not to be confused with *Army Forum*) that was explicitly modeled on *Delphi* (e.g., specific questions were asked and answers were not distributed until all answers were received) and also had a voice channel [Hiltz and Turoff 1978, 65]. This original IFF bent toward very structured conferences changed as the group used conferencing systems more [Price 1975].

7.5.9   MAILBOX

One of the earliest uses of CMC was on the *MAILBOX* system, which was developed by Scientific Time Sharing Corporation (STSC) of Bethesda, Maryland, by at least 1973. This was used for accessing common data on some IBM 370/158 machines in Bethesda from locations in 20 cities. Various degrees of confidentiality were supported. There was a related program called **NEWS** that was apparently a noninteractive information distribution service. *MAILBOX* produced one of the first examples of an effect of conferencing on the structure of the organization using it: instead of a pyramidal hierarchy, groups or teams formed to handle tasks as needed [Price 1975].

7.5.10   PLATO

The **NOTES** conferencing software of the *PLATO* conferencing system is the direct ancestor of both **VAXnotes** and **notesfiles**, and was operational about 1974. The *PLATO* system itself (named after the Greek philosopher) was operational in the late 1960s [Kolstad 1988]. This software runs on a CDC machine at the University of Illinois at Urbana-Champaign (UIUC) and was developed by David Woolley [Umpleby 1971]. The associated **PNOTES** software is for personal notes — i.e., mail [Kolstad 1988].

There was a predecessor to **NOTES**: this was **DISCUSS**, which was implemented by Stuart Umpleby and coworkers by 1971 [Umpleby 1971]. *PLATO* itself is intended for computer-assisted instruction and was originally developed by Donald Bitzer [Price 1975].

Access
David Woolley
+1-612-824-7814
Chrysalis Software, Inc.
Minneapolis, MN 55409
U.S.A.

7.5.11   NOTEPAD

NOTEPAD is conferencing software designed for business use and has a very simple user interface. It is marketed through InfoMedia Corporation (InfoMedia), which is led by Jacques Vallee, who is known for his early work with IFF and *PLANET* and has had a strong influence on its design. **NOTEPAD** is widely used in business and government to coordinate projects, mostly through the use of closed conferences [Meeks 1985]. It was written in 1978 for **TOPS-20** and is used by numerous government agencies and large corporations [Cook 1987].

7.5.12   eForum

eForum was produced by Network Technologies International, Inc., which owns Network Technologies, Inc. (NETI) of Ann Arbor, Michigan, and was strongly modeled after face-to-face meetings. There are four different levels of security of conferences, ranging from public to invitation only with password [Meeks 1985]. There is a related distributed document production system called **Docu-Forum** [Cook 1987].

7.6   *Communities*

Meanwhile, another networking technology was being developed based on dialup telephone links instead of dedicated connections. One reason for this is that large amounts of traffic are required before leased lines become as economical as dialup connections.

Two of the earliest products of this technology were *ACSnet* and *UUCP*, both of which survive in modified forms, using the SUN-III and UUCP protocols. The dialup networks produced the most distributed of the conferencing systems: *USENET* and *FidoNet*.

CSNET started as an attempt to bring the collaborative advantages of the *ARPANET* to researchers who did not have access to it by using dialup mechanisms similar to those of *UUCP*. *MAILNET* developed for similar reasons. *BITNET* made IBM's internal mainframe networking technology available to the academic community and spread even to some non-IBM hosts. It also spread outside the United States as *NetNorth* and *EARN*.

7.7   *Influences*

Some influences can be seen across several networks.

7.7.1   Internets

Internets required new protocol suites, such as XNS, TCP/IP, and the ISO-OSI protocols. The spread of XNS has, some say, been stifled by the secrecy of its originating company. The TCP/IP protocols are by far the most widely implemented of these three due to the accessibility of their specifications, their long history of practical use, and the backing of the U.S. government. Some of the ISO-OSI protocols were implemented in 1983 on *CDNnet* in Canada, the first **Ean** network, and spread rapidly in Europe the following year. Other implementations, particularly of X.400, have followed, especially in Europe. Most of the ISO protocols are either adaptations of CCITT protocols or are, like them, oriented toward virtual circuits.

7.7.2   Host Size

Hosts on early networks were usually either mainframes or minicomputers. A few networks, such as *BITNET*, continue this tradition. Internets usually have many workstations on their LAN components, so the average size of their hosts is smaller. Personal computers are sometimes connected to internets like the *Internet*, and some appear on the dialup networks. Users of IBM PCs have found a network of their own in *FidoNet*. At least one network, *MFEnet*, was developed primarily for access to supercomputers, and that was also one of the purposes of *NSFNET*.

7.7.3   Tragedy of the Commons

Historians and sociologists recognize a phenomenon known as the *tragedy of the commons*. If a whole town's sheep are allowed to graze on a single common area of grass and the villagers have economic advantages in increasing their own flocks, the commons may eventually become overgrazed. Consider local telephone systems, which are increasingly used for data access to computers. Computer users have increasing need of such use and use increasingly fast modems that require more bandwidth from the system. This bandwidth comes from the general pool of circuits that is also used for voice transmissions. An average data connection uses more bandwidth than a voice connection but costs the same, and there is more pressure for increasing data use. This situation leads to overgrazing. To deal with this problem, many local telephone companies have instituted excess charges on data connections or time charges.

Networks frequently encounter economic limits as traffic increases. Dialup networks such as *USENET* end up spending a considerable amount of money on telephone charges, usually with only a few machines carrying most of the burden. Redistribution of the burden and eventual technological improvements are the usual methods of alleviation, short of dissolution of the network. Networks such as the *ARPANET*, which use fixed links, cannot automatically increase their capacity. In this case, traffic congestion, rather than increased costs, is the primary effect. This is a straightforward case of the tragedy of the commons and has led, in the case of the *ARPANET*, to its demise. Networks that charge for traffic can eventually increase their capacity, but there is often a lag between need and availability. These are examples of commons that can be increased. Even in the *ARPANET* example, the same users will end up using other networks, such as *NSFNET*, and even the same protocols. One set of physical links is being exchanged for another.

Transmission bandwidth is another kind of commons. This is already an issue in India, where one network, *OILCOMNET*, avoids use of satellite transmission because another, *NICNET*, plans to make very heavy use of it. The problem is exacerbated by the proximity of the numerous ground stations planned. The use of more than one geosynchronous satellite might help, but there are only a limited number of slots in that orbit because satellites require a minimum separation to avoid interference; these slots are already carefully allocated by an international commission.

For the moment, technology will continue to provide new commons and new ways to make more efficient use of existing ones. For example, with sufficient synchronization, it is possible to use satellites in nongeosynchronous orbits; this is commonly done in the Soviet Union already, because of its far northern location. Yet there are probably eventual limits required by the third law of thermodynamics, if nothing else: a minimum amount of energy is required to transmit information, some of it is lost as heat, and the planet's atmosphere can only absorb so much heat.

7.8 *Future*

Most developments in new services are currently limited by the speeds of existing networks. Thus, most future developments of services will be driven by increases in speeds and storage space. These, in turn, will be technologically driven and physically limited, and there will no doubt be accompanying administrative and sociological effects.

7.8.1 Speed Increases

In a few years, Integrated Services Digital Network (ISDN) service will be commonly available from most telephone services. This will permit 64Kbps digital data transmission, with possibly 9600bps links to end users. Meanwhile, 38.4Kbps modems that work over old-style analog telephone connections are expected to be available in 1989, and 9600bps modems are already widely used. At this time, 1.544Mbps (T1) links (often by microwaves) are available to anyone who wants to pay the price. The spread of long-distance fiber-optic links makes 100Mbps technologically possible, and its use in wide area networks is likely to occur soon.

Not yet quite possible is Fiber Distributed Data Interface (FDDI) in gallium arsenide (GaAs) instead of silicon; this will run at about 1Gbps, another order of magnitude increase in speed. ANSI X3T9 is working on a standard for 1.6Gbps.

It is interesting to compare the fastest currently feasible long-distance speed, 100Mbps, with previous technologies:

- It is an order of magnitude faster than 10Mbps Ethernet.
- It is two orders faster than the T1 links used in *NSFNET*.
- It is three orders faster than *ARPANET*'s 56Kbps links.
- It is four orders (10,000 times) faster than the 9600bps links currently used in *EUnet*, *JUNET*, and *USENET*.

Of course, one must remember that these faster links will normally be multiplexed among several users or virtual circuits. Even 100Mbps isn't extremely fast when compared to the video refresh speed of an average high-speed bit map display (about 30Mbps). A few machines transferring images could saturate such a network. Also see the comments on dynamic video simulation in the following section.

7.8.2   Speed Limits

Networks faster than about 30Mbps to 100Mbps will not be CSMA/CD like Ethernet or 802.3 because it is too difficult to detect the presence of a packet without making its size so large that throughput is lost. For this reason, FDDI is a token ring.

The maximum transfer speed a protocol can support is the maximum packet size times the maximum number of simultaneous packets (the window) divided by round trip transmission time. This is already a problem for UUCP: its g protocol sends three tiny (64 byte) packets and waits for an acknowledgment. Modems such as Telebit Trailblazers that get speeds faster than 9600bps on UUCP transmissions do so by spoofing the sender by immediately acknowledging outgoing UUCP packets and bundling them into larger segments for transmission (the modem on the other end must know to unbundle them, of course). The t protocol for use over TCP and the f protocol for use over X.25 have been invented to avoid this problem by using larger packets and leaving checksums to the higher or lower layers.

Latency may be due to processing overhead (on the host, in a modem, or in the network) or to a more basic limit: the speed of light. Round trip transmission time to geosynchronous orbit is about half a second. Consider TCP running over a network like *ARPANET* that has a maximum window size of eight packets. A maximum packet size of 64Kbytes and a smaller packet size of 64bytes at both geosynchronous satellite distance and at a terrestial distance of 6,000 miles (twice U.S. transcontinental distance) are shown in Table 7.1. Although increased use of satellites for data networks was predicted as long ago as 1974 [Roberts 1974] and is happening today (witness *WIDEBAND, NORDUnet, ITESM,* and *NICNET*), the latency involved does limit the possible speeds.

Use of parallelism might be a way to squeeze more throughput out of links [Shein 1987]: instead of sending one bit across a channel, use several channels and send several bits. Given an arbitrary number of channels and arbitrarily large files to send, throughput could be arbitrarily high. But files are usually of limited size, and interactive traffic usually consists of only a byte at a time, each one being echoed. For large files, large windows could have an effect similar to that of massive parallelism, but for interactive traffic, neither large window sizes nor parallelism can help much.

Of course, if there is reasonable confidence in the data link and the capability of the link and the data sink to absorb data as fast as it is transmitted, or the nature of the data being transferred can tolerate losses, as in voice or video, one can dispense with acknowledgments and just send packets continuously. This is essentially what analog television and telephone do. One might say that real-time transfer tends to be analog.

Fortunately, most fast links will be shared among several virtual circuits, but eventually these limits may be a problem.

Future wide area networks may be internets in order to localize addressing information and because of economic considerations. Traffic between networks will have to pass through gateway machines. Such a gateway must at least transmit every bit that passes through it, and it must examine each packet to decide where to send it. If 100 million packets entered a gateway in a second, many more machine instructions would be needed to handle the packet. No currently available computers can handle a billion instructions per second in a single CPU. Perhaps massively parallel machines could handle the load. Given two 100Mbps networks connected through a gateway, assuming a packet size of 64 bytes, something like 10 million instructions per second would be needed. This is plausible, since such machines are already available [Shein 1987].

Table 7.1. *Speed of light limits on TCP throughput*

	Geosynchronous (90,000 miles)	Continental (6,000 miles)
64Kbytes	8Mbps	120Mbps
2Kbytes	256Kbps	3.84Mbps
64bytes	8Kbps	120Kbps

Note: TCP over a network with a maximum window size of eight packets.

7.8.3   Effects on Layering

Many protocol suites and layering models such as ISO-OSI and TCP/IP were first designed when computers were much faster than the communication links that were available to connect them. The 56Kbps links used in the *ARPANET* were state of the art at the time and could handle traffic from a relatively large number of hosts. CPU speeds were only a few million instructions per second (MIPS) at most, and most users connected to the machines over 9600bps or slower terminal lines. Protocol suites with many layers assumed that it was cost-effective to devote CPU cycles to optimizing the use of slow network links.

In addition to raw network speed increases, the speed and complexity of user interfaces continue to increase, involving high-resolution bit-mapped displays with windows, graphics, and images. It is likely that CPU speeds of 15 or 20 MIPS will become common by 1990. This is about an order of magnitude faster than the CPU speeds of ten years ago. But 100Mbps is three orders of magnitude faster than 56Kbps, and transport mechanisms of 1Gbps or faster are being planned.

It is possible that protocol suites of many layers will become less acceptable if network speeds cease to be the bottleneck. Already some network file systems use minimal transport layers, and there is a European trend toward X.400 over TP0 over X.25 (bypassing ISO-IP and TP4). Outboard protocol processors have been used by some for years as a solution, and FDDI is being designed to be implemented in silicon [Chesson 1987]. Of course, this involves a protocol between the outboard processor and the CPU, but research has been done on this problem [Cheriton 1988]. It is not a new idea, having been used in the original design of the *ARPANET* in 1969.

The traffic that must be multiplexed over the faster links is also increasing rapidly. And there is life yet in the old methods: a current version of TCP can saturate a 10Mbps Ethernet with traffic traveling at 9Mbps between two machines that still have 40 percent idle CPU time [Jacobson 1988]. Other speeds obtained with existing infrastructure may be faster than expected. There have been claims of 400Mbps with TCP over HYPER-channel [Borman 1988]. Only time will tell what effect increased speeds will have on protocol design and implementation.

7.8.4   Storage

By 1989 it will be possible to buy a half-height Winchester disk drive that will fit inside a personal computer, hold 800Mbytes, and cost less than $5,000. That amount of storage five years ago cost about $20,000 and came in a drive the size of a clothes washing machine. Mountable shockproof volumes up to 800Mbytes are available. It is possible to get a 100Mbyte drive the size of a pack of cigarettes [Shein 1987].

Write once read many (WORM) compact disk (CD) drives are already available. They hold a large fraction of a gigabyte on removable media that cost about a hundred dollars apiece. Fully writable CDs will be common by 1990. Unfortunately, they don't use the same technology as WORM drives. Also, the technology to master read only CDs is very expensive. Nonetheless, it might be convenient to configure a system (perhaps a file server) with many cheap read-only drives to contain basic references, such as the operating system and utilities, the *New Oxford English Dictionary*, or the *Whole Earth Catalog*, and one medium size writable drive [Shein 1987]. The writable drive could be used to save snapshots of entire sets of sources, programs, or documents instead of using complicated schemes of compressing records of development activity [Yost 1985].

7.8.5   Mobility

With satellite, packet radio, and cellular telephone technology, as well as portable computers, it is quite possible to develop whole networks of mobile machines [Kahn 1987].

7.8.6   Services

Fast transport technology is available and is starting to be used [Kahn 1987]. Data storage is becoming very cheap. New services such as the following might become widely available.

Continent-wide distributed file access. Experiments show that this is not laughable even over 9600bps links [Shein 1987]. Carnegie-Mellon University (CMU) is considering expanding its *Andrew* distributed file system to a national scale [Spector 1988].

WAN shared memory. Given sufficiently high transmission speeds, network communication can be treated by the same mechanisms as interprocess communications over a local area network. This is a currently popular area of research and has been done in at least one large network, *Tandem*. It is also the logical modern application of the original *ARPANET* goal of resource sharing. The network itself will be invisible to the user in the same way that the various spinning platters and chips that make up a disk subsystem are already invisible. Recent performance research in this area has been done on *Memnet* [Delp et al. 1988].

Massive database access. Would it not be possible to have the Library of Congress online and mounted for direct access over a national network? Optical character recognition devices are becoming increasingly sophisticated, so even putting many books online is not an insurmountable problem. For that matter, with sufficient bandwidth and storage space, graphic images could be used uninterpreted [Shein 1987]. Of course, there is no point in doing this for single books, when the *New Oxford English Dictionary* will be available on a few CDs [Gonnet and Tompa 1987; Raymond and Tompa 1988].

Integrated voice, images, and text. Multimedia mail is currently limited mostly by bandwidth and is in use on the *Internet*, as a result of the NSF project. Simple uses such as matching a face from a library with a mail source address are already common in some places.

Dynamic video simulation. Supercomputers can do sophisticated dynamic video simulation, and workstations can display detailed images: the missing link is a fast enough network connection. This means about 480Mbps for a mega pixel display and a refresh rate of 30 frames per second, neglecting data compression [Kahn 1987].

Cyberspace. Comprehending the kinds, locations, sizes, and details of the massive amounts of information that will be available will be a serious problem. Perhaps William Gibson's idea of a "consensual hallucination" of a three-dimensional graphic space with symbolic representations of various interesting entities will become not only plausible but necessary [Gibson 1984]. This is only a straightforward extrapolation of the current popularity of two-dimensional iconic interfaces such as those of the Apple Macintosh. The effects of *cyberspace* on the perceived identities of its inhabitants have already been discussed in Section 3.3.2.

New interfaces. People can receive and perhaps interpret data visually at speeds fast enough to take advantage of the transmission speeds that are already available on workstations on local area networks and that will soon be widely used on wide area networks. But people can speak or type only at speeds an order of magnitude slower. Will widespread desire to interact with masses of information at high speeds lead to new interface technologies? There is speculation [Delaney 1969; Gibson 1984] and research in this area [Brand 1987].

New services that could not be invented before the technology became widely available. Without bit map displays, iconic interfaces are not possible. Without mice, menu choices are not convenient. Without sufficient bandwidth, what as yet unknown services are hidden?

There is every indication that services or tools and the people who use them mutually affect each other in a process of *co-evolution* [Engelbart and Lehtman 1988a]. New services mean new social and psychological structures, which will in turn produce new services not previously thought of.

7.8.7   Providers

When CPU cycles and storage space were the main things being provided by computers, computer centers developed. Now that everyone can have those things on a personal machine, computer centers may tend to become information distributors, making organization of information a major goal. In other words, computer centers may merge with libraries [Shein 1987].

Libraries will probably keep local caches of core texts and update them from authoritative repositories. WORM mastering technology will probably be affordable to large universities, which can then produce their own online versions of locally available texts and make them available to other libraries and their users. Duplication of texts will become much easier by the same process [Shein 1987].

Newspapers have extensive print morgues. Movie studios have back stocks of films even larger than they currently make available on videocassettes. If they could charge per transmission, they might make these films available over networks. Similarly, television networks have much more footage in their video morgues than they broadcast [Shein 1987].

Museums have extensive and varied collections. Some combination of textual indexing and video and audio transmission might be usable for making much of this information more accessible. Similar techniques could be used for operas or other art forms, given enough bandwidth [Shein 1987].

Manufacturers of sound CDs will eventually be affected by truly writable CD drives because it will become possible and easy to copy music CDs. This controversy already exists over digital audio tape (DAT), which also may become a cheap computer storage device.

7.8.8   Computer Equipment Availability

Whole computer systems will become available as cheap surplus [Shein 1987]. Large universities already have warehouses of old terminals because they have moved on to workstations. Terminals aren't usually very interesting to people used to personal computers, and old minicomputers or mainframes aren't very practical for the average house, due to power and maintenance requirements. But soon older workstations such as Sun-2s will be considered outdated in favor of Sun-4s and other faster machines. These older workstations are usually capable of supporting exactly the same services as newer, faster ones, so a home user might be quite happy to buy an old one as surplus equipment. This may also apply to disk drives, WORM drives, or other peripherals.

Cheap **UNIX** boxes are already widely available and are getting faster and cheaper all the time, as the recent growths of *USENET* and *EUnet* demonstrate.

MS-DOS users can now connect to the outside world easily, not only because of the various *FidoNet* programs, but also because of **UUPC**, a public domain version of **UUCP** for **MS-DOS**. **UUPC** also provides hooks that make getting *USENET* news easy.

7.8.9   Users

Doubtless old-style services such as text electronic mail and news will continue indefinitely. But it only takes about 60Mbytes to get a full *USENET* news feed for the default expiration time of two weeks, and that much storage costs only a few hundred dollars in 1989. Already, the kinds and numbers of machines on that network and others are expanding rapidly. *USENET* doubled in size from August 1987 to June 1988, as measured in number of hosts, number of articles, and megabytes of data; *EUnet* apparently saw similar growth. Many more people are gaining access to what previously required the backing of a large company to afford. And many people inside large companies who would not have used networks previously are doing so now. The executive who can't or won't type may become a relic [Mills 1984].

There has already been a trend for several years for networks such as *EUnet*, *EARN*, and *JUNET* to gain users who are not directly associated with computer science. So far, these new users are mostly in other academic departments at universities or at technologically oriented companies. This sort of expansion is being explicitly encouraged in the United States through *NSFNET* and related developments. Researchers in other areas, such as Southeast Asia and Latin America, have discovered the utility of computer networks for collaboration.

But networking has already broken out of its original academic bounds. In France, the *Minitel* system reaches about six million people, which is a sizable fraction of the entire population of about 55 million. In Japan, groups such as COARA promote the use of conferencing systems and networks by businesses and the general public. Older commercial services such as *The Source* are being interconnected by forwarders such as *DASnet*. Some of the new services that faster speeds will permit will attract still more nontechnical users. There is no reason why CMC will not eventually be as widely used and commonly accepted as the telephone, television, or paper mail are now.

7.8.10   Connectivity

Pressure from users and the desire of research organizations to promote communication have resulted in the connection of previously separate networks. Already most publicly accessible networks and large conferencing systems are interconnected so that mail can be exchanged among them, forming one large metanetwork that covers the world: the *Matrix*.

Meanwhile, internetworks such as the *Internet* and *PHYSNET* continue to increase in size. The number of networks in the same niche tends to decrease: *MAILNET* is no more, and *CSNET* and *BITNET* have decided to merge. As networks spread, they carry their protocols with them. New networks tend to adopt working protocols from already existing networks. Thus, the number of protocols seems to be diminishing: if *BITNET* adopts TCP/IP and *EARN* adopts ISO-OSI, will NJE and RSCS vanish? (Probably not, since *BITNET* is putting IP underneath NJE, and there is still *VNET*). Already, XNS appears to have ceased to expand outside of XEROX. And, of course, the Commission of the European Communities (CEC), the U.S. government, and other governments insist that any equipment sold to them must soon be compatible with ISO-OSI [NBS 1988; Passmore and Horn 1988; Shaw 1988].

The general trend is toward internetworks of increasing size and homogeneity of protocols. Eventually there may be one worldwide network used for electronic mail, conferencing, file transfer, and remote login, just as there is now one worldwide telephone network and one worldwide postal system.

7.8.11   Administration

If such a worldwide homogeneous network develops, it will almost certainly be run by government PTTs in every country of the world, with the probable exception of the United States, where it will be run by the regional

Bell Operating Companies (BOCs) and the long-distance carriers. The European PTTs have been trying to achieve this end for years (see the discussions in the RARE, *EARN*, and *DFN* sections in other chapters), and the March 1988 U.S. Federal District Court decision by Judge Harold Greene permitting the BOCs to run electronic mail services will no doubt speed the process [Scott 1988].

Interestingly, that court decision did not allow the BOCs to run conferencing systems. They can transfer information but not originate it; this even seems to rule out directory services. Store and forward transfer was declared equivalent to direct transmission, permitting mail and voice mail service, but this does not cover conferencing. Therefore, at least in the United States, there seems to be a future for independent conferencing services. In France, most of the information provided by *Minitel* comes from private companies, not the government. Historically, networks such as *EUnet* have developed in spite of what governments wanted. In less politically liberal areas of the world, data communication networks are sometimes seen as a direct threat to the monopoly of the government communications agency, and perhaps to the control of the government itself [Hiltz and Turoff 1981, 750]. This view of computer networks as subversive might be correct, although the same technology may as readily be used by governments to enforce their power.

Will the future be characterized by government provision of transmission services and private provision of the information transferred? That seems likely, if only because governments are unlikely to be able to provide sufficient information to satisfy the entire population except in very controlled societies.

7.9   *Bibliographic Notes*

Many useful historical papers and some prognostications for the future may be found in Partridge 1988.

7.10   *References*

Abramson 1970. Abramson, N., "The Aloha System," *AFIPS Conference Proceedings*, pp. 281–285, AFIPS Press, Montvale, NJ, 1970.

Abramson 1985. Abramson, N., "Development of the ALOHANET," *IEEE Transactions on Information Theory*, vol. IT-1, pp. 119–123, March 1985.

Abramson and Kui 1975. Abramson, N., and Kui, F.F., *Computer-Communication Networks*, Prentice-Hall, Englewood Cliffs, NJ, 1975.

Barber 1976. Barber, D.L.A., "A European Informatics Network: Achievement and Prospects," *IEEE '76 (Toronto, August 1976)*, pp. 44–50, IEEE, New York, 1976.

BBN 1988. BBN, "MILNET and ARPANET Maps," BBN, Cambridge, MA, 31 January 1988.

Boggs et al. 1980. Boggs, D. R., Schoch, J. F., Taft, E. A., and Metcalfe, R. M., "Pup: An Internetwork Architecture," *IEEE Transactions on Communications*, vol. COM-28, no. 4, pp. 612–624, April 1980.

Borman 1988. Borman, David, "Fast TCP?," *Proceedings of the Internet Engineering Task Force*, IETF, 1988.

Brand 1987. Brand, Stewart, *The Media Lab: Inventing the Future at MIT*, Viking, New York, 1987.

Bryant 1988. Bryant, Paul, Personal communications, 13 September 1988.

Bush 1945. Bush, Vannevar, "As We May Think," *The Atlantic*, vol. 176, no. 1, pp. 101–108, Atlantic Monthly Co., Boston, July 1945.

Cerf 1988. Cerf, Vinton G., Personal communications, August 1988.

Cheriton 1988. Cheriton, David, "VMTP: Versatile Message Transaction Protocol; RFC1045," *ARPANET Working Group Requests for Comments*, February 1988.

Chesson 1987. Chesson, Greg, "Protocol Engine Design," *Proceedings of the Summer 1987 USENIX Conference (Phoenix, Arizona, 8–12 June 1987)*, pp. 209–215, USENIX Association, Berkeley, CA, 1987. Also in Partridge, *Innovations in Internetworking*, 1988.

Cook 1987. Cook, Gordon, "A Survey of Computer Mediated Communications: Computer Conferencing Comes of Age," Gartner Group, Inc., Stamford, CT, 9 November 1987. This paper was published in a series available only to subscribers who paid a substantial fee.

DARPA 1983. DARPA, "A History of the ARPANET: The First Decade," Bolt Beranek and Newman, Cambridge, MA, April 1983. Defense Tech. Info. Center AD A1 15440.

Delaney 1969. Delaney, Samuel R., *Nova*, Bantam, November 1969. Originally published by Doubleday, August 1968.

Delp et al. 1988. Delp, Gary S., Sethi, Adarshpal S., and Farber, David J., "An Analysis of Memnet: An Experiment in High-Speed Shared-Memory Local Networking," *Proceedings of the ACM SIGCOMM '88 Workshop (Stanford, 16–19 August 1988)*, pp. 165–174, ACM SIGCOMM, New York, 1988.

Dennett et al. 1985. Dennett, Stephen, Feinler, Elizabeth J., and Perillo, Francine, "ARPANET Information Brochure," DDN Network Information Center, SRI International, Menlo Park, CA, CA, December 1985.

Deparis et al. 1976. Deparis, M., Duenki, A., Gien, M., Louis, J., LeMoli, G., and Weaking, K., "The Implementation of an End-to-End Protocol by EIN Centres: a Survey and Comparison," *Proceedings of IEEE '76 (Toronto, August 1976)*, IEEE, New York, 1976.

Devillers 1988a. Devillers, Yves, Personal communications, 5 October 1988.

Devillers 1988b. Devillers, Yves, Personal communications, December 1988.

Elsner 1988. Elsner, Frank, Personal communications, 16 August 1988, 4 November 1988.

Engelbart and Lehtman 1988a. Engelbart, Douglas, and Lehtman, Harvey, "Working Together," *BYTE*, vol. 13, no. 13, pp. 245–246, 250, 252, December 1988.

Engelbart and Lehtman 1988b. Engelbart, Douglas, and Lehtman, Harvey, "The NLS/Augment Architecture," *BYTE*, vol. 13, no. 13, pp. 247–248, December 1988.

Featheringham 1977. Featheringham, Tom, "Teleconferences: the Message is the Meeting," *Data Communications*, vol. 6, no. 7, pp. 37–41, July 1977.

Flowers 1966. Flowers, *Report on Future Provision for Computing in Universities*, HMSO, London, 1966.

Gibson 1984. Gibson, William, *Neuromancer*, Ace, New York, 1984.

Gien 1988. Gien, Michel, Personal communications, 4 August 1988.

Gonnet and Tompa 1987. Gonnet, G. H., and Tompa, Frank Wm., "Mind Your Grammar: A New Approach to Modelling Text," *Proceedings of the 1987 Very Large Database Conference (Brighton, U.K.)*, pp. 339–346, 1987.

Grudin 1988. Grudin, Jonathan, "Perils and Pitfalls," *BYTE*, vol. 13, no. 13, pp. 261–262, 264, 266, December 1988.

Hiltz 1977. Hiltz, Starr Roxanne, "Communications Medium," *Technological Forecasting and Social Change*, vol. 10, no. 3, pp. 225–238, 1977.

Hiltz 1978. Hiltz, Starr Roxanne, "The Human Element in Computerized Conferencing Systems," *Computer Networks*, vol. 2, no. 6, pp. 421–428, December 1978.

Hiltz and Turoff 1978. Hiltz, Starr Roxanne, and Turoff, Murray, *The Network Nation: Human Communication via Computer*, Addison-Wesley, Reading, MA, 1978.

Hiltz and Turoff 1981. Hiltz, Starr Roxanne, and Turoff, Murray, "The Evolution of User Behavior in a Computerized Conferencing System," *Communications of the ACM*, vol. 24, no. 11, pp. 739–751, November 1981.

Hiltz and Turoff 1985. Hiltz, Starr Roxanne, and Turoff, Murray, "Structuring Computer-Mediated Communication Systems to Avoid Information Overload," *Communications of the ACM*, vol. 28, no. 7, pp. 680–689, July 1985.

Jacobson 1988. Jacobson, Van, "Congestion Avoidance and Control," *Proceedings of the ACM SIGCOMM '88 Workshop (Stanford, 16–19 August 1988)*, pp. 314–329, ACM SIGCOMM, New York, 1988. Also in Partridge, *Innovations in Internetworking*, 1988.

Kahn 1987. Kahn, Robert E., "Networks for Advanced Computing," *Trends In Computing*, pp. 34–41, October 1987.

Karn 1988. Karn, Phil, "Improving your TCP: 'Karn's Algorithm'," *ConneXions—The Interoperability Report*, vol. 2, no. 10, p. 23, Advanced Computing Environments, Mountain View, CA, October 1988.

Kolstad 1988. Kolstad, Rob, Personal communications, 1 December 1988.

Lauck et al. 1986. Lauck, Anthony G., Oran, David R., and Perlman, Radia J., "Digital Network Architecture Overview," *Digital Technical Journal*, no. 3, pp. 10–24, September 1986.

Lederman et al. 1988. Lederman, Sol, Harrenstien, Ken, and Stahl, Mary, Personal communications, 22 November 1988.

Linstone and Turoff 1975. Linstone, Harold A., and Turoff, Murray, *The Delphi Method*, Addison-Wesley, Reading, MA, 1975.

McQuillan et al. 1972. McQuillan, John, Crowther, John, Cosell, Bernard, Walden, D. C., and Heart, Frank, "Improvements in the Design and Performance of the ARPA Network," *Proceedings of the 1972 Fall Joint Computer Conference*, pp. 741–754, IEEE, New York, 1972.

McQuillan and Walden 1977. McQuillan, J. M., and Walden, D. C., "The ARPA Network Design Decisions," *Computer Networks*, vol. 1, pp. 243–289, 1977.

Meeks 1985. Meeks, Brock N., "An Overview of Conferencing Systems," *BYTE*, vol. 10, no. 13, pp. 169–184, December 1985.

Mills 1984. Mills, Miriam K., "SMR Forum: Teleconferencing—Managing the 'Invisible Worker'," *Sloan Management Review*, vol. 25, no. 4, pp. 63–67, Summer 1984.

NBS 1988. NBS, "Government Open Systems Interconnection Procurement Specification (GOSIP)," Institute for Computer Sciences and Technology, National Bureau of Standards (NBS), Gaithersburg, MD, 24 August 1988.

Partridge 1988. Partridge, Craig, *Innovations in Internetworking*, ARTECH House, Norwood, MA, October 1988.

Passmore and Horn 1988. Passmore, L. David, and Horn, Jeffrey, "GOSIP to Govern Federal Nets," *Network World*, vol. 5, no. 9, pp. 1, 35, 38–40, 29 February 1988.

Pouzin 1982. Pouzin, Louis, *The CYCLADES Computer Network—Towards Layered Network Architectures*, vol. 2 of Monograph Series of the ICCC, Elsevier, New York, 1982.

Pouzin 1988. Pouzin, Louis, Personal communications, 27 August 1988.

Price 1975. Price, Charlton R., "Conferencing via Computer: Cost Effective Communication for the Era of Forced Choice," in *The Delphi Method*, ed. Murray Turoff, Addison-Wesley, Reading, MA, 1975.

Quarterman and Hoskins 1986. Quarterman, John S., and Hoskins, Josiah C., "Notable Computer Networks," *Communications of the ACM*, vol. 29, no. 10, pp. 932–971, October 1986.

Raymond and Tompa 1988. Raymond, Darrell R., and Tompa, Frank Wm., "Hypertext and the Oxford English Dictionary," *Communications of the ACM*, vol. 31, no. 7, pp. 871–879, July 1988.

Roberts 1974. Roberts, Lawrence G., "Data by the Packet," *IEEE Spectrum*, vol. 11, no. 2, pp. 46–51, February 1974.

Schwartz 1987. Schwartz, Mischa, *Telecommunication Networks*, Addison-Wesley, Reading, MA, 1987.

Scott 1988. Scott, Karyl, "Greene Loosens Reins on BOCs," *Network World*, vol. 5, no. 11, pp. 1, 52, 14 March 1988.

Shaw 1988. Shaw, S. J., "TCP/IP Still Rules Federal Nets," *Network World*, vol. 5, no. 11, pp. 1, 46–48, 14 March 1988.

Shein 1987. Shein, Barry, Personal communications, June–July 1987.

Spector 1988. Spector, Alfred Z., "Nationwide File Systems: Rationale and Challenges," Information Technology Center, Computer Science Department, Carnegie Mellon University, Pittsburgh, PA, August 1988.

Spratt 1986. Spratt, E. Brian, "Networking Developments in the U.K. Academic Community," *Proceedings of the International Conference on Information Network and Data Communication (Ronneby Brunn, Sweden, 11–14 May 1986)*, IFIP TC.6, Elsevier, Amsterdam, 1986.

Tanenbaum 1988. Tanenbaum, Andrew S., *Computer Networks*, 2d ed., Prentice-Hall, Englewood Cliffs, NJ, 1988.

Tazelaar 1988. Tazelaar, Jane Morrill, "Groupware," *BYTE*, vol. 13, no. 13, p. 242, December 1988.

Turoff 1980. Turoff, Murray, "Management Issues in Human Communication Via Computer," in *Emerging Office Systems*, ed. Robert M. Landau, James H. Bair, Jean H. Siegman, pp. 233–257, Ablex Publishing Corporation, Norwood, NJ, 1980. Based on Proceedings of the Stanford University International Symposium on Office Automation.

Turoff 1982. Turoff, Murray, "Interface Design in Computerized Conferencing Systems: A Personal View," in *Human Factors and Interactive Computer Systems*, ed. Yannis Vassiliou, pp. 243–259, Ablex Publishing Corporation, Norwood, NJ, 1982. Proceedings of the NYU Symposium on User Interfaces (26–28 May 1982).

Turoff 1985. Turoff, Murray, "Information, Value, and the Internal Marketplace," *Technological Forecasting and Social Change*, vol. 27, no. 4, pp. 357–373, July 1985.

Umpleby 1971. Umpleby, Stuart, "Structuring Information for a Computer-Based Communications Medium," *AFIPS Conference Proceedings*, vol. 39, pp. 337–350, 1971.

Volk 1989. Volk, Rüdiger, Personal communications, December 1988 – January 1989.

Wells 1984.   Wells, M., "The JANET Project," *University Computing*, vol. 6, pp. 56–62, 1984.

XEROX 1980.   XEROX, *The Ethernet, A Local Area Network: Data Link Layer and Physical Layer Specification*, Xerox Corporation, Stamford, CT, October 1980.

Yost 1985.   Yost, David, "A Rich Man's SCCS," *Proceedings of the Summer 1985 USENIX Conference (Portland, Oregon, 11–14 June 1985)*, pp. 229–245, USENIX Association, Berkeley, CA, 1985.   Also in Partridge, *Innovations in Internetworking*, 1988.

Zander 1987.   Zander, Prof. Karl, Personal communications, 6 October 1987.

8   *Standards Bodies*

The groups that produce and influence standards for protocols and protocol models are important. Some of them are described in this chapter.

One of the main sources of confusion in trying to understand network standards is that they are produced by overlapping sets of standards groups. This is particularly noticeable among the worldwide bodies and those of the United States, Europe, and Japan. Some of those groups and their analogies with one another are sketched in Table 8.1. No attempt is made to describe all organizations involved in standardization in every country in either Table 8.1 or the text.

In the interest of brevity, explicit cross-references among sections in this chapter are omitted. The order of the sections is that of Table 8.1. Major sections correspond to rows: e.g., Section 8.1. *Formal Standards Bodies* corresponds to the row labelled "Formal." Subsections match columns: e.g., Section 8.1.1. **Worldwide** corresponds to the column labelled "World." Specific standards bodies are under third level heads and can also be located through the index.

8.1   *Formal Standards Bodies*

Certain groups exist to produce standards and are acknowledged to be formal standards bodies. These are mostly international or national bodies. Many are governmental but some are private consortia of corporations.

Table 8.1. *Standards analogies*

Type	World	United States	Europe	Japan
Formal	ISO IEC	ANSI IEEE, EIA	CEN/CENELEC ECMA	JISC
PTT	CCITT	FCC	CEPT	MPT
Government				
Legislatures	UN	Congress	CEC	Diet
Policy		FCCSET		MITI
Direction	CCRN	FRICC	RARE	
Standards	CCITT	NIST	COSINE	INTAP
Implementation		IAB, CAB, DSAB, IETF	ROSE, RARE Working Groups	INTAP
Industry	X/OPEN OSF	COS	SPAG	POSI

8.1.1　Worldwide

The most important formal standards bodies are those of worldwide scope.

8.1.1.1　*ISO*

The International Organization for Standardization (ISO) is the main non-PTT standardization body that handles networking issues. It is not associated with the United Nations (UN) and is instead composed of the national standards bodies of member countries, currently 89 of them. There are three levels of proposed or actual ISO standards: Draft Proposal (DP), Draft International Standard (DIS), and International Standard (IS) [Tanenbaum 1988, 29–30]. ISO often adopts CCITT recommendations. Standards may also be proposed by national bodies, such as the Institute of Electrical and Electronics Engineers, Inc. (IEEE).

> **Access**
> International Organization for Standardization
> +41 22 34 12 40
> 1 Rue de Varembé
> Case postale 56
> CH-1211 Geneva 20
> Switzerland

ISO standards can usually be ordered from national standards bodies such as the American National Standards Institute (ANSI).

8.1.1.2   *IEC*

The International Electrotechnical Commission (IEC) is composed of one committee from each country. Each committee is supposed to be representative of all electrical interests in the country. These committees may or may not be the same as those that represent their countries to ISO. IEC and ISO have an agreement to pursue complementary activities and thereby to cover all areas that need standardizing. IEC usually does electrical and electronic standards, while ISO does everything else [Fredriksson et al. 1987, 236–238]. Sometimes the two form a joint technical committee (TC) or working group (WG), as happened when the IEEE 1003.1 (POSIX) operating system interface standard was moved into the international standardization arena.

Access

International Electrotechnical Commission
+41 22 34 01 50
3 Rue de Varembé
P.O. Box 131
CH-1211 Geneva 20
Switzerland

8.1.2   United States

8.1.2.1   *ANSI*

The American National Standards Institute (ANSI) is the promulgator of basic standards such as ASCII. ANSI is the usual U.S. delegate body to ISO. ANSI is not an arm of any government and is private and nonprofit. Some corresponding groups in other countries are the British Standards Institute (BSI) in the United Kingdom, Association Française de Normalisation (AFNOR) in France, and Deutsches Institut für Normung (DIN) in Germany [Tanenbaum 1988; McNamara 1988, 336].

Access

ANSI Sales Department
+1-212-642-4900
1430 Broadway
New York, NY 10018
U.S.A.

8.1.2.2   *IEEE*

The Institute of Electrical and Electronics Engineers, Inc. (IEEE) has a Standards Office that handles topics such as those of IEEE 802 for LAN standards. IEEE may act as the national U.S. standards body in representation to ISO or IEC.

Access

IEEE Standards Office
+1-212-705-7960
Telex: 237936
The Institute of Electrical and Electronics Engineers, Inc.
345 East 47th Street
New York, NY 10017-2394
U.S.A.

IEEE Service Center
+1-201-981-0060
+1-201-562-5346 (credit cards)
445 Hoes Lane
Piscataway, NJ 08854
U.S.A.

8.1.2.3   *EIA*

The Electronic Industries Association (EIA) establishes standards for serial data interfaces such as RS-232-C, EIA-232-D, EIA-422-A, and EIA-423-A [McNamara 1988, 337].

Access

EIA Sales Order Department
+1-202-457-4966
Electronic Industries Association
2001 Eye Street N.W.
Washington, DC 20006
U.S.A.

8.1.3   Europe

8.1.3.1   *CEN/CENELEC*

CEN/CENELEC is a Joint European Standards Institution formed in 1984 from the combination of the European Committee for Standardization (CEN) (for national standards organizations) and the European Committee for Electrotechnical Standardization (CENELEC) (for national electrotechnical committees). The purpose of CEN and CENELEC is to produce Harmonization Documents (HD) in areas where the national bodies disagree and eventually to produce European Standards (EN).

Like its two component organizations, CEN/CENELEC has members from both the European Community (EC) and the European Free Trade Area (EFTA) (see RARE for a listing of the countries in these regions). It cooperates closely with CEPT in the areas of information technology (IT) and telecommunications [Fredriksson et al. 1987, 221].

Access

European Committee for Standardization (CEN)
+32 3 519 68 11

European Committee for Electrotechnical Standardization (CENELEC)
+32 2 519 68 50

Rue Bréderode 2
B-1000 Brussels
Belgium

8.1.3.2   *ECMA*

The European Computer Manufacturers Association (ECMA) is interested in portability of data and programs among dissimilar computers. It is a nonprofit organization and does not itself produce hardware or software. It was founded in 1960 by Compagnies des Machines Bull (Bull), IBM World Trade Europe Corporation (IBM Europe), and International Computers and Tabulators Limited (ICL) in cooperation with other European computer manufacturers. ECMA is a liaison member of both ISO and IEC and also promulgates its own standards [Fredriksson et al. 1987, 255 – 256].

Access

European Computer Manufacturers Association
+41 22 35 36 34
Rue du Rhône 14
CH-1204 Geneva
Switzerland

8.1.4   Japan

8.1.4.1   *JISC*

The Japanese Industrial Standards Commission (JISC) produces Japan Industrial Standards (JIS), which affect such things as character codes for use in Japan to handle the Japanese language. These are described in Section 15.3.1.

8.2   *PTTs*

Telephone companies have formed several bodies that recommend guidelines. These bodies do not themselves produce formal standards, but their guidelines are often used by formal standards bodies in producing actual standards. These bodies range from the worldwide, such as CCITT, to the continental, such as CEPT, to national bodies such as the FCC and MPT.

8.2.1   World

8.2.1.1   *CCITT*

The Comité Consultatif International de Télégraphique et Téléphonique (CCITT), or International Consultative Committee for Telephony and Telegraphy, is an agency of the International Telecommunications Union (ITU) of the United Nations (UN). CCITT is closely associated with the national telephone companies. CCITT recommends specifications of networking protocols and related standards. These are readily recognized by name because they all start with the prefix X. as in X.400 [Fredriksson et al. 1987; McNamara 1988, 337].

> **Access**
> International Consultative Committee for Telephony and Telegraphy
> +41 22 99 51 11
> Place de Nations
> CH-1211 Geneva 20
> Switzerland
>
> **For CCITT books and catalogs, contact:**
> United Nations Bookstore
> +1-212-963-7680
> Room GA 32B
> United Nations General Assembly Building
> New York, NY 10017
> U.S.A.

8.2.2   United States

8.2.2.1   *FCC*

Detailed communications regulatory issues in the United States are handled by the Federal Communications Commission (FCC). The FCC is somewhat like Japan's MPT, but it is not equivalent to CEPT or CCITT, or to any national European PTT, and there is no national PTT in the United States. Some policy decisions are made by the judicial branch of the federal government, as in the famous decision of U.S. Federal District Court judge Harold Greene to break up the telecommunications monopoly of AT&T. See Appendix B for other legal issues dealing with the FCC.

8.2.3   Europe

8.2.3.1   *CEPT*

The Conférence Européenne des Administrations de Postes et des Télécommunications (CEPT), or European Conference of Postal and Telecommunications Administrations is the European equivalent of CCITT.

Access
European Conference of Postal and Telecommunications Administrations
+41 31 62 20 79
Seilerstrasse 22
Case postale 1283
CH-3001 Bern
Switzerland

8.2.4 Japan

Some comments on the current Japanese telecommunications situation can be found in Appendix A. There are also a few comments on Japanese laws in Appendix B.

8.2.4.1 *MPT*

The Ministry of Posts and Telecommunications (MPT) oversees all telecommunications policy in Japan and handles most of the functions that are within the purview of the FRICC and the FCC in the United States. There is a separate association for amateur radio, but it is approved by MPT [Shapard 1988].

8.3 *Government*

National governments play strong roles in determining standards by passing laws, through agencies concerned with standards, by purchasing power, and by organizing implementations. Their most basic role is in setting national policy.

8.3.1 World

8.3.1.1 *UN*

The United Nations (UN) has several agencies that affect networking standards, most notably CCITT.

8.3.1.2 *CCRN*

The Coordinating Council on Research Networks (CCRN) is intended to coordinate European networking needs and has two co-chairs: William Bostwick, the chair of FRICC, and James Hutton, the Secretary General of RARE [Vaudreuil 1988]. Both FRICC and RARE are described in sections below in this chapter.

8.3.2   United States

8.3.2.1   *Congress*

The Congress has to approve any federal government funding in the United States, although the executive branch of government, i.e., that of the President, can and does recommend policy and has a set of standing committees for that purpose. These are the FCCSET committees.

8.3.2.2   *FCCSET*

There are several Federal Coordinating Council for Science, Engineering, and Technology (FCCSET) committees operating out of the Office of Science and Technology Policy (OSTP) of the Executive Office of the President of the United States. The Computer Research and Applications Committee completed a "systematic review of the status and directions of high performance computing and its relationship to federal research and development" and published a report in November 1987 [FCCSET 1987, 1]. This report was published largely because of a bill submitted by Senator Albert Gore requesting such a report.

The report found that the United States was lagging behind other countries in establishing a national research network to connect every research institution. It included the following:

- A proposal to upgrade existing facilities, particularly the *Internet* originally established by DARPA, to interconnect the existing research networks in the United States
- A suggestion that link speeds and number of sites connected should be increased
- A suggestion that a general national research network should be established with speeds up to 3Gbps within 15 years beginning in 1988

One result of this report was the establishment of FRICC, which solidified earlier cooperation among affected government agencies [Vaudreuil 1988].

> **Access**
> Executive Office of the President
> Office of Science and Technology Policy
> Washington, DC
> U.S.A.

8.3.2.3   *FRICC*

The Federal Research Internet Coordinating Committee (FRICC) was established in December 1987 as an information and cooperative group by the U.S. Department of Defense (DoD), the National Aeronautics and Space

Administration (NASA), the National Science Foundation (NSF), the Department of Health and Human Services (HHS), and the Department of Energy (DoE), under the guidance of William Bostwick of DoE [Vaudreuil 1988]. All five of these federal agencies had existing networks with overlapping purposes and clienteles. FRICC allows them to conserve scarce budgetary resources by reducing duplication of effort and to increase services by pooling resources. The agencies had been coordinating their efforts to some extent for years, but several circumstances led them to produce a more formal structure:

- A unified group was needed to communicate with CCRN, and, in turn, RARE, the European association of research networks.
- Great pressure was being applied by Congress to shrink the federal budget in order to reduce the deficit. For example, a single satellite link to Japan or Australia can cost $200,000 a year. Clearly it is in the interests of the participating agencies to share a single link.
- The National Research Internet (*NRI*) recommended by the FCCSET report to Congress is similar to the Defense Research Internet (*DRI*) that the members of FRICC were already working on. FRICC was formed very soon after the FCCSET report of November 1987 [FCCSET 1987].

In addition to the chair, the other members of FRICC are Mark Pullen of DARPA, Anthony Villasenor of NASA, Stephen Wolff of NSF, John Cavallini from HHS, and Daniel Hitchcock from DoE. FRICC is closely related to the FCCSET Subcommittee on Computer Networking, Infrastructure, and Digital Communications in pursuing similar goals and in having many common members, but the two groups are distinct and independent. The IAB is also distinct and complementary to FRICC. The immediate plan of FRICC is to produce a Research Interagency Backbone (*RIB*).

8.3.2.4   *NIST*

The National Institute of Standards and Technology (NIST), formerly known as the National Bureau of Standards (NBS) is an agency of the U.S. Department of Commerce (DoC). NIST publishes Federal Information Processing Standards (FIPS) that are used by agencies of the federal government in writing a Request for Proposals (RFP). NIST will often write a FIPS corresponding to some existing national or international standard, the difference usually being that the FIPS will specify almost everything that was left optional in the other standard.

Access
National Institute of Standards and Technology
Technology Building
Gaithersburg, MD 20899
U.S.A.

8.3.2.5   *NIST ISO-OSI Workshops*

The NIST ISO-OSI Workshops are intended to promote the development and implementation of ISO-OSI standards and protocols in the United States.

8.3.2.6   *IAB*

The Internet Activities Board (IAB) exists to determine the needs of the *Internet* and to propose technical methods to achieve them. It is composed of several task forces that work in specific areas, such as the IETF. The IAB chair is David Clark of MIT, its vice chair is Jon Postel of ISI, and its representative to FRICC is Barry Leiner of NASA RIACS [Vaudreuil 1988]. Since the IAB is responsible for design of both the *Internet* (TCP/IP) protocols and of the *Internet* itself [Cerf 1988], Clark and Postel also have the titles of Internet Architect and Deputy Internet Architect. The IAB tries to focus on research issues [Gross 1988a], although some of its task forces are concerned with operational issues (see IETF).

There is a parallel organization, the DSAB, that concentrates on distributed computing and distributed operating systems. The chair of the IAB is a member of the DSAB, and the chair of the DSAB is a member of the IAB [Comer 1988, 7].

The IAB was formed by DARPA about 1983 to oversee and coordinate work under its Internet Research Program (IRP). Delegation into task forces was decided on at the outset. Areas such as gateway algorithms, end to end services, and privacy were to be covered. The chairs of the various task forces would compose the IAB. The expansion and success of the *Internet* brought the involvement of other federal agencies and, after a FCCSET report, was part of the reason for the formation of FRICC, which is similar in intent and composition to the IAB [Gross 1988a].

Access
Dave Clark
ddc@lcs.mit.edu

8.3.2.7   *DSAB*

The Distributed Systems Architecture Board (DSAB) is concerned with distributed computing and distributed operating systems. It is chaired by Douglas Comer of Purdue. The chair of the DSAB is a member of the IAB, and the chair of the IAB is a member of the DSAB. These two groups have some joint task forces [Comer 1988, 7].

Access
Douglas Comer
comer@purdue.edu

8.3.2.8   *IETF*

The Internet Engineering Task Force (IETF) is the largest of the task forces of the IAB. The IETF chair, Phill Gross of the Corporation for National Research Initiatives (CNRI), a private corporation, is on the IAB.

Activities of IETF are mostly delegated to working groups, of which there are currently 18, on topics including Routing; Domains; Performance; PDN Routing; TELNET; *Internet* Authentication; Host Requirements (chaired by Bob Braden of ISI); CMIP-Over-TCP (CMOT) Network Management (chaired by Lee LaBarre of MITRE); SNMP Extensions (chaired by Marshall Rose of The Wollongong Group (TWG)); *Internet* Management Information Base (MIB) (chaired by Craig Partridge of BBN); and SLIP (with three co-chairs).

Many of the recently formed groups have been established at the request of interested parties who have approached IETF. IETF requires a written charter stating the group's goals and expected duration, a reasonably small group of core participants who actively communicate by electronic mail, and a working paper (usually an RFC) to document results. Interim reports are also expected at IETF plenary meetings, as are written status reports in the *IETF Proceedings*.

IETF plenary meetings are held four times a year and are three days long. The first day and the morning of the second day are devoted to working group breakout sessions, and the rest of the time is devoted to network and working group status reports and to technical presentations. The resulting *Proceedings* include minutes of the plenary sessions, written working group reports, and all presentation foils. These can be obtained from SRI-NIC. Thirteen working groups met and reported at the IETF meeting of June 1988 at the U.S. Naval Academy. Topics discussed included a report of 200Mbps TCP throughput by Dave Borman of Cray, congestion control work by Van Jacobson, Canadian plans for an *NRCnet* modeled on *NSFNET*, plans for the *DRI* to replace the *ARPANET*, the status of FRICC, and a report on the current state of *NSFNET* by Hans-Werner Braun of Merit.

The ancestor of the IETF was the Gateway Algorithms and Data Structures Task Force (GADS), which dated from the origin of IAB and had as chair David Mills of the University of Delaware (Delaware). GADS was originally intended to stick to research in routing and other internet layer topics, but the growth of the *Internet* soon led the task force to emphasize ongoing operational topics. Evolution of the EGP protocol became increasingly important (for example, see Chapter 11).

The IAB meeting of January 1986 made the decision to divide GADS into two groups: the Internet Architecture Task Force (INARC), to pursue research goals, with David Mills as chair, and IETF, to handle nearer term engineering and technology transfer issues. The original IETF chair was Mike Corrigan, then the technical program manager of the Defense Data Network (*DDN*).

The beginnings of *NSFNET* led to vendors of gateways for the *NSFNET* regional networks attending IETF meetings, altering its composition from its original similarity to GADS. NSF had its own NSFNET Routing Group, but that merged with IETF in March 1987, doubling the size of the latter group. About that time, Mike Corrigan moved to the Office of the Assistant Secretary of Defense (OASD), and the present chair of the IETF took office. The increased size and wider composition of the group led to the formation of working groups to concentrate on specific areas, starting with routing, domains, and performance, and expanding to the present 18 groups. Many of the original working groups were established by the IETF chair [Gross 1988a]. In the two and a half years from 1986 to the end of 1988, there were 11 IETF meetings [Gross 1988b].

Access

There are two primary IETF mailing lists: ietf-interest@venera.isi.edu and ietf-tf@venera.isi.edu. If you want to join the interest list, send a request directly to westine@isi.edu. To join the main IETF list, you should send a note to gross@sccgate.scc.com, with a brief statement explaining your interest in the IETF.

Many of the working groups now have mailing lists of their own. For additional information on the IETF or any of its working groups, contact:

Phill Gross
gross@sccgate.scc.com

8.3.3   Europe

8.3.3.1   *CEC*

The Commission of the European Communities (CEC) often sets policy that affects all its member countries. The most far-reaching of these may be the decision to remove most trade barriers among those countries by the year 1992 in order to produce a continental European common market.

8.3.3.2 *RARE*

RARE (Réseaux Associés pour la Recherche Européenne) is an association of European research networks and their users. But RARE is not a network itself: its purpose is to promote network services for the research community in European countries, and especially to promote international interconnections of such services [Olthoff 1987, 1]. The eventual specific goal is an international European ISO-OSI infrastructure supplied, if possible, by the national PTTs [RARE 1987a; RARE 1988]. Users should then have international facilities available that offer the same communication functionality on a European scale as in domestic service [Olthoff 1987, 1].

Administration and Funding

RARE is a membership organization funded by dues from its national members [Hutton 1988]. The policy-making body of RARE is the Council of Administration (COA), which is composed of a single representative appointed by each national member. It meets three times a year and also handles budgets and accounts and sets up and monitors technical working groups. Detailed management is done by the RARE Executive Committee (REC). The Secretariat does general coordination, including that for the technical working groups, and publicity [Olthoff 1987, 4]. The working groups carry out the technical activities of the organization, usually meeting three or four times a year. The number of potential users of the services RARE promotes is probably at least 500,000 [Hutton 1988]. RARE considers this to be too many for academics to handle, making professional carriers preferable [Kaufmann and Ullmann 1987]. Professional paid staff are also employed.

The 1988 REC was composed of Klaus Ullmann, President; Jürgen Harms, Vice President; Kees Neggers, Treasurer; Bob Cooper, Member; Fernando Liello, Co-opted Member [Hutton 1988]. The Secretary-General is James S. Hutton. The Secretariat is in Amsterdam, currently at the Scientific Research Centre Watergraafsmeer (WCW). This is the same facility that houses CWI, the host organization of *cwi.nl* (*mcvax*), the main host of *EUnet*. Numerous other organizations are housed at WCW, including the National Institute for Nuclear and High-Energy Physics (NIKHEF), which, along with the Foundation for Fundamental Research of Matter (FOM), is the host for RARE.

Membership

There are four classes of membership: Full National Members, Associate National Members, International Members, and Liaison Members.

Table 8.2. *RARE Full National Members (October 1987)*

Country	Type	Organization	Representative
Austria	EFTA	ACONET	Manfred Paul
Belgium	EC	ABUT/BVT	Paul van Binst
Denmark	EC	UNI-C	Peter Villemoes
Finland	EFTA	FUNET	Marcus Sandiemi
France	EC	OFRIR	Guy Pujolle
Germany	EC	DFN	Klaus Ullmann
Greece	EC	ARIADNE	C. Halatsis
Iceland	EFTA	SURIS	Johann Gunnarsson
Ireland	EC	HEANET	Michael Walsh
Italy	EC	GARR	Enzo Valente
Luxembourg	EC		Pierre Decker
Netherlands	EC	SURF	Kees Neggers
Norway	EFTA	RUNIT	Petter Kongshaug
Portugal	EC	RIUP	Vasco Freitas
Spain	EC	IRIS	José Barberá
Sweden	EFTA	UHÄ	Mats Andersson
Switzerland	EFTA	SWITCH	Jürgen Harms
(Turkey	Other		Semih Bilgen)
United Kingdom	EC	JANET	Bob Cooper
(Yugoslavia	Other		Tomaz Kalin)

Source: [Hutton 1988]
Note: Parentheses indicate eligible nonmembers with expressed interest.

Full National Members are national academic and research network organizations (one per country). If there is no such national network, a country may be represented by a delegate from the academic or research community. Countries eligible to be full national members are listed in its constitution but may be classed for convenience as follows:

- All countries in the European Community (EC)
- Countries in the European Free Trade Area (EFTA), which is composed of Western European or neutral countries that are not part of the EC
- Others, such as Turkey and Yugoslavia. These countries are closely associated with Western Europe for economic or political reasons but are not part of the EC or EFTA.

Note that no Soviet bloc countries are included (unless Yugoslavia may be so characterized), and none without land area in Europe, as traditionally defined geographically. In Table 8.2, the country, its type, the member organization, and the representative are shown. For countries that have as yet only expressed interest in joining, parentheses are used.

Associate National Members may be organizations that are doing networking and that agree with the objectives of RARE but cannot be full national members because they are based in countries not on the preceding list. There are such members in Hungary and Korea.

International Members could be European organizations that are international in scope and that agree to the objectives of RARE but that do not fit in the previous categories. Current International Members include CERN, *EARN*, ECFA, NORDUNET, ECMWF, ESONE, and EUUG (for *EUnet*) [Hutton 1987].

Liaison Members are other organizations involved in networking. *BITNET* and *CSNET* are jointly the only current members in this category.

Associate, International, and Liaison members may appoint nonvoting representatives to RARE activities and organizations. Although RARE is a very European organization, it has influence far beyond the continent, due to its leadership in promoting ISO-OSI standards and protocols.

There are national or regional networks that readily fit into the RARE scheme, such as *DFN* in Germany and *NORDUnet* in the Nordic countries. *DFN* was originally pure ISO-OSI. Others, such as *SURFnet* in the Netherlands, do not use ISO-OSI protocols yet (DECNET, in this case), but are nonetheless closely associated with RARE philosophically [Spiegel 1987] (and usually as members as well). *JANET* in the United Kingdom uses the Coloured Book protocols, but the founding president of RARE, Peter Linington, was head of the JNT, and the current JNT head, Bob Cooper, is a member of the RARE COA [Hutton 1988]. JNT requires Coloured Book protocols for computer equipment sold in that country. This is because some widely used existing services are based on those protocols; the situation is similar to that of TCP/IP in the United States. There is a strong U.K. commitment to ISO-OSI but no rush to convert prematurely [Kille 1988]. Thus, interconnection to *JANET* is not a technical problem, especially since there are already gateways in place at UCL for mail and CERN for file transfer, but it is a procurement problem. The United Kingdom, like all other EC countries, will have to require ISO-OSI protocols in a few years [Kaufmann and Ullmann 1987]. Related problems exist for *EARN*, as detailed in the *ILAN* section in Chapter 19.

Existing European Continental Networks

Talks took place in Brussels in July 1987 and through mid-1988 between RARE and the existing European continental networks *EARN*, *EUnet*, and *HEPnet* about possible use of a common infrastructure. Agreement in principle was reached among the networks and with RARE. However, the networks were not in complete agreement with the PTTs about charging. PTT rates vary by an order of magnitude between European countries and are generally an order of magnitude higher than in the United States (see Appendix A). Some PTTs—e.g., in Germany—have attempted volume charges; most want to charge the individual user, but international and domestic rates are often radically different (by as much as 100 percent or even 600 percent [Carpenter 1988]). These problems already affect the topology of existing networks and could have further effects. See the *EARN* section later in this chapter and the *DFN* section in Chapter 13 about these problems.

Each of the networks that participated in the Brussels RARE meeting has produced a migration plan for conversion to ISO-OSI protocols. Those existing networks as they are currently constructed do not fit into the RARE scheme well, since they do not use ISO-OSI protocols, nor do they even all use the same protocols, and most make significant use of leased lines rather than depending entirely on the PTT PDNs. This leads to the question of whether those networks will be replaced by the eventual ISO-OSI network or whether they will be converted to become part of it. The RARE position appears to be that there is no objection to the continued existence of those networks as separate administrative entities, but they are encouraged to use ISO-OSI protocols and to interconnect transparently with other such networks. RARE wants network communications to be provided by "organizations dedicated to that purpose, and not be dependent on informal agreements between participating organizations" [RARE 1987a; RARE 1988].

There are currently legal restrictions on third party information transfer in many European countries: a private network cannot relay traffic between two public networks because that would violate the government monopoly of such services. Liberalization is in progress, however [Carpenter 1988]. See Appendix B.

This set of questions remains among the most prominent in European networking, arising in almost any discussion of European-wide services. For a discussion of possible problems with the RARE "multinational" approach, as compared to the *EARN* "international" approach [Jennings 1987], including some discussion of PTT rate problems, see the *EARN* section.

Overseas Interconnections

Most RARE participants want interconnections with networks, particularly national research networks, on other continents, and this is a stated goal of RARE itself: "universal coverage of Europe is essential, and this should be extended to give access to as much of the world as possible" [RARE 1987a; RARE 1988]. *EARN*, *HEPnet*, and *EUnet* already maintain such connections. Resolution of this duplication of effort may be a RARE task.

The United States presents a particular problem for interconnection: *NSFNET* uses TCP/IP, which RARE considers to be a stopgap solution. Thus, many people do not want an *NSFNET* node on the European continent (although there is already a connection to *ARISTOTE* at INRIA in France and plans for connections to *NORDUnet* and *JANET*); they prefer an ISO-OSI transatlantic connection. Others feel that a TCP/IP connection to *NSFNET* is desirable because those protocols are widely used in Europe, even for some international connections. FRICC has recently been formed in the United States and is analogous to RARE politically, although it is not multinational. Both FRICC and RARE cooperate in CCRN, which is intended to handle this sort of problem.

Protocols

The particular kind of ISO-OSI protocol stack RARE advocates is TP0 directly over X.25. Some observers in the United States might have expected TP4 over ISO-IP over X.25, but this is not recommended by RARE, partly due to a feeling that the European PTTs provide sufficiently good service that a protocol like TP4 that does end to end error checking and retransmission at the transport layer would be redundant. If error checking is needed at the transport layer, TP1 is available for that purpose. X.25 with the 1984 and 1988 additions can provide full Connection Oriented Network Service (CONS). X.121 addressing plus NSAP addressing is adequate for a large network. There is a desire to avoid the proliferation of gateways that might accompany the continent-wide internetwork produced by ISO-IP. Using X.25 directly makes it one big single network. RARE specifically does not want to produce an international backbone to which national networks would connect; it wants to connect and unify all the national networks. Some comments on the sorts of protocol conversion that may be necessary between the RARE type of wide area network and local area networks already in place in Europe may be found in the *DFN* section.

RARE has proposed quality of service targets for the eventual continental network [RARE 1988]. Three measures are indicated for the two different states of an empty network and of busy hour performance on 90 percent of the days.

Standards

RARE is a member of the European Workshop for Open Systems (EWOS), which works on functional standards and selects options to use with them, in cooperation with the European standards organization CEN/CENELEC [Olthoff 1987, 2]. EWOS is somewhat analogous to the NIST workshops in the United States. There is an even more closely associated project, COSINE, and RARE is sometimes thought of as the action arm of COSINE.

RARE Working Groups

In some cases where RARE feels immediate action is needed, it sponsors development tasks directly, organized in working groups.

WG.1   Message Handling System (MHS) is in charge of a variety of activities, including a MHS Pilot Project, coordination with COSINE, and mapping between X.400 and RFC822 [Olthoff 1987, 13–14]. The MHS Pilot Project involves experimental networks in member countries; these are known as the RARE Experimental R&D MHS Networks. This project started in 1987, and the purpose is to test implementations of X.400 [Olthoff 1987, 3]. It is funded largely by CEC and NORDUNET. WG.1 provides initial MHS specifications, which are refined in COSINE specifications, which are then tested in implementations in the RARE MHS Pilot Project. The RARE and COSINE work is thus complementary [Olthoff 1987, 22–24]. There are also related projects in participating countries, such as the MHS projects **GIPSI** in France and **Kromix** of *DFN* in Gemany. Digital has developed an MHS product. Many of these are based on the **Ean** implementation of X.400. *DFN* has made extensive modifications for correct X.400 support.

WG.2   File Transfer, Access and Manipulation (FTAM) is involved in setting up an international FTAM infrastructure [Olthoff 1987, 14–15].

WG.3   Information Services and Directories is involved with providing information on resources such as the computer facilities available through the networking facilities being developed [Olthoff 1987, 16, 32].

WG.4   Network Operations and Management is involved with the network layer—i.e., X.25—management and operations [Olthoff 1987, 17–18, 32].

WG.5   Full Screen Services is involved in the short, medium, and long run, respectively, with improving the performance of Triple-X, development of an ISO Virtual Terminal (VT) standard, and providing standards for windowing and other bit-mapped screen management [Olthoff 1987, 18–19].

WG.6   Medium and High Speed Communication and ISDN cooperate with COSINE in high-speed networking and ISDN development [Olthoff 1987, 19–20, 32].

WG.7   PTT and CEPT Relations has a descriptive title [Olthoff 1987, 32].

WG.8   Management of Network Application Services is interested in communicating with the managements of national networks and of international networks such as *EARN* and *EUnet*, and of course cooperates closely with COSINE [Olthoff 1987, 20–21].

History

The germ of RARE and COSINE came from Professor Karl Zander of the Hahn-Meitner Institut (HMI) in Berlin. He was one of the principals in starting *DFN*, as well as in earlier German networking projects including both *BERNET* and *HMI-NET*. He instigated a series of meetings in late 1983 and early 1984 in an attempt to encourage similar and coordinated projects in the rest of Europe and elsewhere. A more general workshop for the same purpose was proposed in 1984, and such a workshop was held in Luxembourg on 13–15 May 1985 [Olthoff 1987, 3]. It was sponsored by the following groups:

- Cooperation Européenne dans la domaine de la recherche Scientifique et Technique (COST)
- European Committee for Future Accelerators (ECFA) for the High Energy Physics (HEP) community
- European Science Foundation (ESF)

The meeting was hosted by the Commission of the European Communities (CEC).

During this workshop, representatives of countries and of the sponsors proposed an association to foster European research networking, and funding for it seemed likely. This was the beginning of RARE [Olthoff 1987, 3–4]. RARE itself has since organized a European Networkshop every year.

RARE was formally chartered on 13 June 1986 under Dutch law. Initial funding came from the Dutch Ministry of Education and the CEC. The original Secretariat for RARE was provided by James Martin Associates (JMA), an international consulting firm based in Amsterdam. The initial organization was done by Frank van Iersel. A constitution was accepted in spring 1986, and James Hutton of the Rutherford Appleton Laboratory (RAL) was hired on 1 March 1987 to head the organization. (Hutton had been a major proponent of the 1985 workshop and was chairman of the ECFA networking subgroup before being hired by RARE [Carpenter 1988].) The move to WCW occurred on 18 September 1987 [Olthoff 1987, 4].

Access
raresec@nikhefh.hep.nl
+31 20 592 5078
Fax: +31 20 592 5155
Telex: 10262 hef nl

James S. Hutton
RARE Secretary-General
JSH@nikhefh.hep.nl

RARE Secretariat
c/o Postbus 41882
NL 1009 DB Amsterdam
Netherlands

8.3.3.3   *EWOS*

The European Workshop for Open Systems (EWOS) bring together participants from industry, government, and academia to discuss standards.

8.3.3.4   *COSINE*

COSINE, or Cooperation for Open Systems Interconnection in Europe, is a consortium of European countries, organized as a Eureka project in July 1987 [Olthoff 1987]. Its purpose is to create a market pull for ISO-OSI products.

Administration and Funding

As a Eureka project, COSINE is funded by its member countries. Administration is divided between the COSINE Policy Group (CPG) and RARE. CPG represents national governments and the CEC, while RARE represents the actual and potential user community of the services being specified and implemented. RARE has a COSINE Project Management Team (CPT) that delegates tasks to RARE working groups and contracts to specific institutions in order to produce reports that are then submitted to CPG for approval [Olthoff 1987, 7 – 8].

Composition

There are currently 18 countries participating in COSINE in addition to CEC: Austria, Belgium, Denmark, Federal Republic of Germany, Finland, France, Greece, Iceland, Ireland, Luxembourg, Netherlands, Norway, Portugal, Spain, Sweden, Switzerland, Turkey, and the United Kingdom. These are all the Full National Members of RARE, plus Turkey. There is some possibility of least favored region funding, perhaps for Greece, Turkey, Corsica, Portugal, and Spain [Hutton 1987].

Standards

Initial areas of standardization include remote login (Triple-X), file transfer (FTAM), mail (X.400 MHS), and directory services [Olthoff 1987, 25]. Other problems to be addressed eventually include gatewaying LANs to WANs and various supplier problems pertaining both to suppliers of equipment and suppliers of communication services [Hutton 1987]. Much of the work is contracted by CPG to RARE, which carries it out through its working groups [Olthoff 1987, 26 – 30].

COSINE draws from specifications set forth by ISO, CCITT, CEN/CENELEC, and CEPT. There is coordination with European Workshop for Open Systems (EWOS), which is a formalized platform for communicating about options. COSINE also tends to parallel SPAG, the manufacturer's group somewhat, although any connection is mostly indirect: CEN/CENELEC uses some of the results of SPAG, and COSINE adopts some of the results of CEN/CENELEC.

History

COSINE is derived from a call in early 1985 by François Mitterrand, president of France, for European countries to "coordinate their efforts to strengthen the overall technological position of Europe in the Eureka programme" [RARE 1987b; Olthoff 1987, 6]. Eureka, unlike ESPRIT, (see ROSE later in this chapter) is focused on technological projects, not precompetitive research. Eureka projects are also funded directly by participating countries, not by the EC, although the CEC does contribute some funding to this project. Some ESPRIT projects are conducted by giving a piece to one company in each EC country and sometimes letting the companies keep proprietary rights; Eureka projects usually do not work that way. COSINE is also a purely standards project: it might or might not use the results of ESPRIT projects such as ROSE or THORN, but it does not intend to implement anything itself.

Mitterrand's call bore fruit at the European Conference of Ministers in Hannover in November 1985, where a German proposal for a European Research Network was accepted as a Eureka project. It was later renamed COSINE, and RARE was asked to produce a plan for the establishment of the project. The resulting plan was accepted by the CPG in June 1986 and contracted in July 1987. In August 1988, the CEC decided to fund COSINE with 37 million ECU (European Currency Units), which is about 40 million U.S. dollars. This is in addition to the direct funding from the Eureka countries.

Access
N. K. Newman
+32 2355976
Telex: 21877 COMEU B
Secretariat
COSINE Policy Group
DGXIII-A2
Rue de la Loi 200
B-1049 Brussels
Belgium

8.3.3.5   *RARE Working Groups*

The RARE Working Groups are coordinated by RARE and focus on specific technical areas.

8.3.3.6   *ROSE*

ROSE (Research Open Systems for Europe) was the principal development project of the Information Exchange System (IES) [Blumann et al. 1986] of the European Strategic Programme for Research in Information Technology (ESPRIT) of the Commission of the European Communities (CEC). IES and work on the ROSE implementations started in 1984 with the goal of providing an infrastructure for collaborative research and development projects within ESPRIT and eventually for other projects of other kinds in Europe. It was also a proving ground for the use of the ISO-OSI protocols in an environment of heterogeneous machines and both wide and local area networks [Quarterman and Hoskins 1986].

Funding came from the CEC and went to five industrial partners that did the work: Bull of France, GEC and ICL of the United Kingdom, Olivetti of Italy, and Siemens of West Germany. Some tasks were subcontracted.

Services eventually expected under ROSE included mail, conferencing, file transfer (including text files), remote command execution, and remote login. The **UNIX** operating system was chosen as the first implementation system. Initially, existing implementations of protocols already in widespread use on **UNIX**, such as UUCP, were used. The intention was to start with UUCP in **4.2BSD** and gradually replace it layer by layer from the bottom up with ISO-OSI protocols. There was a version of **uucico** that used X.25. The ISO-OSI protocols and options were chosen from those recommended by SPAG [SPAG 1985].

Remote terminal access was to be accomplished by Triple-X PADs; file transfer by ISO8571 (FTAM); mail by X.400; session as ISO8326 and ISO8327; transport as ISO8072 with TP0, TP2, and TP3 over X.25 and TP4 over CSMA/CD protocols such as Ethernet. The internet layer was ISO8473, and the network layer was mostly X.25 with X.75.

The end to end addressing convention to be used in ROSE with the ISO-OSI protocols was a three-level hierarchy of eight octets for the name of the remote network, eight octets for the system on the LAN, and two octets for the transport selector. This allowed gateways between networks to be the only machines that need know about the interconnection topology of the networks. The transport selector could allow choosing UUCP instead of the ISO-OSI session service. A prototype network was set up in 1986 [Quarterman and Hoskins 1986].

The **GIPSI** X.400 implementation done for ROSE by INRIA, CNET, and Bull of France was the initial one used in the French network *ARISTOTE*. ROSE itself is no longer active, but it was very useful for industry in gaining experience with ISO-OSI protocols [Devillers 1988].

8.3.4   Japan

8.3.4.1   *Diet*

The Japanese Diet, or parliament, decides major issues of policy, including whether or not to introduce competition into both the domestic and international telecommunications market.

8.3.4.2   *MITI*

The Ministry of International Trade and Industry (MITI) is a policy-making body in Japan that has strong effects on Japanese industry. It encouraged and authorized the formation of INTAP [INTAP 1987a].

8.3.4.3   *INTAP*

INTAP, the Interoperability Technology Association for Information Processing, Japan, was established on 18 December 1985 in Japan by authorization of MITI. INTAP is a nonprofit research and development group whose goal is "to promote and contribute to the development of Interoperability Technology for Information Processing" [INTAP 1987a]. It does this with activities ranging from research and development to testing and verification to public relations. For example, the project on interoperable database systems has an expected life span of seven years starting in 1984 and a budget of about 15 billion yen. INTAP is interested in implementing ISO-OSI protocols and standards [INTAP 1987a]. There is an INTAP ISO-OSI conformance test center, which was established in September 1987 by MITI [INTAP 1987b]. One of the first protocols to be tested and demonstrated was FTAM [INTAP 1987c].

The board of directors is composed of representatives from many major Japanese corporations, as well as institutions such as the Japanese Standards Association (JSA) [INTAP 1986].

> **Access**
> Interoperability Technology Association for Information Processing, Japan
> +81-03-505-6681
> Fax: +81-03-505-6689
> Akasaka 7th Avenue, Bldg. 6F
> 7-10-20, Akasaka
> Minato-ku, Tokyo 107
> Japan

8.3.4.4   *MPT/MITI Study Groups*

MPT and MITI both sponsor study groups, such as one on international telecommunications. That group is particularly interested in *Nihongo networking*, which means networking using the Japanese language. For more details, see Section 14.3.1.

8.4   *Industry*

Private companies sometimes form bodies that recommend standards or guidelines.

8.4.1   World

8.4.1.1   *X/OPEN*

The X/OPEN Group is a group of leading computer manufacturers that has produced a document intended to promote the writing of portable applications indirectly based on the **UNIX** operating system. The group closely follows both the AT&T System V Interface Definition (SVID) and POSIX (IEEE 1003), and it cites the /usr/group 1984 Standard as contributing. However, the *X/OPEN Portability Guide (XPG)* the group publishes covers a wider area than any of those other documents.

> **Access**
> Mike Lambert
> mgl@xopen.co.uk
> uunet!mcvax!inset!xopen!mgl
> +44 256 843 142
> X/Open
> Abbot's House
> Abbey Road
> Reading, Berkshire RG1 3BD
> United Kingdom

8.4.1.2   *OSF*

The Open Software Foundation (OSF) is primarily oriented toward the **UNIX** operating system but is also interested in standardizing network areas such as window systems, transport layer interfaces, and network file systems.

> **Access**
> Open Software Foundation
> +1-617-621-8700
> 11 Cambridge Center
> Cambridge, MA 02139
> U.S.A.

8.4.2   United States

8.4.2.1   *COS*

The Corporation for Open Systems (COS) is a vendor group that was established in the United States in 1985 to attempt to resolve incompatibilities in

ISO-OSI implementations. COS does testing and verification and certifies implementations for conformance [Kahn 1987]. This is similar to the function of SPAG in Europe and POSI in Japan.

Access
Corporation for Open Systems
+1-703-883-2796
1750 Old Meadow Road, Suite 400
McLean, VA 22102-4306
U.S.A.

8.4.3   Europe

8.4.3.1   *SPAG*

The Standards Promotion and Application Group (SPAG) is a consortium of European manufacturers concerned with choosing option subsets of ISO-OSI protocols for use by its members. It publishes these in a *Guide to the Use of Standards* (GUS) [SPAG 1985]. It was formed in 1983 and is an ESPRIT industry group [Fredriksson et al. 1987, 229]. It is somewhat similar to COS in the United States and to POSI in Japan.

Access
Standards Promotion and Application Group SA
+32 2 219 10 20
1 – 2 Avenue des Arts, Bte. 11
B-1040 Brussels
Belgium

8.4.4   Japan

8.4.4.1   *POSI*

POSI, or Promoting Conference for OSI, is a Japanese industry group whose purposes are to disseminate policy for ISO-OSI standards among its member corporations, to promote information exchange and cooperation with overseas groups, and to provide feedback to INTAP. It is approximately equivalent to SPAG in Europe or COS in the United States [INTAP 1987a; INTAP 1987c].

8.5   *Academia*

Professional societies and journals are influential in developments in the field that lead to standards.

8.5.1   Professional Societies

Most people involved in academic or research networking are members of one or more of three professional societies, ACM SIGCOMM, the IEEE Communications Society, or IFIP TC6.

8.5.1.1   *SIGCOMM*

The Special Interest Group on Data Communication (SIGCOMM) of the Association for Computing Machinery (ACM) has as chair Vint Cerf and vice chair A. Lyman Chapin.

> **Access**
> SIGCOMM
> Association for Computing Machinery
> 11 West 42nd Street
> New York, NY 10036
> U.S.A.
>
> Dr. Vinton Cerf
> Corporation for National Research Initiatives
> 1895 Preston White Drive Suite 100
> Reston, VA 22091
> U.S.A.

8.5.1.2   *IEEE-CS*

The IEEE Communications Society (IEEE-CS) runs several conferences and publishes several journals listed later in this chapter.

> **Access**
> IEEE Communications Society
> +1-212-705-7900
> 345 East 47th Street
> New York, NY 10017-2394
> U.S.A.

8.5.1.3   *IFIP TC6*

The International Federation for Information Processing (IFIP) is a federation of technical organizations or groups of such organizations that was formed in 1960. There are numerous technical committees [Fredriksson et al. 1987, 397–403]. The most relevant to this book is IFIP Technical Committee 6 (IFIP TC6) on Data Communication. Some conferences and workshops that are held by this technical committee or its working groups are listed later in this chapter.

Access
IFIP Technical Committee 6
+41 22 28 26 49
International Federation for Information Processing
16 Place Longemalle
CH-1204 Geneva
Switzerland

8.5.2   Journals

Many journals occasionally publish notable papers in computer networking. Some of these are *IBM Systems Journal, Proceedings of the IEEE, Communications of the ACM (CACM),* and *Software—Practice and Experience.* Other journals publish such papers more frequently and are listed in this section [Partridge 1988].

8.5.2.1   *TOCS*

ACM Transactions on Computer Systems (TOCS) is an ACM publication that began in 1982.

8.5.2.2   *CCR*

Computer Communication Review (CCR) is the quarterly publication of ACM SIGCOMM. Proceedings of SIGCOMM Symposiums are published as special issues of *CCR,* which began publication in 1970. The current editor is Craig Partridge.

8.5.2.3   *Computer Networks*

Computer Networks and ISDN Systems is a North Holland (Elsevier) publication that began in 1980 and was originally titled *Computer Networks.* Its current editor is Philip H. Enslow, Jr.

8.5.2.4   *JSAC*

IEEE Journal on Selected Areas in Communications (JSAC) is an IEEE journal that began publication in 1982 and publishes a series of special issues on selected topics in communications.

8.5.2.5   *IEEE Transactions*

IEEE Transactions on Communications (IEEE Transactions) is another IEEE journal. It began publication in 1952 and has a general scope of all topics in communication.

8.5.2.6   *Telecommunications Policy*

Telecommunications Policy is published by Butterworths in the United Kingdom.

8.6   *Conferences*

People who produce technology and standards often meet in conferences. There are enough such meetings that they could consume most of one's time without the need of anything else.

8.6.1   Academic

There are numerous academic conferences associated with computer networking. Some of them are listed here.

8.6.1.1   *SIGCOMM*

The ACM SIGCOMM Symposium is held annually in the summer. This may be the largest of the academic conferences.

8.6.1.2   *INDC*

An International Conference on Information Network and Data Communication (INDC) is held annually in the spring by IFIP TC6.

8.6.1.3   *IWCMHSDA*

Working Group 6.5 (IFIP WG 6.5) holds an annual fall International Working Conference on Message Handling Systems and Distributed Applications (IWCMHSDA) in conjunction with IFIP TC6.

> **Access**
> IFIP65@ics.uci.edu
> IFIP65@vax.runit.unit.uninett
> IFIP65@UCI.BITNET
> IFIP65@CERNVAX.BITNET
> MCI Mail: 357-8979
> Telex: 650-357-8979 MCI UW

8.6.1.4   *ISDN in Europe*

European members of IFIP TC6, in cooperation with the European International Council of Computer Communication (ICCC) governors, held a conference, ISDN in Europe, about the Integrated Services Digital Network (ISDN), hosted by the Netherlands PTT at The Hague in April 1989.

Access
ISDN in Europe
Ir. A. Boesveld
+31 70 43 33 78
Fax: +31 70 43 32 93
Telex: 31111 ptt nl
PTT
Hoofddirectie Technische Zaken
Postbus 30 000
2500 GA The Hague
Netherlands

8.6.1.5   *IEEE-LANs*

The IEEE Conference on Local Area Networks is held annually by IEEE. The name is self-explanatory.

8.6.1.6   *IPCCC*

International Phoenix Conference on Computers and Communications (IPCCC) is an annual IEEE conference, with proceedings of refereed papers, held in the spring in Scottsdale, Arizona.

Access
Arizona State University
College of Engineering and Applied Sciences
Center for Professional Development
Tempe, AZ 85287
U.S.A.

8.6.2   Workshops

A few limited attendance workshops are held to allow people who are highly involved in developing or implementing networking technology to meet and discuss projects and approaches in a relatively informal atmosphere. Some are invitation-only and are mentioned here only to indicate that they do exist, that they do have an influence, and that there are parallel events of this type in different parts of the world. Those appropriate to attend will probably be invited.

8.6.2.1   *ANW*

Developers associated with academic networks around the world meet annually in the fall in the International Academic Networking Workshop (ANW) invitation-only series of workshops.

8.6.2.2   *RARE Networkshops*

RARE Networkshops have been held at least annually since 1985 [RARE 1987c]. They are limited to RARE members.

8.6.2.3   *JNT Workshops*

The JNT in the United Kingdom holds annual workshops.

8.6.3   Industry

Industry conferences tend to be either all-inclusive or organized around a particular protocol suite. The protocol suite tends to be either TCP/IP or ISO-OSI.

8.6.3.1   *INTEROP*

Advanced Computing Environments (ACE) presents a TCP/IP conference, INTEROP, with technical sessions, tutorials, and a vendor exhibition in the fall of each year. The group also publishes a monthly newsletter called *ConneXions—The Interoperability Report*, which covers TCP/IP, ISO-OSI, and other networking issues. The editor is Ole J. Jacobsen.

> **Access**
> Advanced Computing Environments
> +1-415-941-3399
> 480 San Antonio Road, Suite 100
> Mountain View, CA 94040
> U.S.A.

8.6.3.2   *OMNICOM OSI Conference*

OMNICOM presents an OMNICOM Open Systems Interface Conference in the fall of each year.

> **Access**
> Omnicom, Inc.
> 800-666-4266
> +1-703-281-1135
> Fax: +1-703-281-1505
> Telex: 279678 OMNI UR
> Conference Registrar
> 115 Park Street S.E.
> Vienna, VA 22180-4607
> U.S.A.

8.6.3.3   *CeBIT*

The Hannover Fair, or CeBIT, is a large annual spring vendor exhibit in Hannover, Germany, that has a marked networking component.

Access

Hannover Fairs USA Inc.
+1-609-987-1202
103 Carnegie Center
Princeton, NJ 08540
U.S.A.

8.6.3.4   *Networking Forum*

The Networking Forum was begun by the Institute for Networking Design (IND), which held two symposia in 1987: one in Tokyo (April 30) and another in Oita (October 28–29). The third was held on 22–23 April 1988 in Tokyo. MITI and MPT jointly sponsored the 1988 Networking Forum, which was very successful [Aizu and Nakamura 1988]. There were 31 vendors at the exhibition, which was attended by about 8,000 people; technical sessions were attended by about 1,000 people [Aizu et al. 1988].

8.6.3.5   *DATA SHOW*

The annual DATA SHOW is held in Tokyo each October [Shapard 1988; INTAP 1986].

8.6.4   Users

Some users of networks and conferencing systems are not specialists in that technology, either as academics or as vendors, but they nonetheless want to affect its course to some extent. Many of these groups hold conferences at which people who have known each other through computer mediated communications meet face to face. Users of networks that are strongly associated with a particular vendor's hardware tend to go to the user group conferences associated with that vendor's hardware—e.g., DECUS for Digital *(SPAN, HEPnet, EASYnet)* and SHARE for IBM *(BITNET)*. Some networks are strongly associated with particular operating systems, and their users tend to go to related conferences, such as USENIX and Uni-Forum for *USENET* and *UUCP* and EUUG for *EUnet*. One conference was invented specifically for its network: the International *FidoNet* Conference. The few conferences and groups mentioned here are unusual in some way, such as being primarily academic (ISTE), more involved with networking technology than most (USENIX), or associated with conferencing systems rather than networks (ENA).

8.6.4.1   *ISTE*

The International Symposium on Telecommunications in Education (ISTE) is held annually in the summer by the International Council for Computers in Education (ICCE). The 1989 symposium (August 21–24 in Jerusalem) is cosponsored by the Israel Association for Computers in Education (IACE), a Special Interest Group of the Information Processing Association of Israel (IPAI).

Access

ISTE Organizing Committee
FEIN@HUJIAGRI.BITNET
+972 03 654541
Telex: 033 544
c/o International Ltd.
P.O. Box 29313
Tel Aviv 61292
Israel

8.6.4.2   *USENIX*

The USENIX Association (USENIX) is "The Professional and Technical **UNIX** User's Group" and is the oldest (founded in 1976) and largest group of users of the **UNIX** operating system. It holds two annual technical conferences, an annual vendor exhibit, and many workshops, and it maintains relations with similar groups in other countries. It publishes a bimonthly newsletter and a set of manuals for the **4.3BSD** operating system; it also distributes software tapes. It is a nonprofit corporation under the laws of the State of Delaware, with eight unpaid directors on a board that meets four times a year and is elected every two years by the membership, and has an office with paid staff in Berkeley, California.

In addition to funding networking experiments such as *UUNET*, USENIX had the first Ethernet exhibit network at a major conference. Since many networking implementations are done on **UNIX** and this is the major technical association related to **UNIX**, many networking papers have been presented at USENIX conferences. Since the summer of 1988, all submissions have been refereed, and full papers have usually been required, making this more of an academic conference. USENIX also started publishing a quarterly refereed technical journal, *Computing Systems*, in 1988. The editor is Mike O'Dell.

Access

Ellie Young
Executive Director
ellie@usenix.org
+1-415-528-8649
USENIX Association
2560 9th Street, Suite 215
P.O. Box 2299
Berkeley, CA 94710
U.S.A.

8.6.4.3   *ENA*

The Electronic Networking Association (ENA) holds an annual spring conference on uses of conferencing systems and networks. Unlike most conferences related to networking, this one is organized by the users, and most of the users involved use conferencing systems, not academic networks. ENA began in 1985 as an online discussion group called *Symposium* that had a very unusual feature for that time: it took place concurrently on more than one commercial conferencing system, including *EIES* and *CompuServe*. This was largely due to the efforts of one person, Lisa Carlson, who downloaded messages from each system and uploaded them to all the others, thus inventing a technique called *porting*.

A face-to-face meeting of about 50 people was held in April 1985 in Greenwich Village, and ENA was named. All the participants at the original meeting were from the United States, except for one Israeli who happened to be in the States at the time. There have been annual meetings since, each including people from Canada, the United Kingdom, and Japan. The fourth meeting, held in May 1988 in Philadelphia, featured speakers from as far away as France and the Soviet Union.

This is a very loosely structured organization, and its specific goals are unclear. In spite of or because of this, it has so far achieved a high level of communication among network users and has promoted connections to places that were previously unreachable. Nonetheless, ENA primarily consists of people from only one of the two major computer conferencing communities: that of the commercial systems. Many ENA members have never even heard of *USENET*.

Access

Ed Yarrish
Treasurer
+1-215-821-7777
Electronic Networking Association
c/o Executive Technology Associates, Inc.
2744 Washington Street
Allentown, PA 18104-4225
U.S.A.

8.7   *Bibliographic Notes*

Useful overviews of players in the telecommunications, networking, and standards worlds may be found in Tanenbaum 1988, pp. 28–30; Stallings 1985, pp. 12–14; and Stallings 1987a, pp. 6–12. Descriptions of standards bodies related to ISO-OSI standards may also be found in Knightson et al. 1988, pp. 12–19. For the standards themselves, see in particular Stallings

1987a and Knightson et al. 1988 for ISO-OSI standards. For DoD (TCP/IP) standards, see Comer 1988 and Stallings et al. 1988. For LAN standards, see Stallings 1987b and McNamara 1985. And for the lower layers, see McNamara 1988. For European and international groups, the indispensable reference is Fredriksson et al. 1987, which lists far more organizations than have been mentioned here, describes them, gives access information, and has contextual essays.

8.8   *References*

Aizu and Nakamura 1988.   Aizu, Izumi, and Nakamura, Hiroyuki, "Institute for Networking Design," Institute for Networking Design, Tokyo, May 1988.

Aizu et al. 1988.   Aizu, Izumi, Nakamura, Hiroyuki, Kitaya, Yukio, and Carlson, Lisa, "The Business of Networking in Japan: Past, Present and the Future," *Proceedings of ENA Conference (Philadelphia, 13 May 1988)*, Electronic Networking Association, 1988.

Blumann et al. 1986.   Blumann, W., Cadwallader, R., Diediw, A., Lovelock, J., Power, D., Pozzana, S., and Saury, C., "Implementation of OSI Protocols in the ESPRIT Information Exchange System," in *ESPRIT '85: Status Report of Continuing Work*, pp. 1387–1398, Elsevier, Amsterdam, 1986.

Carpenter 1988.   Carpenter, Brian, Personal communications, October 1988.

Cerf 1988.   Cerf, Vinton G., "IAB Recommendations for the Development of Internet Network Management Standards; RFC1052," *ARPANET Working Group Requests for Comments*, April 1988.

Comer 1988.   Comer, Douglas, *Internetworking with TCP/IP Principles, Protocols, and Architecture*, Prentice-Hall, Englewood Cliffs, NJ, 1988.

Devillers 1988.   Devillers, Yves, Personal communications, 5 October 1988.

FCCSET 1987.   FCCSET, "A Research and Development Strategy for High Performance Computing," Executive Office of the President, Office of Science and Technology Policy, Washington, DC, 20 November 1987.

Fredriksson et al. 1987.   Fredriksson, E. H., Bus, J. C. P., and Wedgwood, C. G., *Information Technology Atlas Europe*, Elsevier, Amsterdam, 1987.

Gross 1988a.   Gross, Phill, "The Internet Engineering Task Force," *ConneXions — The Interoperability Report*, vol. 2, no. 9, Advanced Computing Environments, Mountain View, CA, September 1988.

Gross 1988b.   Gross, Phill, Personal communications, September 1988.

Hutton 1987.   Hutton, James S., "RARE," *Proceedings of the International Academic Networkshop (Princeton, New Jersey, 9–11 November 1987)*, 1987.

Hutton 1988.   Hutton, James S., Personal communications, September 1988, 14 December 1988.

INTAP 1986.   INTAP, "INTAP Profile," Interoperability Technology Association for Information Processing, Tokyo, November 1986.

INTAP 1987a.   INTAP, "Introduction to INTAP: Toward the Interoperability of Information Processing," Interoperability Technology Association for Information Processing, Tokyo, October 1987.

INTAP 1987b.   INTAP, "OSI Conformance Test Center," Interoperability Technology Association for Information Processing, Tokyo, October 1987.

INTAP 1987c.   INTAP, "Demonstration Brochure of OSI FTAM," Interoperability Technology Association for Information Processing, Tokyo, October 1987.

Jennings 1987. Jennings, Dennis M., "Computing the best for Europe," *Nature*, vol. 329, no. 29, pp. 775–778, October 1987.

Kahn 1987. Kahn, Robert E., "Networks for Advanced Computing," *Trends In Computing*, pp. 34–41, October 1987.

Kaufmann and Ullmann 1987. Kaufmann, Peter, and Ullmann, Klaus, Personal communications, 7 October 1987.

Kille 1988. Kille, Steve, Personal communications, September 1988.

Knightson et al. 1988. Knightson, Keith G., Knowles, Terry, and Larmouth, John, *Standards for Open Systems Interconnection*, McGraw-Hill, New York, 1988.

McNamara 1985. McNamara, John E., *Local Area Networks*, Digital Press, Bedford, MA, 1985.

McNamara 1988. McNamara, John E., *Technical Aspects of Data Communication*, 3d ed., Digital Press, Bedford, MA, 1988.

Olthoff 1987. Olthoff, Ruud, "RARE Annual Report 1987," RARE, Amsterdam, 1987.

Partridge 1988. Partridge, Craig, Personal communications, August–November 1988.

Quarterman and Hoskins 1986. Quarterman, John S., and Hoskins, Josiah C., "Notable Computer Networks," *Communications of the ACM*, vol. 29, no. 10, pp. 932–971, October 1986.

RARE 1987a. RARE, "Statement of the RARE position on the provision of Network Services," RARE, Amsterdam, 13 October 1987.

RARE 1987b. RARE, "COSINE Information Bulletin," RARE, Amsterdam, September 1987.

RARE 1987c. RARE, "Proceedings of the Valencia Networkshop," *Computer Networks and ISDN Systems*, vol. 13, no. 3, 1987.

RARE 1988. RARE, "Statement of the RARE position on the provision of Network Services," *DFN Mitteilungen*, no. 11, pp. 6–7, March 1988.

Shapard 1988. Shapard, Jeffrey, Personal communications, September 1988.

SPAG 1985. SPAG, *Guide to the Use of Standards*, Standards Promotion and Application Group SA, Brussels, 1985.

Spiegel 1987. Spiegel, Dr E. van, "Speech by Dr E. van Spiegel, director-general for science policy, Ministry of Education and Science, at the official opening of the RARE secretariat," Ministerie van Onderwijs en Wetenschappen, Amsterdam, 18 September 1987.

Stallings 1985. Stallings, Richard, *Data and Computer Communications*, Macmillan, New York, 1985.

Stallings 1987a. Stallings, William, *The Open System Interconnection (OSI) Model and OSI-Related Standards*, vol. 1 of *Handbook of Computer Communications Standards*, Howard W. Sams, Indianapolis, 1987.

Stallings 1987b. Stallings, William, *Local Network Standards*, vol. 2 of *Handbook of Computer Communications Standards*, Macmillan, New York, 1987.

Stallings et al. 1988. Stallings, William, Mockapetris, Paul, McLeod, Sue, and Michel, Tony, *Department of Defense (DOD) Protocol Standards*, vol. 3 of *Handbook of Computer Communications Standards*, Macmillan, New York, 1988.

Tanenbaum 1988. Tanenbaum, Andrew S., *Computer Networks*, 2d ed., Prentice-Hall, Englewood Cliffs, NJ, 1988.

Vaudreuil 1988. Vaudreuil, Gregory M., "The Federal Research Internet Committee and the National Research Internet," *Computer Communication Review*, 1 July 1988.

II *The Matrix*

9 *The Matrix*

This second half of this book describes the *Matrix* itself, giving details of specific current networks and conferencing systems and interconnections between them.

9.1 *Organization of Part II*

The networks and conferencing systems described are representative of those found throughout the world. An attempt has been made to find and describe all the largest and most widespread systems. However, it is probable that some have been overlooked, and lack of inclusion here does not indicate lack of importance. Examples of smaller systems are included, but no attempt has been made to even name them all because there are so many of them. The ones described here were chosen mostly because the author encountered information about them. In fact, the most general criterion for inclusion of any system in this book is the same as for Quarterman and Hoskins 1986: they are those that the author noticed.

9.1.1 Geographically

Approaches to networking differ markedly in different parts of the world. This part of the book allows discussions of regional attitudes and of networks specific to certain areas. Geographical areas are sometimes presented in chronological priority—i.e., those areas that first participated in the development of networking technology and of actual working networks are presented first. Where chronological selection is too difficult, as among the nations of Europe, alphabetical order is used instead.

For each geographical region, noncommercial systems are presented first, followed by commercial systems; the order of presentation of networks within a region is otherwise arbitrary. Small conferencing systems of one or a few machines are placed under the geographical section for their physical location, regardless of the geographical distribution of their users. This is to avoid largely irrelevant decisions about which are international systems and which are not. In the cases of gateway systems such as *UUNET* or *DASnet*, which do not support any direct user accounts for subscribers on their machines, either the physical location of the machine or the geographical affiliation of the sponsoring organization is used. Systems that make a point of international connectivity are mentioned in Section 10.4. Chapter 11 is about the *Internet*, basically because that material is too large to fit anywhere else. Some of the larger commercial systems are grouped together in Chapter 21 so that their common features can be discussed. Appendix A discusses the public data networks that are often used as infrastructure by the other systems.

9.1.2   Within Sections

Each system is characterized according to the topics introduced in the previous chapters of the book. Except as otherwise appropriate, the order of presentation is that of Chapter 6.

One kind of information emphatically *not* provided is pricing information for commercial services. That information varies too quickly to be appropriate for a book, and it can be obtained directly from the various services through the contact information provided. Costs of public data networks are, however, listed in Appendix A.

Details of user interfaces are usually not given for the following reasons:

- It is impractical to use every network listed.
- A good taxonomy and comparison of user interfaces would be a book in itself.
- The results would be too subjective to be of much use.

However, there are some comments on CMC interfaces in Chapter 3, Chapter 4, and Chapter 7.

9.1.3   Interconnections

Where possible, each section on a network that supports electronic mail contains a table of likely mail routing syntaxes and gateways that may be used to send mail to other such networks. In general, the idea is to identify a gateway between a pair of networks and the syntax needed to pass mail through it; some hosts on some networks are sufficiently sophisticated to be able to deduce an appropriate gateway from the domain syntax of the target host name.

Placeholders in italics are used for the most common tokens in network addresses, namely *user*, *host*, *gateway*, and *domain*.

In addition, there are abbreviations for sets of domains specific to particular networks, as summarized in Table 9.1. These are defined in the sections for each such network. Note that several of these domain systems, particularly {DNS} and {NRS}, are not limited to their original networks.

Sometimes several syntaxes or gateways are given for mailing between a pair of networks. They are given in order of desirability—i.e., the first one is the best to use, but it may not be implemented on less sophisticated hosts. For example, a host may recognize certain domains and know gateways to use to reach them, so users do not have to specify gateways explicitly for those domains. But less sophisticated hosts may not be able to do this.

Remember that gateways are subject to change, new networks are being implemented, and addressing syntaxes change. In particular, overuse of a gateway may cause it to vanish or to start charging for its services. Thus, it is best to test any item given in any of these tables before sending large messages using it. Where no syntax or gateway is given, or where the syntax or gateway given does not work, a likely approach would be to try sending mail through a host that is widely known for being a gateway among several networks; some such hosts are discussed in Section 10.4.

9.2   *Interconnection Difficulties*

Although the noncommercial metanetwork is closely connected, that is not because such interconnection is easy. Different underlying protocols, such as those of TCP/IP, ISO-OSI, DECNET, XNS, UUCP, or SUN-III, mean that interconnection for most services would require protocol conversion, and that is not commonly done.

Table 9.1. *Domain abbreviations*

Abbreviation	Networks (top level domain)
{ACSNET-domain}	ACSnet (**OZ.AU**)
{SUN-III}	ACSnet, AUSEAnet, TCSnet
{Ean-domain}	CDNnet, Ean networks
{DNS}	Internet, CSNET, NSFNET, NRI, EUnet, UUCP
{JUNET-domain}	JUNET (**JUNET**)
{XEROX-domain}	XEROX Internet
{JANET-domain}	JANET (**UK**)
{NRS}	JANET, HEANET, SPEARNET

9.2.1   The Service: Electronic Mail

There is one service that is converted and interconnected almost universally: electronic mail. This is the glue that holds the *Matrix* together.

Mail has a simple format:

The *body* contains the actual text of the message. The sender may or may not prepend salutations and append closing remarks and signatures in the style of paper post. Most mail systems consider the body to be straight text, although a character set or line lengths may be enforced, and Japanese systems such as *JUNET* distinguish several character sets within it. X.400 recognizes a hierarchical structure of data of various types. As far as the average user is concerned, mail that can be sent reliably among most of the systems described in this book must have a simple text body with 7 bit bytes, lines less than 80 characters long, and a single character set. The most prevalent character set is USASCII. The size of the entire message is usually limited, often to 100,000 bytes.

The *header* contains important information such as the addresses of the sender and recipients and a subject line, all provided by the sender, as well as a message identifier and date provided by the local mail system. These are used by a local mail agent in deciding how and whether to send the mail. The subject line and date can usually be passed through most mail systems essentially unchanged. The message identifier is handled by the mail systems themselves and should not be supplied or changed by the user. The header elements the user must be concerned with are those containing addresses — e.g., the *From:*, *To:*, *Cc:*, *Bcc:*, *Reply-To:*, and *Sender:* header lines of RFC822 [Crocker 1982].

The *envelope* is used by a particular mail delivery system in routing and point to point delivery. This part is usually not seen by the users. Distinctions between the header and the envelope are often unclear.

Mail can be used to carry other services, because binary files can readily be encoded in text that will pass through most mail services in the body of mail messages. It is quite common to transfer source files, object files, binary graphics images, and other kinds of data by this means. The encoding used must be known to the sender and recipients, but this can often be done by using a commonly available format and noting its type in the subject header.

9.2.2   The Problem: Addresses

Ideally, there would be one addressing syntax known to all networks and hosts worldwide. But the current mess is not ideal. The benefits and problems with source or system routing, domains or attribute lists, and other subjects related to naming, addressing, and routing were discussed at length in Section 5.3. Following is a brief summary and some practical implications of the systems in actual use.

9.2.2.1   *Syntax*

Network addresses usually have two parts. (1) The *local part* specifies a mailbox for a specific user, or sometimes a distribution alias or a file to put mail in. The meaning of the local part is determined by the system specified by the host part. (2) The *host part* traditionally specifies a particular machine, as in LISTSERV@BITNIC.

There are several ways of specifying these parts—i.e., there are several commonly used separators:

user@host	The at sign is used in *BITNET, JANET, Internet*, and many other networks. It may be the most prevalent separator.
host::user	This double colon syntax is used in Digital's *EASYnet* and other networks such as *MFEnet* and *INFNET*. Note that the order of the local and host parts is opposite that used with the at sign.
host!user	This exclamation point syntax (more commonly called *bang syntax*) is used in the *UUCP* network. It is unusual in more than one way because there is often more than one element, due to the source routing used on that network.
host1!host2!host!user	Chains of *UUCP* hosts may be indicated by separating exclamation points.
<@host2:user@host>	This is *Internet* RFC822 source routing and can be used to accomplish the same thing as *UUCP* source routing. It is used and implemented much less often, however.

user%host@host2   The percent sign here is used to do source routing similar to that of RFC822. This syntax is not required by formal mail system specifications (except Grey Book), but it is very widely used. It depends on the general rule that the local part to the left of the at sign is interpreted locally, so the message will reach host2, and that many hosts know to interpret the percent sign as a secondary at sign, so host2 will know to send the mail on to the destination host.

The most obvious question is which syntax to use. The answer depends on the source network and host, the target network and host, and any intermediate networks.

9.2.2.2   *Precedence*

Consider an address such as

host1!host2!hostx!user@hosta

This might be constructed by a user on the *UUCP* network to reach a user on hosta on the *BITNET* network. This may work, as long as all the intermediate hosts know only about UUCP bang syntax. But suppose host2 also understands at sign syntax. The part it sees in the mail envelope will be

host!user@hosta

Does this mean

"hostx!user"@hosta

that is, send to hosta and expect hosta to do something appropriate with the local part host!user? If hosta doesn't understand bang syntax (which it won't, being on *BITNET*), the mail will fail.
    Or does it mean

hostx!"user@hosta"

that is, send to hostx and expect hostx to do something with the local part user@hosta? If hostx is an old-style *UUCP* host, it won't understand at signs, and again the mail will fail.
    The problem can be even worse. On **TOPS-20**, an exclamation point is a comment delimiter, and pairs of them are used to surround comments.

Thus

> host1!host2!host3!hostx!user@hosta

was read as

> host1host3user@hosta

Putting quotes around the left-hand side could avoid this problem. Even stranger things could happen when addresses with odd numbers of exclamation points were listed, as in a *Cc:* list:

> hostx!userx@hosta, hosty!usery@hostb

would be read as

> hostxusery@hostb

This could be very confusing to the sender if an error message came back from hostb for an essentially random user name [da Cruz 1988]. The best way around these problems is to stick to one major syntax and to convert completely at gateways.

Some systems actually use spaces in user names. These often also accept an underscore instead of a space, or quotes around the whole user name, but the sending user has to know this. Some systems, such as *DASnet*, use brackets in their addresses, while other systems, such as *Telex*, do not permit those characters in addresses. The user has to know the appropriate substitute characters (in this case parentheses) that a gateway will transliterate.

There is, in general, no way to tell what precedence to use merely from the syntax of a mail address. And there is, in general, no way to tell what precedence a host *will* use. There is no way to tell without being told what address format can be used to reach a given user on a given system successfully. The gateway tables in this book may be of use in getting around these problems. A generally accepted addressing syntax is the only real solution.

9.2.2.3   *Domains*

A simple host part requires a global flat namespace and a global host table for the network to which it applies. Large, complex, or quickly changing networks can't afford this restriction. Thus, domain naming systems were invented to provide hierarchical namespaces so that each part of the space could be managed by an administrative organization associated with the hosts in it.

The archetypical domain naming systems are *Internet* DNS [Mockapetris 1986; Crocker 1982] and *JANET* NRS [Kille 1984]. They both use at signs in their syntax—e.g., respectively matrix@longway.tic.com and postmaster@uk.ac.ucl.nss. The host part is known as the *domain part* in a domain system. The domain part is *not* constructed by taking a host name and appending a domain; everything to the right of the at sign is the domain. That is, it is incorrect to say that in the above example longway is the host name and tic.com is the domain. It is true that tic.com is a domain, but longway.tic.com is also a domain, and one that refers to a specific host. That is, longway.tic.com is the host name in the domain naming system. That the name longway happens to be the old-style UUCP name for the same host is an irrelevant coincidence. If you can name a host and assume a domain to append, as in longway and *UUCP*, it's not a real domain.

Domains are not networks, despite early misconceptions on that subject [Crocker et al. 1977] and unfortunately common misuse today. A domain is an administrative entity, while a network is a technological one. A domain may include parts of many networks, and a network may include parts of many domains. The domain addresses relay.cs.net and uunet.uu.net are real; the hosts they name are the main administrative machines for *CSNET* and *UUNET*, respectively. But to name each host on *CSNET* host.cs.net would be an incorrect use of domains; the individual hosts are administered by local organizations, not by the network.

Unfortunately, this distinction has not been grasped by many network administrators, and the tables in this book include some theoretically incorrect but practically necessary examples of confusion between domains and networks. The most common ones are the use of host.uucp and host.bitnet to refer to hosts on the *UUCP* and *BITNET* networks, respectively.

9.2.2.4   *Order*

There are three kinds of ordering problems:

Local and domain parts	Depending on the syntax, the local part may come first (user@domain) or last (host::user).
Precedence	Which of several syntactically significant operators to evaluate first may be unclear (hostx!user@hosta).
Domain order	The order of elements of a domain may be different on different networks. *JANET* and other Grey Book networks use left to right order, while the *Internet* and other DNS networks use right to left order.

9.2.2.5   *Length, Case, and Character Sets*

Some networks impose very tight limits on the length of host names — e.g., old-style *UUCP* host names should not be longer than seven characters.

Most networks consider the host or domain part of an address to be case insensitive — i.e., user@host is the same as user@HOST. But old-style *UUCP* host names are case sensitive. The local part is sometimes case sensitive.

Europeans often use ISO8859 [ISO 1987] or other variants of ASCII to encode characters that do not occur in USASCII but that are used in their languages. These sometimes occur in local parts of network addresses. Since such characters are not alphabetic or numeric in USASCII, but instead are what are usually considered separator characters, such as the vertical bar character (|), such addresses may not be able to pass through all mail systems. Conversion into and out of different kinds of EBCDIC can also have peculiar effects, as has been noted on *BITNET*.

9.2.3   The Method: Gateways

In the current state of the networking world, one must often know a set syntax and a gateway or set of gateways to send mail through to get from one network to another. Mixing basic syntaxes should be avoided whenever possible. Mixing ones with opposite precedence, such as using ! and @ in the same address, is just asking for trouble. The tables in this book list likely syntaxes and gateways.

9.2.3.1   *Examples*

user%host.uucp@uunet.uu.net

or

user%domain@uunet.uu.net	Usually works to get mail from the *Internet* to the *UUCP* network
uunet!domain!user	Usually works to get mail from the *UUCP* network to the *Internet*
host!user@domain	Almost certainly fails to do either

9.2.3.2   *X.400 as a Solution*

The CCITT/ISO X.400 message handling protocol set handles a superset of all these addressing syntaxes and might, if generally implemented, solve all these problems. But universal adoption of X.400 is not near, and meanwhile the current mess must be dealt with.

9.2.3.3   *Abbreviations versus Directories*

Many host systems or networks allow local abbreviations of host names or whole addresses. For example, john@here.cs.bigu.edu might be abbreviated from hosts inside the domain bigu.edu as john@here.cs and from hosts inside cs.bigu.edu as john@here. A user who corresponded with that address frequently might establish a local abbreviation so that just john could be used. But trying to use any of john, john@here, or john@here.cs from otherhost@there.cc.stateu.edu would almost certainly fail, or, worse, john@here might be interpreted as john@here.cc.stateu.edu and the mail might be misdelivered without warning.

Fully qualified names should always be used when trying to address anyone not extremely local (that is, on the same machine) and for location independent uses such as writing on business cards. A directory that allows looking up John Whoever and finding an appropriate mail address is a useful idea. A few such services are described in this book, but they are not generally available.

9.2.4   Postal and Telephone Addresses

Many users complain that they do not want to have to remember a complicated syntax such as user%host@domain in order to reach other users, and it is true that what is necessary is often complex. A bit of perspective is useful.

9.2.4.1   *Postal Addresses*

Consider a postal address:

        S. W. Smith
        P.O. Box 12345
        42 Big Long Avenue
        Austin, TX 78711

First, notice that there are two punctuation characters here that people usually don't think of as such: space and newline. If you drop a space or two, you have a different address:

        S. W. Smith
        P.O. Box 1234542
        Big Long Avenue
        Austin, TX 78711

If you reverse the order of a couple of elements separated by newlines, e.g.,

S. W. Smith
42 Big Long Avenue
P.O. Box 12345
Austin, TX 78711

the mail gets delivered to the post office box, not the street address. If you convert a newline into a space, e.g.,

S. W. Smith
P.O. Box 12345 42 Big Long Avenue
Austin, TX 78711

the postal carrier might try to find a P.O. Box 12345 at 42 Big Long Avenue, not at the postal branch office indicated by the zip code.

Depending on the address, other characters such as commas also play syntactical roles. But considering only space and newline, two is the same number of syntactically significant characters found in a typical domain address, such as matrix@longway.tic.com. But the domain address is shorter.

Computer users want to be able to just type "John" and reach a user. Most of them realize that that is too simplistic and that to reach me they would have to type "John Quarterman." But which one? There are several in England. Well, there can't possibly be more than one in town, so "John Quarterman, Austin, Texas" should work. But there are, in fact, two in Austin, so it is necessary to use a full postal address.

Thus, postal addresses are not simpler than electronic addresses, and electronic addresses are often shorter. The common opposite perception is more a matter of what people are used to than of reality.

9.2.4.2 Telephone Numbers

Telephone numbers are another case in point: many people find them easier to remember than electronic mail addresses. But a typical U.S. number, (212) 555-1212, contains three syntactically significant characters (the two parentheses and the dash), its length is syntactically significant, and the strings of numbers in it are recognizable only because everyone has seen them frequently. The corresponding international address is +1 212 555 1212. It uses different separator characters, plus and space, but has all the same problems.

Telephone numbers represent probably the worst user interface of any commonly used communication system. They are certainly much worse than the average domain address, but they are easy for many people to use and remember simply because of constant and chronic practice.

9.2.5   Newsgroups and Mailing Lists

Electronic mail is not the only service that gets gatewayed. Many *USENET* newsgroups are gatewayed into mailing lists on other networks such as *BITNET* and the *Internet*, and many mailing lists are gatewayed between mail networks. However, this is mostly done by automatic gateways or by people who specifically take care of the task, and the average user doesn't need to know much about it.

In the commercial world, contents of conferences are often manually carried between different systems: this is known as *porting*. It doesn't require much special knowledge beyond what a user will learn from having accounts on more than one system.

But users often do need to know specialized details to get mail between networks, and that is why the gateway tables in this book were composed. Confusion results from different user interface software, from different addressing syntaxes peculiar to specific networks, from attempts to represent one network's syntax in another's, and from attempts to encapsulate one network's syntax inside another's. The moral of all this is that there is no magic formula to get mail between any two points in the *Matrix*. It's a jungle with trails that may cross and conflict, lead to the wrong place, or become overgrown [Quarterman and Hoskins 1986].

9.2.6   The Barrier: Charging

Beyond the technical problems of interconnecting networks, there is a financial one: somebody has to pay. Costs are often hidden on the noncommercial networks, but they are explicit on the commercial ones. Gatewaying between noncommercial and commercial networks presents a special problem in that the gateway operator has to pay for both directions. A solution used in *DASnet* is to allow only certain users on the noncommercial network to use the gatewaying service and to charge them for it. But this is not a general solution to the problem, and the barrier remains, although it may be lower. See Chapter 6, Chapter 21, and Appendix A for more discussion of financial problems and Chapter 3 for some other barriers.

9.3   *Bibliographic Notes*

Computer networks and conferencing systems are constantly changing, so the state of the world will constantly diverge from what is published in this book. This is a major reason why access information is provided at the end of each section on a system. Electronic sources of documentation are often also cited. And whatever printed documents are available (and that were found) are noted, with the corresponding citations appearing at the end of each chapter.

A good general introduction to actual functioning networks is Landweber et al. 1986. Some speculations on research networks may be found in Jennings et al. 1986 and Jennings 1987. There are some useful comparative network papers in Compton 1986. A short introduction to some major networks, intended for undergraduates, may be found in Nassar 1988.

Detailed host lists for many networks accessible from North America (including *BITNET*, the *Internet*, *CSNET*, and *SPAN*), together with brief descriptions and some tutorial essays on mail, domains, and other relevant topics, may be found in LaQuey 1989. Host lists, descriptions, and brief tutorials for the three continental European networks, *EUnet*, *EARN*, and *HEPnet*, may be found in Karrenberg and Goos 1988. And Frey and Adams 1989 is a quick desk reference for many networks worldwide.

Finally, the entire first part of this book serves as a quick reference for services, uses, protocols and protocol suites, history, and standards. The index can be used to locate specific text.

9.4 *References*

Compton 1986. Compton, Mark, ed., *UNIX REVIEW*, vol. 4, no. 1, January 1986.

Crocker 1982. Crocker, David H., "Standard for the Format of ARPA Internet Text Messages; RFC822," *ARPANET Working Group Requests for Comments*, 13 August 1982.

Crocker et al. 1977. Crocker, David H., Vittal, John J., Pogran, Kenneth T., and Henderson, D. Austin, Jr., "Standard for the Format of ARPA Network Text Messages; RFC733," *ARPANET Working Group Requests for Comments*, 21 November 1977.

da Cruz 1988. da Cruz, Frank, Personal communications, October–November 1988.

Frey and Adams 1989. Frey, Donnalyn, and Adams, Rick, !:/@ *A Guide to Electronic Mail Networks and Addressing*, O'Reilly & Associates, 981 Chestnut Street, Newton, MA 02164, 1989.

ISO 1987. ISO, "Information Processing—8-bit Single-Byte Coded Graphic Character Sets—Part 1: Latin alphabet No. 1; ISO8859-1," ISO, Geneva, 15 February 1987.

Jennings 1987. Jennings, Dennis M., "Computing the best for Europe," *Nature*, vol. 329, no. 29, pp. 775–778, October 1987.

Jennings et al. 1986. Jennings, Dennis M., Landweber, Lawrence H., Fuchs, Ira H., Farber, David J., and Adrion, W. Richards, "Computer Networking for Scientists," *Science*, vol. 231, no. 4741, pp. 943–950, 28 February 1986.

Karrenberg and Goos 1988. Karrenberg, Daniel, and Goos, Anke, *European R&D E-mail Directory*, European UNIX systems User Group, Buntingford, Herts., England, December 1988.

Kille 1984. Kille, S. E., *The JNT Mail Protocol (Grey Book)*, Joint Network Team, Rutherford Appleton Laboratory, Chilton, Didcot, Oxfordshire, England, March 1984.

Landweber et al. 1986. Landweber, Lawrence H., Jennings, Dennis M., and Fuchs, Ira, "Research Computer Networks and Their Interconnnection," *IEEE Communications*, vol. 24, no. 6, pp. 5–17, June 1986.

LaQuey 1989. LaQuey, Tracy Lynn, *Users' Directory of Computer Networks*, Digital Press, Bedford, MA, 1989.

Mockapetris 1986. Mockapetris, Paul, "Domain System Changes and Observations; RFC973," *ARPANET Working Group Requests for Comments*, January 1986.

Nassar 1988. Nassar, Hamed, "Computer Networks Serving University Needs," *The Virtual Times*, vol. 3, no. 3, EE Department, New Jersey Institute of Technology, Newark, NJ, November 1988. A brief introduction to real computer networks for undergraduates, available by electronic mail from the author at hxn8477%njitx.decnet@njitc.njit.edu; bellcore!argus!mars!nancy; CompuServe: 74000,130; Fidonet: 1:107/701.

Quarterman and Hoskins 1986. Quarterman, John S., and Hoskins, Josiah C., "Notable Computer Networks," *Communications of the ACM*, vol. 29, no. 10, pp. 932–971, October 1986.

10 *Worldwide Networks*

Two kinds of organizations have proven most successful at running world-wide computer networks: private corporations and loosely organized cooperatives. National governmental research and military networks are usually limited by international borders, and commercial networks often can't cope with different tariff restrictions and language barriers. Many companies plan to have government PTTs support international computer networks by mutual agreements just as they now support international telephone, telegraph, and postal services, but current examples are few.

10.1 *Research*

These networks are primarily used for scientific research.

10.1.1 Antarctic research stations {AQ}

The only continent not described in the following chapters is Antarctica, but even that most remote place on earth is connected by regular electronic data communications.

The U.S. Antarctic Palmer, Siple, and South Pole research stations are connected by Kermit through the NASA ATS3 satellite to a Digital **VMS** machine in Florida. This machine is then reached by researchers of several projects sponsored by NSF at the University of Maryland (Maryland), AT&T Bell Laboratories (Bell Labs), and Stanford University (Stanford). The Antarctic link is leased from ITT Antarctic Services of Paramus, New Jersey [da Cruz 1987].

The link in Florida is on private property in Malabar, which is about 25 miles south of Cape Canaveral. It is supported by contracts from NASA and from NSF, the latter relating to oceanographic research vessels and polar research programs. There is a direct DDCMP connection to *SPAN*, and some researchers reach the machine from that network or through it from *BITNET* or the *Internet* [Eden 1988].

Data sent from Antarctica includes meteorological information collected by various instruments (some later used by the National Weather Service for forecasting, and some used for research on topics such as the hole in the ozone layer), as well as supply inventories and orders (to keep the stations operating). Software is sent in the other direction. Most data are processed on a Digital PDP-11/70 and transferred from there, although some IBM PC connections are also made for PC software and inventory databases [da Cruz 1987]. Connections are made daily. The satellite is visible from Antarctica for five hours a day, although there are large interruptions due to atmospheric conditions [Eden 1988].

Data connections have been in use since 1980 with Palmer and Siple stations. Kermit has been used since 1984, starting with the South Pole base [Eden 1988].

Access

If you need access, you probably already know the proper channels.

10.1.2   HEPnet

HEPnet, or High Energy Physics Network, originated in the United States but has since spread to most places where High Energy Physics (HEP) is done. *HEPnet* is also a major continental European network, as discussed in the next chapter, and extends to Japan as well. The total number of reachable hosts worldwide was estimated to be about 1,000 by the end of 1987 [Carpenter et al. 1987] and 5,000 by the end of 1988 [Blokzijl 1988].

The core facilities of *HEPnet* in the United States are the major HEP laboratories, i.e., Argonne National Laboratory (ANL), Brookhaven National Laboratory (BNL), Fermi National Accelerator Laboratory (FNAL), Lawrence Berkeley Laboratory (LBL), and the Stanford Linear Accelerator Center (SLAC) [LaQuey 1988]. The links among these facilities form the backbone of the network. Universities connect to it with 9600bps or 56Kbps leased lines. These facilities are linked by the *ESnet* X.25 backbone, currently running at 56Kbps. The *HEPnet* Review Committee has called for an early upgrade to T1 speeds [HEPnet 1988].

The DECNET protocols are widely used on *HEPnet*. This choice is apparently attributable to a number of factors:

- Most importantly, Digital equipment is widely used by physicists. This gave DECNET a decided advantage over Coloured Book, even in Europe, as in *Starlink*.
- TCP/IP is not used because the huge files physicists like to exchange made use of the early *ARPANET* and *Internet* impractical, and there was no developed TCP/IP network in Europe.
- DECNET services are considered very satisfactory by physicists.
- DECNET higher level protocols can run over a variety of network protocols and media, most importantly Ethernet and X.25; the latter is particularly important in Europe.

HEPnet DECNET areas (equivalent to network numbers) are coordinated with *SPAN*, although *HEPnet* is not part of *SPAN*.

HEPnet also supports a circuit switched network of terminal connections to remote computers through laboratory switches, both by direct leased lines and by the X.25 network. High Energy Physicists are also frequent users of *BITNET* [Price 1988].

Interconnections

Interconnections from *HEPnet* are shown in Table 10.1. The quotation marks shown in the table are necessary.

There are plans for *ESnet* to replace *HEPnet* and *MFEnet* [LaQuey 1988]. Backbone services for *HEPnet* have been provided by *ESnet* since the spring of 1988 [Price 1988].

Access
Larry Price
LEP@ANLHEP.BITNET
Argonne National Laboratory

10.1.3   PHYSNET

PHYSNET, or Physics Community Network, is the combination of many DECNET based physics research networks that share the same network layer address space (even though they use many different DECNET area numbers) and are thus an internet in the same sense that *NSFNET* or the *Internet* are internets. The networks comprising *PHYSNET* include *HEPnet*, *SPAN*, and *NRAO* [Wells 1987], as well as more local networks such as *CITNET* and *THEnet*. *PHYSNET* is often referred to as just *HEPnet* (as in some *BITNET* mailers [Nussbacher 1988]) or *SPAN* [Wells 1988a; Wells 1988b]. This network has no overall administration, although NASA and ESA have been instrumental in coordinating area numbers for it. Although several of the constituent networks have been operational for many years, the term

Table 10.1. *HEPnet interconnections*

Network	Syntax
Internet	LBL::"*user*@{**DNS**}"
BITNET	LBL::"*user*@*host*.BITNET"
EASYnet	LBL::"*user*%*host*.DEC@decwrl.dec.com"
Starlink	19457::jbvad::*user*

PHYSNET was apparently first used in 1985 [Chartrand and Demar 1985]. The name originated in the United States, but the network is worldwide because at least two of its constituents, *SPAN* and *HEPnet*, are.

10.2   *Cooperative*

This category is probably the loosest, not only because of the laissez-faire policies of some of the networks included in it, but also because of their widely varying administrative structures, ranging from the nearly pure anarchy of *UUCP* to the libertarian *USENET* to the semicorporate structure of *BITNET* to the detailed and almost priestly hierarchy of *FidoNet*. The common factor is that they are run by at least a subset of their own users, not by any outside agency. And most of them allow anyone with the necessary technical capabilities to join. Finally, most of their funding comes from the sites, hosts, or users they connect.

10.2.1   BITNET

BITNET (Because It's Time NETwork) [Fuchs 1983] is a cooperative network serving more than 2,300 hosts at several hundred sites in 32 countries, as shown in Table 10.2. Although the network is technologically one, and any user of any host on it can send mail to any user on any other host on it, administration and policies vary in the constituent parts. Generally, the membership is similar to that of *UUCP* and *USENET*, except that it is more limited to academic institutions. *BITNET* also resembles *CSNET* somewhat, but it is not as centralized and has never been supported by the government.

The major services supported are mail, mailing lists, and file transfer. *BITNET* has a very sophisticated automatic mailing list maintainer called **LISTSERV** and an archive server called **NETSERV**. The underlying protocol is NJE, as in *VNET*.

Table 10.2. *BITNET growth*

Country	1 May 1986	1 May 1988	1 August 1988
BITNET			
United States	844	—	1,461
Mexico	1	—	5
Argentina	1	—	—
Chile	0	—	4
Totals			
Countries	3	4	3
Sites	—	—	397
Hosts	846	—	1,470
NetNorth			
Canada	91	166	167
Asianet			
Japan	7	—	46
Singapore	1	—	6
Taiwan	0	—	2
Korea	0	—	1
EARN			
Countries	17	24	24
Sites	—	500	—
Hosts	363	600	644
Users	—	30,000	—
All of *BITNET*, *NetNorth*, and *EARN*			
Countries	21	30	32
Sites	—	—	974
Hosts	1,306	—	2,377

Sources: 1986 and May 1988 figures courtesy Henry Nussbacher.
August 1988 figures courtesy Ben Yalow, Roger Watt, Paul Bryant,
and Henry Nussbacher.
Note: BITNET connected hosts by network and country

In addition to the batch services, there is also a basic ability for any user to send a message of one line, not exceeding 160 characters, to any user on any machine. This is used to build an interactive chat facility. It is even used to build a sort of *anonymous FTP* facility by having a daemon trap messages to a specific user and interpret them as file system commands, the results of which will be sent back by the usual file transfer mechanism. The same daemon services may be reached by RFC822 mail or file transfers to the same pseudo-users. The main services *BITNET* does *not* have are remote login and general file transfer. (Although remote login is supported between **VM** hosts with **Passthru** as in *VNET* [da Cruz 1988].) A user can send any file to any other user, but a user cannot request a file from any user except the special transfer pseudo-users; a user cannot even request files from the user's own account on another machine [Nussbacher 1987]. NJE uses BSC at the link level [Klein 1988]. Although NJE allows for bidirectional traffic and multiplexing, the BSC line driver in RSCS does not. RSCS also has no provisions for dynamic adaptation for failed links, although **JES2/NJE** does dynamic routing.

In North America, work is in progress for using TCP/IP underneath NJE, while in Europe there are plans for migration to ISO protocols. In Israel, migration to TCP/IP and eventually to ISO-OSI is already in progress.

There are three main constituents of the network:

- *BITNET* in the United States and Mexico, as well as in Japan, Singapore, Taiwan, and Korea (the Asian parts are sometimes known as *Asianet*)
- *NetNorth* in Canada
- *EARN* in Europe (including *ILAN* in Israel), with some African links into Abidjan, Ivory Coast, and Algiers, Algeria.

GulfNet extends through several Persian Gulf states but is not yet connected to the other networks. The distinctions among the constituent networks are purely political, and mail can be freely exchanged between any two hosts. See the sections on the above-mentioned constituent networks for administrative, political, and historical details.

Interconnections

Interconnections from *BITNET* to other networks are shown in Table 10.3. Methods of preparing messages to be sent to other networks vary widely among *BITNET* hosts. From many hosts and for many target networks and domains, the mail interface allows the sender to specify an ordinary domain address. Sometimes it is necessary to prepare a message in a file in Batch Simple Message Transfer Protocol (BSMTP) format and send it to a special user on a gateway host. This is indicated in Table 10.3 by entries with two lines: the first line contains the gateway address, and the second gives the address format to use within the BSMTP file. BSMTP format is described in Chapter 4.

Once a BSMTP file has been prepared, it is still necessary to use an operating system-specific method to send it. Rather than give details for all of those methods here, I would like to recommend that you obtain better mail user interface software, which is mostly available for free. For details, send "GET GATEWAYS BSMTP" to a **NETSERV** (see below).

Table 10.3. *BITNET interconnections*

Network	Syntax
BITNET	*user@host*
Internet	*user@domain*.**{DNS}**
Internet	SMTP@INTERBIT
	user@domain.**{DNS}**
HEPnet	*user@host*.HEPNET
HEPnet (Japan)	*user@host*.HEPNET.JP
MFEnet	MFEGATE@ANLVMS
SPAN	*user%host*.span@vlsi.jpl.nasa.gov
SPAN	*user%host*.span@star.stanford.edu
Ean	*user@domain*.**{Ean-domain}**
UUCP (U.S.)	MAILER@PSUVAX1
	h1!h2!*host*!*user*@PSUVAX1
UUCP (Canada)	MAILER@UWOCC1
	h1!h2!*host*!*user*@UWOCC1
EUnet (W. Germany)	BSMTP@UNIDO
	user@domain@UNIDO
EUnet (Europe)	MAILER@MCVAX
	user@domain
XEROX Internet	*user*.**{XEROX-domain}**@xerox.com
EASYnet	*user%host*.dec.com@decwrl.dec.com
VNET	*user*@vnet
JANET	*user%domain*.**{JANET-domain}**
JANET	*user%domain*.**{JANET-domain}**@ac.uk
JANET	*user%***{JANET-domain}**.*domain*@ac.uk
JANET	MAILER@UKACRL
	user%domain.**{JANET-domain}**
CDNnet	*user@domain*
CDNnet	*user%domain*@ean.ubc.ca
ACSnet	SMTP@INTERBIT
	user@domain.**{ACSNET-domain}**
INFNET	MAILER@IBOINFN
JUNET	*user%domain*.**{JUNET-domain}**@csnet-relay.csnet
PeaceNet	cdp!*user*%labrea@stanford
DASnet	TO: XB.DAS@STANFORD
	SUB: [*host*]*user*!subject

An extensive table of gateways not only to other networks but also to specific domains is maintained by Henry Nussbacher on behalf of BITNIC. *BITNET* is one of the largest worldwide networks, having hosts and gateways in countries from Singapore to Iceland to the Ivory Coast. Many of the entries in Table 10.3 are derived from the *BITNET* table, but only a selection is presented here, mostly for large international networks, plus a few examples for smaller systems. The full table can be obtained by sending mail to a **NETSERV** machine with a first line of

GET BITNET GATES

Be aware that this is a rather large file (about 25,000 bytes) and that retrieving it will cost somebody: do it only if you really need it. In general, this file will be more useful to *BITNET* users in getting to other networks than for users of other networks in reaching *BITNET*.

To reduce traffic, it is best to use the **NETSERV** nearest you, which can be located by sending

QUERY SERVICE

to NETSERV@BITNIC.BITNET. For a listing of other information available from a **NETSERV**, send it a message containing

HELP

The various **NETSERV** machines exchange files among themselves and keep very similar sets of files, so one is much as good as another.

If no more specific method is known for reaching a given network from *BITNET*, it may be worth trying to send through SMTP@INTERBIT. This is a logical host name that is translated into a real host name appropriate for the sender's location. Its original purpose was to provide gatewaying service to the *Internet*, but since the hosts participating in the *INTERBIT* scheme are likely to have more sophisticated software than most, they are a good bet for reaching other networks as well. Here is how you would reach some networks from *BITNET*:

Internet	For the *Internet*, see above about *INTERBIT*.
JANET	The three methods given for reaching *JANET* in Table 10.3 are in order of desirability. Many *BITNET* hosts will recognize the top level *UK* domain directly and know a gateway to reach it. Others may need to be told to send such mail to *ac.uk*. And particularly anachronistic hosts may need to be told the gateway name in *BITNET* form, as *UKACRL*. In that case, the supplied syntax is what goes in the RFC822 *To:* header line, while the *BITNET* mail envelope address has MAILER@UKACRL instead. The entire file must be sent as a PUNCH file to user MAILER at *EARN* node UKACRL with class M.
VNET	A *VNET* user must first obtain permission from the *VNET* administration before sending or receiving mail involving other networks.
EUnet	Generally, access to *EUnet* should be through *MCVAX*; only German hosts can be reached through *UNIDO*.
DASnet	The method of reaching *DASnet* subscribers uses the *DASnet* method of putting the target address in the subject header.

A good example of a **NETSERV** is **KERMSRV** on *CUVMB.BITNET*. This is the primary distribution server for **Kermit** software and documentation. It replies to hundreds of requests a day, originating from all over the world. It is sufficiently sophisticated to be able to return a response in the format of a request — e.g., as an NJE interactive message, as electronic mail, or as a virtual card deck [da Cruz 1988].

Access

See the previous information about **NETSERV** and the sections on the constituent parts of the network later in this book: *BITNET* in the United States, *NetNorth* in Canada, *EARN* in Europe, *ILAN* in Israel, and *GulfNet* in the Persian Gulf states.

10.2.2   USENET

USENET began in 1979 and is thus one of the oldest cooperative networks [Daniel et al. 1980; Emerson 1983; Tokuda et al. 1986]. It is also one of the largest networks by almost any measure, having about 265,000 users and 9,700 hosts on five continents, as shown in Figure 10.1, and ranging from individuals to people at the largest corporations and universities. In fact, one of its key distinguishing features is that essentially anyone and any organization can join. Its name is usually taken to mean "User's Network." This network is unusual in a number of ways, most remarkably because it supports only one basic service, *news*, a distributed conferencing service, and does not support electronic mail (the closely associated network *UUCP* supports mail but not news).

Administration

USENET is one of the most decentralized networks: all a new machine needs to join in most regions is another machine to communicate with [Todino and O'Reilly 1988a]. Although registration in the general maps is advisable, there is no central authority that determines access. There is also no central funding source or mechanism: each host pays for its own transmission costs and generally passes through traffic originating at other hosts. This has led to a general consensus that commercial use of the network is frowned upon. Product announcements are usually permitted, but advertisements are not. There is no way to enforce such policies directly. Instead it is done by public opinion and direct complaints: anyone posting an advertisement will get direct mail complaining about it and will see postings on the network showing that many people think the original posting was a bad idea. Since people and companies don't generally like bad publicity and castigation by their colleagues and customers, this usually works. In extreme cases, people have proposed putting pressure on the

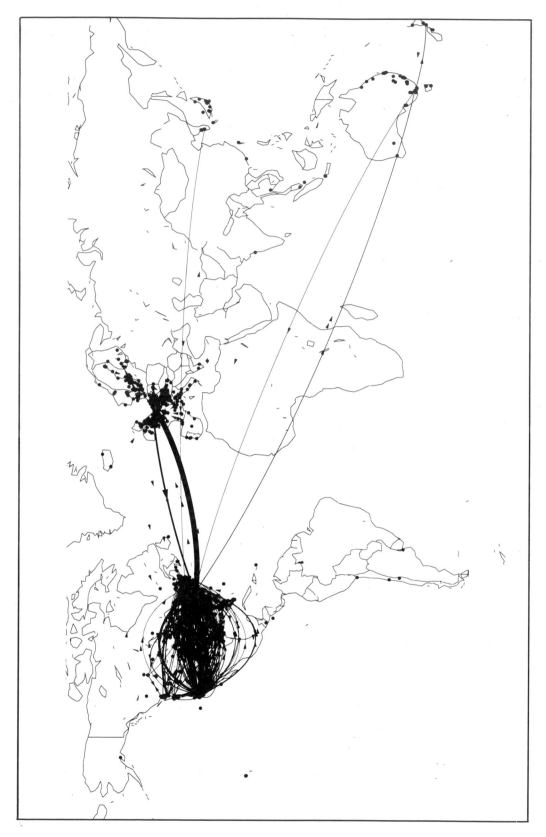

Figure 10.1. *USENET worldwide map (June 1989) [Reid 1989a]*

administrators of machines neighboring the machine from which the offending message was posted in an attempt to remove the posting machine from the network. Apparently this has never actually been done.

The greatest degree of organization in the network is found in the *backbone*, shown in Figure 10.2 and Figure 10.3. This consists of the machines with the greatest amount of traffic and thus the highest costs. (The European backbone is shown in the *EUnet* section in Chapter 13.) Since these hosts bear much of the burden of the network, their administrators tend to take a strong interest in the state of the network. The exact influence of the backbone is unclear, but it is involved in the organization of both the distribution and the content of news. There is a backbone on each continent, with trees radiating from its nodes. There may be redundant links among the nodes of those trees as well.

Speed

Most backbone (and many other) links currently run at about 11000bps. The average speed of slower links is probably close to 2400bps. More than 90 percent of all messages reach 90 percent of all hosts for which they are intended within one day.

Articles and Newsgroups

The element of information is called an *article*. Its format, as given in RFC1036 [Horton and Adams 1987] is modeled after that of *ARPANET* mail, as given in RFC822 [Crocker 1982]. That is, articles are lines of 7 bit ASCII text with a header prepended. The *From:*, *Date:*, and *Subject:* header lines are used in common with RFC822, although RFC1036 makes more requirements on *From:* and *Date:* than does RFC822. There are additional header lines peculiar to news articles, some of which are mentioned later in this section.

Articles are grouped according to topics in *newsgroups*, of which there are about 350. Newsgroup names are intended to reflect the topics to be discussed in them.

news.announce.important	Used for important announcements that are intended for everyone on the network
news.announce.newusers	Used for new users of the network

These are both *moderated* newsgroups: that is, when a user posts an article, the news software arranges to mail it over a mail network (usually *UUCP*) to a *moderator*, who decides whether or not to post it on the basis of considerations such as relevance, interest, clarity, and nonredundancy.

Some other newsgroups play roles in the administration of the network.

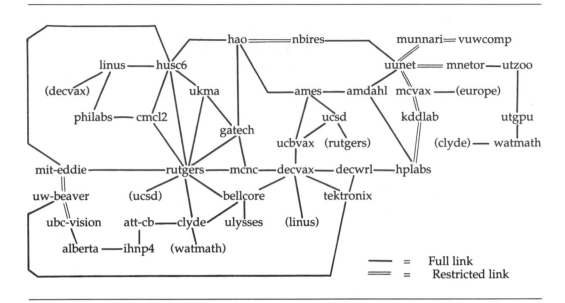

Figure 10.2. *USENET backbone topology (3 April 1988) [Spafford 1988a]*

news.groups	Newsgroups are created or deleted according to decisions made after discussion in this newsgroup.
comp.mail.maps	This is used to distribute maps of the *UUCP* network, with *USENET* hosts marked as annotations. These moderators form another group interested in *USENET* organization. Most newsgroups are not moderated, and postings to them are distributed directly.

The current top level newsgroups in *USENET* and their subjects are as follows [Spafford 1988b]:

comp	Computer science, software source, hardware and software systems
sci	Technical discussions about established sciences
misc	Topics that don't fit under another top level group
soc	Social issues and socializing
talk	Debates, lengthy discussions, few resolutions
news	The news network and the software that implements it
rec	Hobbies and recreational activities

Distributions

In Japan and Europe, the services of *USENET* are administered jointly with those of *UUCP* in the networks *JUNET* and *EUnet*, respectively, and there are large amounts of data that do not normally travel outside of Europe or Japan. Yet much news does travel the world, and much of the structure of

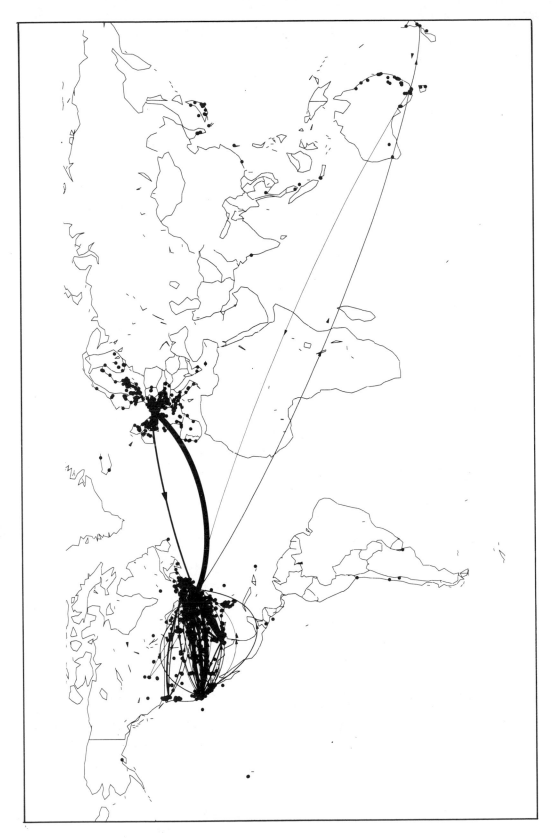

Figure 10.3. USENET *backbone map (June 1989) [Reid 1989a]*

Table 10.4. *USENET distributions*

Distribution	Geography
world	Everywhere
eunet	EUnet (Europe)
att	AT&T
can	Canada
na	North America
usa	United States
ca	California
ba	San Francisco Bay Area
ga	Georgia
ne	New England
tx	Texas
austin	Austin, Texas

USENET is reflected throughout the world. No explicit gatewaying is required to post an article that will travel to various parts of the world (although most users know that the main gateways to Europe, Japan, and Australia are *mcvax*, *kddlab*, and *munnari*, respectively). Rather, *distributions* are used. Some current distributions are shown in Table 10.4. Many states, provinces, and cities have their own distributions. Many companies maintain internal distributions, and often there is a distribution just for the machine of posting; these most local distributions are not really part of USENET proper.

Distributions are specified by the header line *Distribution:* in the outgoing article. For example, in

Distribution: world

the *world* distribution is used (this is also the default when no distribution is specified), and the article will go everywhere that *USENET* does. Accidental use of this distribution by naive users can cause problems, as in the canonical case of car for sale advertisements posted in New Jersey that aren't of any interest to people in Australia or Europe, particularly considering that people on those other continents have to pay for articles received from North America. Thus, most news posting software asks the user posting to such a distribution whether broadcast to the whole world is really intended. Also, not all newsgroups are accepted everywhere.

Protocols and Management

Articles are transferred by a flooding algorithm: each host sends each article to each other host with which it communicates. There are two mechanisms for preventing loops, each involving a header line in each article as well as an expiration mechanism:

Path: longway!ames!mailrus!mcgill-vision!gate — This *Path:* header is updated at each host to reflect the host from which the article was just received, and thus reflects the entire path the article has traveled from the originating host to the receiving host. The receiving host will not send the article back out to any host that appears in this header.

Message-ID: <1064@mcgill-vision.UUCP> — This header line is set when the article is posted and is never changed; it is required not only for news articles, but also by RFC822. It is supposed to be unique throughout the network. This is usually accomplished by having it include the host name and a sequence number for articles posted from that host, or the time of day, as in the above example. This header line is used to construct a history file on each host of all articles received on that host. If an article with the same *Message-ID:* as one in the history file is seen, it is considered to be a duplicate and is thrown away. This is not quite as good a loop-prevention mechanism as the *Path:* header because someone has paid to transfer a duplicate article, but it protects against corrupted *Path:* lines and broken software on other hosts.

Expires: 24 Apr 88 23:44:56 GMT — Since hosts do not have unlimited storage, news articles are usually *expired* after some rather short period, by default 14 days. Expired articles are also removed from the history file. It is possible to set the expiration date of an article with the *Expires:* header line, but this should be done only for important articles.

There are also some fine-tuning mechanisms:

Outgoing   Each host has lists of the hosts it communicates with and of the newsgroups and distributions to send to each of those hosts. If an outgoing article's newsgroup and distribution are not included in the lists for a given destination host, the article is not sent to that host.

Incoming   Each host also has a list of the newsgroups and distributions it will accept. Thus, a host may decide not to accept an article it has received. Once again, someone has to pay for transferring the article anyway, so this situation is to be avoided by tuning the specifications on the source host. It is also possible to reject articles that were posted more than a specified time ago, on the theory that they must be retransmissions from hosts that have been down. The posting rejection time is usually the same as that for article expiration because expired articles are also removed from the history file, and such retransmissions would thus not be rejected as duplicates.

The transport layer is UUCP for most links, although many others are used, including Ethernets and long-haul packet switched networks; sometimes UUCP is run on top of other transport layers, and sometimes UUCP is not used at all.

Naming, Addressing, and Routing

Every *USENET* host has a name. That host name and the name of the poster are used to identify the source of an article. Those hosts that are on both the *UUCP* mail and *USENET* news networks usually have the same name on both networks, but mail addresses have no meaning on *USENET*. Mail related to *USENET* articles is usually sent via *UUCP* mail; by definition, it cannot be sent over *USENET*. The two networks have always been closely related, but there are far more hosts on *UUCP* than on *USENET* and far more connections between hosts. In Australia, the two networks do not even intersect except at one host.

Interconnections

Since *USENET* is not a mail network, there are no mail gateways in the usual sense. However, *USENET* newsgroups are commonly interconnected with mailing lists on other networks because users on those networks want to participate in the discussions in the newsgroups, but their networks don't support the news service. Meanwhile, implementations of news for non-**UNIX** machines are becoming increasingly prevalent. For example, one of the largest machines on *USENET*, with about 30,000 users, is *CUNYVM.CUNY.EDU* [Reber 1988], which is best known as the root of the *BITNET* tree. It runs news and is connected as part of *USENET* as well. Here is how you would reach some networks from *USENET*:

Internet   The machine that does the most gatewaying between *Internet* mailing lists and *USENET* newsgroups is known as *ucbvax* on *USENET* and as *ucbvax.berkeley.edu* on the *Internet*. It bursts digested mailing lists into individual articles.

BITNET   Although many newsgroups are being gatewayed with *BITNET* mailing lists, there appears to be no single machine that does most of the gatewaying.

EASYnet   The main gateway for *EASYnet* is *decwrl* or *RHEA*, also known as *decwrl.dec.com*. Of course, the user does not have to know the names of these gateways, or even that they exist. Specialized software at the gateways handles the conversions between news and mail automatically.

Uses

USENET users pursue both technical and social ends, many of them organized by the newsgroup structure. But others are more general than that. At least one newsgroup has produced a series of conventions of its participants, not to mention t-shirts. There are even feuds between newsgroups, as in the long-running attempts of some *soc.women* participants to ban all male posters from that newsgroup; this has included the tactic of creating *soc.men*. More recently, *comp.society.women* has been created as a moderated newsgroup.

No description of *USENET* would be complete without mention of some of the notorious April Fool's Day jokes. These are derived from the ease of forging articles (such forgeries are usually readily detectable by a skilled eye). The most notorious example happened in 1984, when one "Konstantin Chernenko" announced that *kremvax*, *moskvax*, and he, mcvax!moskvax!kremvax!chernenko, were joining the network. Many users believed it, and the resulting follow-up articles and mail replies were numerous and interesting [Neumann 1984]. A more recent example, in 1988, was a purported warning by a well-known backbone host administrator about such April Fool's Day jokes: it was itself a forgery.

Effects

Relationships, marriages, conventions, lost friendships, software packages, papers, and books have resulted at least partly because of the use of *USENET*; many of them would not have happened without the network.

History

Jim Ellis and Tom Truscott were graduate students at Duke University (Duke) when they originated the idea of *USENET* in 1979 [Spafford 1988c]. According to an early description [Daniel et al. 1980], "A goal of *USENET* has been to give every **UNIX** system the opportunity to join and benefit from a computer network (a poor man's *ARPANET*, if you will)." The transport mechanism was UUCP, as distributed with the newly released Seventh Edition **UNIX** from AT&T Bell Laboratories. Access was limited to **UNIX** source licensees, as they were the only ones who could legally have the **UUCP** software (binary **UNIX** distributions had not been thought of yet).

The news software was not part of the Seventh Edition distribution but rather was written by Steve Bellovin, then a graduate student at the University of North Carolina (UNC) at Chapel Hill. The first two hosts were called *unc* and *duke*. A third host, *phs*, was added by 1980; it was administered by Dennis Rockwell, who also participated in the late 1979 planning sessions. Steve Bellovin rewrote the original shell script implementation into the **C** programming language, but this was never released beyond the original universities. Stephen Daniel did another C implementation, which, after modifications by Tom Truscott, became **A news** and was later distributed widely, although it was never intended for more than a hundred hosts and a few articles per day [Spafford 1988c].

The originators soon invited others to join, partly by distributing a flyer [Ellis et al. 1980] at the next USENIX conference, 29 January through 1 February 1980 in Boulder, Colorado. The news software was distributed on the June 1980 USENIX Delaware Conference distribution tape [Daniel et al. 1980]. The USENIX Association is the oldest and largest group of users of the **UNIX** operating system. The name *USENET* was coined by James Ellis as a variant of "Usenix Network." The name USENIX itself is derived from **UNIX**, which is a pun on **Multics** [Organick 1975], the name of a major predecessor operating system. (The pun indicates that in areas where **Multics** tries to do many things, **UNIX** tries to do one thing well.) Alternative names for the network were considered, such as *CHAOSNET, ARACHNET*, and *Spidernet*, but most of them were already taken. The users would have liked a name including the word **UNIX** but that was not considered appropriate because of AT&T's trademark. Later, Mark Horton or Matt Glickman claimed *USENET* meant "User Network." Since the users had gained quite a bit of control from the founders (the existence and popularity of the newsgroup *net.jokes* attested to this), the new meaning was appropriate [Truscott 1988]. Even that meaning has changed slightly to "User's Network," which is the one most commonly accepted today.

According to Daniel et al., "New systems will probably find that the rapid access newsletter is the initially most significant service" [Daniel et al. 1980]. Newsgroups were originally thought of as "newsletters" partly because of the analogy with *;login:*, the USENIX paper newsletter, which was in a brief hiatus when *USENET* was started. Newsgroups were seen as a logical extension of mailing lists when those grew to have too many participants. Initially, there were only *NET.general NET.v7bugs*, with *NET.test* following soon afterward. There was no newsgroup hierarchy originally: that was added by Stephen Daniel. For example, you could subscribe to "ALL,!ALL.play," meaning everything but newsgroups with *play* as the second component.

Early traffic was low: "The articles from the Usenet Epoch (lets call it 00:00 Jan 1 1980) to 1982 would fit comfortably on a single 800bpi tape, not to mention our 200 megabyte /usr/spool filesystem. Once we might have retrieved them, but they are surely gone now" [Truscott 1988]. All the articles from 1982 to the end of 1987 fill 26 reels of 6250bpi tape, as recorded by Tom Truscott. Enough individual articles have survived from the early years to show that even then the network had a mix of technical and social discussions, although the latter have outgrown the former in recent years. Growth, as measured in machines, users, newsgroups, articles, and data transferred and stored, has been the biggest historical problem with this network [Durlak et al. 1987].

The first of several news software rewrites to cope with growth of the network was done in 1981 at the University of California at Berkeley (UCB) by graduate student Mark Horton and high school student Matt Glickman. This was **B news**, first released to the public as **B news 2.1** in 1982. Mark Horton remained the principal maintainer through **B news 2.10.1** in 1984 [Spafford 1988c].

One of the effects of growth is articles that duplicate information in other articles, as when one article asks a question and many people post similar answers. This happens both because of the inherent delay of network propagation and because of new users who do not realize the likelihood that their articles will be duplicates in such a case. More users also lead to more unfocused or vituperative discussions, as well as other problems such as possible posting of licensed or copyrighted material. Moderation was introduced in 1984 as a solution to this problem after a great deal of debate. The idea was derived from the moderated mailing lists that had existed on the *ARPANET* for many years. The first moderated newsgroup was *mod.announce*, which was an alternative to *net.general*, a newsgroup formerly intended for general discussions throughout the network, but that had become useless because of the above problems.

Initial code for moderation was in **B news 2.10.1**, the last version released by Mark Horton, and depended on the first element of a moderated newsgroup's name being *mod*. **B news 2.10.2** was released by Rick Adams of the Center for Seismic Studies (CSS) in Arlington, Virginia, and completed on 18 September 1984. Adams added code that handled moderated newsgroups without depending on the *mod* keyword on 15 September 1986 and released **B news 2.11** in late 1986 [Horton and Adams 1987]. The distinction between distributions and newsgroups was not in early news software; it was also added in. The purpose is to allow users to limit individual postings to geographical areas appropriate to them, while still keeping such articles in newsgroups appropriate to their general topics.

Actual use of this software involved changing the names of newsgroups, and the opportunity was taken to change the names of *all* newsgroups in order to give them a more rational structure. This was the only time this has ever been done. There were originally only two main top level newsgroup elements, *net* and *mod*, and some others that indicated distributions. The name changes were done in two phases, each affecting about half of all newsgroups. The unmoderated newsgroups were changed in September 1986, and the moderated newsgroups were changed in April 1987.

Basically the same structure is still used, but some top level names and many more newsgroups have since been added [Durlak et al. 1987].

The most controversial decision involved in the newsgroup renaming was the creation of the *talk* top level name and the moving of many newsgroups to names under it. This was desirable because the number of non-technical newsgroups and their volume had become large enough that many backbone hosts did not want to carry them: a separate top level category for them would make that easy. Many users complained that this would cause the death of those newsgroups [Durlak et al. 1987]. Instead, a kind of alternative backbone, called the *jawbone*, was developed to carry them. The current *alt* and *bionet* top level newsgroups [Gilmore and Spafford 1988] are also results of this reorganization, and are also generally not carried by the backbone. Interestingly, some newsgroups that the backbone refused to carry, such as *net.rec.drugs*, have been created under new names as *alt* groups. There was an attempt before the reorganization to form a *funny bone* to carry such newsgroups, but that disappeared in the reorganization [Durlak et al. 1987].

The decisions to rename the newsgroups and to divide them into classes the backbone would carry and ones it would not led to a great deal of antipathy toward the reputed *backbone cabal* that made the decisions [Durlak et al. 1987]. This group actually comprised the administrators of the machines carrying most of the traffic, and thus paying most of the bills, and they considered the changes necessary to keep the network working. This was probably the high point of the backbone's power, for three main reasons: (1) the group deliberately encouraged the creation of an alternative backbone; (2) technological advances, such as much faster modems and *NSFNET*, have made the backbone less necessary; and (3) organizational developments such as the *inet* distribution (see below) and *UUNET* have also reduced the need for a backbone.

B news 2.11 included enhanced mechanisms for batching together groups of articles for transmission and for compressing them before transmission, as well as other features. This is the most common version of news software in use, but the distributed nature of the network means that there is no way to compel hosts to upgrade. There are still versions of **B news 2.9**, and maybe even **A news**, in use. Fortunately, **B news 2.11** is relatively clever at dealing with problem articles produced by such old software.

Geoff Collyer and Henry Spencer of the University of Toronto (Toronto) produced an alternative version of the basic news software, called **C news**, which they made available in 1987. Its main purpose was speed and reliability [Spencer and Collyer 1987]. This is not the only alternative version of the software in current use. The **notesfiles** software was developed at the University of Illinois at Urbana-Champaign (UIUC) by two graduate students, Ray Essick and Rob Kolstad, starting in 1979 [Kolstad 1988]. They were inspired by the UIUC CDC *PLATO* **NOTES** system. The **notesfiles** software was first released to the public at the January 1982 USENIX conference in Santa Monica. This software originally spread separately from the news software. But even though different interchange formats and internal organizations were used, the *notes* and *USENET* networks were connected within six months of the **notesfiles** announcement [Kolstad 1988] and are now considered to be a single network, carrying most of the same newsgroups (or *notesfiles*) [Spafford 1988c].

Another new top level newsgroup is *inet*. This is used to distribute news over networks such as the *Internet*, producing marked savings by allowing messages to exist as one *USENET* news article per machine instead of many mail messages in individual users' mailboxes. UUCP can be used over TCP/IP, and there is even a way to do it so that its functions that duplicate those of TCP are not used. However, the usual method of transporting news over TCP/IP is the Network News Transfer Protocol (NNTP) [Kantor and Lapsley 1986].

The many problems with *USENET* (e.g., reader overload, old software, slow propagation speed, and high and unevenly carried costs of transmission) have raised the possibility of using the experience gained in *USENET* to design a new network to replace it. These problems have been considered so bad that the network has been declared almost dead several times. But it is not dead yet, due largely to technology having kept up with growth. For example, Spencer Thomas wrote a program that used **Lempel-Ziv** [Welch 1984] compression, and Rick Adams applied it to news transmission in **B news 2.10.2** [Adams 1988]. As shown in Table 10.5, effective transfer speeds in 1988 were an order of magnitude greater than they were in 1983. Of course, not every host connects to every other one at 12000bps yet, but most of the backbone hosts do, and they have always been the biggest bottleneck. Table 10.5 does not take into account cost-cutting factors such as more efficient news software, *PC Pursuit*, *UUNET*, or NNTP. It is not clear what the next advance will be, but DS1 and DS3 (1.544Mbps and 45Mbps) speeds are becoming increasingly plausible. In fact, faster speeds are already in use on some links: some backbone hosts exchange news over *NSFNET*, with effective speeds of 40Kbps or more.

Most of the *USENET* problems are hard to measure, but numbers of hosts and users, as well as volume of total articles, have been estimated since 1986 by a project headed by Brian Reid [Reid 1988b]. These are shown in Table 10.6, with the earlier figures coming from various sources [Frey and Adams 1987]. Details from that project on growth in recent years are shown in Table 10.7. The readership numbers are based on actual readers,

Table 10.5. *USENET technological improvements*

Date	Advance	Effective bps	Factor	Comment
1979	—	300	1×	**news** and **notesfiles** invented
1980	—	300	1×	**A news** distributed
1981	1200bps	1200	4×	
1982	—	1200	1×	**B news 2.1, notesfiles**, *EUnet*, *SDN*
1983	—	1200	1×	**4.2BSD, System V, vnews**
1984	Moderation	1700	1.4×	**B news 2.10.1, rn**, *JUNET*, compression, revised moderation and distribution, **B news 2.10.2**
1985	2400bps	3400	2×	
1986	NNTP	3400	1×	**4.3BSD, B news 2.11**, jawbone
1987	—	3400	1×	**System V.3**, *UUNET*, newsgroup reorganization completed
1988	12000bps	12000	3.5×	Telebit Trailblazers

Sources: [Spafford 1988d; Truscott 1988; Kolstad 1988]

Table 10.6. *USENET growth*

Date	Newsgroups	Articles/day	MBytes/day	Hosts	Readers
1979	3	2	—	3	10?
1980	3?	10	—	15	20?
1981	—	20	0.05	150	—
1982	—	35	—	400	—
1983	—	120	—	600	10,000?
1984	—	225	—	900	—
1985	—	375	>1	1,300	—
1986	241	946	2.0	2,200	53,000
1987	259	957	2.1	5,200	100,000
1988	381	1,933	4.4	7,800	141,000

Sources: [Spafford 1988d; Reid 1988a]

not just users, in a continuing survey of about 7 percent of all *USENET* hosts.

Comparing these figures with those of Table 10.5, we see that the hardest years were about 1983–1986, when growth had exceeded the capability of the original technology and further developments had not yet alleviated the problem. Disk space has also been a problem because all those data have to be stored on the machine for users to read. Cost per megabyte has diminished rapidly, however, and with developments such as 800Mbyte half-height Winchester drives for a few thousand dollars expected by 1989, an IBM PC could easily have enough space for the current traffic.

Table 10.7. *Recent USENET growth*

Month	News-groups	Mes-sages-	Mbytes	HC12	HC3	HC1	Sam-ple	Reader est.	User est.
Apr 1986	241	28,388	59.512	2,193	2,193	2,315	249	53,000	380,000
May 1986	244	27,476	59.155	2,618	2,618	2,352	296	59,000	420,000
Jun 1986	243	20,706	49.024	2,951	2,951	1,724	293	75,000	500,000
Jul 1986	236	19,521	46.218	3,052	2,828	1,692	320	95,000	640,000
Aug 1986	241	19,057	44.846	3,354	2,311	1,641	351	78,000	630,000
Sep 1986	262	19,652	45.593	3,607	2,506	1,765	320	82,000	660,000
Oct 1986	298	20,579	49.490	3,878	2,502	1,816	328	88,000	640,000
Nov 1986	314	18,259	43.233	4,104	2,550	1,684	354	88,000	590,000
Dec 1986	242	17,396	44.914	4,358	2,585	1,656	356	84,000	620,000
Jan 1987	252	26,809	62.321	4,683	2,653	2,056	347	79,000	570,000
Feb 1987	250	29,410	62.735	5,053	2,873	2,223	362	90,000	590,000
Mar 1987	259	28,223	62.036	5,376	3,149	2,238	398	90,000	550,000
Apr 1987	—	—	—	5,200	2,765	2,238	412	86,000	570,000
May 1987	259	29,689	61.272	5,052	2,945	2,249	435	105,000	550,000
Jun 1987	269	32,349	71.316	5,323	3,453	2,359	452	120,000	530,000
Jul 1987	262	33,493	77.531	5,519	3,514	2,585	476	118,000	640,000
Aug 1987	265	26,689	57.344	5,675	3,552	2,302	497	125,000	720,000
Sep 1987	312	32,665	74.395	5,929	3,711	2,632	514	134,000	810,000
Oct 1987	319	33,161	69.593	6,195	3,871	2,837	534	131,000	770,000
Nov 1987	321	40,843	82.451	6,368	4,064	2,797	589	140,000	730,000
Dec 1987	328	34,839	77.438	6,615	4,130	2,854	596	129,000	770,000
Jan 1988	330	50,593	110.838	6,925	4,363	3,337	645	137,000	840,000
Feb 1988	—	—	—	7,362	4,838	3,498	632	143,000	850,000
Mar 1988	347	53,144	121.561	7,362	4,398	3,498	641	142,000	910,000
Apr 1988	381	57,979	130.945	7,810	4,803	4,152	809	141,000	880,000

Source: [Reid 1988a]
Note: All data were measured at *decwrl*.
> *Newsgroups* is the number of newsgroups that had nonzero traffic during the measurement interval.
> *Messages* is observed messages per month.
> *Mbytes* is megabytes of data per month.
> *HC12, HC3,* and *HC1* are three different ways of computing the "host count."
> *HC12* is the total number of distinct hosts mentioned in *Path:* lines in the past 12 months.
> *HC3* is the total number of distinct hosts mentioned in *Path:* lines in the past 3 months.
> *HC1* is the total number of distinct hosts in *Path:* lines in the past 30 days.
> *Sample* is the number of sites submitting **arbitron** reports.
> *Reader est.* is an estimate of the total number of readers.
> *User est.* is an estimate of the total number of users.

Regardless of how fast machines can transfer or store news, there is still the problem of readers being able to keep up with masses of material [Durlak et al. 1987]. The original user interface was called **readnews** and was line oriented. A screen-oriented interface called **vnews** was written by Kenneth Almquist and released in 1983. It is similar to the interface to the **notesfiles** software, and it allows moving among several menus, can list contents of newsgroups, and is quite fast. The **rn** interface was written by Larry Wall of JPL and NASA and was originally released in 1984 [Spafford 1988c]. It provides ways to read, discard, or otherwise process articles based on patterns (regular expressions and logical expressions) specified by the user. One of its most popular commands is the K command, which allows skipping all articles with the subject of the current one, even in later reading sessions. All news reading interfaces allow the user to subscribe or unsubscribe to individual newsgroups at will, without having to go through a system administrator (assuming the host system itself subscribes to the desired newsgroups). All of them also allow a user who is reading a particular article to post a follow-up news article, to reply by mail (usually over the *UUCP* network), to save the article to a file, to mark it as unread so it will be seen again while the user is reading news, or to mark it as read so that it will not be seen again.

Relations between *USENET* and USENIX have been obscure since 1980, when Thomas Truscott said, "It is hoped that USENIX will take an active (indeed central) role in the network" [Truscott 1988]. Michael Tilson of Human Computing Resources (HCR) in Toronto proposed about 1982 that USENIX buy a Digital PDP-11 to use as a central node for *USENET*, but the USENIX board of directors has been wary of assuming any direct responsibility or control for a network as amorphous as *USENET*. Nonetheless, USENIX is willing to attempt technical improvements to the network and did sponsor the **Stargate** experiment, to use part of the vertical blanking interval on a satellite television transmission to carry news [Weinstein 1985; Weinstein 1986]. There were political problems with this service, such as the unpopularity of its decision not to permit forwarding of articles received from it. USENIX declared the technological experiment a success in February 1987 and left the operational service to survive as it might [Durlak et al. 1987]. Tilson's idea was later revived in an updated form as *UUNET*, which was sponsored by USENIX and is discussed elsewhere in this book.

Access

The *UUCP* map includes *USENET* map information as annotations. A list of legitimate netwide newsgroups is posted to several newsgroups monthly. Volunteers keep statistics on the use of the various newsgroups and on frequency of posting by persons and hosts. These are posted to *news.lists* once a month, as is the list of newsgroups. Important announcements are posted to two moderated newsgroups, *news.announce* and *news.announce.newusers*, which are intended to reach all users (the current moderators are Mark Horton and Gene Spafford, respectively).

For information on the network, contact:

uunet!usenet-request usenet-request@uunet.uu.net

10.2.3   UUCP

The name of the *UUCP* network comes from that of its transport protocol, UUCP, and is an acronym for **UNIX** to **UNIX** Copy Program [Nowitz 1979]. The network began shortly after the distribution of the **UUCP** program in 1978 with Seventh Edition **UNIX** from AT&T Bell Laboratories (Bell Labs), and is thus one of the oldest dialup networks in the world. It currently extends throughout the world and mostly connects machines that run the **UNIX** operating system [Ritchie and Thompson 1974; Ritchie and Thompson 1978; Quarterman et al. 1985; Bach 1987; Leffler et al. 1989].

Administration

UUCP is also possibly the most decentralized network in the world. It is largely a dialup network, and each host pays for each call it makes. There is no central authority determining access: all that is required for a connection is the software, a modem, and another host to connect to. There is a map, and a host that is not registered in it will be hard to find, but there is no authority that requires such registration. Information for the map is collected by a group of volunteers known as the UUCP Project [Summers-Horton and Horton 1985]. The map is posted monthly in the *USENET* newsgroup *comp.mail.maps*. There is a directory of personal addresses on the *UUCP* network [Kiessig 1986]. It is a commercial venture unrelated to the UUCP Project.

This *UUCP* mail network is often confused with the *USENET* news network. Although mail and news are combined under one administration in some areas—e.g., in *EUnet* in Europe and in *JUNET* in Japan—they are distinct in North America, and all the connected networks throughout the world that support mail over *UUCP* may be considered one network in the same way that there is a worldwide *BITNET*, even though there are separate administrations for *EARN* in Europe and *NetNorth* in Canada.

The topological nature of the network varies between continents, from the almost random connections of North America to the near tree structure of *EUnet*.

Scope

The hardware used in the *UUCP* mail network ranges from small personal computers through workstations to minicomputers, mainframes, and supercomputers. The network extends throughout most of North America and many other parts of the world. Including *JUNET* and *EUnet* hosts (which are listed in the *UUCP* maps), there are probably more than 10,000 hosts on the network, and possibly a million users, making it one of the largest networks of any kind. This is attributable to three circumstances:

ease of connection, low cost, and its close relationship with the *USENET* news network. The speed of links varies from 1200bps up to at least 11000bps. That higher speed is becoming more common, but 2400bps is still probably the most used speed for the links with the heaviest traffic.

User Services

Mail is the only service provided throughout the network [Horton 1986]. In addition to the usual uses of mail, much traffic is generated as responses to *USENET* news. There are also some *UUCP*-based mailing lists [Spafford 1988e]. These mailing lists permit a feature that *USENET* newsgroups cannot readily supply: limited access per person rather than per host. Also, they are more economical for low traffic discussions, since traffic can be directed to those specifically interested in it. There has never been any remote login facility associated with this network, although the **cu** and **tip** programs are sometimes used over the same telephone links.

Protocols

The UUCP protocol is mostly used over dialup RS-232-C links (with the g protocol) in North America. In Europe, it is sometimes used over X.25 (with the f protocol). There are adaptations for use over TCP/IP (the t protocol). The most basic services are file transfer and remote command execution. Mail is built on top of those by transferring a file and then executing a command with the name of the destination as an argument. Remote command execution can be made to work over successive links by arranging for each job in the chain to submit the next one. This is how mail through multiple links is done. Several programs do file transfer over multiple hops this way as well: unfortunately, they are incompatible with each other [Todino and O'Reilly 1988b].

Management

There is no facility at the transport level for routing beyond adjacent systems or for error acknowledgment. All routing and end to end reliability support is done explicitly by application protocols that are implemented using the remote command execution facility. The *UUCP* mail network is one of the few major networks which uses source routing: the usual syntax is hosta!hostb!hostc!host!user. There is a program, **pathalias** [Honeyman and Bellovin 1986], that can compute reasonable routes from the *UUCP* map, and there is software that can automatically look up those routes for users. The widespread use of sophisticated mail relay programs such as **sendmail** and **MMDF** has increased reliability. Still, many hosts have none of these new facilities, and the sheer size of the network makes it unwieldy. Many *UUCP* hosts are adopting *Internet* DNS domains [Horton 1984;

Horton et al. 1984]. The *UUCP* maps contain entries for *UUCP zone* domains, and there are official gateways from the *Internet* to many of these domains. To a casual mail user, it is often not clear what network a given host with a domain name is on. The domain name conversion was made earlier in *EUnet* and more thoroughly in both *EUnet* and *JUNET*.

Interconnections

The UUCP protocol is commonly used for international connections, even to networks such as *ACSnet* in Australia that do not use UUCP internally, because UUCP connections are so easy to set up. At the moment, the *UUCP* machine in North America that has the most international connections appears to be *uunet*, which talks to, for example, *mcvax* for *EUnet*, *kddlab* for Japan, *kaist* for Korea, and *munnari* for Australia. This is an unusual development because *UUNET* charges for its services.

Effects

This network provides mail service to a great many people and institutions that would otherwise not have that service. A greater level of information exchange has resulted, particularly with people in small companies, and not only among those whose only direct network connection is to the *UUCP* network, but also with people on other networks. The *UUCP* network is especially closely associated with *USENET*, and the two networks together provide a very useful method of communication.

History

File transfer and remote command execution were the original intent and main use of the UUCP protocol. There was an assumption that any pair of communicating machines had direct dialup links—i.e., no relaying was done through intermediate machines. By the end of 1978, 82 hosts within Bell Labs were connected by UUCP. Although remote command execution and file transfer were heavily used, there is no mention of mail in the standard reference [Nowitz and Lesk 1979]. There was another similar network of "operational" hosts with UUCP links that apparently were outside Bell Labs but still within the Bell System. The two networks intersected at one Bell Labs machine.

Both of these early networks differed from the current *UUCP* network in assuming direct connections between communicating hosts and in not having mail service. The *UUCP* mail network proper developed from the early networks and spread as the **UUCP** programs were distributed as part of the **UNIX** system.

Future

This network is likely to continue to grow, and domain names will probably become more widespread.

> **Access**
> UUCP Project
> uucp-query@cblpf.ATT.COM
> cblpf!uucp-query
> uucp-query@cblpf.UUCP
>
> Much information about *UUCP* is published in *USENET* newsgroups. See also *UUNET*.

10.2.4   FidoNet

FidoNet is a cooperative network that has connected personal computers, originally IBM PCs or compatibles running **MS-DOS**, since 1983.

Administration

The network is administered by the coordinators of the nodes at the various levels of its routing hierarchy, with assistance from the International FidoNet Association (IFNA). *FidoNet* is not designed to be a commercial venture, but some system operators (sysops) make minimal charges to recover the cost of mail and conferencing services, which are the main services provided. No one is paid for time spent administering the network, and the machines are typically owned by the sysops. In Europe, systems are often owned or supported by commercial organizations or well-organized clubs.

The network currently has about 220 conferencing areas; the conferencing software is called **echomail**. It extends throughout the world and is arranged in a tree structure, divided into zones by continental areas. Most nodes are in the United States and tend to be clumped in metropolitan areas such as St. Louis, Boston, and Chicago. But there are many nodes in Europe, a few in Indonesia, and even some in South Africa. About 2,500 machines are connected, and the network is growing anywhere from 20 to 75 percent a year, depending on whom you ask and what measure is used. Basically anyone with an **MS-DOS** machine can connect. There are recent ports of *FidoNet* software and compatible programs for Apples, Amigas, and other kinds of personal computers.

Protocols

Many links are at 1200bps or 2400bps, but most long-distance links with high traffic are now 9600bps. Most connections are by the Fido protocol, which is a dialup protocol similar to UUCP that was invented for this network [Bush 1986]. It uses a variant of **XMODEM** for data consistency [Jennings 1983] and also sometimes uses **ZMODEM**. Some nodes now also speak UUCP, using a public domain implementation that became available in 1987, and there are gateways into the *UUCP* mail network and the *Internet*.

Management

The network is arranged in a tree structure [Jennings 1985a] of three basic tiers (zones, nets, and nodes), with two intermediate tiers:

Zones
: The major zones are 1 for North America, 2 for Europe, Africa, and the Middle East, and 3 for Asia. Zone 7 is sometimes used for *Alternet*, which is a splinter network in the U.S. Northeast that is connected to *FidoNet* but is administratively separate from *FidoNet* and IFNA; neither zone 7 nor any *Alternet* nodes are found in the map maintained by IFNA. There are other splinter networks.

(Regions)
: This is an intermediate tier that has been added for administrative convenience.

Nets
: These usually correspond to major metropolitan areas. There are about 400 nets.

(Hubs)
: These are machines that form another intermediate tier. They usually spring up within metropolitan areas to offload machines of the net tier.

Nodes
: These are the final leaf systems. There are about 4,000 nodes.

(Points)
: But these are a further level for people whose machines do not run a full bulletin board system but who send or receive a great deal of mail or echomail.

Echomail, like all traffic in *FidoNet* (except files, under certain conditions), travels as mail. It is distinguished by special control words in the body of the mail message. Mail usually travels from the originating node machine to the net machine corresponding to the destination node. For example, node 105/302 sends mail for node 152/3 to node 152/0, which will forward it by a local call. The idea is for calls into a region to be batched through one machine in order to maximize use of long-distance telephone calls. Sometimes the reverse is done: all nodes on a net send outbound mail through the net host. All traffic for a point travels through its superior node and any superior points.

The distinction between the three main tiers and the intermediate ones is mainly that the former are reflected directly in addresses as used by users and the latter are used transparently for routing. A *FidoNet* address is composed of the user's name, a net (a region or host), and a node (a Fido), e.g.,

user Net *net_number* Node *node_number*

where Net and Node are required literal words, and the spaces are also required. Intercontinental mail is specified by also including a zone, e.g.,

user Zone *zone_number* Net *net_number* Node *node_number*

There is a shorthand form that separates the zone and the net with a colon and the net and the node with a slash, as in

user 1:151/299

Points are sometimes distinguished like this:

user 1:151/299.0

The three different separators are used because each level was added one by one, and there was a desire to preserve the ability to use the old form of just net/node, as in 151/299, while expanding the hierarchy at both ends.

A complete node list is updated and distributed weekly from Phoenix by David Dodell. The intercontinental connection from North America — i.e., zone 1 — to the other zones is in Portland, Oregon, and is run by Randy Bush (<randy@oresoft.uu.net>). Mail from the United States to Europe usually takes from 24 to 48 hours. There is no extra charge for the overseas links.

Interconnections

There is a *FidoNet* DNS domain that has been registered with the *Internet* since March 1988: *FIDONET.ORG* (it was originally called *IFNA.ORG*). This domain applies only to *FidoNet* proper, not to any of the splinter networks. Ironically enough for a network totally dependent on a static host table, the *Internet* domain is done totally dynamically by domain nameservers. Some gateways have the domain names *castle.fidonet.org*, *fidogate.fidonet.org*, and *ankh.fidonet.org*. *FidoNet* nodes are also known by transliterations of their *FidoNet* numeric addresses, as in

f299.n151.z1.fidonet.org

or

p0.f299.n151.z1.fidonet.org

Interconnections from *FidoNet* to other networks are shown in Table 10.8 and described below:

Table 10.8. *FidoNet interconnections*

Network	Syntax
Internet	UUCP *gateway* ARPA: *user@domain*
UUCP	UUCP *gateway* To: host1!host2!*host*!*user*
BITNET	UUCP *gateway* UUCP: host1!psuvax1!*host*.bitnet!*user*

UUCP To get to the *UUCP* network, a *FidoNet* user sends mail to a gateway such as *fidogate.fidonet.org*, known as *1:125/406* on *FidoNet*. The mail is addressed to user UUCP, and the first line of text is

      UUCP: host1!host2!*host*!*user*

      The literal leading keyword *UUCP*: is required. If UUCP source routing is used, the path must be relative to the gateway as a *UUCP* host. Some gateways support domain addressing.

BITNET There is no direct gateway, but indirecting through the *BITNET* and *UUCP* gateway *psuvax1* may work.

Internet It may be possible to get to the *Internet* by indirecting through *UUCP*, but there is now a more direct route through the gateway *castle.fidonet.org*, or *1:152/201*, which understands domain addresses when used in the first line of text after the leading keyword *ARPA:*.

Uses

There are some unusual uses of this network. Some people at the UN are trying to make much of their collected information available to the general public over *FidoNet*. For example, there is a UN directory of databases that is kept in Geneva and a UN yearbook compiled by UNICEF. Other uses made possible by the grass roots nature of the network range from political polling to postal chess to medical collaboration. It is popular in social service work. Another interesting use of it is a conference of handicapped people (gatewayed to *USENET* and *BITNET* and elsewhere). For many shut-ins, this is the only way they can communicate with each other, and much information is exchanged that is of great value to disabled people [da Cruz 1988].

  The Fifth International *FidoNet* Conference (FidoCon) was held in June 1988 in Ede, Netherlands, the Sixth in August 1988 in Cincinnati, Ohio, and the Seventh in August 1989 in San Jose, California, with a local branch of the network set up in the conference hotel. These conferences provide a forum for users of the network to meet each other face to face.

History

The original *FidoNet* software, called **Fido**, was developed by by Tom Jennings in 1983 [Jennings 1985b] as basically an extension of the Fido Bulletin Board System (Fido BBS). The new software provided unattended electronic mail transfer between nodes of the new network. Exchange of conferencing messages and access to *USENET* newsgroups by personal computer users was added later. The software was distributed as shareware but without sources. A problem with this software was that it required the machine to go into a transfer-only mode that prohibited use for other purposes. Thus, most nodes were accessible as bulletin board systems during the day and transferred data between themselves at predetermined times during the night. One effect of this was to limit the speed of mail: often it was one day per hop.

Another mailer called **SEAdog**, named for System Enhancement Associates (SEA), was developed by Tom Henderson in 1986 [Henderson 1986] and is a commercial product. It allows demand calling, which is known on *FidoNet* as *crash mail*. Henderson also wrote **arc**, which allows **Lempel-Ziv** data compression to speed effective transfer rates, just as is done on *USENET*. **Arc** is in the public domain. Other, more recent mailers include **Opus, Binkley, Dutchie, D'Bridge, FrontDoor, Tabby** for the Apple Macintosh, and **Pandora** for the Atari ST. There are about 30 *FidoNet* mailer software packages. Most of them are shareware, but **Opus** is in the public domain; it is also a front end and BBS system, not a router, and is partly written in assembler. **Binkley** is written in **C**.

There are several BBS software packages for *FidoNet*, including **Fido, Opus, QBBS,** and **TBBS**. Any of these can use any of the above mailers. **QBBS** is single tasking. **TBBS** allows up to 16 simultaneous users on an **MS-DOS** system. Increasing use is being made of Intel 386 systems.

The most controversial recent development is the formation of splinter groups that are displeased with IFNA. IFNA continues to be active in the network and in FidoCon.

Access

A gateway between *USENET* and *FidoNet* is administered by:

Tim Pozar
1:125/555
"tim pozar"@f555.n125.z1.fidonet.org

An *Internet* and *UUCP* gateway is run by:

Lee Damon at FidoNode 1:105/302
nomad@castle.fidonet.org
fidohost@castle.FIDONET.ORG
verdix!castle!fidohost
agora!castle!fidohost
{tektronix,hp-pcd}!orstcs!castle!fidohost
{verdix,agora,{tektronix,hp-pcd}!orstcs}!castle!nomad
{verdix,agora,{tektronix,hp-pcd}!orstcs}!castle!fidohost

For the dialup number of a Fido node in your area, contact your local IBM PC user group or:

IFNA
+1-314-576-4067
P.O. Box 41143
St. Louis, MO 63141
U.S.A.

IFNA also publishes a weekly newsletter called *FidoNews*, which appears not only on *FidoNet*, but also in the newsgroup *comp.org.fidonet* on *USENET*. It has the unusual editorial policy of publishing everything submitted. It is also not in any known digest format, so reading it online is painful; apparently it is intended to be printed.

10.2.5   Ean

There are several networks in Europe and elsewhere that use the **Ean** implementation (first developed for Canada's *CDNnet*) of X.400 and other ISO-OSI protocols. They have an address format with a usual user presentation form that resembles *Internet* DNS domains but with an internal format of X.400 attribute lists [Kille 1986; Kille 1987]. The *Ean* networks originally used top level domains corresponding to network names, such as *cdn* for *CDNnet* in Canada and *dfn* for *DFN* in Germany. ISO3166 codes are now used instead [Demco 1988].

Interconnections

Interconnections from *Ean* are shown in Table 10.9. There, {**Ean-domain**} stands for top level domains used in the *Ean* networks to specify national networks. These now correspond to ISO3166 two letter country codes. Hosts on the *Ean* networks recognize most major domain systems directly and do not ordinarily require explicit specification of gateways by users.

10.3   *Company*

These networks are wholly owned and operated by single companies for their own internal uses.

Table 10.9. *Ean interconnections*

Network	Syntax
Ean	*user@domain.*{**Ean-domain**}
Internet	*user@domain.*{**DNS**}
JANET	*user@domain.*{**JANET-domain**}
XEROX Internet	*user.*{**XEROX-domain**}@xerox.com
EASYnet	*user%host.*dec@decwrl.dec.com
VNET	*user%host*@ibm.com
BITNET	*user@host.*bitnet
ACSnet	*user@domain.*{**ACSNET-domain**}
UUCP	*user@host.*uucp
JUNET	*user%domain.*{**JUNET-domain**}@relay.cs.net

10.3.1   VNET

VNET is IBM's internal network, which provides services such as mail, remote login, and file transfer for company employees.

Administration and Funding

The VNET Project Team, which was formed in 1978, maintains and sets network guidelines. There is also a *VNET* corporate office that was established in 1982. The network is funded by IBM and within a few years grew from a few hundred hosts to 2,297 as of 26 November 1986 [Nussbacher 1987].

IBM maintains its own internal security to limit access to *VNET*. For a person within IBM to be able to send or receive mail, it is necessary to obtain an account on a *VNET* node. In addition, to exchange mail with external networks, it is necessary to register. Most professionals within IBM are *VNET* users, although a relatively small number are registered to talk to the outside world via gateways. An outsider need not be registered to send mail to *VNET*, but the person receiving the mail inside IBM must be registered. Many of the people in the Research Division (Yorktown Heights, New York; Almaden, California; and Zurich, Switzerland) and the various Scientific Centers are registered; most of the others in IBM are not.

Composition

VNET is actually two distinct networks. The *RSCS* network [Hendricks and Hartman 1979] is the mail and file transfer part of *VNET* and had approximately 2,200 nodes as of September 1986. The Passthru VM (*PVM*) network provides a remote login facility for *VNET* [Nussbacher 1987]. There were about 1,100 *PVM* nodes as of September 1986. *VNET RSCS* and *PVM* nodes are found in North and South America, Africa, the Middle East, Europe,

Australia, and Asia. The *VNET PVM* nodes are perhaps not a pure subset of the *VNET RSCS* nodes, but for all practical purposes they can be considered as such.

Protocols

The NJE protocols are used for mail transfer, in their **RSCS** implementation. These are the same as the ones *BITNET* uses. *VNET* links are typically 9600bps leased lines, though they vary from 2400bps to T1 speeds.

Other IBM Networks

There are other internal IBM networks — for example, *VIBTS* (VTAM Integrated Bulk Data Transfer System) is a fast network composed of mostly T1 microwave links. *VIBTS* is for transferring memory images during debugging and other activities that require fast access to huge files. Another example is *CCDN*, which is used solely for remote login.

History

VNET and the NJE protocols began in 1972 as an ad hoc project of some IBM employees who felt that the available alternatives did not meet their needs. IBM eventually adopted the new network, and in this sense NJE is the UUCP of IBM.

> **Access**
> postmaster@IBM.COM

10.3.2   XEROX Internet

The initial part of the *XEROX Internet*, the *RIN* (XEROX Research Internet) had developed by 1976. *CIN* (Corporate Internet) split from *RIN* about the middle of 1985. *CIN* and *RIN* are highly interconnected and connect many company sites around the world. *CIN* is intended to be a stable backbone network for various corporate needs, and *RIN* is primarily intended to serve research and development.

Both *CIN* and *RIN* support many thousands of machines. Grapevine [Schroeder et al. 1984], a very large distributed mail and name system for *RIN*, supports about 4,000 users around the world. *CIN* has its own distributed mail system and about 8,000 users. There are sites in Japan, England, and Canada, as well as many within the United States.

Administration of the networks is distributed among several groups within XEROX. *RIN* is administered for the most part by the XEROX Palo Alto Research Center (PARC), while *CIN* is primarily run by other divisions within the XEROX Corporation. Both *RIN* and *CIN* are funded by the XEROX Corporation.

The services offered by *RIN* and *CIN* include remote login, file transfer, mail, remote procedure call, distributed file system, and distributed computation, among others.

Both *CIN* and *RIN* use XNS. *RIN* also uses PUP and TCP/IP on some of its networks. *RIN* is the faster of the two and has 56Kbps leased lines and T1 microwave links.

Naming and addressing are handled differently for internal and external users. The mail system in *RIN* is called Grapevine, and the name system in *CIN* is called Clearinghouse.

Interconnections

The *XEROX Internet* communicates with the outside world via two hosts on the *Internet*, *Xerox.COM* and *parcvax.Xerox.COM*. *Xerox.COM* (formerly *Xerox.ARPA*) is the mail gateway between the *Internet* and Grapevine, and *parcvax.Xerox.COM* is used for TELNET and FTP. Several mail gateways transparently connect *RIN* to *CIN*. Certain aliases are maintained at the *Xerox.COM* gateway for ease of external addressing—e.g., internally, Postmaster@Xerox.COM is aliased to Postmaster.PA. In Table 10.10, **{XEROX-domain}** stands for a *XEROX Internet* registry, such as *PA* for Palo Alto.

Access
Postmaster@Xerox.COM

10.3.3 EASYnet

Digital Equipment Corporation (Digital) maintains an internal engineering network called *EASYnet*. Digital began its network endeavors as one of the pioneers of the *ARPANET*. The company went on to develop its own network protocols and software, called DECNET, and to make it available to Digital customers by 1976. *EASYnet* was started in 1978.

The basic network capabilities provided by DECNET include intersystem file access and transfer, electronic mail, intersystem resource sharing, interprocess communications, adaptive routing, and remote login. These are enhanced by *EASYnet* services such as ELF (a Digital Employee Locator Facility), Videotext Infobases, online network conference discussions (interactive bulletin boards), system monitoring, and communications for general operational issues.

EASYnet is administered by Digital's Digital Telecommunications organization. Funding comes from the business functions of the Corporation. *EASYnet* primarily uses DECNET. It also uses other protocols, such as TCP/IP. Reliability is reported to be at least as good as that of the

Table 10.10. *XEROX Internet interconnections*

Network	Syntax
RIN (Grapevine)	User.registry (e.g., JDoe.PA)
CIN (Clearinghouse)	Name:Domain:Org (e.g., John Doe:OSBU North:Xerox)

ARPANET. *EASYnet*'s speed is maintained by 10Mbps Ethernets and 128–156Kbps backbone intersite links, with lower speed links to sites with lower traffic requirements. Addressing is the same as for the *Internet*, e.g.,

    user%host.DEC@decwrl.DEC.COM

For *UUCP*, the correct way of addressing is

    {ucbvax, decvax, allegra, ...}!decwrl!enetnode.dec.com!user

EASYnet has more than 34,000 hosts. Assuming two-thirds of Digital's employees are users, there are 80,000 users of the network. It is international in scope, extending throughout North America, the Caribbean, Europe, the Near East, Australia, New Zealand, and the Far East.

Access
postmaster@decwrl.dec.com

10.3.4   Tandem

Tandem's network is unusual among those described in this book not because it is a company network, nor because of its worldwide extent, nor because of its heavy traffic (its administration claims it to be the second most heavily used network in the world), but because it is not interconnected to the other networks. This is one consequence of its being based on proprietary protocols and a proprietary operating system. Because it is a closed system, it can appear to the users as a distributed operating system. But this means that security can be a problem—thus, there are no outside links.

This is an example of an *enterprise network*, which is one used to support all functions of a corporation. This network is used for everything from sales to manufacturing, from accounting to administration, from programmers to executives. The network is used more than telephones, and the company depends on it as many others depend on telephones. According to one of its administrators, "If the network were to cease running, the company would too, and immediately."

Administration and Funding

Administration is by a full time staff of six people in the States and three in Germany. They provide 24 hour support without anyone having to work after midnight by taking advantage of the time zone difference between California and Germany:

0800 – 1800	Handled by the U.S. staff at work (Pacific time)
1800 – 2400	Handled by the U.S. staff on call from home
2400 – 0800	Handled by the German staff at work, where it is 0900 – 1700 their time

Funding is done entirely by the company, with internal charges to departments for modems and links to recover costs. Half of each link is normally charged to each end, except for links to the backbone, which are considered to be a premium service due to additional speed; in that case, the nonbackbone end is charged the entire cost. The backbone itself is run as overhead out of the fees collected.

Composition

The network is organized around a backbone with two nodes west of the Pacific (Melbourne, Australia, and Singapore), two in Europe (Frankfurt, West Germany, and London, England), and six in the United States (Washington, D.C.; Chicago, Illinois; Austin, Texas; Santa Clara, California; and two in Cupertino, California) [Madsen and Foley 1985a]. About 40 to 50 million packets are sent over the backbone each day, and about 4.5 million mail messages are sent each month. The mail messages average about 15 to 20 lines apiece. There are 198 nodes in 21 countries in all, including Australia, New Zealand, and Hong Kong.

Services

Services include electronic mail, distribution lists, order entry, and customer engineering dispatch. Network administration lists more than a hundred distinct applications. Users are addressed by real names with underscores for spaces, such as

Jane_Doe

or aliases, such as

    Payroll

with no accompanying host name needed. An underlying nameservice is transparent to the user. The database for this nameservice is available for searches by personal names, office locations, node locations, and other keys [Madsen and Foley 1985b].

The company has voice mail, but it is not much used. Incoming telephone messages are either immediately transcribed into electronic mail or are taken as voice mail. In the latter case, an electronic mail message is sent to notify the user of the presence of the voice mail message.

The electronic mail service is particularly interesting and is the most widespread service in the network, extending to sales offices in Sweden, Canada, and Mexico [Madsen and Foley 1985b]. Automatic replies, forwarding, and filing into folders by subject are implemented. Delivery in 30 seconds to any host on the network anywhere in the world is the norm. A user can get to the home mailbox transparently from any host on the network, be it in New Zealand or California. This is because mail is implemented in two parts, as a client ("requester") that implements the user interface and that uses an IPC mechanism to transfer messages to and from a second part, which is a server on the home machine. The same programs and the same access methods are used regardless of the location of the client.

Although the mail implementation is not intended to be a conferencing system as such, it has distribution lists with many of the properties of a conferencing system. There is certified mail, so that a message is returned when a user receives mail, and there is a distribution list option that allows a sender to be informed if any recipient has *not* read a message after three days. A mail message sent as a reply to a previous mail message includes the text of the previous message. This would tend to lead to an unbounded mushrooming of the size of mail messages, but the system is clever enough to prevent that by sending only an indication that the previous message is to be included. This can work because one copy of each mail message is kept on each system with a mailbox of an addressee. Thus, a copy can be assumed to be present on the original sending system. Distribution lists are kept to a reasonable size by the same technique.

There are three levels of service:

- Person to person
- Company
- Third class, or junk mail

And there are three kinds of user interface:

- Conversational and line oriented; favored by technical personnel
- Screen and form oriented; favored by administrators
- IBM 3270; used by those who use IBM machines

Protocols

The protocol set is called EXPAND [Madsen and Foley 1985a; LaPedis and DeBra 1987] and is proprietary, although the network layer protocol is related to X.25. Management protocols allow a new host to be added without central assistance; other hosts learn about the presence of the new host from their neighbors in a ripple effect. Dead hosts are handled similarly.

The network is arranged around the backbone in nested rings [Madsen and Foley 1985a]. There are four classes of nodes in the network:

Backbone nodes are machines that are dedicated to moving information and to being always available for that purpose. Backbone links are mostly at 56Kbps, but there are several T1 (1.544Mbps) links. Most of them are leased lines, although there are three Very Small Aperture Terminal (VSAT) links. A T1 backbone is being installed in the United States. There are at least two backbone paths between any pair of backbone nodes.

Class A nodes support critical applications such as accounting and manufacturing. Each is connected directly to one backbone node and directly or indirectly (through other Class A nodes) to another backbone node. Class A nodes are not allowed to leave the network without being scheduled to do so.

Class B nodes support field and service offices, and their main application is mail. Each one is no more than two hops away from a backbone node, if possible, and each has an alternate path to the backbone.

Class C nodes are primarily client nodes that do not support basic network applications. They are used for development work and customer education. They may not always be connected to the network and are sometimes used as test machines, with deliberate overloads and crashes. Class C nodes are connected in rings or spurs of Class C nodes and have no nodes of other classes dependent on them.

Local links range from copper to fiber optics to T1 laser links to T2 microwave; the maximum speed is 45Mbps over fiber optics.

The network is implemented as a large distributed operating system. The machines to be linked were already running a multiprocessor operating system in order to implement their major feature of fault tolerance.

Extending this operating system to handle processors on multiple machines was easier than extending a single processor operating system would have been. The basic mechanism used is pairs of messages — a request and a reply — i.e., essentially remote procedure call, implemented as an extension of the basic message passing facilities of the operating system [Madsen and Foley 1985b].

Interconnections

Although there are no incoming connections to the network from any other, there are outgoing connections to *Telenet, TYMNET, Worldnet, CompuServe, Telex,* and many specialized services based on X.25. Employees can use services such as Bank of America's home banking service transparently from anywhere on the network.

History

This network began in 1979 and grew with no centralized management until 1981, when there were about 40 nodes. A star topology around a few central machines at corporate headquarters was first attempted, in order to make processing orders easy. This proved insufficiently robust, since downtime on the central machines isolated the whole network, and there were no redundant links to replace one that isolated a single machine. A network support group was formed in 1981 to address this sort of problem, and rings of nodes were established within four months. The network grew further to include 200 nodes by 1985 [Madsen and Foley 1985a].

The current mail system is about five years old, and is based on a previous one dating back to about 1978.

Plans

There are plans to migrate to X.400 for mail. A T1 backbone also is planned. ISDN may be used eventually.

Access

Dave Foley
+1-408-725-6338
Fax: +1-408-725-6660
Tandem Computers Incorporated
19191 Vallco Parkway 4-15
Cupertino, CA 95014-2599
U.S.A.

10.3.5   HP Internet

The *HP Internet* is a TCP/IP company internetwork of Hewlett-Packard (HP). The *HP Internet* is part of the *Internet*, had 6,500 hosts by September 1988 and 12,000 hosts and 200 routers by March 1989. It extends to locations in the United States, the United Kingdom, France, Germany, Switzerland [Kincl and Michaels 1988], Australia, Singapore, Japan, Mexico, Canada, and Italy [Kincl 1989]. The *HP Internet* is generally believed to be the largest TCP/IP network operated by a single organization (although the *Internet* is, of course, larger).

Administration

The network is administered by HP's Corporate Telecommunications and Office Systems (CTOS). CTOS has responsibility for the overall network and the backbone connections. Telecommunication groups at the various sites are responsible for the local networks that are interconnected and for some local connections [Kincl 1989].

Services and Effects

As evidenced by the very rapid growth of the network, there was a need for it within the company. Testimonials to profitable uses of the network are numerous, including software distribution, source code sharing between Cupertino, California, and Fort Collins, Colorado, reduced travel due to better communication and remote access, and projects completed more quickly because of fast interactive remote access [Kincl and Michaels 1988].

Protocols

There were many existing local area networks within the company, and interconnecting them seemed a logical goal. Doing so with data link layer bridges such as Vitalink's TransLAN was considered but eventually rejected in favor of using IP routers. Routers were preferred for a variety of reasons, among them the existing model of the *Internet*, the need for a testbed for TCP/IP company products, and a desire for experience with networking products from diverse vendors, which was expected to be useful later with ISO-OSI protocols. The gateway vendor eventually chosen was cisco.

Underlying network technology includes Ethernet, 802.3, X.25, broadband, and serial links ranging from 9600bps RS-232-C to 1.544Mbps T1 (usually broken into twenty-four 56Kbps channels) and satellite links. HP already owned the satellite and X.25 facilities; the latter are mostly used whenever there is insufficient traffic to justify dedicated links [Kincl and Michaels 1988]. In the San Francisco Bay Area, the connections go over

HP's microwave network. Long-haul links use leased lines from various vendors. There is a 10Mbps microwave connection to Stanford and from there to *NSFNET* [Kincl 1989].

History

By August of 1985, HP found that the use of UUCP connections (over 1200bps dialup or 9600bps X.25 links) for corporate mail was too expensive and too slow. A faster, interactive, and less expensive service was sought. The first five sites were interconnected in July 1986, and there were a thousand hosts in 20 divisions by January 1987. Also an *Internet* connection was added in August 1987 by a satellite connection to *CSNET* [Kincl and Michaels 1988].

Plans

Connections to company sites in Malaysia, Hong Kong, and Spain are planned [Kincl 1989]. Redundant links will also be added to supplement those already in place as need for redundancy or more bandwidth arises [Kincl and Michaels 1988].

> **Access**
> Network Marketing Center
> Hewlett-Packard
> 19420 Homestead Road
> Cupertino, CA 95014
> U.S.A.

10.4 *The Backbone of the World*

Most of the traffic *among* networks and conferencing systems is carried by surprisingly few machines. All of them are described elsewhere, but it is worthwhile to mention some of them together here. It is quite possible that not all such machines are included in the following list.

10.4.1   relay.cs.net (csnet-relay)

The machine *relay.cs.net* has connections to other machines in a large number of countries around the world. It is the central *CSNET* machine and is often used to reach the *Internet*. It is located at Bolt Beranek and Newman (BBN) in Cambridge, Massachusetts.

10.4.2   psuvax1 (PSUVAX)

One of the major gateways between *BITNET* and *UUCP* is *psuvax1* at Pennsylvania State University (PSU).

10.4.3   berkeley.edu (ucbvax)

The machine known as *berkeley.edu* or *ucbvax* is a VAX-11/750 at the University of California at Berkeley (UCB). It gateways many *Internet* mailing lists with *USENET* newsgroups. Until 1988, it was the primary such gateway, but the load has since been distributed more widely.

10.4.4   rutgers.edu (rutgers)

The machine *rutgers.edu* at Rutgers University (Rutgers) acts as an *Internet* nameserver for many domains that are not directly on the *Internet*. It also has the old-style *UUCP* name of *rutgers*.

10.4.5   UUNET (uunet.uu.net, uunet)

The *UUNET* service connects *UUCP* (where it is known as *uunet*) and the *Internet* (where it is known as *uunet.uu.net*). It has subscribers in many countries and connects to *JUNET*, *EUnet*, *ACSnet*, *SDN*, and other networks throughout the world. It currently consists of a single Sequent Symmetry multiprocessor in Arlington, Virginia.

10.4.6   DASnet (das.net, das.com, dasnet)

The *DASnet* machine connects many conferencing systems and commercial mail systems together and with the academic and research networks. Its connections are too numerous to list here. *DASnet* is located in Campbell, California.

10.4.7   cwi.nl (mcvax)

The central machine in *EUnet* is *mcvax* or *cwi.nl* in Amsterdam. It connects European countries together, to the world, and to numerous other networks, such as *EARN* and *BITNET* (it is known as *MCVAX* on those networks), the *Internet*, *JUNET*, *SDN*, and *ACSnet*.

10.4.8   munnari.oz.au (munnari)

A machine in Melbourne, *munnari.oz.au* or *munnari*, connects Australia and *ACSnet* to the world, including numerous networks, such as *UUCP*, *JUNET*, *SDN*, and *EUnet*. It is also a key machine in the southwestern Pacific.

10.4.9   kaist.ac.kr (kaist)

Korea and *SDN* are connected to the world, particularly to *CSNET* and *UUCP*, by *kaist* or *kaist.ac.kr* in Seoul. It also connects much of the western Pacific together in *PACNET*.

10.4.10   ccut.cc.u-tokyo.junet (u-tokyo)

The Japanese *CSNET* link is to *u-tokyo* or *ccut.cc.u-tokyo.junet*, which is a key machine on *JUNET* and connects to *uunet*.

10.4.11   kddlab.kddlabs.junet (kddlab)

There is also a commercial (i.e., not educational) international Japanese link — *kddlab* or *kddlab.kddlabs.junet* — owned by the government telephone company and located in Tokyo.

10.4.12   cunyvm.cuny.edu (CUNYVM)

CUNYVM at City University of New York (CUNY) is the primary *BITNET* gateway with the *Internet*, where it is known as *cunyvm.cuny.edu*. There are also regional gateways for this purpose, and they should be used where appropriate. To send mail outward from *BITNET*, the logical host *INTER-BIT* should be used rather than any specific gateway to the *Internet*.

10.4.13   CERN (FRMOP22, cernvax)

The Organisation Européenne pour la Recherche Nucléaire (CERN). or European Laboratory for Particle Physics, near Geneva, Switzerland, connects several networks, including *EARN* (and through it *BITNET* and *Net-North*), *EUnet* (and through it *UUCP*), *HEPnet* (and thus *SPAN*), and all MHS *(Ean)* networks in Europe. The *EARN* node *FRMOP22* is the European equivalent of *CUNYVM* in the States. It has connections to all European *EARN* hosts, as well as a 56Kbps link to the United States. Most traffic between *EARN* and *BITNET* or the *Internet* passes through this node. The Swiss national *EUnet* backbone machine is *cernvax*. More references to

CERN appear in the *HEPnet* section in this chapter and the CERN section in Chapter 13.

10.5   *Bibliographic Notes*

References for worldwide networks are few, but some of interest are Jennings 1987 and Landweber et al. 1986. There is some information on actual networks among the technical information in Tanenbaum 1988 and Partridge 1988.

10.6   *References*

Adams 1988.   Adams, Rick, Personal communications, 16 May 1988.

Bach 1987.   Bach, M. J., *The Design of the UNIX Operating System*, Prentice-Hall, Englewood Cliffs, NJ, 1987.

Blokzijl 1988.   Blokzijl, Rob, Personal communications, October – November 1988.

Bush 1986.   Bush, Randy, "A Basic FidoNet Technical Standard," IFNA, St. Louis, MO, 10 September 1986.

Carpenter et al. 1987.   Carpenter, B. E., Fluckiger, F., Gerard, J. M., Lord, D., and Segal, B., "Two Years of Real Progress in European HEP Networking: A CERN Perspective," *Computer Physics Communications*, vol. 45, pp. 83 – 92, August 1987.

Chartrand and Demar 1985.   Chartrand, Greg, and Demar, Philip, "DECnet and the High Energy Physics Network," *DECUS US Chapter SIGs Newsletters*, vol. 1, no. 1, pp. NTW-17 – NTW-19, FERMILAB, P.O. Box 500, Batavia, IL 60510, September 1985.

Crocker 1982.   Crocker, David H., "Standard for the Format of ARPA Internet Text Messages; RFC822," *ARPANET Working Group Requests for Comments*, 13 August 1982.

da Cruz 1987.   da Cruz, Frank, "Kermit in Antarctica," *Kermit News*, vol. 2, no. 1, p. 6, November 1987.

da Cruz 1988.   da Cruz, Frank, Personal communications, October – November 1988.

Daniel et al. 1980.   Daniel, Stephen, Ellis, James, and Truscott, Tom, "USENET — A General Access UNIX Network," Duke University, Durham, NC, Summer 1980. This is a slightly modified copy of the original flyer of January 1980.

Demco 1988.   Demco, John, Personal communications, August 1988.

Durlak et al. 1987.   Durlak, Jerome, Yigit, Ozan, and O'Brien, Rory, "USENET: An Examination of the Social and Political Processes of a Cooperative Computer/Communications Network Under the Stress of Rapid Growth," *Proceedings of the Canadian Communications Association (Montreal, 20 May 1987)*, UQAM, Montreal, 1987.

Eden 1988.   Eden, Paul, Personal communications, November 1988.

Ellis et al. 1980.   Ellis, James, Truscott, Tom, and Daniel, Stephen, "Invitation to Join a General Access UNIX Network," USENIX Association, Boulder, CO, January 1980. About 40 copies of this flyer were distributed; none still exist.

Emerson 1983.   Emerson, Sandra L., "USENET: A Bulletin Board for UNIX Users," *BYTE*, vol. 8, no. 10, pp. 219 – 236, October 1983.

Frey and Adams 1987. Frey, Donnalyn, and Adams, Rick, "USENET: Death by Success?," *UNIX REVIEW*, vol. 5, no. 8, pp. 55–60, August 1987.

Fuchs 1983. Fuchs, Ira H., "BITNET: because it's time," *Perspectives in Computing*, vol. 3, no. 1, pp. 16–27, IBM Corporation, March 1983.

Gilmore and Spafford 1988. Gilmore, John, and Spafford, Gene, "Alternative Newsgroup Hierarchies (Updated: 11 March 1988)," *news.lists, news.groups, news.announce.newusers*, USENET, 3 April 1988.

Henderson 1986. Henderson, Thom, SEAdog Electronic Mail System Version 3, Thom Henderson, April 1986.

Hendricks and Hartman 1979. Hendricks, E. C., and Hartman, T. C., "Evolution of a virtual machine subsystem," *IBM Systems Journal*, vol. 18, no. 1, p. 111, 1979.

HEPnet 1988. HEPnet, "High Energy Physics Computer Networking, Report of the HEPNET Review Committee," Department of Energy, Washington, DC, June 1988.

Honeyman and Bellovin 1986. Honeyman, Peter, and Bellovin, Steven M., "Pathalias or the Care and Feeding of Relative Addresses," *Proceedings of the 1986 Summer USENIX Conference (Atlanta, 9–13 June 1986)*, pp. 126–141, USENIX Association, Berkeley, CA, 1986.

Horton 1984. Horton, Mark, "What is a Domain?," *Proceedings of the Summer 1983 USENIX Conference (Salt Lake City, Utah, 12–15 June 1984)*, pp. 368–372, USENIX Association, Berkeley, CA, 1984.

Horton 1986. Horton, Mark R., "UUCP Mail Interchange Format Standard; RFC976," *ARPANET Working Group Requests for Comments*, February 1986.

Horton and Adams 1987. Horton, Mark R., and Adams, Rick, "Standard for Interchange of USENET Messages; RFC1036," *ARPANET Working Group Requests for Comments*, December 1987.

Horton et al. 1984. Horton, Mark, Summers-Horton, Karen, and Kercheval, Berry, "Proposal for a UUCP/Usenet Registry Host," *Proceedings of the Summer 1983 USENIX Conference (Salt Lake City, Utah, 12–15 June 1984)*, p. 373, USENIX Association, Berkeley, CA, 1984.

Jennings 1987. Jennings, Dennis M., "Computing the best for Europe," *Nature*, vol. 329, no. 29, pp. 775–778, October 1987.

Jennings 1983. Jennings, Tom, "Extending XMODEM/MODEM File Transfer Protocol to support DOS," IFNA, St. Louis, MO, 20 September 1983.

Jennings 1985a. Jennings, Tom, "Fido's Internal Structures," IFNA, St. Louis, MO, 13 September 1985.

Jennings 1985b. Jennings, Tom, "FidoNet Electronic Mail Protocol," IFNA, St. Louis, MO, 8 February 1985.

Kantor and Lapsley 1986. Kantor, Brian, and Lapsley, Phil, "Network News Transfer Protocol; RFC977," *ARPANET Working Group Requests for Comments*, February 1986.

Kiessig 1986. Kiessig, Richard, *UUCP Network Directory*, vol. 2, no. 2, Spring 1986. (P.O. Box 50174, Palo Alto, CA 94303)

Kille 1986. Kille, S. E., "Mapping between X.400 and RFC822; RFC987," *ARPANET Working Group Requests for Comments*, June 1986.

Kille 1987. Kille, S. E., "Addendum to RFC 987 (Mapping between X.400 and RFC-822); RFC1026," *ARPANET Working Group Requests for Comments*, September 1987.

Kincl 1989. Kincl, Norman, Personal communications, 10 March 1989.

Kincl and Michaels 1988. Kincl, Norman, and Michaels, Robert, "Inside Autonomous System 71 — The HP Internet," *ConneXions — The Interoperability Report*, vol. 2, no. 9, pp. 2–7, Advanced Computing Environments, Mountain View, CA, September 1988.

Klein 1988.   Klein, Ben, "Networking at CUNY: an Overview," *CUNY University Computer Center Communications*, vol. 14, no. 3/4, pp. 15–21, CUNY, New York, March/April 1988.

Kolstad 1988.   Kolstad, Rob, Personal communications, 1 December 1988.

Landweber et al. 1986.   Landweber, Lawrence H., Jennings, Dennis M., and Fuchs, Ira, "Research Computer Networks and Their Interconnnection," *IEEE Communications*, vol. 24, no. 6, pp. 5–17, June 1986.

LaPedis and DeBra 1987.   LaPedis, Ron, and DeBra, Corinne, "Network Noted," *Communications of the ACM*, vol. 30, no. 3, p. 195, March 1987.

LaQuey 1988.   LaQuey, Tracy Lynn, *Users' Directory of Computer Networks*, Office of Telecommunication Services, University of Texas System, Austin, July 1988.

Leffler et al. 1989.   Leffler, Samuel J., McKusick, Marshall Kirk, Karels, Michael J., and Quarterman, John S., *The Design and Implementation of the 4.3BSD UNIX Operating System*, Addison-Wesley, Reading, MA, 1989.

Madsen and Foley 1985a.   Madsen, Kent, and Foley, David, "When the shoe's on the other foot: A look at Tandem's corporate network," *Data Communications*, vol. 14, no. 9, pp. 183–193, August 1985.

Madsen and Foley 1985b.   Madsen, Kent, and Foley, David, "How multi-processor nodes can become more sociable," *Data Communications*, vol. 14, no. 10, pp. 279–294, September 1985.

Neumann 1984.   Neumann, Peter G., "Spring Fever—Ape Rills are Flowing (or Fooling?)," *Software Engineering Notes*, vol. 9, no. 4, pp. 6–8, ACM SIGSOFT, July 1984.

Nowitz 1979.   Nowitz, D. A., "Uucp Implementation Description," in *UNIX Programmer's Manual, Seventh Edition*, vol. 2, pp. 577–591, Holt, Rinehart and Winston, New York, 1983.

Nowitz and Lesk 1979.   Nowitz, D. A., and Lesk, M. E., "A Dial-Up Network of UNIX Systems," in *UNIX Programmer's Manual, Seventh Edition*, vol. 2, pp. 569–576, Holt, Rinehart and Winston, New York, 1983.

Nussbacher 1987.   Nussbacher, Henry, "Conversion Plans from RSCS to Tcp/Ip for Israel Academic Network," *TCP-IP@SRI-NIC.ARPA*, Israeli University Telecommunications Subcommittee, Tel Aviv, 7 July 1987.

Nussbacher 1988.   Nussbacher, Henry, "BITNET GATES Version 88.09," BITNET/EARN NETSERV, 25 August 1988.

Organick 1975.   Organick, Elliot I., *The Multics System: An Examination of Its Structure*, MIT Press, Cambridge, MA, 1975.

Partridge 1988.   Partridge, Craig, *Innovations in Internetworking*, ARTECH House, Norwood, MA, October 1988.

Price 1988.   Price, Larry, Personal communications, 7 December 1988.

Quarterman et al. 1985.   Quarterman, John S., Silberschatz, Abraham, and Peterson, James L., "4.2BSD and 4.3BSD as Examples of the UNIX System," *ACM Computing Surveys*, vol. 17, no. 4, pp. 379–418, December 1985.

Reber 1988.   Reber, Pat, "NETNEWS: A Mainframe Bulletin Board," *CUNY University Computer Center Communications*, vol. 14, no. 5–6, pp. 29–31, CUNY, New York, May–June 1988.

Reid 1988a.   Reid, Brian, "Network Maps (DECWRL netmap 1.5)," DEC Western Research Lab, Palo Alto, 19 June 1988.

Reid 1988b.   Reid, Brian, "USENET Readership Summary Report for Mar 88," *news.groups, news.lists*, USENET Measurement Project, DEC Western Research Laboratory, Palo Alto, CA, 3 April 1988.

Ritchie and Thompson 1974.   Ritchie, D. M., and Thompson, K., "The UNIX Time-Sharing System," *Communications of the ACM*, vol. 7, no. 7, pp. 365–375, July 1974. This is the original version, which describes Sixth Edition UNIX.

Ritchie and Thompson 1978. Ritchie, D. M., and Thompson, K., "The UNIX Time-Sharing System," *Bell System Technical Journal*, vol. 57, no. 6, part 2, pp. 1905–1929, July/August 1978. This version describes Seventh Edition UNIX.

Schroeder et al. 1984. Schroeder, M. D., Birrell, A. D., and Needham, R. M., "Experience with Grapevine: The Growth of a Distributed System," *ACM Transactions on Computer Systems*, vol. 2, no. 1, pp. 3–23, February 1984. Also in Partridge, *Innovations in Internetworking*, 1988.

Spafford 1988a. Spafford, Gene, "The USENET Backbone (Updated: 3 April 1988)," *news.misc, news.config*, USENET, 4 April 1988.

Spafford 1988b. Spafford, Gene, "List of Active Newsgroups (Updated: 2 April 1988)," *news.lists, news.groups, news.announce.newusers*, USENET, 3 April 1988.

Spafford 1988c. Spafford, Gene, "USENET Software: History and Sources (Updated: 2 April 1988)," *news.admin, news.announce.newusers*, USENET, 3 April 1988.

Spafford 1988d. Spafford, Gene, "USENET," *IETF Proceedings*, IETF, Washington, DC, October 1988.

Spafford 1988e. Spafford, Gene, "Publicly Accessible Mailing Lists (Updated: 14 April 1988)," *news.lists, news.announce.newusers*, USENET, 17 April 1988.

Spencer and Collyer 1987. Spencer, Henry, and Collyer, Geoff, "News Need Not Be Slow," *Proceedings of the Winter 1987 USENIX Conference (Washington, D.C., 21–23 January 1987)*, USENIX Association, Berkeley, CA, 1987.

Summers-Horton and Horton 1985. Summers-Horton, Karen, and Horton, Mark, "Status of the USENIX UUCP Project," *Proceedings of the Winter 1985 USENIX Conference (Dallas, Texas, 23–25 January 1985)*, p. 183, USENIX Association, Berkeley, CA, 1985.

Tanenbaum 1988. Tanenbaum, Andrew S., *Computer Networks*, 2d ed., Prentice-Hall, Englewood Cliffs, NJ, 1988.

Todino and O'Reilly 1988a. Todino, Grace, and O'Reilly, Tim, *Using UUCP and Usenet*, O'Reilly & Associates, Inc., Newton, MA, 1988.

Todino and O'Reilly 1988b. Todino, Grace, and O'Reilly, Tim, *Managing UUCP and Usenet*, O'Reilly and Associates, Inc., Newton, MA, 1988.

Tokuda et al. 1986. Tokuda, T., Landweber, L. H., Faber, D. J., Horton, M. R., Tokuda, H., Adrion, W. R., and Horton, K. S., "Toward the network community for R&D (kenkyuukaihatsuyou no network community wo mezashite)," *BIT Magazine*, vol. 18, no. 2, p. 122, 1986. Transcript of a panel discussion, in Kanji.

Truscott 1988. Truscott, Thomas, Personal communications, 16 February 1988.

Weinstein 1985. Weinstein, Lauren, "Project Stargate," *Proceedings of the Summer 1985 USENIX Conference (Portland, Oregon, 11–14 June 1985)*, pp. 79–80, USENIX Association, Berkeley, CA, 1985.

Weinstein 1986. Weinstein, Lauren, "Project Stargate," *EUUG Spring '86 Conference Proceedings (Florence, Italy, 21–24 April 1986)*, European UNIX systems User Group, Florence, Italy, 1986.

Welch 1984. Welch, Terry A., "A Technique for High Performance Data Compression," *IEEE Computer*, vol. 17, no. 6, pp. 8–19, June 1984.

Wells 1987. Wells, William C., "PHYSnet/CITnet/HEPnet/NRAO/SPAN — Physics Community DECnet Mail," Data Communication and Network Services, University of California at Berkeley, 14 September 1987.

Wells 1988a. Wells, William C., "HEPNET, PHYSNET and SPAN," *info-nets@think.com*, BITNET, Internet, Berkeley, CA, 6 June 1988.

Wells 1988b. Wells, William C., Personal communications, 12 September 1988.

11   *The Internet*

The *Internet* is all of the following:

- A worldwide network, because some of its component parts extend to several continents
- A largely North American network, because that is where most of its hosts are
- A set of U.S. networks, because that is where it started and where most of its networks still are

The networks described in this chapter are the constituent parts of the *Internet* that are either worldwide or located in the United States. These are not all the parts of the *Internet*: there are others elsewhere in the world, and many of them are described in other chapters. The *Internet* has recently developed many connections outside of North America, including links to *ARISTOTE* in France, *NORDUnet* in the Nordic countries, *EUnet* through Amsterdam to Western Europe, *JUNET* in Japan, *ACSnet* in Australia and to New Zealand.

However, the primary association of those others is shared protocols and name and address spaces, with only minimal administrative connections. Many people confuse using the *Internet* Domain Name System (DNS) with being in the *Internet*. Thus, it is useful to give a few examples of networks that are and are not part of the *Internet*. Among those that are part of the *Internet* are *NORDUnet*, *DREnet*, and *EUnet*. Among those that are *not* part of the *Internet* are *UUCP*, *BITNET*, *NetNorth*, *EARN*, *HEPnet*, and *JANET*.

11.1   *Internet*

The *Internet* is an internetwork of many networks all running the TCP/IP protocol suite [Leiner et al. 1985], connected through gateways, and sharing common name and address spaces [Cerf and Cain 1983]. It exists to facilitate sharing of resources at participating organizations (which include government agencies, educational institutions, and private corporations) and collaboration among researchers, as well as to provide a testbed for new developments in networking. This is the system on which the TCP/IP protocols were developed. The *Internet* is very large, not only covering the United States, but also extending into Canada, Europe, and Asia (the Philippines, Korea, and Japan). Some of its constituent networks such as *CSNET*, are themselves very large, and some, such as *NSFNET*, have many component networks of their own. Estimates of numbers of hosts range from 40,000 to 500,000 and of numbers of users from 500,000 to more than a million [NNSC 1988a]. There are at least 400 connected networks.

The *Internet* has been known under several names:

ARPA Internet was its original name, after the Advanced Research Projects Agency (ARPA) of the U.S. Department of Defense (DoD), which was its original funding agency. The oldest network in the *Internet*, the *ARPANET*, was also named after this agency.

DARPA Internet was often used as the name of the *Internet* when ARPA changed its name to Defense Advanced Research Projects Agency (DARPA).

TCP/IP Internet is sometimes used to avoid calling it only after DARPA, now that it is funded by several government agencies and numerous companies and managed by several agencies, including a new coordinating body, FRICC.

Federal Research Internet is sometimes used for the same reason.

The network is usually known simply as the *Internet*, however, without a distinguishing adjective but with a capital *I*. An *internet* with a lowercase *i* refers to any internetwork. With a capital *I*, *Internet* refers to a specific internet, usually the one described in this section. There is also the *XEROX Internet*, which uses different protocols and may be older, but that network is mostly limited to a single company. Other networks, such as *BITNET, UUCP, EUnet*, and *ACSnet*, are not part of the capital-*I Internet*. It is not sufficient for a network or a host to have a DNS domain name to be part of the *Internet*; use of IP and integration into the *Internet* IP address space, as well as a connection at the IP level, are also necessary. *CSNET* is a special case: part of it is part of the *Internet*, and part of it is not.

Administration

Practical coordination of the entire *Internet* is provided by the *DDN* Network Information Center (NIC) at SRI International (SRI) in Menlo Park, California (sometimes known as SRI-NIC) and the Network Operations Center (NOC) at Bolt Beranek and Newman (BBN) in Cambridge, Massachusetts. The main backbone networks of the *Internet*, *MILNET* and *NSFNET*, are funded mostly by government grants. The campus area networks are funded mostly by local organizations. There are generally no per user or per message charges.

Protocols and Services

All hosts and networks in the *Internet* use the TCP/IP protocols, and most support TELNET for remote login, FTP for file transfer, SMTP for mail, and numerous other smaller services (date, time, system status, *Internet* directory, etc.). The DNS domain name system is widely used, but *MILNET* has mostly not converted from the previous system involving a static host table. *MILNET* long-haul links are mostly 56Kbps, while *NSFNET* currently uses T1 1.5Mbps links.

There are several unusual networks in the *Internet*. *WIDEBAND* uses geosynchronous satellites to provide paths between the East and West coasts of the United States that are faster than the usual *MILNET* land lines. *SATNET* provided satellite links to Italy, Great Britain [Tanenbaum 1988, 9–12], and Norway, but it has been replaced by leased lines. *PRNET* has nodes on mobile vehicles that communicate with packet radio. *AMPRNET* also uses packet radio, but its users are ham radio operaters rather than traditional researchers.

Many companies, schools, and government agencies have local networks that are part of the *Internet*. These include Ethernets, token rings, broadband networks, and *ARPANET*-style PSN networks. Some *Internet* networks run the TCP/IP protocol suite on top of X.25 on public data networks. There are even point to point connections over terminal lines, HYPERchannel links, dialup links, and T1 microwave links. These point to point links are usually used to connect higher speed networks. Thus, the speed of such local networks may vary from 1200bps to HYPERchannel speeds or higher.

Many campus-size organizations actually have several local networks. Since there is no need for people outside of the local organization to know the details of such internal networking arrangements, and since there is also a limit on the number of networks that the *Internet* core gateways can handle, many organizations arrange that their networks appear logically as one network to the rest of the *Internet* with subnets that are known only locally [Mogul and Postel 1985].

Gatewaying between *MILNET* and *ARPANET* is illegal, except through half a dozen government approved gateways. These gateways are rather slow and were often bottlenecks in 1986 and 1987, although part of the problem was some overloaded links, which have since been upgraded or replaced. Also, there was a program at one point whereby private companies were encouraged to provide hardware for additional gateways; this was known as the "adopt a gateway" program.

Interconnections

Interconnections from the *Internet* are shown in Table 11.1. There, {DNS} stands for the top level domains used in the *Internet* DNS, including *COM, EDU, GOV, ORG, MIL, NET, ORG,* and *US,* as well as many ISO3166 two letter country codes. The old temporary top level domain *ARPA* is being phased out. Note that these domains also apply to many hosts that are not on the *Internet* but do have domains that are known to the *Internet.*

Due to the use of *MX records* referring to gateways to the networks connected to the *Internet,* users can reach many hosts on many networks by mail as if they were on the *Internet,* simply by using domain names for them:

HEPnet	Around January 1989, *LBL.GOV,* the gateway to *SPAN* and *HEP-net,* was expected to become *GW.LBL.DOE.GOV.*
JANET	Access to *JANET* through *nss.cs.ucl.ac.uk* is somewhat controlled, due to the cost of the transatlantic link. For details, send a message with no text to authorisation@nss.cs.ucl.ac.uk. Alternatively, *JANET* may be reached through *BITNET* and *EARN* by sending through a *BITNET* gateway such as *cunyvm.cuny.edu.*
VNET	The indicated syntax will result either in sending the mail directly to the IBM employee or in generating a message that the person needs to register for *VNET* use.
DASnet	Although the *DASnet* gateway machine has two registered domains (*das.com* and *das.net*), three nameservers, and a forwarder, this knowledge will be of little use unless the user is a subscriber to the *DASnet* service or corresponding with one.
PeaceNet	An exception to the above rule about *DASnet* is *PeaceNet,* which has a group account and allows all its users to be reached as indicated. It can also be reached without going through *DASnet.*

Intermail is a free gateway to several commercial systems. Run by the Information Sciences Institute (ISI), *Intermail* can forward to *GTE Telemail, MCI Mail,* and *Dialcom* systems such as *COMPMAIL, NSF-MAIL* for the National Science Foundation (NSF), and *ONR-MAIL* for the Office of Naval Research (ONR). ISI prefers that use of this gateway be limited to DARPA sponsored research activities and other approved government business. *Internet* users can get the files

Table 11.1. *Internet interconnections*

Network	Syntax
Internet	*user@domain.***{DNS}**
BITNET	*user%host*.bitnet@cunyvm.cuny.edu
SPAN	*user%host*.span@vlsi.jpl.nasa.gov
SPAN	*user%host*.span@star.stanford.edu
HEPnet	*user%host*.HEPNET@LBL.GOV
HEPnet	*user%host*.HEPNET@LBL.BITNET
ACSnet	*user@domain.***{ACSNET-domain}**
UUCP	*user%host*.uucp@*gateway*
UUCP	*host!user*@uunet.uu.net
Ean	*user%domain.***{Ean-domain}**%ubc.csnet@relay.cs.net
XEROX Internet	*user.***{XEROX-domain}**@xerox.com
XEROX RIN	User.registry@Xerox.COM
	(eg. JLarson.PA@Xerox.COM)
XEROX CIN	Name.foreignRegistry@Xerox.COM
	(eg. JDoe.osbunorth@Xerox.COM)
EASYnet	*user%host*.dec@decwrl.dec.com
VNET	*user%host*@ibm.com
JANET	*user%domain.***{JANET-domain}**@nsfnet-relay.ac.uk
JANET	*user%domain.***{JANET-domain}**@cunyvm.cuny.edu
Starlink	*user*@starlink.jodrell-bank.manchester.ac.uk
Starlink	*user*@star.jb.man.ac.uk
JUNET	*user%domain.***{JUNET-domain}**%japan.csnet@relay.cs.net
DASnet	*user*@das.com
DASnet	*user*@das.net
PeaceNet	*user*@de3mir.das.net
PeaceNet	*user*%cdp.uucp@parcvax.xerox.com

```
PS:<INC-PROJECT>COMPMAIL-ARPAMAIL-FORWARDING.TXT
PS:<INC-PROJECT>MCI-MAIL-ARPAMAIL-FORWARDING.TXT
PS:<INC-PROJECT>TELEMAIL-ARPAMAIL-FORWARDING.TXT
```

from *c.isi.edu* by *anonymous FTP*. People on other networks can ask for them from

    intermail-request@isi.edu

For a brief synopsis of the format, see the section on *Dialcom* in Chapter 21.

History

The *ARPANET* is the oldest of the networks in the *Internet*, becoming operational in 1969. The *Internet* was formed in 1983 when *ARPANET* was divided into two networks, *ARPANET* and *MILNET*, and the Defense

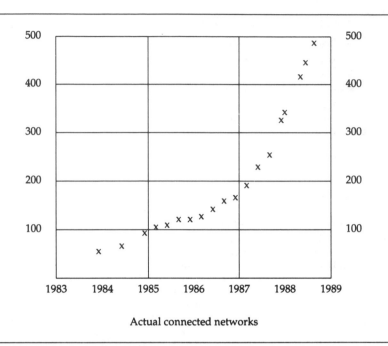

Figure 11.1. *Internet growth (1983 – 1988) [Brescia 1988]*

Communications Agency (DCA), which manages both networks, mandated the use of TCP/IP for all hosts connected to either [Lederman et al. 1988]. *CSNET* and *NSFNET* have already made major changes to the structure of the *Internet*. There were plans to retire *ARPANET* during 1988 and 1989, leaving *MILNET* and *NSFNET* providing major backbone connectivity and picking up connections to many of the hosts formerly on *ARPANET*. However, the direct replacement for *ARPANET* is *DRI* [Lederman et al. 1988].

The size of the *Internet* has grown exponentially since 1983, as shown in Figure 11.1 and Figure 11.2. One of the main reasons for the early popularity of the *Internet* and of the TCP/IP protocols was the implementation of those protocols for the Berkeley Software Distribution (BSD) of the **UNIX** operating system [Ritchie and Thompson 1978], which was in use at 90 percent of all university Computer Science Departments in the United States and elsewhere [Comer 1988, 6]. This implementation was done by the Computer Systems Research Group (CSRG) of the University of California at Berkeley (UCB), partly based on an earlier implementation by Rob Gurwitz at BBN. The leader of the original CSRG TCP/IP implementation was William N. Joy, now with Sun Microsystems, Inc. (Sun), and the first

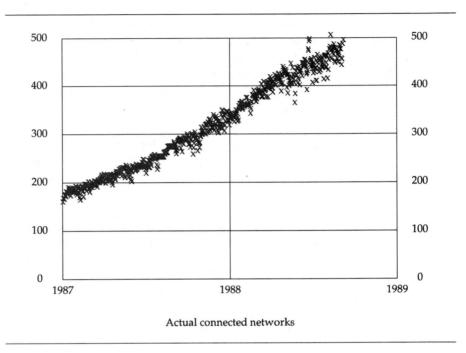

Figure 11.2. *Recent Internet growth (1987 – 1988) [Brescia 1988]*

general distribution was in **4.2BSD** in 1984, under the leadership of Samuel J. Leffler [Quarterman et al. 1985]. The currently available release is **4.3BSD**, coordinated by Marshall Kirk McKusick and Michael J. Karels, who are leading future developments [Leffler et al. 1989]. The more recent explosive growth of the *Internet* is probably more related to the general availability of inexpensive hardware and good implementations of the protocols, many of which are derived from **4.3BSD**, even for other versions of **UNIX**, or for **MS-DOS, VMS**, or gateway boxes.

Plans

The Department of Commerce (DoC), the General Services Administration (GSA), and NIST have published a Government Open Systems Interconnection Procurement Specification (GOSIP) that mandates eventual conversion to ISO-OSI protocols for all U.S. government networking procurements [NBS 1988; Passmore and Horn 1988]. This is unlikely to have any strong effect on the use of TCP/IP on the *Internet* for at least two years [Shaw 1988], although there are signs of increased involvement of *Internet* researchers in ISO-OSI protocol and implementation development—e.g., **CMOT**.

A Defense Research Internet (*DRI*) is being implemented to be the successor to the *ARPANET*, and a Research Interagency Backbone (*RIB*) is being planned, both of which are to lead to a National Research Internet (*NRI*). All three of these efforts are described in Chapter 12, along with *CSNET* and *NSFNET*; *MILNET* is described later in this chapter. See also *NORDUnet*, *NRCnet*, *ARISTOTE*, *JUNET*, *ILAN*, and *SDN*. Several U.S. federal government bodies, such as the IAB, FCCSET, FRICC, and DCA, have varying degrees of policy, technological, or operational effect on the *Internet* and these follow-on projects. Those bodies are described in Chapter 8.

Access

Many *Internet* hosts support a command called **whois** that can be used to look up directory information. Failing that, it is possible to TELNET to *SRI-NIC.ARPA* (eventually *NIC.DDN.MIL* [Lederman et al. 1988]) and type WHOIS. That host is run by the NIC at SRI.

A great deal of information can be obtained by *anonymous FTP* (login anonymous, password guest) from *SRI-NIC.ARPA*, particularly from the files in the *NETINFO:* directory. The TCP/IP protocol specifications are online in documents called Requests for Comments (RFC) in the *RFC:* directory.

Most of this information can also be obtained by mail. For details, send mail as follows:

To: SERVICE@SRI-NIC.ARPA
Subject: HELP

DDN Network Information Center
SRI International
Room EJ291
333 Ravenswood Avenue
Menlo Park, CA 94025
U.S.A.

11.1.1   PRNET

PRNET, or Experimental Packet Radio Network, is in the San Francisco Bay Area. Its purpose is to provide a testbed for development of packet radio protocols and technology [Su and Mathis 1988; Kahn 1975]. There are base stations in Berkeley, Mission Ridge, Menlo Park, and elsewhere. These communicate with mobile vans. There is a connection to the *ARPANET* at SRI International (SRI) of Menlo Park, and thence to the *Internet* [Tanenbaum 1988, 9–12; IEEE 1978].

The project was proposed by SRI in 1979 and funded by DARPA for development starting in December 1979, eventually for four and a half years in all. There were other participants from academia and industry, organized in the Packet Radio Working Group (PRWG) and led by an implementer's group (IG) composed of representatives from BBN, Rockwell

International (Rockwell), SRI, and DARPA, who met every three to six months. Each IG company had responsibility for specific areas: BBN for station software; Rockwell for radio software; and SRI for network interface software (and final testing of the network) [Klemba 1985].

During this project, SRI addressed the *ARPANET* problem of a fixed number of IMPs and a fixed number (four) of host interfaces on each IMP by inventing and implementing a *port expander* that allowed a single IMP port to connect up to eight hosts [Klemba 1985]. This problem was resolved more completely by the implementation of the TCP/IP protocols and the *Internet*, which were developed in part in order to connect *PRNET* hosts to the *ARPANET* in a fashion other than requiring an apparently direct IMP connection for each host.

Access
Telecommunications Science Center
+1-415-326-6200
Telex: 334-486
Computer Science and Technology Division
SRI International
333 Ravenswood Avenue
Menlo Park, CA 94025
U.S.A.

11.1.2   AMPRNET

The Amateur Packet Radio Network (*AMPRNET*) is developed and used by shortwave radio amateurs (hams). By 1985, there were about 30,000 of them around the world with equipment capable of transmitting data reliably; no doubt there are many more now [Karn et al. 1985]. Some of them associate in the TCP/IP network *AMPRNET*, which has a Class A network address and a domain, *ampr.org*, registered with the *Internet*, although *AMPRNET* is not actually interconnected with the *Internet*. There are about a thousand systems registered in *ampr.org* [Karn 1988a].

Protocols

The modem used for encoding data into radio signals is called a Terminal Node Controller (TNC). It is possible to use many TNCs on a single frequency, producing a virtual network similar to a network like Ethernet on cable, except that collision detection is impossible because a TNC cannot monitor the channel while transmitting (its own transmissions drown any incoming signal), one node cannot necessarily hear all other nodes, and the error rate can be much higher [Karn 1988a]. Obviously, some sort of robust error correcting protocol is needed to support a network over this sort of infrastructure. One possibility is AX.25 [Fox 1982], which is a noninteroperable variant of X.25 that has been used since 1982 [Karn 1988a].

TCP/IP for packet radio has been developed experimentally since at least 1985 by Richard Bisbey and David Mills [Karn 1985a]. Their work mostly involved adapting existing hardware and software and inspired Phil Karn to develop a package (**KA9Q**, after Karn's call sign) specifically designed for amateur packet radio that runs on the machines commonly available to hams—i.e., IBM PCs [Karn 1987]. It has been ported to many other environments and is free for noncommercial use, although it is not in the public domain. **KA9Q** uses IP (and ICMP, TCP, UDP, TELNET, FTP, and SMTP) over AX.25 with ARP for address mapping and also supports SLIP [Karn et al. 1985]. This work has led to detection of problems in the TCP protocol and its implementations and of solutions involving routing [Karn 1985b] and speed improvements [Karn 1988b].

History

Amateur packet radio was first used in Canada in the late 1970s after Canada liberalized its relevant rules [Karn 1988c]. There were earlier packet radio networks, most notably *Aloha* and *PRNET*. *AMPRNET* is different for several reasons. Amateur operators must be licensed by the FCC but have access to a wide range of frequency bands, although they may not use them for commercial purposes and cannot use them anonymously. Amateur radio is already being used for voice, Morse code, teletype, television, and facsimile, and is being propagated by methods ranging from line of sight transmission to bouncing off the moon. Hams are amateurs, not academics or business people (some of them may be those things in other endeavors but not in ham operations). A ham outfit does not require a van to carry it or a large grant to buy it, although it may also not be very fast: about 1200bps is the common data speed, although some operate at speeds as high as 56Kbps. *AMPRNET* has developed in the age of the personal computer, and many hams are computer amateurs (*hackers*, not *crackers*) as well [Levy 1984]. However, as in *PRNET*, the links in use may vary over time [Karn 1988a].

Perhaps the most distinguishing feature of amateur packet radio is its low cost. A TNC can be bought for about $100, and a radio that can be used with it to handle 1200bps costs about $400 [Karn 1988c].

Access
Phil Karn
karn@thumper.bellcore.com

11.1.3   Los Nettos

Los Nettos is a regional network created and supported by its members beginning in 1988. It is part of the *Internet* but is not funded by *NSFNET*. This is the only such regional network in the United States. The initial members were the Computer Science Department of the California Institute of Technology (Caltech), Trusted Information Systems (TIS), the Computer Science Department of the University of California at Los Angeles (UCLA), the University Computing Services of the University of Southern California (USC), and the Information Sciences Institute (ISI). As many as 30 member sites were expected within two years (by 1990), extending from Santa Barbara to San Diego [Postel 1988]. Connections are desired to individual campuses and research centers in southern California, as well as to long-haul networks [ISI 1988].

Los Nettos has no financial or administrative ties to DARPA, NSF, DoE, DoD, or any other federal government agency. It is funded and operated by the member organizations, each of which supplies a representative to a board of directors that produces a budget, sets fees, and determines rules for membership. There is also an administrative committee that handles details and submits reports to the board for approval. Sites are being added in groups in order to keep the topology of the network reasonable. There is a technical committee that assists in this. The initial board of directors consists of Chuck Seitz, Caltech; Jon Postel, ISI; Steve Crocker, TIS; Len Kleinrock, UCLA; and Dick Kaplan, USC.

The board has delegated operational authority to ISI, which invoices members, deposits received funds into a bank account set up for the purpose, and uses them later to pay for T1 lines, gateways, and other necessary equipment, which it also orders on behalf of new members. Purchasing is centralized in order to get volume discounts and to make part swapping for maintenance easy by keeping ownership under one body. Costs per member in August 1988 were $25,000 to $35,000 for connection and $2,500 to $3,500 per month afterward [ISI 1988].

The TCP/IP protocol suite is used. All the links are T1, or 1.5Mbps, and thus this is a high-speed network.

There are connections to *ARPANET* and *WBNET*. It will be an initial *DRI* site and may be connected to the *NSFNET* backbone before that [Postel 1988]. *Los Nettos* will also be a "special member" of *CERFnet* [ISI 1988].

Access

Jon Postel
POSTEL@ISI.EDU

Walt Prue
PRUE@ISI.EDU

11.1.4   CERFnet

CERFnet, the California Education and Research Federation network, will use the TCP/IP protocols in a regional internetwork in southern California (the name *SURFnet* was already taken by another network) [Postel 1988]. About 180 hosts were connected to the network in November 1988 [Armstrong 1988a], even though it was still becoming fully operational [Armstrong 1988b]. The purpose of the network is "to advance science and education . . . by assisting the interchange of information among research and educational institutions, by means of high-speed data communications techniques" [CERFnet 1988].

Administration and Funding

CERFnet is administered by the board of officers of the California Education and Research Federation (CERF); these are elected by a set of representatives, one from each subscribing academic institution [Armstrong 1988b]. The current officers are Susan Estrada, San Diego Supercomputer Center (SDSC), chair; Brent Auernheimer, California State University Fresno (CSUF), vice chair; David Walker, University of California at Irvine, secretary; Russel Utterberg, California State University (CSU), CO/SWRL Facility, Seal Beach, treasurer [CERFnet 1988]. The management location is at the SDSC, to which applications for access should be sent.

Funding was undetermined as of the end of 1988 [Armstrong 1988b], but *CERFnet* anticipates full funding from NSF for the first year of operations, with partial NSF funding for the second and third years. The remainder is to come from industrial participation, or perhaps from the academic participants [Armstrong 1988a]. The network is to be self-supporting after the third year.

Services and Protocols

In addition to the TCP/IP protocols and all the usual services that come with them, as well as supercomputer and database access, *CERFnet* plans a monthly electronic newsletter. The DECNET protocols also will be used. Link speeds range from 9600bps to T1 (1.544Mbps).

History and Plans

CERF was founded by Susan Estrada and colleagues in January 1988, for the same purpose as *CERFnet*, with specific goals for faster supercomputer access (permitting many scientific projects that could not previously be undertaken), access to multiple supercomputer centers (because they have different databases and software), and some experimentation with the network itself [Armstrong 1988b]. A proposal for initial support as an *NSFNET* regional network has been made to NSF. *CERFnet* will have wider membership than *Los Nettos* and varying grades of access and link speeds. *Los Nettos* will be a "special member" of *CERFnet* [ISI 1988]. *CERFnet* has 38 sites committed [Armstrong 1988a], all California centers of higher education or research [CERFnet 1988], and may have more eventually [Armstrong 1988a].

Access

Karen Armstrong
External Relations Representative
armstrongk@Luac.Sdsc.Edu

Susan Estrada
Chairperson
ESTRADAS@SDS.SDSC.EDU

CERFnet
+1-619-534-5067
San Diego Supercomputer Center
P.O. Box 85608
San Diego, CA 92138-5608
U.S.A.

11.2   *DDN*

The Defense Data Network (*DDN*) is a TCP/IP internet that is a subset of the *Internet* and that is operated and funded by the U.S. Department of Defense (DoD). Management is done by the Defense Data Network Program Management Office (DDN/PMO), which is an Office of the Defense Communications Agency (DCA).

DDN is composed of the networks *ARPANET* and *MILNET*, plus *DISNET* (Defense Integrated Secure Network) *SCINET* (Sensitive Compartmented Information Network) and *WINCS* (WWMCCS Intercomputer Network Communication Subsystem) of the World Wide Military Command and Control System (WWMCCS) [Perillo 1986]. There are local networks in the *Internet* at military installations such as the Ballistics Research Laboratory (BRL).

There were plans in the late 1970s to replace the original U.S. military network *AUTODIN* with one called *AUTODIN II*, but the proven reliability, survivability, and availability of *ARPANET* technology led to the demise of that project in favor of *DDN*, which was formed when *MILNET* split from *ARPANET* in 1983.

There are other classified networks, not part of *DDN*, such as *WIN* (Top Secret Network) Some still run NCP. *SCINET*, *WINCS*, and *Secretnet* will merge to form *DISNET*.

The Canadian Defence Research Establishment network *DREnet* is also connected to the *Internet*.

Access

Information on *DDN* may be obtained from SRI-NIC by the mechanisms mentioned in the section on the *Internet*. Users of *BITNET*, *NetNorth*, or *EARN* should first check a local **NETSERV**, and *CSNET* users should first check with the *CSNET* **Info-Server** on *sh.cs.net* before requesting information directly from SRI-NIC.

11.2.1   MILNET

MILNET is a long-haul military production network that is not normally used for networking research, although it is part of the *Internet*. It is intended to be a stable operational network, and service disruptions are kept to a minimum. There are about 1,500 hosts and gateways, most in the continental United States, as shown in Figure 11.3, with some in Hawaii, the Philippines, Korea, and Japan, as shown in Figure 11.4, and Europe (the latter on *MINET*), as shown in Figure 11.5. There are a few dozen Terminal Access Controller (TAC) nodes that provide only client access. Access to *MILNET* is determined by the U.S. Department of Defense (DoD).

Administration and Funding

ARPANET and *MILNET* are the main constituents of the *DDN* (Defense Data Network) which is a subset of the *Internet*. Management of *MILNET* is by the Defense Data Network Program Management Office (DDN/PMO) of the Defense Communications Agency (DCA). Funding is by DoD.

Protocols

MILNET uses the TCP/IP protocols, except *MILNET* has not yet adopted DNS domain nameservers and still uses static host tables for host name to address mapping. Like *ARPANET* PSNs, *MILNET* PSNs are connected by 56Kbps leased lines. There is a classified segment of *MILNET* in addition to the readily accessible part.

History

MILNET was built using the results of the *ARPANET* research. It split from the *ARPANET* in October 1983 but is still connected to the *ARPANET* by gateways at the internet layer. These gateways were originally intended at least to be able to limit traffic between the networks to mail only, but they

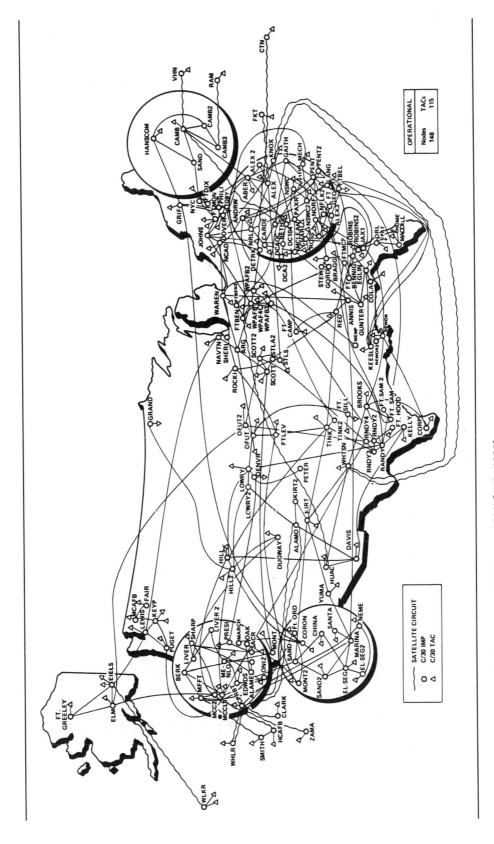

Figure 11.3. *MILNET in North America map (31 January 1983)* [DCA1988]

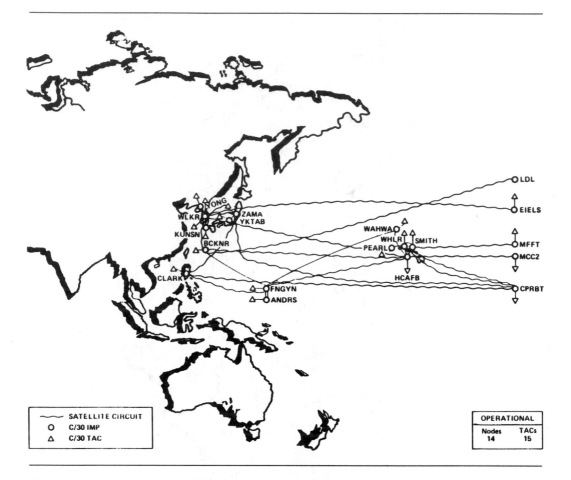

Figure 11.4. *MILNET in the Pacific map (31 January 1988) [DCA1988]*

actually always passed all traffic as if the networks had not been divided (except for a performance penalty). Nonetheless, their PSNs formed two disjoint sets, and the two networks could easily be separated if the need were to arise. These gateways formed a severe bottleneck in 1986 and 1987, due to a shortage of transcontinental links, confusion of routing with *NSFNET*, and especially lack of CPU power. When *ARPANET* was retired in 1988 and 1989, *MILNET* and *NSFNET* became the backbone networks of the Internet.

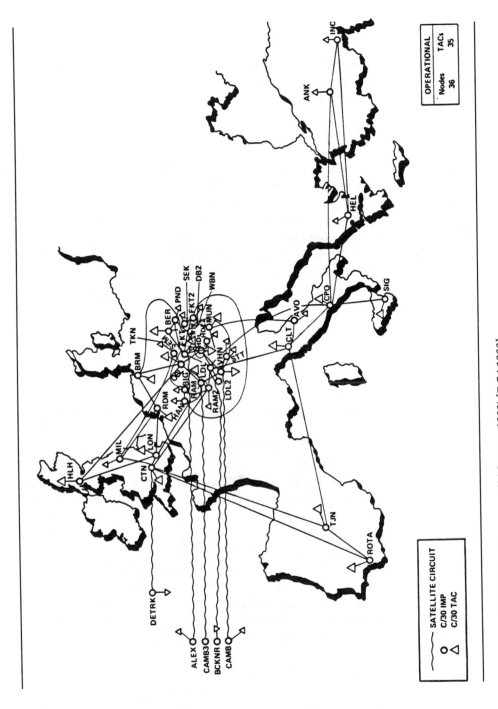

Figure 11.5. *MILNET in Europe map (31 January 1988) [DCA1988]*

11.2.2   DRI

The Defense Research Internet (*DRI*) was proposed in 1988 to replace the *ARPANET*, which had become too slow and expensive. *DRI* will multiplex traffic onto *RIB* [Vaudreuil 1988].

11.2.3   RIB

The immediate technical plan of FRICC is to form the *RIB* (Research Interagency Backbone) which consists of fiber-optic 45Mbps DS3 links connecting Washington, Boston, New York, Los Angeles, San Francisco, San Diego, Pittsburgh, Chicago, and Denver. The participating agencies will be connected to the backbone with 1.544Mbps T1 leased lines. Bids have been received for the backbone, but no selection had been made as of 6 September 1988. Protocols and switches to handle 45Mbps speeds are to be developed on *DRI*, which is intended to be the replacement for the *ARPANET*.

11.3   *NRI*

The National Research Internet (*NRI*) is being planned by a network working group of several committees authorized by the Office of the President of the United States. The relevant committees are collectively known as the Federal Coordinating Council for Science, Engineering, and Technology (FCCSET), and their purpose is to coordinate activities in the various federal agencies. One of them is the FCCSET Committee on Very High Performance Computing (VHPC) and is aimed at the supercomputer activities.

NRI will interconnect the networks owned by the various federal agencies in order to promote resource sharing and collaboration among researchers. This differs from *NSFNET*'s purpose in that it attempts to satisfy most if not all needs for scientific networking (*NSFNET* is more directed toward providing access to supercomputer centers). Also, *NSFNET* will be one of the networks connected by *NRI*. The *NRI* project is administered by the FCCSET Network Working Group (NWG). The network will be funded by various federal agencies. Accounting methods are still under study.

The TCP/IP protocol suite will be used. The main focus of development will be on gateway standards in order to facilitate interconnection of the networks. The links used will presumably be fast, and the TCP/IP protocols will promote reliability.

Access

Access restrictions among the various agency networks may become an issue, and prior arrangement with the administration of a network may be necessary before a given resource on it may be used by a user of a different network.

11.4   *CSNET*

CSNET was established in January 1981 to facilitate research and advanced development in computer science or engineering by providing a means for increased collaboration among those working in the field [Denning et al. 1983; Comer 1983; CSNET 1985; Edmiston 1983]. Membership restrictions are now more general, and include industrial, academic, government, and nonprofit institutions "engaged in computer-related research or advanced development in science or engineering" [CSNET CIC 1988]. Use of *CSNET* for commercial gain is explicitly prohibited. *CSNET* is a metanetwork built of several physical networks and protocols but serving a single community [Landweber 1982]. Access to the research community of the *Internet* is the principal benefit provided by *CSNET* to its members [Rugo 1988].

The network is mostly confined to the United States and Canada, but it has links to international members and affiliates in Australia, Finland, France, Germany, Israel, Japan, Korea, New Zealand, Sweden, Switzerland, the United Kingdom [CSNET CIC 1988], and the People's Republic of China. There are about 180 hosts in all, as shown in Figure 11.6. Many serve as gateways into internal company networks or national networks. Perhaps thousands of hosts on such networks can be reached through *CSNET*. *CSNET* is considered an *NSFNET* mid-level regional network [Partridge 1988], although it is not directly connected to the *NSFNET* backbone.

Administration

All parts of *CSNET* are administered by the CSNET Coordination and Information Center (CSNET CIC) at Bolt Beranek and Newman (BBN) in Cambridge, Massachusetts [CSNET 1985]. CSNET CIC provides technical, operational, administrative, and end user support. The University Corporation for Atmospheric Research (UCAR), under contract to NSF, oversees BBN's operation of the CIC, with advice from the *CSNET* executive committee, which consists of representatives from member organizations [Rugo 1988].

Funding

NSF provided initial funding for the establishment of *CSNET*. The total project budget was $5 million over the five years 1981 through 1985. Even though there is no current funding from NSF and the network has been

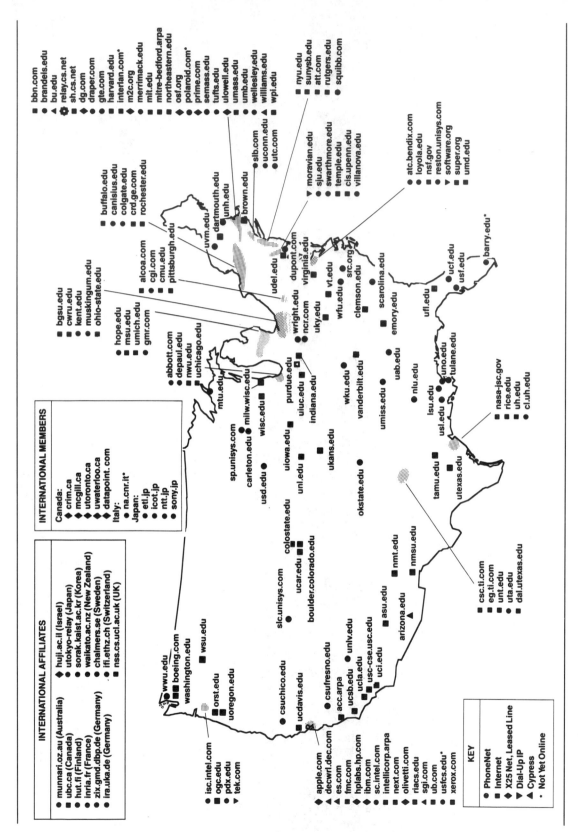

Figure 11.6. *CSNET map (15 December 1988) [CSNET CIC 1989]*

self-supporting since 1985, CSNET CIC continues to operate with a no-cost contract with NSF [Partridge 1988]. Annual dues are collected from member organizations with rates set according to several classifications (usually either academic or industrial). Member organizations also have to pay for hardware and communication costs directly [Rugo 1988].

Services

General *CSNET* information, source code, and information on other networks and conferences can be retrieved from *sh.cs.net* via several methods.

- The **Info-Server** program [Partridge 1987] automatically provides distribution of requested documents in response to requests sent to

  info-server@sh.cs.net

  For more information on the Info-Server service, send a message with the command HELP in the body of the message. These documents are also available via *anonymous FTP* from *sh.cs.net*.
- The User Name Server provides information such as name, address, telephone numbers, and electronic mail addresses for *CSNET* sites and users [Landweber et al. 1983a; Landweber et al. 1983b; Solomon et al. 1982]. It is accessed in several ways:

  electronic mail to registrar@sh.cs.net

  TELNET to sh.cs.net (login ns, no password)

  voice telephone, +1-617-491-2777

- Traveller Telnet Access allows users access to an account on *relay.cs.net* via a phone call or the *Telenet* PDN. The user can then TELNET to any host on the *Internet* [Lanzillo 1988].
- CSNET-FORUM, a mailing list digest containing general information, announcements, and discussions, is distributed to *CSNET* members monthly, and previous copies are kept available online through the Info-Server. Nonmembers may request the CIC to send copies to their electronic address.
- *CSNET News*, a quarterly news digest, presents information of interest to the *CSNET* community and network.

The *CSNET* Service Host, *sh.cs.net*, is a Sun-3/280 file server providing these services [Swindell 1988].

Protocols

The only service supported on all of the parts of *CSNET* is mail, transferred in *Internet* RFC822 format. But *CSNET* is a metanetwork composed of several parts that vary in their additional services, lower level protocols, speed, reliability, and other qualities. Some of these parts do support remote login, file transfer, and other services.

Component Networks

Six networks allow connection to *CSNET*: *PhoneNet*, *X25Net*, *ARPANET*, *Cypress*, *Leased Lines*, and *Dial-up IP*.

PhoneNet is the original *CSNET* network service and is a store and forward electronic mail network. It is a star centered around *relay.cs.net*, which is located at CSNET CIC. (There were originally two relay hosts, one on each coast, with the other at Rand, but this duplication of effort turned out not to be cost-effective [Partridge 1988].) *PhoneNet* sites run **MMDF2**, **PMDF**, or **CMDF** software. Connections are made with modems through the public telephone system, usually at 1200bps or 2400bps [CSNET CIC 1988]. The original *PhoneNet* software was Multi-channel Memo Distribution Facility (**MMDF**) [Szurkowski 1980; Crocker et al. 1979; Crocker et al. 1983]. Its current version is **MMDF2**. Pascal Memo Distribution Facility (**PMDF**) is a subset of **MMDF** and is distributed by *CSNET* to its members. C Memo Distribution Facility (**CMDF**) implements the *CSNET PhoneNet* mail transfer protocol by queuing mail to *relay.cs.net* and passing messages to and from the mail daemon **sendmail**. **CMDF** is a **UNIX** alternative to the **Pascal PMDF** system [Long 1987].

X25Net uses TCP/IP on top of X.25 [Comer and Korb 1983; Korb 1983a] and is part of the *Internet* [Landweber et al. 1986]. This service was developed at Purdue University (Purdue) and was implemented in the fall of 1982 [Comer 1983]. It was intended to allow full TCP/IP services for subscribers without a direct *ARPANET* connection [Comer 1988]. It has since also become the common method for international members to connect to *CSNET*, since they can use their local X.25 PDN to reach *Telenet* in the United States [CSNET CIC 1988; Korb 1983b]. Gatewaying to the *Internet* was previously done by *relay.cs.net* but is now done with two cisco AGS gateways [Swindell 1988].

ARPANET members have a connection to the *ARPANET* or the *Internet*. Many organizations have joined *CSNET* to increase the availability of a preexisting *ARPANET* connection. *CSNET* has permission from DARPA to permit researchers who are not working directly on government contracts to access the *ARPANET* [Rugo 1988].

Cypress is a network built from a leased line protocol of the same name, using **UNIX** systems as switching nodes [Comer and Narten 1988]. The network provides *Internet* access through gateways at Purdue and has been operational since 1985 [Rugo 1988].

Leased Lines currently provides full *Internet* connectivity to a number of *CSNET* sites, most of which are in the greater Boston area. Several link level protocols are used to support TCP/IP.

Dial-up IP has recently been introduced by *CSNET*. It is an implementation of SLIP that allows IP connections over dialup telephone links to *relay.cs.net* [Lanzillo and Partridge 1989]. All of the usual TCP/IP services are supported above IP, and mail delivery is more immediate because SMTP can be used. Users of this method of connection thus have the same services as *X25Net* sites. It is anticipated that many *PhoneNet* sites will convert to *Dial-up IP* [Lanzillo 1988]; 9600bps modems will be provided for this type of connection [Swindell 1988].

Interconnections

CSNET has adopted DNS domain syntax for all hosts, even on *CSNET PhoneNet*. The center of the *CSNET PhoneNet* star, *relay.cs.net*, a Sun Microsystems 3/60 workstation [Swindell 1988], provides domain name service and knows how to route mail messages to the *Internet*. It also advertises *MX records* for all *CSNET* hosts that are not directly accessible from the *Internet* so that hosts on either network can reach hosts on the other transparently.

History

The developers of *CSNET* noticed that electronic mail was the most popular service on the *ARPANET*. They proposed a network to provide electronic mail only and used it to connect institutions that did not have *ARPANET* access to those that did.

In May 1979, Lawrence Landweber, then chairman of the University of Wisconsin (Wisconsin) Computer Science Department, initiated discussions for the "feasibility of establishing a Computer Science Department research computer network" [Comer 1983; Landweber 1983] with representatives from NSF, DARPA, and six other institutions. There was a shortage of experienced and qualified computer science personnel at the time, especially those familiar with networking; this was caused by the recent rapid growth of the field and was similar to the situation in the United Kingdom when *JANET* was formed. A proposal was suggested to NSF for evaluation of establishing a network that would benefit schools by improving research facilities. An initial proposal was made to NSF in December 1979 [Comer 1983] but was deferred in favor of funding further study.

A planning group for this purpose met in May 1980. It consisted of representatives from 14 universities, EDUCOM, and the Rand Corporation (Rand) [Comer 1983; Landweber 1980]. Universal access by U.S. academic Computer Science Departments was desired, as was use of existing facilities wherever possible; thus use of existing *ARPANET* connections and of PDNs was wanted, but some sites would not have access to either, or would not be able to afford them, so an inexpensive dialup telephone connection method was needed. "The term *PhoneNet* came into use for the set of *CSNET* sites constituting this 'imaginary' network" [Comer 1983]. The revised proposal was submitted in October 1980 and approved in January 1981 [Barney 1982]. CSNET CIC has been operating since June 1982.

Reliable mail delivery has been a major *CSNET* service from the beginning [O'Brien and Breeden 1983; O'Brien and Long 1984]. With time, *CSNET* users began to realize that electronic mail was not enough, and *X25Net* and eventually *Dial-up IP* were developed. The network originally used old-style *ARPANET* syntax (e.g., user@host) but has completely moved to current *Internet* DNS domain name syntax [Partridge 1986].

The success of *CSNET* led to the proposal of *NSFNET* [Jennings et al. 1986] and continues to be relevant in the development of academic and research networking both in the United States and abroad [Jennings 1987].

Plans

CSNET will continue to provide reliable networking service to the scientific research community. Expanding interest in research networking is providing new growth opportunities for *CSNET*. *CSNET* is considering merging with *BITNET*, and such a merger was recommended by the *CSNET* executive committee on 19 October 1988 and by the *BITNET* board of trustees on 25 October 1988. The intent was to provide combined organization for the existing services of the two networks plus new services, thus reducing redundancy and allowing another step toward a single national research network. The plan needed approval by a vote of the *BITNET* site representatives and by the UCAR board of trustees [Breeden 1988]. This has been done, and implementation plans were being discussed in April 1989, using the name *ONEnet*.

Access
CSNET CIC
cic@sh.cs.net
+1-617-873-2777 (24 hour hotline)
10 Moulton Street
Cambridge, MA 02238
U.S.A.

11.5   *NSFNET*

NSFNET, the National Science Foundation Network, is a general purpose internet providing access to scientific computing resources, data, and information, initially organized and partly funded by the National Science Foundation (NSF). It is a three level internetwork consisting of the following levels:

- The backbone: a transcontinental network that connects separately administered and operated mid-level networks and NSF funded supercomputer centers
- Mid-level networks (three kinds): regional, discipline based, and supercomputer consortium networks [Wolff 1987a]
- Campus networks (whether academic or commercial) connected to the mid-level networks

Although originally intended specifically to connect supercomputer centers, *NSFNET* now provides other services as well [Wolff 1987a] and has in fact become the national U.S. research network, especially since the demise of *ARPANET*. It provides the general academic community with the kind of networking infrastructure that *ARPANET* provided to a few networking researchers and the kind of services that *CSNET* extended to computer science researchers in general. It uses the ideas of resource sharing, which motivated the *ARPANET*, and of collaboration among researchers, which partly grew out of the development of the *ARPANET*. The TCP/IP protocols are used on the backbone and on most of the mid-level and campus networks, and *NSFNET* is part of the *Internet*. Some of the *NSFNET* networks other than the backbone use internet and transport protocols other than IP and TCP, such as DECNET (e.g., *THEnet*) or the *MFEnet* NSP protocols. Thus, *NSFNET* is actually a metanetwork.

Administration

There is no combined administration for all three levels of the *NSFNET* internetwork hierarchy. Administration of the *NSFNET* backbone is divided functionally among several groups:

- Policy for *NSFNET* is the responsibility of the Division of Network and Communications Research and Infrastructure (DNCRI) [NSF 1986], which is part of the Computer and Information Science and Engineering Directorate (CISE) of NSF. The current director of DNCRI is Steve Wolff.

- Management and operation of the *NSFNET* backbone are the responsibility of Merit, Inc. (Merit), a nonprofit membership consortium of eight Michigan universities. Merit is located in Ann Arbor, Michigan [Braun 1988a].
- End user support to the research community is provided by a Network Information Center (NIC), the NSF Network Service Center (NNSC), at BBN Systems and Technologies Corporation (formerly BBN Laboratories) in Cambridge, Massachusetts, in a cooperative agreement with the University Corporation for Atmospheric Research (UCAR) [Roubicek 1988].

There is a Cooperative Agreement (rather than a grant or a contract) between Merit and NSF about *NSFNET*. The Project Director is Eric Aupperle, who is also Director of the *Merit* Computer Network. The Principal Investigator is Hans-Werner Braun. The Chairman of the Board of Directors of Merit, Inc., is Douglas Van Houweling, who is also Vice Provost for Information Technology at the University of Michigan. Two committees carry out the work. The Executive Committee is chaired by Douglas Van Houweling, and the Technical Committee is chaired by Hans-Werner Braun. Direct responsibility for specific areas is taken by three groups:

- Internet Engineering is headed by Hans-Werner Braun.
- A Network Operations Center (NOC), headed by Dale Johnson, provides 24-hour coverage seven days a week.
- Information Services, headed by Jim Sweeton, offers a complete set of online communications and information. In addition, a 24-hour WATS line facilitates trouble reporting and general status information delivered to mid-level and campus NOCs. The machine *nis.nsf.net* is a general document repository for the entire *NSFNET* community, permitting documents to be sent in response to queries. The program that provides online information and communications services is called **GRASP** and is a merging of IBM's **GRAND** with Stanford's production data management system **SPIRES**.

There are two IBM 4381 mainframes located on the Ann Arbor campus of the University of Michigan (Michigan): one for the NOC and one for Information Services (*nis.nsf.net*) [Braun 1988a]. Merit also sets policy and provides funding for the *Merit* Computer Network.

The Project Manager of NNSC is Richard D. Edmiston (who is also the Director of *CSNET*). He is assisted by Karen Roubicek, Director of NNSC User Services, and Craig Partridge, Director of NNSC Technical Services. The liaison from UCAR is William Curtis [Partridge 1988].

There are corresponding NOCs for some of the regional networks, and sometimes also NICs, such as the one for *NYSERNet*. There may also be campus level operations, support, and information centers. Ideally, people with questions or problems should start at their most local center and work upward only if the more local centers can't provide adequate answers. The highest level NIC and NOC help get other such centers working properly so that they can handle part of the load. However, a user who doesn't know who to call locally can call NNSC (which may redirect the user to an appropriate local center) [Partridge 1988].

Funding

Merit obtained management responsibility for *NSFNET* in November 1987 after submitting a proposal [Merit 1987a] that outlined its plan to reengineer the *NSFNET* backbone [Mills and Braun 1987]. NSF funded Merit with a five year, $14 million award for this project. The State of Michigan Strategic Fund also contributed $5 million. Merit established joint study agreements with IBM and MCI on network research and development. As part of this effort, MCI provided leased lines for the backbone and provided expertise in circuit switched technology [Hoffman 1988], while IBM provided hardware and software for the *NSFNET* backbone nodes and for network management and information services. Although funding from NSF covers part of the costs of the MCI links (as well as staffing the NOC in Ann Arbor), both MCI and IBM are contributing noticeable facilities and services to the project [Braun 1988a].

NSF funds UCAR and BBN for operation of NNSC. NSF provides initial and partial funding for many mid-level networks in hopes that they will eventually become self-supporting through participation of state or regional organizations, industry, and the university campuses that they serve [Wolff 1987b]. The expectation is that such subsidies will end after two or three years, as they did for *CSNET* [Partridge 1988].

NSFNET Backbone

The current *NSFNET* backbone connects 13 network hubs with 1.544Mbps T1 physical links, as shown in Figure 11.7. Since September 1988, each physical link has been multiplexed into three 448Kbps logical links between each pair of nodes, adding up to 1.344Mbps, which is the effective speed of a 1.544Mbps T1 link after framing is taken into account [Braun 1988a]. The packet switch nodes of the backbone are Nodal Switching Subsystems (NSS) supplied by IBM. Each NSS is composed of nine IBM RT/PCs (running an IBM version of **4.3BSD UNIX**), each connected to two token ring networks for redundancy. The NSS appears to the user as a single loosely coupled multiprocessor system [Braun 1988a]. Within each NSS a Routing

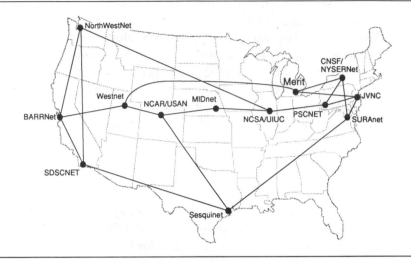

Figure 11.7. *NSFNET T-1 data network topology (8 February 1989) [Merit 1989]*

Control Processor (RCP) mediates routing information between more than one NSS. The backbone routing software at each NSS is an IBM implementation of the Intermediate System to Intermediate System (IS-IS) Intra-Domain Routing Exchange Protocol that was forwarded by ANSI to ISO for standardization. It uses the Shortest Path First (SPF) algorithm, also called link state routing protocols, as opposed to distance vector routing protocols. The IS-IS protocol is based on work done at Digital Equipment Corporation (Digital) and was selected by ANSI for intradomain routing [Braun 1988b].

Routing between the the *NSFNET* core and the mid-level networks is done via the Exterior Gateway Protocol (EGP), which was previously developed on the *Internet*.

Multiple routes through different administrations have led to the development of *policy based routing*, which is based on recognition of the autonomy of mid-level networks; communication among the managers of those networks and of the backbone; and the addition of some protection capability in the backbone to use information contributed by the mid-level networks [Rekhter 1988].

The backbone and each regional network has its own *autonomous system* number, as in the old scheme, but some new features are visible. There is the idea of *peer networks* — i.e., other backbones, such as that of *NSI* or *MILNET* for *DDN* — which are peers of the *NSFNET* backbone [Rekhter 1988; Braun 1988c; Braun 1988b]. There are also plans to replace the current version of EGP, version 2, with version 3 [Gardner and Karels 1988], which will have more sophisticated facilities [Braun 1988a]. It is hoped that EGP will eventually be replaced completely by something that also distributes much of the work to the regional gateways [Braun 1988b].

See Chapter 5 for discussions of the various routing protocols (EGP, RIP, and HELLO) and the routing daemon (**gated**).

The software controlled circuit switching equipment installed at each site is an Integrated Digital Network Exchange (IDNX), an intelligent T1 communications processor also provided by IBM. These 13 nodes interconnected by T1 trunk lines will eventually provide subrate T1 multiplexing, dynamic alternate routing, and dynamic bandwidth allocation and are controlled from the *NSFNET* NOC.

Internet DNS domains are used (although not on the backbone). NNSC runs a backup domain server for those parts of *NSFNET* that have requested it. NNSC also advises sites about the DNS protocols and installation and the use of related software [Waitzman and Karels 1988].

There is also a test and engineering network that is a ring from Merit in Ann Arbor, Michigan; to IBM Technical Computing Systems (TCS) in Milford, Connecticut; to IBM Research in Yorktown, New York; to MCI in Reston, Virginia; and back to Merit in Ann Arbor. An unusual experimental service on this test network is packet video. This encapsulates video frames in UDP datagrams for slow motion display through **X11** Release 2. There are hopes that this can be used for video conferencing by multicasting images from each participant to each of the others for display in separate windows [Braun 1988a].

Mid-Level Networks

Each *NSFNET* mid-level network has a subsection following this *NSFNET* section. Most of the information on them was taken from publications of NNSC and Merit. Some contact information was obtained from the file contacts-sites on the *Internet* host *sh.cs.net* in the directory nsfnet. These networks are listed in Table 11.2. Most are regional networks, three are supercomputer consortium networks, and one (*USAN*) is a discipline-oriented network. There is a subsection below on each of these networks. In addition, *CSNET* is now considered an *NSFNET* regional network [Partridge 1988]. There are approximately 200 institutions linked in some way to *NSFNET*.

Interconnections

In addition to the mid-level networks connected to the *NSFNET* backbone and the campus networks reachable through them, *NSFNET* also connects to *ARPANET*, *BITNET*, *CSNET*, and *UNIDATA*. *BCnet* and *CDNnet* (and thus the rest of Canada) are connected by a link from *NorthWestNet* at the

Table 11.2. *NSFNET mid-level networks*

BARRNet	San Francisco Bay Area Regional Research Network[2]
JVNCNet	John von Neumann Center Network[1]
Merit	Merit Computer Network[2]
MIDnet	Midwest Network[2]
NCSAnet	National Center for Supercomputing Applications Network[1]
NorthWestNet	Northwestern States Network[2]
NYSERNet	New York State Educational and Research Network[2]
PSCnet	Pittsburgh Supercomputer Center Network[1]
SDSCnet	San Diego Supercomputer Center Network[1]
Sesquinet	Texas Sesquicentennial Network[2]
SURAnet	Southeastern Universities Research Association Network[2]
THEnet	Texas Higher Education Network[2]
USAN	University Satellite Network[3]
WESTNET	Mountain States Network[2]

[1]Supercomputer consortium network
[2]Regional network
[3]Discipline-oriented network

University of Washington (Washington) to the University of British Columbia (UBC). A connection from Cornell to *Onet* at the University of Toronto (Toronto) was recently established. There are rumors of a connection to University College London (UCL) for *JANET* in the United Kingdom. There is a test connection to INRIA at its Sophia Antipolis location (near Nice) for *ARISTOTE*, a request for connection from *NORDUnet*, and interest from *ITESM* in Mexico and elsewhere. Mail relay methods to reach *NSFNET* are the same as for the *Internet*, of which it is a subset.

History

The history of *NSFNET* properly starts with the academic and research networking in the United States that began with *ARPANET* and continued with networks such as *THEORYNET* and *CSNET*. In mid-1984, NSF established the Office of Advanced Scientific Computing (OASC). Several reports of the NSF and National Academy of Sciences in the early 1980s summarized a growing concern over the lack of supercomputing environments (due to no network access or funding) for researchers in science and engineering. The OASC's first efforts included initiating two programs, one to develop supercomputer centers and another to build a national network that would provide access to these centers and eventually become a general purpose national academic network [Denning 1985a; Denning 1985b; Jennings et al. 1986; Landweber et al. 1986]. These programs would combine to help develop new specialized NSF supercomputer centers and support for existing centers.

The following five NSF centers were funded in 1985:

- John von Neumann Supercomputer Center (JVNC) at Princeton University
- San Diego Supercomputer Center (SDSC) on the campus of the University of California at San Diego (UCSD)
- National Center for Supercomputer Applications (NCSA) at the University of Illinois
- Theory Center, a production and experimental supercomputer center at Cornell University (Cornell)
- Pittsburgh Supercomputing Center (PSC) located in Pittsburgh and managed by Carnegie-Mellon University (CMU), Westinghouse, and the University of Pittsburgh

The initial list of planned member institutions for *NSFNET* included these supercomputer sites and the then-existing supercomputer center consortia networks (the SDSC and JVNC networks), National Center for Atmospheric Research (NCAR) satellite network sites (*USAN*), and *ARPANET* sites.

The general strategy at the beginning, or first phase, of *NSFNET* was that NSF should take advantage of these existing networks to create a "network of networks" (an internet) rather than a separate new computer network, as in the current, second phase. Agreement was reached between NSF and DARPA in October 1985 to allow mutual access by users of *ARPANET* and NSF supercomputer centers. NSF supported additional *ARPANET* connections and installation of *ARPANET* connections at the supercomputer sites. This provided an immediate high level of connectivity for supercomputer users.

Initial engineering of *NSFNET* was performed by the University of Illinois at Urbana-Champaign (UIUC) and a NOC managed by Cornell. The NNSC, involving BBN and UCAR, began at this time. BBN and some of the personnel involved were considered appropriate because of their experience providing similar services for *CSNET*. High-level technical assistance and consulting were provided by the Information Sciences Institute (ISI). "Supplemental technical and engineering services are also provided by the University of Delaware, the University of Maryland, and the University of Michigan" [NSF 1986].

The original backbone nodes consisted of Digital LSI-11/73 gateway systems with 512Kbytes of memory. The software system, called the **Fuzzball** [Mills 1988], consisted of an operating system and application programs for network protocol development, testing, and evaluation. The **Fuzzball** was used primarily as a packet switch/gateway, while the application programs were for network monitoring, management, and control.

The installation of the reengineered backbone project undertaken by Merit, IBM, and MCI for NSF took place during the winter and spring of 1988. The new backbone was operational by 1 July 1988, at a time when *NSFNET* was growing at a rate of 100 percent per year [Van Houweling 1988]. This reengineering involved the upgrade to T1 links by MCI and the replacement of the original backbone nodes' **Fuzzball** gateways with IBM NSS and IDNX nodes, as well as the addition of other sites to the *NSFNET* backbone. During the first full month of operation after the old backbone was completely dismantled, August 1988, the new *NSFNET* backbone carried twice as much traffic as the old one had in its last full month, June 1988, before any of the new backbone was in operation [Partridge 1988].

Future

Future phases of the Merit reengineering plan for *NSFNET* will include full implementation of dynamic resource allocation capabilities by March 1989. There was also a proposal for T3 capability by 1990, but no funding has yet been forthcoming. Support of ISO-OSI protocols is also expected. Perhaps *NSFNET* will become a general national higher education network [EDUCOM 1987] or will lead to a national research network [Bell 1988a; Wolff 1987a]. *NSFNET* continues to be taken into account in the thinking of those working with other national research networks, such as *DFN* in Germany [Bell 1988b] and *NRCnet* in Canada, with international networks such as *EARN*, *HEPnet*, and *EUnet*, and with international networking projects such as RARE [Jennings 1987], as well as with CCRN and FRICC.

Access

For general questions about *NSFNET*, contact NNSC:

NSF Network Service Center (NNSC)
nnsc@nnsc.nsf.net
+1-617-873-3400
BBN Systems and Technologies Corporation
10 Moulton Street
Cambridge, MA 02238
U.S.A.

NNSC publishes a free quarterly newsletter, *NSF Network News*. It also has reports and information on network operations, as well as electronic mailing lists, and it provides information through *anonymous FTP* to host *nnsc.nsf.net*: log in as user anonymous with password guest. In addition, NNSC provides information through an **Info-Server**: send mail to info-server@nnsc.nsf.net; leave the *Subject:* line blank and include two text lines:

REQUEST: NSFNET
TOPIC: HELP

For technical questions, contact Merit:

Merit Computer Network
nsfnet-info@merit.edu
800-66-MERIT (24-hour operational number)
800-666-3748 (same in real numbers)
1075 Beal Avenue
Ann Arbor, MI 48109
U.S.A.

Further network information is provided by the host *nis.nsf.net*. This includes general written network information (text and graphics) as well as network statistics.

The Merit NSFNET Information Services group publishes a monthly newsletter, *Link Letter*, providing technical information to the networking community. Subscriptions for the electronic mail version can be submitted to:

NSFNET-Linkletter-Request@Merit.EDU

For further information about *NSFNET* policies, contact:

Program Director
Division of Network and Communications Research and Infrastructure
Computer and Information Science and Engineering Directorate
National Science Foundation
1800 G Street NW
Washington, DC 20550
U.S.A.

11.5.1   NSFNET Supercomputers

The supercomputer centers currently on the *NSFNET* backbone are listed here. Most of this information was taken from *NSFNET* newsletters and *NSFNET* monthly reports.

John von Neumann Supercomputer Center (JVNC) was founded in 1985 by the Consortium for Scientific Computing located in Princeton, New Jersey. It currently has two Cyber 205 supercomputers, and plans to obtain the ETA-10 Class VII supercomputer. In addition to supercomputer resources, JVNC also provides access to its network, *JVNCNet* [Hughes 1988].

National Center for Atmospheric Research (NCAR) Scientific Computing Division (SCD) is located in Boulder, Colorado, and provides access to a Cray X-MP/48 supercomputer and a Cray-1A supercomputer. The NCAR computing facility is devoted to joint and independent projects of NCAR and various universities. These include developing and running large mathematical models that simulate natural phenomena and archiving and manipulating large data sets.

Pittsburgh Supercomputing Center (PSC) in Pittsburgh, Pennsylvania, provides supercomputer resources, network connectivity to *NSFNET*, and maintenance of *PSCnet*. PSC is a joint project of Carnegie-Mellon University (CMU) and the University of Pittsburgh and is managed by Westinghouse Electric Corporation. The supercomputer at PSC is a Cray X-MP/48 [Benton 1987].

San Diego Supercomputer Center (SDSC) is at the University of California at San Diego (UCSD) and is administered by GA Technologies, Inc. An alliance of 19 universities (in California, Hawaii, Maryland, Michigan, Utah, Washington, and Wisconsin) and six research institutions provide policy guidance. The supercomputer at SDSC is a Cray X-MP/48 running **CTSS**. There is also a Scientific Computer Systems SCS-40 minisupercomputer. Researchers can access SDSC through *SDSCnet*, which links 24 remote sites by 56Kbps terrestrial or satellite links [Love 1987].

Access
SDSC consultant
+1-619-534-5100

National Center for Supercomputer Applications (NCSA), located at the University of Illinois at Urbana-Champaign (UIUC), operates a Cray X-MP/48 supercomputer running **CTSS** and a Cray-2S/4-128 running **UNICOS**. The X-MP/48 replaced a Cray X-MP/24 in November 1986 and is expected to be converted to **UNICOS** by mid-1989. The Cray-2S/4-128 was added in October 1988 [Catlett 1988a]. Network access to NCSA is provided by *NSFNET*, *NCSAnet*, *ARPANET*, *BITNET*, *Telenet*, local HYPER-channel and ProNET networks, direct dial telephone, and T1 connections to industrial laboratories at AMOCO Corp., Motorola, Inc., Eli Lilly & Co., Eastman Kodak Co., and Cray Research, Inc. (Cray) [Catlett 1988a]. TCP/IP is implemented on the Cray machines, allowing all the usual services, such as TELNET and FTP. The Supercomputing Center Peer Review Board (PRB) comprises 12 members representing 12 institutions and makes decisions on time allocations for the supercomputer systems. The Interdisciplinary Research Center (IRC) of NCSA offers a Visitor's Program, an Academic Affiliates Program, and a Scientific Visualization Program in efforts to further the exchange of ideas and experiments among supercomputer users [Paoli 1987].

Cornell Center for Theory and Simulation in Science and Engineering (Theory Center), located in Ithaca, New York, was founded by Cornell physicist and Nobel Laureate Kenneth Wilson and was the first NSF supercomputer center opened, in May 1985. Wilson's efforts helped launch the NSF program to set up the supercomputer centers. The Theory Center offers an IBM 3090 600/E, an IBM 4381, and two FPS 164 processors at its primary supercomputing resource, the Cornell National Supercomputer Facility

(CNSF). Programs associated with the Cornell Theory Center include the Cornell Program of Computer Graphics, the Strategic User Program, the Visitor's Program, the Smart Nodes Program, and the Corporate Research Institute. The Theory Center serves as the *NSFNET* gateway for *NYSERNet*. The Theory Center's Network Information and Support Center (NISC) developed **gated**, the gateway daemon used in the *NSFNET* backbone nodes [Leary 1987].

Access

For the monthly newsletter, *ForeFronts*, contact:

Ruth Binkowski
+1-607-255-7969

11.5.2 BARRNet

The San Francisco Bay Area Regional Research Network, *BARRNet*, serves northern California as a regional internet, as shown in Figure 11.8.

Administration

BARRNet is organized under charter and member agreements with two types of members: (1) Participating Institutions (voting nonprofit educational and research organizations and government research facilities) and (2) Affiliate Institutions (other, nonvoting qualifying organizations).

Composition

The following seven sites currently compose the *BARRNet* backbone:

- NASA Ames Research Center (ARC) in Sunnyvale
- University of California at Berkeley (UCB)
- University of California at Davis
- University of California at Santa Cruz (UCSC)
- University of California at San Francisco (UCSF)
- Stanford University (Stanford) in Palo Alto
- Lawrence Livermore National Laboratory (LLNL), which joined in August 1988

Lawrence Berkeley Laboratory (LBL) and the Stanford Linear Accelerator Center (SLAC) are connected through the respective campus networks. The U.S. Geological Survey (USGS) in Menlo Park and the XEROX Palo Alto Research Center (PARC) were added as "stub" members off the backbone network in September 1988. Scheduled fall 1988 additions also included the Monterey Bay Aquarium Research Institute (Monterey,

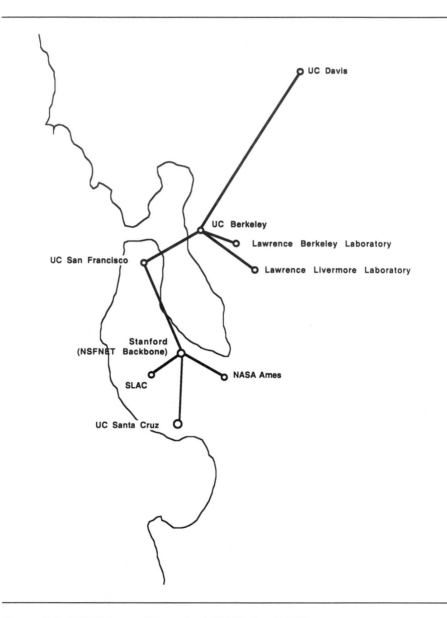

Figure 11.8. *BARRNet map (November 1988) [Catlett 1988b]*

California), Apple Computer, Hewlett-Packard Labs, 3Com, Excelan-Kinetics, and SRI [Yundt 1988].

Stanford and UCB have the two largest campus networks in *BARRNet*. The Stanford network (IP Class A network 36) has about 75 subnets, 2,000 IP hosts, and 11,000 users. More than two dozen research programs at

Stanford use *BARRNet* for remote supercomputer access [Yundt 1988]. The UCB campus network (IP Class B network 128.32) had 99 subnets and about 2,876 hosts in September 1988, with perhaps 20,000 users [Wells 1988].

Protocols

BARRNet uses TCP/IP and operates at T1 channel transmission speeds between campus networks on the backbone. Stub networks connect at either T1 or 56Kbps.

Interconnections

Since July 1988, there has been a T1 link to the new *NSFNET* backbone at Stanford. Various *BARRNet* members support other external connections. The 56Kbps *ARPANET* link at UCB continues to serve most of the University of California sites. Some *BARRNet* sites, such as Stanford, have their own *ARPANET* links [Wells 1988]. All *BARRNet* sites operate their own *UUCP* gateways. NASA ARC provides a gateway to *SPAN*. Advertising of routes to and from all external networks is managed and carefully controlled by a technical committee.

History

BARRNet was established in mid-1986 and became operational in May 1987. The first external TCP/IP link from *BARRNet* was a 56Kbps *ARPANET* link at UCB.

   BARRNet's first link to the interim *NSFNET* was a 56Kbps link between UCB and the SDSC; this link was in use between 12 February 1988 and 14 July 1988 [Wells 1988].

   BARRNet was the first regional network to provide full bandwidth T1 transmission speeds on a packet switched backbone. This was partly because of the availability of T1 facilities in northern California. More importantly, *BARRNet* chose to use full channel T1 because those planning it believed innovative uses (including new remote supercomputer applications) would be hampered at lower bandwidths. The relatively small geographical area to be covered helped make it practical [Ferrin et al. 1986; Frost 1988; Wasley 1988].

   Curiously enough, of all the *NSFNET* regionals that existed before the *NSFNET* T1 backbone transition, *BARRNet* was the last to connect to the new *NSFNET* backbone [Frost 1988].

Plans

About 15 additional sites have expressed an interest in joining, including one or more in Nevada, so substantial growth in numbers and geographic coverage is expected through 1989 [Yundt 1988].

Access

Bill Yundt
BARRNet Executive Director
gd.why@forsythe.stanford.edu
+1-415-723-3909

Tom Ferrin
BARRNet Deputy Director
tef@cgl.ucsf.edu
+1-415-476-1100

David Wasley
BARRNet Technical Director
dlw@violet.berkeley.edu

11.5.3   CICNet

CICNet, the Committee on Institutional Cooperation Network, was expected to be operational in January 1989 and to be connected to *NSFNET* as a mid-level regional network. It is a T1 (1.544Mbps) TCP/IP backbone network connecting 11 institutions of higher education in the seven U.S. midwestern states (Illinois, Indiana, Iowa, Michigan, Minnesota, Ohio, and Wisconsin) [Wolfe 1988a].

Administration

CICNet is incorporated as CICNet, Inc., with Executive Director Barbara Wolfe. There is a board of directors, consisting of one representative from each participating institution, plus the executive director of *CICNet* and the director of the Committee on Institutional Cooperation (CIC) (from which the network takes its name). The current directors and member institutions are George F. Badger, Jr., University of Illinois at Urbana-Champaign (UIUC); Alison Brown, Ohio State University; Thomas H. Brown, University of Illinois, Chicago (UIC); Daniel W. DeHayes, Indiana University (IU); Robert L. Graves, University of Chicago (UC); Fred H. Harris, University of Iowa; Paul M. Hunt, Michigan State University (MSU); V. Rama Murthy, University of Minnesota (Minnesota); Tad B. Pinkerton, University of Wisconsin, Madison (UWM); Peter G. Roll, Northwestern University (Northwestern); Douglas Van Houweling, University of Michigan (Michigan); Roger G. Clark, CIC; and Barbara B. Wolfe, executive director.

A NOC and a NIC are expected to be implemented eventually. Meanwhile, there is a *CICNet* Technical Working Group with representatives from several of the major campuses [Wolfe 1988a]. Most management will be distributed to member campuses, under the responsibility of the corresponding board member, and the *CICNet* NOC will communicate directly only with those campus NOCs and with the *NSFNET* NOC. There is a technical representative for each campus, appointed by the campus board member, and these together form the Network Technical Group (NTG). Similarly, there is a campus NIC and a campus information officer [Wolfe 1988b].

History and Plans

Planning began in 1987, and a small grant was received for that purpose from NSF on 1 July 1988, as well as commitments for funding from the above mentioned 11 institutions of higher education. Implementation of the network began in October 1988, with MCI as the long-distance carrier and Ameritech Communications Incorporated (ACI) as one of the primary business partners [Wolfe 1988a]. Requests for information for routers and for Digital Access and Cross-connect System (DACS) had been sent out and responses received by September 1988. These were evaluated by the Technical Working Group [Wolfe 1988b], and cisco routers were chosen [Wolfe 1988c]. Requests for quotation for DS1 services were also sent out, and responses were expected in that month [Wolfe 1988b].

NSF has committed $1.2 million to *CICNet* over two fiscal years [Wolfe 1988d] in the expectation that *CICNet* will be the major access medium for institutions of higher education in the seven states it reaches. As usual, NSF expects *CICNet* to become self-sufficient [Wolfe 1988a]. At the September 1988 meeting of the *CICNet* board of directors, the members set an expected figure of $60,000 from each campus over the two years of the NSF grant; this would be matched by an equal amount from NSF, for a total of $1,320,000. Participation of *CICNet* in FARNET (Federation of American Research NETworks) was approved at the same meeting [Wolfe 1988c].

Southern Illinois University (SIU) will be connected to *CICNet* by a 56Kbps link to UIUC as soon as the original 11 members are connected [Wolfe 1988c].

Access

The monthly *CICNet Bulletin* is written by Barbara Wolfe, the executive director, and distributed in both paper and electronic form.

Barbara Wolfe
Executive Director
bbwolfe@vx.acss.umn.edu
bbwolfe@umnacvx.bitnet
+1-612-633-9438
CICNet, Inc.
Room 100
2520 Broadway Drive
Lauderdale, MN 55113
U.S.A.

11.5.4   JVNCNet

JVNCNet is a consortium network that connects several supercomputers at the John von Neumann Supercomputer Center (JVNC) in Princeton, New Jersey, to seven Northeast states (New Jersey, Pennsylvania, New York, Connecticut, Rhode Island, Massachusetts, and New Hampshire). There are 24 *JVNCNet* sites. A regional research community is served directly, and an international one is served through connections to *NSFNET* and other networks [Heker 1988a].

Administration

Administration of *JVNCNet* is divided into the following functional areas [Heker 1988a]:

- *JVNCNet* Network Information Services interacts with *NSFNET* NNSC and Merit and provides telephone and electronic mail support to *JVNCNet* users.
- *JVNCNet* Operations interacts with the *NSFNET* NOC staff and provides operations support to *JVNCNet* site network organizations.
- Network Installation and Maintenance handles adding new links and keeping old ones running.
- Network Engineering measures various network performance characteristics.

Protocols

JVNCNet Phase I is the current network. It is composed of nine T1 links arranged in stars around JVNC and MIT, connected by one T1 link. Twelve 56Kbps links (including ten terrestrial and two satellite links) branch in trees from those centers, with two paths stretching between the two centers [Heker 1988a].

Interconnections

JVNCNet is connected to *ARPANET*, *BITNET*, and *TYMNET* [Brunell 1988]. A connection to *NORDUnet* was in place in late 1988 [Heker 1988b].

History

JVNCNet Phase I was the first operational version of the network.

Plans

A connection to *JANET* was expected by 28 February 1989 [Heker 1988b]. *JVNCNet* Phase II is expected to be complete in the summer of 1989. It consists of more than a dozen T1 (1.544Mbps) links arranged around endpoints

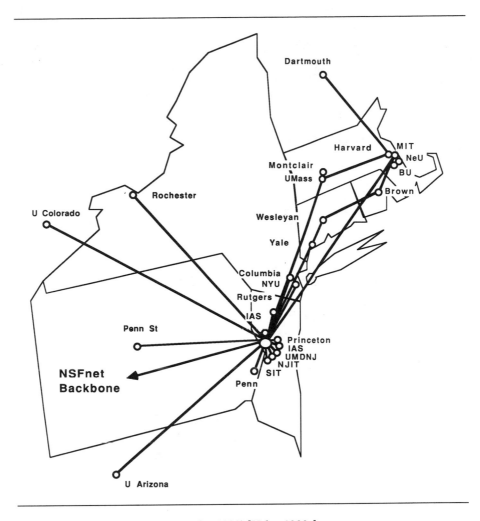

Dartmouth

MIT
NeU
Harvard
BU
Montclair
UMass
Brown
Rochester
Wesleyan
U Colorado
Yale

Columbia
NYU
Rutgers
IAS

Penn St
Princeton
IAS
UMDNJ
NJIT
SIT

NSFnet
Backbone
Penn

U Arizona

Figure 11.9. *JVNCNet map (September 1988) [Heker 1988a]*

at Boston and Philadelphia, as shown in Figure 11.9. There is a direct link
between those endpoints, a path of five links, and other, redundant links.
Connections to sites branch off these main paths in stars and trees of T1
links, with some 56Kbps leaf connections, as can be seen in Figure 11.9.
TCP/IP is used, with IGRP and RIP for internal routing protocols and EGP
for an external routing protocol [Heker 1988a]. The first planned conversions from Phase I to Phase II were for Rutgers, Stevens, UMDNJ, and NJIT,
all in March 1989 [Heker 1988b].

Access

JVNCNet NIC
JVNCNet-nic@jvnca.csc.org
+1-609-520-2000

JVNCNet Network Operations
JVNCnet-noc@jvnca.csc.org
+1-609-520-2000

Sergio Heker
heker@jvnca.csc.org
+1-609-520-2000

Doyle Knight
knight1d@jvnca.csc.org
+1-609-520-2000

11.5.5   Merit

The *Merit* Computer Network is managed by Merit, Inc. (Merit), the consortium of Michigan universities; the network is shown in Figure 11.10. It began in 1972 (with planning since 1969) as an interuniversity network for the State of Michigan and is now an *NSFNET* regional mid-level network. Initial funding was provided by NSF and the State of Michigan. The network became self-supporting after a few years by means of funding from the member universities.

Merit is not a TCP/IP network: it uses much older locally developed protocols. In addition, it provides X.25 services. IP has recently been implemented on this network, due to an NSF grant, but TCP is still under development, and network operations are supported by the Merit protocols [Braun 1988a].

By 1986, the network had grown to almost 300 nodes. Much of this growth was in the parts of the network within university campuses, such as *UMnet* at all three campuses of the University of Michigan (Michigan), *WSUnet* at Wayne State University (Wayne State), *ZOOnet* at Western Michigan University, and *MSUnet* at Michigan State University (MSU). These more local parts of *Merit* are separately funded and administered, but all use the technology developed for the Merit protocols and buy hardware for them from the University of Michigan Computing Center. The other member universities are Central Michigan University, Oakland University, Eastern Michigan University, and Michigan Technological University.

Most long-distance lines run at 9600bps, although a few digital lines are 56Kbps links, notably the one from Ann Arbor to Detroit. There are links to *Telenet* (and through it to *Datapac*) and *Autonet* (and through it to *TYMNET*) at 4800bps each [Aupperle 1987]. The *NSFNET* connection is in Ann Arbor, which is also the location of Merit's facilities for management of *NSFNET* under its cooperative agreement with NSF.

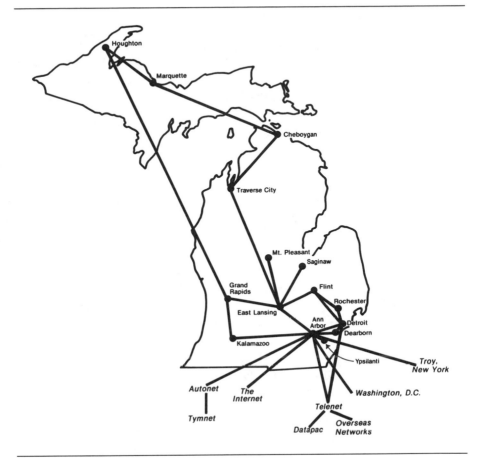

Figure 11.10. *Merit map (November 1987) [Merit 1987b]*

Access

Eric Aupperle
eaupperle@merit.edu
+1-313-764-9423

Hans-Werner Braun
hwb@mcr.umich.edu
+1-313-763-4897

For a detailed description of *Merit*, contact:

merit_computer_network@merit.edu
or
+1-313-764-9423
and provide a U.S. mail address.

See also the Merit publications listed under *NSFNET*.

11.5.6   MIDnet

MIDnet was initiated in the spring of 1985 after discussions with NSF. A formal proposal was submitted to NSF in May 1986, and the network was fully operational in September 1987 [Gale 1987]. *MIDnet* connects to the *NSFNET* backbone at the University of Nebraska, Lincoln (UNL) and at the National Center for Supercomputer Applications (NCSA) at Urbana-Champaign, Illinois. *MIDnet* has hosts at 15 midwestern universities and is arranged in a ring spanning the states of Iowa, Illinois, Missouri, Arkansas, Oklahoma, Kansas, and Nebraska, as shown in Figure 11.11. All the links are 56Kbps leased lines [Gale et al. 1988]. The common protocols are TCP/IP, although participating institutions may also support others, such as DECNET or SNA. Participating organizations are also responsible for protocol conversion.

MIDnet is governed by a board of directors consisting of an institutional representative from each of the participating institutions, plus the director of *MIDnet* [Gale 1988]. The initial director of *MIDnet* was appointed by the Principal Investigator of the original NSF startup grant, Dr. Douglas Gale of the Computing Resource Center of UNL. The initial NSF grant is for three years, after which *MIDnet* is expected to be self-supporting. The board of directors is responsible for raising funds, and member fees are currently $5,000 per year. The MIDnet Network Information Center (MID-NIC) is located at UNL and is responsible for operating and supporting the network [Gale et al. 1988].

Access

Doug Gale
doug@unlcdc3.bitnet
+1-402-472-5108

Doug Finkelson
dmf@westie.unl.edu
+1-402-472-5032

11.5.7   MRNet

MRNet, or Minnesota Regional Network, is an *NSFNET* regional network that was organized in 1987 and became operational in the spring of 1988. The TCP/IP protocols are used exclusively throughout, and the backbone is an Ethernet. It connects organizations such as Carleton College, Control Data Corporation (CDC), Cray Research, Inc. (Cray), ETA Systems, Inc. (ETA), Honeywell, the Mayo Foundation, the Minnesota Supercomputer Center, Inc. (MSC), Network Systems Corporation (NSC), St. Olaf College, the University of Minnesota (Minnesota), and 3M Corporation. These

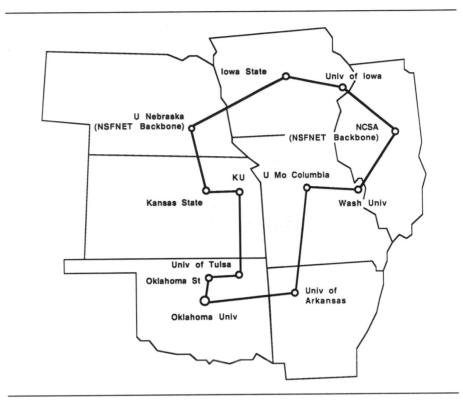

Figure 11.11. *MIDnet map (November 1988) [Catlett 1988b]*

include a large proportion of the U.S. supercomputer industry. Each of these 11 sites has one host on the backbone, and there is an additional NIC host for *MRNet* itself. There are more than a thousand hosts at the member organizations.

The network is managed by the MRNet Organization, which is currently an informal gathering of member representatives. There was an initial NSF grant, but member organizations pay dues to cover operating expenses. The current membership fees are $500 per year, and members pay for their lines directly. By January 1989, all expenses were to be paid by the member organizations [Finseth 1988].

Link speeds range from 9600bps through 56Kbps to the 10Mbps Ethernet links that connect MSC and Minnesota. *MRNet* has a 56Kbps link to the *NSFNET* backbone via UIUC. MSC also has a 56Kbps *ARPANET* link, which is available for use by *MRNet* members. The *NSFNET* and *ARPANET* links are load-shared with EGP [Finseth 1988]. There are also *BITNET* and *USENET* connections [MRNet 1988].

Access

Mahlon Stacy
Chairman
mcs@bru.mayo.edu
+1-507-284-4558
Minnesota Regional Network
c/o Mayo Foundation
Medical Sciences 1-18
Rochester, MN 55905
U.S.A.

Craig A. Finseth
fin@uf.msc.umn.edu
+1-612-624-3375
Minnesota Supercomputer Center, Inc.
1200 Washington Avenue South
Minneapolis, MN 55415
U.S.A.

11.5.8   NCSAnet

NCSAnet (National Center for Supercomputing Applications Network) is a regional network that connects to the NCSA supercomputers and to the *NSFNET* backbone; it is a mid-level network of *NSFNET* [Catlett 1988c]. There are currently ten *NCSAnet* sites in Indiana, Illinois, and Wisconsin, as shown in Figure 11.12.

There are two *NCSAnet* hubs, one at NCSA and the other at the University of Illinois, Chicago (UIC), with a T1 line between them whose costs are shared by all its users. Central management is done by NCSA, with a high level of interaction with the network staffs at UIC and UIUC [Catlett 1988d].

The hubs and the direct links to them appear as Ethernets, so users have the greatest choice of router hardware. The T1 link between hubs uses Proteon routers; the one at NCSA is also used to connect some smaller institutions. The upper layer protocols are TCP/IP [Catlett 1988d]. The NCSA hub has a T1 link to Indiana University, a 56Kbps leased line to the University of Wisconsin, Milwaukee, and a 14.4Kbps link to the Fermi National Accelerator Laboratory (FNAL). The Chicago hub has T1 connections to Northwestern University and the University of Chicago (UC) and 56Kbps links to the Argonne National Laboratory (ANL), the Illinois Institute of Technology, and the University of Notre Dame. There are plans for several more connections, such as to Purdue University (Purdue) and Bradley University [Catlett 1988a]. The *NSFNET* backbone connection is at UIUC, as are those to *MIDnet*, *MRNet*, and *ARPANET* [Catlett 1988d].

NCSA was one of the sites on the original *NSFNET* backbone [Roubicek 1988]. The first NSF grant was to UIC for connections to the UC,

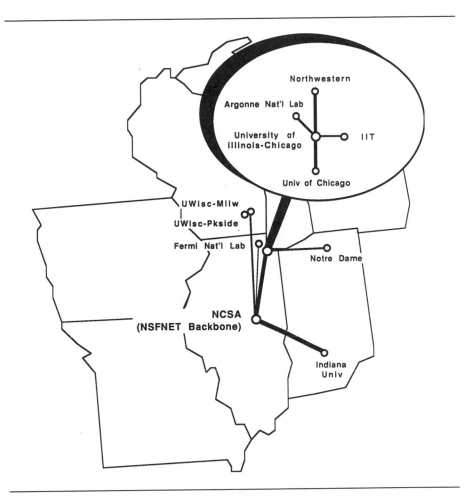

Figure 11.12. *NCSAnet map (November 1988) [Catlett 1988b]*

Northwestern University (both connected in early 1986), and Indiana University (connected in mid-1987). Near the end of the original grant, UIC and NCSA shared in the purchase of a T1 line (operational January 1988) that would allow faster access to NCSA by Chicago area universities than the 56Kbps links they were likely to pay for themselves. Some of the money saved by not having private long-distance links could then be used for faster links to the Chicago hub [Catlett 1988d].

Access

NCSAnet NIC/NOC
network@ncsa.uiuc.edu
+1-217-244-1144

Charlie Catlett
catlett@ncsa.uiuc.edu
+1-217-333-1163

Joel Replogle
replogle@ncsa.uiuc.edu
+1-217-244-0072

11.5.9   NorthWestNet

NorthWestNet received NSF approval in June or July 1987 and provides network service to the six northwestern states (North Dakota, Montana, Idaho, Washington, Oregon, and Alaska), as shown in Figure 11.13. The connection to Alaska (Fairbanks) is by satellite and makes this probably the largest *NSFNET* regional network (except for *CSNET*). The rest of the network is arranged in a loop, with 56Kbps links between the University of Oregon (UO) at Eugene, Oregon State University (ORST) in Corvallis, the Oregon Graduate Center in Beaverton, Boeing Computer Services (BCS) in Bellevue, the University of Washington (Washington) in Seattle, Washington State University (WSU) in Pullman, and the University of Idaho (Idaho) in Moscow. The remaining part of the circuit is done with 9600bps lines from Idaho to Montana State University in Bozeman, on to North Dakota State University (NSU) in Fargo, and back to UO. These latter links use Fujitsu modems for an effective rate of 19.2Kbps. All run TCP/IP over Proteon routers, which also support DECNET; two cisco routers have also been installed [Markwood 1988]. The primary connection to *NSFNET* is a T1 digital radio link from Washington to SDSC. There is a backup secondary satellite link from ORST to NCAR [Skelton 1988].

    NorthWestNet is managed by BCS, under contract to the Western Interstate Commission for Higher Education (WICHE). (BCS also has a contract with NASA to manage the NASA *PSCN* network.) There are also two committees, the management committee and the technical committee, each composed of one representative from each node [Markwood 1988]. Fees are currently $5,000 for nonprofit organizations and $25,000 for for-profit ones, of which BCS is the only one so far. BCS has also contributed a block grant of $170,000 of Cray X-MP time [Markwood 1988].

    NorthWestNet originated as a result of the collaboration of three current participants: WICHE (formed in 1955), the Northwest Academic Forum (NAF), and BCS [Markwood 1988]. *NorthWestNet* is expected to develop a nonprofit organization within three years, the Northwest

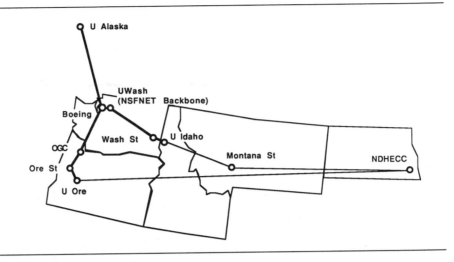

Figure 11.13. *NorthWestNet map (November 1988) [Catlett 1988b]*

Academic Computing Consortium (NWACC). NWACC is supposed to extend the facilities of *NorthWestNet* to smaller universities, undergraduate institutions, government laboratories, and commercial companies [Markwood 1988].

Access

Dick Jonsen
jonsen@colorado.bitnet
+1-303-497-0200

John Skelton
skelton@orstate.bitnet
+1-503-754-2498

Carol Olden
Olden@uwacdc.bitnet
+1-206-543-6384

Ellen Jensen
EllenJ@uwacdc.bitnet
+1-206-543-7732

11.5.10   NYSERNet

NYSERNet, Inc. (NYSERNet) was organized in 1985 as a collaborative effort of a group of universities, the State of New York, several commercial corporations, and NSF. The network it formed, *NYSERNet*, currently covers New York State with a T1 backbone infrastructure and reaches certain areas in neighboring states with 9600Kbps and 56Kbps links. There were 27 sites connected in August 1988, as shown in Figure 11.14 [Schoffstall 1988].

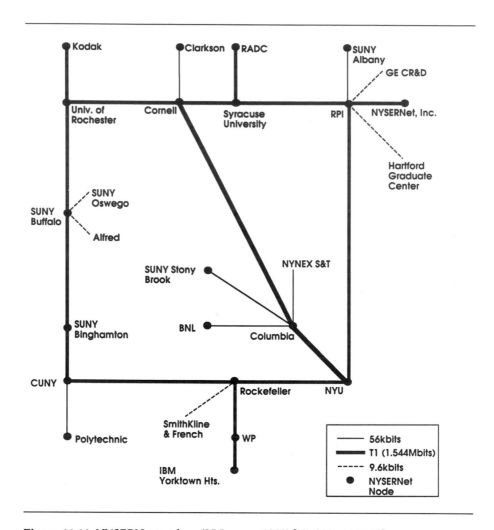

Figure 11.14. *NYSERNet topology (25 January 1989) [NYSERNet 1989]*

Users can obtain information from *NYSERNet* Network Information and Support Center (NYSERNISC) at host *nisc.nyser.net*. NYSERNet has a monthly newsletter, *NYSERNet News* [NYSERNet 1988a; NYSERNet 1988b] and a quarterly technical meeting, as well as user and site consulting [Schoffstall 1988]. In addition to the usual TCP/IP services, *NYSERNet* is working on electronic library access protocols and is encouraging institutions that can provide network services to join. Current members with such services include the Cornell National Supercomputer Center and the NorthEast Parallel Architecture Center.

NYSERNet was heavily involved [NYSERNet 1988c] in the development of the TCP/IP management protocol Simple Gateway Monitoring Protocol (SGMP) [Davin et al. 1987] and its successor, the current standard, Simple Network Management Protocol (SNMP) [Case et al. 1988]. NYSERNet implemented both network monitoring protocols and distributes Network Management Station (NMS) for them [Fedor et al. 1988].

There are direct links to both *ARPANET* and *NSFNET*, and *NYSERNet* is an *NSFNET* mid-level regional network. A principal gateway between *NSFNET* and *BITNET* is *cunyvm.cuny.edu*, the root of the *BITNET* tree.

Access
NYSERNISC
info@nisc.nyser.net
nisc@nisc.nyser.net
+1-518-283-8860

Martin Lee Schoffstall
schoff@nisc.nyser.net
+1-518-283-8860

William L. Schrader
wls@nisc.nyser.net
+1-518-283-8860

11.5.11   OARnet

OARnet, the Ohio Academic Resources Network, is a general purpose regional network that connects most of the academic institutions in the state of Ohio [Brown 1988]. Uses include library access, collaborative research, and supercomputer access. Ohio information resources to be connected to *OARnet* include Online Computer Library Catalog (OCLC), Chemical Abstracts, and Meade Data (Lexis). Other *OARnet* organizations include Battelle Memorial Institute and NASA Lewis.

Administration

OARnet is currently unincorporated, and its administrative structure is part of the Ohio Supercomputer Center (OSC), having the same board of governors.

There is a NOC and a NIC, both run by Ohio State University (Ohio State). The NOC operates 24 hours a day and seven days a week, while the NIC has somewhat more restricted hours. Operational policies are determined by a Statewide Network Users' Council (SNUC) with representatives from each campus and three standing committees: a technical committee (OARtech), which provides engineering advice and assistance to the NOC; an operations committee, which reviews NOC and NIC services; and a policy committee, which makes recommendations on acceptable use and other such issues.

Funding

State schools with supercomputer users are provided free connections through a state agency. Some private schools have been provided free connections by NSF, which also funds the connection between *OARnet* and the *Internet*. Most funding for network operations is provided by the Ohio Board of Regents as part of the budget for OSC.

Protocols

Most *OARnet* links are 56Kbps connected with Proteon routers. Three protocols are supported: TCP/IP, DECNET, and NJE. The preferred protocol suite of the *OARnet* community is ISO-OSI, with TCP/IP being the appropriate migration path for nodes currently using DECNET and NJE. The connection between *OARnet* and the *Internet* is through a T1 1.544Mbps link to *CICNet*.

History

OARnet was originally conceived as a high-speed access network for OSC and was operational in the summer of 1987. The first nodes unrelated to supercomputer access were connected 18 months later.

> **Access**
> OARnet NIC/NOC
> info@nisc.oar.net
> +1-614-292-9248
>
> Alison Brown
> Ohio Supercomputer Center
> 1224 Kinnear Road
> Columbus, OH 43212
> U.S.A.

11.5.12   PSCnet

PSCnet is the network of the Pittsburgh Supercomputing Center (PSC). It connects to sites in Pennsylvania and also in Michigan, Oklahoma, and Maryland, as shown in Figure 11.15.

> **Access**
> Jim Ellis
> ellis@morgul.psc.edu
> +1-412-268-4960
>
> Eugene Hastings
> eugene.hastings@morgul.psc.edu
> +1-412-268-4960

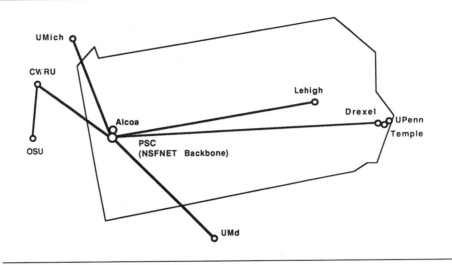

Figure 11.15. *PSCnet map (November 1988) [Catlett 1988b]*

Mike Levine
levine@morgul.psc.edu
+1-412-268-4960

11.5.13   SDSCnet

SDSCnet is the consortium network of the San Diego Supercomputer Center (SDSC) and is modeled after *MFEnet*. *SDSCnet* is connected to *MFEnet*, *HEPnet*, *SPAN*, *BITNET*, and *TYMNET*. *SDSCnet* nodes use mostly 56Kbps terrestrial and satellite links centered on SDSC, as shown in Figure 11.16.

The first *SDSCnet* link was put in place in January 1986, shortly after the Cray X-MP to which it connected arrived. The *MFEnet* NSP protocols were used because they were well known at SDSC, due to its involvement in *MFEnet*. There have also been some TCP/IP and DECNET connections. The maximum number of sites was about two dozen, but this has since decreased as some have moved to other *NSFNET* regionals that support TCP/IP. *SDSCnet* itself now supports migration paths for other protocol suites, providing TCP/IP TELNET and client and server FTP service, as well as DECNET *SET HOST* remote login service on the Cray. The X11 windowing system is the most recent addition to the network. Eventual ISO-OSI migration is expected [Maisel and Love 1988].

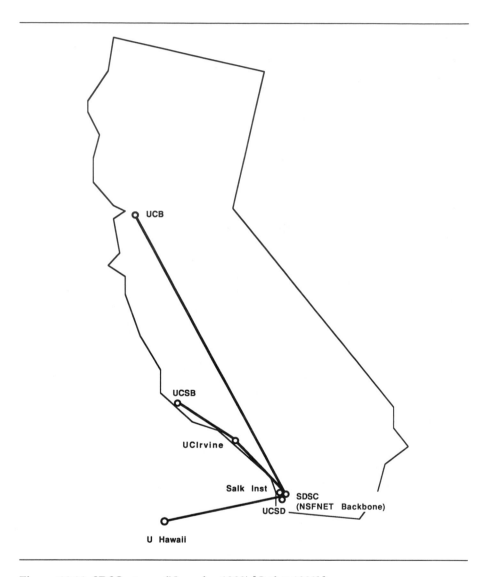

Figure 11.16. *SDSCnet map (November 1988) [Catlett 1988b]*

Access

Paul Love
loveep@sds.sdsc.edu
+1-619-534-5043

Fred McClain
mcclain@sds.sdsc.edu
+1-619-534-5045

11.5.14   Sesquinet

The Texas Sesquicentennial Network, *Sesquinet*, connects research sites in Texas to each other and to the *NSFNET* backbone, using TCP/IP. It has six nodes at research institutions, primarily in the Houston area, as shown in Figure 11.17. It is currently preparing a proposal to expand the network to include the entire state of Texas; 15 total sites were expected by the end of 1988 [Almes 1988]. Policy for *Sesquinet* is established by a steering committee chaired by Guy Almes of Rice University (Rice) [Almes 1987].

Sesquinet uses cisco AGS systems connected via 56Kbps leased lines. One external gateway connects to the *ARPANET*. *Sesquinet* connects to the *NSFNET* backbone by a link between this gateway and NCAR [Almes 1987]. There are plans for upgrading links to T1 or to 448Kbps speeds (the latter by multiplexing DS1 circuits) and for a connection to the *NSN* (NASA Science Network) in 1989 [Almes 1988].

In 1986, Rice proposed an *ARPANET* connection for its campus network, to be funded by NSF; this was granted and implemented. The proposal for *Sesquinet* was made in the same year (the one hundred fiftieth anniversary of the founding of the Republic of Texas; hence the name) by a group of mainly Houston area research institutions. It was approved by NSF in the spring of 1987 and implemented that summer [Almes 1987].

Access

Guy Almes
almes@rice.edu
+1-713-527-6038

Farrell Gerbode
farrell@rice.edu
+1-713-527-4005

11.5.15   SURAnet

SURAnet, or Southeastern Universities Research Association Network, connects the 12 southeastern states of Maryland, Virginia, West Virginia, Kentucky, Tennessee, Alabama, Mississippi, Louisiana, Florida, Georgia, South Carolina, and North Carolina, plus the District of Columbia, as shown in Figure 11.18. It is has been operational since 1987 and is a network project of the Southeastern Universities Research Association (SURA), an association of 35 research universities in the southeastern United States. *SURAnet* is managed by Glenn Ricart, Henry Schaffer, and Morty Taragin, the principal authors of the original proposal to NSF for a 60Mbps network in the early 1980s. SURA's computer committee is known as the Network Committee. *SURAnet* provides access to supercomputers at the University of

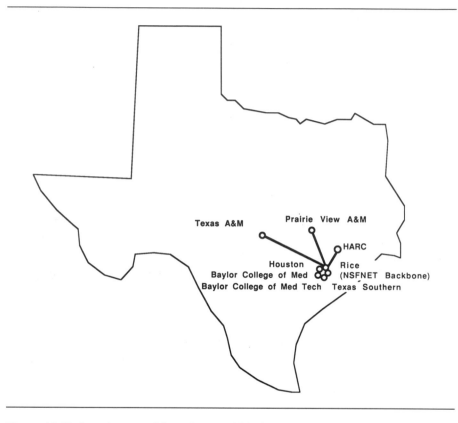

Figure 11.17. *Sesquinet map (November 1988) [Catlett 1988b]*

Georgia (UGA), Florida State University (FSU), Virginia Tech, and the University of Alabama.

Access

Dr. Jack Hahn
hahn@umdc.umd.edu
+1-301-454-5434

Glenn Ricart
glenn@umd5.umd.edu
+1-301-454-4323

Computer Science Center
University of Maryland
College Park, MD 20742
U.S.A.

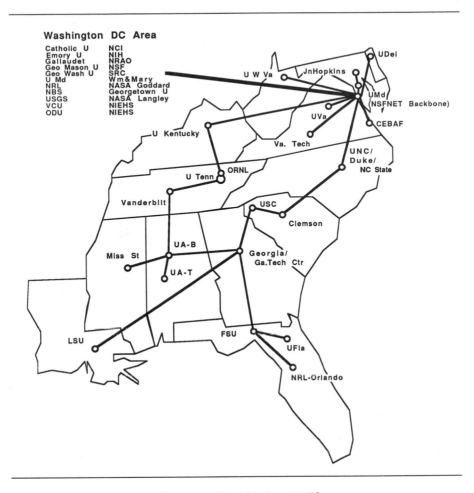

Figure 11.18. *SURAnet map (November 1988) [Catlett 1988b]*

11.5.16 THEnet

THEnet, the Texas Higher Education Network, is a state network with several thousand hosts at more than 40 academic, medical, research, and corporate institutions in Texas, as shown in Figure 11.19 [LaQuey 1988a]. There is a backbone, consisting of Digital and cisco routers connected with 9600bps and 56Kbps leased lines [LaQuey 1988b]. Many (about 950) of the hosts use DECNET. Others, particularly in the campus networks, use TCP/IP. *THEnet* has been an *NSFNET* mid-level regional network since April 1988 [LaQuey 1988a].

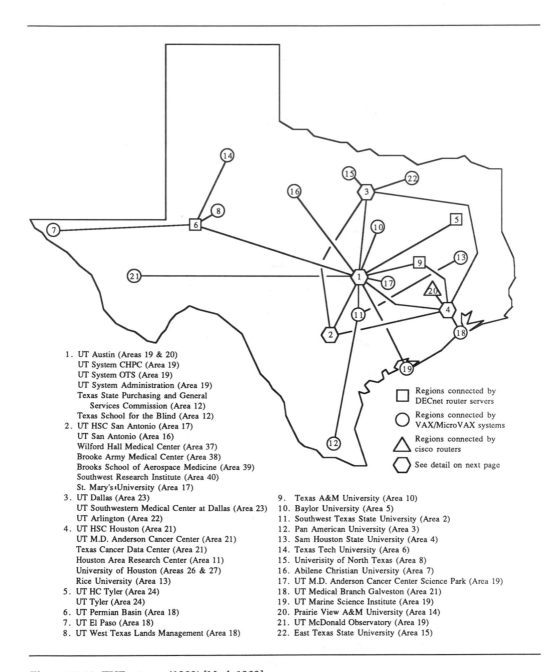

1. UT Austin (Areas 19 & 20)
   UT System CHPC (Area 19)
   UT System OTS (Area 19)
   UT System Administration (Area 19)
   Texas State Purchasing and General
     Services Commission (Area 12)
   Texas School for the Blind (Area 12)
2. UT HSC San Antonio (Area 17)
   UT San Antonio (Area 16)
   Wilford Hall Medical Center (Area 37)
   Brooke Army Medical Center (Area 38)
   Brooks School of Aerospace Medicine (Area 39)
   Southwest Research Institute (Area 40)
   St. Mary's University (Area 17)
3. UT Dallas (Area 23)
   UT Southwestern Medical Center at Dallas (Area 23)
   UT Arlington (Area 22)
4. UT HSC Houston (Area 21)
   UT M.D. Anderson Cancer Center (Area 21)
   Texas Cancer Data Center (Area 21)
   Houston Area Research Center (Area 11)
   University of Houston (Areas 26 & 27)
   Rice University (Area 13)
5. UT HC Tyler (Area 24)
   UT Tyler (Area 24)
6. UT Permian Basin (Area 18)
7. UT El Paso (Area 18)
8. UT West Texas Lands Management (Area 18)

9. Texas A&M University (Area 10)
10. Baylor University (Area 5)
11. Southwest Texas State University (Area 2)
12. Pan American University (Area 3)
13. Sam Houston State University (Area 4)
14. Texas Tech University (Area 6)
15. Univeristy of North Texas (Area 8)
16. Abilene Christian University (Area 7)
17. UT M.D. Anderson Cancer Center Science Park (Area 19)
18. UT Medical Branch Galveston (Area 21)
19. UT Marine Science Institute (Area 19)
20. Prairie View A&M University (Area 14)
21. UT McDonald Observatory (Area 19)
22. East Texas State University (Area 15)

□ Regions connected by DECnet router servers

○ Regions connected by VAX/MicroVAX systems

△ Regions connected by cisco routers

⬡ See detail on next page

Figure 11.19. *THEnet map (1989) [Nash 1989]*

Administration and Funding

The network is administered by the Office of Telecommunication Services of the University of Texas (Texas) System. Each organization connected to *THEnet* is responsible for its own network and communication expenses. The UT System provides the backbone for the network.

History

THEnet evolved out of three main projects. In 1984, the University of Houston and Texas A&M University established a 9600bps DECNET link between their two institutions. At the same time, but independent of this project, the University of Texas Health Science Center (UTHSC) at San Antonio established DECNET connections to the other UT System medical institutions and to the University of Texas at Austin. The third project, the creation of the *UTSN* (University of Texas System Network) in 1986, provided access to a Cray X-MP/24 supercomputer located at the UT System Center for High Performance Computing (CHPC) in Austin. The *UTSN* forms a backbone to which other institutions of higher education in Texas can connect. Access to other networks besides *THEnet* (the *Internet*, *NSFNET*, *BITNET*, *CSNET*, and *SPAN*) is also provided.

Access

Stuart Vance
stuart@thenic.the.net

Tracy LaQuey
tracy@thenic.the.net

THEnet Network Information Center
+1-512-471-2444
Office of Telecommunication Services
University of Texas System
Balcones Research Center
10100 Burnet Road
Austin, TX 78758-4497
U.S.A.

11.5.17 USAN

USAN, the University Satellite Network, connects eight universities to NCAR via KU-band satellite links that use Very Small Aperture Terminal (VSAT) technology. These institutions, shown in Figure 11.20, are the University of Maryland (Maryland), the University of Miami, the University of Michigan (Michigan), Oregon State University, the University of Wisconsin (Wisconsin), the Institute for Naval Oceanography, the Naval Research Laboratory, and Woods Hole Oceanographic Institute [Choy 1988]. The nominal speeds are 56Kbps to NCAR and 224Kbps in the broadcasts to each

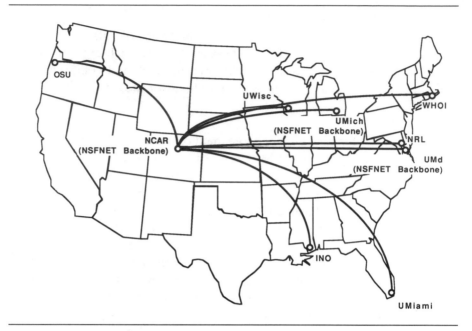

Figure 11.20. *USAN map (November 1988) [Catlett 1988b]*

of the sites [Braun 1988a]. File transfers from NCAR to the seven remote sites have been measured at up to 70Kbps; transfers from the remote sites to NCAR have been measured at up to 45Kbps [NNSC 1988b].

NCAR is part of the *NSN* and also has 9600bps links to *BITNET* and *SPAN*. NCAR supports a *SPAN* and *Internet* gateway that translates remote login, file transfer, and mail between DECNET and TCP/IP.

Splitting of *UCARnet* and *USAN* was implemented in 1987. In 1987, the NCAR SCD provided approximately 650 academic researchers and 350 NCAR researchers with supercomputer access by means of the *Internet* to the computing facility at NCAR. An unusual service is **UNIDATA**, a UCAR software package that is used by the atmospheric sciences community to provide weather data and other services. It is widely used over *NSFNET* and has users on other parts of the *Internet*.

Access

Joe Choy
choy@windom.ucar.edu

11.5.18   WESTNET

WESTNET extends to the five mountain states of Colorado, New Mexico, Arizona, Utah, and Wyoming [Burns and Wood 1988], with 16 academic sites, as shown in Figure 11.21. There are also four industrial sites, including New Mexico Technet (NMT), Los Alamos National Laboratory (LANL), the Air Force Weapons Laboratory, and Ford Aerospace. Potential nodes include the Idaho National Engineering Laboratory and several in Colorado, New Mexico, and Arizona.

This is a TCP/IP internet, using cisco routers to connect the long-haul links, which are mostly 56Kbps. State networking activity is burgeoning in this region, and *WESTNET* connects many such efforts, such as:

> *NMT* (New Mexico Technet), a TCP/IP and DECNET optical fiber network extending throughout the Rio Grande valley, founded in 1983 as a nonprofit corporation, and funded by NSF, DoE, and the State of New Mexico. It supports the state government as well as academic institutions and the national research laboratories LANL and Sandia National Laboratory (SNL) [Burns and Wood 1988].
>
> **Access**
> Marlin Mackey
> Director, NMT
> irwin@unmb.bitnet
>
> *CSN* (Colorado SuperNet), a 56Kbps TCP/IP network established in 1986 as a nonprofit corporation by the Colorado Advanced Technology Institute (CATI) and connecting many universities in Colorado [Burns and Wood 1988].
>
> **Access**
> Ken Klingenstein
> Director, CSN
> kjk@spot.colorado.edu

WESTNET connections to these state networks permit traffic to go directly between them without going over the *NSFNET* backbone. This reduces the hop count and helps avoid congestion. Such regional networking activity may lead to coordination of the funding that will be needed when the NSF start-up grant expires after three years from the original grant, which was received in March 1988. Most of the universities were actually connected to the *NSFNET* backbone before that: universities in Colorado since the fall of 1986; the University of Wyoming since the fall of 1987; New Mexico universities since the winter of 1988; Arizona and Utah since April 1988. There is

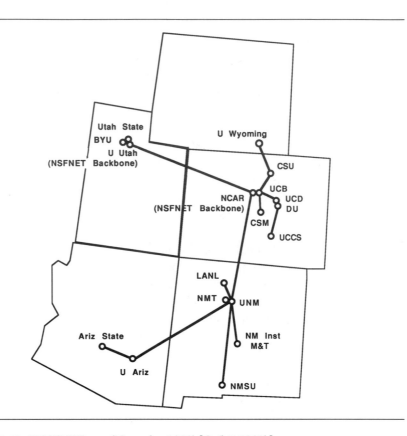

Figure 11.21. *WESTNET map (November 1988) [Catlett 1988b]*

no gateway to *HEPnet* at LANL; apparently the DECNET and TCP/IP networks there are separate. However, the University of Arizona (UA) in Tucson and the University of Colorado at Boulder (Boulder) are also on *JVNCNet*, and the University of Utah (UU) is on *SDSCnet* [Burns and Wood 1988].

There are currently two *NSFNET* connections. The primary one is from UU in Salt Lake City, for Utah and Arizona. UU has an IBM NSS connected to the *NSFNET* backbone with T1 links to NCAR, to the University of Washington (Washington) for *NorthWestNet*, and to *NYSERNet*. This NSS is also connected to a cisco router, which has three 56Kbps serial ports, one to Brigham Young University (BYU) in Provo, Utah, one to Utah State in Logan, Utah, and one to UA. The secondary *NSFNET* connection is a T1 link from NCAR in Boulder, Colorado, to UCB for Colorado, New Mexico, and Wyoming [Burns 1988].

Access

Pat Burns
pburns@csupwb.colostate.edu
+1-303-491-1575

David C. M. Wood
dcmwood@spot.colorado.edu
+1-303-492-4905

11.6   *References*

Almes 1987. Almes, Guy, "SESQUINET," *NSF Network News*, no. 2, p. 5, NNSC, Cambridge, MA, November 1987.

Almes 1988. Almes, Guy, Personal communications, 29 August 1988.

Armstrong 1988a. Armstrong, K., Personal communications, 23 November 1988, 6 December 1988.

Armstrong 1988b. Armstrong, K., "Responses to Questionnaire," CERFnet, San Diego, 17 October 1988.

Aupperle 1987. Aupperle, Eric M., "Merit: Michigan's Universities' Computer Network," Merit, Ann Arbor, MI, November 1987.

Barney 1982. Barney, Clifford, "CSNET Unites Computer Scientists," *Electronics*, IEEE, New York, 20 October 1982.

BBN 1988. BBN, "MILNET and ARPANET Maps," BBN, Cambridge, MA, 31 January 1988.

Bell 1988a. Bell, C. Gordon, "Gordon Bell calls for a U.S. research network," *IEEE Spectrum*, vol. 25, no. 2, pp. 54 – 57, February 1988.

Bell 1988b. Bell, C. Gordon, "Für ein amerikanisches Forschungsnetz," *DFN Mitteilungen*, no. 12, pp. 8 – 12, June 1988.

Benton 1987. Benton, Vivian M., "The Pittsburgh Supercomputing Center," *NSF Network News*, no. 1, p. 3, NNSC, Cambridge, MA, July 1987.

Braun 1988a. Braun, Hans-Werner, Personal communications, September 1988.

Braun 1988b. Braun, Hans-Werner, "The NSFNET Routing Architecture," Merit, Ann Arbor, MI, 24 April 1988.

Braun 1988c. Braun, Hans-Werner, "NSFNET Inter Autonomous Domain Routing," Merit, Ann Arbor, MI, 9 September 1988.

Breeden 1988. Breeden, Laura, "CSNET Executive Committee, BITNET Board Approve Network Merger," *CSNET-FORUM Digest*, vol. 4, no. 6, 10 November 1988.

Brescia 1988. Brescia, Mike, Personal communications, September 1988.

Brown 1988. Brown, Alison, Personal communications, November 1988.

Brunell 1988. Brunell, Mats, "NORDUNET and the NORDUnet network," NORDUNET, September 1988.

Burns 1988. Burns, Pat, Personal communications, September 1988.

Burns and Wood 1988. Burns, Pat, and Wood, C. M., "WESTNET," *NSF Network News*, no. 4, pp. 3, 4 – 5, NNSC, Cambridge, MA, June 1988.

Case et al. 1988. Case, J., Fedor, M., Schoffstall, M., and Davin, J., "A Simple Network Management Protocol; RFC1067," *ARPANET Working Group Requests for Comments*, August 1988.

Catlett 1988a. Catlett, Charlie, Personal communications, 23 September 1988.

Catlett 1988b. Catlett, Charlie, "NSFNET Regional Network Maps," National Center for Supercomputing Applications, Urbana-Champaign, Illinois, November 1988.

Catlett 1988c.   Catlett, Charlie, "The NSFnet: Beginnings of a National Research Internet," *Academic Computing*, December 1988.

Catlett 1988d.   Catlett, Charlie, "NCSAnet," *NSF Network News*, no. 4, pp. 3, 8–9, NNSC, Cambridge, MA, June 1988.

CERFnet 1988.   CERFnet, "The California Education and Research Federation," CERFnet, San Diego, October 1988.

Cerf and Cain 1983.   Cerf, Vinton G., and Cain, Edward, "The DoD Internet Architecture Model," *Computer Networks*, vol. 7, no. 5, pp. 307–318, October 1983.

Choy 1988.   Choy, Joe, Personal communications, September 1988.

Comer 1983.   Comer, Douglas, "The Computer Science Research Network CSNET: A History and Status Report," *Communications of the ACM*, vol. 26, no. 10, pp. 747–753, October 1983.

Comer 1988.   Comer, Douglas, *Internetworking with TCP/IP Principles, Protocols, and Architecture*, Prentice-Hall, Englewood Cliffs, NJ, 1988.

Comer and Korb 1983.   Comer, Douglas, and Korb, John T., "CSNET Protocol Software: The IP-to-X.25 Interface," *Communications Architectures & Protocols SIGCOMM '83 Symposium (March 1983)*, pp. 154–159, ACM SIGCOMM, New York, 1983.

Comer and Narten 1988.   Comer, Douglas, and Narten, Thomas, "UNIX Systems as Cypress Implets," *Proceedings of the Winter 1988 USENIX Conference (Dallas, Texas, 9–12 February 1988)*, pp. 55–62, USENIX Association, Berkeley, CA, 1988.

Crocker et al. 1983.   Crocker, D.H., Reilly, G.B., and Farber, D.J., "MMDF—An Inter-Network Memo Distribution Facility," *Digest of Papers from the IEEE Computer Society International Conference (26th COMPCON, March 1983)*, pp. 314–315, IEEE Computer Society Press, New York, 1983.

Crocker et al. 1979.   Crocker, D.H., Szurkowski, E.S., and Farber, D.J., "An Internetwork Memo Distribution Capability—MMDF," *Proceedings of the Sixth Data Communications Symposium (November 1979)*, IEEE, New York, 1979.

CSNET 1985.   CSNET, "Fourth Anniversary Issue," *CSNET News*, no. 8, Summer 1985.

CSNET CIC 1988.   CSNET CIC, "Profile: CSNET—The Computer Science Network," *ConneXions—The Interoperability Report*, vol. 2, no. 3, pp. 8–11, Advanced Computing Environments, Mountain View, CA, March 1988.

CSNET CIC 1989.   CSNET CIC, "CSNET Map," CSNET CIC, Cambridge, MA, 15 December 1989.

Davin et al. 1987.   Davin, J., Case, J., Fedor, M., and Schoffstall, M., "A Simple Gateway Monitoring Protocol; RFC1028," *ARPANET Working Group Requests for Comments*, November 1987.

Denning 1985a.   Denning, Peter J., "The Science of Computing: Computer Networks," *American Scientist*, vol. 73, no. 2, pp. 127–129, March/April 1985.

Denning 1985b.   Denning, Peter J., "The Science of Computing: Supernetworks," *American Scientist*, vol. 73, no. 3, pp. 225–227, May–June 1985.

Denning et al. 1983.   Denning, Peter J., Hearn, Anthony C., and Kern, C. William, "History and Overview of CSNET," *Proceedings of the SIGCOMM '83 Symposium (March 1983)*, pp. 138–145, ACM SIGCOMM, New York, 1983.

Edmiston 1983.   Edmiston, Richard D., "An Overview of the Computer Science Network (CSNET)," *Digest of Papers from the IEEE Computer Society International Conference (26th COMPCON, March 1983)*, pp. 310–313, IEEE Computer Society Press, New York, 1983.

EDUCOM 1987.   EDUCOM, "A National Higher Education Network: Issues and Opportunities," Educom Networking and Telecommunications Task Force (NTTF Paper Number 1), May 1987.

Fedor et al. 1988.   Fedor, Mark S., Schoffstall, Martin Lee, and Yeong, Wengyik, *SNMP: Network Management Station (NMS) and Agent/Server Implementation; Version 3.0*, NYSERNet, Inc., Troy, NY, 1988.

Ferrin et al. 1986.   Ferrin, Tom, Wasley, David, and Yundt, William, "The Northern California Regional Research Network," proposal to the National Science Foundation (Robert L. Street, Principal Investigator), March 1986.

Finseth 1988.   Finseth, Craig A., Personal communications, November 1988.

Fox 1982.   Fox, T., "Amateur Packet Radio Link Layer Protocol AX.25," American Radio Relay League, 1982.

Frost 1988.   Frost, Cliff, "NSFNet change(d)," *NETGROUP@violet.berkeley.edu*, BARRNet, Berkeley, CA, 21 July 1988.

Gale 1987.   Gale, Doug, "MIDNET," *NSF Network News*, no. 3, p. 5, NNSC, Cambridge, MA, November 1987.

Gale 1988.   Gale, Doug, Personal communications, 30 August 1988.

Gale et al. 1988.   Gale, D. S., Finkelson, D., Kutish, G., Meyer, M., Farnham, C., and Fluehr, D., "MIDnet 1986 & 1987 Annual Report," Computing Resource Center, University of Nebraska-Lincoln, January 1988.

Gardner and Karels 1988.   Gardner, Marianne L., and Karels, Mike, "Exterior Gateway Protocol, Version 3, Revisions and Extensions; IDEA009," *Internet Working Group IDEAs*, February 1988.

Heker 1988a.   Heker, Sergio, "Regional Networks: JVNCNet Phase II," *Proceedings of the TCP/IP Interoperability Conference (Santa Clara, California, 26 – 30 September 1988)*, ACE, Mountain View, CA, 1988.

Heker 1988b.   Heker, Sergio, Personal communications, 18 January 1988.

Hoffman 1988.   Hoffman, Ellen, "Physical connections for NSFNET backbone ready for operation," *Link Letter*, vol. 1, no. 3, p. 1, Merit, Ann Arbor, MI, 30 April 1988.

Hughes 1988.   Hughes, Heidi, "The John von Neumann Supercomputer Center," *NSF Network News*, no. 3, p. 4, NNSC, Cambridge, MA, March 1988.

IEEE 1978.   IEEE, *IEEE Proceedings*, IEEE, New York, November 1978. A special issue on packet switching that contains a number of classic papers.

ISI 1988.   ISI, "The Los Nettos Status Report," Information Sciences Institute, Marina del Rey, CA, 17 August 1988.

Jennings 1987.   Jennings, Dennis M., "Computing the best for Europe," *Nature*, vol. 329, no. 29, pp. 775 – 778, October 1987.

Jennings et al. 1986.   Jennings, Dennis M., Landweber, Lawrence H., Fuchs, Ira H., Farber, David J., and Adrion, W. Richards, "Computer Networking for Scientists," *Science*, vol. 231, no. 4741, pp. 943 – 950, 28 February 1986.

Kahn 1975.   Kahn, R. E., "The Organization of Computer Resources in a Packet Radio Network," *Proceedings of the National Computer Conference (May 1975)*, pp. 177 – 186, AFIPS Press, Montvale, NJ, 1975.

Karn 1985a.   Karn, P., "TCP/IP: A Proposal for Amateur Packet Radio Levels 4 and 3," *Proceedings of the Fourth ARRL ARCNC*, 1985.

Karn 1985b.   Karn, P., "Addressing and Routing Issues in Amateur Packet Radio," *Proceedings of the Fourth ARRL ARCNC*, 1985.

Karn 1987.   Karn, P., "The KA9Q Internet (TCP/IP) Package: A Progress Report," *Proceedings of the Sixth ARRL ARCNC*, 1987.

Karn 1988a.   Karn, Phil, "Amateur Packet Radio and TCP/IP," *ConneXions — The Interoperability Report*, vol. 2, no. 9, pp. 8 – 15, Advanced Computing Environments, Mountain View, CA, September 1988.

Karn 1988b.   Karn, Phil, "Improving your TCP: 'Karn's Algorithm'," *ConneXions — The Interoperability Report*, vol. 2, no. 10, p. 23, Advanced Computing Environments, Mountain View, CA, October 1988.

Karn 1988c.   Karn, Phil, Personal communications, 5 December 1988.

Karn et al. 1985.   Karn, P., Price, H., and Diersing, R., "Packet radio in the Amateur Service," *IEEE Journal on Selected Areas in Communications*, vol. SAC-3, no. 3, pp. 431–439, May 1985.

Klemba 1985.   Klemba, Keith S., "The Packet Radio Project Final Report," SRI International, Menlo Park, CA, 2 January 1985.

Korb 1983a.   Korb, J.T., "A Standard for the Transmission of IP Datagrams Over Public Data Networks; RFC877," *ARPANET Working Group Requests for Comments*, September 1983.

Korb 1983b.   Korb, J.T., "Public Network Interconnection in CSNET," *Digest of Papers from the IEEE Computer Society International Conference (26th COMPCON, March 1983)*, pp. 318–319, IEEE Computer Society Press, New York, 1983.

Landweber 1980.   Landweber, Lawrence H., "CSNET, The Computer Science Research Network," proposal to the National Science Foundation, September 1980.

Landweber 1982.   Landweber, Lawrence H., "Use of Multiple Networks in CSNET," *CSNET Design Notes*, no. DN-1, 1982.

Landweber 1983.   Landweber, Lawrence H., "The Computer Science Network: History, Status, and Future," *Computer Compacts*, vol. 1, no. 1, pp. 9–13, North-Holland, Amsterdam, February 1983.

Landweber et al. 1986.   Landweber, Lawrence H., Jennings, Dennis M., and Fuchs, Ira, "Research Computer Networks and Their Interconnnection," *IEEE Communications*, vol. 24, no. 6, pp. 5–17, June 1986.

Landweber et al. 1983a.   Landweber, L.H., Litzkow, M., Neuhagen, D., and Solomon, M., "The CSNET Name Server (Extended Abstract)," *Digest of Papers from the IEEE Computer Society International Conference (26th COMPCON, March 1983)*, pp. 316–317, IEEE Computer Society Press, New York, 1983.

Landweber et al. 1983b.   Landweber, L.H., Litzkow, M., Neuhengen, D., and Solomon, M., "Architecture of the CSNET Name Server," *Proceedings of the SIGCOMM '83 Symposium (March 1983)*, pp. 146–153, ACM SIGCOMM, New York, 1983.

Lanzillo 1988.   Lanzillo, Leo, "Traveller Telnet Access," *CSNET-FORUM Digest*, vol. 4, no. 3, Cambridge, MA, 7 September 1988.

Lanzillo and Partridge 1989.   Lanzillo, Leo, and Partridge, Craig, "Implementation of Dial-up IP for UNIX Systems," *USENIX 1989 Winter Conference Proceedings (San Diego, 30 January–3 February 1989)*, USENIX Association, Berkeley, CA, 1989.

LaQuey 1988a.   LaQuey, Tracy Lynn, Personal communications, September 1988.

LaQuey 1988b.   LaQuey, Tracy Lynn, *Users' Directory of Computer Networks*, Office of Telecommunication Services, University of Texas System, Austin, July 1988.

Leary 1987.   Leary, Pat, "Cornell Theory Center," *NSF Network News*, no. 2, p. 3, NNSC, Cambridge, MA, November 1987.

Lederman et al. 1988.   Lederman, Sol, Harrenstien, Ken, and Stahl, Mary, Personal communications, 22 November 1988.

Leffler et al. 1989.   Leffler, Samuel J., McKusick, Marshall Kirk, Karels, Michael J., and Quarterman, John S., *The Design and Implementation of the 4.3BSD UNIX Operating System*, Addison-Wesley, Reading, MA, 1989.

Leiner et al. 1985.   Leiner, Barry M., Cole, Robert, and Postel, Jonathan B., and Mills, David, "The DARPA Internet Protocol Suite," *IEEE Communications*, March 1985.

Levy 1984.   Levy, Stephen, *Hackers: Heroes of the Computer Revolution*, Anchor Press/Doubleday, Garden City, NY, 1984.

Long 1987. Long, Daniel, "CMDF Version 1.2," *CSNET-FORUM Digest*, vol. 3, no. 7, 14 December 1987.

Love 1987. Love, Paul, "The San Diego Supercomputer System," *NSF Network News*, no. 1, p. 3, NNSC, Cambridge, MA, July 1987.

Maisel and Love 1988. Maisel, Merry, and Love, Paul, "SDSCnet," *NSF Network News*, no. 5, pp. 5, 10–11, NNSC, Cambridge, MA, October 1988.

Markwood 1988. Markwood, Dick, "NorthWestNet," *NSF Network News*, no. 5, pp. 5, 9–10, NNSC, Cambridge, MA, October 1988.

Merit 1987a. Merit, "Management and Operation of the NSFnet Backbone Network," Merit, Ann Arbor, MI, 1987.

Merit 1987b. Merit, "Merit Computer Network Map," Merit, Ann Arbor, MI, November 1987.

Merit 1989. Merit, "NSFNET T-1 Data Network New Topology Map," Merit, Ann Arbor, MI, 8 February 1989.

Mills 1988. Mills, Dave, "The Fuzzball," *Proceedings of the ACM SIGCOMM '88 Workshop (Stanford, 16–19 August 1988)*, pp. 115–122, ACM SIGCOMM, New York, 1988.

Mills and Braun 1987. Mills, David L., and Braun, Hans-Werner, "The NSFNET Backbone Network," *Proceedings of the ACM SIGCOMM '87 Workshop (Stowe, Vermont, 11–13 August 1987)*, vol. 17, no. 5, pp. 191–196, ACM SIGCOMM, New York, 1987.

Mogul and Postel 1985. Mogul, J., and Postel, J., "Internet Standard Subnetting Procedure; RFC950," *ARPANET Working Group Requests for Comments*, August 1985.

MRNet 1988. MRNet, "Minnesota Regional Network," MRNet, Rochester, MN, 1988.

Nash 1989. Nash, Donald L., "Texas Higher Education Network Map," Office of Telecommunication Services, University of Texas System, Austin, 1989.

NBS 1988. NBS, "Government Open Systems Interconnection Procurement Specification (GOSIP)," Institute for Computer Sciences and Technology, National Bureau of Standards (NBS), Gaithersburg, MD, 24 August 1988.

NNSC 1988a. NNSC, "Measuring the Size of the Internet," *NSF Network News*, no. 5, pp. 1–2, NNSC, Cambridge, MA, October 1988.

NNSC 1988b. NNSC, "The NCAR Scientific Computing Division," *NSF Network News*, no. 3, p. 4, NNSC, Cambridge, MA, March 1988.

NSF 1986. NSF, "Project Solicitation for Management and Operation of the NSFNET Backbone Network," National Science Foundation, Washington, DC, 1986.

NYSERNet 1988a. NYSERNet, "Membership in NYSERNet: Information for Prospective Members," NYSERNet, Inc., New York, 1988.

NYSERNet 1988b. NYSERNet, "NYSERNet Topology," *NYSERNet News*, vol. 1, no. 8, p. 3, NYSERNet, Inc., New York, June 1988.

NYSERNet 1988c. NYSERNet, "Internet Network Management: Simple Network Management Protocol," NYSERNet, Inc., New York, 1988.

NYSERNet 1989. NYSERNet, "NYSERNet Topology," NYSERNet, Inc., New York, 25 January 1989.

O'Brien and Breeden 1983. O'Brien, Michael T., and Breeden, Laura, "A Brief History and Description of CSNET," *Proceedings of the Summer 1983 USENIX Conference (Toronto, Ontario, 13–15 July 1983)*, USENIX Association, Berkeley, CA, 1983.

O'Brien and Long 1984. O'Brien, Michael T., and Long, Daniel B., "CSNET Grows Up," *Proceedings of the Winter 1984 USENIX Conference (Washington, D.C., January 1984)*, USENIX Association, Berkeley, CA, 1984.

Paoli 1987.   Paoli, Peggy, "The National Center for Supercomputing Applications," *NSF Network News*, no. 2, p. 3, NNSC, Cambridge, MA, November 1987.

Partridge 1986.   Partridge, Craig, "Report From the Internet NIC on Domains," *CSNET-FORUM Digest*, vol. 2, no. 2, 19 February 1986.

Partridge 1987.   Partridge, Craig, "The CSNET Information Server: Automatic Document Distribution Using Electronic Mail," *Computer Communication Review*, vol. 17, no. 4, pp. 3–10, October/November 1987.

Partridge 1988.   Partridge, Craig, Personal communications, August–November 1988.

Passmore and Horn 1988.   Passmore, L. David, and Horn, Jeffrey, "GOSIP to Govern Federal Nets," *Network World*, vol. 5, no. 9, pp. 1, 35, 38–40, 29 February 1988.

Perillo 1986.   Perillo, Francine, Personal communications, 10 July 1986.

Postel 1988.   Postel, Jon, Personal communications, August 1988.

Quarterman et al. 1985.   Quarterman, John S., Silberschatz, Abraham, and Peterson, James L., "4.2BSD and 4.3BSD as Examples of the UNIX System," *ACM Computing Surveys*, vol. 17, no. 4, pp. 379–418, December 1985.

Rekhter 1988.   Rekhter, Jacob, "EGP and Policy Based Routing in the New NSFNET Backbone," T. J. Watson Research Center, IBM Corporation, Yorktown, NY, 6 March 1988.

Ritchie and Thompson 1978.   Ritchie, D. M., and Thompson, K., "The UNIX Time-Sharing System," *Bell System Technical Journal*, vol. 57, no. 6, part 2, pp. 1905–1929, July/August 1978. This version describes Seventh Edition UNIX.

Roubicek 1988.   Roubicek, Karen, Personal communications, September 1988.

Rugo 1988.   Rugo, John, Personal communications, September 1988.

Schoffstall 1988.   Schoffstall, Martin, Personal communications, 23 September 1988.

Shaw 1988.   Shaw, S. J., "TCP/IP Still Rules Federal Nets," *Network World*, vol. 5, no. 11, pp. 1, 46–48, 14 March 1988.

Skelton 1988.   Skelton, John E., Personal communications, 30 August 1988.

Solomon et al. 1982.   Solomon, Marvin, Landweber, Lawrence H., and Neuhengen, Donald, "The CSNET Name Server," *Computer Networks*, vol. 6, no. 3, pp. 161–172, July 1982.

Su and Mathis 1988.   Su, Zaw-Sing, and Mathis, James E., "Internetwork Accommodation of Network Dynamics: Reconstitution Protocol," SRI International, Menlo Park, CA, February 1988.

Swindell 1988.   Swindell, David, "New Equipment for the CSNET CIC," *CSNET-FORUM Digest*, vol. 4, 3, 7 September 1988.

Szurkowski 1980.   Szurkowski, Edward S., "MMDF Dial-Up Link Protocol," *CSNET Design Notes*, no. DN-4, April 1980.

Tanenbaum 1988.   Tanenbaum, Andrew S., *Computer Networks*, 2d ed., Prentice-Hall, Englewood Cliffs, NJ, 1988.

Van Houweling 1988.   Van Houweling, Douglas E., "Higher Education's Role in NSFNET," *EDUCOM Bulletin*, vol. 23, no. 2/3, pp. 32–35, Spring/Fall 1988.

Vaudreuil 1988.   Vaudreuil, Gregory M., "The Federal Research Internet Committee and the National Research Internet," *Computer Communication Review*, 1 July 1988.

Waitzman and Karels 1988.   Waitzman, David, and Karels, Mike, "NNSC Expands Domain Backup Service," *NSF Network News*, no. 4, p. 5, NNSC, Cambridge, MA, June 1988.

Wasley 1988.   Wasley, David, Personal communications, September 1988.

Wells 1988.   Wells, William C., Personal communications, September 1988.

Wolfe 1988a.   Wolfe, Barbara B., "CICNet Bulletin 1," CICNet, Inc., August 1988.

Wolfe 1988b.   Wolfe, Barbara B., "CICNet Bulletin 2," CICNet, Inc., September 1988.

Wolfe 1988c.   Wolfe, Barbara B., "CICNet Bulletin 3," CICNet, Inc., October 1988.

Wolfe 1988d.   Wolfe, Barbara B., Personal communications, November 1988.

Wolff 1987a.   Wolff, Steve, Personal communications, 24 March 1987.

Wolff 1987b.   Wolff, Steve, "Steve Wolff Comments on NSFnet's Progress," *NSF Network News*, no. 1, pp. 1, 8, NNSC, Cambridge, MA, July 1987.

Yundt 1988.   Yundt, William H., "1987 Annual Report to the NSF—Bay Area Regional Research Network," BARRNet, Stanford, CA, March 1988.

12   *North America*

Two countries are listed in this chapter on North America: the United States and Canada (Mexico appears in Chapter 18 on Latin America, and the *Internet* has already been described in the previous chapter). Canada and the United States have long had similar (but not identical) sets of networks, including several (*USENET*, *UUCP*, *BITNET*, and *NetNorth*) that differ between the two countries only in administration.

12.1   *Continental North American Networks*

There are a few networks that cover the continent. Two that are described here are *UUCP* and *USENET*. There is also *UUNET*, which serves as a gateway between those networks and the *Internet*, which was described in the previous chapter.

12.1.1   UUCP N.A.

Most of what has been said above about *UUCP* in the world applies to North America as well, but the part of the network on that continent is more loosely organized than elsewhere. Partly because this network is so decentralized, it is useful to describe the routings and gateways to and from other networks.

Connectivity

In North America, connections between hosts tend to be made for any of several reasons, including the following:

> *Low telephone costs.* This may mean physical proximity, as in a local dialing area with no volume tariffs. Many cities have a few hosts that make most of the long-distance calls and allow others to pass mail through them, as long as the number and sizes of such messages stay low. But it may also mean interstate, because those are often lower at night than nonlocal intrastate rates.
>
> *Personal acquaintances.* Many connections are made to people's previous schools or employers or to machines of friends. These account for many transcontinental connections.
>
> *Short paths.* A machine that already has many connections is a desirable machine to connect to. Each locality tends to have at least one such machine, as already mentioned. Such machines often connect to each other, forming something similar to the *USENET* backbone, and many of the *USENET* backbone machines carry large mail loads as well. But there is even less organization as to which mail will be carried than there is for news, both because mail is much more private than news and because there are far more *UUCP* mail connections than *USENET* news connections.

Note that some new services, such as *UUNET*, meet at least two of these qualifications, and thus produce warps in the network.

Interconnections

Interconnections from *UUCP* to other networks are shown in Table 12.1.

UUCP hosts with domain names can be reached from many other networks as *user@domain*.{**DNS**}. From a *UUCP* host that understands domains, a user may often reach a host on another network that uses domains, such as *ACSnet*, without explicit use of gateways. A likely gateway from *UUCP* to almost anywhere is *uunet*, known in domain form as *uunet.uu.net*.

There is a map of the *UUCP* network that lists gateways to many domains on many networks. That map is distributed monthly in *USENET* newsgroup *comp.mail.maps* and is also available from many major *USENET* and *UUCP* hosts, such as *uunet*, for *UUCP* transfer. The usual way of obtaining the map is through being on *USENET*. *UUCP* hosts that are not also *USENET* hosts usually forward mail for addresses they don't understand to a host that is known to keep the full map; there is usually such a smart gateway host nearby. There would be little or no advantage to a user

Table 12.1. *UUCP interconnections*

Network	Syntax
UUCP	*user*@*domain*.**{DNS}**
UUCP	h1!h2!*host*!*user*
Internet	*gateway*!*domain*.**{DNS}**!*user*
JANET	*user*@*domain*.**{JANET-domain}**
JANET	*user*%*domain*.**{JANET-domain}**@cs.ucl.ac.uk
JANET	*gateway*!cs.ucl.ac.uk!*domain*.**{JANET-domain}**!*user*
JANET	*user*%*domain*.**{JANET-domain}**@cunyvm.cuny.edu
JANET	psuvax1!cunyvm.bitnet!*domain*.**{JANET-domain}**!*user*
JANET	*user*%*domain*.**{JANET-domain}**@ukc.uucp
JANET	ukc!*domain*.**{JANET-domain}**!*user*
Ean	*gateway*!*domain*.**{Ean-domain}**!*user*
XEROX Internet	parcvax!*user*.**{XEROX-domain}**
EASYnet	decwrl!*host*.dec.com!*user*
VNET	*gateway*!ibm.com!*user*%*host*
BITNET	psuvax1!*host*.bitnet!*user*
ACSnet	uunet!munnari!*domain*.**{ACSNET-domain}**!*user*
JUNET	*user*%*domain*.**{JUNET-domain}**@uunet.uu.net
JUNET	uunet!*domain*.**{JUNET-domain}**!*user*
FidoNet	*user*@*fnode*.*nnet*.*zzone*.fidonet.org
FidoNet	*gateway*!*zone*!*net*!*node*!*user*
FidoNet	*gateway*!*net*!*node*!*user*
DASnet	sun!daslink!dasnet!*user*
DASnet	*user*@*domain*.das.net
PeaceNet	uunet!pyramid!cdp!*user*
PeaceNet	ihnp4!hplabs!cdp!*user*

on another network in obtaining the *UUCP* map, since it is basically for sending mail within and from the *UUCP* network, and it changes rapidly. Such a user should send mail to a *UUCP* user through one of the well-known gateway hosts that use up-to-date copies of the map—for example, *uunet*.

JANET   Sophisticated *UUCP* hosts can recognize *JANET* domains directly without explicit specification of a gateway by the user. If a gateway is required, *cs.ucl.ac.uk* can be tried. One can also go through *BITNET* by using *cunyvm.cuny.edu*, perhaps by routing through *psuvax1*. Finally, routing through *ukc* will work for subscribers to their service.

CDNnet   A gateway from *UUCP* to *CDNnet* is *ubc-ean*.

FidoNet   There are two ways to reach *FidoNet* hosts:

The old way:

Use the *FidoNet* net and node numbers, as in

gateway!net!node!user
or
gateway!zone!net!node!user

depending on software configurations. The tokens in italics represent numbers.

The new way:

Use the fidonet.org domain, as in

*gateway!fnode.nnet.zzone.*fidonet.org!*user*

The tokens in italics represent numbers here, too, but they are prefixed with the literal ASCII characters f, n, and z (for fidonode, net, and zone, respectively). The host *fidogate.fidonet.org* is a likely gateway. To send to a *FidoNet* user at fidonode 1:24/666, a likely path would be

fidogate.fidonet.org!f666.n24.z1.fidonet.org!sysop

On hosts fully supporting domain *syntax*, this can be expressed as

sysop%f666.n24.z1.fidonet.org@fidogate.fidonet.org

And from hosts that fully support domain *semantics* — i.e., that know how to find gateway hosts appropriate to domains — this can be used:

sysop@f666.n24.z1.fidonet.org

This last way is the simplest and best. Note that the user sysop is the *FidoNet* equivalent of postmaster.

DASnet   The *DASnet* syntax will be useful only for those who are either subscribers to its service or are corresponding with subscribers.

Access

See the section about *UUCP* as a worldwide network for access information.

12.1.2   USENET N.A.

USENET covers North America rather completely. The backbone is depicted in Figure 12.1, with the whole network in Figure 12.2. See also the section on *USENET* worldwide.

12.1.3   UUNET

UUNET is a subscription network relay service for traffic on the *UUCP* and *USENET* networks, and for traffic between *UUCP* and the *Internet*. There were about 400 subscribers by mid-1988, including not only a large number of machines in North America, but also many backbone machines on national networks around the world, in places such as Europe, Australia, Indonesia, Malaysia, Hong Kong, Korea, Japan, Chile, Argentina, and India, as shown in Figure 12.3.

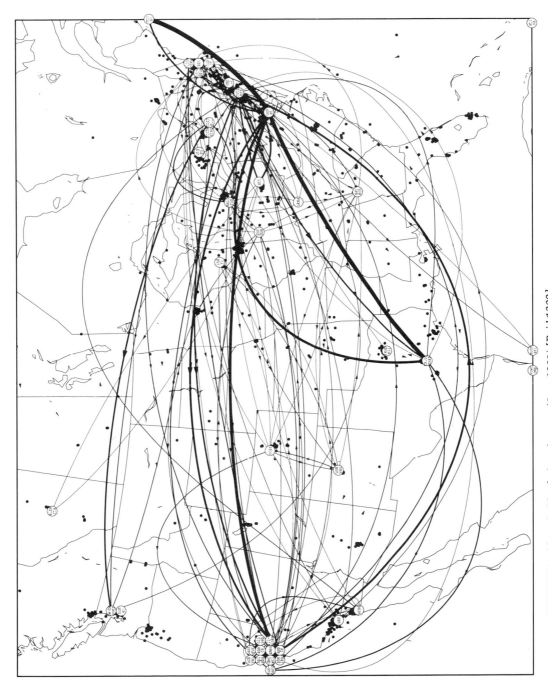

Figure 12.1. *USENET backbone in North America map (June 1989) [Reid 1989]*

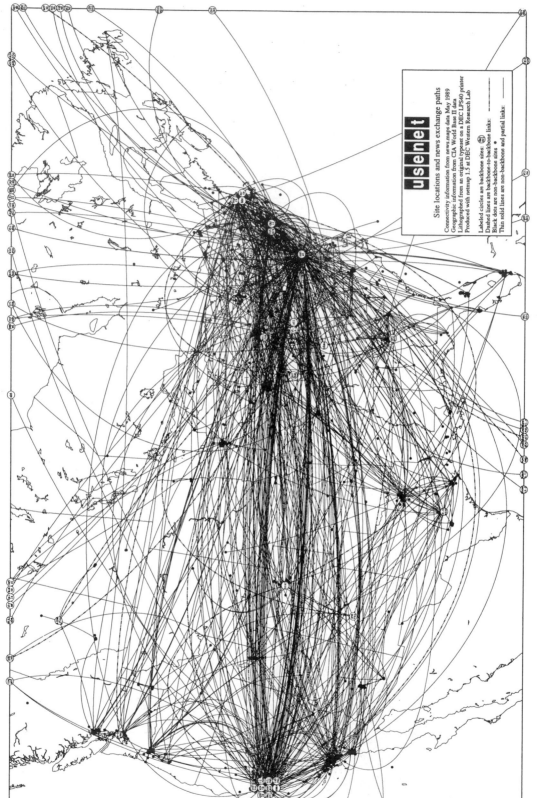

usenet

Site locations and news exchange paths

Connectivity information from news.maps data May 1989
Geographic information from CIA World Base II data
Lithographed from an original typeset on a DEC LPS40 printer
Produced with netmap 1.5 at DEC Western Research Lab

Labeled circles are backbone sites:
Dashed lines are backbone-to-backbone links:
Black dots are non-backbone sites
Thin solid lines are non-backbone and partial links:

Figure 12.2. *USENET in North America map (June 1989)* [Reid 1989]

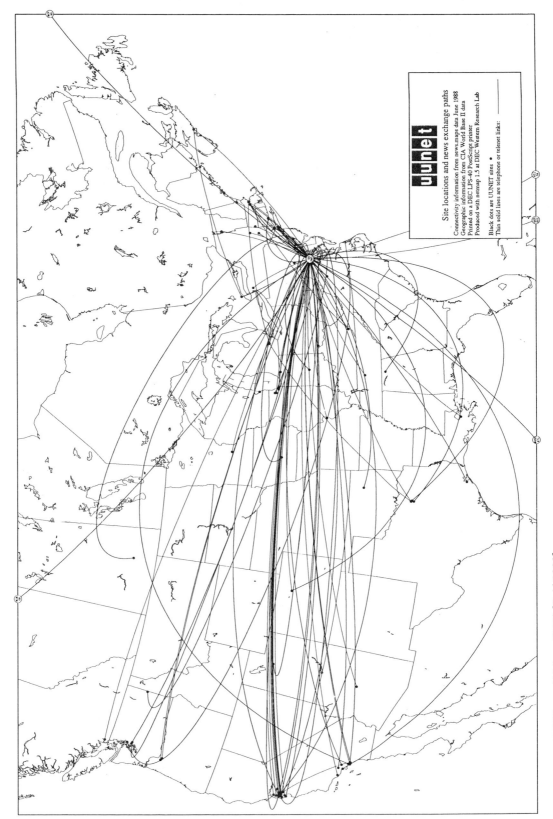

Figure 12.3. *UUNET map (19 June 1988) [Reid 1988]*

Services

The most basic function of *UUNET* is to transfer mail and news quickly among hosts on the *UUCP* and *USENET* networks in North America; the *UUNET* machine is known as *uunet* on those networks. But the quick international transfers it provides are another major service. And a major reason for all the international subscribers is that *UUNET* provides a gateway-ing service with the *Internet*. This is done by a connection to the *NSFNET* mid-level network *SURAnet*. The *UUNET* is known in the *Internet* by the DNS domain name *uunet.uu.net*. *UUNET* acts as a domain forwarder for many domains that do not have other *Internet* connections; it is also capable of registering new domains and of providing nameservice.

The *UUNET* machine has archives of many things online for users to transfer to their machines by UUCP or *anonymous FTP*; these include *comp.unix.sources* archives, sources for the news software, the latest *UUCP* maps, GNU's not UNIX (GNU) (a public domain rewrite of **UNIX** sponsored by the Free Software Foundation (FSF), founded by Richard M. Stallman), **Kermit** sources, and *Internet* RFCs [Adams and Salus 1988]. Users do not have personal accounts on the *UUNET* machine, only UUCP login accounts for their machines. The few dozen user accounts on *UUNET* are for people related to the service itself. *UUNET* in general originates no information (similarly to *DASnet*) and is in effect a common carrier.

Administration

UUNET is a nonprofit corporation with a board of three directors, one third of whom are appointed by the board of directors of the USENIX Association. The CEO is Rick Adams, the inventor of the service. There is a small paid staff, including one person each for financial matters and membership services.

Protocols

Physically, *UUNET* is a single machine in Arlington, Virginia. It was originally a Sequent Balance 21000 with ten (later 14) NCR 32032 CPUs but was upgraded in October 1988 to be a Sequent Symmetry with four Intel 80386 CPUs. The configuration of 16 September 1988 had about a gigabyte of disk space, 24Mbytes of memory, 32 serial ports, an X.25 board, and a 6250bpi tape drive for backups. The 32 serial ports were divided into ten for incoming WATS lines, twelve for direct dialup, and three for outgoing WATS lines. All of the modems were Telebit Trailblazer-Pluses. The WATS service was supported by a T1 connection to Sprint. The X.25 board was for a 56Kbps connection to *TYMNET*. The *Internet* connection was by a local TCP/IP Ethernet connection to the *ARPANET* PSN of the Center for Seismic Studies (CSS). The overseas connection to *cwi.nl* (*mcvax*) in Amsterdam was through a 9600bps leased line running SLIP and TCP/IP; an upgrade to 64Kbps was on order. There were 421 *UUNET* subscribers, about 200 connect hours a day, about 190Mbytes of data transferred a day, and something like 10,000 mail messages a day, not counting *Internet* traffic. About 200 subscribers got news feeds. Total income was about $50,000 a month, with expenses of $49,000 a month ($20,000 for *TYMNET*, $15,000 for Sprint, $5,000 for the machine, lease payments, and miscellaneous) [Adams 1988]. No staff were yet on salary, although the revenue was sufficient.

Subscribers are charged hourly connection charges and a monthly flat fee. The hourly charges vary with the methods of connection, which include the following:

TYMNET	Some users connect through *TYMNET*'s 1200bps or 2400bps dialup to a local number and from there by X.25.
WATS	In North America, an AT&T 800 number can be used to avoid long-distance tolls.
Direct dialup	Many users connect directly to a local number in Arlington through various long-distance carriers, balancing whatever long-distance charge is thus incurred with a lower hourly charge from *UUNET*. Some international users do this.
PDN	Many international users come in through their local national X.25 PDN and through *TYMNET*.

Dialup speeds range from 1200bps to 2400bps to 9600bps to even faster rates up to 11000bps supported by the Telebit Trailblazer modems, which have the UUCP g protocol in firmware. Mail is usually transferred from one subscriber to another within a day.

UUNET charging is actually quite similar to that of *EUnet*, although *UUNET* lacks the multilevel hierarchy of that network. Subscribers may produce that kind of hierarchy themselves, however, by dividing costs among hosts they in turn feed.

Interconnections

Because of *UUNET*'s direct connections to many national networks around the world and to the *Internet*, it is capable of relaying mail from its subscribers to almost any known network. Return addresses will involve the host name *uunet* in old-style underlying *UUCP* source routing, or *uunet.uu.net* in DNS format.

The methods a user should use to send mail through *UUNET* are the more sophisticated of those listed for the *UUCP* network in North America, including the DNS domain forms. For example, to reach a host on *BITNET*, if the host has a domain name, all that is necessary is to use it directly, e.g., *user*@CUNYVM.CUNY.EDU

If the host does not have a domain name, one could explicitly route it through a known *BITNET* gateway, but it is better to use the pseudodomain *BITNET* and let *UUNET* route it:

user@*host*.BITNET

This all depends on how the user's host is set up for sending mail, of course. In general, a subscriber should set up the subscribing machine to know to send otherwise unresolved mail traffic to *UUNET* automatically for further routing; this is the assumption in the above examples.

History

UUNET began as an experiment proposed by Rick Adams and Mike O'Dell to the board of directors of the USENIX Association (USENIX). The USENIX membership had for years been asking its board to do something to improve the level of service available on the *UUCP* and *USENET* networks. The board did not see taking a direct organizational role in either network as consonant with the purposes of the Association, but it had previously sponsored experiments in technological improvements, including the following:

- The UUCP Mapping Project, whose purpose is to keep up-to-date maps of machines on both networks for use in routing, especially through databases composed from the maps by the **pathalias** program [Honeyman and Bellovin 1986]. This project continues today, although USENIX funding for it, which had always been at a low level, ceased in 1986.
- Stargate was an attempt to carry news over the vertical blanking interval of a television signal through a geosynchronous satellite with a footprint covering North America, thus reducing both traffic delays and costs to subscribers over telephone dialup. USENIX declared that experiment technologically successful in January 1987 and ceased funding it at the end of February 1987.

UUNET was viewed as another in this series of experiments. It was a particularly promising one, due to Adams's two years of experience running the *USENET* and *UUCP* backbone machine *seismo* at the CSS in Arlington, Virginia, and due to the off-the-shelf nature of the equipment needed. USENIX approved the new service as an experiment in January 1987 [Adams and Salus 1987]. Another key ingredient (5 June 1987) was approval from ARPA to perform gatewaying between the *Internet* and the *UUCP* and *USENET* networks for an initial period of three years, as an experiment.

Adams and USENIX negotiated an initial loan of a machine from Sequent for 90 days and a contract with *TYMNET*. USENIX provided a loan of $35,000 for initial operations, with a time limit of 31 July 1987 for demonstrated performance. The service was first advertised on *USENET* on 11 April 1987, and the machine first became operational and began transferring messages on 14 May 1987 [Frey and Adams 1987]. Early subscription services were run from the USENIX office in Berkeley, California, with technical support from Rick Adams in Virginia and political support from the USENIX board. The initial equipment loan was extended another 90 days by Sequent, and USENIX agreed to extend its financial loan because the first three month test period was promising but inconclusive. USENIX declared the experiment successful on 27 October 1987 [Salus 1988] and started successful negotiations for a loan to buy the machine and ancillary equipment, such as the X.25 interface. The former backbone machine, *seismo*, retired from forwarding service on 1 September 1987.

Subscriptions and revenue continued to climb, and membership services were moved to Arlington to be closer to actual operations. Eventually, observing that *UUNET*'s cash flow promised to outstrip that of the parent association, the USENIX board decided on 22 June 1988 to form a separate corporation for *UUNET*. However, since USENIX continued to guarantee the loan, and since it did not choose to abandon its original purpose of influencing the level of service on the *UUCP* and *USENET* networks, USENIX retained a third of the positions on the board of directors of the new corporation. The nonprofit nature of the service was retained.

Rick Adams originally intended the name *UUNET* to be analogous to that of *EUnet*, taking the E to be for Europe and changing it to U for United States. He later noticed that the UU prefix corresponded to that of UUcp, UUX, UUcico, and other similar UUCP programs [Adams 1988]. Since USENIX, a North American organization, considers *UUNET* to be a North American service, the latter derivation is possibly most appropriate.

Effects

There have been mail and news relays like *UUNET* before, but they were all done as contributions from their parent companies, and most of them eventually succumbed to traffic overload or were kept functional by a single person in addition to a real job, causing them to become less useful when that person moved. *UUNET*, while nonprofit, does collect funds to cover its costs. This means that increased traffic is likely to lead to increased capability of the hardware, and paid staff positions mean that there will more likely be continuity of service.

Another advantage is that *UUNET* will connect to a machine of almost anyone who will pay the price. This is unlike most *USENET* backbone machines, which are already sufficiently loaded that they cannot take on more direct feeds. In congested regions such as the San Francisco Bay Area, shown in Figure 12.4, this can mean that the only news feed available by traditional means is from a machine three or four hops off the backbone, possibly leading to a day or more of delay. A machine faced with this situation can subscribe to *UUNET* and be directly connected to the backbone. Also, *UUNET* carries all newsgroups, including the alternative ones [Dunne 1987]. Because *UUNET* has not yet been declared a common carrier, there are a few legal glitches: certain organizations in South Africa cannot be allowed to connect, and no organizations in the USSR and certain Soviet bloc countries are permitted, due to U.S. government restrictions.

UUNET is a point of failure for *UUCP* and *USENET*, especially because of its great popularity, but this problem is widely accepted by administrators of systems on those networks. The reliability of the Sequent hardware and the commitment of a well-financed corporation to keep the machine running help alleviate fears.

Future

Future possibilities include penetration of new markets by advertising. As of mid-1988, there had never been any paid advertisements for the service, so most subscribers came from the existing *USENET* and *UUCP* communities. Currently, the overseas links are paid for entirely by the other end from *UUNET*. For example, the links between *uunet* and *mcvax* cost about $7,000 per month at the end of 1987, all being paid by *EUnet*. At that time, if *UUNET* were to have paid half of all the overseas links to it, the cost would have been about $5,000 per month. *UUNET* decided in Spring 1989 that it had sufficient cash reserves be able to afford to carry its end. Subscriptions and revenue continued their generally linear increases into mid-1989.

Access
UUNET Communications Services
uunet-request@uunet.uu.net
uunet!uunet-request
+1-703-876-5050
Fax: +1-703-876-5059
3110 Fairview Park Drive, Suite 570
P.O. Box 2324
Falls Church, VA 22042
U.S.A

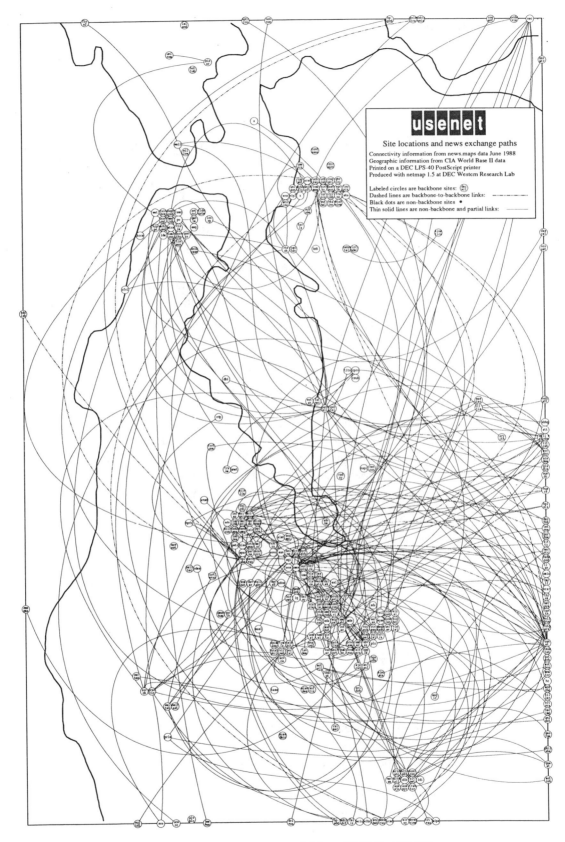

Figure 12.4. *USENET around San Francisco Bay map (19 June 1988) [Reid 1988]*

12.2   *United States {US}*

The networks and conferencing systems in the United States are too numerous to list in an introductory paragraph: probably several of every kind of system exist in this country. Details down to the host level may be found on some of the larger academic and research networks in Kroll 1987, LaQuey 1988, and LaQuey 1989, which also include many useful maps. Everything except the maps may be obtained by *anonymous FTP* from several hosts on the *Internet*. Other particularly useful concentrations of information on networks are kept on hosts on the *Internet, CSNET, BITNET,* and *UUNET* and are largely accessible by automatic reply to electronic mail inquiries. Directories of users are kept by the *Internet, CSNET, NEMR, DASnet,* and *PeaceNet*.

There is a national domain, *US*, which is intended for hosts and sites that do not fit under the other *Internet* DNS domains, such as *COM, EDU, GOV*, or *ORG*, and is administered by a different group than the other top level domains. Subdomains of *US* are handled strictly geographically, with second level domains being U.S. Postal Service two letter state abbreviations, such as CA for California (unrelated to the top level domain *CA* for Canada) or TX for Texas, and third level domains being Western Union city mnemonics or the full name of the city, as in AUSTIN.TX.US. A host that already has a domain name does not need another one under *US*. A rather unusual feature of this top level domain is that SRI-NIC is administering it right down to the city level: users are permitted to run nameservers for organizations below that level, but all registration and administration of city and state domains is done directly by SRI-NIC [Postel and Westine 1988a; Postel and Westine 1988b]. Much of the rest of the world also uses the *US* domain to hide the other DNS domains (*COM, EDU*, etc.) as pseudo second level domains, as in EDU.US.

Access
US Domain Registrar
WESTINE@ISI.EDU

12.2.1   **BITNET U.S.**

BITNET had its beginnings in 1981 when the first two hosts, *CUNYVM* at City University of New York (CUNY) and *YALEVM* at Yale University (Yale), were connected on 5 May 1981 [Cotter 1988]. The network was originally used primarily for collaboration and communications among systems programmers at university computation centers. Since existing IBM networking software was used, *BITNET* was initially a network of IBM hosts. The basic premise for establishing *BITNET* was to provide a communica-

gure 12.5. *BITNET U.S. map (25 April 1988) [BITNIC 1988]*

tions network among universities with no special requirements, restrictions, or fees for membership. Today *BITNET* is used by scholars and administrators from a variety of different disciplines.

Scope

As of 13 July 1988, there were 397 U.S. member sites with a total of 1,461 hosts [Nussbacher 1988], as shown in Figure 12.5. The scope is the United States plus one host in Mexico and one in Buenos Aires, Argentina (since November 1987). There are direct links to *NetNorth* and *EARN*.

Hosts in Asia are often distinguished as *Asianet*, shown in Figure 12.6, but are sometimes included as part of *BITNET*. There are many hosts in Japan. A connection to Singapore was established in January 1987 and was originally a dialup link; this is a new facility on the network. That connection is now over a satellite. Taiwan and Korea are also connected. *GulfNet* will be a cooperating member of *BITNET* — i.e., nonvoting but with similar services.

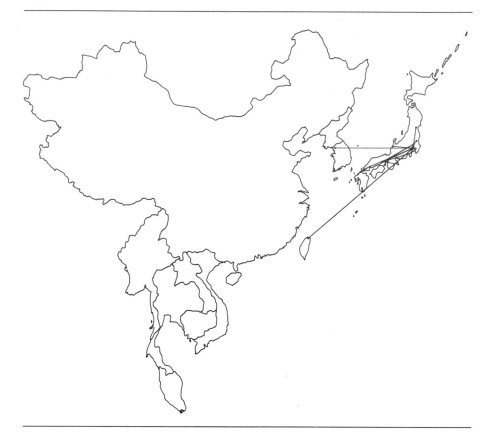

Figure 12.6. *Asianet map (25 April 1988) [BITNIC 1988]*

Services

Services provided include the following:

- Electronic mail (currently mostly using RFC733 domain format for external use—i.e., *user@host*.BITNET—but partly changing to more modern DNS format)
- File transfer
- Interactive messages

Administration and Funding

User services are provided by *BITNET* Network Information Center (BITNIC) under contract to BITNET, Inc., which was incorporated in May 1987. Services provided include an online directory, electronic newsletters, end user documentation, workshops, seminars, and conference presentations. It is possible to retrieve most of this information through *LISTSERV@BITNIC.BITNET*. In addition to these direct user service functions provided by BITNIC, BITNET, Inc. provides administrative support by negotiating for software and equipment discounts and by archiving network procedures and policies. BITNIC and other *BITNET* functions are supported by membership fees.

Protocols

BITNET uses the Network Job Entry (NJE) protocol, and most hosts use the **RSCS** implementation of it on **VM** or **JES/NJE** on **MVS**. As the network has grown, software to emulate the protocols has been developed by commercial vendors and members of the *BITNET* community. Emulation software is being used at non-IBM sites for the DEC 10/20, VAX (**UNIX** and **VMS**), CDC Cyber, and Unisys environments.

The machine that is the root of the tree is *CUNYVM*. If this node goes down, the network will still run, but it will be split into several networks in the western, central and southern, and northeastern United States and elsewhere. *EARN* will also be disconnected. *NetNorth* will remain connected to the northeastern U.S. section. Because this is a store and forward network, files and mail that need to pass through *CUNYVM* will be queued at the nodes nearest it.

Interconnections

Hosts are interconnected by leased phone lines supporting 9600bps data transmission. The mail and file delivery delay ranges from minutes to hours. An unusual feature of *BITNET* is that there is usually exactly one path between any two hosts, and the whole network is organized in a tree, rooted at CUNY. This can occasionally have complications, as when, in March 1987, the static routing tables that are distributed monthly turned out to be too much for the link between *PSUVM* at Pennsylvania State University (PSU) and *OHSTVMA* at Ohio State, and had to be put on a tape and mailed. The eventual workaround was to generate the needed data on the other side of the link.

Gateways exist between *BITNET* and *CSNET* and the *Internet*; there is also restricted access to *VNET*. *CUNYVM* is even on *USENET* [Reber 1988] and is probably the machine with the most users on that network. The gateway between *BITNET* and the *Internet* was *WISCVM* at the University of Wisconsin (Wisconsin) for most of the history of the network, until 15 December 1987. Since that time, that task has been taken over by a set of machines distributed around the continent starting with *CUNYVM* and known collectively on *BITNET* as *INTERBIT*. The original (December 1987) group of *INTERBIT* participants included CUNY, Cornell University

(Cornell), and the Massachusetts Institute of Technology (MIT) [Yalow 1988]. The idea is that mail from any *BITNET* host to any *Internet* host can be sent to *INTERBIT*, which is an alias on the local host and points to *CUNYVM*. Any *INTERBIT* participant on the path between the sending host and *CUNYVM* may intercept the mail and forward it to the *Internet*. Similarly, any mail from an *Internet* host can be sent to the nearest known *BITNET* gateway, such as *cunyvm.cuny.edu*. Unfortunately, this facility requires nameserver *MX records* or the equivalent, and most of the likely *BITNET* gateways did not initially support them. Thus, most users on *BIT-NET* cannot mail to hosts with domain names unless those names are listed in the static host table kept at *SRI-NIC.ARPA* or are directly on the *Internet* and have *A records* recorded with the DNS nameservers there [Yalow 1988]. Large numbers of hosts on the *Internet, UUCP, EUnet, ACSnet*, and other networks are therefore inaccessible by direct domain addressing from *BIT-NET*, although such hosts may be reached by indirect addressing through a gateway that understands *MX records*. Also, the TCP/IP available at the time from IBM for **VM** supported only 20 character host names. For these reasons, actual implementation was slow, not being completed until late 1988. IBM has indicated, however, that support for *MX records* is forthcoming [Yalow 1988]. See the section on *BITNET* worldwide for addressing syntax and gateway details from the user's point of view.

The actual connection to the *Internet* from *CUNYVM* is through five 56Kbps circuits to *NYSERNet* [NYSERNet 1988; Klein 1988], a constituent network of *NSFNET*. *NYSERNet* is in turn connected to the *ARPANET* through a 56Kbps link at the University of Rochester and another at Cornell.

History

According to some sources, the original acronym expansion was "Because It's There," referring to the fact that *BITNET* was based on the NJE protocols that came at no extra cost with IBM mainframe systems [da Cruz 1988]; this is quite similar to the origin of the *UUCP* network. It is not clear why the explanation was changed to "Because It's Time."

There were originally no membership fees, with each site required only to provide a connection to an adjacent site. Government support provided funding for the support sites. IBM originally provided funds for BITNIC, but that funding ended in 1987. Much technical support was provided in the early days by EDUCOM and CUNY. This was largely coordinated by CUNY's *BITNET* Development and Operations Center (BITDOC), which maintained a support center computer (*BITNIC*). **BITSERVE** was a help facility organized and operated by BITDOC at CUNY to offer a *BIT-NET* news service, a user directory, a list of *BITNET* sites and computers, and information on conferences, software, and special facilities available to *BITNET* members. **LISTSERV** has since superseded **BITSERVE**. The original version of **LISTSERV** was written by Ricardo Hernandez of BITDOC. The current version is by Eric Thomas.

Plans

A merger between *BITNET* and *CSNET* [Breeden 1988] has been decided upon by their boards and members. This is desirable because their clients are often the same universities and companies and because it would result in less confusion now that the regional networks of *NSFNET* are becoming more prevalent and connecting to those same computer centers. The resulting merged network will probably be called *ONEnet*. *BITNET* itself is certified as a mid-level component *NSFNET* network. There is a project called *BITNET II* sponsored by NSF that is building a network that uses **RSCS** over TCP/IP; the existing *BITNET II* links are integrated into the *Internet* through *NSFNET* and use DNS domain names. *BITNET* in general is moving toward domain names—that is, real domain names such as *CUNYVM.CUNY.EDU* instead of *CUNY.BITNET*. *CSNET* already uses TCP/IP for many of its nodes and DNS domain names for all of them.

Access

BITNET Network Information Center (BITNIC):

INFO%BITNIC.BITNET@CUNYVM.CUNY.EDU
NETSERV%BITNIC.BITNET@CUNYVM.CUNY.EDU
LISTSERV%BITNIC.BITNET@CUNYVM.CUNY.EDU

To join:

EDUCOM Networking Activities
+1-609-734-1878
P.O. Box 364
Princeton, NJ 08540
U.S.A.

12.2.2   MFEnet

MFEnet, or Magnetic Fusion Energy Network, uses several underlying network and transport protocols to support access to several supercomputers, including one at Lawrence Livermore National Laboratory (LLNL) and one at the Supercomputer Computations Research Institute (SCRI) at Florida State University (FSU). The basic purpose of the network was originally to connect physics departments doing research in nuclear fusion, specifically in Magnetic Fusion Energy (MFE), but the Department of Energy (DoE) has since expanded it to reach all the DoE energy research programs [LaQuey 1988]. Access is restricted to DoE-funded researchers.

Scope

There are about 120 hosts on the network, all in the continental United States except for one in Japan. All of the U.S. national laboratories and many universities are reached. Five supercomputers are reachable: a Cray 1, a Cray X-MP/2, two Cray 2s, and a Cyber 205 [Leighton 1988a].

Administration and Funding

MFEnet is funded and administered by the DoE and is managed from the National MFE Computer Center (NMFECC) of LLNL [NMFECC 1988].

Services and Protocols

Mail, file transfer, remote command execution, and remote login are all supported on at least parts of the network. There are also specialized remote procedure calls for interactive graphics terminals. The links use special purpose protocols developed at LLNL and collectively called NSP. NSP is implemented on the Digital **VMS** and Cray **CTSS** operating systems and provides remote login, file export, remote printing, and electronic mail [LaQuey 1988]. The use of nonstandard protocols has led to interoperability problems with other networks. Therefore, DoE is changing *MFEnet* to use the NSP suite over the IP protocol and intends an eventual move to the ISO-OSI protocols, such as CLNS. The replacement for *MFEnet* is referred to as *MFEnet II* [Leighton 1988a].

The existing links range from 9600bps to 56Kbps leased lines to 112Kbps satellite links. Speed between any two hosts depends greatly on the intervening links. Reliability is high. Addressing is specific to the NSP protocol. There are mail gateways to the *Internet* and several other networks [Leighton 1988a].

History

This network originated in the mid-1970s to allow access to a Cray 1 at LLNL [Jennings et al. 1986]. There are plans for *ESnet* to provide the high-speed backbone carrier for *MFEnet* and *HEPnet*, as well as a transition to *MFEnet II* [Leighton 1988b; Leighton and NMFECC 1988].

Access

National MFE Computer Center
University of California
Lawrence Livermore National Laboratory
P.O. Box 5509
Livermore, CA 94550
U.S.A.

12.2.3   ESnet

ESnet, or Energy Science Network, is a network for all DoE energy research programs [Leighton and NMFECC 1988]. It is a backbone network intended to support *HEPnet* and *MFEnet* in the United States, at least for DoE use [Leighton 1988a]. Access is restricted to projects sponsored by DoE.

Administration and Funding

ESnet is funded by the DoE and installed and operated by the NMFECC of LLNL. Representatives from each of the DoE energy research programs are appointed by the DoE Office of Scientific Computing (OSC) to the *ESnet* steering committee, which handles policy issues and wrote the *ESnet* program plan [ESnet 1987].

Scope and Phases

Plans for *ESnet* were completed by early 1987 [Leighton 1988b].

Phase 0   There are X.25 links to the Fermi National Accelerator Laboratory (FNAL), Brookhaven National Laboratory (BNL), Oak Ridge National Laboratories (ORNL), Florida State University (FSU), Lawrence Berkeley Laboratory (LBL), Lawrence Livermore National Laboratory (LLNL), Massachusetts Institute of Technology (MIT), and the Organisation Européenne pour la Recherche Nucléaire (CERN). This was Phase 0, which was in place in early 1988 [Leighton 1988b].

Phase I   A 56Kbps leased line IP backbone was operational in the fall of 1988, connecting NMFECC at LLNL, LBL, Argonne National Laboratory (ANL), Princeton Plasma Physics Laboratory (PPPL), the University of Texas at Austin (UT Austin), FSU, Los Alamos National Laboratory (LANL), and General Atomics Corporation (GAC) in San Diego. This was Phase I.

Phase II   More sites were to be added to the high-speed backbone during the last months of 1988, including CEBAF, FNAL, MIT, ORNL, and University of California at Los Angeles (UCLA). Some of these sites will be disconnected from *MFEnet*. This is Phase II.

Phase III   During 1989 and Phase III more sites will be disconnected from *MFEnet* and connected to *MFEnet II*.

Through Phase III, *ESnet* will consist of *MFEnet*, *MFEnet II*, and the X.25 backbone. The *ESnet* Phase 0 X.25 links will be absorbed into the backbone eventually, leaving only *ESnet* [Leighton and NMFECC 1988].

Protocols

Network technologies underlying IP on *MFEnet II* include Ethernet, point to point DMV, and HYPERchannel [Collins et al. 1987]. Both X.25 and IP will be provided in *ESnet*, which will support TCP/IP, DECNET, and the

MFEnet NSP protocols (initially on *MFEnet* and eventually over IP) in various component networks [LaQuey 1988].

Interconnections

Overseas links are planned to the following:

CERN	A 64Kbps satellite connection will upgrade the current X.25 PDN link.
Germany	A second 64Kbps satellite connection will have internal German connections by PDN.
Europe	A more general European access method is desired.
Japan	The existing *MFEnet* 9600bps link to Nagoya, Japan, is usable, but with restricted access. A 64Kbps satellite link is being considered [Leighton 1988b].

Access

National MFE Computer Center
University of California
Lawrence Livermore National Laboratory
P.O. Box 5509
Livermore, CA 94550
U.S.A.

12.2.4   NSI

The NASA Science Internet (*NSI*) is the National Aeronautics and Space Administration (NASA) metanetwork that includes the DECNET Space Physics Analysis Network (*SPAN*) and the TCP/IP internet NASA Science Network (*NSN*). There are also other DECNETs within NASA, such as those managed as part of flight projects. And there is the Canadian *DAN* DECNET, which uses an address space uncoordinated with *SPAN*. *NSI* would like to pull all of these together [Jones and Hart 1988]. The *SPAN* Data Systems Users' Working Group (DSUWG) and the NSN Users' Working Group (NSNUWG) have already been merged to form a NSI Users' Working Group (NSIUWG) [Jones 1988a].

Administration and Funding

It is impossible to understand NASA networks without understanding something about NASA's internal organization and networking history. A few of NASA's 17 centers are responsible for most of the networking activities. This is in keeping with the idea of lead centers promulgated by former NASA director Hans Mark.

MSFC (Marshall Space Flight Center) in Huntsville, Alabama, traditionally does administrative networks.

GSFC (Goddard Space Flight Center) in Greenbelt, Maryland, traditionally does networks for manned space flight missions.

JSC (Johnson Space Center) in Houston, Texas, has a 9600bps SNA network for administrative computing called *NASAnet*. This is in keeping with a policy that centers reserve the right to handle their own needs.

JPL (Jet Propulsion Laboratory) in Pasadena, California, did a tracking network for unmanned space missions. This was in keeping with a general policy of individual centers doing their own test range networks, with the whole planet being considered a range in this case. This network was later folded into the Space Shuttle communications network for economy.

ARC (Ames Research Center) at Moffett Field, California, has been involved with the *ARPANET* since 1970, when NASA agreed to fund 20 percent of an ILLIAC IV and to make it available as a research computer over the *ARPANET* [Roberts 1974]. An IBM 360/67 was also connected, and it was the only **TSS** machine on the network. The ILLIAC IV came with a Burroughs 6700 and a Digital PDP-10 and PDP-11. Since these machines had different word sizes and formats, ARC did extensive format conversion. The well-known *Internet* and *EASYnet* gateway *decwrl* is connected to one of ARC's *ARPANET* PSNs.

Headquarters in Washington, D.C., has traditionally seen computer communications as an administrative function. Thus, communication budget pays for Federal Telephone System (FTS) bills, for *Fax*, and for voice conferencing. The headquarters also started the *NPSS* (NASA Packet Switch System) which consists of X.25 links, some of them over PDNs. This is run by GSFC and is used for NASA mail, with a directory at MSFC. The main supplier is *Telenet*. There are also some *NPSS* point to point links. These could be used by centers to supply their own layer 3 protocols and thus to build their own networks. This is how *SPAN* began, connecting GSFC, MSFC, JSC, JPL, and, later, ARC.

Separate sources of funding are primarily responsible for many of the separate networking projects:

Code T (Program Support Communications) funds the Program Support Communications Network (*PSCN*), which serves as the physical infrastructure for *SPAN*, *NSN*, and all the networks mentioned below. It is partly an outgrowth of the dedicated links formerly associated with *NPSS* and partly a reaction to intercenter networks such as *SPAN* that had been developed by the centers using those links. *PSCN* is a circuit switched network—i.e., a collection of leased lines and microwave links. *PSCN* is managed from MSFC [Jones and Camp 1988], and the T1 links were paid for by MSFC. Tail circuits and services have been paid for by users since fiscal year 1989 (beginning October 1988) [Jones 1988b]. *NSI* is the user paying for one 56Kbps circuit to the European Space Operations Centre (ESOC) in Darmstadt, West Germany.

Code R (Office of Aeronautics and Space Technology) funds the Numerical Aerodynamics Simulation Network (*NASNET*), which is intended to promote aerospace technology competitive with that of Europe. This TCP/IP network is configured as a star centered on ARC (and connecting to, for example, Lewis in Cleveland and Langley in Virginia) for fast interactive access to several supercomputers, including a Cray YMP, two Cray 2s, and an ETA-10. It uses Digital Vitalink bridges. Although *NASNET* is also run from ARC, it is not run by the NSIPO (NASA Science Internet Project Office), and *NASNET* is *not* part of *NSI*.

Code S (Office of Space Station) has three networks planned based on SNA, DECNET, and TCP/IP.

Code E is the *OSSA (Office of Space Science and Applications)* of NASA headquarters, headed by Anthony Villasenor. OSSA does basic research in hard sciences. OSSA funds *NSI* and makes policy decisions and interagency agreements. *NSI* is managed by the NSIPO at ARC. ARC was asked by headquarters to do *NSI* because of its history of internetworking.

The purpose of the *NSI* project, which is headed by William P. Jones, is to coordinate all the networks that are involved, while consolidating OSSA science requirements; network engineering involving *PSCN* requirements, gateways, and other internetwork requirements; and network technology research and development, such as ISO-OSI migration [Jones and Camp 1988].

NASA is a participant in FRICC, with representative Anthony Villasenor of OSSA, and in the Research Interagency Backbone Group (RIG). *NSI* is also a participant in the California Federation of Research Internets (CFRI).

Interconnections

NSI is connected to *ARPANET, BARRNet, NSFNET, CSNET, BITNET, HEPnet, UUCP, USENET,* and numerous other networks. ARC funds the *NSFNET* connection between JVNC in Princeton, New Jersey, and INRIA in Sophia Antipolis, France.

Protocols

A *PSCN* T1 backbone was ordered 1 March 1988 and was installed as of November 1988. Engineering for this backbone was done by the Huntsville office of Boeing Computer Services (BCS), from OSSA requirements provided by NSIPO [Jones 1988b]. There is some redundancy in the links. The

T1 backbone is managed as pools of 56Kbps links allocated to data, voice, and other uses and switched dynamically as the need arises. Links can also be taken from pools other than the one allocated for a given purpose if the need is strong enough. Switching is done by about 14 roadrunner switches, which switch in a few seconds. There are eight earth stations.

NSI primarily uses this fast *PSCN* backbone, but there are also a few slow links, such as one at 9600bps to Rockwell in Anaheim. Some such links use SLIP, others use IP over X.25, such as one to Kansas State University (KSU), and others use Proteon routers. There are some Annex terminal servers and *MILNET* TACs, as well as nine MICOM terminal switches inside ARC [Jones and Hart 1988].

Plans

There are plans for eventual transition of both *NSN* and *SPAN* to use ISO-OSI protocols [Jones 1988c].

Access

William P. Jones
jones@nsipo.arc.nasa.gov
+1-415-694-6482
MS 233-17

James P. Hart
hart@orion.arc.nasa.gov
+1-415-694-6251
MS 240-9

NASA Ames Research Center
Moffett Field, CA 94035
U.S.A.

12.2.5   NSN

The NASA Science Network (*NSN*) is a TCP/IP based internetwork that serves NASA flight projects and all NASA disciplines. As of October 1988, *NSN* served about 25 backbone hosts, with an eventual expected internet population of 10,000 hosts [Jones and Hart 1988]. Its backbone is shown in Figure 12.7. *NSN* uses the *PSCN* infrastructure and is part of the NASA Science Internet (*NSI*), along with *SPAN*.

NSN is managed by the NASA Science Internet Project Office (NSIPO) at Ames Research Center (ARC) on behalf of the Office of Space Science and Applications (OSSA) [Jones and Camp 1988] and in cooperation with the NSN Users' Working Group (NSNUWG) [Jones 1988b].

NSN was developed by ARC beginning in 1987, partly in support of the Goddard Space Flight Center (GSFC) Pilot Land Data System (PLDS). *NSN* was originally intended to be a network for land scientists in analogy

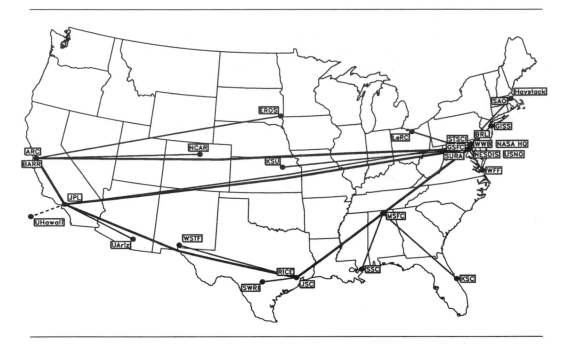

Figure 12.7. *NASA Science Network Gateway Interconnections (January 1989) [NSIPO 1989a]*

to the way *SPAN* was a network for space physicists [Jones 1988b]. The TCP/IP protocols were used (mostly over Ethernets) to permit scientists to use a variety of vendor hardware, and this work led to the *NSI* emphasis on connection of networks (internetworking) rather than just connection of hosts (networking) [Jones 1988c]. The principal architect of *NSN* is Marc Siegel of ARC [Jones and Hart 1988].

Access

Marc Siegel
msiegel@ames.arc.nasa.gov

William P. Jones
jones@nsipo.arc.nasa.gov
+1-415-694-6482
MS 233-17
NASA Ames Research Center
Moffett Field, CA 94035
U.S.A.

12.2.6   SPAN

SPAN, the Space Physics Analysis Network, is a multimission, correlative data comparison network serving projects and facilities of the American NASA and having extensions to Japan, Canada, and many countries in Europe in addition to extensive links in the United States [Green 1988]. These agencies have traditionally set up data collection networks to serve specific space missions, but *SPAN* is mission independent, general purpose, low cost, and easy to connect to. (However, it is sometimes used to support specific missions, such as the ICE mission to the Giacobini-Zinner comet [Sanderson et al. 1986] and the encounter with Halley's Comet [Green and King 1986].) It is an operational network in the sense that it is not intended to promote the development of network technology, but it is a research network in that it provides an infrastructure for space-related research. It was not created to access supercomputers, but supercomputers are becoming more available through it.

There were about 100 hosts on *SPAN* in September 1986 [Quarterman and Hoskins 1986], about 500 by the end of 1987, and around 2,400 in November 1988 [Sisson 1988]. Figure 12.8 shows the *SPAN* backbone. All *SPAN* hosts must run DECNET [Sisson 1988]. Outside of NASA, there are many participating universities and laboratories, such as Los Alamos National Laboratory (LANL). There are many local area networks indirectly connected to *SPAN*. There is a transatlantic X.25 link between Marshall Space Flight Center (MSFC) in Huntsville, Alabama, and the European Space Operations Centre (ESOC) of the European Space Agency (ESA) in Darmstadt, West Germany. A 19.2Kbps link was installed in September 1986 from Goddard Space Flight Center (GSFC) to Germany. There are DECNET circuits (running on X.25) running from GSFC to Kyoto University (KU) in Kyoto, Japan, Cerro Tollo Inter-American Observatory in Santiago, Chile, and the Canadian *DAN*, in Ontario, Canada. By early 1989, there were to be additional circuits with DECNET over X.25 to the National Space Development Agency (NASDA) in Tokyo [Sisson 1988].

Administration

Guidance for the network is provided by the users through the Data Systems Users' Working Group (DSUWG) and project scientists [Green and Zwickl 1986]. Direct administration is done by project managers, network managers, and routing center managers [Green et al. 1987a], particularly by the National Space Science Data Center (NSSDC) at GSFC. NSSDC has many useful publications, including a node directory [Ha et al. 1988] and a security guide [Lopez-Swafford and Gary 1987].

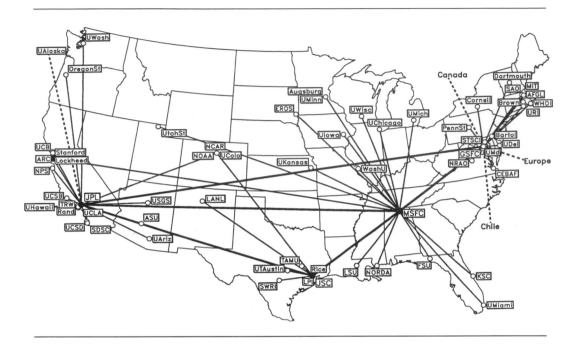

Figure 12.8. *SPAN backbone map (January 1989) [NSIPO 1989b]*

Funding

As a general rule, *SPAN* backbone and tail circuits in the United States are funded by various offices of NASA. For example, NASA science communications requirements are usually met with 9600bps circuits as a baseline for service. Higher bandwidth or more extensive services require more project-oriented funding. Participating organizations pay for their own host computers and network interfaces [Sisson 1988].

Protocols

SPAN is currently based on DECNET Phase IV and will migrate to Phase V for ISO-OSI compatibility as it becomes available. Lower layers are mostly provided by *PSCN* [Peters 1986]. Local Ethernets are also used. The backbone of the network consists of redundant 56Kbps links among five routing centers, at Goddard Space Flight Center (GSFC) in Greenbelt, Maryland; Johnson Space Center (JSC) in Houston, Texas; Jet Propulsion Laboratory (JPL) in Pasadena, California; Marshall Space Flight Center (MSFC) in Huntsville, Alabama; and Ames Research Center (ARC) at Moffett Field, California. The backbone to European *SPAN*, or *E-SPAN* [Sanderson 1988; Sanderson et al. 1988], is a 19.2Kbps link between GSFC and MSFC. Each routing center is the center of a 9.6Kbps/56Kbps link to other institutions on the network [Sisson 1988].

DECNET addresses consist of 16 bits, 6 of which specify an area, while the other 10 specify a node within the area. Since there are only 64 possible areas, management of area numbers is very important. Within Digital's DECNET-based company network, *EASYnet*, all area numbers are in use; thus direct gateways between *EASYnet* and other DECNETs are problematic. But there are many wide area DECNET networks, and *SPAN* management at GSFC is the focal point for coordination and distribution of area numbers for most of these. A major task of *SPAN*'s routing centers is the assignment of nodes to their respective area number [Sisson 1988]. (ESA provides a similar forum in Europe and acts in coordination with *SPAN*.)

Interconnections

Interconnections from *SPAN* are shown in Table 12.2. The quotation marks shown in the table are necessary.

SPAN can be reached from *Telenet*, and there are gateways to *BITNET*, *Internet* [Quarterman and Hoskins 1986], and *JANET*. There is a direct gateway to *NSFNET* at NCAR [Koblinksy and Choy 1988]. In addition, *SPAN* and *HEPnet* are interconnected and share the same address space [LaQuey 1988]. It is possible to reach *SPAN* from many other networks [Sisson and Posinski 1988]. There is a document specifically about reaching *SPAN* from *JANET* [Hapgood 1986].

History

Planning for *SPAN* began in 1980, and operations commenced in 1981 [Green et al. 1987b]. Much of the original hardware, such as the routing computers at each routing center, came from NASA. *SPAN* was originally oriented toward researchers in Solar Terrestrial and Interplanetary Physics but is now expanding to serve other disciplines. DECNET was used because it came with **VMS** on Digital VAXes, which were much less expensive than the machines previously used for NASA research. Later, **4.3BSD UNIX** and TCP/IP began to be widely used in some of the centers (see *NSI* and *NSN* earlier in this chapter) [Jones and Hart 1988].

Plans

Migration to ISO-OSI protocols as implementations become available is planned.

Table 12.2. *SPAN interconnections*

Network	Syntax
Internet	LBL::"*user*@{**DNS**}"
Internet	JPL::"*user*@{**DNS**}"
BITNET	LBL::"*user*@*host*.BITNET"
EASYnet	LBL::"*user*%*host*.DEC@decwrl.dec.com"

Access

Access is limited to researchers in appropriate areas, and unauthorized access is a federal offense.

Cindy Posinski
Pat Sisson
NETMGR%NCF.SPAN@JPL.NASA.GOV
NCF::NETMGR
+1-301-286-7251
SPAN Network Information Center
National Space Science Data Center
Code 630.2
NASA Goddard Space Flight Center
Greenbelt, MD 20771
U.S.A.

There is an extensive bibliography about *SPAN*, as well as the actual documents, available by contacting

NSSDCA::REQUEST
REQUEST@NSSDCA.GSFC.NASA.GOV

or by sending a postal address and a list of desired documents to the Request Coordination Office at the above address.

12.2.7   NRAO

NRAO is the U.S. National Radio Astronomy Observatory network. It uses DECNET and is integrated into the *PHYSNET* address space [Wells 1987].

Access
BRAUN%AIPS@HAMLET.CALTECH.EDU
+1-505-772-4335

12.2.8   CITNET

CITNET is the California Institute of Technology Network. There is a host, *CIT-HAMLET.ARPA*, which is also on *ARPANET* and *BITNET*. Many of the machines run **VMS** and the **Software Tools** mail system from Lawrence Berkeley Laboratory (LBL). There are direct connections to *NRAO* and

HEPnet using DECNET, and *CITNET* is integrated into the *PHYSNET* address space [Wells 1987].

Access
Postmaster@Hamlet.CALTECH.EDU
POSTMAST@CALTECH.BITNET

12.2.9   EIES

EIES (pronounced "eyes") is one of the oldest conferencing systems in the world, having begun operations in October 1976 [Hiltz 1978]. It has a broad range of users and uses, from research to military and from government to personal. There are about 2,000 users, mostly in the United States, but others are from 17 other countries.

Administration

EIES is owned and operated by the New Jersey Institute of Technology (NJIT) and supported by fees collected from its users.

Services and Protocols

Services include most interactive conferencing ones, from mail to lists to true conferencing. Particular emphasis is given to supporting group decision-making processes. The software is called **EIES 1** and is widely known for its extremely rich feature sets. These features are used in experiments conducted by NJIT and reported in the academic literature. *EIES* must be the most widely studied conferencing system in the world.

Interconnections

Interconnections from *EIES* to other networks are done through *DASnet*.

History

The first year, through October 1977, was a pilot test phase. There were field trials sponsored by NSF from November 1977. NSF funding ended 1 April 1980 [Hiltz and Turoff 1981].

 EIES was designed for communication among geographically dispersed scientists [Hiltz 1978]. It was originally strongly modeled on specific existing mechanisms, such as *Delphi* [Price 1975]. The **EIES** conferencing software is similar to that of **Discussion, PLANET,** and **Confer,** but its principal ancestor is **EMISARI** [Hiltz and Turoff 1981]. Unlike **EMISARI, EIES** was not limited to crisis situations but was for research. There was a shift toward more generality [Hiltz 1980], and new services have been invented, such as the *Information Market Place* [Turoff 1985; Turoff and

Chinai 1985]. There is a recent strong emphasis on *not* merely automating existing mechanisms [Turoff 1980; Turoff 1985]; and on providing mechanisms by which the user, more than the developer, may determine the form of interaction [Hiltz and Turoff 1985] in order to prevent information overload, which was a problem encountered rather early, by 1981 [Hiltz and Turoff 1981, 749].

EIES has spawned many other projects, such as *CARINET* and *SFMT*.

Plans

The planned successor system, EIES 2, is intended to be **UNIX** based and thus portable over a variety of hardware. There is another planned system called Tailorable EIES (TEIES) that will run only on **VM** on IBM hardware. Unlike EIES 2, which may be distributable, TEIES is intended to be a single machine system.

> **Access**
>
> Bob Arms
> Operations Manager
> +1-201-596-3437
> Operations Manager
> EIES
> New Jersey Institute of Technology
> Newark, NJ 07102
> U.S.A.
>
> For protocols and interconnections:
>
> James Whitescarver +1-201-596-2937

12.2.10   BST

BST (Big Sky Telegraph) is a conferencing system founded and operated by Frank Odasz and Regina Odasz, both of whom are education professors at Western Montana College, a teacher's college in Dillon, Montana. Funding comes from several organizations, including US West. This is an unusual system in that it is primarily rural, intended to connect 116 one-room schoolhouses to aid in teacher recertification (i.e., teaching teachers). The system, which is used to teach real courses, was first used on 1 February 1988. The sysop is Elaine Garrett [Hughes 1988].

BST was implemented by David Hughes, a longtime conferencing expert, who was also the first person to teach a course for college credit using a conferencing system, in 1981, for Colorado Technical College, over *The Source*. Hughes was concerned about the state of computing in academia, especially in rural colleges. Because of his emphasis on growth potential, the *BST* machine was always multiuser. *BST* is an Intel 386-based machine running **XENIX**. The conferencing software is a version of the

xbbs bulletin board program customized by Hughes. He chose **xbbs** instead of **Participate, Confer, Caucus,** and other possibilities because of concern for ease of use by new users and usability on a multiuser system (i.e., **UNIX**). For the same reason, an incoming WATS line was installed from the beginning (there were three other dialup lines). Many of the modems were mailed to the schools with instructions. *BST* also runs the **Foxbase** database program (an augmented version of **DBASE-3**), which was a key factor in the choice of SCO **XENIX** as the version of **UNIX** to use. The availability of a database on the conferencing system is very important so that teachers can handle data on the same system they use for taking courses and communicating with each other [Hughes 1988].

Part of the software customization was to make the user interface use a metaphor of a small town, where, for example, the main menu was referred to as "main street." Hughes was greatly concerned with getting new users with no experience in this technology to post messages, not just read them. The specific measure he looked for was 50 percent messages per calls—i.e., every other call should result in a posted message. (Over the lifetime of a previous system in Colorado Springs, the *Old Colorado City Electronic Cottage*, a single line bulletin board system running **TBBS**, Hughes logged 50,000 calls and 26,000 messages from 8,600 users.) The actual percentage on *BST* was about 60 percent, in tens of thousands of calls. This indicated that the initial users really were using the system. The first users were later encouraged to help teach other users, and use of the system spread quickly. Another set of groups using *BST* is the Women's Resource Centers of Montana, which is thinking of starting its own system. The Economic Development Corporation (EDC) of Montana applied to US West in 1988 for a grant to start its own system and was referred by US West to *BST* as a model, which it ended up using. Frank Odasz is teaching representatives from each of seven counties how to do this sort of conferencing and database use, in a formal course. Other courses taught on *BST* by other teachers include English 101, involving many students reviewing each other's papers and using pen names for anonymity. The system has become so popular that three gubernatorial candidates visited it during the 1988 campaign. There is interest in Wyoming, Colorado, and other states as well [Hughes 1988].

Hughes installed another Compaq machine in the summer of 1988. This one runs **MS-DOS** and has voicemail, an optical scanner, Fax, and various other unusual services and devices attached to it. Marge Rolando of the Office of Public Instruction of the state Department of Education has transferred most of a large library of Apple software from a mainframe to this machine. She uses *BST* herself, and orders for other software can be made through it [Hughes 1988].

There are no *UUCP* connections [Shapard 1988].

There is a similar service in Colorado that is sometimes used to connect rooms of schools that do have telephones, but only one; this is often cheaper and more flexible than wiring the buildings. A business shortwave license is used for this rather than a ham license.

Hughes also runs a system called *Chariot* in Colorado Springs [Shapard 1988].

Access
David R. Hughes
uunet!hpda!hplabs!hp-lsd!oldcolo!dave
+1-719-636-2040
6 North 24th Street
Colorado Springs, CO 80904
U.S.A.

12.2.11   Confer

Confer is a conferencing system at the University of Michigan (Michigan) based on the **Confer** software developed by Dr. Robert Parnes. The system has been operating since 1975 and was originally intended to be only for students and faculty, but access has since been granted to many outsiders. The Professional Development Office (PDO) does this as a nonprofit service for educational groups. There are membership and connection time fees for individuals. The system is accessible through *Telenet*, *Datapac*, *Autonet*, and *Merit* [Morabito 1986].

The current version of the software, **Confer II**, available since 1979, is marketed by Advertel Communication Systems, Inc. (Advertel), which also supports a system using it at the Computing Services Center of Wayne State University (Wayne State). Other users include the Society for Motion Picture and Television Engineers and the Kellogg Foundation [Advertel 1988].

Access
For the PDO *Confer* system, contact:

Professional Development Office
+1-313-763-9497
University of Michigan
School of Education
610 East University
Ann Arbor, MI 48109
U.S.A.

For the WSU *Confer* system, contact:

Computing Services Center
Wayne State University
Detroit, MI
U.S.A.

For the **Confer II** software, contact:
Dr. Robert Parnes

President
+1-313-665-2512
Advertel Communication Systems, Inc.
2067 Ascot Road
Ann Arbor, MI 48103
U.S.A.

12.2.12　Army Forum

U.S. Army Forum (*Army Forum*) is a conferencing system based on **Confer** software [U.S. Army Forum 1984] that has been operational since 1983 [Advertel 1988]. There were about 400 users in June 1984, with 25 conferences, collectively called *FORUMNET* or the *Skunkworks*. Administration is by a staff at the Department of Army (DoA) headquarters. The host machine is at Wayne State University (Wayne State) in Detroit [U.S. Army Forum 1984].

The primary goal is force modernization—i.e., developing new operations, strategies, and tactics, getting them to the field, getting them understood there, and getting feedback to headquarters. Participants include both commissioned and noncommissioned officers, as well as civilians. Normal command boundaries are deliberately crossed in the *Skunkworks* in developing ideas, but the regular chain of command is responsible for making decisions based on those ideas. The intensity and length of discussion possible is something that would be prohibitive if all the participants had to be in one place [U.S. Army Forum 1984]. See the previous section on *Confer*. *Army Forum* should not be confused with the historical system *FOORUM* by the Institute for the Future (IFF).

Access

Director
U.S. Army Forum
Department of the Army
The Pentagon
Washington, DC
U.S.A.

12.2.13   PeaceNet

PeaceNet was formed in September 1985 with an original and continuing focus on the peace movement. *PeaceNet* sees computer conferencing as community and organization and hopes to be a community infrastructure for peace organizations in the United States and elsewhere.

Administration

PeaceNet is owned and operated by the nonprofit corporation Institute for Global Communications (IGC) of San Francisco, which is a division of the Tides Foundation, a public charity. The staff is quite small: two programmers, two system managers, two billing people, and two company administrators. There were about 2,300 users in May 1988, but a total of 3,800 were wanted by the end of 1988 for economic self-sustenance. Most users reach the machine by *Telenet*; this means a typical access speed of 1200bps or perhaps 2400bps. One third of *PeaceNet*'s operating budget goes to *Telenet*.

Services and Uses

General conferencing services and electronic mail are the basic services. There are more than 200 conference topics, ranging from socially responsible investing to presidential candidates to nuclear weapons to an extensive set on Central America. The latter are known as the Central America Resource Network (CARNet) and are a project of the Western States Central America Network (WestCAN). Despite the similarity of acronyms, this should not be confused with *CARINET*, which is a conference on *EIES*. There is also an unusual relational database service based on **Informix** and **notesfiles**. Databases currently being compiled include lists of peace groups, speakers, and foundations. There are mail interconnections with numerous other systems through *DASnet*. IGC distributes a quarterly paper newsletter called *NetNews*, and there is a corresponding online conference, as well as an online user directory.

The peace movement is taken to include the ecological movement, and thus IGC has taken on *EcoNet*, whose primary goal is "to tie together local, national, and international ecology and development groups to allow for collaborative action on critical issues" [Zaunbrecher 1987]. *EcoNet* was formed in July 1987 by the Farallones Institute (Farallones) of Occidental, California, as a conference on Apple's *OnTyme* system. Health is another related issue, and *HomeoNet* is another recent project of IGC, started in October 1987. There is close cooperation with Amnesty International (A.I.), particularly regarding its action alerts [Miller 1987]. They are jointly developing tools for coordinating events and have collaborated in the production of a series of concert tours by internationally famous musicians in support of A.I.

Interconnections

Interconnections from *PeaceNet* to other networks are shown in Table 12.3. They are mostly done through *DASnet*. The user enters the indicated addresses at the same *To:* and *Cc:* prompts as for sending mail to people on the local machine. The prefixes in the right-hand column of the table, including the colons, are required. That is, the colon takes the function of the at sign (@) in RFC822 mail, with reverse order of the local and host parts. For some networks, mostly (but not entirely) the ones for which gatewaying charges are not required, the at sign is used. Apparently, true DNS syntax is allowed for the *Internet*, but RFC733-style network domain tags are used for the rest, even for networks such as *JANET, CSNET*, and *ACSnet*, which have real domain names for all of their hosts. The syntax for *Dialcom* uses the colon for source routing, as if it were a UUCP exclamation point (!).

History and Future

PeaceNet originally ran on Apple's *OnTyme* system. It is currently a Plexus P35 running **UNIX** and conferencing software written by the Association for Progressive Communications (APC), an umbrella organization that IGC helped found, partly in order to coordinate the concerts mentioned above and partly composed of musicians. IGC hopes to promote the development of local autonomous but connected systems in other parts of the world and is currently setting up a machine in Nairobi, Kenya. It will also use APC software. That software is being ported to machines based on the Intel 386 CPU due to overload of the current machines; this work is partly supported by the MacArthur Foundation.

IGC has already helped set up *GreenNet* in London and its hourly UUCP connection with the *PeaceNet* machine, as well as *UPGCN* in San José, Costa Rica [Graham 1987]. IGC is also involved in connecting the Soviet Union through *SFMT*.

Access

Mark Graham
PeaceNet Director
mgraham%cdp.uucp@parcvax.xerox.com
uunet!hpda!hplabs!cdp!mgraham
cdp!mgraham%labrea@stanford.bitnet
DASnet: [DE3MIR]mgraham
DASnet: igc:mgraham
+1-415-923-0900
Fax: +1-415-923-1665
Telex: 154205417 ID: igc:mgraham

Table 12.3. *PeaceNet interconnections*

Network	Syntax
Charges for these	
AT&T Mail	attmail:*user*
AT&T Land Mail	landmail (with a special message format)
BIX	bix:*user*
CARINET	carinet:*user*
DC Meta (THE META NETWORK)	dcmeta:*user*
Dialcom	dialcom:*host*:*user*
TCN (Dialcom host 41)	tcn:*user*
IMC (Dialcom host 42)	imc:*user*
EasyLink	easylink:*user*
EIES	eies:*user*
GeoNet	geo*host*:*user*
MCI Mail	mci:*user*
NWI	nwi:*user*
The Source	source:*user*
TWICS	twics:*user*
UNISON	unison:*user*
No charges for these	
ACSnet	*user@host*.acsnet
Internet	*user@*{**DNS**}
BITNET	*user@host*.bitnet
CSNET	*user@host*.csnet
EASYnet	*user@host*.dec
Ean	*user@host*.ean
GreenNet	gn:*user*
JANET	*user@host*.janet
JUNET	*user@host*.junet
Portal	portal:*user*
UUCP	*user@host*.uucp
WELL	well:*user*

Institute for Global Communications
3228 Sacramento Street
San Francisco, CA 94115
U.S.A.

12.2.14   DASnet

DASnet is a gateway machine that connects diverse networks. It is named after DA Systems of Campbell, California, which has owned and operated it since its beginning in July 1987 [Licalzi 1987]. A *DASnet* subscriber specifies an already existing account on one of the commercial services for *DASnet* to deliver mail to. This avoids the problem of the user having to dial up and log in on each system. It is also possible to reach many of the noncommercial networks.

There are few direct users of *DASnet*: it gateways mail and conferences from other systems but originates little of its own. Batch file transfer between subscribers is being designed; both ASCII and binary (where possible) transfers will be implemented. *DASnet* provides a printed directory of subscribers [Fisher 1987]. Some services, such as *TWICS*, *EIES*, and *UNISON*, provide online copies. *DASnet* is experimenting with a mail directory lookup service similar to the *SRI-NIC.ARPA* WHOIS service, but allowing search keys for information in addition to users' names. *DASnet* subscribers are also listed in the independent National Electronic Mail Registry (*NEMR*) [Data Channels 1987].

Each *DASnet* subscriber pays a monthly connection fee and a per message fee. A subscriber can send mail to any user of any of the gatewayed networks. This is usually done by sending mail to a special *DASnet* account on the mail system of the sending user. The user names the target system and user mailbox in the *Subject:* line, if the originating mail system has one, or in the first line of text. The user usually sees the outgoing message like this:

```
From: source-system-mailbox
To: source-system-DASnet-mailbox
Subject: DASnet-address!actual subject

<text>
```

The *DASnet* address usually looks like this:

```
[host]user
```

where *host* is an alphabetic (or sometimes numeric) code for the target system and *user* is whatever user identifier the target system requires. This format is used for historical reasons, having been invented at DA Systems in about 1983 for their CIM applications.

The exclamation point in the *Subject:* line indicates that everything before it is to be used for addressing; anything after it on that line is ignored for addressing purposes, although the destination user will see it. For systems that do not provide a return receipt requested service, *DASnet* interprets two exclamation points in the *Subject:* line as a request for that service. The user is usually notified when the message is received by the target system [Gorin 1987], but some systems, such as *MCI Mail*, permit receipts to be returned when the recipient reads the message.

When a message passes through the *DASnet* machine, *DASnet* replaces the contents of the *Subject:* line that the sender provided with a *DASnet* code for the sender's system and the sender's mailbox identifier on that system.

The target system automatically makes the *From:* line contain the name of the *DASnet* gateway mailbox on the target system [Gorin 1987]. The target user sees the incoming message like this:

    From: target-system-DASnet-mailbox
    To: target-system-mailbox
    Subject: DASnet-address!actual subject

    <text>

All the recipient has to do to respond is to reply as to any other message, being sure to use the given *Subject:* line. Subscribers are charged for each message they receive from nonsubscribers [Link-Up 1987].

Attempts by two nonsubscribers to gateway between two networks through *DASnet* will fail, with no message returned. In other words, this is not a general gatewaying service but is only for those who pay subscription fees. This kind of system is sometimes called a *forwarder* or *refiler*. However, *DASnet* sells group subscriptions, and several other systems, such as *PeaceNet*, *UNISON*, *GeoMail*, and *TWICS*, subscribe to *DASnet* for their users [Link-Up 1987]. *DASnet* subscribers can get *to* anyone on any of the gatewayed networks.

Some services have mail systems that are sophisticated enough to allow better user interfaces. These include the following:

- *BIX* lets the user specify a *DASnet* address of the above form, a domain address, or a couple of other forms in the *To:* or *Cc:* fields.
- *UNISON* allows the user to select a target system from a menu using *DASnet*'s network directory information. The system then prompts the user for appropriate addressing information for the target system. Searches for information in the network directory by company, network, or system name are possible.
- *PeaceNet* allows addresses in the *To:* and *Cc:* fields and does not require putting them in the *Subject:* line.

DASnet has subscribers throughout the world, and currently links 11 conferencing systems: *EIES, PeaceNet, EcoNet, DC Meta, The Source, Portal, WELL, TWICS, NWI, UNISON,* and *BIX*; seven commercial mail systems: *MCI Mail, AT&T Mail, Dialcom, GeoMail, Telemail, EasyLink,* and *Envoy 100*; and one noncommercial mail network: *UUCP*. (Through *UUCP* it is possible to reach many networks that use domains, such as *EUnet* and *JUNET*.) It is possible to reach the *Telex* and *Fax* networks indirectly through *GeoMail* [Rubenking 1988], as well as various networks that support domain addressing. DA Systems says that 2.5 million people can be reached through its service, plus another 2 million through the Fax connection. The number of direct subscribers is unknown. Two prominent systems that declined to connect are *GEnie* and *CompuServe* [EMMS 1987].

All connections are by dialout modems, at either 1200bps or 2400bps, often over PDNs. *DASnet* claims a maximum of eight hours to transfer a message from one subscriber's system to another's. The *DASnet* service uses IBM PCs and clones running the **QNX** operating system, which is multiuser and multitasking. These machines (there are seven of them) are connected over an Ethernet. The operating system allows easy migration of tasks between machines for load balancing. A few individual subscribers use **MS-DOS** software supplied by *DASnet*, but most have accounts on the services listed above. *DASnet* ordinarily dials up the subscriber's machine (between 1 and 24 times daily, increasing with traffic) and communicates using the local mail or conferencing software [Gorin 1987]. It can deal with **Caucus, CoSy, Participate, UNIX** mail systems, UUCP, **VMS Mail**, and **WYLBUR**. Proprietary *DASnet* protocols are used for transfers from the *DASnet* gateway accounts on the subscriber services to *DASnet* machines. There are basically two of these protocols, and both have error checking. Some subscriber machines cannot support these protocols, and *DASnet* may in those cases resort to reading back mail as it is sent. A future possibility is to put a PC at the customer's site.

DASnet has a **UNIX** machine on the *UUCP* network, *daslink*. Another machine, *dasnet*, appears in the *UUCP* maps, but it is actually a deliberate illusion for routing purposes. There are two registered *Internet* DNS domains, *das.net* and *das.com* (with three nameservers and a forwarder). But it is pointless to attempt to provide a gateway syntax table here because the user interface to the gatewaying facility depends on the network the user is sending from, as there are no direct subscriber general purpose accounts on the *DASnet* machines [Gorin 1987]. (There are a few special purpose logins for subscribers that use *DASnet* software to exchange messages).

DA Systems began as a Computer Aided Design (CAD) company in 1974 and moved into computer integration manufacturing [Data Channels 1987]. Apparently *DASnet* originated when DA Systems personnel invented it for their own use in communicating while doing other business. The company plans to attract more business subscribers to the service. It is experimenting with clarified billing methods (e.g., allowing the end user to see each hop and each address of each hop). Connections to other services are still sought.

Access

DA Systems, Inc.
+1-408-559-7434
Telex: 910-380-3530
1503 East Campbell Avenue
Campbell, CA 95008
U.S.A.

12.3   *Canada {CA}*

There are systems of every kind in Canada, including commercial mail services, academic conferencing systems, national and regional research networks, and regional internets.

Since November 1987, mail service under the domain *CA* has been coordinated for all of the following national mail networks in Canada: *Net-North*, *CDNnet*, *DREnet*, and *UUCP*, with links to *CSNET*, *NSFNET*, the *Internet*, *BITNET*, and European *Ean* networks. Many of the sites connected are shown in Figure 12.9.

The *CA* domain is registered with the *Internet* and has DNS nameservers, as well as *UUCP* map entries for **pathalias**, *NetNorth* and *CDNnet* routing tables, etc. The information is actually kept in a neutral form, and it is the responsibility of the various networks to translate to their format. The *Internet* DNS nameservice was originally provided by *CSNET*, but since August 1988 the primary nameserver for the *CA* domain has been operated by *CDNnet* at *relay.ubc.ca*, and the *Internet* connection is through a leased line link to the *NSFNET* backbone node at the University of Washington (Washington) in Seattle [Demco 1988a]. Registration of *CA* was done by John Demco of the University of British Columbia (UBC) and *CDNnet*. Administration may eventually be taken over by an organization such as the National Research Council (NRC) [Demco 1987a].

The domain name *CA* was chosen because RFC920 [Postel and Reynolds 1984], X.400, X.500, and ISO9594 all recommend use of ISO3166, which specifies two letter country codes. Subdomains are intended to be mostly geographical, with second level domains being the common Canadian two letter provincial codes [Demco 1987b]. However, as of August 1988, most second level subdomains were not geographical, instead representing national organizations. All universities are considered to be national organizations [Demco 1988a]. It is hoped that all participating organizations will choose subdomains in accordance with the recommendations of X.500 and ISO9594. ''The use of nationally recognized abbreviations is recommended, especially since subdomain names will be widely

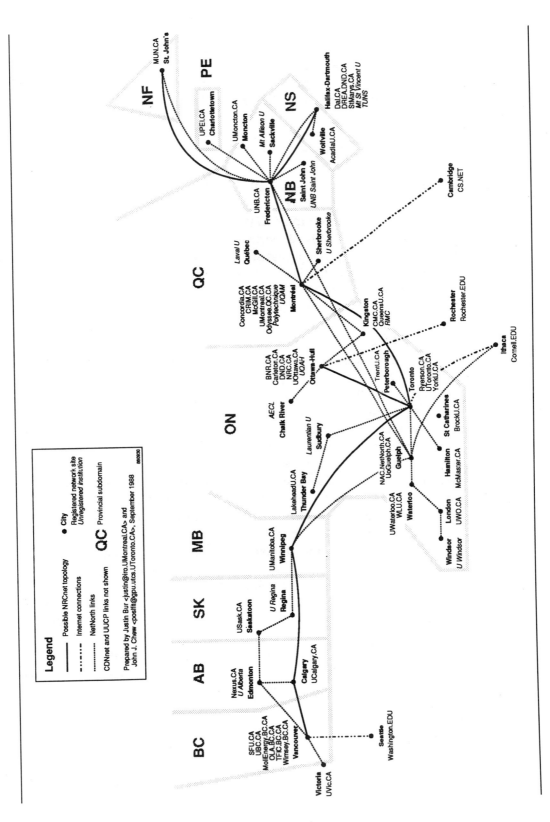

Figure 12.9. *Major network sites in Canada (3 September 1988)* [Bur 1988]

distributed and will appear on letterheads and on business cards" [Demco 1987c]. There were about 40 domains registered in November 1988: 30 educational, 10 commercial, and 2 government [Prindeville 1988a]. There are also some Canadian hosts in the top level *Internet* DNS domains *COM*, *EDU*, etc.

The NRC is also considering developing a national research network, *NRCnet*, similar to *NSFNET*. Meanwhile, *DREnet* is integrated into the *Internet*, and the Ontario regional network *Onet* and the British Columbia regional network *BCnet* are, as well, through *NSFNET* (the same *NSFNET* connection serves both *BCnet* and *CDNnet*). These and other Canadian regional networks, for example *CRIM* or *RISQ* in Quebec, are likely to participate in *NRCnet*. *CRIM* is connected to the *Internet* through *CSNET*: both *CRIM* and *Onet* are likely to assist in providing nameservice for the *CA* domain [Vachon 1988a]. These regional networks use a variety of protocols, including TCP/IP, DECNET, X.25, and X.400 [Prindeville 1988b].

Information of mid-1989 indicates that the new national network may be called *NRNet*.

The cost of leased lines in Canada is a problem [Hunter and Curley 1988], especially compared to the cost of lines to the United States. This makes policy-based routing important so that Canadian traffic can be made to traverse Canadian transcontinental links [Prindeville 1988a]. Canadian law permits passing data out of the country and back in if it is processed in the foreign country: does IP forwarding count as processing, or does adding *Received:* lines to mail [Prindeville 1988b]? The Canadian federal communication policy-making body, the Canadian Radio-Television and Telecommunications Commission (CRTC), says that the government intends to control only the basic services offered by common carriers. The specific issue of computer networks has apparently never been raised. An operational *NRCnet* may force the issue [Demco 1988a].

Major portions of the *USENET* news network are also in Canada. There is a large DECNET network called *DAN* (Data Analysis Network) which is roughly equivalent to *SPAN* but does not use a coordinated address space. There are various special purpose networks run by banks, airlines, governments, the military, and private companies [Taylor and Heyworth 1988].

There are several unusual Canadian conferencing systems, such as *Web*, *NCCN*, and *CoSy*, and at least one large commercial system, *Envoy 100*. The Canadian PDN *Datapac* is the oldest in the world, and there are also other Canadian PDNs.

Access

Send a message to the *CDNnet* archive server, archive-server@relay.ubc.ca, with contents

send ca-domain introduction

or

send ca-domain application-form

To retrieve a list of the *CA* subdomain registrations, send to the same address with contents

index ca-domain

The actual registrations are available as well, e.g.,

index ca-domain ca.ubc

Or mail a message to infoserver@sh.cs.net containing

Request: info
Topic: domain.CA

For general information on Canadian networking developments, contact:

Listmaster@CS.McGill.CA

12.3.1   CDNnet

The primary purpose of *CDNnet* is to provide network services to the Canadian research, education, and advanced development community [Demco 1988a]. This is the original **Ean** X.400 network, the first X.400 network in the world [Prindeville 1988a]. The first intermachine messages were exchanged on *CDNnet* in 1983 [Neufeld et al. 1985; Kawaguchi et al. 1985; Uhlig 1986]. The network is independent of the Canadian Department of Defense; *CDN* is a common abbreviation for Canada [Demco 1988a].

Administration and Funding

CDNnet is administered by CDNnet Headquarters at the University of British Columbia (UBC). Policy decisions are made by a committee of the whole consisting of one representative from each member organization and by an executive committee elected from the committee of the whole. The executive committee recently decided to allow commercial enterprises to support their research and educational clients over the network [Demco 1988a].

Funding for the network has come from membership dues and a grant from the Natural Sciences and Engineering Research Council (NSERC). The grant was for three years ending in 1988 and was used for cooperative research and development of the **Ean** X.400 software between UBC and Sydney Development Corporation (SDC). (SDC owns the commercial rights to the **Ean** software.) Support for *CDNnet* was included in the grant, but annual contributions to the network decreased for each year as membership increased. The network was expected to be completely supported by membership dues by the end of 1988. Annual dues have been collected since 1987, with rates set according to the type of organization (educational, government, nonprofit, or commercial) and according to the number of *CDNnet* hosts at an organization. Organizations pay the telecommunications costs for connections to other organizations. *CDNnet* does not have usage charges except to recover the costs associated with gateways and bridges to other networks [Gilmore and Neufeld 1985].

Scope

The exact number of hosts is difficult to count because the **Ean** software allows a single Message Transfer Agent (MTA) to span a number of CPUs. Estimated numbers of MTAs over several years are given in Table 12.4, with 175 hosts as of August 1988. One *CDNnet* institution has nine colleges. The host that is probably the busiest, *ean.ubc.ca*, processed about 5,000 messages a day in August 1988, up from 2,500 in August 1987 and 2,000 in October 1986.

Most machines are Digital VAX or Sun file servers (about 60 percent **UNIX** and 40 percent **VMS**), with perhaps 20 to 30 active users on each. Thus, there could be as many as 5,250 users. Registration in the *CDNnet* user directory is optional, but there are about 3,000 entries. A guess at the composition of the user clientele would be 60 percent research, 30 percent students, and 10 percent administration [Demco 1988a].

Services

Mail is the basic application service provided. X.400 also provides receipt notification, which is widely used in *CDNnet* and in the other **Ean**-based networks. This is implemented in **Ean** as follows. If the sender requests this service, a receipt report will be returned to the sender when the recipient displays the body of the message. The **Ean** implementation also provides mailing lists, although X.400 (1984) does not. Such lists are mostly redistributions of *Internet* mailing lists or *USENET* newsgroups. *CDNnet* is working on exploiting the X.400 capability of handling multimedia body parts to send Fax and display it on a bitmap display or print it on a **PostScript** printer.

X.400 implementations other than **Ean** are also used, including **QK/MHS** from Queen's University (Queen's) (the forerunner of the IBM commercial product) and commercial products from Data General and Consumers Software, the last being an implementation for the IBM PC.

USENET news (**B News 11**) is available on at least part of the network. There is a directory service for locating users of *CDNnet* and other **Ean**-

Table 12.4. *CDNnet growth*

Year	Institutions	Hosts	Messages/day at *ean.ubc.ca*
1984	12	14	—
1985	19	24	—
1986	23	44	2,000
1987	23	76	2,500
1988 (August)	32	175	5,000

based networks. Remote login is available via Triple-X (X.28/X.29/X.3) to hosts with X.25 service.

Protocols

The network currently uses the **Ean** implementation of X.400, although other X.400 software may be approved as it becomes available. The **Ean** implementation conforms to CCITT and ISO specifications at the session (CCITT X.215, CCITT X.225, and ISO8327), transport (TP0: CCITT X.214, CCITT X.224 class 0, ISO8072, and ISO8073), and network (X.25, PSTN, DECNET, etc.) layers. TTXP is also used as a network layer; it is based on the specifications of *CSNET*'s MMDF, was developed by *CDNnet*, and is usable over either asynchronous or Triple-X links. Some parts of the network also use TCP/IP, with TCP being used as a network layer. **Ean** implementations exist for **4.2BSD, VMS, System V**, and soon **VM/CMS**.

Most long-haul links are X.25 at 2400bps, though they vary from 1200bps to 9600bps (the range offered by the Canadian PDN *Datapac*). There are some leased lines, such as the 19.2Kbps one to the *NSFNET* backbone. Inside organizations, Ethernet is widely used. Mail delivery is usually accomplished within minutes. Reliability is very high within the network and somewhat less to other networks. Gateways seem to be inherently less reliable than bridges [Demco 1988a].

Management

Small organizations usually have only one link, which is usually directly to CDNnet Headquarters. Larger organizations usually also have connections to other organizations. The network is thus a star with extra connections. This simple arrangement is kept because there is no automated routing table maintenance, so links have to be listed manually, although use of X.500 to handle host and routing information is being investigated; testing was expected to be complete by the end of 1988, with deployment in 1989. Host naming is done with a particular subset of X.400 attributes that maps easily into RFC822. A small measure of security is provided for in the X.400 mail system by allowing MTAs to exchange their names and passwords when establishing a session.

Interconnections

There are gateways from *CDNnet* to *CSNET, BITNET,* and *UUCP,* as well as close connections to the other *Ean* networks. The *Internet* can be reached indirectly through *CSNET* or *NSFNET,* and *EUnet* through either *UUCP* or the European *Ean* networks. The syntaxes to use are those in the *Ean* addressing table.

Internally, *CDNnet* addresses are represented in binary form as X.400 Originator/Recipient (O/R) names, often with X.500 attributes. *CDNnet* users use subdomain-style addressing most of the time, although they may specify X.400 O/R addresses directly if necessary in the "keyword=value;" form originally suggested by *DFN*.

Most *CDNnet* hosts are registered under the *CA* domain, with DNS domains, and may thus be reached readily from any network that recognizes that format. However, networks such as *BITNET,* whose gateways do not understand *MX records* may need to indirect through *ean.ubc.ca,* as in

user%domain@ean.ubc.ca

There are also a few hosts still using the old *CDN Ean* top level domain; these also require indirection. From the X.400 world, *CDNnet* must still be addressed using a combination of O/R address attributes, which is not recognized by CEN/CENELEC:

DD.=u; DD.=d; PRMD=CA;

There are plans to change to support standard attribute only addresses for *CDNnet* mailboxes.

Standards

Canada has been a leader in communications standards for some time. It had the first public X.25 network, *Datapac,* and the first X.400 implementation, **Ean**. For that matter, the telephone is a Canadian invention.

CDNnet has been committed from the outset to use international standards wherever possible for the usual reasons, such as vendor independence. The network began when it was first possible to consider such a commitment because it coincided with the standardization of X.400. **Ean** and *CDNnet* have influenced standards bodies by demonstrating that X.400 actually does work: the ISO-OSI protocol suite is not very mature, but some within *CDNnet* believe that the only way to fix that is to actually do something about it.

Using a new and untried protocol suite, and one that is different from that used in the huge country across the border, was an audacious decision and a difficult one to implement. Protocol converters were necessary from the outset, as was constant explanation of why something different from *ARPANET* or *BITNET* protocols was being used. These conversions and explanations are not only for the benefit of the continental neighbors, but also for that of many Canadians. For example, *NRCnet* may use TCP/IP before moving to ISO-OSI protocols, even though some think *CDNnet* has demonstrated that this is not necessary.

Canada is a bilingual country. This has made the language independence of the international standards more attractive than English-only formats such as RFC822. It is also reflected in modularity of software design, and may have simplified the task of creating an Arabic **Ean** user agent (UA). There was originally an entirely French UA for use at French-speaking Canadian universities. Strangely enough, the users felt more comfortable with a UA with English commands and French online help, so this was produced instead.

History

The people with the idea for *CDNnet* were Paul Gilmore and Gerald Neufeld, both of the UBC Computer Science Department. The first NSERC grant began in November 1981. Much later work has been done by John Demco.

Canada is too small to develop everything itself, leading to a desire to adapt developments from elsewhere. It has strong ties to both the United States and Europe: Canadian researchers participated in *CYCLADES*, the early French research network, and have long followed *ARPANET* developments; Canadians are also quite influential in *UUCP* and *USENET*. These ties allow Canadian researchers to comprehend developments in both regions readily, while still keeping sufficient distance for perspective. There is more of an international perspective than in the States, and perhaps more of a tendency to act than to debate than in Europe.

Access

John Demco
Marilyn Martin
postmaster@relay.ubc.ca
+1-604-228-6537

CDNnet Headquarters
University of British Columbia
309-6356 Agricultural Road
Vancouver, BC V6T 1W5
Canada

Or send text "help" to <archive-server@relay.ubc.ca>.

12.3.2   NetNorth

The NetNorth Consortium and the network that it operates began in 1983. As of August 1988, it provided communications for 57 member institutions throughout Canada and 167 NJE nodes, from Vancouver Island to Newfoundland [Watt 1988]. Many of the nodes act as mail gateways to non-NJE systems internal to member organizations, many of which have campus TCP/IP or DECNET networks, or both. *NetNorth* was designed using the same technology and several of the same basic assumptions as *BITNET*, such as the links being arranged in a tree structure; see the section on *BITNET* in the United States earlier in this chapter for details. Link speeds in *NetNorth* range from 2400bps to 9600bps and are adequate for the traffic.

Administration

The *NetNorth* Directors are responsible for running the Consortium and the network, and they ordinarily delegate administration to an Executive Committee of Executive Directors. Members are organizations, not individuals. Each member designates, by whatever means it finds appropriate, a *NetNorth* Director for management and planning and a *NetNorth* Representative for technical, procedural, and operational matters. A single person can perform both roles. The *NetNorth* Directors collectively elect the Executive Directors. A NetNorth Administration Centre (NAC) coordinates membership applications, provides basic software, maintains node and name lists, and exchanges them with *BITNET* and *EARN* network coordination centers. NAC is managed by the University of Guelph (Guelph). The Consortium is funded through fees from the membership.

Members are institutions of five kinds, all of which must be Canadian:

A   Universities or colleges that are full voting members of the Association of Universities and Colleges of Canada (AUUC) or the Association of Canadian Community Colleges (ACCC)

B   Other nonprofit research or educational institutions; a part of a Class A organization that is not a member may become a Class B member

C   Federal or provincial governmental organizations, or nongovernmental organizations whose purpose is to support the purposes of Class A organizations

D   Commercial organizations that frequently conduct joint research with Class A members

E   Other institutions of interest to Class A members.

This is the very model of the membership and representation of an academic and research network, spelled out more clearly than is done for many other networks. These rules are partly derived from those of *BITNET* and *EARN* [Nussbacher 1988]. They are detailed here as an example of such rules.

Interconnections

Direct links exist to *BITNET* in the United States and indirectly through the United States to *EARN* in Europe. Those three networks are essentially one network technologically, although they differ widely in administration. *NetNorth* and *BITNET* are connected by a 9600bps leased line between Cornell University (Cornell), *CORNELLC*, and the University of Guelph (Guelph), in Ontario, *CANADA01*. There are no formal plans at this time for any other connections. For interconnection details, see the section on *BITNET* worldwide in Chapter 10.

History

There was a predecessor network, *OUnet*, or Ontario Universities Network [Watt 1988]. Planning for *OUnet* started among six members in 1982. There were eight members by 1983. Since one was not a university and one was not in Ontario, *OUnet* was no longer appropriate, and *NetNorth* was formed instead.

From 1984 through 1987, IBM Canada provided three-year grants in support of *NetNorth*. These went to the following institutions:

- Guelph to fund the connection between *NetNorth* and *BITNET* and to operate the NAC
- University of New Brunswick (UNB) to fund the connections within the eastern provinces and to Guelph
- University of Alberta (Alberta) to fund the connnections within the western provinces and to Guelph

Plans

The University of Toronto (Toronto) has proposed to the *NetNorth* Executive Committee to shift the *NetNorth* connection to *BITNET* to a 56Kbps link from *UTORVM* at Toronto to *CORNELLC* at Cornell. This would involve rearranging the tree structure of *NetNorth* slightly—i.e., some new links would have to be installed—but Toronto proposes to bear all necessary expenses at no cost to *NetNorth*. This new link would also provide direct

NetNorth connections to *NSFNET* and the *Internet*, and is related to the *BITNET II* TCP/IP plans of *BITNET* in the United States (*NetNorth* would eventually use NJE over IP on the international link) [Toronto 1988a]. See also *Onet* (not to be confused with *OUnet*) later in this chapter.

Access
AdminSec@NAC.NetNorth.ca

12.3.3   DREnet

DREnet is an internet linking sites and systems involved in research for the Canadian Department of National Defence (DND). There are 9 *DREnet* sites, 11 networks, and more than 45 hosts (excluding personal computers and dedicated gateways) [Bradford 1988]. There are concentrations of *DREnet* machines in Dartmouth, Nova Scotia, which is the location of Defence Research Establishment Atlantic, and in Ottawa, where Defence Research Establishment (DRE) headquarters is located. There are also machines in Toronto [Prindeville 1988a].

Protocols

The current primary long-haul network in the *DREnet* internet is *XDRENET*. *XDRENET* uses TCP/IP over an X.25 PDN. All *DREnet* hosts are currently registered under the DND.CA domain, either directly or in subdomains. The nameserver for DND.CA is at *ncs.dnd.ca*. *DREnet* is currently connected to *ARPANET* with a BBN Butterfly gateway.

History

DREnet began in 1983 as *DRENET*, an *ARPANET*-like PSN and TCP/IP network linking Defence Research Establishments in Ottawa, Ontario, and Dartmouth, Nova Scotia. This network was connected to the *ARPANET* via an LSI-11 gateway in 1984 (this machine has since been retired). Growth in demand for network services led to the development of *XDRENET* [Bradford 1988].

Plans

Several new sites and networks are planned in 1989. *DREnet* is scheduled to be retired in the very near future, and sites currently on it will join *XDRENET* [Bradford 1988].

Access
Bob Bradford
DREnet Coordinator
netcoor@ncs.dnd.ca

12.3.4   NRCnet

The Canadian National Research Council (NRC) is considering developing a national research network on the model of *NSFNET* in the United States and of national research networks in European nations. This new network, *NRCnet*, would provide more and faster services than the existing Canadian national networks *NetNorth* and *CDNnet*. The proposal [Hunter and Curley 1988] is to provide a transcontinental leased line backbone connecting regional networks [Woodsworth 1988a], such as *BCnet* in British Columbia [Leigh 1988], *Onet* in Ontario [Toronto 1988b], and *CRIM* in Quebec [Vachon 1988b]. This would allow researchers to communicate with each other easily and efficiently and would also allow access to supercomputer centers and other specialized facilities [Prindeville 1988a].

The model is actually in three levels, as in *NSFNET*: backbone, mid-level (mostly regionals), and campus networks connected to the mid-level networks [Woodsworth 1988b]. A minimum of five nodes on the backbone is expected, with a maximum of nine [Taylor and Heyworth 1988]. About ten major initial participating institutions and about 1,000 users are expected, growing to 80 institutions and 30,000 users by 1991 [Hunter and Curley 1988].

NRCnet is mainly intended to be a production network. But there is also a need to support networking development, both for itself and in order to attract private sector involvement [Woodsworth 1988a], which is considered very important in encouraging technological development [Taylor and Heyworth 1988]. This goal may be met by allocating a subset of the network for development [Prindeville 1988a].

Administration and Funding

Management is to be directed by a consortium or corporation of users and other participants, such as communications carriers. There is already a project team reporting to the Vice-President for Engineering of NRC and headed by Andrew Woodsworth [Woodsworth 1988a]. There are plans for a steering committee, a regional network committee, a technical advisory board, a Network Operations Centre (NOC), and one or two Network Information Centres (NICs) [Taylor and Heyworth 1988; Hunter and Curley 1988].

Complete self-sufficiency within five years after a start date early in 1989 is desired [Prindeville 1988a].

NRCnet Backbone

The protocols most desired for the backbone by most of the potential participants are TCP/IP, but there is a lobby for X.25 and immediate use of ISO-
OSI protocols at UBC and *CDNnet* [Demco 1988b]. There is some chance
that IBM will donate equipment and its **ACIS** version of the **4.3BSD UNIX**
operating system [Heyworth 1988a]. There have been two major proposals
for the composition of the backbone:

- One from Toronto is modeled on *NSFNET*, with 56Kbps or T1 (and
  perhaps eventually DS3 or 45Mbps) TCP/IP links and IBM PC/RT
  nodes [Taylor and Heyworth 1988; Heyworth 1988a; Hunter and Curley 1988]. The specific model is *NYSERNet*, the *NSFNET* regional in
  the New York State area [Taylor and Heyworth 1988; Hunter and Curley 1988].
- One from UBC involves T1 X.25 links (above which all the other
  desired protocols can be supported) [Leigh 1988].

No decision has yet been made, and NRC is sending out a Request for Proposals (RFP) [Prindeville 1988a].

While *NetNorth* and *CDNnet* provide only batch services such as mail
and file transfer, *NRCnet* would provide others, such as remote supercomputer and database access [Demco 1988b; Taylor and Heyworth 1988]; multimedia document transfer involving text, graphics, pictures, and voice;
conferencing using words and pictures; and remote process control [Hunter
and Curley 1988].

Regional Networks

There are low-speed higher education mainframe terminal access networks
in most provinces, but these are too slow and of too limited service to be
used in building *NRCnet*. But there are also other existing or potential
regionals that may become involved [Woodsworth 1988b]. Networking in
the provinces of Alberta, British Columbia, Quebec, and Ontario is discussed in the subsections on *AHEN*, *BCnet*, *CRIM*, and *Onet*, respectively.
All of those networks are expected to become *NRCnet* regionals. Developments in other provinces are described here.

> *Saskatchewan.* There are campus networks at the University of
> Saskatchewan and the University of Regina. Those universities are
> interested in building a provincial network, especially for super-
> computer access. Other potential members are the Plant Biotech-
> nology Institute of NRC, SED Systems, and the Saskatchewan
> Research Council. Funding is a problem [Woodsworth 1988b].

Manitoba. There are campus networks at the University of Winnipeg and the University of Manitoba, the latter of which expects to support TCP/IP and Ethernet on its mainframe soon. There is a 9600bps RJE network linking all institutions of higher education, using Dataroute and microwave links. Other organizations interested in a network are CIIT of NRC, the Freshwater Institute of DFO, and Agriculture Canada [Woodsworth 1988b].

New Brunswick and Prince Edward Island. There has been a 19.2Kbps terminal access and file transfer network co-operated by New Brunswick and Prince Edward Island for many years. Higher speeds are a budgetary problem [Woodsworth 1988b].

Nova Scotia. There is a 9600bps and 19.2Kbps leased line DECNET network in the metropolitan Halifax area that has been operational since 1987. It connects Dalhousie University (Dalhousie), Mount Saint Vincent University, Saint Mary's University, the Technical University of Nova Scotia, the Applied Microelectronics Institute, and Digital Canada (Dartmouth Branch). There is also an Ethernet campus network at Dalhousie. There are more than 80 hosts in all on this DECNET. Dalhousie also has a TCP/IP network that is expected to be connected by a low-speed link to Acadia University in Wolfville. Other university and government research laboratory connections to these are expected. A study by Systemhouse (also sponsored by the Provincial Department of Industry, Trade and Technology) about a provincial network was just completed [Jones 1988d], and there is a possibility that Industry, Science and Technology Canada (ISTC) may help fund and implement such a network. Potential sites include universities in the Halifax area and federal research laboratories [Woodsworth 1988b].

Newfoundland. There is no present network, but the province is proposing a high-speed network to connect university and government research institutions, plus a link to Nova Scotia. The likely funding agency is the Atlantic Canada Opportunities Agency (ACOA). There is at least one campus network being installed, at Memorial University. This is based on fiber optics and will support TCP/IP and DECNET [Woodsworth 1988b].

Interconnections

There are internal NRC networks such as *IRAPnet* and *DIVnet* [Hunter and Curley 1988]. The Canopus *DAN* network is the Canadian part of *SPAN* [Woodsworth 1988c], and NRC has gateways to *NetNorth*, *CDNnet*, *UUCP*, and *USENET* [Hunter and Curley 1988]. *CDNnet* has supported the *NRCnet* proposal since early 1987 and expects to use *NRCnet* as infrastructure [Demco 1988b]. The regional networks *BCnet* and *Onet* have connections to *NSFNET*, and *CRIM* has a *CSNET* connection to the *Internet* [Prindeville 1988b; Vachon 1988a].

History

There was a previous proposal known as *Supernet*, brought forth by the Atmospheric Environment Service (AES) and primarily concerned with selling excess capacity of a Cray to federal government users. The previous proponents of *Supernet* now mostly expect to use *NRCnet* for this purpose [Taylor and Heyworth 1988], at least if *NRCnet* runs at T1 speeds. Another previous proposal was for an *NRN* (National Research Network) [Toronto 1988b], but this was just an early name for *NRCnet* [Prindeville 1988b].

Plans

The network is intended to become self-sufficient within five years [Woodsworth 1988a]. Migration to ISO-OSI protocols is expected eventually [Taylor and Heyworth 1988]. *NRCnet* might play a strong role in finding a path from TCP/IP to ISO-OSI [Woodsworth 1988c].

Access

Dr. Andrew Woodsworth
Project Manager, NRCnet
WOODSWORTH@NRCDAO.NRC.CA
WOODSWORTH@NRCDAO.BITNET
PSI%302068100434::WOODSWORTH
+1-604-388-0024
Telex: 049-7295

Research Officer
National Research Council
Herzberg Institute of Astrophysics
Dominion Astrophysical Observatory
5071 West Saanich Road
Victoria, BC V8X 4M6
Canada

There is a mailing list about *NRCnet*. To subscribe, send a request to list-request@ean.ubc.ca, listmaster@cs.mcgill.ca, or listserv@ualtavm.bitnet with

Subject: subscribe NRCNET-L (your name here)

12.3.5   AHEN

AHEN, or Alberta Higher Education Network, connects various organizations in Alberta, including school boards, hospitals, and oil exploration companies. There were 40 machines on the network in April 1988 [Woodsworth 1988c]. An existing satellite link allows access from the University of

Ottawa (Ottawa) to a Cyber 205 at the University of Calgary (Calgary) [Woodsworth 1988b].

AHEN is apparently also known as *AdhocNet* [Kieffer 1988], and a domain *adhocnet.ca* was recognized by *BITNET* and *NetNorth* in 1987 and 1988, but never in the *CA* top level domain recognized by other networks, such as *CDNnet*.

Plans

The current network uses low-speed links. A proposal for a faster (T1, or 1.544Mbps) network is being developed, based on a high-speed backbone link between Calgary (where there is a Convex and perhaps soon a Cray) and the University of Alberta (Alberta) in Edmonton (where there may soon be a Myrias Canadian-made supercomputer). There are also some ETA-10 supercomputers at oil companies in Calgary. There is interest in compressed video educational networking involving the Alberta Telecommunications Research Centre (ATRC). This may use the same network or may require another [Woodsworth 1988b].

Access
Rom Kieffer
Kieffer@UCNET.UCALGARY.CA
Kieffer%UCNET.UCALGARY.CA@UNCANET.BITNET
+1-403-220-6210
Academic Computing Services
University of Calgary
Calgary, AB
Canada

12.3.6   BCnet

BCnet, or British Columbia network, is a regional network headquartered at the University of British Columbia (UBC), also home to *CDNnet* [Demco 1988b]. The *BCnet* hub at UBC is connected to the following [Leigh 1988]:

UBC with a 10Mbps Ethernet link

Simon Fraser University (Simon Fraser) with a 1.544Mbps T1 broadband connection

University of Victoria (UVic) with a 224Kbps British Columbia Telephone (BCTel) link

TRIUMF cyclotron computing environment with a 2.048Mbps European T1 fiber-optic cable link

British Columbia Advanced Systems Institute (ASI) with a 19.2Kbps line to Simon Fraser

Dominion Astrophysical Observatory (DAO) of NRC [Woodsworth 1988b]

Microtel Pacific Research Corporation (Microtel) [Woodsworth 1988c], a commercial member.

Protocols

TCP/IP, DECNET, and X.25 are all used [Prindeville 1988a], supported by Digital Vitalink bridges and Proteon routers over a varied infrastructure including microwave, fiber optics, and coaxial cable [Woodsworth 1988b].

Interconnections

A 19.2Kbps connection to the *NSFNET* backbone at the University of Washington (Washington) was operational on 26 May 1988 [Leigh 1988]. There is a 2400bps *HEPnet* link to Stanford [Woodsworth 1988b].

History

Initial costs were provided by ASI, which is funded through an Educational Research and Development Agency (ERDA) agreement that provides matching federal and provincial funds [Woodsworth 1988b].

Plans

Likely future *BCnet* participants include the Institute of Ocean Sciences (IOS) near Victoria [Taylor and Heyworth 1988] and British Columbia Institute of Technology (BCIT) [Martin 1988]. Other new members are also sought. Self-sufficient operation is expected soon; members will be charged about $30,000 per year, to support an annual budget of about $200,000 [Woodsworth 1988b]. *BCnet* will be an *NRCnet* regional.

Access

Dennis O'Reilly
dennis_oreilly@mtsg.ubc.ca
+1-604-228-3072
BCnet Manager

J. L. Leigh
jack_leigh@mtsg.ubc.ca
Director
Computing Centre
University of British Columbia
6356 Agricultural Road
Vancouver, BC V6T 1W5
Canada

12.3.7   CRIM

CRIM is named after the Centre de recherche informatique de Montréal (CRIM), or Computer Research Institute of Montreal, a nonprofit research corporation funded by various agencies including the government of Quebec, Quebec universities, and private companies. The *CRIM* network has existed since mid-1986 [Vachon 1988b] and is a metropolitan 56Kbps star network using DECNET and connecting various local area networks at universities in the Montreal area [Taylor and Heyworth 1988]. The institutions other than CRIM currently participating in the *CRIM* network are the Université du Québec à Montréal (UQAM), the Université de Montréal, Concordia University (Concordia), McGill University (McGill), the Ecole Polytechnique, and SIRICON [Vachon 1988b].

Protocols

Each participating institution has a DECNET area number, and DECNET is the basic protocol suite supported. For TCP/IP, IP is encapsulated in NSP transport packets so that it can be carried along with DECNET traffic [Prindeville 1988b]. Application level interoperability is provided by Digital **Ultrix** (**UNIX**) systems that run both DECNET and TCP/IP [Vachon 1988b].

Interconnections

McGill has had a 9600bps TCP/IP leased line to *CSNET* at BBN in Cambridge, Massachusetts [Prindeville 1988a] since September 1987, paid for by CRIM. CRIM established a similar connection directly, at 19.2Kbps, in October 1988, using IP through a cisco router. Since the end of November 1988, this new link has replaced the McGill link for *Internet* access from *CRIM*. It is unclear whether the McGill link will remain [Vachon 1988a].

The *CRIM* network is one of the Canadian regional networks that *NRCnet* is intended to connect, and there is communication between CRIM and NRC about this.

History

The main network connecting CRIM universities before the *CRIM* network was *NetNorth*, which only connected machines in the computer centers, leaving other machines in the Computer Science and Engineering departments cut off. Although departments of two universities, Computer Science at Montreal and Electrical Engineering of Concordia, joined *CDNnet*, and thus gained mail access, the other universities and departments did not.

To alleviate this isolation, CRIM decided to encourage campus Ethernet networks and later connected them with 56Kbps leased lines to an Ethernet at CRIM, producing the *CRIM* network. The services desired on it were mail, file transfer, and remote login, which could all be provided by either DECNET or TCP/IP. The use of these two protocols was split between **VMS** and **UNIX** users, respectively [Vachon 1988b].

There is also a separate academic X.25 terminal access network called *UQ* at the Université du Québec (Quebec) [Prindeville 1988b]. Links run from 9600bps to 19.2Kbps and connect all components of the University of Quebec, including those at Chicoutimi, Hull, Montreal, Quebec, Rimousi, Rouyn-Noranda, and Trois-Rivieres. (Contact either M. Pierre Cormier, UQAM, <S602@uqam.bitnet> or M. Josef Komenda, UQ at Quebec City, <ccsjoko@uqhull.bitnet> [Vachon 1988a]).

Plans

A likely additional site is NRC's Biotechnology Research Institute (BRI) in Montreal [Prindeville 1988b]. CRIM plans to expand the network to include all other universities in Quebec, including Université Laval, Université Sherbrooke, and all of the branches of the Université du Québec (Quebec). TCP/IP will be used directly over those new links, and eventually over the existing ones. This is possible using cisco or similar routers, while simultaneously supporting DECNET [Vachon 1988a]. Higher speeds and access to planned supercomputing facilities in Montreal are also being discussed [Prindeville 1988a].

Some Quebec universities would like a provincial network modeled after *Onet* [Woodsworth 1988b]. CRIM has formed a steering committee to accomplish this, using the existing *CRIM* network as the core and building on the new connections mentioned above. The members of the committee come from the potential sites of the new network, *RISQ*. crossref QCnet RISQ crossref Qnet RISQ It was expected to be operational in 1989. Both TCP/IP and DECNET will probably be supported, and access will eventually be provided to government, educational, and private research organizations in the province. The *UQ* network may be incorporated, but *RISQ* will provide more services. CRIM will probably run a NIC, while McGill would run a NOC. *CRIM* will be an *NRCnet* regional [Vachon 1988a].

Access
Mario Vachon
Network Analyst
vachon@crim.ca
+1-514-848-3980
Fax: +1-514-848-8892

Bernard Turcotte
Assistant Vice President Systems Management and Director, Operation CRIM
turcotte@crim.ca
+1-514-848-3990
Centre de recherche informatique de Montréal
1550, db de Maisonneuve ouest
Bureau 1000
Montréal, PQ H3G 1N2
Canada

Alan Greenberg
Director
Telecommunications and Computing Centre
alan@vm1.mcgill.ca
+1-514-398-3705
McGill University
Computer Centre
805 Sherbrooke Street West
Montreal, PQ H3A 2K6
Canada

12.3.8   Onet

The Ontario Network (*Onet*) is a TCP/IP network that connects the campus networks of six universities in Ontario [Hares 1988]. One of its purposes is to provide access to a Cray supercomputer at the University of Toronto (Toronto); this machine is operated by the Ontario Centre for Large Scale Computation (OCLSC), which has partly sponsored many of the connections [Woodsworth 1988b].

Another participating organization is the Ontario Centres of Excellence (OCE) program [Taylor and Heyworth 1988]. These Centres have resources that the universities in the area wish to access, and the Centres also could benefit by communication among themselves. The OCE are Ontario Laser and Lightwave Research Centre (OLLRC); Information Technology Research Centre (ITRC); Manufacturing Research Corporation of Ontario (MRCO); Ontario Centre for Materials Research (OCMR); Institut de Science Terrestre et Spatiale (ISTS), or Institute for Space and Terrestrial Science; Waterloo Centre for Groundwater Research (WCGR); and Telecommunications Research Institute of Ontario (TRIO) [Heyworth 1988b].

The six universities currently participating in *Onet* are Toronto, the University of Waterloo (Waterloo), McMaster University (McMaster) (with three registered IP numbers), the University of Western Ontario (UWO), Queen's University (Queen's), and York University (York). In addition, there are two government research facilities: the ITRC and ISTS [Prindeville 1988a].

Protocols

Although *Onet* is basically a TCP/IP network, some DECNET functionality is supported, at least at Toronto [Woodsworth 1988c]. The links are 19.2Kbps leased lines to the university Computing Centres, using cisco routers [Woodsworth 1988b]; 56Kbps is being considered for the future [Prindeville 1988a].

Interconnections

There is a link from Toronto to the *NSFNET* backbone at Cornell [Heyworth 1988a; Toronto 1988b] at 56Kbps [Woodsworth 1988b] with a Proteon router; it has been operational since October 1988 [Hares 1988]. The University of Toronto has proposed to *NetNorth* that the *NetNorth* connection to Cornell (and thus to *BITNET* and *NSFNET*) be shifted to Toronto in order to provide faster connectivity over the Toronto 56Kbps connection, at no cost to *NetNorth* [Toronto 1988a]. This might involve use of the *BITNET II* software (NJE over IP), and possibly direct participation in *BITNET II* [Prindeville 1988a].

Plans

Other institutions are considering joining *Onet*, including the Universities of Guelph and Carleton [Prindeville 1988a] and the National Research Council (NRC) in Ottawa. Another network (perhaps a branch of *Onet*) might develop in the Ottawa-Hull region because of the concentration of research agencies there [Woodsworth 1988b]. *Onet* will be an *NRCnet* regional.

Access

Warren Jackson
+1-416-978-8948
University of Toronto

Lee Oattes
<oattes@gpu.utcs.toronto.edu>
University of Toronto

Jeff Honig
<jch@tcgould.tn.cornell.edu>
Cornell University Theory Center

Allan Heyworth
heyworth@utoronto.bitnet
Office of the Vice President of Research
University of Toronto
Toronto, ON
Canada

12.3.9   Web

The *Web* is a national Canadian nonprofit conferencing system formed in 1987. There are about 300 users who pay hourly connect charges (usually for connections at 2400bps). Administration is done by full-time staff of the NIRV Centre, which is a nonprofit organization established to help voluntary organizations make more effective use of new technology.

The basic services are conferencing (both interactive and batch) and mail, as well as mailing lists, all supported by **Picospan** software. There are connections from the *web* machine to *uunet* (and thus to the *UUCP* mail network and to the *Internet*), and to *BITNET* (as *WEB.UUCP*), *PeaceNet*, and *GreenNet*. The latter two systems are similar in purpose and clientele to the *Web*.

Uses of the *Web* have included conferences on the Contadora Group's Central America Peace Plan; a listing of the top 30 toxic substances, drawing input from chemical experts across the country and discussing tips on how to deal with the government; and checks on infractions of environmental laws by ordinary citizens. In the latter two cases, the system allowed people with varying but related expertise to communicate easily and quickly and to perform tasks that would otherwise have been difficult, if not impossible (this specific kind of use of CMC was predicted in 1977 [Hiltz 1977]). These are only a few of the many examples of positive social change being realized by users of the *Web*.

> **Access**
> Web
> +1-416-925-1322
> P.O. Box 125 Station P
> Toronto, ON M5S 2Z7
> Canada
>
> You can reach the system directly through its *Datapac* gateway address 95400842 (reverse charging available via *TYMNET* and *Telenet*) and log in for a free trial.

12.3.10   NCCN

The Native Computer Communications Network (*NCCN*) is a computer network used to connect Native people and organizations dealing with Native issues in Canada. It is based on *USENET* software and is deliberately decentralized: there is no central or controlling node. Initial funding, in December 1986, came from the Innovations Program of Employment and Immigration Canada (IPEIC) with a matching contribution from York University (York). Initial testing was done in Ontario.

There are currently six hosts and about 40 users. Eighty more hosts are expected when funding is available. Initial setup costs for a fill site (given an existing computer) are for about 40Mbytes of disk space and for **XENIX** software. A leaf node would require only 20Mbytes and could run **MS-DOS** software. Later costs are mostly telephone charges and may be less than costs of previous communications media, especially in isolated areas. Most links are at 2400bps.

The services provided are mail, news, and file transfer, based on UUCP and *USENET* news. Redundant links are used to avoid centralized control. This may or may not also be less expensive, but it promotes self-replication of the network and greater participation. Because many (40 percent) of the organizations serving Native peoples already own computers, and most of them were IBM PCs or clones, *NCCN* runs on those machines. Specifically, the machines are IBM PC/XTs and PC/ATs (and clones). Leaf nodes may run **MS-DOS** (**UUPC** and other transfer agents are being considered); all others run **XENIX**.

NCCN is connected to *USENET* through the gateway *yunccn*, receiving a partial feed of *USENET* newsgroups.

There are about half a million Natives and Metis in Canada and about 30,000 Inuit. These peoples have had a greater share of social problems compared with the rest of Canadian society, including high rates of unemployment, alcoholism, crime, and illiteracy. Recently, however, many young Native people are trying to overcome these problems within their communities through building up the local economies and reinstituting traditional education and cultural pursuits. *NCCN* is a means to link Native councils, businesses, and other organizations in order to foster greater self-reliance among Canada's Native peoples.

Access
The Native Computer Communications Network
Native/Canadian Relations Theme Area
Faculty of Environmental Studies
Room 217A, Lumbers Building
York University
4700 Keele Street
North York, ON M3J 1P3
Canada

12.3.11   CoSy

The *CoSy* conferencing system has been operational since April 1983 at the University of Guelph (Guelph) using the **CoSy** conferencing software developed at Guelph. By December 1985, there were about 400 users in 28 different countries [Meeks 1985]. As of December 1988, there were about 3,000 users in 28 different countries [Ellis 1988].

The software is designed to be easy for the new user and efficient in its resource usage. The same software is used in *BIX*. It is mostly modeled on in-person meeting structures. The **CoSy** software originally ran on **UNIX** but has since been ported to Digital **VMS** and IBM **VM**, as well as **XENIX**. Numbers of software site licenses, by operating system, are 30 **UNIX**, 52 **VMS**, 8 **XENIX**, and 4 **VM**. These are mostly in Canada and the United States, but there are sites in the Netherlands, Spain, England, Scotland, Australia, New Zealand, Indonesia, and Japan. Licensees are mostly academic, but there are companies ranging from small to very large [Ellis 1988].

Guelph decided in October 1988 to sell the **CoSy** software but did not expect a transfer to any of the potential buyers to take place before the end of the first quarter of 1989 [Ellis 1988].

Access
Director Communications Services
+1-519-824-4120
University of Guelph
Guelph, ON N1G 2W1
Canada

12.3.12   Envoy 100

Envoy 100 is a Canadian commercial mail system [Prindeville 1988a]. It has the usual features, such as online editing, uploading, and delivery receipt acknowledgment. Its 1200bps dialup access is supported with PAD or IBM 3780 interfaces. A service called EnvoyPost gateways mail to Canada Post, with a limit of four pages per message. Another, called EnvoyCourier, delivers up to 30 pages within three hours [Datapac 1988].

Envoy 100 has a *DASnet* connection and an X.400 gateway; *CDNnet* also is looking into interconnecting to it [Demco 1988a]. There has been a gateway to *Telemail* since 1985 [Vachon 1988a].

Access
Telemarketing
+1-613-560-3880
800-267-7400
Telecom Canada
410 Laurier Avenue West
Box 2410, Station D
Ottawa, ON K1P 6H5
Canada

12.4   *References*

Adams 1988.   Adams, Rick, Personal communications, July, September 1988.

Adams and Salus 1987.   Adams, Rick, and Salus, Peter, "UUNET Progress Report," *;login:*, vol. 12, no. 4, pp. 28–29, USENIX Association, Berkeley, CA, July/August 1987.

Adams and Salus 1988.   Adams, Rick, and Salus, Peter, "UUNET Communications Service," *;login:*, vol. 13, no. 4, p. 23, USENIX Association, Berkeley, CA, July/August 1988.

Advertel 1988.   Advertel, "An Introduction to Confer II," Advertel Communication Systems, Inc., Ann Arbor, MI, 1988.

BITNIC 1988.   BITNIC, "BITNET Maps," BITNIC, New York, 25 April 1988.

Bradford 1988.   Bradford, Bob, Personal communications, 9 December 1988.

Breeden 1988.   Breeden, Laura, "CSNET Executive Committee, BITNET Board Approve Network Merger," *CSNET-FORUM Digest*, vol. 4, no. 6, 10 November 1988.

Bur 1988.   Bur, Justin, "Major Network Sites in Canada," CRIM, Montreal, 3 September 1988.

Collins et al. 1987.   Collins, M., Hain, T., Lund, P., Masarro, H., and Nitzan, R., "Subnet Functional Specifications," National MFE Computer Center, Livermore, CA, 10 December 1987.

Cotter 1988.   Cotter, Holland, "Birth of a Network: a History of BITNET," *CUNY University Computer Center Communications*, vol. 14, no. 1–2, pp. 1, 10, CUNY, New York, January–February 1988.

da Cruz 1988.   da Cruz, Frank, Personal communications, October–November 1988.

Data Channels 1987.   Data Channels, "Gateway Service Provides Connectivity Between Public, Private E-Mail Systems," *Data Channels*, p. 6, 15 July 1987.

Datapac 1988.   Datapac, *DATAPAC Directory*, Telecom Canada, Ottawa, March 1988. Revision 136.

Demco 1987a.   Demco, John, "CA domain," *can-inet@mc.lcs.mit.edu*, CSNET, 22 November 1987.

Demco 1987b.   Demco, John, "The Canadian Domain .CA," *CSNET Info-server*, CSNET CIC, Cambridge, MA, 25 November 1987.

Demco 1987c.   Demco, John, "The Canadian Domain," *CDNnet Archive Service*, CDNnet, Vancouver, 7 December 1987.

Demco 1988a.   Demco, John, Personal communications, August 1988.

Demco 1988b.   Demco, John, "CDNnet and NRCnet," *CDNnet Reports*, no. 2, p. 2, Summer 1988.

Dunne 1987.   Dunne, Kenis McGough, "UUNET Provides International Network Access," *CommUNIXations*, vol. 7, no. 4, pp. 15–16, /usr/group, Santa Clara, CA, July/August 1987.

Ellis 1988.   Ellis, Marg, Personal communications, 28 November 1988.

EMMS 1987.   EMMS, "E-Mail Refiler Connects 18 Systems," *EMMS*, vol. 11, no. 14, pp. 5–9, 15 July 1987.

ESnet 1987.   ESnet, "ESnet program plan," National Technical Information Services (NTIS), ESnet, June 1987.

Fisher 1987.   Fisher, Sharon, "Dasnet to Link 18 E-Mail Services," *Info World*, vol. 9, no. 27, p. 5, 6 July 1987.

Frey and Adams 1987.   Frey, Donnalyn, and Adams, Rick, "USENET: Death by Success?," *UNIX REVIEW*, vol. 5, no. 8, pp. 55–60, August 1987.

Gilmore and Neufeld 1985.   Gilmore, Paul, and Neufeld, Gerald, "A Strategy for a National Electronic Messaging System for Research in Canada," *Proceedings Canadian Information Processing Society National Meeting (Montreal, June 1984)*, Canadian Information Processing Society, Montreal, 1985.

Gorin 1987. Gorin, Amy, "DASnet Links Many E-Mail Systems," *PC Week*, vol. 4, no. 28, pp. C3, C48, 14 July 1987.

Graham 1987. Graham, Mark, "University for Peace Global Computer Network," *NetNews*, vol. 1, no. 5, p. 1, IGC, San Francisco, Winter 1987.

Green 1988. Green, J. L. , "The Space Physics Analysis Network," *Computer Physics Communications*, vol. 49, pp. 205–213, 1988.

Green and King 1986. Green, J. L., and King, J. H., "Behind the Scenes During a Comet Encounter," *Eos*, vol. 67, no. 9, p. 105, March 1986.

Green et al. 1987a. Green, J. L, Peters, D. J., Heijden, N. Van der, and Lopez-Swafford, B., "Management of the Space Physics Analysis Network (SPAN); Second Edition," *NSSDC Technical Reports*, National Space Science Data Center, NASA Goddard Space Flight Center, Greenbelt, MD, January 1987.

Green et al. 1987b. Green, J. L., Thomas, V. L., Lopez-Swafford, B., and Porter, L. Z., "Introduction to the Space Physics Analysis Network (SPAN); Second Edition," *NSSDC Technical Reports*, National Space Science Data Center, NASA Goddard Space Flight Center, Greenbelt, MD, January 1987.

Green and Zwickl 1986. Green, J. L., and Zwickl, R. D., "Data System Users Working Group Meeting Report," *Eos*, vol. 67, no. 8, pp. 100–101, February 1986.

Hapgood 1986. Hapgood, M. A., "Access to the Space Physics Analysis Network (SPAN): A Guide for JANET users," *RAL Technical Reports*, Rutherford Appleton Laboratory, Chilton, Didcot, Oxfordshire, England, October 1986.

Hares 1988. Hares, Susan, Personal communications, September 1988.

Ha et al. 1988. Ha, T., Sisson, P. L., Thomas, V. L., and Green, J. L., "Space Physics Analysis Network Node Directory (The Yellow Pages); Third Edition," *NSSDC Technical Reports*, National Space Science Data Center, NASA Goddard Space Flight Center, Greenbelt, MD, March 1988.

Heyworth 1988a. Heyworth, Allan, "A status report on the U of T activities," Office of the Vice-President Research, University of Toronto, 11 April 1988.

Heyworth 1988b. Heyworth, Allan, "Ontario Centres of Excellence information," Office of the Vice-President Research, University of Toronto, 25 April 1988.

Hiltz 1977. Hiltz, Starr Roxanne, "Communications Medium," *Technological Forecasting and Social Change*, vol. 10, no. 3, pp. 225–238, 1977.

Hiltz 1978. Hiltz, Starr Roxanne, "The Human Element in Computerized Conferencing Systems," *Computer Networks*, vol. 2, no. 6, pp. 421–428, December 1978.

Hiltz 1980. Hiltz, Starr Roxanne, "Experiments and Experiences with Computerized Conferencing," in *Emerging Office Systems*, ed. Robert M. Landau, James H. Bair, Jean H. Siegman, pp. 187–204, Ablex Publishing Corporation, Norwood, NJ, 1980. Based on Proceedings of the Stanford University International Symposium on Office Automation.

Hiltz and Turoff 1981. Hiltz, Starr Roxanne, and Turoff, Murray, "The Evolution of User Behavior in a Computerized Conferencing System," *Communications of the ACM*, vol. 24, no. 11, pp. 739–751, November 1981.

Hiltz and Turoff 1985. Hiltz, Starr Roxanne, and Turoff, Murray, "Structuring Computer-Mediated Communication Systems to Avoid Information Overload," *Communications of the ACM*, vol. 28, no. 7, pp. 680–689, July 1985.

Honeyman and Bellovin 1986. Honeyman, Peter, and Bellovin, Steven M., "Pathalias or the Care and Feeding of Relative Addresses," *Proceedings of the 1986 Summer USENIX Conference (Atlanta, 9–13 June 1986)*, pp. 126–141, USENIX Association, Berkeley, CA, 1986.

Hughes 1988. Hughes, David, Personal communications, 30 November 1988.

Hunter and Curley 1988. Hunter, Art, and Curley, John, "National Research Computer Network (NRCnet)," Division of Marketing, National Research Council, Ottawa, 4 June 1988.

Jennings et al. 1986.   Jennings, Dennis M., Landweber, Lawrence H., Fuchs, Ira H., Farber, David J., and Adrion, W. Richards, "Computer Networking for Scientists," *Science*, vol. 231, no. 4741, pp. 943–950, 28 February 1986.

Jones 1988d.   Jones, Peter, "Nova Scotia's Networks," *NRCNET-L@UALTAVM.BITNET*, National Research Council, Ottawa, 12 October 1988.

Jones 1988a.   Jones, William P., "NSI project quarterly accomplishments," *ISO Newsletter*, OSSA, NASA, Washington, DC, 10 November 1988.

Jones 1988b.   Jones, William P., "NASA Science Internet Transitions to Project Status," *ISO Newsletter*, OSSA, NASA, Washington, DC, 8 November 1988.

Jones 1988c.   Jones, William P., "NASA Science Network," *ISO Newsletter*, OSSA, NASA, Washington, DC, 9 November 1988.

Jones and Camp 1988.   Jones, William P., and Camp, Warren Van, "Internetworking for NASA Science Programs," *Information Systems Newsletter*, no. 14, pp. 36–38, OSSA, NASA, Washington, DC, August 1988.

Jones and Hart 1988.   Jones, William P., and Hart, James P., Personal communications, 16 November 1988, 21 November 1988.

Kawaguchi et al. 1985.   Kawaguchi, Kenichi, Sato, Katsushi, Sample, Rick, Demco, John, and Hilpert, Brent, "Interconnecting Two X.400 Message Systems," *Proceedings of the Second International Symposium on Computer Message Systems (Washington, D.C., September 1985)*, pp. 15–26, IFIP, Washington, DC, 1985. Also in Uhlig, *Computer Message Systems—85*, pp. 17–28.

Kieffer 1988.   Kieffer, Rom, "Calgary activities," *NRCNET-L@UALTAVM.BITNET*, NetNorth, UUCP, CDNnet, Calgary, 10 May 1988.

Klein 1988.   Klein, Ben, "Networking at CUNY: an Overview," *CUNY University Computer Center Communications*, vol. 14, no. 3/4, pp. 15–21, CUNY, New York, March/April 1988.

Koblinksy and Choy 1988.   Koblinksy, C. J., and Choy, J., "NASA/NSF/NCAR Computer Gateway," *EOS*, vol. 69, no. 36, p. 833, American Geophysical Union, Washington, DC, 6 September 1988.

Kroll 1987.   Kroll, Carol Engelhardt, *Users' Directory of Computer Networks*, Office of Telecommunication Services, University of Texas System, Austin, Texas, July 1987.

LaQuey 1988.   LaQuey, Tracy Lynn, *Users' Directory of Computer Networks*, Office of Telecommunication Services, University of Texas System, Austin, July 1988.

LaQuey 1989.   LaQuey, Tracy Lynn, *Users' Directory of Computer Networks*, Digital Press, Bedford, MA, 1989.

Leigh 1988.   Leigh, J. L., "BCnet Status," Computing Centre, University of British Columbia, Vancouver, 18 April 1988.

Leighton 1988a.   Leighton, Jim, Personal communications, November 1988.

Leighton 1988b.   Leighton, Jim, "Networking and Engineering Overview," *NMFECC Buffer*, vol. 12, no. 1, pp. 12–16, National MFE Computer Center, Livermore, CA, January 1988.

Leighton and NMFECC 1988.   Leighton, Jim, and NMFECC, "MFEnet II Five Year Planning: Short Range (1–3 years)," National MFE Computer Center, Livermore, CA, 1988.

Licalzi 1987.   Licalzi, Pamela, "DA Systems Adds Message Transfer," *Computer Systems News*, pp. 32, 35, 2 July 1987.

Link-Up 1987.   Link-Up, "New DA Systems Service Links E-Mail Networks," *Link-Up*, vol. 4, no. 9, pp. 1, 28, November/December 1987.

Lopez-Swafford and Gary 1987.   Lopez-Swafford, B., and Gary, P., "SPAN: network security guide," *NSSDC Technical Reports*, National Space Science Data Center, NASA Goddard Space Flight Center, Greenbelt, MD, January 1987.

Martin 1988.   Martin, Marilyn, Personal communications, 25 November 1988.

Meeks 1985.   Meeks, Brock N., "An Overview of Conferencing Systems," *BYTE*, vol. 10, no. 13, pp. 169–184, December 1985.

Miller 1987. Miller, Debbie, "Save a Life: The Urgent Action Network," *NetNews*, vol. 1, no. 5, p. 4, IGC, San Francisco, Winter 1987.

Morabito 1986. Morabito, Margaret, "Confer: An Electronic Roundtable," *Link-Up*, vol. 3, no. 7, pp. 8–9, Learned Information, Inc., Medford, NJ, July/August 1986.

Neufeld et al. 1985. Neufeld, Gerald, Demco, John, Hilpert, Brent, and Sample, Rick, "EAN: an X.400 message system," *Proceedings of the Second International Symposium on Computer Message Systems (Washington, D.C., September 1985)*, pp. 1–13, IFIP, Washington, DC, 1985. Also in Uhlig, *Computer Message Systems — 85*, pp. 3–15.

NMFECC 1988. NMFECC, "Annual Review 1987," *NMFECC Buffer*, vol. 12, no. 1, pp. 1–24, National MFE Computer Center, Livermore, CA, January 1988.

NSIPO 1989a. NSIPO, "NASA Science Network Gateway Interconnections," NASA Science Internet Project Office, Moffett Field, CA, January 1989. Prepared for NSIPO by Sterling Software.

NSIPO 1989b. NSIPO, "SPAN North American Sites," NASA Science Internet Project Office, Moffett Field, CA, January 1989. Prepared for NSIPO by Sterling Software.

Nussbacher 1988. Nussbacher, Henry, Personal communications, 8 August 1988.

NYSERNet 1988. NYSERNet, "NYSERNet Topology," *NYSERNet News*, vol. 1, no. 8, p. 3, NYSERNet, Inc., New York, June 1988.

Peters 1986. Peters, D., "Riding the PSCN backbone with SPAN," *Information Systems Newsletter*, no. 5, p. 18, OSSA, NASA, Washington, DC, March 1986.

Postel and Reynolds 1984. Postel, Jonathan B., and Reynolds, Joyce, "Domain Requirements; RFC920," *ARPANET Working Group Requests for Comments*, October 1984.

Postel and Westine 1988a. Postel, Jonathan B., and Westine, Ann, "US Domain Policy and Procedures — July 1988 (Revised)," SRI-NIC, Menlo Park, CA, CA, July 1988.

Postel and Westine 1988b. Postel, Jonathan B., and Westine, Ann, "US Domain Questionnaire for Host Entry," SRI-NIC, Menlo Park, CA, CA, July 1988.

Price 1975. Price, Charlton R., "Conferencing via Computer: Cost Effective Communication for the Era of Forced Choice," in *The Delphi Method*, ed. Murray Turoff, Addison-Wesley, Reading, MA, 1975.

Prindeville 1988a. Prindeville, Philip A., "Pleins feux sur les réseaux canadiens (Networking in Canada)," *ConneXions — The Interoperability Report*, vol. 2, no. 11, pp. 2–6, Advanced Computing Environments, Mountain View, CA, November, 1988.

Prindeville 1988b. Prindeville, Philip A., Personal communications, November 1988.

Quarterman and Hoskins 1986. Quarterman, John S., and Hoskins, Josiah C., "Notable Computer Networks," *Communications of the ACM*, vol. 29, no. 10, pp. 932–971, October 1986.

Reber 1988. Reber, Pat, "NETNEWS: A Mainframe Bulletin Board," *CUNY University Computer Center Communications*, vol. 14, no. 5–6, pp. 29–31, CUNY, New York, May–June 1988.

Reid 1988. Reid, Brian, "Network Maps (DECWRL netmap 1.5)," DEC Western Research Lab, Palo Alto, 19 June 1988.

Roberts 1974. Roberts, Lawrence G., "Data by the Packet," *IEEE Spectrum*, vol. 11, no. 2, pp. 46–51, February 1974.

Rubenking 1988. Rubenking, Neil J., "DASnet Links 21 E-Mail Services and FAX," *PC Magazine*, vol. 7, no. 1, p. 46, 12 January 1988.

Salus 1988. Salus, Peter, "UUNET Progress Report," *;login:*, vol. 13, no. 1, p. 18, USENIX Association, Berkeley, CA, January/February 1988.

Sanderson 1988. Sanderson, T., "The European Space Physics Analysis Network," *Proceedings from the 21st ESLAB Symposium (Bolkesjo, Norway)*, no. ESA SP-275, European Space Agency, 1988.

Sanderson et al. 1988. Sanderson, T., Albrecht, M., Benvenuti, P., Franks, J., Hapgood, M., Green, J. L., Harvey, C., Heijden, N. v.d., Jabs, E., and Veldman, G., "The European Space Physics Analysis Network," *ESA Bulletin*, 1988.

Sanderson et al. 1986. Sanderson, T., Ho, S., Heijden, N., Jabs, E., and Green, J. L., "Near-realtime data transmission during the ICE-Comet Giacobini-Zinner Encounter," *ESA Bulletin*, vol. 45, no. 21, 1986.

Shapard 1988. Shapard, Jeffrey, Personal communications, September 1988.

Sisson 1988. Sisson, Pat, Personal communications, 30 November 1988.

Sisson and Posinski 1988. Sisson, P., and Posinski, C., "Accessing SPAN from Non-SPAN Nodes," National Space Science Data Center, NASA Goddard Space Flight Center, Greenbelt, MD, October 1988.

Taylor and Heyworth 1988. Taylor, Roger, and Heyworth, Allan, "NRCnet: A National Network for Canada's Research Community," Division of Informatics, National Research Council, Ottawa, 7 June 1988.

Toronto 1988a. Toronto, "A Proposal to the NetNorth Executive Committee," University of Toronto, October 1988.

Toronto 1988b. Toronto, "A Proposal in Support of a National Research Network," University of Toronto, January 1988.

Turoff 1980. Turoff, Murray, "Management Issues in Human Communication Via Computer," in *Emerging Office Systems*, ed. Robert M. Landau, James H. Bair, Jean H. Siegman, pp. 233–257, Ablex Publishing Corporation, Norwood, NJ, 1980. Based on Proceedings of the Stanford University International Symposium on Office Automation.

Turoff 1985. Turoff, Murray, "Information, Value, and the Internal Marketplace," *Technological Forecasting and Social Change*, vol. 27, no. 4, pp. 357–373, July 1985.

Turoff and Chinai 1985. Turoff, Murray, and Chinai, Sanjit, "An Electronic Information Marketplace," *Computer Networks and ISDN Systems*, vol. 9, pp. 79–90, 1985.

Uhlig 1986. Uhlig, R. Ed., *Computer Message Systems—85*, Elsevier, Amsterdam, 1986.

U. S. Army Forum 1984. U. S. Army Forum, "U.S. Army Forum: A Way to Tap Experience and Wisdom Off-line," *Government Executive*, vol. 16, no. 6, pp. 55–57, June 1984.

Vachon 1988a. Vachon, Mario, Personal communications, November 1988.

Vachon 1988b. Vachon, Mario, Personal communications, 23 September 1988.

Watt 1988. Watt, Roger, Personal communications, July–August 1988.

Wells 1987. Wells, William C., "PHYSnet/CITnet/HEPnet/NRAO/SPAN— Physics Community DECnet Mail," Data Communication and Network Services, University of California at Berkeley, 14 September 1987.

Woodsworth 1988a. Woodsworth, Andrew, "NRCnet Proposal," *CDNnet Reports*, no. 2, pp. 1, 4, Summer 1988.

Woodsworth 1988b. Woodsworth, Andy, "Regional Networks in Canada," *NRCNET-L@UALTAVM.BITNET*, National Research Council, Ottawa, 7 October 1988.

Woodsworth 1988c. Woodsworth, A. W., "NRCnet Meeting (21 April 1988)," NRC, Ottawa, 29 April 1988.

Yalow 1988. Yalow, Ben, Personal communications, June–September 1988.

Zaunbrecher 1987. Zaunbrecher, Dusty, "From EcoNet," *NetNews*, vol. 1, no. 1, p. 4, IGC, San Francisco, July 1987.

13   *Europe*

If Europe were treated exhaustively, this chapter could easily be a book in itself. But there has been no attempt to describe here every development in every European country. Criteria for inclusion have had to be somewhat arbitrary, so lack of a lengthy description of any particular country or system is merely a sign of time or space constraints for this book, not of the lack of importance of the system or the country.

Europe acts in concert (perhaps in counterpoint) on many issues. The same may be said for certain regions of this continent, and this chapter is arranged accordingly:

- European Networking Concerns
- Continental European Networks
- European Community (EC): Belgium, Denmark, France, the Federal Republic of Germany, Greece, Ireland, Italy, Luxembourg, Netherlands, Portugal, Spain, and the United Kingdom
- Nordic Countries: Denmark, Finland, Iceland, Norway, and Sweden
- European Free Trade Area (EFTA): Switzerland, Austria, Yugoslavia, and Turkey
- Eastern Europe: the Union of Soviet Socialist Republics, Poland, the German Democratic Republic, Czechoslovakia, Hungary, Romania, Bulgaria, and Albania

Networks that span a whole region are discussed first in the corresponding section, followed by descriptions of individual countries and the networks within them.

13.1   *European Networking Concerns*

Terminal access by X.25 PDN is very common in Europe (and in much of the rest of the world, other than the United States). Speeds range up from about 2400bps and are commonly 9600bps in some places, such as France (although the actual available bandwidth may be less). This availability leads to wide use of per-link file transfer programs such as **Kermit** [Huitema 1987a].

PDN access charges are usually by volume—i.e., per packet. This causes some of the large research networks, such as the British network *JANET*, to use leased lines instead. Although *JANET* uses X.25, nonetheless, some other large networks do not: none of the three existing continental European networks is exclusively based on X.25. This is partly because the PTT services are optimized for terminal traffic and their tariffs and bandwidths are not as appropriate for handling bulk services such as large file transfers or remote graphics; also, protocol conversion is needed to communicate with machines on TCP/IP or DECNET local area networks [Carpenter et al. 1987]. General mail and file transfer protocols, software, and services are often developed on research networks, so they have usually been developed for leased line networks, not for PDNs; the German network *DFN* is an exception. PDN rates vary widely, not only within a country, but also for access to other countries. From France, access to other European countries costs about three times as much as internal access, to the United States about ten times more, and to Japan perhaps fifteen times more [Huitema 1987a]. Rationalization of the rates of these X.25 networks, of the protocols and software used on them, and of the interconnections of higher level networks built on top of them is one of the reasons for the formation of RARE (see Chapter 8). The section on RARE, as well as those on the three existing continental European networks—*EUnet*, *EARN*, and *HEPnet*—contain some discussion of the political effects of PDN rate differences. Some specific examples of rates may be found in Appendix A.

ISDN is expected to solve some of the current PTT bandwidth problems, but it is not clear when it will be generally available, what protocol interfaces will be available, or what the tariffs will be [Carpenter et al. 1987].

Rationalization of naming conventions and namespaces is also a general European problem, since at least four or five major protocol suites are used, and even those with similar naming syntaxes may differ in details. Converting between the different orders used in *JANET* Grey Book NRS and *Internet* (and *EUnet*) DNS is relatively easy. Converting between X.400 and NRS or DNS is more difficult, but a standard and software do exist [Kille 1986]. Another point of agreement is the use of ISO3166 two letter country codes as top level domain names. Mechanisms also exist for transferring mail with networks based on other protocol suites, such as DECNET (*HEPnet*) and NJE (*EARN*). Even though interconnection is possible for at least mail, the diversity of protocol suites and naming conventions used is still a major European problem. Specification, implementation, and use of ISO-OSI protocols is widely awaited as the solution [Carpenter et al. 1987].

13.2   *Continental European Networks*

There are three widely used networks that span the continent, as well as an association of research networks.

13.2.1   EUnet

The European **UNIX** network, *EUnet*, is a "pan-European cooperative R&D network" [Karrenberg 1988a, 1]. The purpose of the network is to provide its users with modern communication facilities, particularly electronic mail and news and interconnections to other networks.

EUnet began as an extension or application of the software and protocols used in *USENET* and *UUCP* in North America, and most hosts, as on those networks, run **UNIX**. But *EUnet* is not restricted to **UNIX** hackers: it is widely used by mathematicians, computer science researchers, and others in the European research and development community to communicate with each other and similar people worldwide. Users tend to be in small or medium size companies or university departments that have their own computing facilities. The network is an important means of technology transfer between industry and academia. It extends throughout Western Europe, as shown in Figure 13.1, and is one of only three widely used European-wide computer networks, the other two being *EARN* and *HEPnet*. Talks are in progress among those three networks and with RARE about coordinating and integrating networking services throughout Europe, possibly including shared intercontinental gateways and infrastructures [Karrenberg 1988b].

Administration

Mail and news are closely tied together in *EUnet*: the backbone hosts and administrators are the same for both, and a single name is used for the combined mail and news network. The administration of the network is much more organized than for *UUCP* and *USENET* in North America, and there has always been a much stronger relationship between *EUnet* and the European UNIX systems Users Group (EUUG) than there has ever been between

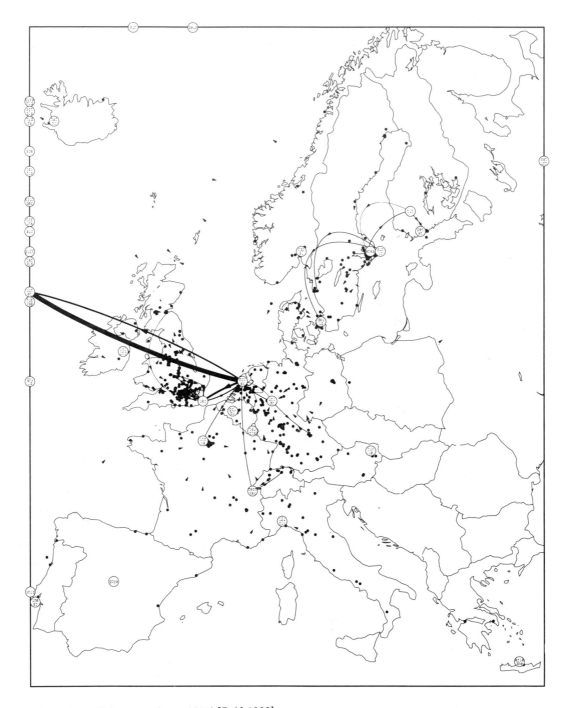

Figure 13.1. *EUnet map (June 1989) [Reid 1989]*

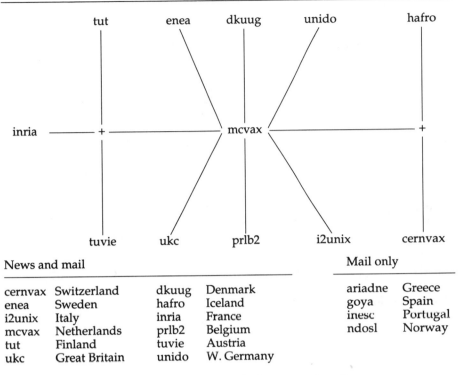

News and mail

cernvax	Switzerland	dkuug	Denmark
enea	Sweden	hafro	Iceland
i2unix	Italy	inria	France
mcvax	Netherlands	prlb2	Belgium
tut	Finland	tuvie	Austria
ukc	Great Britain	unido	W. Germany

Mail only

ariadne	Greece
goya	Spain
inesc	Portugal
ndosl	Norway

Note: All the hosts in the figure subscribe to both news and mail

Figure 13.2. *EUnet backbone topology (April 1988) [Spafford 1988]*

USENET or *UUCP* and USENIX or UniForum (the two organizations in North America most similar to EUUG). Many of the "soapbox" discussion newsgroups are not carried (due to their high costs in transatlantic and European traffic), and there are many newsgroups that are distributed only within Europe or within a country. In the latter case, the national language and character set are frequently used.

English is the lingua franca of the network, though many other European languages are used. There is one *EUnet* backbone host in each member country in Europe, as shown in Figure 13.2 [Spafford 1988]. *EUnet* had 1,221 sites in 19 countries in Western Europe as of May 1988, as shown in Table 13.1. Of those, 153 subscribed to news (all subscribed to mail). Each backbone host organizes communications within its country, often by maintaining direct connections to all other hosts in the country. National backbones increasingly hide the internal national organization of the network from the rest of the world, usually by using domain names; the same

Table 13.1. *EUnet growth*

Country	June 1986	17 April 1987	October 1987	May 1988	November 1988
Austria	7	19	23	30	33
Belgium	17	11	16	20	22
Denmark	36	38	46	61	74
Finland	47	45	53	56	56
France	94	68	96	136	136
Germany	90	107	140	184	206
Greece	1	4	7	7	9
Iceland	0	1	11	11	14
Ireland	6	9	6	6	14
Italy	28	25	28	32	46
Luxembourg	0	0	2	2	1
Netherlands	129	93	110	128	165
Norway	7	6	20	20	36
Portugal	0	0	1	1	1
Spain	0	0	1	1	23
Sweden	108	123	144	173	196
Switzerland	50	29	29	37	45
United Kingdom	276	208	244	315	351
Yugoslavia	0	1	1	1	2
Totals					
Mail hosts	896	787	978	1,221	1,430
News hosts	—	—	132	153	—
Gigabytes/month					
cwi.nl (*mcvax*)	0.550	>1	>1	2.5	—

Sources: Courtesy of Teus Hagen, Piet Beertema, Marc Nyssen, Daniel Karrenberg, and José Mañas
Note: Connected sites by country

thing sometimes happens inside large organizations such as universities. This makes the exact number of hosts unknown and essentially unknowable and is the reason why the numbers of sites shown in Table 13.1 do not increase nearly as fast as the increase in throughput shown.

Figure 13.3 compares recent *EUnet* and *USENET* growth. It shows that the traffic growth curves for the two networks have been very similar and that the growth curve for numbers of *USENET* hosts is also very similar to that for numbers of *EUnet* hosts. There are not enough data available to plot a similar curve for *EUnet* hosts, but the few data points shown fit the expectation of less increase in *EUnet* hosts because the numbers for *USENET* are actual counts of hosts posting news articles, while those for *EUnet* are for registered domains.

The backbone hosts also communicate among themselves across international boundaries. The whole set of backbone hosts is the backbone of the network. There is a central host to which all backbone hosts have

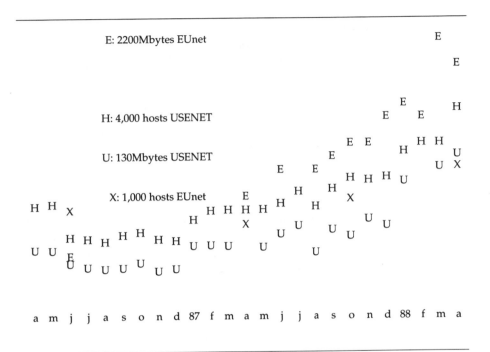

Figure 13.3. *EUnet and USENET recent growth [Reid 1988; Beertema 1988a]*

connections and which carries all the intercontinental news and most of the intercontinental mail traffic; this host has always been *mcvax* at the Centrum voor Wiskunde en Informatica (CWI), or Centre for Mathematics and Computer Science, in Amsterdam. The domain name of *mcvax* is *cwi.nl*. Administration for this machine and for much of *EUnet* is done by Piet Beertema and Daniel Karrenberg of CWI. Traffic through that host in May 1988 amounted to 2.5Gbytes per month, increasing by about 100Mbytes per month, and up from about 1Gbyte per month a year previously, according to the administration of *cwi.nl*. These figures do not include exchange of network maps or file transfers with *uunet*. They also do not include mail traffic among European countries, since most of that passes directly between the national backbone machines: that traffic probably amounts to several hundred more megabytes per month, perhaps producing a total network throughput figure of about 3Gbytes per month. The network is growing by more than 100 percent per year in both sites and throughput.

The administrators of the backbone hosts hold meetings (usually at EUUG meetings), where they determine concerted strategies and tactics. They have succeeded in implementing *Internet* DNS domains throughout the network (or at least throughout the backbone), completing the job in mid-1987. The top level domains used are the ISO3166 two letter country codes, following RFC920 [Postel and Reynolds 1984]. These domains have even been accepted on some other networks in Europe, largely at the instigation of *EUnet*.

When a single legal or political entity is needed to speak for the network, EUUG does so. For example, EUUG has funded the first part of a study about protocol migration strategies for the network and is holding discussions with the Commission of the European Communities (CEC) about its potential involvement. It must be emphasized, however, that there are no formal agreements or contracts among the backbone administrators or with EUUG: the entire network is essentially run by volunteer labor. This works well enough for a cooperative network and helps avoid bureaucratic overhead costs and minimize any potential liabilities [Karrenberg 1988b]. EUUG publishes a printed directory of *EUnet*, and of *EARN* and *HEPnet* [Karrenberg and Goos 1988].

Funding

Funds are provided by the owners of the individual hosts and by the individual users. The service is nonetheless quite affordable, due to the low overhead mentioned above [Karrenberg 1988b]. There is a flat fee of about two pounds per site per month. The cost of the news connections with North America (primarily through *uunet*) is shared proportionately among the *EUnet* backbone hosts according to the number of news hosts each feeds. They each in turn share it equally among all the hosts in their country. Thus, no host bears a disproportionate burden. Mail is charged to the originating host on a message by message and link by link basis. This is not possible, however, for intercontinental links and links to nonchargeable networks. The originating host usually brings these charges to the attention of the senders of the mail in some manner.

The European PDNs charge per segment (maximum 64 bytes) for use of X.25. There is also a negligible connection time charge and an initial connection charge, but the per-packet charge accounts for more than 80 percent of the costs. Rates for X.25 connections are lower in Europe than in North America, and usually lower than equivalent North American telephone rates for similar distances and connection times. But despite uniformity in charging units, X.25 tariffs vary widely within Europe. Mail originating outside of Europe in some cases must be paid for by a *EUnet* backbone host, particularly when gatewaying to a national noncharging network. This makes bulk mailings rather annoying to the gateway administrators.

Protocols

The basic application protocols are news and mail as in *USENET* and *UUCP*, plus remote login where X.25 or TCP/IP links are used. *EUnet* originally used UUCP over dialup telephone links like those of *USENET* and *UUCP* in North America. This arrangement did not last more than about six months, as it quickly became evident that X.25 links were more practical (faster and cheaper) in Europe for long-distance links. Many *EUnet* links between backbones and outside Europe are now UUCP (using the f protocol, without much of the usual g protocol error checking) over X.25. However, recent technological developments have made international phone links more attractive than X.25. With the Telebit Trailblazer modem, international links can be up to seven times less expensive than X.25 links; leased lines can be even less expensive (but use of these modems requires PTT approval, which is not yet forthcoming in some countries). *EUnet* is currently switching interbackbone links to leased lines where cost-effective. For example, there is a leased line between *mcvax* and *inria* in Paris. For other interbackbone links, a mixture of X.25 for mail and phone lines with Trailblazer modems for news is being considered. Ordinary UUCP telephone dialup links are still the most common for local links and to leaf nodes. Ninety percent of all mail and news traffic arrives within one day. Reliability is quite high.

The SLIP protocol, which allows TCP/IP over serial lines, may be used over some interbackbone links in place of X.25 because of its advantage of speed (4800bps is the practical limit for X.25 links), especially over some of the faster digital telephone links now becoming available (up to 64Kbps at about 25 cents a minute). TCP/IP is also sometimes used over X.25 with RFC877 encapsulation. Over TCP, NNTP is often used for news transfer and SMTP for mail transfer.

Speed

Most X.25 links are effectively about 4800bps, though the nominal rate most commonly used is 9600bps. Many dialup telephone links are still 2400bps, but Trailblazers with their effective data rate of 10Kbps or more are becoming increasingly popular. In the Netherlands, these modems are used almost exclusively. Each European PTT has to certify these modems separately, however, and in some countries this has not been done.

Naming, Addressing, and Routing

Old-style UUCP source routing such as hosta!hostb!*host*!*user* is now usually used only to support DNS domain syntax (although users can still use source routing directly if they wish to). Routing is managed by the backbone hosts, each of which knows the organization within its own country and which hosts are in which country. Routing information is automatically exchanged daily between the backbone hosts and between Europe and the United States, Japan, Korea, Australia, Malaysia, New Zealand, and Israel. If mail is sent from a nonbackbone host that lacks a direct link to the destination host, the mail is forwarded to the national backbone host, which relays it. Because domains are geographical, at least to the extent of there being one domain per country, each backbone host need only know the hosts within its own country domain and a path to the backbone host for each other country domain: there is no need to know anything about the internal structure of other country domains. In fact, routing is delegated further, since the internal structure of a given subdomain may be known by a host other than the national backbone host, which then need only know the appropriate nameserver host for the subdomain. In this context, the *Internet* DNS top level domains *EDU, COM, GOV, ORG, MIL,* and *NET* are considered to be U.S. top level domains (in fact, subdomains of the X.500 top level domain *US*) and are routed accordingly.

Interconnections

There are connections from *EUnet* to *EARN, JANET, DFN,* and other networks within Europe, plus intercontinental connections to Japan (*JUNET*), Korea (*SDN*), Australia (*ACSnet*), Malaysia (*RangKoM*), New Zealand, and Israel, and to *CSNET* and *UUCP* in North America. Many of these links also carry *USENET* news traffic.

There is no need for any user on *EUnet* to directly specify a gateway to any other network. At most, a user must get internetwork mail to a *EUnet* national backbone host: all those machines know how to route it from there. For example, a user might get mail to a *BITNET* host by sending it to

    backbone!*host*.bitnet!*user*

where backbone would be the name of a backbone host. From most *EUnet* hosts, even this is not necessary. Just using straightforward domain syntax will work:

    user@host.bitnet

or

    user@{**DNS**}

The latter example works for *BITNET* or *EARN* hosts that have DNS domain names.

The default gateway to *UUCP* and the *Internet* in North America and also to many other places is *mcvax*, which connects to *uunet* for those two specific networks. A national backbone host that has no direct connection to a target network usually forwards mail for that network through *mcvax*. But a *EUnet* user does not need to know these details. Incoming mail from other networks may in general be sent to *mcvax*, which will often route it through the appropriate national backbone host. For example, incoming mail from *EARN* might be sent to *MCVAX*, which is the *EARN* name of *mcvax*. That machine might determine that mail for, for example, Germany would be better sent through *unido*, the German backbone machine, which also has a direct *EARN* connection. So *MCVAX* would send the mail back through *EARN* to *UNIDO*, thus bypassing the expensive *EUnet* connection from *mcvax* to *unido*. Also, *MCVAX* can't charge the cost of the *EUnet* link to the originator of the message on *EARN*, but the cost of the *EARN* path between *MCVAX* and *UNIDO* doesn't have this problem. *EUnet* traffic in general is not forwarded through *EARN*, of course; this applies only to traffic originating on *EARN*.

History

EUnet was started by Teus Hagen, Peter Collinson, and Keld Simonsen at the April 1982 EUUG meeting in Paris. It originally connected machines in the Netherlands, Denmark, Sweden, and the United Kingdom but quickly spread throughout Western Europe.

Plans

A number of problems in *EUnet* are under intensive discussion [Devillers 1988a]. These include the following:

- Setting up fixed charges without increasing costs for the smallest sites
- How to charge IP traffic, especially considering expected traffic increases due to FTP
- How to make reserve funds to cope with the increase in traffic and the necessary increase of the bandwidth
- How several newly installed links between Europe and the United States will affect *EUnet*. (Will they draw academic sites away from *EUnet*, thus decreasing revenues?)
- What will be the effects of the emerging European academic networks, such as those being encouraged by RARE and NORDUNET?

Many of these problems are not sufficiently well defined yet to have solutions.

Although *EUnet* users express no immediate need to move to ISO-OSI protocols, there is a detailed plan for such migration [Karrenberg 1988a]. This plan was developed with sponsorship from EUUG and the EC.

There is no great difficulty in supplying mail service with X.400 in its 1988 revision, and other services that X.400 provides would then also be available. But news is another matter: there is no equivalent ISO-OSI standard, and there are problems with an implementation using X.400.

Services	There are no facilities for retrospective subscription to newsgroups, cross-posting of articles, geographically limited newsgroup distributions, or easy unsubscription.
Mechanisms	Compression for transmission and storage of a single copy per machine are not provided for.

In other words, X.400 could provide mailing list service, but not true news or conferencing.

The migration plan would set up a small parallel network for use in developing implementations to the point of usability. There would be application layer gateways for mail and news, preferably connecting to the existing network through existing national backbones. There may also be use of ISODE to provide ISO-OSI service over existing *EUnet* TCP/IP links.

The protocols to be used would be TP0 over X.25 for wide area network (WAN) connections, largely for interoperability with other networks that use that configuration. For a local area network (LAN), the more likely configuration would be TP4 over CLNS, which has the advantage of existing **UNIX** implementations and an expected one for **4.4BSD**, as well as requirement by the U.S. government GOSIP report [NBS 1988], which will encourage further implementations. One can also run X.25 over the LAN and use the WAN protocol stack [Karrenberg 1988a].

About Spring 1989, *EUnet* began setting up a continental TCP/IP network, tentatively called Réseau IP Européen (*RIPE*). This uses T1 links from Amsterdam to France and *FNET*, Stockholm and *NORDUnet*, thus also connecting most of the transatlantic links to *NSFNET*.

Access

New hosts must register with their national backbone host administrator, and inquiries within Europe should be addressed to the same place. Elsewhere, for direct inquiries to EUUG, contact:

EUUG Secretariat
mcvax!euug
euug@cwi.nl
Owles Hall
Buntingford
Herts. SG9 9PL
United Kingdom

13.2.2   EARN

The charter and statutes of *EARN*, the European Academic Research Network, state that it is a network for Europe, the Middle East, and Africa. It has hosts in every Western European country, plus Austria, Yugoslavia, Cyprus, Turkey, Israel, Algeria, and the Ivory Coast, as shown in Figure 13.4. Recent voting has ratified Morocco, Tunisia, and Egypt as full members and India as an associate member, and negotiations are in progress on whether to accept connection requests from Bulgaria, Hungary, and the Soviet Union [Nussbacher 1988a; Greisen 1988].

EARN links more than 600 hosts at more than 500 institutions and has more than 30,000 users, as shown in Table 13.2.

Administration and Funding

Administratively, *EARN* is an association registered in France. There is a board of directors consisting of one representative from each member country. Each institution in a country with computers connected to *EARN* is an *EARN* member. Most directors are elected by all of the *EARN* members in a country, although some are appointed by their ministry of education. The board of directors in turn elects an executive committee whose members have two year terms, and a president, who is currently Dennis Jennings of University College Dublin (UCD). There is also a technical committee and a membership committee, both appointed by the executive committee. Management offices are located in Dublin and Paris. Central *EARN* administrative and technical services are handled by one central computer in each European country.

Internal national financing is up to the *EARN* nodes in each country and varies. Each country pays for one international line to another country in Europe. The cost of a common link to the United States and the administrative costs of the network are met by fees collected from the national *EARN* members and are based on gross national product. The money is eventually collected from the member organizations and is not charged back to the individual users. Money for internal national operations is collected by similar means. The total amount involved is about 1.2 million European Currency Units (ECU) per year, or about 1.5 million U.S. dollars.

Protocols and Services

EARN is similiar to *NetNorth* in that it is based on the same technology as *BITNET* and is technically an integral part of the latter network, sharing the same namespace and being coordinated in the same tree structure of links. The services supported are those listed in the section on *BITNET* worldwide, and the underlying protocol is NJE. In *EARN* as in *BITNET*, most

Figure 13.4. *EARN map (25 April 1988) [BITNIC 1988]*

sites are in large computer centers at universities and government research facilities, plus some large companies. Many *EARN* hosts are IBM **VM** or Digital VAX **VMS** machines.

Interconnections

There are gateways to several national academic networks, such as *JANET* in the United Kingdom and *HEANET* in Ireland. Gateways to *EUnet* include *MCVAX* in Amsterdam and *UNIDO* in Dortmund, Germany. The current transatlantic link is between Montpellier, France, and New York. The link to Abidjan in the Ivory Coast is also from Montpellier, as are the ones to Israel (*ILAN*) and Izmir, Turkey. Gateways between *EARN* and other networks are mostly the same as for *BITNET*. For example, to send mail from the *Internet* to *EARN*, an address format might be

Table 13.2. *EARN growth*

Country	1 May 1986	1 May 1988	1 August 1988
Algeria	0	—	0
Austria	6	—	13
Belgium	13	—	27
Denmark	13	—	19
Finland	7	—	23
France	39	—	103
Germany	130	—	197
Greece	2	—	5
Iceland	0	—	1
Ireland	4	—	5
Israel	38	—	47
Italy	31	—	76
Ivory Coast	0	—	1
Luxembourg	0	—	1
Netherlands	39	—	58
Norway	1	—	5
Portugal	1	—	2
Spain	8	—	19
Sweden	8	—	24
Switzerland	22	—	40
Turkey	0	—	11
United Kingdom	1	—	1
Yugoslavia	0	—	1
Totals			
Countries	17	24	24
Sites	—	500	—
Hosts	363	600	644
Users	—	30,000	—

Sources: May 1986 figures courtesy Henry Nussbacher; August 1988
courtesy Paul Bryant and Henry Nussbacher
Note: Connected hosts by country

user%host.BITNET@CUNYVM.CUNY.EDU

See the gatewaying information given in the section on *BITNET* worldwide.

History

EARN was formed in 1983 on the model of *BITNET*. IBM funded transatlantic links between *BITNET* and *EARN* until April 1987. Between 1983 and 1987, IBM invested $15 million in *EARN* for support ranging from much of the equipment to support personnel. The links to Israel and Turkey were from Pisa, Italy, until May and June 1988, respectively. There was formerly an additional transatlantic link between Darmstadt in West Germany and Washington, D.C.; this was removed in mid-1988.

Plans

EARN will migrate to the ISO-OSI protocols, such as X.400 [Bryant 1987; Salminen 1988a]. This is partly because of deficiencies of the NJE protocols (as detailed in the sections on *BITNET* worldwide and *ILAN*). It is also because *EARN* must obtain permission from the PTT in each European country in order to operate there; in most European countries, switching third party communications is a government monopoly. The European Conference of Postal and Telecommunications Administrations (CEPT) has made future operation conditional both on a surcharge to be paid to the national PTTs and on conversion of *EARN* to the ISO-OSI protocols. (Some countries have opposed this surcharge, and some PTTs are dropping it.) Also, all European countries are expected to convert other networks to ISO-OSI, and *EARN* wishes to interoperate with them. Implementations of the ISO-OSI protocols are now becoming available. Digital Europe, IBM, and Northern Telecom will be supplying hardware, software, and technical support for the transition. The initial plan is to operate the currently used NJE protocol over ISO session service to preserve the current application services. ISO higher level protocols, in particular X.400, will be introduced a little later.

Any migration will be coordinated with RARE. Talks are taking place among the three widely used continent-wide European computer networks, *EARN*, *EUnet*, and *HEPnet*, together with RARE, about convergent migration plans and potential shared infrastructure.

However, the purposes of RARE and *EARN* are not necessarily identical, since the former's main end is the promotion of standards in coordination with the PTTs, while the latter's function is to supply a working network and to further academic research. This is best seen in the different approaches to charging: *EARN* considers annual flat fees to institutions that are known in advance to be important, rather than per-user usage charges such as PTTs usually use. Also, *EARN* is very interested in building a uniform system extending throughout the EC, rather than expecting users to negotiate different rates and services with each national PTT. And *EARN* is oriented toward being a backbone network connecting national and campus networks into a continental internetwork, along the lines of *NSFNET* in the United States [Jennings 1987].

Meanwhile, *BITNET* in the United States has plans involving the TCP/IP protocol suite. *ILAN* in Israel is already implementing a TCP/IP migration plan with further plans for eventual ISO-OSI migration. A major consideration in the latter case is the diversity of operating systems used in

Israel. The international *EARN* backbone is composed exclusively of IBM machines for which there are ISO-OSI implementations, making it much more practical for *EARN* to migrate directly to ISO-OSI. The *EARN* board of directors recognizes that it cannot direct internal national migration plans and merely requires protocol converting gateways to be in place for continued connection to *EARN*. This exemption will probably be taken advantage of by the United Kingdom, for *JANET*, and in Ireland, for *HEANET*, both of which use the Coloured Book protocols. Israel will be another such case. Exceptions are also explicitly allowed for DECNET protocols, in order to accommodate networks such as *HEPnet* that are international and to which *EARN* interconnections are important.

The main problem with immediate ISO-OSI conversion is the lack of availability of implementations of the necessary protocols. The networks are to be based on the national X.25 PTT networks, but those mostly support only the 1980 version of X.25, while the 1984 version is necessary for most of the ISO-OSI protocols. So *EARN* will initially support a private international X.25 network supplying X.25 (1984). Implementations of the transport protocols TP0 and even TP4 exist, as do ones of the X.400 mail protocol and partial ones of the FTAM file transfer protocol. But VTP for remote login and JTP for remote job entry are not generally implemented. Thus, X.400 will be the first application layer protocol to be promoted, both in new implementations and in interconnection with the existing *Ean* network. The point system is at IBM in Heidelberg. All ISO-OSI protocols used on *EARN* will be coordinated with the recommendations of CEN/CENELEC and RARE.

Access

Country coordinators are available for each of the 18 countries currently connected to *EARN*. The large majority of nodes have a mailbox named INFO. Users on other networks may be able to use the domain address:

INFO%*host*.BITNET@CUNYVM.CUNY.EDU

European Academic Research Network
Office of the President
Computer Center
University College, Belfield
Dublin 4
Ireland

13.2.3 HEPnet Europe

HEPnet is a shorthand name for the coordinated set of networking facilities used by High Energy Physicists in Europe. *HEPnet* is also a worldwide network and is described as such in Chapter 10. However, there are some specifically European characteristics of it, and those are discussed here.

Administration

HEPnet in Europe is organized around a coordinating committee with a chair from Organisation Européenne pour la Recherche Nucléaire (CERN). This committee was formed in 1988, and the current chair is François Fluckiger. There is also a user requirements committee [Fluckiger 1988].

Composition

Networking for High Energy Physics (HEP) is partly done over networks dedicated to physicists, such as *INFNET* in Italy or *PHYNET* in France, and over multidisciplinary networks such as *JANET* in the United Kingdom [Fluckiger 1988]. These various components are interconnected through a set of international leased lines dedicated to HEP; most of them connect to CERN [Blokzijl 1988]: from the CEN in Saclay, France; from the Institut National de Physique Nucléaire et Physique des Particules (IN2P3) in Lyons, France; from Rutherford Appleton Laboratory (RAL) in Oxford-Didcot, United Kingdom; from the Laboratoire d'Annecy-Le-Vieux de Physique des Particules (LAPP), or Particle Physics Laboratory, in Annecy-Le-Vieux, France; two lines from the Instituto Nazionale Fisica Nucleare (INFN) in Bologna, Italy; from CIEMAT in Madrid, Spain; from the Massachusetts Institute of Technology (MIT) in Cambridge, Massachusetts, United States; and a DoE sponsored satellite link from the Fermi National Accelerator Laboratory (FNAL) in Batavia, Illinois, United States. A line from the National Institute for Nuclear and High-Energy Physics (NIKHEF) in Amsterdam, Netherlands, will soon be operational and will also link the Nordic countries through *NORDUnet*. There are also leased lines from CERN to several organizations in Switzerland, including the University of Geneva (UG), the Schweizerisches Institut für Nuklearphysik (SIN), or Swiss Institute for Nuclear Physics, in Zurich, and the Eidgenossische Technische Hochschule (ETH), or Federal Institute for Technology, also in Zurich.

In addition to the leased lines to CERN, there are leased lines from RAL in the United Kingdom and from INFN in Italy to the Deutsches Elektronen SYnchrotron (DESY), or German Electron Synchrotron, in Hamburg, Germany. There is a link from Italy to the United States. *SPAN* is reachable through various European sites as well as through MIT. There are also DECNET links using intermittent X.25 PDN connections from Austria, Portugal, and Germany.

Protocols

The network is large enough that the DECNET address space limitation is a problem (see Poor Man's Routing (PMR) in Chapter 5).

Most of the dedicated links operate at 64Kbps. Most use X.25, sometimes using multiplexers for the coexistence of other protocols. These links and the networks they connect form an overall X.25 infrastructure with a common HEP X.25 addressing scheme. The main service offered over this infrastructure is DECNET. SNA, NJE, and Coloured Book protocols are also used. Physicists also use *EARN* extensively.

To cope with the current diversity of protocols, which is inevitable to serve an amorphous and demanding user population, application converter projects have been conducted by the community [Fluckiger 1988]. The first of these, General Internetwork File Transfer Protocol (GIFT), is a multiprotocol file transfer converter developed jointly by INFN, RAL, Oxford University (Oxford), CERN, and Stichting Academisch Rekencentrum Amsterdam (SARA), or Foundation Academic Computing Center Amsterdam, beginning in 1985. It allows conversion among any pair of *JANET* Blue Book, CERNNET FTP, TCP/IP FTP, DECNET FTP, and CDC RHF. Translation takes place during a file transfer without intermediate storage of the file. GIFT has been in operation at CERN since 1985 and at SARA since 1988 [Fluckiger 1988].

The second project, Mail Internet Transfer Protocol (MINT), is a CERN project for mail conversion, operational since 1986 [Carpenter et al. 1987]. It handles conversions between any pair of the following: **UNIX** *UUCP* mail, DECNET **VMS** mail, *EARN* NJE mail, X.400 MHS, *Internet* RFC822 and DNS mail, and the IBM **MVS WYLBUR** mail system [Fluckiger 1988].

Plans

Plans are well advanced for the introduction of 2Mbps links.

CERN was an early proponent of the *Ean* networks and of the use of X.400. There is a general policy within *HEPnet* for the use of ISO-OSI services, whenever available on a commercial basis and at least equivalent to alternative solutions in terms of functionality, performances, and cost-effectiveness. The use of DECNET turns out to be fortuitous in this respect, because Digital is heavily involved in ISO-OSI protocol development and implementation, and DECNET Phase V is expected to be interoperable with ISO-OSI. It is, however, expected that ISO-OSI can never replace proprietary or ad hoc solutions for all of the sometimes very demanding applications of *HEPnet* [Fluckiger 1988].

Access
Brian Carpenter
brian@priam.cern.ch
brian@cernvax.bitnet

Denise Heagerty
denise%priam.cern@cwi.nl
denise@cernvax.bitnet
mcvax!cernvax!denise
HEPNET: vxcern::denise
JANET: denise%cern.priam@uk.ac.ean-relay
CERN: denise@priam.cern
+41 (022) 83 49 75
Telex: 419000 CER CH

DD Division
CERN
CH-1211 Genève 23
Switzerland

13.2.4   Ean Europe

The objective of the *Ean* networks is to establish communication links for the European research community, in cooperation with RARE.

Most of the sites connected inside the same country are linked by 9600bps leased lines. Interdomain links consist mostly of X.25 public switched networks, with some using 9600bps lines. Mail delivery in minutes to hours is usual, with medium reliability.

Naming, addressing, and routing are the same as for *CDNnet*. Methods for reaching *Ean* networks from non-*Ean* networks vary greatly depending on the network of origin and the locations of the sender and the addressee. A gateway at CERN connects *EARN* (and *BITNET*), *EUnet* (and *UUCP*), and the *Ean* networks.

The **Ean** implementations of the X.400 protocols have spread so rapidly into new nations that it is interesting to track their progress (see Table 13.3). There are actually no *Ean* networks as such in the United Kingdom or Australia: these are merely gateways into the national networks, in much the same way as Australia also has *UUCP* gateways. In March 1987, there was one host in Denmark, three in Finland, one in Iceland, six (at five institutes) in Norway, and six (at five institutes) in Sweden [Carlson 1987]. As of October 1987, there were 15 hosts in Switzerland, 30 in France, 65 in Germany, and about 30 elsewhere in Europe [Kaufmann and Ullmann 1987]. There were ten hosts at CERN alone by the end of 1987 [Carpenter et al. 1987].

The German network *DFN* is not strictly **Ean**-based. *CDNnet* in Canada, the progenitor of all the others, may not remain solely **Ean** as other X.400 implementations become available. Meanwhile, the **Ean** implementation is being improved by its original developers [Demco 1988].

Table 13.3. *Timetable for the European Ean networks*

Country	Network	Domain Old	New		Date	
Canada	CDNnet	CDN	CA		April	1983[1]
			CA	1	March	1984[1]
Norway	UNINETT	UNINETT	NO	7	October	1984
Switzerland	CERN	CERN	CH	2	November	1984
United Kingdom	UK	UK	GB	27	November	1984
Sweden	SUNET	SUNET	SE	9	December	1984
Switzerland	CHUNET	CHUNET	CH	17	June	1985
Germany	DFN	DFN	DE	22	August	1985
Ireland	IRL	IRL	IE	12	November	1985
Italy	OSIRIDE	I	IT	3	December	1985
Spain	IRIS	E	ES	3	December	1985
Australia	AU	AU	AU	23	December	1985
Netherlands	NL	NL	NL	17	March	1986

Source: Courtesy John Demco
[1]First message
[2]Test network

Access

Trond Skjesol
skjesol@vax.runit.unit.no

Alf Hansen
alf_hansen@vax.runit.unit.no
RUNIT-D
N-7034 Trondheim-NTH
Norway

Brian Carpenter
CERN
CH-1211 Genève 23
Switzerland

CDNnet Headquarters
cdnnet-hq@ean.ubc.ca
Computing Centre
University of British Columbia
Vancouver, BC V6T 1W5
Canada

13.3   *European Community*

The European Community (EC) is the most active in networking of the European regions. The countries within it are discussed in alphabetical order.

13.4   *Belgium {BE}*

Although there is a local branch of *EARN* in Belgium, its academic and IBM mainframe orientation has prevented it from spreading widely. *EUnet*, meanwhile, has benefited from the popularity of **UNIX** machines and IBM PCs, both of which can readily be connected, regardless of whether they are at academic institutions or not. The network in Belgium that covers the whole country is *EUnet*, or its national branch, described below [Nyssen 1987].

13.4.1   EUnet in Belgium

The first Belgian site on *EUnet* was Vrije Universiteit Brussel (VUB), or the Free University of Brussels, which connected to *mcvax* by a 300bps link in 1983 [Nyssen 1987]. The Belgian backbone host since 1985 has been *prlb2* at the Philips Research Laboratory Brussels (PRLB), in Watermael Boitsfort. Although most network management is done by volunteers, they tend to be members of the Belgian UNIX Users Group (BUUG), which occasionally performs some political functions for the network. Unlike many national branches of *EUnet*, the Belgian branch does not have a specific separate name. There were 20 registered Belgian *EUnet* sites as of May 1988; the number of hosts is probably at least three times as large, due to the use of domains and of local area networks. Most connections are by UUCP over X.25 at 2400bps over the national PTT. Eventual conversion to other protocols is expected, and Belgium is participating in the *EUnet* migration plan that is being developed in cooperation with RARE, *EARN*, *HEPnet*, and the EC [Karrenberg 1988b]. Services are the same as those of *EUnet* mail and news.

There is a gateway to *EARN*, *kul-cs*. The two networks cooperate in the top level domain *BE* for Belgium. Domain addressing and local subdomains are widely used in Belgium as a solution to routing problems. Because of this, all the hosts on all the networks reachable through *prlb2* and *mcvax* are addressable directly in domain format.

Access
Marc Nyssen
Secretary of the BUUG
marc@minf.vub.be
+32 02 478.15.20

Eenheid Medische Informatica
Faculteit Geneeskunde en Farmacie
Vrije Universiteit Brussel
Laarbeeklaan 103
B-1090 Brussels
Belgium

13.5 *Denmark*

Denmark is both a member of the EC and a Nordic country. To avoid describing it in both categories, it appears below under Nordic Countries.

13.6 *France {FR}*

France has long been a center of networking activity, since at least the development of *CYCLADES* and participation in *EIN*, as well as *RPC* and *COSAC*, all already described in Chapter 7.

There are a number of current French networks, ranging from the research networks *SMARTIX*, *PHYNET*, and *ARISTOTE*; to the academic network, *REUNIR*; to the French branches of *EUnet* (*FNET*, with backbone node *inria*) and *EARN*; to the very large and popular *Minitel* network.

There are visible groupings among these networks [Devillers 1988b].

- *FNET* and *ARISTOTE* are managed from the Institut National de Recherche en Informatique et Automatique (INRIA), or the National Research Institute for Computer Science and Automation, and are partly funded by it as well. These two networks are gatewayed, and there is a gateway from *ARISTOTE* to *SMARTIX*.
- The academic network *REUNIR* is closely associated with *EARN*. Half of the funds for *EARN* come from the national ministry of education and the national research center CNRS, which also funds *REUNIR* for eventual development of X.400 service.
- The committee Organisation Française des Réseaux integrés de la Recherche (OFRIR) is composed of members from *ARISTOTE*, *REUNIR*, and *FNET* and discusses French positions for representation in RARE and COSINE; the formal representation is from *REUNIR* [Devillers 1988a].
- The PDN *TRANSPAC* is a subsidiary of the French PTT, France Telecom, and *TRANSCOM* is a service provided by the PTT. These are widely used by all networks in France. *TRANSPAC* is an X.25 PDN. *TRANSCOM* provides a 64Kbps V21 non-ISDN interface. An

ISDN service called *numeris* is also becoming popular, with strong promotion from France Telecom. It is currently available in Brittany and in Paris La Defense, a business district of Paris. Extensions to greater Paris and then to the rest of France are expected in 1989 and 1990 [Devillers 1988a].

- *Minitel* is in a class by itself.

The *FR* domain and DNS domain names are supported on most of the current networks (except *Minitel*).

The current networks are presented in subsections below in order according to these groupings.

13.6.1   FNET

FNET is the French national branch of *EUnet*, providing news and mail service. It has come to be considered indispensable by many of its participants [Devillers 1988c].

FNET is closely associated with the French research network *ARISTOTE*. On those two networks, there were 120 hosts as of May 1988, of which 30 were at public research laboratories, 29 were at universities, 7 were at private research organizations, 24 were at computer manufacturers, 19 were at software vendors, and 14 were of user groups, some of them at private companies [Huitema 1988a]. The total number was reduced to 80 by December 1988, mostly by arranging to have only one host per site. There were about 6,500 users by that date [Devillers 1988a]. Fifteen sites received news in December 1987 [Devillers 1988c].

Administration

Management is primarily done from the Institut National de Recherche en Informatique et Automatique (INRIA), in cooperation with the Association Française des Utilisateurs d'UNIX (AFUU), or French UNIX Users' Group. At one time, AFUU funded a student to write software for *FNET*, but no more [Devillers 1988a].

INRIA pays for much of the cost of the backbone, *inria* or *inria.inria.fr*, because it is housed at INRIA and its chief administrator, Yves Devillers, is paid as head of the international gateway service that interconnects *FNET*, *ARISTOTE, REUNIR, EARN, CSNET*, and other networks [Devillers 1988a]. AFUU also contributes funds for *FNET*. Nonetheless, a fee of 4,000 francs per year was proposed, starting in 1988, with a fee of 1,500 francs for those academic institutions and public research organizations that help support the network by rendering services. This proposed fee schedule has not met with much resistance.

The above fees are for mail. Similar arrangements are being considered for news, with the additional problem that, while twice as many sites would like to receive news as are doing so currently, few of the potential sites would be willing or able to pay for all of the costs of a full news feed [Devillers 1988c]. The expense is mostly in the link between INRIA and the subscriber, at 20,000 to 35,000 francs per year, and in sharing the cost of the link between *inria* and *mcvax*, which comes to about 12,000 francs per site per year for 16 sites. (The transatlantic link from *mcvax* to *uunet* comes to only about 1,800 francs per site per year because there are about 150 sites in all of *EUnet* sharing the cost.) Filtering of unwanted newsgroups is being improved in order to reduce the cost of transmissions from INRIA to the subscriber to around 2,000 to 5,000 francs per year [Devillers 1988a]. A similar problem has been encountered in *Dnet* in Germany and also occurs in *EUnet* in general.

FNET, ARISTOTE, and REUNIR are jointly represented to RARE within the framework of OFRIR, with REUNIR as the formal French representative [Devillers 1988b].

Protocols

Most internal links are carried over *TRANSPAC*, with an effective rate of about 4800bps. The protocol most used on *FNET* is UUCP.

The *EUnet* backbone is *inria.inria.fr*, with a leased line to *mcvax* in Amsterdam. That machine saw 150Mbytes of traffic in June 1986, 500Mbytes in November 1987 [Devillers 1988c], and 1000Mbytes in November 1988, as measured at transport level [Devillers 1988a]. Most of the traffic is news transmissions: 50Mbytes per site per month, actually transferred compressed as 25Mbytes.

Mail only, as measured with **sendmail** for the first eight months of 1988, accounted for 774Mbytes and 263,246 messages total, for averages of 96Mbytes and 35,000 messages per month. Of the eight-month total of 774Mbytes, a quarter was domestic and the rest foreign, as shown in Table 13.4.

History

The first *FNET* UUCP connections were put in place in 1983 at the Conservatoire National des Arts et Métiers (CNAM) by Humberto Lucas. By 1984, three sites (CNAM, the Institut de Recherche et Coordination en Acoustique et Musique (IRCAM), or Research Institute for Coordination in Acoustics and Music, and INRIA) established a telephone link to *mcvax*. This was changed to use X.25 a few months later. CNAM ran the French backbone until June 1986, with INRIA providing a backup. When Lucas left CNAM, INRIA took over backbone services. The Agence de l'Informatique (ADI)

Table 13.4. *FNET mail traffic*

	Megabytes	Networks
French domestic traffic (25%)	195	FNET
Foreign traffic (75%)	579	—
Worldwide	20	X.400
Europe (43%)	250	EUnet, EARN
Australia	0.5	ACSnet
Japan	2.6	JUNET
North America (53%)	306	UUNET, CSNET, Internet, etc.
Total traffic (100%)	774	

Source: [Devillers 1988a]
Note: Totals over the first eight months of 1988

that had formerly run the gateway between *CSNET* and *COSAC* was dismantled in January 1987, and INRIA absorbed that service as well. Operational costs became a serious problem as early as the end of 1986, as traffic doubled annually. Volume billing to users was instituted only in 1987. An annual subscription for mail and a fixed annual cost for news were introduced in 1988.

An X.400 MTA was running by April 1987 at GIPSI, which is a consortium of INRIA, Centre National d'Etudes des Télécommunications (CNET), and Honeywell-Bull (Bull), located at INRIA. This was soon connected to *FNET* for software testing, using an X.400 to RFC822 translation that preceded RFC987. *ARISTOTE* began with the use of *COSAC* and has remained interconnected with *FNET*. In addition to the **GIPSI** software, the **mailway** product developed later at INRIA's Sophia Antipolis campus is also used, to provide full RFC987 gateway functions. The backbone machine is a Digital VAX-11/785. It was initially shared with several research groups, but they eventually left it, partly because of the load induced by the networking activities. Even though it is now dedicated to mail and news, the load is an increasing problem [Devillers 1988a].

The leased line to *mcvax* was in place by March 1988 [Devillers 1988c].

Plans

Because *FNET* has become so important to the people and organizations that use it, there are current plans for improving it in several areas, specifically the following [Devillers 1988c]:

Speed   Repeated connections by the UUCP **uucico** program over dialup or X.25 PDN in PAD to PAD mode are becoming less supportable (largely due to management) as mail traffic

	increases. Instead the use of TCP/IP over leased lines and IP over X.25 on private or public networks has been identified as a solution. Direct gateways to other networks, such as *EARN* (*BITNET*) and the *Internet*, are also being considered [Devillers 1988a].
Reliability	Mail and news sometimes get lost or mangled, primarily because of the underlying transport protocol. UUCP has never been known as a reliable delivery mechanism because, although its link mechanisms will usually get a file from one machine to another, the file may still get lost on either end due to spool directory corruption, system crashes, or PAD failure.
Costs	Most new hosts use *TRANSPAC*; such connections can be made easily and quickly because *TRANSPAC* is so widespread. But PDN tariffs are based on usage, and when traffic for a site increases, costs become a problem. Not only the magnitude is a problem, but also the variability: many organizations need to budget expenses in advance. Leased lines become attractive in this situation, although management efforts are not to be neglected.
Durability	Like the rest of *EUnet*, *FNET* is run by volunteers. The fragility of *EUnet* itself is a concern and is a continuing item on the agendas of meetings of the *EUnet* national representatives. Protocol and software interoperability is also a concern. And *FNET* is largely a network for research and development: such networks never seem to have a balanced budget (*CSNET* would appear to be an exception, but it has had trouble finding money to update its equipment). A permanent organization is needed to handle development and distribution of new links and software, to fix operational problems, to disseminate information, to aid connection of new sites, to collect fees, and to organize meetings.

Leased lines are expected to be useful in a number of ways, including lowering the cost per megabyte of transmission, limiting bills for large sites, and reducing the contribution of INRIA in running the network.

In addition to managing the *FR* domain, *FNET* also allocates a batch of Class C IP network numbers to *FNET* and other sites in France. These network numbers are registered in the *Internet* address space. There is already a small (ten hosts and eight sites with local area networks) TCP/IP network within *FNET*. This is expected to expand as IP is used over X.25 (using **sun-sunlink** and **sps7-dpx2000**). There is cooperation with *REUNIR*, which is also using TCP/IP. Interconnections to the presently forming European TCP/IP network and to the *Internet* are current issues.

New services are being planned, such as an archive server and directories accessible through mail. File transfer and some *Minitel* services are wanted. User assistance has become an important topic and has taken the forms of documentation, tutorials, and workshops.

Finally, there is an ISO-OSI migration plan, funded by the ministry for industry. This involves an X.400 product (based on **mailway** and including X.500 directory service) to be made available to academic and public research sites free of charge and to commercial sites for a fee. Software distribution and network management and security are part of the plan, as is migration of news service. An experimental network will be used for testing; 18 to 24 months are expected until final product delivery [Devillers 1988a].

Access

Yves Devillers
Yves_Devillers@inria.inria.fr
mcvax!inria!devill
+33 39 635511
INRIA
Domaine de Voluceau
B.P. 105
F. 78150, Le Chesney
France

AFUU
+33 1 4670 9590
Telex: 263 887 F
11 Rue Carnot
94270 Le Kremlin Bicetre
France

13.6.2   ARISTOTE

ARISTOTE is an acronym for Association de Réseaux Informatique en Système Totalement Ouvert et Très Elaboré, or Association of Information Networks in a Completely Open and Very Elaborate System; Aristote also is the name Aristotle in French. Interconnection with French and European research networks has always been a basic goal, as has the use of protocols that conform to CCITT and ISO standards and the use of PDNs for transport [Huitema 1987b]. Development is coordinated with RARE and COSINE [Huitema 1988a].

Administration

The network is organized as a French nonprofit association, whose purpose is to be a sort of club within which French research institutions can associate in order to develop networking technology [Huitema 1987b]. The principal administrative bodies are the Committee of Directors, the Assembly of Members, and technical working groups on specific subjects [Huitema 1988a].

The following institutions were members of *ARISTOTE* as of May 1988 [Huitema 1988a]:

CNES (Centre National d'Etudes Spatiales), or the National Space Studies Center

CEA (Commissariat à l'Energie Atomique), or the Atomic Energy Commission

CNET (Centre National d'Etudes des Télécommunications), or the National Telecommunications Research Center

EDF-DER (Division Etude et Recherche), the research center of Electricité de France (EDF), is heavily involved in networking research, participating in OFRIR and *ARISTOTE* [Devillers 1988a]

INRIA (Institut National de Recherche en Informatique et Automatique), or the National Research Institute for Computer Science and Automation

IN2P3 (Institut National de Physique Nucléaire et Physique des Particules), or the National Institute of Nuclear Physics and Particle Physics

CCVR (Centre de Calcul Vectoriel pour la Recherche), or the Vector Calculus Center for Research

EMSE (Ecole des Mines de Saint-Etienne), or the School of Mines of Saint-Etienne

LAS-CNRS (Laboratoire d'Automatisme et d'Analyse des Systèmes), or the Laboratory of Automation and Systems Analysis, of the Centre National de la Recherche Scientifique (CNRS), or National Center for Scientific Research

There are actually three classes of members [Huitema 1988a]. Full Members are French public research and development institutions and are listed above. Associate Members are public agencies and user groups that accept the goals of *ARISTOTE*, such as CERN. Correspondent Members are mostly from industry, e.g., Bull and CISI, both of which have expressed an interest in becoming associate members [Devillers 1988a]. Participation by industrial members in development of *ARISTOTE* recommendations is considered important for production of products satisfactory to users [Huitema 1988a].

The total number of hosts connected is unknown because many of the participating organizations have large internal networks.

Protocols

Low-speed (4800bps to 9600bps) and international transmissions are done with X.25 over *TRANSPAC*, the French PDN. Faster connections may eventually use the PTT's *TELECOM-1* X.21 satellite service and ISDN network called *numeris* (available in early 1989): experiments are in progress at CEA. Another possibility is the 64Kbps digital packet switched X.21 *TRANSCOM* service, also provided by the PTT.

Services

Remote login	Although some members' internal networks support TCP/IP, this is done with X.25 over *TRANSPAC* or over Ethernet at local installations. Sometimes X.25 is carried over Ethernet, and sometimes X.29 is converted to UCB rlogin or the ARPA TELNET protocols running over TCP/IP. The ISO VTP remote login protocol, based on X.25 or ISO-IP, is not supported yet [Huitema 1988b].
Mail (X.400)	This service began with the **GIPSI** implementation by INRIA, CNET, and Bull for *ROSE* [Devillers 1988b]. A test version was in use among CEA, CNES, EMSE, and INRIA by 1985. The actual service uses a mix of research products developed by INRIA, CNET, and EMSE; industrial products from Digital and Bull; and specialized X.400 servers provided by service companies [Huitema 1987b]. There is a mail gateway to *FNET* **UNIX** RFC822 mail at INRIA. This was developed by Christian Huitema and can be used over X.25 (1980); a full X.400 gateway would require TP0 and X.25 (1984) [Devillers 1988b].
Directory service	*ARISTOTE* is used as a testbed for **THORN**, the ESPRIT name and directory service [Huitema 1988c] that can be used to register domains, users, and mailboxes.

Interconnections

There is a gateway at INRIA between *ARISTOTE* and *FNET* (the French part of *EUnet*), which uses DNS domains and is connected to the *UUCP* network as well as to *CSNET* [Huitema 1988a] and the *Internet*. The gateway implements the RFC987 mapping between X.400 and RFC822, so from networks such as *EUnet* and *CSNET* that use DNS addressing, there is no syntactical distinction for *ARISTOTE*. All hosts on *ARISTOTE* are in the top level domain *FR*, but there is no specific domain for the network itself. Each organization will typically have its own subdomain, as in

   user@host.cea.fr

This is, of course, the proper way to use domains.

   A gateway service from the U.S. TCP/IP-based *Internet* has recently been set up. By making a TELNET connection to a bridge provided by INRIA (*kwai.inria.fr*, IP address 192.5.60.25), one can gain access to the X.29 service and connect to French hosts. A reverse service is also available. A nameserver was provided by the end of 1988 for direct routing of messages, or automatic identification of gateways through *Internet* DNS *MX records* [Huitema 1988b]. See also *RIPE* under *EUnet* in this chapter.

One can also reach any *ARISTOTE* machine through a *TRANSPAC* public PAD, which can usually be reached by a local telephone call, perhaps using a *Minitel* terminal, of which there are millions in France.

History

Remote login has been operational since late 1987, while X.400 mail service became usable in 1988.

Access
Christian Huitema
huitema@mirsa.inria.fr
INRIA
Centre de Sophia Antipolis
06565 Valbonne Cedex
France

13.6.3   SMARTIX

SMARTIX was intended as an experiment and as a way to solve internal needs within the Centre National d'Etudes des Télécommunications (CNET), or French National Telecommunications Research Center [Devillers 1988a].

Administration and Funding

Funding for *SMARTIX* is by the French government, led by CNET and involving INRIA, Agence de l'Informatique (ADI), Bull, and Centre National de la Recherche Scientifique (CNRS) in development and technology transfer.

Services

Services include the following:

- Babel Tex, a documentation management product
- Access to services such as *Telex*, teletex, and *Minitel*
- File servers, long-term archiving service (over optical disks), and backup service
- Conferencing on top of X.400

Protocols

SMARTIX is a generalization of the ideas of *COSAC*. It uses the **COSAC Version 5** commercial implementation of X.400 and **P400**, a commercial implementation by Telesystem.

Interconnections

SMARTIX has direct X.400 access to *ARISTOTE* and through that network to *FNET*, from which *EUnet*, *CSNET*, the *Internet*, and numerous other networks may be reached [Huitema 1988a].

> **Access**
> Projet SMARTIX
> CNET (PAA/TIM)
> 38-40 Rue Général Leclerc
> F-92131 Issy-les-Moulineaux
> France

13.6.4   PHYNET

PHYNET is a network for nuclear physicists in France. It is thus similar to *INFNET* in Italy and to *HEPnet* in Europe and the world. *PHYNET* uses X.25 leased lines [Carpenter et al. 1987]. Higher level protocols are mostly DECNET, and remote job entry to IBM mainframes is used [Devillers 1988a].

> **Access**
> Victor Hajjar
> prevost@smdphpe.cea.fr
> CEA
> Saclay
> France
>
> Paul-Andre Pays
> pays@emsesmc.uucp

13.6.5   REUNIR

REUNIR is a heterogeneous metanetwork connecting many French universities and research institutions [Connes and Ippolito 1986]. The name means "to reunite" in French and is an acronym for Réseau des Universités et de la Recherche, or Network of Universities and Research. The basic purpose of *REUNIR* is operational support of other research, unlike *ARISTOTE*, whose purpose is more research in networking itself.

Administration

Administration is done by two principal directors, assisted by the host administrators, a user group, and a technical team. *REUNIR* cooperates with RARE and COSINE, particularly in the development of X.400 and FTAM. *REUNIR* represents France in COSINE, in cooperation with other French networks in OFRIR [Devillers 1988a].

Scope

The basic participants are the national universities and the Centre National de la Recherche Scientifique (CNRS), or National Center for Scientific Research. There are ten central sites and about 50 smaller ones [Leguigner and Devillers 1988]. There are some other specialized centers, most notably the following:

- National Agronomical Research Institute (INRA)
- Organization for Scientific Research in Overseas Countries (ORSTOM)
- Health and Medical Research Institute (INSERM)
- International Cooperation Center in Agronomical Research for Development (CIRAD)

The number of hosts is unknown because most of them are within these organizations.

Services and Protocols

The services supported on the network (though not necessarily available throughout it) are mail, file transfer, remote login, and some number crunching and document archive services. Although uniform use of ISO-OSI protocols is intended eventually, the current network is composed of several heterogeneous parts, including the following:

- Private X.25 networks interconnected over *TRANSPAC*
- SNA networks connecting mainframes (this is the central part of the network)
- Local area networks interconnected by MAC level gateways or by IP over X.25
- HYPERchannel links

The *REUNIR* connections between these networks tend to be either X.25 over *TRANSPAC* or with leased lines provided by the PTT, sometimes using the *TELECOM-1* X.21 satellite service. Although *REUNIR* has a strong commitment to use the PTT X.25 network, *REUNIR* is willing to use the MDNS being set up by COSINE [Leguigner and Devillers 1988]. Speeds range from 4800bps to 2Mbps.

Interconnections

REUNIR is connected to *EARN* at Montpellier and to *FNET*, the French part of *EUnet*. There are other specialized connections from various member agencies.

Plans

REUNIR has funding from the national ministry of education and CNRS to produce an X.400 network to eventually replace *EARN* for their uses. *REUNIR* is officially starting X.400 services and conducts large-scale experiments of various X.400 products. It is beginning to use TCP/IP as an interim solution.

Access

Mrs. Janine Connes
CIR059@FRORS31.BITNET
+33 1 45 51 77 70
Fax: +33 1 45 51 73 07
Telex: 260 034 F
CNRS
15 Quai Anatole France
75700 Paris Cedex
France

Mr. Jean-Claude Ippolito
IPPOLIJ@FRMOP11.BITNET
+33 67 54 41 33
Fax: +33 67 52 37 63
Telex: 490 459 F
Centre National Universitaire Sud de Calcul (CNUSC)
950 Route de Saint-Priest
BP 7229
34084 Montpellier Cedex
France

13.6.6   Minitel

Possibly the largest network or conferencing system in the world is France's *Minitel*, with four million videotex terminals in use [Devillers and Pays 1988]. (The official but little used name is *Teletel*, after the French word for *videotex*.) This is compared with a total of about a million users of the large commercial services in the United States [Lytel 1987].

Administration and Funding

The *Minitel* network is administered by the government telephone company, France Telecom (FT), and funded by fees from the users [Lytel 1987].

Services

Services range from quality control and employment databases run by the chamber of commerce of the city of Montpellier [Lytel 1988] to banking, electronic mail and larger conferencing services, and a wide variety of sexually oriented services. Most of the actual information services are provided not by FT, but by private services through *Minitel*. The most popular service, the electronic telephone directory, is provided by FT, however. About half of the *Minitel* terminals are used by businesses, and the largest revenue producing services are those provided to businesses.

Protocols

The French PDN *TRANSPAC* carries all *Minitel* traffic. There are 40,000 to 50,000 subscribers to *TRANSPAC*, and about 5,000 of them provide most *Minitel* services. Each server usually provides many services, and servers range from personal computers to large mainframes in computing centers. Total *TRANSPAC* traffic is about 1.2Gbytes per month, of which about 60 percent, or 720Mbytes per month, is accounted for by *Minitel*. The remaining *TRANSPAC* traffic is accounted for by X.25 host intercommunications and Triple-X PAD ASCII terminal communications. *Minitel* connections use videoPAD. There are special purpose common protocols for graphics, database access, and most other things the network is used for.

The original model terminal is not very high resolution, only 40 columns by 24 lines, and works in page mode, but it gets the job done. There is an industry of more than five providers of an IBM PC compatible dedicated card with a V23 1200bps modem and software to emulate a Minitel 1 under **MS-DOS**. The modem receives at 1200bps but sends at 75bps when used for this emulation, although it sends at 1200bps in ordinary computer communications [Devillers and Pays 1988]. This may encourage people to move some processing such as message composition offline [Lytel 1987]. There are also cards for Apple Macintoshes and Amstrad, Commodore, Atari, and other machines. Conversely, it is possible to buy inexpensive cables and software that allow the use of a Minitel as a modem for a microcomputer [Devillers and Pays 1988].

A second model, Minitel 1B, has 80 columns with full ASCII and can act either as a Minitel 1 or as an ANSI terminal in character mode for editors such as **Emacs**. All *Minitel* services are still in page mode [Devillers and Pays 1988].

History

The first *Minitel* experiment was held in Velizy in July 1981 with 2,500 users. The *Teletel* network over *TRANSPAC* was set up in May 1982. The electronic directory service began in February 1983.

The original method of popularizing the network was rather unusual: the government telephone company, then known as Direction Générale Télécommunications (DGT) (the current FT is a subsidiary of DGT, owned by the state but acting as a private company [Devillers and Pays 1988]) gave the *Minitel* terminals away free as replacements for paper telephone directories, in hopes of eventually recouping their costs in increased telephone revenue. The strategy worked, and FT now gets about $158 million more out of a total new industry of about a billion dollars a year. The total revenue is about one fifth that of the French television industry.

Another reason for the success of the network is that a user of a *Minitel* service is charged on the user's ordinary telephone bill, rather than having to pay directly to the service provider (this is actually true only for *grand public* services, not for all professional services). France Telecom keeps a percentage and passes on the rest. This arrangement, called *service kiosque*, began in February 1984 [Devillers and Pays 1988] and was initially controversial because FT effectively acts as a banker.

Plans

There are plans to expand *Minitel* into other countries. The U.S. regional Bell Operating Companies (BOCs) have recently been permitted by U.S. District Court Judge Harold Greene to offer these services. FT, in the form of its promotional arm, Intelmatique, is providing a network called *Minitel-Net* in Canada and the United States that can be used to connect to France for reasonable rates. A *Minitel* terminal is usually provided and used, but there is PC emulation software, and a color board can be obtained.

Access

David Lytel
CompuServe: 73647,2311
The Source: BDS 605
Delphi: LYTELDA
Unison: DLytel

MinitelNet
800-445-6431
800-445-6842 (in Maryland)
6187 Executive Boulevard
Rockville, MD 20852
U.S.A.

13.7   *Germany, Federal Republic of {DE}*

Germany has a long history of networking development, and *HMI-NET* and *BERNET* have already been described in Chapter 7. Their notable descendant, *DFN*, is described here, as are *AGFNET*, a national X.25 and SNA network, and *Dnet*, the national branch of *EUnet*. The national top level domain *DE* has historically been managed by *CSNET* but was shifted in 1988 to *Dnet*, in cooperation with the German branch of *EARN*, *DEARN* [Goos 1988a; Goos 1988b].

There are at least two notable regional networks, *BERNET* in Berlin and *BELWÜ* in Baden-Württemberg, and these are discussed below. Private X.25 networks connecting the universities are also in place or near completion in the states of Bavaria and Nordrhein-Westfalen, using 9600bps and 64Kbps lines, but these are not described here. There tend to be many state networks, partly because the constitution of the Federal Republic puts education into the domain of the states and allows the federal government only some coordination authority. University operational budgets come from the states, although the federal government may fund physical plants and equipment, as well as research projects such as *DFN* [Volk 1989].

There are tentative plans for the Deutsche Bundespost (DBP), the German PTT, to offer the German research community X.25 services better geared to its needs, such as budgeting with fixed costs. *DFN* is representing the German research community to DBP for this project [Volk 1989].

Access

info@unido.irb.informatik.uni-dortmund.de
mcvax!unido!info

There is an occasional newsletter published by a consortium of people from several German networks. It gives a comprehensive view of all networking activities in Germany:

Neüste Netz Nachrichten
Universität Karlsruhe, Zirkel 2
D-7500 Karlsruhe 1
Federal Republic of Germany

13.7.1   Dnet

Dnet is the German branch of *EUnet*, the European **UNIX** network; the D is for Deutschland—i.e., Germany [Goos 1988a; Goos 1988b].

There were about 146 sites (companies or universities) connected in November 1988, of which 86 subscribed only to mail; the rest also subscribed to news (22 sites got *Dnet* and *EUnet* newsgroups, and another 38 got worldwide *USENET* newsgroups). Approximately a quarter of the sites are universities, but they constitute almost half of the worldwide news participants [Volk 1989]. About 5,000 *Dnet* users are accessible by mail.

Administration

The network is managed by a team of students (currently six: Michael Pickers, Axel Pawlik, Jan-Hinrich Fessel, Bernard Steiner, Frank Wiesenfeller, and Anke Goos) and a responsible university staff member. One of the management team, Anke Goos, a journalism student, is also one of the editors of the *EUnet* directory and of the quarterly publication of the German UNIX Systems User Group (GUUG), *GUUG-Nachrichten*.

The management team provides technical support for the backbone machine *unido* at the Universität Dortmund (Dortmund) as an activity of that university. It also provides administration, accounting, information, and technical counseling for *Dnet* members, as well as maintaining the German part of the *UUCP* map. Responses to requests for information about mail addresses and gateways take a large part of management time. Support for the *EARN* BSMTP gateway is also a substantial project. There is an archive server that provides information for end users. Useful software is also distributed to new sites, such as the f protocol for UUCP over X.25 or the **B news 2.11** *USENET* news software.

Funding

The Computer Science Department at Dortmund provides many facilities, but all costs of the link to *EUnet* are paid by *Dnet* members under formal agreements. There is an academic discount, making commercial access four times more costly than academic access, even though the commercial fees are the same as those in the rest of *EUnet*. The rest of the charging arrangements, including those for transatlantic mail and news, are as for the rest of *EUnet*.

Although there is no financial relationship between GUUG and *Dnet*, *Dnet* presents budget reports to the GUUG board of directors (GUUG Vorstand). Also, members of *Dnet* must be members of GUUG, and thus of EUUG, allowing all members to participate in GUUG and EUUG conferences and workshops at a reduced rate and to receive the quarterly newsletters and other benefits of the two groups.

Protocols

The basic *Dnet* transport protocol is UUCP, as in *EUnet*. Internal German links are mostly over X.25 PDN, the costs of which are distance independent and relatively cheap at high traffic volumes. The network is basically a star (150 of 180 sites are directly connected to *unido*), perhaps largely because of these economic considerations. There are some dialup telephone links at 1200bps and 2400bps, and more than ten X.25 sessions are supported simultaneously. News is imported from the *EUnet* hub machine *mcvax* in Amsterdam and distributed from *unido*. Most mail passes through *unido*, which does mail routing and rerouting using the *UUCP* map so that other *Dnet* hosts do not need to keep the map but can use DNS domain addresses.

Interconnections

The backbone machine *unido* is a Siemens MX500, which is derived from Sequent technology. A leased line to *mcvax* is being ordered, with expectations of running TCP/IP over X.25. Most mail to other European *EUnet* backbone hosts is transferred directly to them and is usually delivered within about half an hour. Mail intended for the United States is sent to *uunet* by a direct link from *unido* and is also transferred within half an hour. There are also gateways from *unido* to *CSNET*, *DFN*, and *EARN*.

History

The earliest *Dnet* experimental connections were established in late 1983. By early 1984, there were 13 nodes connected, with the backbone at Dortmund, where it has since remained. Users were not billed until the spring of 1985, before which much of the cost of international data communications was paid by Siemens. The backbone machine *unido* was originally the departmental Digital VAX, then an MX2 donated by Siemens in the summer of 1986, until it was upgraded in the spring of 1988 [Volk 1989]. A former *Dnet* representative to *EUnet* is Daniel Karrenberg, who is now one of the two people who manage the central *EUnet* backbone host *mcvax*. Karrenberg, a founder of GUUG and *Dnet*, started the original *unido* service along with Klaus Eckhoff and Ralf Nolting, but most of the students currently managing the network are of the second or third generation. The *EUnet* coordinator was usually someone from Dortmund who was involved in running the backbone, e.g., Rüdiger Volk, holder of that position from March 1986 through March 1989 and at the same time the principal responsible university staff person.

Plans

Tariffs in *EUnet* and thus in *Dnet* have historically been set with large organizations in mind and are rather high for individuals with their own machines. A fast growing number of such hosts are connected to *EUnet* through public access machines or other hosts that are directly connected to *EUnet*. They are thus not in the *UUCP* map, nor do they pay for or get *EUnet* services such as international newsgroups, although there is much interest on the part of the owners of these small noncommercial machines in obtaining such services. A revised set of modest prices and a more decentralized network topology were worked out by the *Dnet* management team in the summer of 1988 in order to allow these private machines and shadow hosts to join *EUnet* officially. Germany is the first country in *EUnet* to do this. There is some possibility that a nonprofit organization outside of university control may be formed to manage the network and to be better able to handle funding issues.

There may be a GUUG host for individual members, probably in Munich, perhaps by 1989.

There was to be a cisco router at *unido* at the end of 1988, for using IP over X.25 to some other *EUnet* backbone machines. Consequently, IP services such as SMTP (mail), NNTP (news), and *anonymous FTP* may be supported from *unido*.

Dnet is a participant in *RIPE*, described under *EUnet* in this chapter.

Access
postmaster@uni-dortmund.de
unido!postmaster
postmaster@unido.bitnet
+49 231 755 2444
Informatik — IRB
Universität Dortmund
Postfach 500500
D-4600 Dortmund 50
Federal Republic of Germany

Also, postoffice@uni-dortmund.de reaches not only the postmaster, but also the rest of the management team and the *EUnet* coordinator.

For questions about the gateway bsmtp@unido.bitnet between *BITNET* and *EUnet* contact:

postman@unido.bitnet

For general information about GUUG, contact:

Secretariat
mcvax!unido!guug
+49 089/ 570 76 97
German UNIX Systems User Group (GUUG)
Elsenheimer Str. 43
8000 München 21
Federal Republic of Germany

There is a quarterly GUUG newsletter, *GUUG-Nachrichten*. Contact:

guugn@uni-dortmund.de

13.7.2   DFN

DFN (Deutsches Forschungsnetz) is the national research network connecting *every* university, college, and research laboratory in the Federal Republic of Germany. It had 65 hosts as of October 1987 [Kaufmann and Ullmann 1987]. Its purpose is to develop protocols and implementations in the ISO-OSI suite so that they may be used for resource sharing and collaboration among researchers nationwide and communications with foreign researchers. *DFN* is the German part of RARE.

Administration and Funding

The West German Bundesminister für Forschung und Technologie (BMFT), or Ministry of Research and Technology (MRT), has about 15 to 20 people working on the *DFN* project, though all implementation work is contracted out. MRT also funds *DFN*, with sizable parts of the money going to Gesellschaft für Mathematik und Datenverarbeitung (GMD), or Corporation for Mathematics and Data Processing. The current plan is for MRT funding to end by the end of 1990 [Elsner 1988]. Administration is by DFN-Verein, which is located in Berlin.

Protocols

DFN uses X.400 for mail, plus file transfer and remote job entry using protocols designed for the network but compatible with the ISO-OSI suite. The **Ean** implementation of X.400 was the basis for the current *DFN* implementation, although it has been modified to conform with CEN/CENELEC option sets while still gatewaying with the old **Ean** implementation. The network layer is X.25, which supports remote login. Most links are 9600bps, although higher rates are being planned. There are some connections providing a rate of 64Kbps, Technische Universität Berlin (TUB) to Konrad-Zuse-Zentrum für Informationstechnik Berlin (ZIB) for RJE access to the Cray [Elsner 1988].

DFN is heavily involved in implementation of ISO-OSI protocols, such as TP0, FTAM, and X.400. *DFN* has also produced software to handle protocol conversion at gateways, including the following:

- TP0 over X.25, as used in wide area networks, to TP0 over IEEE 802.3, as used in local area networks
- TP0 over X.25, as used in local area networks, to TCP/IP over IEEE 802.3, as also used in local area networks. (This is required by the practical situation of the many local area networks that use TCP/IP. DFN-Verein has done much examination of the potential of TCP/IP and comparison of it with ISO-OSI [Bauerfeld 1988a; Bauerfeld 1988b].)

Interconnections

Gateways exist to *EUnet*, *EARN*, and *CSNET*, and the domain DFN.DBP.DE is used for incoming DNS traffic. Since the *Ean* networks use X.400 over X.25, no gateway to them is required [Kaufmann 1987]. The same appears to be true of *AGFNET*.

History

There was early German networking activity at the Hahn-Meitner Institut (HMI) in Berlin, where an X.25-based network called *HMI-NET* was developed. There was also an academic network between two universities there. These developments led to *BERNET*, a metropolitan area network in Berlin. In 1982, there was a move to expand *BERNET* to be a northern German network. However, a study conducted by Stanford University recommended a national network to provide *ARPANET*-like services.

DFN was started to implement this idea. There is no communications subnet or leased line dedicated to this network; it uses the national X.25 PDN.

As of September 1986, there were about half a dozen hosts supporting mail, with immediate plans for 30 hosts, 10 **4.2BSD**, 10 **System V**, and 10 **VMS**. By May 1987, there were 40 hosts, and by October 1987 there were 65, connecting every university, college, and research laboratory in the country [Kaufmann and Ullmann 1987]. This is an amazing feat.

Access

DFN-Verein publishes a quarterly magazine, *DFN Mitteilungen*, which contains very useful articles about networking in Germany, Europe, and elsewhere, in German and sometimes in English.

DFN-Verein
dfn-verein@zpl.dfn.dbp.de
s=dfn-verein;OU=zpl;P=dfn;C=de
Pariser Strasse 44
1000 Berlin 15
Federal Republic of Germany

13.7.3   AGFNET

AGFNET is named for Arbeitsgemeinschaft der Grossforschungseinrichtungen (AGF), or the Association of National Research Centers of the Federal Republic of Germany [Birkenbihl and Mertens 1987]. *AGFNET* is a backbone network that connects AGF research centers and German universities. There are currently 12 organizations on the backbone, each with its own network and one host on the backbone. There are about 40 or 50 hosts on all the connected networks, and perhaps 10,000 users [Wunderling 1989].

Administration and Funding

The network is administered and funded by AGF.

Protocols and Services

Most *AGFNET* links are 64Kbps leased lines. *AGFNET* provides X.25 interfaces on the backbone, and these allow the use of different higher level protocols, such as SNA and ISO-OSI, on the same physical links. Two techniques are used for providing X.25 service [Wunderling 1989]:

1. X.25 switches are used on leased lines to connect to private X.25 networks. The switches are made by the German company DATUS.
2. **XI** (X.25 SNA Interconnection) is a program supplied by IBM to run in the communication controllers of IBM machines, such as the IBM 3725 or IBM 3745. **XI** allows X.25 packets to be carried over SNA and presents an X.25 DCE interface to which X.25 DTE interfaces may be connected [IBM].

The method used for a given link depends on the kind of traffic on the link: if there is much SNA traffic, **XI** is normally used; otherwise X.25 switches are used [Wunderling 1989].

The network is used in providing *EARN* NJE service in Germany, as well as for IBM 3270 display applications and for ISO-OSI applications such as X.400 MHS and Triple-X. An unusual feature of this network is its support of multiple protocols (including, in addition to the ones already mentioned, DECNET and TCP/IP) over the same physical links [Wunderling 1989].

Interconnections

There are international links to the Centre National Universitaire Sud de Calcul (CNUSC) in Montpellier, France, and City University of New York (CUNY) in the United States [Wunderling 1989].

History

AGFNET sites tend to be computation centers with IBM mainframes — i.e., the same ones that participate in *EARN*. Several of these sites are large laboratories with several campuses and private wide area SNA networks among them, often using leased lines at 64Kbps. The end of IBM funding for *EARN*, planned for the end of 1987, caused these sites to consider (in June 1987) interconnecting these existing networks to form a German *EARN* (*DEARN*) backbone — i.e., *AGFNET*. Some of *AGFNET* was operating by the end of 1988 [Volk 1989].

Plans

This new technical situation for the backbone also allows migrating *DEARN* to ISO-OSI protocols [Volk 1989].

> **Access**
> Peter Wunderling
> AGFNET Technical Coordinator
> GRZ017@DBNGMD21.BITNET
> +49 228 819960
> Gesellschaft für Mathematik und Datenverarbeitung
> (GMD)
> Z1-Bereich Bonn
> Riemenschneiderstr. 11
> 53 Bonn-Bad Godesberg
> Federal Republic of Germany

13.7.4   BELWÜ

A research network called *BELWÜ* (Baden-Württemberg's Extended Network) in the state of Baden-Württemberg has been operational since February 1988. There are two stages planned:

First stage	Connect 140Mbps optical fiber long-distance trunks to campus Ethernets with bridges. This was demonstrated on 23 February 1988.
Second stage	Extend to campus FDDI networks.

Most of the campuses use Ethernet, but some installations use HYPERchannel (with a Cray 2) and pilot FDDI. Higher level protocols currently tend to be TCP/IP, but *DFN* is participating in the project, and the use of ISO-OSI protocols is expected [Volk 1989].

> **Access**
> Paul Christ
> christ@rus.uni-stuttgart.dbp.de
> Comp. Center
> Universität Stuttgart
> Stuttgart
> Federal Republic of Germany

13.8   *Greece {GR}*

There is a national research network in Greece, *ARIADNE*. The machine *ariadne* serves as the national backbone for *EUnet*.

Access

Kostas Vassilakis
kostas@ariadne.uucp
+30 81 221171
Foundation of Research and Technology
Institute of Computer Science
Iraklion, Crete
Greece

13.8.1   ARIADNE

ARIADNE is a national Greek research network that uses X.25 [Carpenter et al. 1987].

13.9   *Ireland {IE}*

The Republic of Ireland has a long history of networking activity, having been connected to networks such as *COSAC* and being the location of one of the main centers of *EARN*. The Commission of the European Communities (CEC) sponsors a conferencing system in Ireland, *EuroKom*. There is also an educational network, *HEANET*. The national backbone host for *EUnet* is *iclitc* or *einode*. The top level national domain *IE* and gateways between networks in Ireland are supported cooperatively by *HEANET*, *EARN*, *EUnet*, and others. All mail uses *Internet* DNS order [Walsh 1988].

Access

Simon Kenyon
simon@iclitc.uucp
+353 1 956644
ICL Information Technology Centre
Dublin
Ireland

13.9.1   HEANET

The Higher Education Authority Network, or *HEANET*, began in 1985 in Ireland. It is administered and funded by the Irish Higher Education Authority (HEA). The purpose of the network is to provide access to specialized hardware and software, to promote information exchange and cooperation, and to provide access to other networks in other parts of the world [HEA 1986]. The network currently connects seven colleges throughout Ireland; it had 18 hosts as of March 1987 and 30 hosts as of November 1988 [Walsh 1988].

Protocols

HEANET uses both leased lines and *EIRPAC*, the national X.25 packet switching network provided by Telecom Eireann. The Coloured Book protocols are primarily used at higher layers. Various other protocols are also used, mostly in connecting nodes for mail service only. Such protocols and programs include NJE, **PMDF**, and **MMDF** [Walsh 1988]. Services provided include mail (Grey Book), file transfer (Blue Book), and remote login (X.25 PAD). Even though the Coloured Book protocols are used, domain addressing is completely in DNS order — e.g., *user@domain*.IE; the *JANET* (reverse) order is not supported [Walsh 1988]. An "advisory service" is provided to assist in establishing contact with remote hosts on *HEANET* and other networks.

Interconnections

The gateway between *HEANET* and *EARN* is *IRLEARN* at University College Dublin (UCD) [Schafer et al. 1987]. This gateway is also used to reach the *Internet*. UCD also provides a gateway to the X.25-based RARE R&D MHS X.400 networks. The gateway between *HEANET* and *EUnet* is *iclitc* at Trinity College Dublin (Trinity) [Walsh 1988].

History

There were predecessor networking activities in Ireland dating back to 1977 [Walsh 1988].

> **Access**
> ADVISER@IRLEARN.BITNET
> +353 1 693244, ext. 2376
> Advisory Service
> Computer Centre
> University College, Belfield
> Dublin 4
> Ireland

13.9.2   EuroKom

EuroKom provides electronic mail and computer conferencing for participants in the European Strategic Programme for Research in Information Technology (ESPRIT) of the European Community (EC). ESPRIT supports precompetitive research by industry and universities into software technology, Computer Integrated Manufacturing (CIM), microelectronics, and related areas. *EuroKom* supports more than half of all ESPRIT projects as well as several other EC research initiatives. *EuroKom* is currently based on a central machine located in Dublin [Jennings 1988].

EuroKom is integrated into the Irish domain namespace underneath the top level domain *IE*, and users may be reached by addresses of the form *user*@EuroKom.ucd.ie, where *user* is a person's real name, using underscores instead of spaces to separate the first and last names.

EuroKom runs the **PortaCOM** software, a commercial version of the **COM** software that is used in *QZCOM* [Palme 1988].

EuroKom used the *QZCOM* machine in Stockholm until it was transferred to a dedicated computer using **PortaCOM** at the beginning of 1988 [Jennings 1988].

Access
Help_Desk@EuroKom.ucd.ie
John_Conroy@EuroKom.ucd.ie

13.10   *Italy {IT}*

An Italian Research Council (CNR) network is listed in the *BITNET* gateway table under the domain *TO.CNR.IT* [Nussbacher 1988b]. There is a national research network in Italy, *INFNET*, most of whose hosts are reachable under the domain INFN.IT. The machine *i2unix*, named after the Italian UNIX Systems User Group (i2u), serves as the national backbone for *EUnet*.

Access
Alessandro Berni
ab@i2unix.uucp
+39 10 310223
Dipartimento di Informatica Sistemistica e Telematica
Genova
Italy

Carlo Mortarino
i2u@i2unix.uucp
i2u Secretariat
+39 2 2520 2530
Via Monza, 347
20126 Milano
Italy

13.10.1   **INFNET**

INFNET (Instituto Nazionale Fisica Nucleare Network) started as connections between the sites of the Italian National Institute for Nuclear Physics (INFN) and spread throughout the country, with 118 hosts by July 1987. It uses DECNET protocols, and has been connected to *SPAN* since January

1987. Its purpose is similar to that of the French network *PHYNET* and to the European and worldwide network *HEPnet* [Carpenter et al. 1987]. Its hosts are mostly reachable under the top level domain INFN.IT, with the corresponding *BITNET* domain *INFNET*.

> **Access**
> Antonia Ghiselli
> INFNET Network Manager
> VXCNAF::GHISELLI
> GHISELLI@VXCNAF.INFN.IT
> GHISELLI@IBOINFN.BITNET

13.11   *Luxembourg {LU}*

The national *EUnet* backbone hosts are *ceclux* and *tauros*.

> **Access**
> Mr. J. Foidart
> Trevor Luker
> treval@ceclux.uucp
> postmaster@tauros.uucp
> +352 4301 3678 / 4620
> C.E.C. Luxembourg
> Luxembourg

13.12   *Netherlands {NL}*

There are two main networks in the Netherlands: the national branch of *EUnet* and the national research network *SURFnet*, which is also the national branch of *EARN*. The top level domain *NL* is supported on at least *EUnet* and part of *EARN*. *HEPnet* is also widely used in this country.

Although the backbone host for *EUnet* in the Netherlands was *mcvax* (*cwi.nl*) for most of the history of *EUnet*, a new machine, *hp4nl*, took over that function in late 1988. The Dutch network is run by the Netherlands Unix systems User Group (NLUUG): this is the usual situation in most countries that participate in *EUnet*.

> **Access**
> Piet Beertema
> piet@mcvax.uucp
> +31 20 5924112

Centrum voor Wiskunde en Informatica (CWI)
Amsterdam
Netherlands

13.12.1   SURFnet

SURFnet is a network for research and higher education in the Netherlands. There are 85 connected organizations, with 375 hosts [Huizer 1988].

Operations for the physical network are done by the Dutch PTT, but general responsibility for *SURFnet*, including user support and plans for protocol migration, is vested in SURFnet B.V. (SURFnet), which was incorporated on 1 January 1989. Shareholders of that organization are Foundation SURF, which represents the users' interests and holds 51 percent of the shares, and the PTT, with 49 percent [Beertema 1988b]. Samenwerkingsorganisatie computerdienstverlening in het Hoger Onderwijs en Onderzoek (SURF) translates roughly as Cooperational Organization for Computer Services in Higher Education and Research. The acronym came from the original name, which was Samenwerkende Universitaire RekenFaciliteiten (SURF), or Cooperating University Computing Facilities [Beertema 1988b].

Part of the network runs DECNET protocols, and part of it is the national branch of *EARN*, running NJE and donated by IBM to *SURFnet*. Most of the links are at 9600bps. A backbone with twenty-five 64Kbps links and forming a private network using COSINE X.25 specifications should be operational by the fourth quarter of 1989 [Huizer 1988].

The Dutch part of *EARN* is part of *SURFnet*, and that part of *SURFnet* is connected to *EUnet* through *MCVAX*. The main gateways from *SURFnet* to the rest of the world are thus *HEARN* and *MCVAX*. Most of the organizations connected to *SURFnet* have at least one Digital VAX using **JNET** NJE software and acting as an *EARN* gateway for that organization.

RFC822 mail format and DNS domain names are being introduced, using **PMDF** and the **Crosswell** mailer. This is expected to be complete by June 1989. This mail format migration is the first step in migration toward X.400. There are already several X.400 hosts running and used in *SURFnet* participation in the RARE MHS project. A gateway between *EARN* and X.400 was expected by the second quarter of 1989. After this gateway is present and the DNS conversion is complete on *SURFnet*, users should not need to know the names of the gateways to other networks. Routing tables are already centrally distributed [Huizer 1988].

Access

User Support
Maria Heijne
info@hutsur51.bitnet
Erik Huizer
huizer@hutsur51.bitnet

+31 30 310290
Fax: +31 30 340903
SURFnet b.v.
P.O. Box 19035
3501 DA Utrecht
Netherlands

13.13   *Portugal {PT}*

The *BITNET* gateway table lists a domain *PT* for a National Scientific Computation Network [Nussbacher 1988b]. The national Portuguese backbone for *EUnet* is *inesc*.

Access

Henrique B. Silva
Paulo Pinto
Pedro Veiga
postmaster@inesc.uucp
+351 1 545150
Instituto de Engenharia de Sistemas e Computadores
Lisboa
Portugal

13.14   *Spain {ES}*

There is a RARE experimental R&D MHS network in Spain and a national branch of *EUnet*. The top level domain *ES* is officially administered by Interconexion de recursos Informaticos (IRIS) and is used on those two networks and on *FAENET*, the local branch of *HEPnet* [Camacho 1988]. There is at least one regional academic network, *RICA* [Barberá and Martinez 1988].

There are 17 *EARN* hosts at 14 sites, with the national backbone at the University of Barcelona (Barcelona). There is no gateway in the country to any of the other national networks, but traffic can be exchanged through *MCVAX* and *CERNVAX*. Since IBM sponsorship ended in December 1988, IRIS has been funding *EARN* in Spain, under an agreement for ISO-OSI migration, starting with domain addressing [Mañas 1988].

Access
Miguel A. Campos
earnmain@cc.ub.es
earnmain@eb0ub011.bitnet

The national branch of *HEPnet* is called Fisica de Altas Energias NET-work (*FAENET*), or High Energy Physics Network [Camacho 1988].

Access
Antonio Mollinedo
<molli@ciemat.es>
molli@emdjen11.bitnet, molli@emdcie51.bitnet
molli@vm.ciemat.es, molli@dec.ciemat.es
ciemat::molli, PSI%021452120250227::molli
+34 1 346 6176
Fax: 341 346 6005
Telex: 23555 E CIEMA
Unidad Informatica
CIEMAT
Av. Complutense 22
28040 Madrid
Spain

13.14.1   Enet

The Spanish part of *EUnet* is referred to in this book as *Enet*, where the E is for España — i.e., Spain. *Enet* is organized as a star with direct connections to all hosts in the country from a backbone machine, *goya* (*dit.upm.es*), which has international connections, such as to *mcvax*. There are also some private links among Spanish hosts. There were 23 registered sites and 43 hosts in November 1988: 60 percent were commercial and the rest research. Only the backbone host and one other receive news. The sites are in five cities (Madrid, Barcelona, Valencia, San Sebastian, and Bilbao) around the country [Mañas 1988].

Administration and Funding

The backbone machine is at Departamento Ingeniería Telemática (DIT), or Department of Telematics Engineering, at the Universidad Politecnica de Madrid (UPM), or Technical University of Madrid. DIT has two people working part-time in managing the network.

Domestic costs are allocated by having all the nodes within the country call the backbone, so they pay transmission costs directly. The national backbone communicates directly with five other European national backbone hosts, with plans to do so with all of them. There are cooperative agreements with most of those backbone hosts so that traffic is balanced. DIT currently pays for European mail and news exchanged with *mcvax*.

There is close cooperation with IRIS and a gateway to its associated network.

Protocols

The main protocol is UUCP, with the g protocol over dialup links (mostly at 1200bps), the f protocol over the X.25 *IBERPAC*, and the t protocol or SMTP over TCP/IP on local area networks, such as the one at DIT. International links are done over 9600bps links through the national PDN, *IBERPAC*. DNS addressing is used to support domains under *ES*, although some sites can only do bang addressing and depend on the backbone for conversion; the backbone also uses **pathalias**. More domains are expected. The machine that serves as the backbone host and the gateway to the R&D MHS network, *goya*, is a Sun-3/160 with 600Mbytes of disk space. Another main machine at the same location is *ADAN* [Mañas 1988].

History

The first international connection to *EUnet*, from *goya*, was made in the first quarter of 1986 [Mañas 1988]. There were no more nodes until 1988, when growth became explosive. Mail traffic of various kinds measured approximately as follows in October 1988:

UUCP nodes	4Mbytes/month
R&D gateway	3Mbytes/month
International	5Mbytes/month
Intercontinental	2Mbytes/month

Plans

Rapid growth is expected. DIT plans to collect fees to pay back costs incurred in running the backbone. Commercial subscribers will pay both a fixed and a volume dependent rate. Some software to identify mail for this purpose is being tested and is expected to be in use in January 1989.

Better *EARN* and *HEPnet* gateways are being experimented with and were expected to be operational by the end of 1988. There are plans to migrate from the current **Ean** software at the X.400 gateway in accordance with the *EUnet* ISO-OSI plan [Karrenberg 1988a].

Access

José A. Mañas
postmaster@dit.upm.es
+34 1 44 95700, ext. 375
Dpt. Ingeniería Telemática
E.T.S.I. Telecomunicación
E-28040 Madrid
Spain

13.14.2   Ean in Spain

The RARE experimental R&D MHS network in Spain (*Ean* in Spain) is a national Spanish research network that uses X.25 over the national PDN *IBERPAC*, as well as other ISO-OSI protocols [Barberá and Martinez 1988]. There were 22 hosts at 14 sites in November 1988, including one in the Canary Islands [Mañas 1988].

Administration

The network is currently administered by IRIS, which is a national research plan for the harmonization of all Spanish network activities. IRIS is run by Fundacion para el desarrollo de las comunicaciones (Fundesco), a nonprofit organization funded by the Spanish government [Mañas 1988]. The period of the plan is January 1988 through December 1991, with the first two years, through December 1989, managed directly by Fundesco. IRIS represents Spain in RARE and COSINE and is also the Spanish representative in *EARN* and *HEPnet* [Barberá 1988]. IRIS also has official responsibility for the top level domain *ES*, which is used in this and other Spanish networks [Camacho 1988].

IRIS provides some funding for *EUnet* in Spain, partly as encouragement for ISO-OSI speedy migration. IRIS also sponsors *EARN* and *FAENET* in the same way [Barberá and Martinez 1988].

Protocols

The **Ean** software is used in the *Ean* network in Spain, and more recent and complete implementations of X.400 are beginning to be used. Most of the hosts use 9600bps X.25 connections, but a few with low traffic use 1200bps X.28 over dialup connections. The backbone machine for *Ean* in Spain is named after the Escuela Tecnica Superior de Ingenieros de Telecomunicacion, Madrid (ETSITM). This Message Transfer Agent (MTA) runs on a Digital VAX-11/750 with 500Mbytes of disk space. True X.400 connections use the backbone *iris-dcp*, which is a MicroVAX 3600 with 300Mbytes of disk space.

There is a gateway to *EUnet* at the Universidad Politecnica de Madrid (UPM), or Technical University of Madrid, using **Ean** software on *goya*, the *Enet* backbone machine, and on *ADAN*, which is the same machine as *ETISM* [Mañas 1988].

History

A foreign **Ean** connection from DIT was installed in the last quarter of 1985 from *ETSITM* [Mañas 1988].

Plans

There are plans to upgrade links with heavy traffic to use 64Kbps leased lines, with an international link of the same kind to the international infrastructure sponsored by COSINE, specifically to CERN [Mañas 1988]. More and better X.400 implementations are to be used, and experiments with FTAM, perhaps using ISODE, will be performed. Eventually, directory service and management protocols will be implemented [Barberá and Martinez 1988].

Access

José Barberá
Director
barbera@iris-dcp.es
C=es/A= /P=iris/O=iris-dcp/S=barbera

Ignacio Martinez
Technical Coordinator
martinez@iris-dcp.es
S=martinez; O=iris-dcp; P=iris; A= ; C=es

+34 1 435 1214
Fax: +34 1 5227489
Telex: 42608 USEF E
Programa IRIS
Fundesco
Alcalá, 61
E-28014 Madrid
Spain

13.14.3   RICA

RICA is a network among and organized by universities in Andalusia. There were seven hosts and about 1,500 users in September 1988. *RICA* is partly supported by IRIS.

RICA uses **Ean** software for X.400 mail service, as well as DECNET and proprietary protocols such as XODIAC of Data General (DG). The network layer is X.25 [Barberá and Martinez 1988].

13.15   *United Kingdom {GB}*

There are detailed descriptions below of the national United Kingdom research network, *JANET*; of a network dedicated to the use of astronomers, *Starlink*; of *UKnet*, the U.K. branch of *EUnet*; and of a conferencing system, *GreenNet*.

The ISO3166 two letter code for the United Kingdom is *GB*, which is an abbreviation for Great Britain. This is not completely appropriate, as most of the other ISO3166 codes correspond to political entities, not to geographical ones, and because the United Kingdom includes Northern Ireland, which is not part of Great Britain. Nonetheless, *GB* is used in this book as the code for the United Kingdom.

13.15.1   JANET

JANET was established to provide consolidated network links among universities and research institutions in the United Kingdom and network access to the outside world [Spratt 1986]. It was renamed from *SERCnet* on 1 April 1984 [Wells 1984] and is a backbone network that supports an internet.

Scope

The number of hosts counted can vary, depending on factors such as whether PADs are counted, whether those on local area networks are included, and whether only registered ones are counted or an attempt is made to estimate the actual number of connected hosts. As of September 1986, there were about 915 registered hosts including those on local area nets, but there were probably really about 1,500 connected ones. There were only about 20 hosts directly on the *JANET* wide area network. At the end of 1985, the *JANET* switches passed about 24Mbytes of data a day [Spratt 1986].

Administration and Funding

JANET is funded by the Computer Board for Universities and Research Councils (CB). Because of this source of funding, connections are mainly limited to the following:

- Universities
- Laboratories or institutes funded by Research Councils
- Individual members of polytechnics or other institutes of further education that hold Research Council grants
- Polytechnics, which may join the network but are charged

For universities, there is encouragement for connections to be from computer centers, even in cases where individuals or departments have Research Council grants [Wells 1984]; this is notably different from the situation for *EUnet*. No direct charges are made for usage. The annual CB budget for *JANET* and University local area networks was about 3.5 million pounds sterling in 1986. (Not all university LANs are funded by this money.) An additional amount of 5 million pounds was approved by CB in

1986 for three years. This is for upgrading the wide area network switches and trunk lines to use British Telecom (BT) Megastream links, as well as enhancements to the local area networks [Spratt 1986].

Technical and administrative support for the wide area network, such as approval of connections, is supplied by the Network Executive (NE), which is based at the Science and Engineering Research Council (SERC) at Rutherford Appleton Laboratory (RAL). The Joint Network Team (JNT), which predates *JANET*, is primarily involved in development for both the wide area network and the local area networks, in software, hardware, and protocols. These two groups are small (originally three and five people, respectively) and delegate most functions. A combined head of JNT and NE, currently Dr. Robert Cooper, is in turn overseen by the Director of Networking for *JANET*.

There is participation by the user community, particularly in user groups organized by NE at sites with large numbers of users. These user groups also help provide operational support to the users and are organized regionally. There are also Special Interest Groups (SIGs). Each regional or interest group provides a small number of delegates to a national user group, which meets several times a year.

The Network Advisory Committee (NAC) sets and oversees policy. NAC meets in February, June, and October of each year and sometimes more often. It is composed of two members from CB, one representative each from NERC and SERC, the chairman of the user group, a representative of the polytechnics, and the Director of Networking of *JANET*. Both JNT and NE are part of the CB secretariat, and there are three members of NAC on the Board.

Services

Services include mail, file transfer, remote login, and remote job entry. A Name Registration Scheme (NRS) is run on a Prime computer for JNT by the UMRCL. Some supercomputers are accessible over *JANET* through local area networks at their institutions. These are a Cray 1S accessible through an Amdahl Front End system at the University of London Computer Centre (ULCC), and a CDC Cyber 205 at the University of Manchester (Manchester) Regional Computer Centre [Spratt 1986].

Protocols

Local networks connected to *JANET* tend to be either X.25 campus switches, Cambridge Rings (CR82 standard), or Ethernet (or IEEE 802.3). Ethernet and IEEE 802.3 are becoming increasingly popular at the expense of CR82. The long-haul network layer is X.25 over leased lines; some of these lines are digital. Higher layers are based on the Coloured Book protocol specifications.

The packet switches of the wide area network, which is *JANET* proper, are called *JANET* Packet Switching Exchanges (JPSE) and are based on GEC 4000 processors, with software supplied by GEC. Each JPSE is housed at a local NOC, all of which are connected to a Network Control Centre (NCC), which houses a Network Management Unit (NMU). The latter is based on the same equipment as the JPSE. The NOCs handle connection logistics, such as ordering a leased line from BT. The main trunk network is currently running at 512Kbps [Hutton 1988], with some other long-distance links at 64Kbps digital or 48Kbps analog, and subscriber lines are mostly 9600bps.

JANET has a domain name system specified in Grey Book. It is similar to that of the *Internet* DNS, but the order of the domain name parts is opposite, with the root on the left. The system is centrally administered and in full use.

Interconnections

In Table 13.5, **{JANET-domain}** stands for the top level domain *UK*, which is valid in the *JANET* Grey Book, *Internet* DNS, and *Ean* domain naming systems. However, note that *JANET* uses the opposite order of domains from the other two. *JANET* is connected to the following networks:

Internet	To send mail from *JANET* to the *Internet*, the gateway *uk.ac.ucl.cs.nss* at ULCC should be used. But access to it is controlled, due to the cost of the transatlantic link; the gateway has to pay volume charges for traffic in *both* directions. According to mail sent by the mailer daemon on that host, "Contact liaison@uk.ac.ucl.cs.nss for help, or send a text-less message to authorisation@uk.ac.ucl.cs.nss for an automatic message specifically about UK<->US relaying." It is also possible to use the *EARN* gateway at RAL, *uk.ac.earn-relay* (formerly known as *uk.ac.rl.earn* [Bryant 1988]) to reach the *Internet*. Note the order of the domains on the left-hand side of the at sign.
Ean	The *Ean* networks may be reached by using the gateway *uk.ac.ean-relay*. But the French network *ARISTOTE* has a different gateway, *uk.ac.ucl.cs.nss*, and hosts on it use the domain ARISTOTE.FR, not just ARISTOTE. Both gateways allow specification of *Ean* domains in either order. There are three documents available from *uk.ac.ean-relay*: <DOC>ean.usage, <DOC>ean.sites, and <DOCS>ean.ozsites; the latter lists *ACSnet* hosts reachable through *Ean*. They may be retrieved by NIFTP with user name guest and any password.
X.400	For information on reaching X.400 sites other than *Ean*, one can get <DOCS>x400.usage and <DOCS>x400.sites from *uk.ac.ucl.cs* by the same means as for the *Ean* documents mentioned above.

Table 13.5. *JANET interconnections*

Network	Syntax
JANET	*user*@{**JANET-domain**}.*domain*
Internet	*user*%*domain*.{**DNS**}@uk.ac.ucl.cs.nss
Internet	*user*%{**DNS**}.*domain*@uk.ac.earn-relay
CSNET Phonenet	*user*%*domain*.{**DNS**}%relay.cs.net@uk.ac.earn-relay
Ean	*user*%*domain*.{**Ean-domain**}@uk.ac.ean-relay
EARN	*user*%*host*@uk.ac.earn-relay
EARN	*user*%EARN.*host*@uk.ac.earn-relay
BITNET	*user*%BITNET.*host*@uk.ac.earn-relay
UUCP	*user*%*domain*.{**DNS**}@uk.ac.ukc
UUCP	*user*@UUCP.*host*
UUCP	*user*@UUCP.*host*@uk.ac.ukc
UUCP	*user*%host1%*host*.UUCP@uk.ac.ukc
UUCP	"host1!*host*!*user*"@uk.ac.ukc
UUCP	*user*%UUCP.*host*@uk.ac.earn-relay
UUCP	host1!*user*%UUCP.*host*@uk.ac.earn-relay
UUCP	*user*%*host*%UUCP.host2@uk.ac.earn-relay
UUCP	*host*!*user*%UUCP.host2@uk.ac.earn-relay
SPAN	?
ARISTOTE	*user*%*domain*.ARISTOTE.FR@uk.ac.ucl.cs.nss
XEROX Internet	*user*.{**XEROX-domain**}%com.xerox@uk.ac.earn-relay
Easynet	*user*%*host*.dec%com.dec.decwrl@uk.ac.earn-relay
VNET	*user*%vnet.*host*@uk.ac.earn-relay
VNET	*user*%*host*%com.ibm@uk.ac.earn-relay
ACSnet	*user*%*domain*.oz@uk.ac.ukc
ACSnet	*user*%*domain*.{**ACSNET-domain**}%munnari.oz@uk.ac.ean-relay
JUNET	*user*%*domain*.{**JUNET-domain**}@uk.ac.ukc
JUNET	*user*%*domain*.{**JUNET-domain**}%net.cs.relay@uk.ac.earn-relay
INFNET	%cern.decnet.@uk.ac.ean-relay

EARN and *BITNET*   The syntaxes for *EARN* and *BITNET* can be used interchangeably, since the distinctions between those two networks are purely administrative; the RAL gateway *uk.ac.earn-relay* should be used for either. *JANET* users may obtain information on the *EARN* gateway by an interactive call to *uk.ac.janet.news* or by sending a mail message containing the line

GET JANET EARNGATE

to LISTSERV@UK.AC.EARN-RELAY [Bryant 1988]. Problems with the gateway should be reported to US@uk.ac.rl.ib (User Support). There is also a mailing list for *JANET* users of *EARN*: subscriptions to PO2@uk.ac.rl.ib; submissions to EARUNS@uk.ac.rl. Even though mail is sent using these guidelines, it may not arrive because some *BITNET* hosts convert addresses to uppercase, and some destinations expect the local mailbox part of an address to be in lower-case. Also, lines longer than 80 characters will probably be truncated. If this happens to an address line, the mail will be lost.

UUCP and *EUnet*   The main gateway into *UUCP* and *EUnet* is *uk.ac.ukc*. For those target hosts with DNS domain names (all *EUnet* hosts and many *UUCP* hosts), *Internet* DNS domain syntax may be used with that gateway. Old-style *UUCP* names may also be used with the .UUCP suffix — i.e., the *UUCP* pseudo-domain — if the target host is registered in the *UUCP* maps. *UUCP* map information for a host may be obtained by mailing to netdir@uk.ac.ukc with a *Subject:* header containing the name of the target host. Note that *uk.ac.ukc* charges for relay service and requires registration beforehand, although the charges are usually high only for transatlantic traffic; contact uknet@uk.ac.ukc for details. It is also possible to use indirect relaying by using multiple percent signs or old-style *UUCP* bang syntax, but the quotes around everything on the left-hand side of the at sign are necessary for the latter usage; also note the opposite host order. Finally, mail can be sent through the *EARN* gateway at RAL, and indirection in either of the two forms is possible.

SPAN   There is a document specifically about reaching *SPAN* from *JANET* [Hapgood 1986].

JUNET   Although *uk.ac.ukc* is a gateway that knows about *JUNET*, it is also possible to reach some hosts on that network through *CSNET*. But be aware that most *JUNET* hosts do not have permission to use *CSNET*.

Much of the information on *JANET* interconnections is derived from a collection by Tim Clark [Clark 1988]. There are gateways to BT *PSS* and from there to the *IPSS* (International Packet Switched Service) There are also gateways to the *Internet* via University College London (UCL) to *EUnet* via the University of Kent at Canterbury (UKC), and to *EARN* via RAL. All the gateways have access controls because of funding considerations. Routing in the wide area network is via X.25 addresses; this address space is independent of the CCITT X.121 space but conforms to its requirements. Routing between the wide area network and attached networks is via network level relays using extended addressing supported by the Yellow Book protocol.

Plans

SERC set up a one year postgraduate course at UCL to produce networking and distributed systems specialists in order to help alleviate a shortage of such people. The annual Networkshops started by the predecessor of

JANET continue. There is a commitment by the *JANET* community to eventually change to the ISO-OSI protocols, and the plan is given in the White Book [ACOSITG 1987]. *JANET* is a Full National Member of RARE, and the section on RARE in Chapter 8 contains some comments on the relations of *JANET* and RARE.

> **Access**
>
> Network Executive
> Rutherford Appleton Laboratory
> Chilton
> Didcot
> Oxfordshire, OX11 OQX
> United Kingdom
>
> For the Coloured Book protocols, contact JNT at the same address or call +44 235 21900.

13.15.2   Starlink

Starlink is a network for astronomers; its name is derived from that function and from its original star topology. Its purpose is to provide research astronomers in the United Kingdom with interactive computing facilities (both hardware and software). Use in spectral and image work is of particular importance. *Starlink* has made astronomers in the United Kingdom into an integrated community and vastly increased sharing of techniques and software [Wallace 1988].

This is a national network, with hosts in England, Scotland, Wales, and Northern Ireland connected by *JANET* links. There are sites in Armagh, Belfast, Birmingham, Cambridge, Cardiff, Durham, Jodrell Bank (near Macclesfield), Keele, Leicester, Manchester, Oxford, Preston, Queen Mary College London, Royal Greenwich Observatory (near Hailsham), Royal Observatory Edinburgh, Rutherford Appleton Laboratory (RAL) (near Didcot), St. Andrews, Southampton, and University College London (UCL). There are 50 hosts at these 19 sites and 950 users. All the hosts run **VMS**. Eighty-seven percent of the users are research astronomers (both postgraduate and postdoctorate), 10 percent are programmers, and 3 percent are in management and administration.

Administration and Funding

Administration is done by a group at Rutherford Appleton Laboratory (RAL), which is in turn operated through the Astronomy and Planetary Science Board (APSB) by the Science and Engineering Research Council (SERC), which is part of the Department of Education and Science (DES) of the government of the United Kingdom [Lawden 1988]. Local autonomy of the sites and central coordination are carefully balanced. Funding comes from SERC, which receives it from DES.

Services

Mail (**VMS MAIL** and Coloured Book **POST**) is supported and has been important from the beginning, even though mailing lists are not supported. **VMS PHONE** and locally written **TALK** are provided. A locally written **NEWS** utility is present, as is **VAXnotes**, a product purchased from Digital that is becoming widely used both for astronomical research results and technical matters [Terrett 1988]. **PHONE** and **TALK** are discouraged on the grounds that they are intrusive, being interactive, while **NEWS** and **VAX-notes** are encouraged because they are asynchronous facilities that do not interrupt normal work. Remote login and file transfer are supported in DECNET form throughout *Starlink* and with Coloured Book over *JANET*. Red Book RJE is also used. Also, each *Starlink* host has a standard set of application software, called the Starlink Software Collection (SSC), which includes complete astronomical applications packages, subroutine libraries, and system elements. This software is also distributed free to bona fide pure science research institutions outside *Starlink*, currently about 120 worldwide [Starlink 1988a]. There is also a central database of astronomical data.

Protocols

The network uses the DECNET and Coloured Book protocols over Ethernets and *JANET*'s X.25 leased lines. A typical link speed is 9600bps, and mail is usually delivered in minutes. Static host tables and DECNET nameservice are used. There is some redundancy in the long-distance links.

Interconnections

There are DECNET links from *Starlink* to *HEPnet* and *SPAN*. Access to other networks is done through *JANET*.

History

The origin of *Starlink* was a realization in the mid-1970s by U.K. astronomers that they were not able to process data as quickly as new sources (such as satellite astronomy, new ground-based telescopes, multiple dish radio telescope arrays, and automatic scanning of photographic plates) were starting to collect it. Data processing at the time was mostly done in batch on mainframes. Better equipment and sharing of resources, of both hardware and software development, were greatly desired. Professor Michael Disney observed interactive data reduction facilities in use at some overseas sites and proposed a U.K. center to contain an interactive facility of this type so that astronomers could travel to it. A panel he was then asked to chair [Disney 1988] examined the problem and recommended much larger facilities and remote access over networks. A single large central machine was rejected because remote display of image data would not be possible over the network links then available. Personal computers were not adequate either. Machines of intermediate size were thus desired, and the Digital VAX was chosen. The committee recommended the establishment of *Starlink* in 1978. Key software strategies were later formulated in an international workshop. *Starlink* was operational as of 1 April 1980 [Disney and Wallace 1982].

There were six initial hosts, all VAX-11/780s, each at a separate site. *Starlink* originally had its own leased lines, arranged in a star, using DEC-NET over DDCMP. But *SERCnet* was later used for network infrastructure, as was its successor *JANET*. Four VAX-11/750s were added at four additional sites by 1984. The next spurt of growth was seen with the introduction of the MicroVAX, when the network doubled in size. There has been rapid growth in the last few years, with the network gaining about 100 users each year [Starlink 1988b]. All the original 780s and 750s are being retired. A maximum of 20 to 25 sites is expected soon, when all major astronomical centers in the country have been involved; about 1,000 users are expected then. It is hoped that each user will eventually have a personal VAX in a local area network cluster. The use of static name tables kept on *JANET* may be a limit to that growth [Wallace 1988].

Standards

Starlink has been a pioneer in the use of the graphics standard **GKS** since 1980. It does not significantly affect networking standards, due to its small size, but watches Digital's participation in the implementation of ISO-OSI protocols with interest.

Access

Patrick T. Wallace
Starlink Project Manager
PTW%STAR.RL.AC.UK@CUNYVM.CUNY.EDU
PTW@UK.AC.RUTHERFORD.STARLINK
+44 235 445372
Telex: 23159 RUTHLB G.
Rutherford Appleton Laboratory
Chilton
Didcot, Oxfordshire, OX11 0QX
United Kingdom

The Starlink Project publishes a newsletter called the *Starlink Bulletin*.

13.15.3   UKnet

UKnet, the U.K. UNIX Network, is the British part of *EUnet* and provides
similar news and mail services [Collinson 1988].

Administration and Funding

The network is run from the University of Kent at Canterbury (UKC) in
cooperation with the UK UNIX systems Users group (UKUUG). Funding
comes primarily from charges to the user sites, although there have been
grants from government bodies.

Scope

The center of *UKnet* is the machine *ukc* or *ukc.ac.uk*, which also serves as a
gateway to *JANET* and *PSS* and provides connections to much of the rest of
the world both by direct UUCP connections and through *mcvax*. There are
about 350 sites registered with UKC. Some of these are mail gateway
machines into large subnets whose separate machines are invisible to the
world network.

Protocols and Services

UKnet sites fall into several broad categories:

- Standard academic *JANET* sites that communicate with *ukc* using
  Coloured Book protocols. Some of these sites receive news using
  these protocols. Because UKC's mail system is well connected, it is
  used by many sites in the United Kingdom as an intelligent router.
  The UKC link to *JANET* runs at 9600bps [Dallas 1988].
- Academic sites on *JANET* that communicate using UUCP over a login
  line into *ukc*. There were many of these sites in the early days because
  it was not technically possible to install direct X.25 onto their small
  UNIX machines, although it was possible for them to use an X.25 PAD
  in reverse mode. Lee McLoughlin of Imperial College did much work
  in creating a UUCP that would run easily over this type of connection.
  At the start, this form of networking was used by Computer Science
  Departments that were unable to get direct file transfer onto *JANET*
  from their small machines. Internal university politics often played a
  role here, too. Many of these sites did not use the U.K. academic
  domain order at first.
- Commercial sites that communicate with *ukc* using Coloured Book
  protocols over *PSS*. The UKC link is at 4800bps.
- Commercial sites that communicate with *ukc* using UUCP either on a
  telephone line or over *PSS*. These sites generally run standard mailers

using world standard domain order. Telephone connections are mostly at 1200bps with some 300bps; 2400bps has been used since about 1986, although the telephone system is a bit noisy for it. Some Telebit Trailblazers have been used recently [Dallas 1988].

- Many sites that are not directly connected to *ukc*. Some of these run very dumb UUCP mail systems and rely on another host further down the line to perform protocol conversion for them.

The plethora of sites above exclude many private networks in the United Kingdom that are connected "outside" the recognized routes. These are mostly international companies or companies with international connections that do not wish to participate in the U.K. network. It often leads to the annoying situation where mail for U.K. offices travels via the United States.

History

In 1982, telephone connections were made from *mcvax* in Amsterdam, and the network in the United Kingdom fanned out to around 20 sites that were mostly academic. Soon after the start, an ex-student working in the United States established a phone link carrying news and mail. The link lasted for about 18 months until the ex-student moved to another site; communication became patchy and finally ceased in the summer of 1984. In the interim, cost-effective UUCP running over X.25 had been developed by Piet Beertema of CWI and *mcvax*. A connection of this type to *mcvax* became the basic method of communication with the outside world. By December 1984, it became clear that UKC could not afford to pay for this link, and EUUG supplied a large grant to pay an outstanding bill. A UKUUG meeting formalized a charging scheme that was to make the network self-supporting in terms of international communication charges. Sites would contribute toward the cost of these transmission charges in proportion to their usage.

Paradoxically, the meeting generated much interest, and the number of participating sites doubled in the succeeding year. The network has been growing at the rate of ten sites per month ever since.

In October 1984, the Computer Board for Universities and Research Councils (CB), the funding body for computing services in the United Kingdom, provided a funded post called the UNIX Support Officer. CB believed that one of the most important things the Support Officer could do for the U.K. **UNIX** community was to enable access to the worldwide **UNIX** network from *JANET*. This requirement meant that the software supporting the *UUCP* backbone activities had to be upgraded to cope with the need to convert *JANET* Grey Book mail into the RFC822 mail format that is more usual on the *UUCP* network. Of course, reverse translation was also required if users on the *UUCP* network were to send mail to *JANET*. The machine *ukc* at UKC is now performing two parallel functions: those of a *UUCP* backbone site and those of a gateway to *JANET*.

None of this would have been possible without the work put into **MMDF** by Steve Kille at University College London (UCL). It was imperative that a mail system be developed that could handle both domain names ordered in the U.K. Grey Book manner and names sorted in the order that is used by most of the rest of the world—i.e., that of *Internet* DNS. Similar work has been put into **sendmail** in more recent times by Jim Crammond from Imperial College.

In 1986, the network had grown to 100 sites, and it had become apparent that it was no longer possible to hide the load imposed by the network on the Digital VAX-11/780 from the users at UKC. It was also felt that it was about time for the campus mail system to provide a service for the users at UKC rather than for those at other sites. The solution was to run the gateway on a separate machine. CB and the Alvey Commission (Alvey) jointly funded a machine that would be solely responsible for handling the gateway. The Joint Network Team (JNT) were already supporting the X.25 *PSS* gateway.

Plans

Future plans are to install a leased line to *mcvax* and to participate in the *EUnet* migration plan for ISO-OSI protocols.

Access
Peter Collinson
pc@ukc.ac.uk
uunet!mcvax!ukc!pc
+44 0227 66822, ext. 7619
Unix Support Group
Computing Laboratory
The University
Canterbury, Kent CT2 7NF
United Kingdom

13.15.4   GreenNet

This is a political conferencing system similar to *PeaceNet*. It was originally formed as a conference on *GeoNet* but now runs on a Plexus P35 in London and has an hourly UUCP connection with the *PeaceNet* machine. There are about 300 users. There is no direct connection with any of the European Green Parties, but the politics of its users may be similar. One of its notable user organizations is Greenpeace.

Access

GreenNet
+44 1 490 1510
Fax: 01 251 2613
Telex: 851 933524 ref GEO2:GN
26-28 Underwood Street
London N1 7JQ
United Kingdom

13.15.5   COSMOS

COSMOS is an Alvey project in the United Kingdom with a 1.4 million pound budget over three years starting in May 1986. It is for development of mechanisms for group work, including mail and conferencing. Beta test was expected in January 1989. Participants include British Telecom (BT), Computer Sciences Co. Ltd., Queen Mary College, the University of Manchester, and the University of Nottingham. There is some coordination with the **AMIGO** project [Cook 1988; COSMOS 1988a; COSMOS 1988b].

Access

Paul Wilson
wilson@cs.nott.ac.uk
Computer Sciences Co. Ltd.
Computer Sciences House
Brunel Way
Slough SL1 1XL
United Kingdom

13.16   *Nordic Countries*

The Nordic countries are at the same time highly sophisticated technologically and sparsely populated. To overcome the latter problem, they often undertake joint projects, such as *NORDUnet*. There is also quite a bit of activity in each of the countries.

13.16.1   NORDUnet

NORDUnet is an international network connecting the Nordic countries and administered by NORDUNET. This network connects the numerous existing Ethernet networks at Scandinavian universities with a large international backbone Ethernet. There were 2,000 to 3,000 hosts by early 1989 [Brunell 1988; Brunell and Loevdal 1988]. The configuration is a backbone star network centered on Kungliga Tekniska Högskolan (KTH) in Stockholm, Sweden, which is connected to the Swedish national network *SUNET*.

There are *NORDUnet* nodes at UNI-C Lyngby in Denmark for *DENet*; at RUNIT in Trondheim, Norway, for *UNINETT*; and to *FUNET* at CSC in Espoo, Finland [Salminen 1988b].

Administration and Funding

Administration is by NORDUNET, which is a networking program in the Nordic countries that is funded by the Nordic Council of Ministers. There is a steering committee and principles of operation for it. It coordinates development, implementation, and operational projects, documents them, explains them to the public, and evaluates them for new ideas [Carlson 1986]. The participating organizations are the Nordic national networks mentioned above, plus SURIS in Iceland. The goals of NORDUNET are to provide harmonized network services to Nordic research and development users in cooperation with these national networks and to establish good inter-Nordic relations in networking. Projects are of two types: (1) practical infrastructure using existing de facto standard protocols, as in *NORDUnet*; and (2) ISO-OSI pilot networks and experiments leading to eventual migration to ISO-OSI protocols. Specific projects are usually allocated to one of the national members [Brunell 1988].

The NORDUNET program runs from 1986 through 1990, with a total budget of about 10 million Norwegian crowns (NOK). About 3 million NOK are set aside for pilot and research projects. A proposal for a follow-on program has been submitted to the Nordic Council of Ministers, and a decision was expected in the fall of 1988 [Brunell 1988]. Funding for the *NORDUnet* network comes from the four mainland member countries [Salminen 1988c] and from NORDUNET. International links are done by the Scandinavian communications company Scandinavian Telecommunications Services AB (SCANTEL), which was formed in 1987 by the Swedish PTT holding company TeleINVEST, and which is currently owned by all the Nordic countries: 48 percent by Sweden, 16 percent by each of Finland, Denmark, and Norway, and 4 percent by Iceland. In addition to international communications among the Nordic countries, SCANTEL provides connections to the United States through Intelsat [Brunell et al. 1988].

Protocols

The star links are 64Kbps leased lines, using Vitalink Translan bridges and cisco routers. DECNET and NJE links eventually will be handled with **G-Box** routers donated by Digital [Salminen 1988a]. Each of the national locations will then have a bridge to the national network, such as *DENet* in Denmark. The backbone will run all of X.25 (ISO-OSI CONS), ISO-OSI CLNS, TCP/IP (because of its proven serviceability), DECNET (to connect existing installations that use it), and NJE (for *BITNET* and *EARN* [Salminen

1988d]). A Class B IP network number and an autonomous system number registered with SRI-NIC are used, along with subnets. Use of the DECNET protocols will be integrated into the address space managed by *SPAN* and *HEPnet* [Salminen 1988c] using Poor Man's Routing (PMR) and an allocation of noninternational area numbers (47–63) as follows:

Finland	47–49, 61–62
Denmark	50–53
Norway	54–55
Sweden	56–60
Spare	63

Provision of CCITT or ISO-OSI protocols to run over X.25 was expected in early 1989; these are to include XXX, X.400, and FTAM. *EUnet* news will be carried over the backbone. SNMP may be used to manage the TCP/IP and DECNET protocols [Brunell 1988].

The cisco routers were chosen because they already support all of the above protocols (except NJE), as well as XNS and possibly Chaos. There are other similar routers, such as those from Proteon or WellFleet. This ability to use several protocol suites without undue speed constraints was the main reason for the choice of this method of connection [Salminen 1988d].

Interconnections

Connections to *EARN*, *EUnet*, *HEPnet*, *NSFNET*, and possibly *SPAN* are planned [Brunell 1988].

History

Early Nordic networking projects include *Centernet* in Denmark, *FUNET* in Finland, *ICEP* in Iceland, *UNINETT* in Norway, and *SUNET* in Sweden. Annual conferences among the Scandinavian national university network projects have been held since 1980; these were the foundation of NORDUNET, which was formed in 1985. It became an International Member of RARE, with representative Birgitta Carlson, and hosted the May 1986 RARE Networkshop in Copenhagen [Carlson 1986; Carlson 1987]. NORDUNET is a supporter of the goals of COSINE.

The *NORDUnet* project was originally called *X.EARN* because it began with ideas for migration of *EARN* to X.25. The Nordic directors at the *EARN* board of directors meeting of May 1987 in Nice, France, discussed their concern about having to pay for their international leased lines again in 1988 when they were only being used to about 10 or 20 percent capacity by *EARN* traffic. An ability to share those lines with other networks, such as *EUnet*, or with other services, such as access from Finland to the Cray supercomputer at RUNIT in Norway, was desired. The X.25 EARN

(X.EARN) project was formalized in August 1987 at a NORDUNET meeting, during which cost sharing and technical development were planned. Iceland was not involved at this point because it had planned to drop out of *EARN* after 1987.

Rationalization and interconnection of the diverse protocols and services already in use in the Nordic countries were major goals from the beginning, as was ISO-OSI compatibility. The most desired service was the entire TCP/IP protocol suite, with a connection to the United States widely wanted; *EUnet* connections were also much wanted [Brunell et al. 1988]. These goals led to a solution that did not depend on X.25, so the old name is no longer used [Salminen 1988c].

Lines for 64Kbps connections to *NSFNET* in the United States and to the Netherlands [Simonsen 1988a] were ordered by May 1988, and an *NSFNET* connection application had been filed [Salminen 1988c]. The first internal *NORDUnet* link, KTH to RUNIT, was operational in September 1988. Most others were expected to be in use by the end of October 1988, permitting testing of the network before the end of 1988, with full operation by April 1989. The link to Amsterdam was expected to be operational in February 1989 [Loevdal and Brunell 1988]. The *NSFNET* connection will use an Intelsat 56Kbps link from KTH to JVNC in Princeton. The Amsterdam connection is from KTH to CWI, home of *cwi.nl* (*mcvax*), and is expected to carry Nordic traffic for *EUnet*, *HEPnet*, and *EARN*; these connections may have been established by early 1989 [Brunell 1988]. *NORDUnet* is one of the major participants in *RIPE* (see *EUnet* in this chapter). Traffic was passing between *NORDUnet* and *HEPnet* and CERN by May of 1989.

Plans

It is possible that 2Mbps links may eventually be used, perhaps split into several slower channels by Time Division Multiplexing (TDM) [Brunell et al. 1988]. A connection to Iceland is also being discussed. As described in the section on that country, that connection will not be with Ethernet but by IP over X.25. *NORDUnet* is expected to last about three to five years, since its organizers consider that the longest realistic life span for a computer or networking project [Salminen 1988c].

Eventual ISO-OSI migration is being pursued by experiments and pilot services such as FTAM and X.500 directory service (with **THORN**) over **ISODE**; mail gateways are also being developed. Resolution of conflicts between X.121 X.25 addressing and that used by *HEPnet* and others is desired [Brunell 1988].

Access

Arild Jansen
Chairman NORDUNET Steering Committee
z_jansen_a@use.uio.uninett
+47 2 721706
Forbruker- og adminstrationsdepartementet
Plan- og dataavdelningen
P.O. Box 8004 Dep.
N-0030 Oslo 1
Norway

Mats Brunell
Project Manager NORDUNET
matsb@sics.se
+46 8 7521563
Fax: +46 8 7517230
NORDUNET
Swedish Institute of Computer Science
P.O. Box 1263
S-164 28 Kista
Sweden

Einar Loevdal
Technical Coordinator NORDUNET
x_loevdal_e@use.uio.uninett
+47 2 453498
University of Oslo Computing Center
P.O. Box 1059 Blindern
N-0316 Oslo 3
Norway

A mailing list, NDNNET-I, is available from the **LISTSERV** on *EARN* host *FINHUTC*.

13.17   *Denmark {DK}*

There are two main networks in Denmark: *DENet*, an academic and research network, and *DKnet*, the national branch of *EUnet*.

13.17.1   **DENet**

DENet, or Danish Ethernet Network, consists of many local Ethernets in university departments throughout the country, connected together with MAC level bridges over 64Kbps or 128Kbps leased lines. *DENet* provides nationwide access to computers at the Danish Computing Centre for Research and Education (UNI-C) [Sorensen 1988], as well as to many other computers located at institutions under the Ministry of Education (MoE) [Simonsen 1988a]. Both TCP/IP and DECNET are used [Salminen 1988b].

DENet is the Danish part of *NORDUnet*. It was preceded by and replaces *Centernet* [Simonsen 1988a].

History

The terminal network *DENet* provided access to three regional computing centers that were sponsored by the Danish MoE and that were near universities. This was done in cooperation with the national PTT, using X.25 over the PDN *PAXNET* [Carlson 1986]. The three centers were North European University Computing Centre (NEUCC) in Lyngby; Regional Computing Centre at University of Aarhus (RECAU) in Aarhus; and Regional Computing Centre at University of Copenhagen (RECKU) (which assisted DIKU in forming *DKnet*), in Copenhagen. (These centers merged into UNI-C on 1 January 1985 [Simonsen 1988a].) Various computers were connected, including ones made by IBM, CDC, Sperry, and Regnecentralen. There was cooperation with NORDUNET [Carlson 1987].

Access

Jan P. Sorensen
RKUJPS@os1100.uni-c.dk

Peter Villemoes
RKUPV@NEUVM1.bitnet
Network Management

Frode Greisen
NEUFRODE@NEUVM1.bitnet
EARN Management

13.17.2   DKnet

DKnet is the Danish part of *EUnet* and has the same services — i.e., mail and news — plus an archive service that provides access to the latest EUUG software distribution tapes, as well as to the current sources for the essential network software [Simonsen 1988b]. *DKnet* is administered by a subcommittee of the board of directors of Danish UNIX system Users' Group (DKUUG). Unlike EUUG, DKUUG does not just speak for *DKnet* in political matters such as negotiating with other networks; it actually runs the network, including handling its financial affairs. There is a special network account within DKUUG, and the network's managers are responsible for keeping a budget and preventing deficits but otherwise have a free hand. The money is ultimately derived from the individual sites, as for *EUnet*.

The network runs throughout Denmark, with 60 sites receiving mail and 13 receiving news as of May 1988; the total number of machines is about 150. The main backbone machine has four 1200/2400bps modems and two X.25 lines. The total measured traffic through it in February 1988 was about 400Mbytes. The budget for 1988 was about $70,000 U.S., with a site subscription costing about $150 a year, plus an initial hookup charge, also about $150. Each of these charges is applied separately for mail and news. The sites are then responsible for paying directly for any actual communication charges, and DKUUG imposes a surcharge of $3 for each megabyte of news, up to about $100 a month. The cost of international importation of news is divided equally among all Danish news subscribers: this is basically the monthly flat news fee.

In addition to its interconnections to the rest of *EUnet*, through the Danish backbone machine *dkuug*, *DKnet* cooperates with other networks that have branches in Denmark, particularly *EARN* and the Danish MHS research and development network. All the Danish networks use the top level domain *DK* in a cooperative agreement.

In January 1983, Keld Simonsen connected a PDP-11/45 called *diku*, located at the institute of computer science of the University of Copenhagen (DIKU), to the *EUnet* backbone machine *mcvax*. Mail and news were exchanged over a 1200bps autodial modem donated by Selskabet for Rationel Almen Planlaegning (SRAP), Copenhagen, and over an X.25 line loaned from the Regional Computing Centre at University of Copenhagen (RECKU). RECKU is now a part of Danish Computing Centre for Research and Education (UNI-C).

In addition to the original machine, DIKU donated personnel, more modems, and financial administration; in the early days DIKU was the main support of the network. The *diku* machine became successively a VAX-11/750 and a VAX-11/785.

DKUUG has since also become involved in those ways, and formal responsibility was transferred in 1987, when DKUUG hired a person half time to run the backbone, with DIKU still providing technical support. The national backbone functions have been moved to a new machine, *dkuug*, which is a Sun-2/120 on loan from Ericsson/Nokia.

Access

Keld Jorn Simonsen
keld@dkuug.dk
+45 1 13 00 23
DKUUG
Kabbelejevej 27 B
DK-2700 Broenshoej
Denmark

13.18   *Finland {FI}*

There are *BITNET*, *CSNET*, *Ean*, and *EUnet* connections to Finland, but the major internal network is *FUNET*.

Although the *FI* domain has been registered for several years for all networks in Finland, *FUNET* is still in use for the *Ean* network, due to some software problems on some of the machines running **Ean** software [Virtanen 1988]. As of September 1988, *FI* was recognized by most hosts of *FUNET*, and gateways existed among most of the protocols used on it (DECNET, TCP/IP, RJE, UUCP, and X.400) [Salminen 1988b].

The local branch of *EUnet* has two main machines, connected by *FUNET* links, and is managed by the Finnish UNIX Users' Group (FUUG), which has close relations with *FUNET* [Salminen 1987].

The first *EARN* connection to Finland was in 1985 to an IBM 4341 through a 3705 communications controller loaned by IBM, which also provided a leased line from Helsinki University of Technology (HUT) to QZ in Stockholm, Sweden. The system *FINHUTC* runs **LISTSERV**, and *FINHUT* runs **NETSERV** [Salminen 1987].

13.18.1   **FUNET**

The Finnish University Network, or *FUNET*, exists to provide "the best possible network service for the users in the Finnish Universities and Research establishments" [Salminen 1988e]. It is a mostly star-shaped network centered on the Center for Scientific Computing (CSC) located in the Otaniemi Campus of the Helsinki University of Technology (HUT) and extending as far as the University of Lapland, above the Arctic circle [Virtanen 1988]. Although most sites are currently universities, access is not limited to those, and there are increasing numbers of connections from private companies and government agencies. Such nonacademic organizations pay for the costs of their connection links. There is, however, a requirement that use of the national backbone be restricted to that which furthers research and education.

The basic infrastructure is an Ethernet connecting Ethernets (and other kinds of local area networks) at sites with MAC level bridges and network layer routers. There are thousands of hosts using the TCP/IP protocols, ranging from IBM PCs and Apple Macintoshes through the entire range of machine sizes (most running **UNIX**) to IBM mainframes and a Cray X-MP EA 416. There are slightly less than 200 **VMS** VAXes using DECNET. There are about 25 *EARN* hosts using the common infrastructure to communicate with NJE [Salminen 1988e].

Administration

Administration is done by the FUNET Project, which is headquartered at CSC. Most *FUNET* services, such as personnel, servers, and gateways, are located at CSC, HUT, and Tampere University of Technology (TUT).

FUNET Steering Committee:

Matti Ihamuotila <ihamuotila@opmvax.kpo.fi> Chairman, CSC, *EARN* board of directors

Juha Heinaenen <jh@tut.fi> TUT CS laboratory, *Internet* administration

Risto Raitio <raitio@opmvax.kpo.fi> Ministry of Education, COSINE CPG

Lars Backstroem <backstrom@opmvax.kpo.fi> Helsinki University Computing Center, *NORDUnet* Steering Committee

Kaisu Ranta <LK-KR@FINOU.bitnet> Oulu University

Alpo Maekinen, VTT

Tapio Kasanen, PTT

FUNET Project

Markus Sadeniemi <sadeniemi@funet.fi> FUNET Project leader, RARE COA

Harri Salminen <hks@funet.fi> FUNET technical coordinator, *EARN* and *NORDUnet* technical representative

Jyrki Soini <soini@funet.fi> *FUNET* network management: DECNET, *NORDUnet*, and RARE MHS

Vesa Keinaenen <vjk@funet.fi> FUNET/FUUG (at TUT) **UNIX** expert, UUCP, *NORDUnet*, and RARE MHS

Jukka Korpela <jko@hila.hut.fi> HUT, *EARN* country coordinator

Jukka Virtanen <jtv@hut.fi> HUT, *CSNET* technical contact, capital area UUCP

Pekka Kytoelaakso <netmgr@opmvax.kpo.fi> CSC, PMDF and RNEWS distribution, *NORDUnet* and RARE FTAM

There is an official agreement with the Finnish UNIX Users' Group (FUUG) for *FUNET* to provide mail and news transport to FUUG members who are not *FUNET* members; this is acknowledgment of the existing state since the beginning. Unlike many European countries, Finland has no restrictions against non-PTT carriers of third party information traffic. *FUNET* also has good cooperation with the PTT, including a PTT member on the Steering Committee [Salminen 1988e].

Funding

FUNET collects fees from university sites to cover the costs of the national links. The international connections and most purchases and personnel are funded by the Ministry of Education [Salminen 1988b].

Services and Protocols

Services include mail, conferencing (*USENET* news), file transfer, remote job entry, remote login, and interactive graphics [Salminen 1988e]. *FUNET* uses leased lines (at speeds varying from 14.4Kbps to 64Kbps) with Ethernet bridges and routers to connect local Ethernets at Finnish universities. This allows multiple protocols that have proven ability to provide the desired services to be used over this network layer, while providing a pilot environment for experimenting with ISO-OSI protocols. Leased lines are used in preference to PTT X.25 connections because they are fixed cost, usually faster, and often more economical. Fixed costs are particularly important because they obviate any need to bill usage back to the users, because they make budgeting easier, and because they encourage increasing use, which in turn encourages increasing provision of service [Salminen 1988e].

Above this national Ethernet, TCP/IP is the most widely used protocol suite. There is one Class B IP network number for the national Ethernet (and five others associated with a NORDUNET project). It is registered with SRI-NIC, in the *Internet* namespace. The top level domain *FI* is also registered with SRI-NIC, and DNS domain names are widely supported, even on **VMS** DECNET machines, through **PMDF** [Salminen 1987]. The FUNET Project allocates host numbers on it in blocks of 256 and also does subnetting, using cisco routers to provide Proxy ARP for those hosts that still don't understand subnets. Some local organizations have Class C numbers and gateway those networks through Sun or Apollo routers.

DECNET is the second most commonly used protocol suite. Five area numbers are used in a topological arrangement designed to minimize routing traffic and to coordinate with an eventual Scandinavian DECNET using the same address space as *SPAN* and *HEPnet*.

NJE is supported for *EARN*, over both DECNET and UDP over the common Ethernet.

ISO-OSI programs and protocols being tested in the six or seven sites that participate in the pilot project include **Ean, MRX400, MHS** for **VM, ISODE,** and **SUNLINK OSI** over several protocol stacks, including TP0 over CONS (X.25); TP4 over CLNS (ISO-IP) over IEEE802.3; TCP/IP; DECNET; and NJE [Salminen 1988e].

Interconnections

There are direct connections to *EARN*, *EUnet*, *CSNET*, and *NORDUnet*. Most such connections will soon be handled through *NORDUnet*, which will also connect to *NSFNET*, *HEPnet*, and *SPAN*. Various mail formats are converted within *FUNET*. There is a gateway to the national commercial mail network *Elisa*, and X.25 access is possible by PTT with conversion among TCP/IP TELNET, DECNET set host, and CCITT X.29 provided [Salminen 1988e].

History

The original purpose of *FUNET* when it was first established in 1984 was remote login connections to computer center machines by X.25 over *Datapak*. Initial funding came from the Ministry of Education and the PTT [Carlson 1986; Carlson 1987], providing free X.25 access for the first year. Dialup and leased lines were also used, with many different protocols, which led to interoperability problems. The Ministry of Education established the FUNET Project to coordinate and develop networks among Finnish universities and research organizations. Interconnections at first took the form of mail and file transfer gateways on hosts that ran multiple protocols [Salminen 1987].

In 1986, an Ethernet bridge (with a pair of Bridge GS/3M MAC level bridges) was set up between HUT and TUT, marking the beginning of the current *FUNET* [Virtanen 1988]. The network spread rapidly to other universities because of its advantages in services and speed over the previous mechanisms. Still faster links are being negotiated with the PTT, and 2Mbps (T1) was expected to be partly available by the end of 1988 [Salminen 1988e]. *FUNET* is a participant in the Scandinavian *NORDUnet* project and helped inspire it. *FUNET* is also a NORDUNET participant and a Full National Member of RARE.

Access

Markus Sadeniemi
FUNET Project Manager
SADENIEMI@opmvax.kpo.fi
SADENIEMI@FUNET.FI

Harri Salminen
Technical Coordinator
hks@hut.fi
hks@funet.fi
hks@finhutc.bitnet
Funet Project

FUNET c/o VTKK/TLP
P.O. Box 40
SF-02101 Espoo
Finland

Jukka Virtanen
jtv@fingate.bitnet
jtv@hut.fi
Helsinki University of Technology
Computing Centre
SF-02150 Espoo
Finland

13.19   *Iceland {IS}*

The most widespread network in Iceland is the local branch of *EUnet*
[Stefansson 1988]. There are also local nodes on the *EARN* and *Ean* networks; the latter was installed for testing X.400. There are **VMS** hosts that
communicate by DECNET, but their connections to the outside world are
through *EUnet*.

Scope

There are currently about 20 registered *EUnet* hosts in Iceland. Three run
VMS; the rest run **UNIX**. Five organizations get *USENET* news.

Administration

The network is administered by the Icelandic UNIX system Users' Group
(ICEUUG), which also helps fund it by billing sites for usage. Other fund-
ing comes from the Hafrannsóknastofnunin (HAFRO), or Marine Research
Institute, which runs the backbone host, *hafro*.

Services

Mail is available on all sites and hosts. Most *USENET* newsgroups are
received, including those in the *comp*, *news*, and *sci* categories.

Protocols

The network is composed of UUCP links over leased and dialup lines and
X.25 links at speeds ranging from 1200bps to 9600bps. The backbone
machine *hafro* runs **HP-UX** (the Hewlett-Packard (HP) version of **UNIX**),
although it is being changed to run **SunOS** (the Sun version of **UNIX**).

All hosts use *Internet* DNS domains. The top level domain *IS* was
registered with SRI-NIC in 1987 by ICEUUG, in the name of National
Organization for Research Networking in Iceland (SURIS), or the Samtök
um Upplóýsinganet Rannsóknaraðila á Íslandi. ICEUUG assists new sites

in setting up a domain-based mailer in place of the default software where needed.

Interconnections

There are overseas connections from *hafro* by UUCP over X.25 to *mcvax* (Netherlands), *enea* (Sweden), and *ndosl* (Norway).

History

The Icelandic PTT *ICEP* has been operational since 1985 [Carlson 1986; Carlson 1987]. A connection to *EUnet* was first set up when HAFRO got a simple X.28 connection to *enea* in Sweden over *ICEP*. Initially, the connection was set up solely for that institute, but soon after other R&D organizations connected to *EUnet* via *hafro*, and that machine became the official backbone for Iceland.

SURIS has recently received a government grant for setting up a computer network gateway for Iceland. The machine has been ordered and will be a Sun-3/60, probably coupled with a cisco gateway. SURIS, ICEUUG, and HAFRO have agreed that the equipment will be set up at and maintained by the university; *hafro* will eventually be retired as backbone in favor of the new machine. There will be gateways to X.400 services and to the local Ethernet network at the university; the latter will also serve as a gateway to the **VMS** machines there.

The SURIS gateway machine will be connected by TCP/IP over X.25 over a leased line to Sweden. This will allow connection to *NORDUnet*, which in turn will be closely connected to other regions. These connections were to be completed by early 1989.

Access

Helgi Johnsson
hjons@rhi.hi.is

Gunnar Stefansson
gunnar@hafro.is
uunet!mcvax!hafro!gunnar
Marine Research Institute
Reykjavik
Iceland

Marius Olafsson
marius@rhi.hi.is
The University of Iceland
Reykjavik
Iceland

13.20   *Norway {NO}*

The main network in Norway is *UNINETT*. There are national components of quite a few other networks, and these are described in the *UNINETT* section.

13.20.1   UNINETT

UNINETT has been in operation since 1978 and provides PAD connections for remote login, as well as file transfer, conferencing (COM), and mail (MHS) [Carlson 1986; Carlson 1987]. There is also a directory service. As of November 1987, there were 600 users on 11 nodes [Hansen 1987].

Funding has come mostly from the Norwegian Science Research Council (NTNF), with assistance from the participating institutions. *UNINETT* is a participant in NORDUNET.

History

Most of the research effort in *UNINETT* has been in areas such as multimedia messaging, network interconnection, and broadband infrastructure [Carlson 1986; Carlson 1987]. For example, *UNINETT* has had an *Ean* connection since 7 October 1984; this use of the **Ean** X.400 implementation has helped in MHS development. Because of the early start of the network, *UNINETT* could not take advantage of many ISO-OSI protocol specifications. It developed its own Uninett protocols, such as UFTP for file transfer. These are used in some other networks, such as *SUNET*. *UNINETT* also uses other protocols such as DECNET and Coloured Books.

Plans

In addition to the historical network *UNINETT*, there is a specifically ISO-OSI-based research network by the same name. An organization for this new *UNINETT* was set up by the Ministry of Cultural and Scientific Affairs in May 1987. The network is intended eventually to encompass all institutions of higher education in Norway, with perhaps 20,000 employees and 100,000 students. A related pilot project in primary and secondary schools may interconnect. All the usual services (mail, file transfer, RJE, database access, remote login, conferencing, and network management) are wanted. In addition, there is a strong emphasis on reliability (goals of 95 percent of mail delivered nationally within five minutes and 99 percent within an hour), speed (64Kbps links between universities), and support (online help services staffed during regular working hours).

Numerous existing networks extend into Norway. The machine *ndosl* serves as the national backbone for *EUnet*, which has about 600 users on 30 machines in Norway. There are also connections to *EARN* (500 users and four nodes), *HEPnet* (20 users and two nodes), and the *Internet* (200 users and 100 nodes), with *SATNET* gateway *tor.nta.no* at the Norwegian Telecommunications Administration (NTA).

Within the country, there is a national university library network called *BIBSYS*, with 500 users of seven nodes connected over leased lines with Uniscope. Some DECNET links over leased lines with Ethernet are used for supercomputer access by about 600 users from 90 nodes [Hansen 1987].

The hope is eventually to merge all these networks into one ISO-OSI research network. This is to be done in cooperation with COSINE. The first network to be affected is *EARN* [Hansen 1987]. Conversion to a national top level domain of *NO* is also in process. The old *UNINETT Ean* domain is still recognized by *EARN* and *BITNET*. Unfortunately, neither of the former *EARN* gateways to the *UNINETT* domain, *CERNVAX* (as of 10 January 1986) and *UWOCC1* (16 September 1986), pass traffic through anymore [Nussbacher 1987], although there are rumors that *CERNVAX* had resumed as of February 1988.

The *ARPANET* connection to Norway, which had existed for many years, was terminated on 15 August 1988 as part of the retirement of the *ARPANET*. Although there were plans at the time for a Scandinavian connection to the *Internet* (see the section on networks in Iceland), an interruption in such connectivity was caused, lasting through the end of 1988. However, it was still possible to relay mail (via *ENEA.SE*) through either *NORUNIX.BITNET* or *uunet.uu.net*. The usual relaying forms are:

> *user%domain*.NO@NORUNIX.BITNET
> *user%host*.UNINETT@NORUNIX.BITNET
> *user%domain*.NO@UUNET.UU.NET
> *user%host*.UNINETT@UUNET.UU.NET

BITNET and *EARN* users probably noticed no change, since both the *NO* and *UNINETT* top level domains were already relayed through *NORUNIX.BITNET* [Christophersen 1988].

Access
Petter Kongshaug
kongshaug@vax.runit.unit.uninett
kongshaug%vax.runit.unit.uninett@norunix.bitnet
kongshaug%vax.runit.unit.uninett@tor.nta.no
+47 7 592991 (Direct)

Alf Hansen
alf-hansen%vax.runit.unit.uninett@norunix.bitnet
alf-hansen%vax.runit.unit.uninett@uunet.uu.net
+47 7 592982 (Direct)
+47 7 593100 (Switchboard)
Telex: 55620 SINTF N
RUNIT-D
N-7034 Trondheim
Norway

13.21   *Sweden {SE}*

Various component networks in Sweden are organized into the national network *SUNET*. There is a notable academic and research conferencing system, *QZCOM*. The machine *enea* serves as the national backbone for *EUnet*.

Access

Bjorn Eriksen
ber@enea.uucp
+46 8 7567220
ENEA DATA AB
Taeby
Sweden

13.21.1   SUNET

SUNET, or the Swedish University Network, interconnects local and regional networks at universities in Sweden. The goal of *SUNET* is to provide good data communications that are beneficial to the universities. The network is used by researchers and teachers of all disciplines [Wallberg 1988].

Administration

The operation and management is distributed to a few departments at different universities. The network is administered and coordinated centrally by Umeå universitets datorcentral (UMDAC), or Umea University Computing Centre, on behalf of Universitetsoch högskoleämbetet (UHÄ) [Wallberg 1988].

Protocols

The *SUNET* backbone is a star network centered on Kungliga Tekniska Högskolan (KTH), or Royal Institute of Technology, in Stockholm. There are six 64Kbps lines interconnecting local Ethernets to one national

Ethernet. Vitalink Translan bridges connect the Ethernets to the serial lines; cisco routers are used to route IP traffic, and Digital MicroVAXes are used to route DECNET traffic.

There is also an old X.25 network in parallel with the national Ethernet backbone. It consists of local X.25 switches that are connected to the *Datapak* X.25 service of the Swedish PTT, as well as local X.25 PAD units. The X.25 network is used for international traffic, connections to computers outside the university Ethernets, and backup for the backbone DECNET.

Several logical networks are carried over the *SUNET* backbone Ethernet:

- A DECNET network with more than 400 hosts and an address space (area numbers 56−60) coordinated with *NORDUnet*, *SPAN*, and *HEPnet*
- A TCP/IP network with about 1,300 hosts, and one Class B IP network number for each university, registered with SRI-NIC in the *Internet* address space
- An NJE *EARN* subnetwork

SUNET is similar to *NORDUnet* in protocol and network composition.

Mail is transported over all the constituent networks of *SUNET*. There are two interconnected central mail hubs. The first is for SMTP and **VMS** mail at KTH in Stockholm. It also handles *EARN* and *EUnet* traffic. The second one is for **Ean** X.400 mail at the Chalmers Tekniska hogskola (Chalmers), or Chalmers Institute of Technology, in Gothenburg. The main *EARN* gateway is at *SEARN.BITNET* of the QZ UniversitetsData AB (QZ), or Stockholm University Computing Centre. *SUNET* is also connected to *NORDUnet* (at KTH), and connections through *NORDUnet* to *SPAN*, *HEPnet*, and *NSFNET* are planned [Wallberg 1988]. The *HEPnet* connection was operational in May 1989.

History

When *SUNET* began in 1980, the original basic service was remote login by X.25 over the PTT *Datapak* [Carlson 1986; Carlson 1987]. In 1985, the Swedish Science Foundation funded the second stage of *SUNET* development. A Swedish national DECNET was installed with a 64Kbps backbone. On 1 July 1988, *SUNET* became a permanent activity financed by UHÄ [Wallberg 1988]. *SUNET* is a NORDUNET participant, has had an *Ean* connection since 9 December 1984, and is a Full National Member of RARE.

Access

Hans Wallberg
hwg@BIOVAX.UMDC.UMU.SE
hwg@SEUMDC51.BITNET
+46 90 16 56 45
UMDAC
S-901 87 Umea
Sweden

13.21.2   QZCOM

The *QZCOM* directory service of Stockholm University Computing Centre
(QZ), using the COM conferencing protocol and software, has information
on user names and telephones and on electronic and postal addresses,
conferences, and connections to other networks. *QZCOM* has about 1,700
regular users. There are actually two databases: *QZCOM.BITNET* or
QZCOM.QZ.SE is the English-language one, and is mostly used by RARE,
while *QZKOM.BITNET* or *KOM.QZ.SE* is in Swedish. There are plans for
merging the two databases, perhaps by 1 July 1989 [Palme 1988].

Software

The software used in *QZCOM* is called **COM**. **PortaCOM** is a different
implementation of the same facilities [Palme 1984a]. As the name indicates,
PortaCOM is portable to various operating systems, including **VMS**,
Sperry **1100**, CDC **NOS**, Siemens **BS2000**, IBM **MVS/TSO** and **VM/CMS**,
Burroughs **B7800**, and **UNIX**. There are four different levels of security of
conferences, and electronic mail is also supported. Both menus and commands are supported [KOMunity 1987].

   The **COM** and **PortaCOM** software is used at more than 20 locations
in Europe and North America [Palme 1984a]. For example, **PortaCOM** is
used in *EuroKom* [Palme 1987a].

Interconnections

There are mail connections from *BITNET* (*QZCOM.BITNET* or
QZKOM.BITNET), *EUnet*, *JANET*, *CSNET* [Palme 1984a], *NORDUnet*, and
through the latter to *NSFNET* (*QZCOM.QZ.SE* or *KOM.QZ.SE*). Incoming
mail can be sent into conferences, as well as to people's private mailboxes
[Palme 1984b].

History

The original **COM** software was developed for the Swedish National
Research Institute starting in 1977 [Meeks 1985] and was operational in
1978. The new software was influenced by *EIES* and *PLANET*, but the
developers chose to omit features of those previous systems as well as to

select others for use [Palme 1988]. **COM** was completely rewritten in 1982 [Palme 1987a].

PortaCOM was finished by 1984 [Palme 1984a] and was developed by a Swedish company with a contract with the European Community (EC), using EC funds as well as funds from non-EC countries [Palme 1988]. The first implementation of **PortaCOM** was done in Sweden, but ports were later done involving QZ, Josef Stefan Institute (JSI) in Yugoslavia, ENEA of Sweden, Oslo University (OU) in Norway, University of Duesseldorf (Duesseldorf) in Germany, Helsinki University of Technology (HUT) in Finland, University of Aarhus (Aarhus) in Denmark, and CSATA in Bati, Italy, with some financial support from the EC. Further development and marketing were delegated by the EC to QZ [KOMunity 1987].

Plans

There are plans for changing *QZCOM* to the **SuperCOM** software, which is intended to be better than the present **COM** software or the **PortaCOM** software. In particular, it will be decentralized (maintaining conferences across multiple hosts and capable of separating user interface processing from information database handling); support more users (hundreds simultaneously and tens of thousands in all); have a new, hierarchical information organization; be compatible with X.400 while maintaining the present *EARN* and *Internet* compatibility; have a common interface for conferencing, mail, and database functions; and be written in portable code in the **C** programming language on **UNIX** [Palme 1987a]. Beta test is expected in 1989 [Palme 1988].

AMIGO is a European research project in distributed conferencing, planned in the following three phases [Palme 1987a]:

1. Pilot experiments, such as the one described below as **AMIGO** at *QZCOM*
2. Pilot protocols to test basic issues
3. Advanced results, which are not yet implementable [Palme 1988]

AMIGO at *QZCOM* allows access to *QZCOM* information for those who do not have *QZCOM* accounts. Requests should be sent to

DIRECT@QZCOM.BITNET

in RFC822 format (BSMTP for *BITNET*, *EARN*, or *NetNorth*) with the actual commands in the text of the message. Commands are generally of the form

Command (name typelist)

where the literal parentheses are required, as in

DESCRIBE (AMIGO NAME)

In addition, there is a help command, which does not require parentheses. The most basic help command is

HELP

and returns a description of the **AMIGO** service itself [Palme 1987b].

Access
Jacob Palme
jacob_palme_qz@qzcom.bitnet
JPALME@QZCOM.BITNET
+46 8 665 4513
Telex: 10366

13.22   *European Free Trade Area*

The European Free Trade Area (EFTA) is composed of countries that are in some sense neutral in the modern tensions between Eastern and Western Europe and have banded together for economic advantage.

13.23   *Switzerland {CH}*

There is a national Swiss research network, *SWITCH*. The national *EUnet* backbone host is *cernvax* at CERN, the European particle physics research center.

13.23.1   **SWITCH**

SWITCH is a national Swiss research network that uses X.25 [Carpenter et al. 1987].

13.23.1.1   *CERN*

As already noted in Section 10.4, The European Laboratory for Particle Physics, Organisation Européenne pour la Recherche Nucléaire (CERN), is one the networking centers of the world, connecting every European continental network, including *HEPnet*, *EARN*, *EUnet*, and the *Ean* networks. CERN has obtained an unusual relaxation of restrictions on third-party switching from the Swiss PTT for this purpose. CERN is also a testbed for local area networking technology, for interconnection of networks, and for protocol suites, due to its large number of computers, many Ethernet (and 8802/5 token ring) local area networks, and use of CERNNET (a locally-developed set of protocols), TCP/IP, DECNET, SNA, TP4, and X.400. The international character of the institution itself helps it to play a leading role in European networking [Carpenter et al. 1987].

Access

Brian Carpenter
brian@priam.cern.ch
brian@cernvax.bitnet
DD Division
CERN
CH-1211 Genève 23
Switzerland

13.24   *Austria {AT}*

There are local branches of *EARN* and *EUnet* in Austria, plus *ACONET*, an academic and research network, and *UNA*, a university network [Paul and Kunft 1987].

EUnet

Installation of the first Austrian node on *EUnet* was made possible by a grant from the Bundesministeriums für Wissenschaft und Forschung (BMWF), or Ministry of Science and Research. This was done in 1985 using a machine owned by the Institut für Praktische Informatik (IPI), or Institute for Practical Computer Science, of the Technischen Universität Wien (TUW), or Technical University of Vienna. The actual connection was assisted by the Interuniversitären EDV-Zentrums Wien (IUEDVZW), or Interuniversity Division of the Education Center of Vienna, which maintains the current official Austrian *EUnet* backbone node, *tuvie*. This node was officially put into service on 1 August 1986. There were about a dozen *EUnet* hosts in Austria in June 1987 and 30 in May 1988.

The backbone host *tuvie* is a MicroVAX II running Digital's **ULTRIX-32** version of the **UNIX** operating system. It uses UUCP and **sendmail** for *EUnet* mail connections. A news feed was imported starting in 1987 when enough disk space became available. Guest accounts are made available for people who have no other access to *EUnet*. There is also an Ethernet and DECNET connection over *TUNET* (the campus network of TUW) to a

VAX-11/780 on *UNA*. Automatic mail forwarding between *EUnet* and *UNA* is not yet set up but is expected soon. The machine *tuvie* can also be reached for remote login from the Austrian PDN *DATEX-P* and from the local Viennese packet network *PACX*, or Private Automatic Computer Exchange [Paul and Kunft 1987].

> **Access**
>
> Friedrich Plank
> uunet!mcvax!tuvie!plank
> mcvax!tuvie!postmaster
> postmaster@tuvie.uucp
> +43 222 65 87 11 bis 13
> +43 222 58801/3608
> Technical University of Vienna
> EDP-Center, Process Computing Dept.
> Gusshausstrasse 25/0203
> A-1040 Vienna
> Austria

EARN

The first Austrian *EARN* connection was made in May 1985 from the Universität Linz (UL), or University of Linz. There were nine hosts at eight sites by April 1987. All the usual NJE services are supported. The main Austrian node on *EARN* is called *AEARN*, and there is a connection to its German counterpart, *DEARN*, in Darmstadt. There are plans for gateways to *EUnet* and *UNA* [Paul and Kunft 1987].

> **Access**
>
> K000163@AEARN.BITNET
> EARN@AWIWUW11.BITNET

13.24.1   ACONET

ACONET (Akademisches Computer Netz, or Academic Computer Network) is the long-haul research network in Austria. It reaches most institutions of research or higher education in Austria and has connections to *EUnet*, *EARN*, and *DATEX-P*, and to the rest of the world through them. Administration has been done since 28 May 1986 by an organization dedicated to that purpose, named after the network, and located in Vienna.

Services and Protocols

ACONET provides file transfer, remote login, and remote job entry. For the moment, it uses the Dienste vom Datenvermittlungssystem Nordrhein-Westfalen (DVS-NW) protocols, although there are plans to migrate to the CCITT and ISO-OSI protocols as they become available, probably starting with levels 4–6, particularly with TP4.

History

The idea for *ACONET* came from a workshop in June 1981 at the Technischen Universität Wien (TUW), or Technical University of Vienna. The main question at the workshop was how to connect the existing local area research networks with the PDNs. The long-haul network *ACONET* was invented for this purpose. A test network was set up in 1982 and 1983 among the Universities of Graz, Linz, and Vienna. Funding came from the Bundesministeriums für Wissenschaft und Forschung (BMWF), or Ministry of Science and Research. This network was used to implement TP0 above the X.25 service of the Austrian PDN *DATEX-P* [Paul and Kunft 1987].

> **Access**
>
> Walter Kunft
> mcvax!tuvie!kunft
> kunft@tuvie.uucp
>
> Manfred Paul
> mcvax!tuvie!mpaul
> mpaul@tuvie.uucp
>
> Technical University of Vienna
> EDP-Center, Process Computing Dept.
> Gusshausstrasse 25/0203
> A-1040 Vienna
> Austria
>
> ACONET-Verein
> Gußhausstraße 25/0203
> A-1040 Wien
> Austria

13.24.2   UNA

UNA (Universitäts-Netz Austria, or Austrian University Network) uses DECNET protocols to connect Digital computers at Austrian universities.

Services and Protocols

All of the connections for *UNA* are by X.25 over the Austrian PDN *DATEX-P*, using Packet Network System Interface (PSI) software to allow running DECNET. The usual services provided by these protocols are available. X.25 virtual circuits over *DATEX-P* are used to connect DECNET areas, which are then managed by the usual DECNET mechanisms.

Interconnections

The basic connection from *UNA* to the Austrian *EUnet* backbone host *tuvie* is already in place, and automatic gatewaying functions are being added. Connections to *EARN* and *DFN* are also in progress. There has been a connection between the Technischen Universität Wien (TUW), or Technical University of Vienna, and New Zealand since April 1987. Negotiations are in progress for integration with the wide area DECNET address space of *HEPnet*.

History

All Austrian universities already had Digital computers, but Digital donated further hardware and software to ease the establishment of the network. There were also grants from the Bundesministeriums für Wissenschaft und Forschung (BMWF), or Ministry of Science and Research. The desire of the academic sites for immediate service and for a DECNET-based network caused them to develop a closed and separate network instead of an open network.

Plans

There are plans to move away from being a vendor-specific network by taking three steps:

1. Expanding the basic network to include all 15 potential sites. Thirteen were connected in March 1987, so this step is mostly complete.
2. Connecting *UNA* to *EUnet*.
3. Conversion to ISO-OSI protocols, made possible when DECNET Phase V is available. Use of PSI is considered a preliminary for this step because PSI allows use of X.25, X.3, X.28, and X.29, which are not vendor-specific protocols, being CCITT recommendations. This package also allows reaching non-DECNET networks such as *DATEX-P*, and, through it, much of the world. In addition, *DFN* ISO-OSI software is being installed, such as that for remote job entry. There is X.400 testing in progress at Graz.

Eventually, *UNA* may merge with *ACONET* [Paul and Kunft 1987].

13.25 *Yugoslavia {YU}*

There is a PDN in Yugoslavia that may serve as a research network: *SIS*. The national Yugoslav backbone for *EUnet* is *krpan*.

13.25.1 SIS

The Yugoslavia PDN *SIS* is expected eventually to provide electronic mail, remote job entry, file transfer, and videotext. The name appears to come from Social Information System, after a federal law that was passed in 1983 to establish it. It was implemented by the PTT of Slovenia. The equipment used was chosen through an international request for proposals. The supplier chosen was Ericsson/Nokia of Sweden, and the software is **ERIPAX**. It currently provides X.25 (1984). Other equipment comes from Digital, IBM, and Honeywell. All packet switch nodes also emulate IBM SDLC 3270 and IBM BSC 2780/3780 protocols. Various interfaces are supported. Speeds range from 1200bps to 19200bps. Adherence to ISO standards is a basic tenet, as is participation in COSINE and RARE. Apparently there are no international connections and no participation in *IPSS* [Jerman-Blazic 1988].

13.26   *Turkey {TR}*

There is an *EARN* host in Izmir, Turkey, connected to Montpellier, France.

13.27   *Eastern Europe*

The countries of Eastern Europe are described below in geographical order from north to south.

There have been few network connections to the Soviet Union or related countries from other regions. This is partly due to reluctance on the part of the governments of those countries to allow communication of this sort. There are also limitations accompanying export licenses on software and hardware from the United States. The latter have a particular effect on Europe and are a main reason for the paucity of communications between Western and Eastern Europe. The advent of *glasnost* in the Soviet Union seems to be having some effect on the situation, however.

13.27.1   IASnet

IASnet is a "network for Socialist countries" [Alexandrov 1988a]. It is a star network, with the central host at the Institute for Automated Systems (IAS) in Moscow. There are X.25 connections to leading institutes of informatics in Bulgaria, Hungary, East Germany, Poland, Czechoslovakia, Cuba, Mongolia, and Vietnam. These institutes have access to Soviet and foreign databases over the network. Access from IAS to other networks is by X.75 through *RADAUS*, the Austrian PDN run by Radio Austria (RADAUS), and via an X.25 line to *Datapak* (the Finnish PDN). There are conferences in English, Russian, and French [Alexandrov 1988b]. *IASnet* was still being implemented in August 1988 [Alexandrov 1988a].

13.28   *Union of Soviet Socialist Republics {SU}*

There are several large networks in the Soviet Union. *Academnet* connects research and academic institutions to the Institute for Automated Systems (IAS) in Moscow, while *Adonis* does the same for computer centers; the latter appears to be the local equivalent of *EARN* or *BITNET*, and *EARN* has had a connection request from IAS since 1988. There is a connection between Moscow and San Francisco, the so-called San Francisco – Moscow Teleport, or *SFMT*. And the famous hot line between the Kremlin and the White House is a data link, not a voice link.

An unusual example of international connectivity happened on the mornings of 6 and 9 March 1986, when the Soviet spacecraft VEGA-1 and VEGA-2 passed by Halley's comet within about 10,000 kilometers. The IKI spaceflight center in Moscow cooperated with the European Space Operations Centre (ESOC) of the European Space Agency (ESA) in Darmstadt, West Germany, in transferring about 1Mbyte of results over a 9600bps link using Kermit. Part of the data transferred came from a U.S. dust particle mass spectrometer aboard the spacecraft. European and American scientists at ESOC used this information to decide on the closeness to which the ESA craft Giotto would approach the same comet a few days later. Giotto passed within 550 kilometers of Halley's comet on 13 March 1986, with an orbital error of 20 kilometers, compared to the 300 kilometer error that would have obtained without data from VEGA [de Broeck 1987].

The term *data processing distributed systems (DPDS)* is also used in the USSR for wide area computer networking. The main protocols used are X.25, SNA, DNA, and Ethernet. The ISO-OSI reference model is adhered to [Abbasov 1987].

13.28.1   **Academnet**

Academnet connects institutes in the republics of the Soviet Union to the Institute for Automated Systems (IAS) in Moscow. In August 1988, there were connections to Leningrad, Riga, Kiev, Novosibirsk, and Dushanbe. Its purpose is the same as that of *IASnet* — that is, access to Soviet and foreign databases [Novosti 1987; Alexandrov 1988a; Alexandrov 1988b].

13.28.2   **Adonis**

Adonis is run by the Institute for Automated Systems (IAS) in Moscow and connects computer centers in the Soviet Union. It was still being set up in August 1988 [Alexandrov 1988a]. This is apparently an **RSCS** NJE network.

13.28.3   ANAS

The administrative network of the Azerbaijan SSR Academy of Sciences (ANAS) is used for information management among three geographically separated subdivisions of ANAS. It uses X.21 at the physical layer and X.25 at the data link and network layers to connect four CM-4 minicomputers, using Electronica-60, Mera-60, and ISKRA-226 microcomputers as intelligent terminals [Abbasov 1987]. The transport protocol is NSP, and DNA is apparently a USSR standard [Vasilyev 1986; Makhmudov and Abbasov 1986]. Electronic mail, remote login, and other services are supported on *ANAS*.

13.28.4   SFMT

This connection between major cities in the United States and the Soviet Union began as an experiment on *EIES* but was advised to shut down by informal communications from the U.S. government. Formal legal inquiries eventually resulted in formal approval. The link is also approved by the government of the USSR.

The link currently connects the *PeaceNet* machine in San Francisco with a machine named *uniipas* at the Academy of Sciences, Ministry of Communications, Moscow. The international link goes through Helsinki or Vienna on dedicated lines. In Moscow there is a 2400bps dialup modem with MNP error correction, which was delivered from the United States. MNP was necessary due to noisy Moscow telephone lines. There are about 12 people in Moscow with appropriate modems to connect to that one: some of these people are prominent critics of the Soviet government.

> **Access**
> Debbie Miller
> +1-415-931-8500
> San Francisco/Moscow Teleport (SFMT)
> 3278 Sacramento Street
> San Francisco, CA 94115
> U.S.A.

13.29   *Poland {PL}*

There is a Polish connection to *IASnet*.

During the protest years of the early eighties, the union Solidarnosc (Solidarity) used personal computers and floppy disks to transfer information. One advantage was apparently the ease with which a floppy could be made unreadable simply by crushing it.

13.30   *Germany, Democratic Republic of {DD}*

There is a connection to *IASnet*.

13.31   *Czechoslovakia {CS}*

There is a connection from Czechoslovakia to *IASnet*.

13.32   *Hungary {HU}*

There is a connection to *IASnet* and a request for connection to *EARN*. The Hungarian UNIX User's Group has recently joined EUUG, which means that it has also joined *EUnet*.

13.33   *Romania {RO}*

There are no known systems in Romania.

13.34   *Bulgaria {BG}*

There is a connection from Bulgaria to *IASnet* and a request for connection to *EARN*.

13.35   *Albania {AL}*

There are no known systems in Albania.

13.36   *Bibliographic Notes*

A very useful book for understanding the European situation is Fredriksson et al. 1987. It contains not only overviews of the situations in various countries and international bodies, but also access information on a plethora of organizations having to do with computers, networking, and standards. A directory of *EUnet*, *EARN*, and *HEPnet* is published by EUUG for *EUnet* [Karrenberg and Goos 1988].

13.37   *References*

Abbasov 1987.   Abbasov, A. M., "Distributed Data Processing Systems: experience of implementation, analysis, and optimization," Azerbaijan SSR Academy of Sciences, Department of Automated Control Systems, Baku, ASSR, USSR, 1987.

ACOSITG 1987.   ACOSITG, *Transition to OSI Standards (White Book)*, Academic Community OSI Transition Group, July 1987.

Alexandrov 1988a.   Alexandrov, Sergei, Personal communications, August 1988.

Alexandrov 1988b.   Alexandrov, Sergei, Personal communications, May 1988.

Barberá and Martinez 1988.   Barberá, J., and Martinez, I., "IRIS: Spanish Networking Program for the R&D Sector," *Proceedings of the International Academic Networkshop (Jerusalem, 26 – 28 October 1988)*, Programa IRIS, Fundesco, Alcala 61, 28014 Madrid, Spain, 1 September 1988.

Barberá 1988.   Barberá, José, "Brief Description of IRIS," Programa IRIS, Fundesco, Alcala 61, 28014 Madrid, Spain, 1988.

Bauerfeld 1988a.   Bauerfeld, Wulfdieter, "TCP/IP im DFN, Teil I," *DFN Mitteilungen*, no. 11, pp. 9 – 11, March 1988.

Bauerfeld 1988b.   Bauerfeld, Wulfdieter, "OSI statt TCP/IP im DFN, Teil II," *DFN Mitteilungen*, no. 12, pp. 19 – 23, June 1988.

Beertema 1988a.   Beertema, Piet, Personal communications, June 1988.

Beertema 1988b.   Beertema, Piet, Personal communications, December 1988.

Birkenbihl and Mertens 1987.   Birkenbihl, Klaus, and Mertens, Burkhard, "Ein Netz der Grossforschungseinrichtungen," *DFN Mitteilungen*, no. 9/10, November 1987.

BITNIC 1988.   BITNIC, "BITNET Maps," BITNIC, New York, 25 April 1988.

Blokzijl 1988.   Blokzijl, Rob, Personal communications, October – November 1988.

Brunell 1988.   Brunell, Mats, "NORDUNET and the NORDUnet network," NORDUNET, September 1988.

Brunell and Loevdal 1988.   Brunell, Mats, and Loevdal, Einar, "NORDUNET and the NORDUnet overview," NORDUNET, September 1988.

Brunell et al. 1988.   Brunell, Mats, Lunds, Jan Engvald, Salminen, Harri, Soerensen, Jan P., and Torbergsen, Roald, "X.EARN," NORDUNET, 23 March 1988.

Bryant 1987.   Bryant, Paul, "EARN Migration Plans," European Academic Research Network, Rutherford Appleton Laboratory, Didcot, Oxfordshire, England, 20 April 1987.

Bryant 1988.   Bryant, Paul, Personal communications, 13 September 1988.

Camacho 1988.   Camacho, Angel J., "Spanish HEPNET (FAENET) User Guide," Grupo de Altas Energias, Dpto. Fisica Moderna, Universidad de Cantabria, Santander, Spain, December 1988.

Carlson 1986.   Carlson, Birgitta, "NORDUNET: The Nordic Countries National University Networks," *Proceedings of the International Conference on Information Network and Data Communication (Ronneby Brunn, Sweden, 11 – 14 May 1986)*, no. 7, IFIP TC.6, Elsevier, Amsterdam, 1986.

Carlson 1987.   Carlson, Birgitta, "NORDUNET: Cooperation between five Nations," *DFN Mitteilungen*, no. 7, pp. 9 – 12, March 1987.

Carpenter et al. 1987.   Carpenter, B. E., Fluckiger, F., Gerard, J. M., Lord, D., and Segal, B., "Two Years of Real Progress in European HEP Networking: A CERN Perspective," *Computer Physics Communications*, vol. 45, pp. 83 – 92, August 1987.

Christophersen 1988.   Christophersen, Alf, "Changes of .NO and UNINETT addresses," *info-nets@think.com*, BITNET, Internet, Oslo, 31 August 1988.

Clark 1988.   Clark, Tim, *Mail Gateway Hints*, University of Warwick, Warwick, England, 22 January 1988.

Collinson 1988. Collinson, Peter, Personal communications, September 1988.

Connes and Ippolito 1986. Connes, Mrs. Janine, and Ippolito, Mr. Jean-Claude, "REUNIR," REUNIR, Paris, 29 July 1986.

Cook 1988. Cook, Gordon, Personal communications, November 1988.

COSMOS 1988a. COSMOS, COSMOS Information Exchange Network Newsletter, BTI, Ipswich, November 1988.

COSMOS 1988b. COSMOS, "COSMOS, A Research Program into Group Work," BTI, Ipswich, 1988.

Dallas 1988. Dallas, Ian, Personal communications, September 1988.

de Broeck 1987. de Broeck, Paul, "Kermit Aids in Giotto Project," *Kermit News*, vol. 2, no. 1, p. 5, November 1987.

Demco 1988. Demco, John, Personal communications, August 1988.

Devillers 1988a. Devillers, Yves, Personal communications, December 1988.

Devillers 1988b. Devillers, Yves, Personal communications, 5 October 1988.

Devillers 1988c. Devillers, Yves, "Futur Immediat de FNET et de ses Couts," *Tribunix: Bulletin de Liaison de l'AFUU*, vol. 4, no. 18, pp. 8–12, Association Française des Utilisateurs d'UNIX, Supelec, Plateau du Moulon, 91190 Gif-sur-Yvette, France, January/February 1988.

Devillers and Pays 1988. Devillers, Yves, and Pays, Paul-Andre, Personal communications, December 1988.

Disney 1988. Disney, Mike, "Ten years ago...," *Starlink Bulletin*, vol. 1, no. 2, pp. 2–3, Rutherford Appleton Laboratory, June 1988.

Disney and Wallace 1982. Disney, M. J., and Wallace, P. T., "STARLINK," *Quarterly Journal of the Royal Astronomical Society*, vol. 23, no. 4, pp. 485–504, December 1982.

Elsner 1988. Elsner, Frank, Personal communications, 16 August 1988, 4 November 1988.

Fluckiger 1988. Fluckiger, François, Personal communications, November 1988.

Fredriksson et al. 1987. Fredriksson, E. H., Bus, J. C. P., and Wedgwood, C. G., *Information Technology Atlas Europe*, Elsevier, Amsterdam, 1987.

Goos 1988a. Goos, Anke, "Crisis, what Crisis?," *EUUG Newsletter*, vol. 8, no. 4, European UNIX systems User Group, Buntingford, Herts., England, Winter 1988.

Goos 1988b. Goos, Anke, Personal communications, 16 November 1988.

Greisen 1988. Greisen, Frode, "India, USSR etc," *EARN-UG@IRLEARN.BITNET (EARN Users Group Discussion List)*, 2 September 1988.

Hansen 1987. Hansen, Alf, "OSI Introduction in R&D Networking in Norway," *Proceedings of the International Academic Networkshop (Princeton, New Jersey, 9–11 November 1987)*, 1987.

Hapgood 1986. Hapgood, M. A., "Access to the Space Physics Analysis Network (SPAN): A Guide for JANET users," *RAL Technical Reports*, Rutherford Appleton Laboratory, Chilton, Didcot, Oxfordshire, England, October 1986.

HEA 1986. HEA, *Getting Started on the VAX*, HEA, Dublin, Ireland, 1986.

Huitema 1987a. Huitema, Christian, Personal communications, 29 September 1987.

Huitema 1987b. Huitema, Christian, "The ARISTOTE network: status at the end of 1987," *Proceedings of the International Academic Networkshop (Princeton, New Jersey, 9–11 November 1987)*, INRIA, Centre de Sophia Antipolis, Valbonne, France, 2 November 1987.

Huitema 1988a. Huitema, Christian, "Présentation d'Aristote," INRIA Centre de Sophia Antipolis, Valbonne, France, 4 May 1988. Draft A13, Version 5.

Huitema 1988b. Huitema, Christian, Personal communications, September 1988.

Huitema 1988c. Huitema, Christian, "A proposal for a naming, data structures, and name data distribution in RARE," RARE, Amsterdam, March 1988.

Huizer 1988. Huizer, Erik, Personal communications, December 1988.

Hutton 1988.   Hutton, James S., Personal communications, September 1988, 14 December 1988.

IBM.   IBM, "X.25 SNA Interconnection, General Information," IBM.

Jennings 1987.   Jennings, Dennis M., "Computing the best for Europe," *Nature*, vol. 329, no. 29, pp. 775 – 778, October 1987.

Jennings 1988.   Jennings, Dennis M., Personal communications, December 1988.

Jerman-Blazic 1988.   Jerman-Blazic, Borka, "Experiences of Introducing and Developing a Public Data Network," *Proceedings of the Special Conference of the International Council for Computer Communication (New Delhi, 17 – 30 October 1987)*, Elsevier, Amsterdam, November 1988.

Karrenberg 1988a.   Karrenberg, Daniel, "EUnet and ISO Transition Plans," *EUUG Conference Proceedings (Cascais, Portugal, 3 – 7 October 1988)*, pp. 107 – 113, European UNIX systems User Group, Buntingford, Herts., England, 1988.

Karrenberg 1988b.   Karrenberg, Daniel, "EUnet Update," *EUUG Newsletter*, vol. 8, no. 1, pp. 36 – 40, European UNIX systems User Group, Buntingford, Herts., England, Spring 1988.

Karrenberg and Goos 1988.   Karrenberg, Daniel, and Goos, Anke, *European R&D E-mail Directory*, European UNIX systems User Group, Buntingford, Herts., England, December 1988.

Kaufmann 1987.   Kaufmann, Peter, "Eine Zwischenbilanz," *DFN Mitteilungen*, no. 8, pp. 13 – 14, June 1987.

Kaufmann and Ullmann 1987.   Kaufmann, Peter, and Ullmann, Klaus, Personal communications, 7 October 1987.

Kille 1986.   Kille, S. E., "Mapping between X.400 and RFC822; RFC987," *ARPANET Working Group Requests for Comments*, June 1986.

KOMunity 1987.   KOMunity, "PortaCOM Computer Conferencing System," Komunity Software AB, Stockholm, Sweden, 1987.

Lawden 1988.   Lawden, Mike, "Not the Starlink Pie Chart," *Starlink Bulletin*, vol. 1, no. 2, p. 6, Rutherford Appleton Laboratory, June 1988.

Leguigner and Devillers 1988.   Leguigner, Jean-Paul, and Devillers, Yves, Personal communications, December 1988.

Loevdal and Brunell 1988.   Loevdal, Einar, and Brunell, Mats, "Current status for the NORDUnet Implementation," NORDUNET, 10 October 1988.

Lytel 1987.   Lytel, David, "Tout le Monde! C'est la Télématique Française," *Online Access*, pp. 42 – 43, November/December 1987.

Lytel 1988.   Lytel, David, "The Minitel Invasion," *Online Access*, pp. 11, 49, 60, January/February 1988.

Makhmudov and Abbasov 1986.   Makhmudov, Y. A., and Abbasov, A. M., "On Experience in Developing Experimental Networks for Similar minicomputers," *Control Systems and Computers*, no. 4, pp. 80 – 83, Naukova Dumka Publishers, 1986.

Mañas 1988.   Mañas, José A., "Mail Services (a perspective from dit.upm.es)," Dpt. Ingeniería Telemática, E.T.S.I Telecomunicación, Technical University of Madrid, Madrid, 17 November 1988.

Meeks 1985.   Meeks, Brock N., "An Overview of Conferencing Systems," *BYTE*, vol. 10, no. 13, pp. 169 – 184, December 1985.

NBS 1988.   NBS, "Government Open Systems Interconnection Procurement Specification (GOSIP)," Institute for Computer Sciences and Technology, National Bureau of Standards (NBS), Gaithersburg, MD, 24 August 1988.

Novosti 1987.   Novosti, "Publications for Computer Networking," *Soviet Data Center*, July 1987.

Nussbacher 1987.   Nussbacher, Henry, "Re: 'Free Lunch' ?," *MAIL-L@-BITNIC.BITNET*, BITNIC, BITNET, Tel Aviv, 8 February 1987.

Nussbacher 1988a.   Nussbacher, Henry, Personal communications, 8 August 1988.

Nussbacher 1988b. Nussbacher, Henry, "BITNET GATES Version 88.09," BITNET/EARN NETSERV, 25 August 1988.

Nyssen 1987. Nyssen, Marc, "EUnet in Belgium," Vrije Universiteit Brussel, Brussels, 29 September 1987.

Palme 1984a. Palme, Jacob, "The COM and PortaCOM Computer Conference Systems," Stockholm University Computing Centre—QZ, Stockholm, Sweden, 1 August 1984.

Palme 1984b. Palme, Jacob, "COM-RFCMAIL interface," Stockholm University Computing Centre—QZ, Stockholm, Sweden, 30 July 1984.

Palme 1987a. Palme, Jacob, "SuperCOM will replace COM," Stockholm University Computing Centre—QZ, Stockholm, Sweden, 10 July 1987.

Palme 1987b. Palme, Jacob, "QZCOM AMIGO Directory Service," Stockholm University Computer Centre—QZ, Stockholm, Sweden, 12 September 1987.

Palme 1988. Palme, Jacob, Personal communications, October–December 1988.

Paul and Kunft 1987. Paul, M., and Kunft, W., "Datennetze in Österreich," *DFN Mitteilungen*, no. 8, pp. 7–11, June 1987.

Postel and Reynolds 1984. Postel, Jonathan B., and Reynolds, Joyce, "Domain Requirements; RFC920," *ARPANET Working Group Requests for Comments*, October 1984.

Reid 1988. Reid, Brian, "Network Maps (DECWRL netmap 1.5)," DEC Western Research Lab, Palo Alto, 19 June 1988.

Salminen 1987. Salminen, Harri, "Background and goals of FUNET," NORDUNET, Otaniemi, Finland, 13 November 1987.

Salminen 1988a. Salminen, Harri, "Report of the EARN OSI Transition Team," EARN, September 1988.

Salminen 1988b. Salminen, Harri, Personal communications, September 1988.

Salminen 1988c. Salminen, Harri, "NORDUNET report," NORDUNET, 3 May 1988.

Salminen 1988d. Salminen, Harri, "Alternatives for multiprotocol networks," *comp.protocols.tcp-ip*, USENET, 19 July 1988.

Salminen 1988e. Salminen, Harri, "Finnish University and Research Network," *Proceedings of the International Academic Networkshop (Jerusalem, 26–28 October 1988)*, 1988.

Schafer et al. 1987. Schafer, Richard A., Goodman, Sara L., and O'Looney, Martina, *A VM/CMS User's Guide to Electronic Mail*, University College Dublin, 1987.

Simonsen 1988a. Simonsen, Keld Jørn, Personal communications, September 1988.

Simonsen 1988b. Simonsen, Keld Jørn, Personal communications, May 1988.

Sorensen 1988. Sorensen, Jan P., Personal communications, October 1988.

Spafford 1988. Spafford, Gene, "The USENET Backbone (Updated: 3 April 1988)," *news.misc, news.config*, USENET, 4 April 1988.

Spratt 1986. Spratt, E. Brian, "Networking Developments in the U.K. Academic Community," *Proceedings of the International Conference on Information Network and Data Communication (Ronneby Brunn, Sweden, 11–14 May 1986)*, IFIP TC.6, Elsevier, Amsterdam, 1986.

Starlink 1988a. Starlink, "Worldwide Distribution of the Starlink Software Collection," *Starlink Bulletin*, vol. 1, no. 1, p. 1, Rutherford Appleton Laboratory, January 1988.

Starlink 1988b. Starlink, "Starlink user population growth," *Starlink Bulletin*, vol. 1, no. 1, p. 3, Rutherford Appleton Laboratory, January 1988.

Stefansson 1988. Stefansson, Gunnar, Personal communications, August–September 1988.

Terrett 1988. Terrett, Dave, "VAXnotes—electronic conferencing," *Starlink Bulletin*, vol. 1, no. 2, p. 6, Rutherford Appleton Laboratory, June 1988.

Vasilyev 1986. Vasilyev, G. P., *Heterogenous Systems Software*, Finansy i Statistika, Moscow, 1986. In Rus, that is, Ukrainian.

Virtanen 1988.   Virtanen, Jukka, Personal communications, September 1988.

Volk 1989.   Volk, Rüdiger, Personal communications, December 1988–January 1989.

Wallace 1988.   Wallace, Patrick, Personal communications, September 1988.

Wallberg 1988.   Wallberg, Hans, Personal communications, 13 November 1988.

Walsh 1988.   Walsh, Michael E., Personal communications, 12 December 1988.

Wells 1984.   Wells, M., "The JANET Project," *University Computing*, vol. 6, pp. 56–62, 1984.

Wunderling 1989.   Wunderling, Peter, Personal communications, December 1988, January 1989.

14 *Australasia*

This chapter on Australasia describes networks in Australia and New Zealand, plus any other networking activity in the South Pacific, such as rumors of connections to Fiji.

Some international networks, such as *USENET*, extend into this region. Others, described elsewhere, include *AUSEAnet*, which includes countries in Southeast Asia, and *PACNET*, which includes many countries in the Pacific basin.

14.1 *South Pacific Networks*

At least two networks cover the South Pacific: the local part of *USENET* and *SPEARNET*.

14.1.1 USENET in Australasia

The worldwide network *USENET* extends into Australia and New Zealand, as shown in Figure 14.1. In Australia, unlike much of the rest of the world, this network is not supported by the UUCP protocols at all, beyond the single gateway machine *munnari*. Instead, *USENET* news is mostly carried over the *ACSnet* SUN-III protocols.

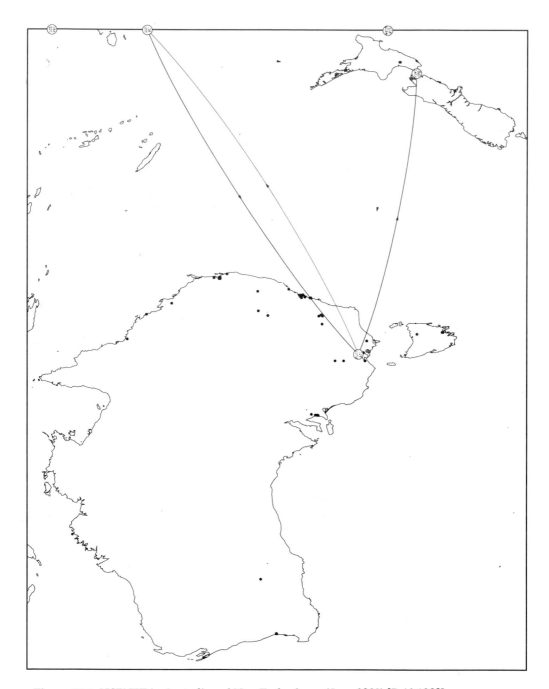

Figure 14.1. *USENET in Australia and New Zealand map (June 1989) [Reid 1989]*

14.1.2   SPEARNET

Universities in Australia and New Zealand formed *SPEARNET* in an attempt to improve computer mediated communications available for teaching and research [Hales and Richards 1987; Carss 1988a]. The name *SPEARNET*, or South Pacific Educational and Research Network, indicates hopes that the network will spread throughout the South Pacific [Rees 1988a]. The network has been partly operational since 1986. It connected eight sites in Australia as of October 1987 and 16 as of August 1988 [Rees 1988b]. All eight New Zealand universities were connected by August 1988. *SPEARNET* in New Zealand is primarily a university network and is the main university network in that country [Hine and Houlker 1987]. There were 22 hosts in December 1987 [Carss 1988b]. Initial services include remote login, file transfer, mail, news, conferencing, and remote job execution. This section describes both the existing network and plans for a national backbone network under the same name.

Protocols

At the moment *SPEARNET* uses the Coloured Book protocols because its proponents see them as a way of promoting international interoperability. The British national research network *JANET*, for which the Coloured Book protocols were developed, is to some extent a model for *SPEARNET*. Like *JANET*, and unlike *ACSnet*, *SPEARNET* has a centralized administration and obtains some funding from the government. Most of the machines on *SPEARNET* are VAXes running **VMS**, although any machine for which an implementation of the Coloured Book protocols exists can join—e.g., there is a Prime system at Massey University (Massey) in New Zealand [McEwan 1988]. Most of the links are by X.25 running over the PDNs *AUSTPAC* (Australia) and *PACNET* (New Zealand), and most links run at 2400bps or 9600bps. International connections between those two countries and to others (such as to *JANET* in the United Kingdom) use the international X.25 network [McEwan 1988].

Interconnections

SPEARNET addressing syntax, as shown in Table 14.1, is straightforward Grey Book at sign syntax with domains in *JANET* order, e.g.,

JOE@NZ.AC.AUKUNI

The actual format is somewhat site dependent because of the connection-oriented nature of X.25-based systems [Rees 1988b].

Table 14.1. *SPEARNET interconnections*

Network	Syntax
SPEARNET	*user@domain*
JANET	SPEARNET%AU.EDU.SYDNEY::*user*
JANET	SPEARNET%AU.EDU.SYDNEY::*user*@{**JANET-domain**}
ACSnet	BUNYIP::"*user@domain*.{**ACSNET-domain**}"
Internet	BUNYIP::"*user@domain*.{**DNS**}"
BITNET	BUNYIP::"*user@host*.BITNET"
INFOPSI	PSI%<X.121>::*user*

JANET	The first syntax indirecting through *AU.EDU.SYDNEY* is a slight variation of standard Coloured Book addressing, which is seen in the second syntax, and can also be used to reach *JANET*.
ACSnet	The syntax to reach *ACSnet* can also be used to reach other networks through *ACSnet*. The machine acting as gateway is *bunyip* or *AU.EDU.UQ.PCC.BUNYIP*. This machine is also known as *uqvax.decnet.uq.oz.au*, a MicroVAX running **Ultrix** in the Computer Centre of the University of Queensland (Queensland). Since every *SPEARNET* site also has an *ACSnet* host, any *SPEARNET* site could theoretically gateway between the two networks, and many do [Elz 1988a].
BITNET	The *BITNET* syntax is for relaying through *ACSnet*. Many *BITNET* hosts can be reached by using their DNS domain addresses, but those that don't have addresses can be reached by using the *BITNET* pseudodomain.

History

In 1984, several university computer centers applied for a grant from Digital for the establishment of a pilot network, knowing that proposals had been granted for similar networks in the United States. The name *SPEARNET* was invented at Queensland, and an announcement was made in March 1986 at a Digital seminar. The Coloured Book protocols were chosen because they were immediately available, even though Digital's implementation of some ISO-OSI protocols was imminent. To pave the way for eventual ISO-OSI conversion, however, X.25 over *AUSTPAC* was chosen as infrastructure rather than the dedicated lines of *JANET* [Hales and Richards 1987]. The original *SPEARNET* gateway to *ACSnet* was *BANANA*, an **Ultrix** MicroVAX in the Department of Computer Sciences.

Plans

The main technical reason why the proponents of *SPEARNET* in Australia want a network different from *ACSnet* is that they want more complete resource sharing capabilities: mail alone is specifically not enough [Carss 1988c]. There are also complaints that *ACSnet* message delivery, charging, and management are too ad hoc [Carss 1988b]. In addition, there is concern that the SUN-III protocols of *ACSnet* run only on **UNIX** [Carss 1988a]. There is no essential tie to either the Coloured Book protocols or **VMS**, and *SPEARNET* is expected to migrate to the ISO-OSI protocols eventually [Rees 1988b; Carss 1988c]. The CEN/CENELEC option sets will probably be used rather than the NBS ones [Carss 1988c].

There is hope that *SPEARNET* will evolve into a national backbone research network, somewhat like *NSFNET* or *BITNET* in the United States, or perhaps like RARE or *EARN* in Europe. A 2Mbps backbone, with costs shared among participating institutions, is recommended by a Joint Working Party of the Australian Committee on Data Processing (ACDP) of the Australian Vice Chancellor's Committee (AVCC) [Carss 1988a]. The specific recommended configuration is a linear network running through Townsville, Brisbane, Sydney, Canberra, Melbourne, Adelaide, and Perth. There is much less emphasis on supercomputer access and much more on database and library access than in *NSFNET* [Carss 1988b]. In addition to the usual services, there is hope that the backbone can also eventually support voice and Fax traffic [Carss 1988c].

Access

For *SPEARNET* in Australia, contact:

Graham Rees
ccrees@uqvax.decnet.uq.oz.au
+61 7 377 3288
Fax: +61 7 371 5896
Manager of Engineering and Communications
Prentice Computer Centre
University of Queensland
St. Lucia QLD 4067
Australia

For *SPEARNET* in New Zealand, contact:

Neil James
Director
Computing Services Centre
Otago University
P.O. Box 56
Dunedin
New Zealand

14.1.3   INFOPSI

The *INFOPSI* network is composed of Digital VAX and MicroVAX machines running Digital's standard Packet Network System Interface (**PSI**) mail software with **VMS**. **PSI** encapsulates DECNET over X.25. As of August 1988, there were about 20 sites in the research and academic world of Australia, and perhaps 50 sites in all, including commercial ones [Rees 1988b]. Many of the links are over *AUSTPAC* [Hales 1987]. There are now a number of sites in New Zealand as well.

All that is required to join *INFOPSI* is a **VMS** system running the **PSI** software and a host name and address list of the hosts on the network. Host names use a form similar to DNS domain names, allowing mail addressing to take forms such as

PSI%ANU.EDU.AU::*user*

where the PSI% prefix indicates the mail handler to use. This is not a store and forward network: the destination host has to be directly reachable, although retries will be done after a diagnostic is printed. There is no known gateway from *INFOPSI* to other networks [McEwan 1988].

There is also a file transfer facility, called **PSI_COPY**, which is similar to FTP [McEwan 1988].

14.2   *Australia {AU}*

Most hosts on at least *SPEARNET* and *ACSnet* can be reached through host names involving the *AU* top level domain.

There is much research regarding networking status [Hales and Richards 1987] and needs [Carss 1988b] in Australia, as well as plans for a national research network [Hales and Richards 1987], perhaps in cooperation with New Zealand [Carss 1988c]; much of this has been discussed previously under *SPEARNET*.

There is an Australian Bibliographic Network (*ABN*) operated by the Australian National Library. The participating libraries exchange catalog information on their holdings. ANL has said it will use the ISO-OSI protocols when implementations become available [Hales and Richards 1987].

Queensland Tertiary Institution Network (*QTInet*), which uses X.25 over leased lines at speeds of 2400bps to 9600bps, connects four and soon all seven institutions of higher education in Queensland [Rees 1988b]. These are known as *tertiary institutions*, hence the acronym in the network's name.

VICNET is a terminal network among the Victorian Colleges of Advanced Education and Institutes of Technology. It originally used statistical multiplexers to connect terminal switches, but migration to X.25 has been in progress since 1986 [Hales and Richards 1987]. There are a number of campus networks in Australia. The usual division is visible between VAX **VMS** machines in large computer centers and **UNIX** in computer science, electrical engineering, and other departments. The former tend to have local area DECNET networks connected to *SPEARNET*, while the latter tend to have TCP/IP networks connected to *ACSnet*. The most common underlying local area network technology in both cases is Ethernet [Hales and Richards 1987, 93].

14.2.1   Queensland

The University of Queensland (Queensland) has extensive DECNET and TCP/IP networks, as well as locally developed Digital MicroVAX II X.25 packet switch software, developed in 1986. There is also an Ethernet with fiber-optic links and terminal servers, as well as a MICOM PBX. There are about 2,000 IBM PCs and Apple Macintoshes on campus. This is the campus that invented *SPEARNET* [Rees 1988b].

14.2.2   Melbourne

The University of Melbourne (Melbourne) has machines ranging from a Cyber 990 and a Digital VAX 8650 cluster through an Elxsi and various smaller machines. Almost all international mail connections from Australia are from this campus and are described under *ACSnet* below.

14.2.3   ACSnet

ACSnet (Australian Computer Science Network) is the main network in Australia and is based on the Sydney UNIX Network (SUN) software developed at the University of Sydney [Dick-Lauder et al. 1984]. The network started in 1979 and connected a machine at Sydney to another at the University of New South Wales. It currently spans the continent and is closely connected to networks elsewhere [Kummerfeld 1985]. The purpose of the network is to support mail traffic and file transfer among researchers, academia, and industry. The underlying transport protocols are also used to support the *USENET* news network in Australia. There is no central administration, but this may change in the future. At present the original developers and the international gateway operator act as coordinators. There is no government funding: each host pays for its own links.

There were about 300 hosts throughout the Australian continent on *ACSnet* as of February 1987 [Hales and Richards 1987]. At least 21 academic institutions were connected to it as of July 1988; twice as many as to the next most popular network, *SPEARNET*, with 11 institutions, and many more than *CSIRONET*, with eight [Carss 1988b]. But connections are not limited to schools: government agencies and private companies are also connected [Hales and Richards 1987].

The original protocols were called SUN-I and supported remote login, file transfer, and multiplexed protocols. Dynamic routing was added in 1980 but was applied only to mail and file transfer. SUN-II was similar but allowed intermittent (dialup) links as well as dedicated ones, plus a method of layering SUN-II on top of other networks (such as *CSIRONET*). For details of the current, SUN-III protocols, see Chapter 4.

The links currently in use include leased lines, dialup lines, X.25, and *CSIRONET*. Most links run at 2400bps. There is a plan to migrate the system to X.400 in the next few years.

ACSnet has a domain naming syntax [Kummerfeld and Dick-Lauder 1985] similar to that for *Internet* DNS domains. The domain *OZ.AU* is registered with the *Internet* and may be interpreted as a subdomain, *OZ*, for *ACSnet*, of the country domain, *AU*, for Australia. There are subdomains within *OZ.AU*, many of which are for distributed organizations. Domains are used for routing in *ACSnet*, so connections between machines determine domains more than anything else. Hosts can register in any subdomain. In practice, this means major hosts are directly in *OZ* and everything else is in subdomains.

Interconnections

{ACSNET-domain} in Table 14.2 stands for the top level domain *OZ.AU*, by which *ACSnet* is known to most of the world.

There are several *UUCP* gateways to North America and Europe, all from Melbourne and all using X.25. The UUCP link to *uunet* is also used to import a *USENET* news feed. There is a *CSNET* link to the United States, as well as *Ean* links to Canada, the United Kingdom, Germany, Norway, and Switzerland. In addition, there are several 1200bps dialup links to North America (New Hampshire, New Jersey, and California). The main gateway machine is *munnari*, or *munnari.oz.au*.

Access

For general information, contact:

postmaster@munnari.oz.au
uunet!munnari!postmaster

For connection requests, contact:

acsnet-request@basser.oz.au
uunet!munnari!basser.oz!acsnet-request

ACSnet Coordinator
Department of Computer Science
University of Sydney
New South Wales 2006
Australia

Table 14.2. *ACSnet interconnections*

Network	Syntax
ACSnet	*user@domain.*{**ACSNET-domain**}
Internet	*user%domain.*{**DNS**}@munnari.oz
JANET	*user%domain.*{**JANET-domain**}@munnari.oz
Ean	*user%domain.*{**Ean-domain**}@munnari.oz
XEROX Internet	*user.*{**XEROX-domain**}%xerox.com@munnari.oz
Easynet	*user%host.*dec.com@munnari.oz
VNET	*user%host*%ibm.com@munnari.oz
BITNET	*user%host.*bitnet@munnari.oz
UUCP	*user%host.*uucp@munnari.oz
JUNET	*user%domain.*{**JUNET-domain**}@munnari.oz

14.2.4   CSIRONET

CSIRONET is a government research network named after the Commonwealth Scientific and Industrial Research Organization (CSIRO).

CSIRONET provides virtual circuits between host machines; link speeds have been 48Kbps since 1974. There were about 160 nodes as of February 1987 [Hales and Richards 1987], but it is unclear which of these were hosts and which were terminals. There were eight academic institutions connected to it as of July 1988 [Carss 1988b].

Services and Protocols

Services include mail, remote login, remote job entry, and file transfer. The protocols are peculiar to the network, but the file transfer protocol is related to the *JANET* Blue Book protocol. Migration to X.25 for the network layer has been in progress since 1984. Some *ACSnet* links run on top of *CSIRONET*.

Interconnections

There are no gateways between *CSIRONET* mail and any other mail network.

History

The name *CSIRONET* was used as early as 1962 to refer to a remote terminal facility that was used to connect to a CDC 3600 at the Black Mountain site of the Division of Computing Research (DCR) in Canberra. Special CDC display terminals were originally used, but a Digital PDP-8 was added for emulation so that less expensive kinds of terminals could be used. Actual jobs were submitted by shipping card decks by air freight. Digital

PDP-11s were installed at various sites in 1971 and interconnected to one in Canberra that was connected to the 3600. Homegrown protocols were used to implement a packet switched network over these links. The central machine was upgraded to a Cyber 76 in 1973; this machine was finally retired in November 1985. Connections to the PDNs *MIDAS* and *TYMNET* were added in the late 1970s to allow overseas access. The PDP-11s were replaced with machines based on Motorola MC68000 CPUs in 1980. An autonomous organization to run the network was established in January 1985 when its original sponsoring department, the DCR, was disbanded [Hales and Richards 1987].

Access
Trevor Hales
Group Leader and Officer-in-Charge
hales@ditmela.oz.au
+61 03 347 8644
Fax: +61 03 347 8987
Telex: AA 152914
Computer Networking Group
Division of Information Technology
CSIRO
55 Barry Street
Carlton, Victoria 3053
Australia

14.2.5   VIATEL

The Australian videotext network *VIATEL* is operated by the Overseas Telecommunications Commission (OTC). It also provides mail, Telex, and banking services and is used by many academic institutions to distribute information about their courses [Hales and Richards 1987].

14.2.6   Keylink 7

The Australian Overseas Telecommunications Commission (OTC) runs *Keylink 7*, which is equivalent to *Dialcom* [Castro 1987].

14.2.7   Keylink T

Telecom Australia runs *Keylink T*, which is equivalent to *Telemail* [Castro 1987]. There is an experimental X.400 link to *ACSnet* [Elz 1988b].

14.3　*New Zealand {NZ}*

There are various networking activities in New Zealand, most of them academic or research in nature. They often involve the seven universities, the Department of Scientific and Industrial Research (DSIR), and the Ministry of Agriculture and Fisheries (MAF). International connections are of particular importance to this country very far away from world centers of research activity [Hine and Houlker 1987].

Various technologies are used in connecting universities to one another. An NJE **RSCS** network spread from the Victoria University of Wellington (VUW) in 1984 to the University of Auckland (Auckland) in 1985. The initial connection was by a leased line, but there was not enough traffic to warrant its continuance, and intermittent X.25 connections over the PDN *PACNET* were substituted [McEwan 1988]. After experiments at the University of Waikato (Waikato) in 1985, DSIR and MAF agreed to join the seven universities in adopting *JANET* Coloured Book protocols, particularly Grey Book mail service, although MAF later pulled out of the agreement due to the cost of the software on some of its machines. There is an internal MAF network, but it has no gateway to it, although there are individual machines on *INFOPSI* and *UUCP* permitting MAF users to log onto those machines and thus to communicate with the rest of the world [McEwan 1988]. A unified national research internet is being attempted. There are currently gateways at VUW between *SPEARNET* and *DSIRnet* (gateway *com.vuw.ac.nz* or *vuwcom*) and between *UUCP* and *ACSnet* (*comp.vuw.ac.nz* or *vuwcomp*). These two machines are connected with TCP/IP over a campus Ethernet [McEwan 1988].

A TCP/IP link from VUW to Waikato is expected in early 1989, in anticipation of the *PACCOM* TCP/IP link from Waikato to Hawaii. There are proponents of developing a nationwide research network from this seed to include all the universities and DSIR, and perhaps other organizations as well [McEwan 1988]. Auckland has been proposing an international *BITNET* connection and an organization and network called *ANN*, for Australasian NJE Network, to affiliate with the *BITNET* organization. The original plans were to use NJE over intermittent X.25 PDN connections (emulating the VUW to Auckland link), but they may use the TCP/IP to Hawaii instead, running NJE over IP and using the **Urep** implementation from PSU. This is similar to an existing link at VUW over a local Ethernet, which has served to indicate the feasibility of the longer link [McEwan 1988].

There is an international SUN-III connection from *vuwcomp* to *munnari* at the University of Melbourne (Melbourne), Victoria, Australia, including a small *USENET* news feed. There are UUCP connections from *vuwcomp* to the University of Calgary (Calgary), Alberta, Canada, and to *uunet* in the

United States. The University of Canterbury (Canterbury) has UUCP links to *watmath* at the University of Waterloo (Waterloo), Ontario, Canada, and to *mcvax* at CWI, Amsterdam, Netherlands, on *EUnet*, but they do not act as a general gateway. There has been a gateway between *SPEARNET* and *CSNET* at Waikato since February 1987, and there are some New Zealand users of the San Diego Supercomputer Center (SDSC). Some links now use the PDN *PACNET* (no relation to the network of the same name that covers the Far East) [Hine and Houlker 1987]. A national administrative database provides ready access to statistics, regulations, policy decisions, and other material for administrators at institutions of higher education [Carss 1988b].

Interconnections

There are two main gateways from New Zealand to the rest of the world: a *CSNET* connection from Waikato and *UUNET* and *ACSnet* connections from VUW. The other five universities are on *SPEARNET* and relay through those two gateways using Grey Book mail. However, the **VMS** Grey Book implementation used at both gateways does not recognize the percent sign as an indication of indirection. To work around this deficiency, the VUW gateway recognizes syntax of the form

postmaster%*user*%*domain*@nz.ac.vuw

and the Waikato one recognizes the form

mailgate%*user*%*domain*@nz.ac.waikato

The special dummy local user *postmaster* or *mailgate* extracts the proper address and forwards the mail. Unfortunately, the two gateways do not agree on other matters: *nz.ac.vuw* expects *Internet* DNS addresses to be in Grey Book order (i.e., with *COM* first), while *nz.ac.waikato* expects the other order (i.e., *COM* last). However, only *SPEARNET* hosts know about Grey Book, and others, such as those on *DSIRnet*, can use DNS order with both gateways. Toward the end of 1988, some *SPEARNET* hosts were moving toward the use of **PMDF** over Blue Book to avoid this Grey Book implementation deficiency [McEwan 1988].

Many hosts on networks in New Zealand can be reached from elsewhere by domain names under the top level domain *NZ*. For *SPEARNET* and *JANET*, NRS order is used, as in

postmaster@nz.ac.vuw.com

For other networks, *Internet* DNS order is often used, as in postmaster@com.vuw.ac.nz

[McEwan 1988]. *UUCP* hosts that only understand bang source routes may route through *vuwcomp*, as in

uunet!vuwcomp!canterbury.ac.nz!postmaster

BITNET does not currently know how to route to *NZ* because the routing involves the gateways between *BITNET* and the *Internet*, which do not know about *MX records*: thus specific indirection such as

user%domain.nz@relay.cs.net

is required [McEwan 1988].

Access

postmaster@comp.vuw.ac.nz

John H. Hine
hine@comp.vuw.ac.nz
uunet!vuwcomp!hine
+64 4 715328
Department of Computer Science
Victoria University
Private Bag
Wellington
New Zealand

John C. Houlker
j.houlker@waikato.ac.nz
+64 71 62 889
Waikato University
Private Bag
Hamilton
New Zealand

14.3.1   DSIRnet

DSIRnet, named for the New Zealand government's Department of Scientific and Industrial Research (DSIR), was operational by 1977. It used protocols developed by DSIR and provided access by IBM 3270 emulation to several large government installations. An SNA emulation was developed to run on top of the DSIR protocols for remote login, job entry, and printing with IBM machines. Since 1980, Digital VAXes have become the most prevalent machines at DSIR (together with PDP-11s and AT&T 3B2 systems). In 1985, an X.25 PAD was added to allow DECNET access;

this also allows mail. A few sites use only DECNET protocols [Hine and Houlker 1987].

One node on *DSIRnet* runs Coloured Book software: *grv.dsir.govt.nz*. Most mail between DSIR and the outside world passes through a 9600bps DECNET link between a DSIR **VMS** VAX located on the campus of Victoria and one of the Victoria University of Wellington (VUW) **VMS** VAXes, *com.vuw.ac.nz*. Both machines run **PMDF** [McEwan 1988].

Access
Stephen White
srghspw@grv.dsir.govt.nz
postmaster@grv.dsir.govt.nz
Division of Information Technology
DSIR
P.O. Box 31311
Lower Hutt
New Zealand

14.4   *References*

Carss 1988a.   Carss, Brian, "Report of the AVCC/ACDP Joint Working Party on Networking: Executive Summary," AVCC/ACDP, Canberra, July 1988.

Carss 1988b.   Carss, Brian, "Report on the Survey of Needs and Uses of Computing Resources in Tertiary Institutions in Australia," AVCC/ACDP, Canberra, July 1988.

Carss 1988c.   Carss, Brian, "A Management Framework for a National, OSI Protocol Based Network for Australasian Tertiary Institutions," AVCC/ACDP, Canberra, July 1988.

Castro 1987.   Castro, Angela, Personal communications, October 1987.

Dick-Lauder et al. 1984.   Dick-Lauder, Piers, Kummerfeld, R.J., and Elz, Robert, "ACSNET—The Australian Alternative to UUCP," *Proceedings of the Summer 1983 USENIX Conference (Salt Lake City, Utah, 12–15 June 1984)*, pp. 11–17, USENIX Association, Berkeley, CA, 1984.

Elz 1988a.   Elz, Robert, Personal communications, July–August 1988.

Elz 1988b.   Elz, Robert, "Re: Access to KEYLINK Network," *info-nets@think.com*, USENET, Melbourne, 26 May 1988.

Hales 1987.   Hales, Trevor, "Australia," *Proceedings of the International Academic Networkshop (Princeton, New Jersey, 9–11 November 1987)*, 1987.

Hales and Richards 1987.   Hales, Trevor, and Richards, Ian, "A Review of Academic and Research Networking in Australia," Division of Information Technology, CSIRO, P.O. Box 1599, Macquarie Centre, North Ryde, NSW 2113, Australia, February 1987.

Hine and Houlker 1987.   Hine, John H., and Houlker, John C., "New Zealand's Academic Networks," *Proceedings of the International Academic Networkshop (Princeton, New Jersey, 9–11 November 1987)*, 1987.

Kummerfeld 1985.   Kummerfeld, R.J., "ACSnet: Current Status and Future Development," *Proceedings of PCCS (Seoul, October 1985)*, PCCS, Seoul, 1985.

Kummerfeld and Dick-Lauder 1985.   Kummerfeld, R.J., and Dick-Lauder, P.R., "Domain Addressing in SUN III," *Proceedings of the EUUG Paris 1985 Conference (Paris, 1985)*, European UNIX systems User Group, Buntingford, Herts., England, 1985.

McEwan 1988. McEwan, Duncan, Personal communications, 7 December 1988.

Rees 1988a. Rees, Graham, "South Pacific Education and Research Network: SPEARNET," *Proceedings of the Special Conference of the International Council for Computer Communication (New Delhi, 17 – 30 October 1987)*, pp. 17 – 33, Elsevier, Amsterdam, November 1988.

Rees 1988b. Rees, Graham, Personal communications, July 1988.

Reid 1988. Reid, Brian, "Network Maps (DECWRL netmap 1.5)," DEC Western Research Lab, Palo Alto, 19 June 1988.

15

Far East

The Far Eastern countries described in this chapter are the Republic of Korea (South Korea), Japan, Hong Kong, Taiwan Province of China, the People's Republic of China, the Democratic People's Republic of Korea (North Korea), and Mongolia.

15.1   *Pacific Networks*

A few networks are intended to cover the entire Pacific basin (eventually).

15.1.1   PACNET

PACNET is a logical grouping of Pacific hosts and organizations [Chon 1985a] that serves as an academic network for the region [Chon 1987]. It covers the Far East, Southeast Asia, and Oceania and is a cooperative network with no centralized administration or funding. South Korea (through *kaist* or *etrivax* on *SDN*) appears to have the most links, being connected directly to Malaysia, Singapore, Indonesia, Australia *(ACSnet)*, and Hong Kong, as well as to *mcvax* in Europe *(EUnet)* and *uunet* in the United States *(USENET* and *UUCP)*. Curiously enough, the only connection to *JUNET* in Japan from any of the *PACNET* countries seems to be through Europe or the United States. *CDNnet*, *CSNET*, and the *Internet* are indirectly reachable through *uunet*. Most connections are 2400bps dialup links. Mail and news are the only services generally supported.

PACNET began with a discussion about computer networks at a UNESCO workshop on 22–24 February 1984. The first organizational meeting was held at the first Pacific Computer Communications Symposium (PCCS) on 22 October 1985. Indirect connections were subsequently established using mailing lists and newsgroups distributed through the United States. The second *PACNET* meeting was held at the Fifth International Academic Networking Workshop (ANW) in Dublin, Ireland, on 10 September 1986. Direct connections among *PACNET* sites were discussed. The 1987 and 1988 *PACNET* meetings were held at the sixth and seventh ANW meetings.

Access
Kilnam Chon
chon@sorak.kaist.ac.kr
uunet!kaist!nmc
nmc%kaist.csnet@relay.cs.net
+82-2-962-5663
Fax: +82-2-962-8835
KAIST
P.O. Box 150
Chongryang
Seoul 131
Republic of Korea

15.1.2   PACCOM

PACCOM is an attempt to build a Pacific regional internet. This is to start with a viable infrastructure based on the emerging fiber-optic cable plant in the Pacific. The majority of these fiber-optic links go through Hawaii, and, partly for this reason, Hawaii is the initial center for this effort. Also, Hawaii is already connected to the *Internet* via a 56Kbps link to the West Coast of the United States, currently to the Jet Propulsion Laboratory (JPL) in Pasadena, California. Hawaii is also home to the largest collection of optical telescopes in the world, and there is substantial scientific interest in having good access to these and other unique research facilities in the State of Hawaii. Current funding for *PACCOM* is provided by the American National Aeronautics and Space Administration (NASA), the National Science Foundation (NSF), and the State of Hawaii.

Initial links are expected to be from Hawaii to Australia and New Zealand. The organizers hope for links to be added in the near future to Japan and to other regions in the Pacific. All links are expected to eventually use fiber optics. TCP/IP will be used, with *Internet* connections. DECNET will be supported over most links, and other protocols may also be used [Nielsen 1988].

Some links had been ordered in late 1988 [Jones and Hart 1988]. The New Zealand link will be at 19.2Kbps to University of Waikato (Waikato) [McEwan 1988], and the Australian one will be to the University of Melbourne (Melbourne) at 64Kbps. A 512Kbps fiber-optic link to the U.S. West Coast is scheduled to be in use by 1 April 1989. This will make Hawaii the westernmost point of the United States to be part of the *Internet* via a high-speed terrestrial connection [Nielsen 1988].

Access
Torben Nielsen
Torben_N_Nielsen@Hawaii.Edu
torben@nsipo.nasa.gov
+1-808-949-6395
Department of Computer Science
2565 The Mall
University of Hawaii
Honolulu, HI 96822
U.S.A.

15.2   *Korea, Republic of {KR}*

The Republic of Korea is the center of *PACNET*, and other international networks such as *BITNET* and *MILNET* extend there. There are also connections to *UUNET* and *CSNET*. The major national network is *SDN*, which supports the top level DNS domain *KR* and is described below.

15.2.1   SDN

The System Development Network (*SDN*) [Chon 1984; Chon 1985b] is a backbone network that interconnects local area networks of major sites. The intent of the network is to provide a facility for computer communications and resource sharing and a test environment for research and development communities in the Republic of Korea. Advanced research is being carried out in network software, international standards, and distributed systems.

Administration and Funding

Technical and administrative support has been provided by the Korea Advanced Institute of Science and Technology (KAIST) since 1983. The Network Management Center, located at KAIST, disseminates information and also maintains international and domestic contacts for administrative matters. Managerial decisions are made by an overseeing committee that consists of representatives of each site. The Electronics and Telecommunications Research Institute (ETRI), the Data Communications Company of Korea (DCCK), and KAIST are the major participants in the management and development of *SDN*.

Each site is charged the cost of its connections. International communications costs are charged proportionally. Expenses of protocol development and management, as well as international communication costs, are covered by national research grants, public corporations, and internal funding of several institutes.

Services

Virtual terminal, file transfer, mail (in both Korean and English), remote command execution, net news, and nameservices are supported.

Protocols

The standard protocol architecture in *SDN* is based on TCP/IP, and UUCP is also supported on all hosts. Some UUCP links run on top of TCP/IP on top of X.25. Links include leased phone lines and X.25 over *DACOM*, the domestic PDN, as well as local area networks. The international connections are based on X.25 and X.28/X.29 PADs. Some links run at 2400bps, but most links run at 9600bps. Reliability is high.

Naming, Addressing, and Routing

The top level domain name *SDN* has been used for years. Second level domains are usually host names. Routing is decided at the host from which the message is issued. In addition to the domain-style name, UUCP-like *host!user* addresses may be used by means of a **pathalias** database.

Internet DNS domain naming is being implemented. The naming structure consolidated as of June 1986 is in conformance with RFC920 [Postel and Reynolds 1984]. The top level domain is *KR* for Korea, with second level domains below it as shown in Table 15.1.

In addition to a *CSNET* connection, *SDN* has *UUCP* connections from the machine *kaist* to *kddlab* in Japan and *indovax* in Indonesia directly, and to *munnari* in Australia and *tataelxsi* in Singapore through *uunet* in the States.

History

SDN was started in 1982 in the Republic of Korea with one node at Seoul National University (SNU) and another at the Korea Institute of Electronics Technology (KIET). The major development issues in *SDN* during the initial period from 1982 to 1984 were setting up the environment for computer communications and adding new nodes. Gateways to *UUCP* in North America were set up in 1983 over X.25 and dialup lines, and there exists now a *UUNET* connection. A *CSNET* link was installed in 1984 using PMDF over X.25.

Table 15.1. *SDN domains*

Domain	Explanation
KR	Top level domain
Second level domains	
RES	Research community
EDU	Educational institutes
COM	Companies
GOV	Government organizations
ORG	General organizations
<network-names>	Other nationwide networks
Third level domains	Names of organizations
Fourth level domains	Usually host names

Plans

The *CSNET* connection will soon be replaced by TCP/IP over the X.25 link.

The *SDN* research community is currently working on migration to ISO-OSI protocols starting from the network and transport layer as well as for VTAM, X.400, CASE, and FTAM. There is a test network for this purpose called *SDN* [Chon 1987]. It is built upon the exisiting *SDN* network and is coordinated by OSI Associations (OSIA). It was scheduled to demonstrate FTAM in 1988 and multimedia mail afterward.

The SDN administrators are also working on *PACNET*.

Access
Kilnam Chon
chon@sorak.kaist.ac.kr
uunet!kaist!nmc
nmc%kaist.csnet@relay.cs.net
+82-2-962-5663
Fax: +82-2-962-8835
KAIST
P.O. Box 150
Chongryang
Seoul 131
Republic of Korea

15.3   *Japan {JP}*

There are several domestic networks in Japan, including the oldest, *N-1*, which connects mainframes, and *NACSIS*, which is used for supercomputer and library access. The most widespread noncommercial network in Japan is *JUNET*. There is a research network, *Sigma*; at least two conferencing systems with international clienteles, *TWICS* and *COARA*; and a booming national conferencing industry, as described later in this section under IND. Numerous international networks, such as *BITNET* and *MILNET*, extend to Japan, and there are connections to *UUNET* and *CSNET*. The Japanese part of *HEPnet* uses the domain *HEP.JP*, at least from *BITNET* [Nussbacher 1988].

A bit of political geography may be useful in understanding Japanese networks. There are more than 120 million Japanese living on a set of islands of only 377,643 square miles, which is more people than in any European nation except the Soviet Union and less land area than in Sweden. Half the population is further concentrated into two areas on the main island of Honshu:

Kanto   The Kanto Plain includes the megalopolis extending from Tokyo to Yokohama and Chiba and including the prefectures of Tokyo (with the city of Tokyo), Kanagawa (with the cities of Yokohama, Kawasaki, and Kamakura), Saitama, Chiba, Ibaraki, and parts of Tochigi and Gumma. These are all within a few hours from the center of Tokyo, and about a third of the entire population of the country lives in them.

Kansai   The Kansai urban area includes Osaka, Kyoto, Kobe, and Nara, and about a fifth of the entire population lives there.

These are not political divisions; the prefectures serve that purpose [Shapard 1988]. But they are convenient practical references and explain the geography of some of the Japanese systems.

The Japanese government is encouraging implementation of campus networks, such as the one at the University of Tokyo *(Kogaku-bu LAN)* described later in this section under *NACSIS*, and is providing money in some cases. This indirectly encourages companies to develop new technology. In addition, the Japanese government is funding two new high-speed international links. It is as yet undecided whether one will go to Europe and the other to the United States or both will go to the United States; it is also undecided to which networks they will connect (*CSNET* and *BITNET* are likely ones). The links are being developed in cooperation with the National Science Foundation (NSF) in the United States. There are also some private internal company international links [Murai 1988].

Until the privatization of Nippon Telegraph and Telephone (NTT) in April 1985 and the corresponding deregulation of the public telephone system allowing it to be used for services such as conferencing systems, there was little communication by personal computer in Japan. But there are now six or seven million personal computers in Japan, of which about 400,000 have modems [Aizu et al. 1988]. Many of their owners subscribe to conferencing systems. A few of those are described here.

The Japanese news media have given a great deal of publicity to conferencing in general, and there has been an accompanying boom of use, some of which may be a media fad. In addition to some of the systems already mentioned, which seem rather well established, there is increasing interest from businesses. Independent electronic mail systems in Japan are mostly used by only a few businesses with a great deal of overseas mail traffic. But conferencing is widely used, especially by personal computer users. The **Participate** and **CoSy** conferencing software has been adapted to handle Japanese, and **Caucus** is being modified for that purpose. *COARA* developed its own software in 1987.

Some systems, such as *TWICS*, have large international clienteles. Another prominent system is *Nikkei MIX* (McGraw-Hill Information Exchange), which uses the **CoSy** conferencing software. It was formed in August 1986 and currently has about 3,500 users [Aizu et al. 1988]. *Space Net*, formed in September 1986 and currently having 4,000 users, uses the **Participate** software [Aizu et al. 1988].

15.3.1   Japanese

The spoken Japanese language is reputed to be relatively straightforward, having more regular syntax than many. The written language is another matter, and one that all networking and CMC efforts in Japan must address.

Written Japanese

There are five writing methods used for the Japanese language [Hadamitzky and Spahn 1981; Shapard 1988]: *Kanji*, or Chinese characters; *Kana*, or syllabaries (in the two forms *Hiragana* and *Katakana*); *Romaji*, or Japanese transliterated in Latin characters; and other uses of foreign alphabets.

1. *Kanji.* These are Chinese characters, which were the original sole basis of written Japanese beginning in about the fourth century. In 1981, 1,945 Kanji were recommended by the Kokugo Shingikai (Japanese Language Council) of the Ministry of Education (extending by 45 a list of 1,900 it had previously recommended on 21 January 1977 (which was up from 1,850 in a 1946 recommendation). These are the *Jôyô Kanji*, or characters for daily use. An additional 92 Kanji for use in personal names were listed in 1951. A few Japanese dictionaries have as many as 10,000 Kanji, and some Chinese dictionaries have 50,000. But only about 3,000 are used in normal Japanese writing, with an additional 1,000 in literary and technical writing; most dictionaries include about 7,000.

Kanji are used more as phonetic signs than as ideographs. They are usually combined with each other and with other writing forms to form words; about 11,000 words are common with the 1,945 Jôyô Kanji (but many of these words involve Hiragana inflections). It is not easy, if even possible, to write readily understandable Japanese using only Kanji because inflectional endings and many words can be expressed only with other writing forms. However, Japanese sometimes refer to *writing in Kanji* to mean using the whole array of writing methods available.

2. *Kana*. There are two Japanese syllabaries, or Kana, called Hiragana and Katakana, with 46 characters each. Although each of the characters in each of these two Kana sets corresponds exactly to a single character in the other in phonetic meaning, both sets are usually used in writing.

2a. *Hiragana*. This is a cursive script, developed during the eighth through twelfth centuries from a cursive form of Kanji. It is sometimes called the *women's hand* because this was formerly the only writing method taught to women. The famous twelfth century Japanese novel, *The Tale of Genji* by Lady Murasaki, was written in Hiragana. This script has since become the usual one for writing native Japanese, or *Yamato*, words, as well as for inflectional affixes and grammatical particles to apply to Kanji.

2b. *Katakana*. Up through the Shogunate days in Japan, men tended to use mostly Kanji. Katakana was developed by Buddhist monks from an angular style of Kanji to assist in writing the phonetics of the Chinese texts that were important sources for their religious tradition. Katakana was used for some official Japanese documents around the time of the Second World War, but it has mostly reverted to its original purpose of transcribing foreign words, especially those borrowed into common usage in the Japanese language. It is also used for onomatopoeia — that is, transcribing sounds — and for telegraph messages.

It is possible to write Japanese solely in either Hiragana or Katakana. However, it is very difficult to do this without ambiguity because of the large number of homophones in the language. These words that sound the same (and thus are written identically in the syllabaries) but have different meanings can only be distinguished in writing by using Kanji.

There are no equivalents of Latin capital letters in Kanji or Kana, and Japanese is written with no blank space between words or sentences. Japanese characters are not proportionately spaced: they are written in a two-dimensional grid, not on lines. The different uses of Hiragana and Katakana are somewhat similar to the use of roman and italic typefaces, respectively, in English, and Katakana is sometimes used for emphasis in phrases that would ordinarily be written in Hiragana (but Hiragana looks more cursive or italic than does Katakana). Boldface Kana fonts exist, and there are several handwriting styles for Kanji. There are about a dozen punctuation marks, as well as two Hiragana and two Katakana characters that are obsolete but nonetheless occur occasionally.

3. *Romaji*. Portuguese and other European contacts in the sixteenth century led to the development of a way of transcribing Japanese phonetically into the Latin alphabet: this is Romaji. Either set of Kana characters can be transliterated directly into or out of Latin characters using 22 Latin characters and two diacritical marks. Thus, Japanese can be written solely in Romaji, but the same problem of ambiguity due to homophones exists as for Kana. There are two slightly different common transliteration methods, *kunrei-shiki rômaji* and *Hebon-shiki rômaji*, or the Hepburn system: the latter is used in this book as being easier for English speakers to pronounce correctly.

4. *Other*. Arabic numerals are the common writing method for numbers in Japanese. One also finds abbreviations, such as for the international communications carrier Kokusai Denshin Denwa (KDD), in Latin characters in Japanese texts, even though the long name is normally written in Kanji. Finally, many technical texts published in Japanese use English (and sometimes other European) words in the Latin alphabet, and some use Greek and Cyrillic alphabets for mathematical notation and Russian words.

A typical technical text in a Japanese journal will use all of these writing methods:

- Traditional Japanese words will be written in Kanji.
- Other Japanese words will be written in Hiragana.
- Foreign words borrowed into common usage will be written in Katakana.
- Romaji will not usually be used because Hiragana is more appropriate.
- Foreign words and names are written in their normal forms in the Latin alphabet (although personal names are sometimes also transcribed into phonetic Kanji equivalents).

Even without Latin or other foreign alphabets, there are four methods of printing used in such a document, not counting Arabic numerals, different typefaces, and punctuation marks.

Encoded Japanese

Although it is possible to do computing in Japan using only Romaji, or even only English, the recent popularity of networks such as *JUNET* and conferencing systems such as *TWICS* has been possible only because they have developed ways of dealing with the full array of Japanese writing methods.

7 bits   Romaji and English are easy enough to deal with, as ASCII is universally used in its original USASCII form. This only takes 7 bits and no modifications to most foreign computing equipment.

8 bits   Hiragana and Katakana are a bit more difficult because they have four dozen characters apiece, making too many (when taken together with ASCII) to represent in 7 bits. But 8 bits are enough, and solutions similar to those used in ISO8859 for European languages would be sufficient.

16 bits   But more than 3,000 Kanji are essential, and about 7,000 are desirable. Eight bits are not enough, but 16 (or even 14) are.

A further complication is that just using 16 bit characters everywhere is not sufficient because ordinary strings of 8 bit bytes containing ASCII characters must still be permitted for computer usage. Thus, there have to be ways of shifting between 8 and 16 bit letters.

There are several standards, official or de facto, for encoding Japanese [Murai and Kato 1987]:

JIS X 0208 is the basic standard in the sense that it is used as the defining reference for all the others and is a Japan Industrial Standard (JIS) (see JISC). It defines codes for Kanji, Hiragana, and Katakana and has the ASCII code embedded; Greek and Cyrillic characters are also included. Each code is of two 7 bit bytes, with the high bits undefined. ASCII control characters are recognized in *either* byte. Kanji characters are divided into two groups. *Level one* includes 3,500 characters and is sufficient for most ordinary texts, including most technical texts. *Level two* has about 3,400 more characters. These are used for naming people and places and for literary terms.

ISO2022 is the ISO equivalent of JIS X 0208, and the latter can be used to encode anything this ISO standard defines.

JIS X 0202 is used to distinguish ordinary ASCII from Kanji. It uses escape sequences involving the ASCII escape character (octal 33, hexadecimal 1B) to shift between the two. Shifting into Kanji is done with the sequence "escape $ @" or "escape $ B". The two sequences introduce two slightly different versions of JIS X 0208, both of which are standard. Shifting into English is done with the sequence "escape (J" or "escape (B". Officially, the former introduces ASCII, and the latter introduces a Roman character set for Romaji. However, the only differences between those two character sets are the graphical representations of a few characters.

JIS X 0201 is an encoding of the Katakana characters in a single byte: this is the only code described here that does not include ASCII characters in its character set. JIS X 0201 is used on some mainframes where introducing two byte encodings was too difficult.

EUC was developed by AT&T UNIX Pacific in an internationalized

version of **UNIX** for Japanese, Chinese, Korean, and Thai. This Extended
UNIX Code (EUC) appears to be becoming the standard Japanese language
representation on **UNIX** systems. EUC assumes that no ASCII code will
have its most significant bit set (which is interesting, considering the ASCII
extensions used in Europe that depend on that bit). Kanji characters are
then distinguished as pairs of bytes with their high bits set.

Digital Kanji is a character encoding used by Digital Japan. It is mostly
compatible with EUC.

Shift-JIS was originally developed for **CP/M** by Microsoft and is now
used on **MS-DOS**. It is the de facto standard used on personal computers
and is sometimes used in **UNIX** environments. Kanji characters are distinguished by being mapped so that the first byte is in one of the ranges
0x81 − 0x94 or 0xe0 − 0xff.

All of these character codes (except JIS X 0201), whether encoded in 16 or 8
bits, have ASCII characters embedded with their usual codes in the low
byte with the high bit off.

Hardware

Ordinary foreign old-style ASCII line-oriented terminals are clearly not adequate for the Japanese language. Kana can be done with special ROMs on
such hardware, but screen resolution is not adequate for Kanji. About 14 by
14 pixel resolution is necessary to adequately represent all Kanji so that they
are readily distinguishable by eye. There is usually no need for radically
different keyboards for Japanese, since words are ordinarily entered in
Romaji, transliterated into Kana, and then converted into Kanji by picking
from a menu of possible Kanji for the Kana homophones. Only two extra
keys are needed for these conversions, since the Kanji menu selection is
done by digit keys.

Software

A great deal of foreign software assumes (at least until recently) 8 bit characters and often even 7 bit characters in 8 bit bytes with the high bit clear.
All such software has to be converted. Fortunately, this has now been done
for much important software, as related in the sections on *JUNET* and
TWICS later in this chapter.

15.3.2   N-1

The earliest large computer network in Japan appears to have been *N-1*
[Ishida 1985], which is an interuniversity network that has been operational
since 1981 [Matsukata 1987].

By March 1987, *N-1* connected about 64 mainframes in large computer centers at about 20 national universities [Murai 1988]. The infrastructure is *DDX-P*, the domestic Japanese X.25 network operated by Nippon Telegraph and Telephone (NTT). Each *N-1* host may make transparent connections to any other host. Transport and higher layer protocols were developed for the network and named N-1 for it; these support multiplexed connections. *N-1* provides remote login and RJE but no mail service. The network is used to share special hardware, such as array processors, and special software, such as **PROLOG/KR**, as well as databases. Line speeds vary from 4800bps to 48Kbps, with 9600bps being the most common.

History and Plans

There were seven computer centers on the network when it began in 1981 after seven years of planning. Since the establishment of *NACSIS* in 1987, *NACSIS* has increasingly been used as infrastructure for *N-1* and may be considered its successor [Matsukata 1987].

The *ULN* (University Library Network) was established in 1984 to connect libraries in universities. It also uses the N-1 protocols, the Network Terminal Protocol (NTP) of which was revised to handle Japanese character codes. *NACSIS* is now being used as the infrastructure for *N-1* [Matsukata 1987].

15.3.3   JUNET

JUNET is the major nationwide noncommercial computer network in Japan. Its purpose is to promote information exchange among Japanese researchers and with researchers outside Japan [Murai and Asami 1985; Murai and Kato 1988]. The network provides a testing environment for research in computer networking and distributed processing, particularly in Japanese character handling, resource name managing, and speed improvements [Murai and Kato 1987]. The network extends throughout the major Japanese islands, with concentrations near Tokyo and Osaka, as can be seen in Figure 15.1; 56 organizations are in the Kanto Plain and 17 in Kansai. There are 87 participating organizations and 250 hosts.

Administration and Funding

The administrators of the major (backbone) hosts on the network administer the network and hold meetings monthly for that purpose. Each host's connection costs are paid by its institution.

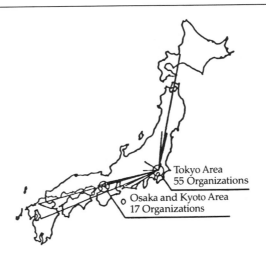

Tokyo Area
55 Organizations

Osaka and Kyoto Area
17 Organizations

Figure 15.1. *JUNET map (August 1987) [Murai and Kato 1987, p. 2, Figure 1]*

Services

JUNET incorporates both news (like *USENET*) and mail (like *UUCP*) in a single network organization (like *EUnet*). There is evidently a tradition in Japan that employees ask their employers for permission before publishing anything publicly; this might explain the small number of Japanese news postings seen outside Japan. But there is a distribution (*fj.all*) of newsgroups that can be seen only inside Japan and that are heavily used. For instance, *fj.kanji* (for Kanji handling) and *fj.micro.mac* are very active. In June 1987, 1,750 articles were posted to the *fj.all* newsgroups, totaling 4Mbytes. Including news originating from non-fj *USENET* newsgroups, 22Mbytes of articles passed through *JUNET* that month. Approximately 85 percent of all traffic is usually news, with about 15 percent mail. Many *JUNET* links are 9600bps; getting the most out of such links has been a particular area of effort in *JUNET*.

Protocols

UUCP is the common protocol, with X.25, telephone dialups, and Ethernets below. Some UUCP links are carried over TCP/IP, and there are many TCP/IP dialup links that use SLIP. The ISO-OSI protocols are not yet used, and there appear to be no immediate plans to use them, although implementations exist within several corporations.

Japanese

JUNET uses JIS X 0208 16 bit codes for external communications between machines, with the high bits of both bytes off and using JIS X 0202 escape sequences. This has the advantages of staying with the JIS and ISO standard character encodings and of allowing the use of some equipment and software (such as old **UNIX** software) that strips the high bit. Conversion is required to communicate with machines using the common operating system de facto encoding standards, EUC and Shift-JIS. The Kana-only JIS X 0201 character set, however, is ignored entirely, since there is nothing it can do that the other character sets cannot and there is no large population of machines using it that *JUNET* wishes to communicate with.

Random access to files and filenames is very important in **UNIX**, in which there is no distinction between text and data files. JIS X 0208 is thus not appropriate for internal use because of the complication of the accompanying JIS X 0202 escape sequences. Certain conventions were developed for handling JIS X 0208 in *JUNET*. ASCII text is the default, and no leading escape sequence is required if text begins with ASCII; this simplifies communication with all-ASCII networks such as *USENET*. The two similar JIS X 0202 escape sequences for shifting into ASCII (for English) or Roman (for Romaji) characters are treated as equivalent. Control characters appearing in Kanji characters can be very difficult to detect during random access, so Kanji codes that would have control characters are not permitted; control characters are permitted only in ASCII codes.

The *USENET* **B news** news software, the **MH** mail handling system, the GNU and Micro **Emacs** text editors, and the X-windows network windowing system were all modified to support Kanji. Bit maps for the set of the 3,500 level 1 Kanji characters were made by hand and posted to *JUNET* so that everyone would have them. The result of all this is shown in Figure 15.2.

Naming, Addressing, and Routing

There is a domain system, and its top level domain is the name of the network, *JUNET*. Second level domains are usually named for organizations such as universities, and third level domains are usually hosts. This scheme is similar to RFC733, the predecessor of the current *Internet* DNS domain system. Routing is done by tables on gateways that are manually updated monthly. Modifications have been made to **sendmail** to support routing by domains.

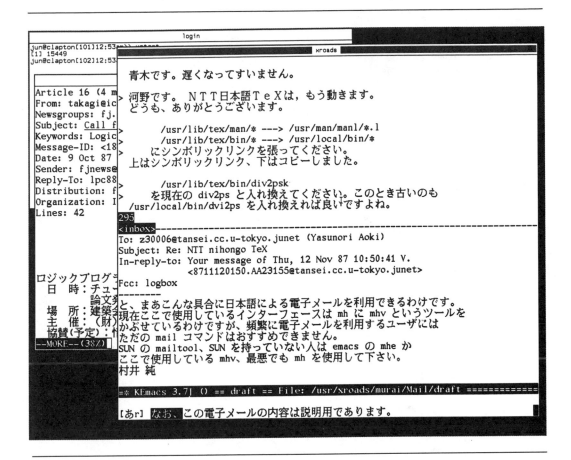

Figure 15.2. *Kanji display in JUNET [Murai and Kato 1987]*

Interconnections

In Table 15.2, **{JUNET-domain}** stands for the top level pseudodomain *JUNET*.

There are two primary international gateways: *kddlab.kddlabs.junet* (or *kddlabs*, as it is known on the *UUCP* network) at Kokusai Denshin Denwa (KDD) and *ccut.cc.u-tokyo.junet* (known as *utokyo-relay* on *CSNET*) at the University of Tokyo. There are links to *mcvax* for *EUnet* in Europe, *uunet* and others for *UUCP* in North America, *munnari* for *ACSnet* in Australia, and *kaist* for *SDN* in Korea. A gateway to *Asianet* (*BITNET* in Japan) is planned.

Many *JUNET* hosts will recognize *JANET* hosts by their domain names and know what to do with them. It is also possible to relay through *BITNET*, using *cunyvm.cuny.edu*.

Table 15.2. *JUNET interconnections*

Network	Syntax
JUNET	*user@domain*.**{JUNET-domain}**
Internet	*user@domain*.**{DNS}**
JANET	*user@domain*.**{JANET-domain}**
JANET	*user%domain*.**{JANET-domain}**@cunyvm.cuny.edu
Ean	*user%domain*.**{Ean-domain}**@ubc.csnet
XEROX Internet	*user*.**{XEROX-domain}**@xerox.com
Easynet	*user%host*.dec@decwrl.dec.com
VNET	*user%host*@ibm.com
BITNET	*user@host*.bitnet
ACSnet	*user@domain*.**{ACSNET-domain}**
UUCP	*user@host*.uucp

History

The network originally linked three universities starting in October 1984. It was connected to Europe in January 1985 by a link between *kddlabs* and *mcvax*.

Access

Jun Murai
jun%xroads.cc.u-tokyo.junet%utokyo-relay.csnet@RELAY.CS.NET
Computer Center
University of Tokyo
2-11-16, Yayoi, Bunkyoku
Tokyo 113
Japan

Akira Kato
kato%cs.titech.junet@relay.cs.net
Department of Computer Science
Faculty of Engineering
Tokyo Institute of Technology
2-12-1, Ookayama, Meguro
Tokyo 152
Japan

15.3.4   NACSIS

The National Center for Science Information Systems (NACSIS) operates a network called Science Information Network, but commonly known as *NACSIS* [Matsukata 1987]. It may be considered the successor to *N-1*.

This is a tree-shaped network with its own packet switches. The direct links to the component institutions are 48Kbps, and speeds of links closer to the root of the tree range up to 768Kbps.

The network connects seven Inter-University Computing Centers throughout the main Japanese islands, giving researchers access to widely separated mainframes and supercomputers. The network uses X.25 and the N-1 protocols, and thus has the same services as the *N-1* network—i.e., remote login and RJE. Experiments are being conducted with Message Handling System (MHS) in order to solve the lack of a mail protocol in N-1.

Because of the expense of ordinary X.25 PTT service for large amounts of data, high-speed leased lines have been ordered from Nippon Telegraph and Telephone (NTT) with a government grant to connect the Computer Center at the University of Tokyo (CCUT), NACSIS, Nagoya University, Kyoto University, and Osaka University. Long-distance links are assumed to be by X.25 and internetworking with local area X.25 links by X.75. Other local area network protocols require protocol conversion.

Some links are converting to IP, which is less expensive and more efficient than X.25 PTT connections. Connection to existing campus networks is also very important, and many of them, such as *Kogaku-bu LAN*, use TCP/IP.

15.3.5   Kogaku-bu LAN

The network established at the Faculty of Engineering at the University of Tokyo (Tokyo) in 1987, *Kogaku-bu LAN*, uses TCP/IP over a Toshiba 100Mbps fiber-optic backbone network to connect Ethernets. The protocols are not FDDI, because the technology precedes FDDI. Instead, the backbone LAN relays IEEE 802.3 packets at the data link layer, making the whole set of networks appear to be one very large Ethernet. The protocol used on the backbone was implemented by Toshiba and is called TOTOLAN/RING. There are also some fiber-optic repeaters connecting individual Ethernets.

Some mainframes, such as those at CCUT, may support as their only TCP/IP application services TELNET and FTP, although SMTP is being added. None of these TCP/IP application programs takes Japanese character sets into account, and some of them assume 7 bit text characters in 8 bit bytes. This problem has mostly not yet been addressed and has been avoided, for example, in FTP by using only binary image mode. Some attempt has been made to adapt the **4.3BSD** client **telnet** program. Mainframe remote login access using Japanese character sets has mostly been managed by putting TELNET in transparent mode and using the character conversion capabilities of the IBM **TSS TIOP2** program on the mainframe [Matsukata 1987].

Currently, 400Mbps fiber-optic technology is being developed; this also requires a special packet switch node to connect to slower networks [Murai 1988].

15.3.6   Sigma

The Sigma Network (*Sigma*) is a research and development testbed network designed for use in the Sigma Project. The Sigma Project is intended to promote increases in software productivity by producing a standard workstation environment for use in Japan. It uses the **UNIX** operating system as a base from which it defines numerous hardware and software parameters. This network is intended to allow quick and easy distribution of the software development environment and of information associated with it. Tests of the network started in the last quarter of 1987, and it was operational in 1988.

Sigma will operate a database retrieval service and a network information center and will produce network management data (including host tables in the format of RFC952 [Harrenstien 1985]), although network management is distributed. The user sites are those of vendors who are cooperating in developing prototype workstations.

Insulation of the users from implementation details is an important goal, and a sophisticated hierarchical naming system has been designed for this purpose. The model is of a single virtual computer with services, users, and files.

The basic underlying protocols are TCP/IP above the following:

- Ethernet on local area networks
- Long-distance X.25 (1980) service with X.21 and V.24 interfaces to the *DDX-P* PDN
- With SLIP over some leased lines, using V.24 and V.52bis [Saito 1987]

15.3.7   TWICS

TWICS is a conferencing system in Tokyo whose purpose is "communication within groups and between individuals inside Japan and abroad who find a globally-oriented Tokyo-based service appropriate to their needs" [Shapard 1988]. Users throughout the greater Kanto metropolitan area connect to *TWICS* by direct telephone calls, while users from other parts of Japan and the world, including North America, South America, Western and Eastern Europe, South Africa, Israel, and the South Pacific, use packet networks. The total number of users is about 500, about half Japanese and half other nationalities; about 82 percent of all members currently reside in Japan. The administration speculates that the users may be further grouped as 30 percent professionals (including engineers, mathematicians, doctors, lawyers, accountants, technical writers, translators, and editors); 30 percent business or corporate people; 30 percent academics, researchers, and educators; and 10 percent students, housewives, etc. Growth is at about 10% a year, without advertising [Shapard 1988].

Administration and Funding

TWICS is owned by the International Education Center (IEC), a nonprofit educational organization specializing in English and Japanese language training, adult continuing education, and cross-cultural activities. It is administered and operated on a commercial basis by TWICS Co., Ltd. (TWICS), a service company also owned by IEC. The relationship with IEC accounts for the international orientation of *TWICS*, for most of the conferences being in English, and for the various research and nonprofit activities supported in addition to the commercial for-profit service. Users pay an annual membership subscription plus fees for usage and value-added services; group subscriptions are available by special arrangement [Shapard 1986]. People living outside Japan may currently get a free membership.

Services

Electronic mail is available, using Digital VAX **VMS MAIL**. Mailing lists also are available but are seldom used. The Participate conferencing system is used as the center of public online activities and for private groups. Conferences are organized according to an island metaphor. Various parts of the island, *Bee Jima*, such as the port, the mountain, and the bush country, represent conferences. *TWICS* is also experimenting with the Caucus conferencing system. While these various facilities are not yet integrated, methods of exchanging information between them are being developed.

Interactive one-to-one conferencing is supported by Participate's **NOW** facility, and one-to-several by VAX **VMS PHONE** and a simple **CB simulator**. A new one-to-several conferencing program called **TALK** is being tested. Interactive one-to-many broadcast service is permitted only to the system operators through the use of the **VMS REPLY** facility.

The service is provided from a single machine, a Digital MicroVAX II running **Nihongo VMS**. The default system language is English, and the default character code is USASCII, but, of course, users can also communicate in Japanese using Kanji. **Nihongo VMS** supports its own Digital Kanji code, which is almost completely compatible with the new EUC **UNIX** standard [Rikitake 1988]. For users whose terminals do not support Digital or EUC Kanji character codes and are therefore limited to the native Shift-JIS Kanji codes of **MS-DOS** and laptop word processors, there is a hardware Kanji filter on two dialup lines.

Interconnections

TWICS is accessible through the Japanese international public packet networks *DDX-P* and *NIS/TYMNET*, as well as through dialup telephone links, at 300bps, 1200bps, or 2400bps. *TWICS* has a group account with *DASnet*, so all users can reach numerous other services around the world by electronic mail. Experiments are being conducted with UUCP connections (using a **VMS** version of the public domain **UUPC** implementation of UUCP) and with X.400 connections to the German network *DFN*, using modified **Ean** mail software.

History

The name *TWICS* was originally an acronym for Two Way Information Communication System and dates from 1983, before direct involvement by IEC. The idea came from Toshiaki Tanaka, who was interested in communications between small and large computers and is president of Sakako Co. (Sakako) (which imports shrimp and sells seafood retail), and David G. Fisher, an IEC faculty member who was interested in the educational applications of computer mediated communications. Initial funding came from Sakako, as did one of the original developers, Makoto Ezure [Shapard 1986]. The first *TWICS* host, a single line BBS, went online in September 1984, and the second host, a multiuser BBS running under **UNIX** on a MC68000-based machine, went online one year later. The current system, the third, has been online since April 1986 [Shapard 1988]. The developer of this service, Jeffrey Shapard, has gathered a very useful list of all the world's PDNs. This list appears in Appendix A.

> **Access**
> Jeffrey Shapard
> Jefu@DCTWCS.DAS.NET
> Bee@DCTWCS.DAS.NET
> +81-3-359-9621
> Fax: +81-3-353-8908
> TWICS Co., Ltd.
> IEC/TWICS
> 1-21 Yotsuya
> Shinjuku-ku
> Tokyo 160
> Japan

15.3.8   COARA

One of the oldest associations of personal computer users in Japan is Compunication of Oita Amateur Research Association (COARA), where *compunication* is a portmanteau word referring to communication by personal computer. A related word is *pasocom tsushin*, or personal computing. There were about 30 initial members when COARA, a regional nonprofit association, was formed in May 1985. Its base is not Tokyo, unlike so many things in Japan, but Oita, 600 miles to the west on the island of Kyushu, outside of either of the major megalopoli (although it only takes about an hour and a half to get there from Tokyo). Apparently some of its members had been using databases before, but they soon discovered the utility of computer mediated communications. They publish a monthly newsletter, *Album COARA*, and meet monthly in person. There are conferences with their own personal meetings, such as *Stiki net*, which consists of most of the women who subscribe. Governor Hiramatsu of Oita Prefecture is a leading user of the *COARA* conferencing system, which is known throughout the country due to extensive news media coverage. The clientele has become international, with subscribers from the Netherlands, the United States, and Switzerland, and more people from elsewhere within the country than from Oita [Aizu et al. 1988].

15.3.9   IND

The most general association for users of conferencing systems in Japan appears to be the Institute for Networking Design (IND), a commercial organization formed in April 1986 by six members in Tokyo. *IND* helped COARA design its Japanese language conferencing system. Unlike COARA, IND is more interested in designing and installing new systems and technologies and in writing about them than in running a single system. For example, IND helped design the first *enterprise network* for a private Japanese company, which was operational in June 1987. This is inside Recruit Corporation, a job recruiting firm that also publishes related magazines.

IND provided marketing and design consulting for a community conferencing system centered in Sendai, which is about 300 miles north of Tokyo and is the main city for the northern part of Honshu. The organizing company, from which the network, *IND*, takes its name, was established in December 1986 by the government and chamber of commerce of the city of Sendai, the government of Miyagi Prefecture, a local bank, and about 120 other companies in the area. There were about 500 members when service was first available in July 1987. The single host system is expected to be upgraded to handle a thousand members soon [Aizu and Nakamura 1988]. About 720 city councils in Japan are providing conferencing and database services to their populaces.

Access

Izumi Aizu
Principal
IZUMI@DCTWCS.DAS.NET

Hiroyuki Nakamura
Vice President
HIRO@DCTWCS.DAS.NET

Institute for Networking Design
+81-03-797-2900
Fax: +81-03-797-2988
2-17-12-502 Higashi, Shibuya
Tokyo 150
Japan

15.4   *Hong Kong {HK}*

There is a national academic network in Hong Kong called *HARNET*.

15.4.1   HARNET

The Hong Kong Academic and Research Network (*HARNET*) became operational in September 1986 [Chow 1987]. As of October 1987, *HARNET* connected five major institutions of higher education in Hong Kong: University of Hong Kong (HKU), Chinese University of Hong Kong, Hong Kong Polytechnic, City Polytechnic of Hong Kong, and Baptist College. There are 18 hosts and about 200 users. Each site does its own administration, although HKU administers about 35 percent. Funding comes from each institution, and international communication expenses are charged back directly to the users.

    HARNET is a star-shaped network around the two machines *hkucs* and *hkucc* at HKU. Links are either UUCP over dialup (1200bps) or PDN (2400bps) or DECNET over leased lines (9600bps). Electronic mail, file transfer, remote login, and *USENET* news are supported. Mail delivery usually takes less than 30 minutes within Hong Kong and about half a day internationally. UUCP source routing is used, and domains are apparently not used. Mapping between DECNET mail and UUCP (RFC822) mail is done by the **sendmail** program on *hkucs*, which runs Digital's **Ultrix** operating system, a variant of **UNIX**.

    International links are supported from the machine *hkucs* to *munnari* (Australia), *uunet* (United States), *kaist* (Korea), *jinan* (Guangzhou, China), and *beijing* (Beijing, China). The latter two are still being planned, while the rest are by X.25 over PDN. All are UUCP links.

Access
Kam P. Chow
uunet!hkucs!chow
Computer Studies
University of Hong Kong
Hong Kong

15.5   *Taiwan, Republic of China {TW}*

There are connections to *BITNET* and *PACNET*.

15.6   *China, People's Republic of {CN}*

There are several connections from the People's Republic of China to the rest of the world:

- A *CSNET* link between Beijing and Karlsruhe, West Germany, described in a subsection below
- A UUCP link to *HARNET* in Hong Kong [Chow 1987]
- A 1200bps Kermit link to Vienna, Austria, from a VAX-11/785 in the High Energy Physics Institute (IHEP) of Academia Sinica through the No. 710 Institute of the former Seventh Machinery Ministry [Zhou 1987]; **Kermit** provides file transfer, remote login, and is used in this instance for electronic mail as well

There is interest in China in development and use of ISO-OSI standards and protocols, as described in a subsection below.

A few networks exist inside China. A Chinese newspaper has reported one at Xian University, and there are links between Nanjing and Yancheng in Jiangsu province [Zhou 1987].

There is no national network in the People's Republic of China, but such a network was apparently originally proposed in the early 1970s by Qian Xuesen [Zhou 1987]. A proposal for a network by 1985 was made at a National Science and Technology Conference in 1978, but there were no direct results.

Interest was revived recently, partly due to a proposal to connect with *BITNET* [Zhenqin 1987] and to produce a national NJE network called *CHINANET*. That network appears not to have been implemented due to organizational difficulties. But there is a *CHINANET* Discussion List on *BITNET* with more than 200 members (both Chinese and non-Chinese) in several countries, including the United States, Canada, Germany, and the United Kingdom. There is also a popular newsgroup, *soc.culture.china*, on *USENET*. Although the original purpose of the newsgroup was to discuss *CHINANET*, it is currently used to discuss many issues of interest to Chinese in the world, and the newsgroup is not gatewayed to the mailing list.

Access

Inquiries regarding the *CHINANET* list should be sent to:

zhou@astro.as.utexas.edu

For information about other, more recent discussions about Chinese networks, contact:

George H. Kemper
Director
X040BK@TAMVM1.BITNET
+1-409-845-4215
Computing Services Center
Texas A&M University
College Station, TX 77843-3142
U.S.A.

15.6.1   Beijing-Karlsruhe

Original planning for this *CSNET* link between Beijing and Karlsruhe, West Germany, goes back to 1983, and a partner for it was found in 1984 [Zorn 1987]. Project organization and funding was done in 1985, and a machine was picked: a VAX-11/780 running **4.2BSD** for the Institute of Computer Applications (ICA) at Beijing Institute of Technology (BIT) and a Siemens 7.760 running **BS2000** for each end of the link. (ICA also belongs partially to the National Machinery Commission (NMC) [Xinhua News Agency 1987; Zhou 1987].) PMDF, the *CSNET PhoneNet* protocol, had to be implemented for **BS2000**. Defining and setting up the transmission link occupied the latter half of 1985 and most of 1986: X.25 is used over a variety of underlying mechanisms, including a satellite link. Most segments run at 9600bps, but there is a 300bps bottleneck.

The connection was actually set up in August and September 1987. The first electronic mail message was successfully sent on 29 September 1987 and said, "Across the Great Wall we can reach every corner of the world" [Zorn 1987]. Funding comes from the government of the German state of Baden-Württemberg and the various Chinese agencies associated with the project [Zhou 1987].

Reaching Beijing from most parts of *CSNET* requires a bit of indirection to get to the host *beijing* through the host *ira.uka.de*:

user%beijing%ira.uka.de@relay.cs.net

Mail is the only service currently supported and has been available since 24 September 1987.

Access

Werner Zorn
zorn%ira.uka.de@relay.cs.net
+49 721 608 3981
Informatik Rechnerabteilung
Universität Karlsruhe
P.O. Box 6980
D-500
Karlsruhe 1
West Germany

Li, Shao-Hong
rzli%beijing%ira.uka.de@relay.cs.net
+86-8414477-5161
+86-8413670
Telex: 22558-NISTI-CN
Institute of Computer Applications
c/o Prof. Wang, ICA
P.O. Box 2418
Beijing
People's Republic of China

15.6.2   Chinese OSI

There is interest in China in development and use of ISO-OSI standards and protocols [Zhao 1988]. The relevant Chinese government standards body is the China State Bureau of Standardization (CSBS). Its standards have the force of national law, and it has decided to develop a complete set of Chinese standards corresponding to the ISO-OSI ones. It has already issued standards on the reference model and on the lower three layers. The China Technical Committee for Standardization of Computer and Information Processing (CTCSCIP) is a technical association corresponding to ISO TC97. There is an Open Systems Interconnection Subcommittee (OSI-SC) that is involved with Chinese versions of standards developed by ISO TC97/SC21 and a Data Communication Subcommittee (DC-SC) corresponding to ISO TC97/SC6. And there is an industry group, China OSI Promotion (COSIP), apparently corresponding to SPAG in Europe or to POSI in Japan.

ISO-OSI services wanted include at least FTAM, MOTIS, and VT, with JTM, directory service, and others slated for eventual development. Chinese language support is a major concern, and the government intends to use the result in its own operations. Reliable encryption is wanted. Implementation projects are mostly targeted at IBM mainframes, Digital minicomputers, and microcomputers using Intel or Motorola CPUs. All products developed will be owned by the Chinese government.

15.7   *Korea, Democratic People's Republic of {KP}*

There are no known networks in the Democratic People's Republic of Korea.

15.8   *Mongolia {MN}*

There is a connection from Mongolia to *IASnet*.

15.9   *References*

Aizu and Nakamura 1988.   Aizu, Izumi, and Nakamura, Hiroyuki, "Institute for Networking Design," Institute for Networking Design, Tokyo, May 1988.

Aizu et al. 1988.   Aizu, Izumi, Nakamura, Hiroyuki, Kitaya, Yukio, and Carlson, Lisa, "The Business of Networking in Japan: Past, Present and the Future," *Proceedings of ENA Conference (Philadelphia, 13 May 1988)*, Electronic Networking Association, 1988.

Chon 1984.   Chon, K., "System Development Network," *Proceedings of TENCON (Singapore, April 1984)*, pp. 133–135, Singapore, 1984.

Chon 1985a.   Chon, K., "National and Regional Computer Networks for Academic and Research Communities in the Pacific Region," *Proceedings of PCCS (Seoul, October 1985)*, pp. 560–566, PCCS, Seoul, 1985.

Chon 1985b.   Chon, K., "SDN: A Computer Network for Korean Research Community," *Proceedings of PCCS (Seoul, October 1985)*, pp. 567–570, PCCS, Seoul, 1985.

Chon 1987.   Chon, Kilnam, "PACNET and Networks in South Korea," *Proceedings of the International Academic Networkshop (Princeton, New Jersey, 9–11 November 1987)*, 1987.

Chow 1987.   Chow, Kam P., "Hong Kong Academic and Research Network (HARNET)," *Proceedings of the International Academic Networkshop (Princeton, New Jersey, 9–11 November 1987)*, 1987.

Hadamitzky and Spahn 1981.   Hadamitzky, Wolfgang, and Spahn, Mark, *Kanji & Kana: A Handbook and Dictionary of the Japanese Writing System*, Charles E. Tuttle Company, Rutland, Vermont; Tokyo, Japan, 1981.

Harrenstien 1985.   Harrenstien, Ken, "DOD Internet Host Table; RFC952," *ARPANET Working Group Requests for Comments*, October 1985.

Ishida 1985.   Ishida, H., "Current Status of the N-1 Inter-University Network with Access to Supercomputers in Japan," *Proceedings of PCCS (Seoul, October 1985)*, PCCS, Seoul, 1985.

Jones and Hart 1988.   Jones, William P., and Hart, James P., Personal communications, 16 November 1988, 21 November 1988.

Matsukata 1987.   Matsukata, Jun, "Computer Networking for Large Computers in Universities," *Proceedings of the ACM SIGCOMM '87 Workshop (Stowe,*

Vermont, 11–13 August 1987), vol. 17, no. 5, pp. 78–87, ACM SIGCOMM, New York, 1987.

McEwan 1988.   McEwan, Duncan, Personal communications, 7 December 1988.

Murai 1988.   Murai, Jun, Personal communications, February 1988.

Murai and Asami 1985.   Murai, Jun, and Asami, Tohru, "A Network for Research and Development Communities in Japan—JUNET," *Proceedings of PCCS (Seoul, October 1985)*, pp. 579–588, PCCS, Seoul, 1985.

Murai and Kato 1987.   Murai, Jun, and Kato, Akira, "Researches in Network Development of JUNET," *Proceedings of the ACM SIGCOMM '87 Workshop (Stowe, Vermont, 11–13 August 1987)*, vol. 17, no. 5, pp. 68–77, ACM SIGCOMM, New York, 1987.

Murai and Kato 1988.   Murai, J., and Kato, A., "Current Status of JUNET," *Future Generations Computer Systems*, vol. 4, no. 3, pp. 205–215, North-Holland, Amsterdam, October 1988.

Nielsen 1988.   Nielsen, Torben N., Personal communications, December 1988.

Nussbacher 1988.   Nussbacher, Henry, "BITNET GATES Version 88.09," BITNET/EARN NETSERV, 25 August 1988.

Postel and Reynolds 1984.   Postel, Jonathan B., and Reynolds, Joyce, "Domain Requirements; RFC920," *ARPANET Working Group Requests for Comments*, October 1984.

Rikitake 1988.   Rikitake, Kenji, "A Proposal for More Flexible VAX/VMS Terminal Device Drivers, to Enhance DEC-J's Share in the Japanese Market," TWICS, Tokyo, 18 April 1988.

Saito 1987.   Saito, Kimio, "The SIGMA Network," *Proceedings of the ACM SIGCOMM '87 Workshop (Stowe, Vermont, 11–13 August 1987)*, vol. 17, no. 5, pp. 88–97, ACM SIGCOMM, New York, 1987.

Shapard 1986.   Shapard, Jeffrey, "TWICS BEELINE: From BBS to 'BEE JIMA'," *ENA NETWEAVER*, vol. 2, no. 6, p. 6, 1 June 1986.

Shapard 1988.   Shapard, Jeffrey, Personal communications, September 1988.

Xinhua News Agency 1987.   Xinhua News Agency, "Beijing-Karlsruhe," *People's Daily*, 9 October 1987.

Zhao 1988.   Zhao, Ziaofan, "OSI Standards in China," *DFN Mitteilungen*, no. 11, pp. 4–5, March 1988.

Zhenqin 1987.   Zhenqin, Li, "Chinanet and BITNET," *USTCAAA News*, Cornell University, 1987.

Zhou 1987.   Zhou, Shudong, "Network Connections to China," *USSSPRC News Letter*, vol. 20, pp. 7–8, U.S. Students and Scholars from the People's Republic of China, 1987.

Zorn 1987.   Zorn, Werner, "How the CSNET China Link was set up between Karlsruhe and Beijing," *Proceedings of the International Academic Networkshop (Princeton, New Jersey, 9–11 November 1987)*, 1987.

16   *Southeast Asia*

This chapter on Southeast Asia includes sections on networks in Indonesia, Brunei, Singapore, Malaysia, the Philippines, Vietnam, Laos, Cambodia, Thailand, and Burma.

In 1988, this area had a series of coordinated activities called SEACOM 88. These activities were organized by the South-East Asia Regional Computer Confederation (SEARCC), which covers Indonesia, Malaysia, the Philippines, Singapore, and Thailand, as well as Hong Kong, India, Pakistan, and Sri Lanka. SEACOM 88 was sponsored by IFIP TC6 [Luhukay 1987]. See *AUSEAnet* for related activities and contact information.

16.1   *Southeast Asian Networks*

One network covers most of Southeast Asia (and other countries): *AUSEAnet*.

16.1.1   **AUSEAnet**

AUSEAnet is a metanetwork for a joint microelectronics Very Large Scale Integration (VLSI) project among the Association of South East Asian Nations (ASEAN) countries and Australia. The ASEAN countries include Thailand, Indonesia, Malaysia, Singapore, Brunei, and the Philippines. The goal is to permit electronic submission of VLSI designs to the fabrication plant in Australia and to exchange information about microelectronics techniques. Funds are provided by the Australian government and will be augmented by the other participant countries.

Indonesia acts as ASEAN regional center of *AUSEAnet* and connects to the host *munnari* in Australia through an international packet switching line. Each participating ASEAN country will have its own network and an international gateway that will poll the Indonesian hub machine, called *indovax*. The national center in Indonesia is at the Network Laboratory (NETLAB), which is part of the Inter-University Center for Computer Science (IUCCS) at the University of Indonesia in Jakarta.

The project started in July 1986 and was operational by November 1986. Four institutional organizations were connected to NETLAB as of July 1986. At least nine ASEAN institutional nodes currently participate in *AUSEAnet*.

AUSEAnet uses UUCP and SUN-III over the international X.25 networks. Outside of Australia it mostly uses UUCP. Most of the links are 1200bps.

Access
Joseph F. P. Luhukay
uunet!indovax!luhukay
+62-21-330308
Telex: 45680-UI-JKT
NETLAB
University of Indonesia
P.O. Box 3442
Jakarta 10002
Indonesia

16.2   *Malaysia {MY}*

The national research network in Malaysia is called *RangKoM*.

16.2.1   RangKoM

The Malaysian Computer Network is known in Malaysia as Rangkaian Komputer Malaysia — hence the short name, *RangKoM* [Awang-Lah 1987]. The current objective is to link most of the universities in Malaysia in order to demonstrate the usefulness of electronic data communications and of this network in facilitating academic discussions and coordination of research projects [Awang-Lah 1988]. There are seven universities and at least 19 government research institutions in Malaysia that will probably eventually be linked; some other organizations may also join. The network will also be used to share resources such as databases and to conduct research in

Table 16.1. *RangKoM hosts by site*

Site	Organization	Hosts	Users	Planned
MIMOS	Malaysian Institute of Microelectronic Systems	5	100	
UM	University of Malaya	10	3,000	
UPM	University of Agriculture	5	2,000	
USMP	University of Science, Penang	2	300	
USMI	University of Science, Ipoh	3	1,000	August 1988
UKM	National University	10	2,000	
UTM	University of Technology	5	1,500	August 1988
ITM	MARA Institute of Technology	5	1,000	August 1988
AFIM	ASEAN Institute of Forest Management	3	50	
Totals		43	9,655	

Source: Courtesy Mohamed b. Awang-Lah, 1 August 1988

information technology. Use of the network for commercial gain is prohibited.

The network is administered by a technical committee consisting of representatives from all participating organizations. Some technical advice is provided by the Malaysian Institute of Microelectronic Systems (MIMOS).

Services supported include electronic mail, file transfer, and *USENET* news. There are some local *USENET* newsgroups.

As of August 1988 the network extended to six sites around the country, with connections to four more planned. Connections were by leased telephone lines or the Malaysian Packet Switched Data Network (*MAYPAC*).

Figures for hosts and users per site are shown in Table 16.1, together with planned dates for further connections. Others not shown and not yet connected include Dewan Bahasa dan Pustaka (DBdP), or the Language and Literature Planning and Development Agency of Malaysia, and Perpustakaan Negara Malaysia (PNM), or the Malaysian National Library. There are also dialup modem connections. Syarikat Telekom Malaysia (STM), or Malaysian Telecom Company (owned by the government and part of the Telecom Department until it was incorporated in 1987) provides both ordinary dialup telephone service and also *MAYPAC*. The Malaysian Circuit Switched Network (*MAYCIS*) may also be used when it is operational, depending on its tariff structure.

RangKoM is initially a metanetwork, with local area networks at participating universities and other organizations connected by UUCP links in a star around MIMOS. It is planned to move to X.25 and TCP/IP for the long-distance connections, making *RangKoM* more of an internet. Academic institutions with campuses in different parts of the country are expected to make their own arrangements for connecting the campuses.

The *MAYPAC* links mostly run at 1200bps to keep costs down, while the leased lines are mostly used at 4800bps or 9600bps depending on line quality, as shown in Table 16.2. Thus, the average speed is about 4800bps. MIMOS forwards any overseas mail within an hour. Most Malaysian hosts poll the machine with *UUCP* name *mimos* every hour. Mail between *mimos* and the University of Malaysia (UM) is forwarded within a minute. On average, mail reaches destinations inside the country within hours.

Internet DNS domain names are used for all hosts and organizations. The top level domain is *MY*, and subdomains are of the two patterns

    host.organization.MY

and

    host.site.organization.MY

UUCP source routing is also supported.

RangKoM is the Malaysian part of *AUSEAnet*. International connections are done through MIMOS using *mimos*, whose domain name is *mimos.ism.my*. There are direct X.25 links to *uunet* (United States), *mcvax* (Netherlands), *munnari* (Australia), *etrivax* (Korea), and *indogtw* (Indonesia). Electronic mail forwarding between foreign countries is prevented unless prior arrangement is made. A *USENET* news feed is received from *UUNET*.

The ASEAN – Australia Economic Cooperation Programme (AAECP) began in June 1986 and provided an opportunity to get *RangKoM* started. AAECP was a three year program to supply hardware and software for microelectronics design plus some funds to set up *AUSEAnet* links. Some parts of *RangKoM* that were related to the AAECP project were funded by it. For example, AAECP provided some Sun-3/110 workstations, and the communication costs associated with them were borne by AAECP. But most operating overhead costs are paid by the government of Malaysia. *RangKoM* sites not involved in AAECP have to pay their own costs.

The network was officially started in June 1987, but few connections were actually in place at that time. A link between the machines *mimos* and *UKM* was in place by October 1987, and others were set up after November 1987. Connection of the rest of the target organizations is expected by 1990.

Table 16.2. *RangKoM links*

Host	Type	bps	Planned
MIMOS	X.25	2400	
UM	SLIP	9600	
UPM	Dialup X.28	1200	
	SLIP	by	August 1988
USMP	Dialup X.28	1200	
USMI	Leased X.28	1200	August 1988
UKM	Leased X.28	1200	
	SLIP		1989
UTM	Leased	9600	August 1988
ITM	Leased	9600	August 1988
AFIM	Dialup	1200	
DBP	Leased	—	1990
PNM	Leased	—	1990

Source: Courtesy Mohamed b. Awang-Lah, 1 August 1988

AAECP may be terminated in June 1989, causing *RangKoM* to be supported completely by the Malaysian government after that. This support may come from each of the participating institutions, which are mostly government agencies, in the form of the operating costs of the links to the central site at MIMOS. Overseas communications would be supported by MIMOS, perhaps with assistance from a special government fund for *RangKoM* as a research project under the sixth Malaysia Plan, for 1990 through 1994. Otherwise, it is likely that international communication costs will be charged back to the users.

A distributed user registry is planned, so it will be possible to send mail to user@rangkom.MY regardless of the actual home machine of the user. Databases related to agriculture and electronics are also planned. Transmission speeds of 64Kbps are planned, and tests were expected by the end of 1988.

Access

Mohamed b. Awang-Lah
mal@mimos.ISM.MY
uunet!mimos!mal
+60-3-2552-700
Telex: MA28145
Malaysian Institute of Microelectronic Systems (MIMOS)
Lot 7.2, Bukit Naga Complex
Off Jalan Semantan
50490 Kuala Lumpur
Malaysia

Administrative requests or inquiries should go to the Director General, MIMOS, at the preceding address.

16.3   *Singapore {SG}*

The Singapore *BITNET* node, *NUSVM*, is the first one in Southeast Asia and is located at the National University of Singapore (NUS). This is a rather large campus, with 14,500 undergraduates, 1,400 graduate students, and several local area networks on campus. The *BITNET* link has been operational since January 1987. The initial connection method was by daily dialup using a dialup feature recently introduced into **RSCS Version 2, Release 2**. A 4800bps leased line was installed by February 1987, and a 9600bps line by January 1988, as traffic increased.

The *BITNET* GATES table shows an entry registered for a domain AC.SG for a Singapore National Network, with gateway *NUSVM.BITNET*. All local telephone calls in Singapore are free, and this actually means all telephone calls, due to the size of the country. So a national dialup network is easy.

There is theoretically Singaporean cooperation in *AUSEAnet*, but actual details are unknown.

There is a UUCP link over X.25 from *tataelxsi* in Singapore to *munnari* in Australia and to *etrivax* in Korea, and perhaps other links to other places. These are *PACNET* connections. There is a link from *tataelxsi* to *nus-cs* in the Department of Computer Sciences at NUS, but there is apparently no internal connection between *nus-cs* and *NUSVM.BITNET*.

Access
POSTMAST@NUSVM.BITNET
Loh, Wai Lung
aawai@NUSVM.bitnet
+65-772-2056
Fax: +65-778-0198
Telex: RS5111-NUSPER
Computer Centre
National University of Singapore
Kent Ridge 0511
Singapore

16.4   *Indonesia {ID}*

The national research network in Indonesia is called *UNInet* (not to be confused with *UNINETT* of Norway). There is a *UUNET* connection from Indonesia to *indogtw*. See also *AUSEAnet* earlier in this chapter.

16.4.1   UNInet

UNInet is a university research network in Indonesia. It is part of a five year plan of the government of Indonesia, in cooperation with many commercial and research organizations. Twelve sites were listed as of 1 August 1988.

The second phase of *UNInet* development began in the summer of 1988 and is ultimately planned to link 45 government sponsored universities in Indonesia. Some links will use the Palapa satellite.

> **Access**
> Joseph F. P. Luhukay
> uunet!indovax!luhukay
> Fax: +62-21-310-2774
> Telex: 45680-ui-jkt
> NETLAB
> University of Indonesia
> P.O. Box 3442
> Jakarta 10002
> Indonesia

16.5   *Brunei {BN}*

There are no known systems in Brunei.

16.6   *Philippines {PH}*

Apparently there's an *AUSEAnet* connection to the Philippines. There is also a *MILNET* connection to Clark Air Force Base there.

16.7   *Vietnam {VN}*

There are no known networks in Vietnam.

16.8   *Cambodia {KH}*

There are no known networks in Cambodia.

16.9   *Laos {LA}*

There are no known networks in Laos.

16.10   *Thailand {TH}*

The national academic network in Thailand is called *TCSnet*.

16.10.1   TCSnet

Since June 1988, four universities in Thailand have been connected in *TCSnet*, or Thai Computer Science Network. The universities are Asian Institute of Technology (AIT), Thammasat University, Chulalongkorn University, all in greater Bangkok, and Prince of Songkhla University (PSU) in Hat Yai and in Pattani, both in southern Thailand. There is one host on each campus, making five hosts in all (or six, counting one at AIT on a local area network). All of the hosts run **UNIX**. About 80 percent of the users are in computer science, with about 20 percent administrators of research projects [Kanchanasut 1988]. There are connections between almost every pair of hosts. AIT is an autonomous, international postgraduate institute providing training and research in engineering and science. There isn't any dedicated funding for the network yet, since telephone calls within the Bangkok area are cheap and traffic is low.

All links within Thailand are by telephone dialup at 1200bps or 2400bps; mail delivery usually takes at least a day [Kanchanasut 1988]. The telephone system is particularly bad during rainstorms, when getting connections is difficult and line noise increases greatly. The Australian SUN-III protocols, invented for *ACSnet*, are used and work rather well under these conditions [Elz 1988]. SUN-III adjusts packet sizes and timeout lengths to the condition of the line and can be made to give up entirely if conditions are too bad. SUN-III will also restart a file transfer that is interrupted by a transmission break rather than retransmitting the whole file. In these ways and in being full duplex, this protocol is unlike the otherwise similar dialup protocol UUCP, and it is better adapted for such conditions. The services provided include mail (using **sendmail**), file transfer, and remote job execution. Berkeley **talk** and **rlogin** are supported on local area networks at AIT, as are X-windows and Sun RPC and NFS. A small amount of *USENET* news is imported from *UUNET*.

There was an early UUCP link from host *ait* at AIT to *munnari* in Australia, beginning early in 1988, but that later was changed to connect to *uunet*. This change was partly because there was only one available serial port on the Sun-3/50 for a modem, and the same modem could not be used for both *munnari* and *uunet*. The link to *UUNET* is by X.25 through *TYM-NET* via the Communication Authority of Thailand (CAT); this is less expensive than direct telephone dialup to the United States. It was hoped that by January 1989, CAT would provide an X.25 gateway and that it would cut the communication cost tremendously.

The Thai language is not written with the Latin alphabet but with a character set that uses several layers of accent marks. It is very difficult to represent adequately on line-oriented terminals. This may be one reason for the lack of development of computing in a country of 60 million people (compared to 15 million in Australia). There was only one undergraduate computer science program in the country by the end of 1988, and its first class was scheduled to graduate in 1989 (there are several postgraduate programs, though). Also, the government did not emphasize this subject or technology until the birth of cheap microcomputers made it difficult to ignore. The language certainly is one reason for the popularity of IBM PCs and clones. Those systems have bit-mapped displays and Thai character display cards, and they are inexpensive. The Thai character set is small enough (44 consonants, 21 vowels, and 4 tonal signs, although there are 5 spoken tones) [Kanchanasut 1988] to fit in 8 bits, and even to coexist with Roman ASCII, so representational problems are not as severe as with Japanese or Chinese. Most machines make do with 7 bits, using escape sequences for accents.

Access
Tomonori Kimura
uunet!ait!tk
+66-2-529-0100, ext. 2709
Division of Computer Science
Asian Institute of Technology
P.O. Box 2754
Bangkok 10501
Thailand

16.11   *Myanmar {BU}*

There are no known networks in Myanmar, formerly known as Burma.

16.12   *References*

Awang-Lah 1987.   Awang-Lah, Mohamed b., "RangKoM—The Malaysian Computer Network," *Proceedings of the International Academic Networkshop (Princeton, New Jersey, 9 – 11 November 1987)*, 1987.

Awang-Lah 1988.   Awang-Lah, Mohamed b., Personal communications, August 1988.

Elz 1988.   Elz, Robert, Personal communications, July – August 1988.

Kanchanasut 1988.   Kanchanasut, Kanchana, Personal communications, August 1988.

Luhukay 1987.   Luhukay, Dr. Joseph F. P., "SEACOMM 88," *Proceedings of the International Academic Networkshop (Princeton, New Jersey, 9 – 11 November 1987)*, 1987.

17   *South Asia*

South Asia includes India, Sri Lanka, Pakistan, Bangladesh, and the Himalayan states.

17.1   *India {IN}*

There are few actual networks in India, but there is much planning activity. Thus, this section includes not only *NICNET*, *OILCOMNET*, and *INDONET*, which exist, but also *ERNET*, which does not yet, but for which extensive planning has been done.

There has also been much use of mailing lists on foreign networks such as the *Internet* and *BITNET*, and of the *USENET* newsgroup *soc.culture.india*, by Indian expatriates in the United States and elsewhere. There are mailing lists corresponding to each of the Indian Institutes of Technology (IITs), for example.

There are a number of special purpose foreign network links, including the following:

- A Kermit link from the International Crop Research Institute for the Semi-Arid Tropics (ICRISAT) in Hyderabad connecting to the agricultural system *CGNET* in Palo Alto, California [Lindsey 1987].
- A link once existed from National Aeronautics Limited to the Information Retrieval Service of the European Space Agency (ESA) databases at Frascati, Italy [Garg 1989a].

- Links to banks [Jolly and Jain 1988]. Many banks, such as Citibank or Hong Kong Bank, have international links and domestic data networks. Some have automated teller machine networks [Garg 1988].
- Links to airlines. Air India and Indian Airlines have passenger reservation data networks and are linked to the international airline system Société International de Télécommunications Aéronautiques (SITA), although the third Indian airline, Vayudoot, does not have such a network yet [Garg 1988].
- A satellite link from Texas Instruments (TI) in Bangalore to the United States. Such private links must be cleared individually with the highest levels of the Indian government [Garg 1988].

There is a great deal of interest from Europe and elsewhere in electronic mail connections to India. This is because there is quite a bit of research collaboration going on between Indian and foreign colleagues. The only other ways of reaching India are the following:

Telephone
: Connections are difficult and noisy, and there is the time zone problem. As always, voice telephone is not good for transferring large amounts of text or data.

Paper mail
: The usual practice is to send up to ten copies of a document in hopes that two or three will arrive in ten days to a month. This is expensive, and the turnaround time is prohibitive (although that is what I finally resorted to for this book).

VIDYANET
: There were negotiations for electronic connections from the National Centre for Software Technology (NCST), Bombay, and the Tata Institute of Fundamental Research (TIFR), Bombay, to a foreign academic network such as *BITNET* or *CSNET*: this was known as *VIDYANET* [Garg 1988]. The word *vidya* in Hindi means knowledge, and *VIDYANET* is thus appropriate for the academic community. However, the January 1989 connection to *UUNET* has obviated much of the need for *VIDYANET*. Also, future connection approvals seem likely to be for *ERNET* [Garg 1989a]. As of August 1988, there were negotiations in progress with *EARN*, and a connection to *JANET* from *ERNET* had been approved by July 1988 (see the section later in this chapter on *ERNET*). NCST, Bombay (one of the key *ERNET* nodes) may be connecting to University College London (UCL) for *JANET* in the United Kingdom, or perhaps with INRIA in Paris or CWI in Amsterdam.

Telex
: The most reliable way to communicate electronically with people in India as of July 1988 was still *Telex*. But connections are intermittent, and this medium is not amenable to sophisticated forms of text or data or to large transmissions [Garg and Ramani 1987].

UUNET
: NCST has had an intermittent connection to *UUNET* in the United States since June 1988 and a reliable one, using Telebit modems, since 12 January 1989.

The Indian host connected to *UUNET* is *shakti*, which is a VAX-8600 running **Ultrix**. It runs a directory information service, not only for NCST, but also for several other Indian sites reachable by mail through it. To use this service, send mail to

uunet!shakti!infoserv

containing the following information:

request: directory
topic: name [name] [name]

The topic line can contain more than one name. For example, to find the mail name of Anant Joshi, try

request: directory
topic: joshi

Uppercase and lowercase distinctions are ignored by the infoserver. Replies are returned by electronic mail [Garg 1989b].

This work is part of the Education and Research Network Project, funded by the Department of Electronics (DOE) of the Government of India, and is assisted by the United Nations Development Program (UNDP). The project is headed by Mr. S. Ramakrishnan of DOE [Garg 1989b].

There are other planned projects or existing networks besides those described in their own subsections below. Some of these are:

Electricity Boards	These use Siemens and other machines such as those of Brwon Boveri. Not only the machines but also the protocols differ, and many of the protocols are proprietary, although DECNET is used in the western region [Garg 1988].
BANKNET	This service was initiated by the Reserve Bank of India, and its first phase was expected to be operational in early 1989, connecting four or five cities in a backbone network of IBM machines. The second phase is expected to have 500 hosts, mostly running **UNIX**, all over India. These are expected to use the ISO-OSI protocols and be connected to the Society for Worldwide Interbank Financial Telecommunication (SWIFT) banking system [Garg 1988].
INFLIBNET	The National Library Network is a proposed network to connect all the libraries in all the universities and major research laboratories. The purchase of many computers will be necessary, since most libraries don't have any [Garg 1989a].

Various other groups are interested in building networks, such as the police and the Steel Authority [Garg 1988].

Access

Anil Garg<uunet!shakti!anil>
H. Shrikumar <uunet!shakti!shri>
S. Ramani <uunet!shakti!ramani>
+91-(22)-6201606
+91-(22)-6201574
+91-(22)-6201488
Telex: 011-78260-NCST-IN
National Centre for Software Technology (NCST)
Gulmohar Cross Road No. 9
Juhu, Bombay 400 049
India

uunet!shakti!infoserv

17.1.1   NICNET

The National Informatics Centre of the Government of India has as one of its functions to provide Management Information Services (MIS) to various agencies in the central and state governments [Seshagiri et al. 1988]. This department is developing a network, *NICNET*, to promote communication among these agencies with mail and file transfer, and especially to provide access to databases kept on four already installed computer systems. Hardware and software are to be shared to reduce overall costs. This is all in direct support of functions of the government such as monitoring projects involving the public, emergency relief, and dissemination of information to the public.

The network is planned to be a four layer hierarchy corresponding to the levels of government in India:

National government. The database machines are NEC S-100s at Delhi, Pune, Bhubaneshwar, and Hyderabad. The Delhi machine is to act as a central coordinating node.

State and union territory governments. These 37 governments are obtaining minicomputers and PC/ATs to use as nodes.

District governments. The 439 districts will probably obtain PC/AT class machines.

Block Development Agencies. These agencies, at the lowest level of government, number 5,000. They are expected to generate most of the data, and they will eventually have terminals or PCs for this purpose.

The databases on the four central machines and elsewhere are to be coordinated by a program and protocol called **UDBMS**. Ideally, **UDBMS** will implement a nationwide distributed database making use of local computing capacity. The long-distance links are to be carried over satellites using a spread spectrum technique that deliberately uses more bandwidth than would be necessary in order to minimize interference. Multiplexing of communications is done by code division multiple access (CDMS) over 5MHz channels. The data channels being multiplexed are 153.6Kbps, and the effective channels are 1200bps or 9600bps. Above all this, X.25 (1980) is used, along with parts of X.25 (1984).

Short links are done synchronously at 4800bps with **PC Link** software or asynchronously at 1200bps. Voice-grade VHF links may be used where land lines are not adequate. Large government offices will eventually have local area networks [Garg and Ramani 1987]. The national PDN, *VIKRAM*, should be fully operational in 1989.

Access
Dr. N. Seshagiri
Director General
+91-621475
Telex: 031-61274-NICS-IN
Director General
National Informatics Centre
CGO Complex, Lodi Road
New Delhi 110 003
India

17.1.2   OILCOMNET

OILCOMNET is a national network used by the Indian oil industry to reduce communication costs [Kumar 1988]. The basic services are electronic mail and retrieval of management information. Eventually, a range of office automation services are wanted. Various word processing and spreadsheet programs are already available. One long-distance link has been established between New Delhi and Bombay. The current link is a 2400bps leased microwave channel. Most users communicate with the backbone machines over 1200bps leased lines through terminals; there are a few nonterminal workstations in Delhi. About 20 organizations, both companies and government agencies, are connected in this manner. This location was chosen for the initial link because these organizations represent more than 10 percent of all economic activity in India. Eventually, the network is planned to have a backbone connecting Delhi, Bombay, Madras, Calcutta, and Gauhati, with many other cities connected in star networks from each of the backbone sites.

The backbone machines are Systems PCA 4000s, which are Indian versions of Data General MV 4000s. There are no high-level network protocols beyond RS-232-C, except on the intercity links (which use X.25 over leased lines). Eventually, use of X.25 is expected on all links, either over leased lines or, if a national PDN arises, using that. Use of satellite connections was considered but rejected on the grounds that signal delay would be a problem and that the available frequencies would become overcrowded due to the popularity of satellite communications among other parties. Also, high frequencies can be blocked by heavy rain, which is common in parts of India, and closely spaced earth stations can interfere with one another.

There are no connections to other networks.

OILCOMNET was first operational about October 1987, but tests began much earlier [Garg 1989a]. The original idea was to have a central batch computer for computational functions and a separate message switching system with 5 bit **Baudot** code interconnections to remote printers. The emergence of personal computers and the recognition of time-sharing led to the current approach.

Access
G. M. Deshpande
Additional Director (CS)
Oil Coordination Committee
2nd Floor, Core-2, SCOPE Complex
7 Institutional Area, Lodhi Road
New Delhi 100 003
India

17.1.3   INDONET

INDONET is a private data network managed by CMC, a public sector company (formerly known as Computer Maintenance Corporation, now involved in software development and known as CMC Ltd. [Garg 1989a]). It uses SNA over leased lines to interconnect IBM machines in five cities. It began in 1986, and there are plans for vigorous expansion [Garg 1988].

Access
Dr. P. P. Gupta
Chairman and Managing Director
CMC Ltd.
1 Kilkori, Ring Road, opposite Maharani Bagh
New Delhi
India

17.1.4 ERNET

The Government of India is developing an academic and research network, *ERNET*, to promote advances in computer communications technology in India [Mathur and Ramakrishnan 1988]. The initial goal is to connect computing resources at eight academic and research institutions, on explicit analogy with *ARPANET, CSNET, CYCLADES, DFN, JANET,* and other national research networks. The network is to be kept open to systems from many vendors by use of the ISO-OSI layering model and protocols. Use of off-the-shelf technology is planned where possible. The participating agencies are the Indian Institutes of Technology (IITs) at Delhi, Kanpur, Kharagpur, Madras, and Bombay, the Indian Institute of Science (IISc) in Bangalore, the National Centre for Software Technology (NCST) in Bombay, and the Department of Electronics (DOE), Government of India, which is responsible for implementing the network. Administration is done by committees derived from the DoE and the project coordinators from each of the participating agencies.

The initial services supported are to be mail, file transfer, remote login, and database access. Some sort of conferencing service is likely.

The *last mile* problem occurs in India, where there is no national PDN (although one, named *VIKRAM*, is planned) and the telephone system is not adequate to the task of supporting a wide area network. Even though **UNIX** machines are popular and prevalent, there is no Indian branch of the *UUCP* network. This is because telephone circuits are too noisy and connections are too difficult to obtain for the current UUCP protocol to manage [Garg and Ramani 1987]. Thus, *ERNET* uses a satellite network for its national backbone, running X.25 over it. To avoid the same problem in metropolitan area networks, those are expected to be based on packet radio. Local area networks will be ordinary IEEE 802.3, with eventual additional use of 802.5. When length requirements make them necessary, fiber-optic links will be used for campus backbones. All these networks are to be joined into an internet by use of ISO-IP; TCP/IP was considered but rejected so that later conversion to ISO-OSI protocols could be avoided. Speeds of all these systems were unknown at the time of writing because they had not yet been implemented; the satellite network was still being designed. However, effective speeds through the satellite links are likely to be 64Kbps [Garg 1988]. For the same reason, there are no interconnections to other networks. Connections with *JANET* were approved by JNT in July 1988, and NCST has had a link with *UUNET* since June 1988. Communications with CERN and similar research organizations abroad are particularly desirable from organizations such as the Tata Institute of Fundamental Research (TIFR), Department of Science and Technology, Government of

India, in Bombay, which might be enticed to join or fund *ERNET* if such connections were available [Garg and Ramani 1987]. In fact, as of August 1988, TIFR had applied to connect a Digital VAX, and possibly a CDC Cyber 170, to CERN with **JNET**, forming a connection to *EARN*.

The idea for Project ERNET was introduced in 1984 in the Indian Seventh Five Year Plan as an area for particular development. Funding came in 1985 from the United Nations Development Program (UNDP) ($6 million U.S.) and the Government of India (30 million rupees). UNDP had also been active in exposing participants to state of the art technology, and thus to the development of the idea. Official approval came in November 1986; implementation started shortly thereafter.

There are plans to extend the initial network not only into local area networks inside the participating agencies, but also into both cities and rural areas. Planned services include graphics transfer protocols and conferencing in several media. Experiments in underlying protocols and in new services are expected. Eventually, it is hoped that such developments will lead to the deployment of networks for use by the general public and industry.

Access

S. Ramakrishnan
Additional Director
Department of Electronics, Govt. of India
A Block, CGO Complex, Lodi Road
New Delhi 110 003
India

Anil Garg
+91-(22)-6201606
+91-(22)-6201574
+91-(22)-6201488
Telex: 011-78260-NCST-IN
National Centre for Software Technology (NCST)
Gulmohar Cross Road No. 9
Juhu, Bombay 400 049
India

17.1.5   Railways

Indian Railways has used computerized reservations since 1987 and is linking them together in a nationwide network that will also be used for managing cargo movements [Garg 1988].

Access
A. J. Kumar
Chief Project Manager
+91-345775
Computerised Railway Reservation System
Northern Railways
Chelmsford Road, I Floor, IRCA Bldg.
New Delhi 110 001
India

17.2   *Sri Lanka {LK}*

Apparently there is an *AUSEAnet* connection in Sri Lanka. *CGNET* also has subscribers there.

17.3   *Pakistan {PK}*

There are no known networks in Pakistan.

17.4   *Bangladesh {BD}*

CGNET has subscribers in Bangladesh.

17.5   *Nepal {NP}*

CGNET has subscribers in Nepal.

17.6   *Bibliographic Notes*

A very useful single source for a perspective on patterns of development in the developing world is the proceedings of a conference held in New Delhi in 1987 [Ramani and Garg 1988]. This work relates the experience of developed countries to the possibilities of developing ones. There are articles by people from Australia, Italy, France, Japan, Korea, Germany, Canada, the United Kingdom, and the United States.

17.7   *References*

Garg 1988.   Garg, Anil, Personal communications, August – September 1988.

Garg 1989a.   Garg, Anil, Personal communications, February 1989.

Garg 1989b.   Garg, Anil, Personal communications, 12 January 1989.

Garg and Ramani 1987.   Garg, A., and Ramani, S., "Options for Networking Academic Centres in India," *Proceedings of the International Academic Networkshop (Princeton, New Jersey, 9 – 11 November 1987)*, pp. 3, 6, 8, 1987.

Jolly and Jain 1988.   Jolly, A. K., and Jain, S. C., "Message Switch System in Indian Banks," *Proceedings of the Special Conference of the International Council for Computer Communication (New Delhi, 17 – 30 October 1987)*, pp. 331 – 336, Elsevier, Amsterdam, November 1988.

Kumar 1988.   Kumar, A. J., "OILCOMNET: An Office Communication and Computing Network for India's Oil Industry," *Proceedings of the Special Conference of the International Council for Computer Communication (New Delhi, 17 – 30 October 1987)*, pp. 358 – 366, Elsevier, Amsterdam, November 1988.

Lindsey 1987.   Lindsey, Georg, "The Green Revolution," *Kermit News*, vol. 2, no. 1, pp. 4 – 5, November 1987.

Mathur and Ramakrishnan 1988.   Mathur, M. N., and Ramakrishnan, S., "Project ERNET: Perspectives, Plan and Approach of an Academic and Research Network Program in India," *Proceedings of the Special Conference of the International Council for Computer Communication (New Delhi, 17 – 30 October 1987)*, pp. 147 – 166, Elsevier, Amsterdam, November 1988.

Ramani and Garg 1988.   Ramani, S., and Garg, Anil, *Proceedings of the Special Conference of the International Council for Computer Communication (New Delhi, 17 – 30 October 1987)*, Elsevier, Amsterdam, November 1988.

Seshagiri et al. 1988.   Seshagiri, N., Kutty, K. K. K., Vijayaditya, N., Sharma, Y. K., Bobde, D. P., and Moni, M., "NICNET: A Hierarchic Distributed Computer Communication Network for Decision Support in the Indian Government," *Proceedings of the Special Conference of the International Council for Computer Communication (New Delhi, 17 – 30 October 1987)*, pp. 367 – 379, Elsevier, Amsterdam, November 1988.

18 Latin America

The utility of computer networks in academic research has become increasingly apparent to many people in this region. There are several efforts to coordinate social scientists working in Latin American studies by the use of computer networks, and Latin American scholars are increasingly interested in building a network infrastructure in and between their countries. The situation somewhat resembles that in Southeast Asia. Several services based elsewhere have conferences dedicated to Latin America, such as CARNet on *PeaceNet*.

18.1 Development Networks

There are several systems and lists devoted to development.

18.1.1 CARINET

CARINET is intended for general network communications by business and development organizations in and among Latin America, the Caribbean, Africa, the Middle East, Asia, Europe, and North America—i.e., most of the world—concentrating on the less industrially developed regions, with users in 32 countries. There is particular emphasis on Latin America, and conferences are carried out in both Spanish and English. *CARINET* first began in 1982 as a conference on *EIES*.

CARINET is based on *EIES* and is accessed primarily by X.25 through the international PDNs; thus most users connect at 1200bps. There is a

DASnet connection. *CARINET* has about 250 users, for a total of 500 in combination with its partner system *CGNET* [Janus 1988; CARINET 1988]. But the people who make use of it are more numerous than its direct users: local government or nongovernmental agencies may interact with farmers, potters, or others who would not use a keyboard themselves, and relay questions and comments through *CARINET* [Hesser 1987].

All funding for *CARINET* is from fees charged to the users [Janus 1988]. *CARINET* is owned by a consortium whose members included (at the time of writing) the Rodale Institute (Rodale), The Daedalus Group, Inc. (Daedalus), Agricultural Cooperative Development International (ACDI), Devres, Inc. (Devres), and Partnership for Productivity (PFP). Many of them provide specialized services through *CARINET*.

In addition to CMC (both interactive and batch), *CARINET* provides a document ordering service called Carinet Information Service (CIS) that provides access for Third World users to U.S. libraries and databases. Technology transfer and cutting of communication and travel expenses are major goals. One of the primary uses of the system is the pooling of the users' expertise in diverse areas such as health, education, argiculture, and small businesses. Some conferences are used for online courses on these subjects.

Not all *CARINET* services are informational only; for example, the USAID Office of Foreign Disaster Assistance (OFDA) uses *CARINET* in coordinating disaster assistance. Also, system staff provide personal user training both in person and over telephones. They will even assist in obtaining and installing terminals, modems, and communication software, as well as in obtaining appropriate telephone service.

CARINET was created by Jerry Glenn and PFP [Hesser 1987], which is a nonprofit corporation specializing in Third World economic development, in response to an approach to networking by Control Data Corporation (CDC) that PFP found unsatisfactory. PFP sold *CARINET* in 1987, when *CARINET* became an independent for-profit corporation.

The main emphasis of the system has always been on actual uses in development—i.e., use by people and organizations already involved in Third World development. The hope is to accelerate development by connecting the people involved in it throughout the world and to provide a means of technology transfer (including the technology of networking) for their use. *CARINET* has been rather successful in doing this, and growth is currently about 40 percent per year [Janus 1988].

Access

531@DDEIES.DAS.NET
+1-202-638-4661
Telex: 160923
Fax: +1-202-628-1813

Noreene Z. Janus
Janus@DDE1NJ.DAS.NET
Carinet: 370
CGNET: CGI104
+1-202-626-8720

CARINET, Inc.
50 F Street NW, Suite 900
Washington, DC 20001
U.S.A.

18.1.2   LASNET

LASNET is an example of a type of thing that is not generally listed in this book: although the name stands for Latin American Studies Network, *LASNET* is neither a network nor a conferencing system; it is a mailing list. It is intended to "expand the use of electronic mail and file transfer in the social sciences, particularly between scholars doing work on Central and South American topics" by putting scholars of and in Latin America in touch with each other. These include historians, social scientists, economists, and linguists of Spanish and Portuguese. The list was started because of a realization on the part of some such scholars that computer networks provided a more economical and convenient way to communicate in pursuit of research than did telephones and paper mail.

Real networks used in *LASNET* include *BITNET*, the *Internet*, *UUCP*, and the *Ean* networks. There are only about 40 members of the list, but they are located in Chile, Norway, France, Israel, and Argentina. The list was started in 1986 at the Institute for Latin American Studies (ILASUT) of the University of Texas at Austin (UT Austin), where it is still maintained, although the originator, Langston Gorée, is now with the United Nations in Brasilia, Brazil. It is conceivable that *LASNET* will eventually be seen as one of the major impetuses for a hemispheric network for nongovernmental and noncommercial users.

Access

Sandy Wheaton
ilasut@emx.utexas.edu
BITNET: ilcj775@UTA3081
UUCP: uunet!cs.utexas.edu!ut-emx!ilasut
+1-512-471-5551

The Institute of Latin American Studies
University of Texas at Austin
Austin, TX 78712
U.S.A.

18.2   *Mexico {MX}*

There are several wide area networks in Mexico. Much networking traffic is supported by the national PDN, *TELEPAC*, and the satellite network *Morelos*, both of which are described in Appendix A.

Commercial application networks are run by the following:

- Petróleos Mexicanos (PEMEX), the government oil monopoly (It has about 70 sites and is built from *TELEPAC* and microwave links [Trujillo 1987], as well as using the *Morelos* satellite network. Currently, 24 channels are used for voice and data, and this is expected to increase to 800 in the next few years [Castañón 1988].)
- IBM, with ten sites connected by leased circuits, and presumably connected to *VNET*
- Banks, with leased circuits and some satellite links
- Some other leased circuit links [Trujillo 1987]

There are two academic networks in Mexico: *UNAM* and *ITESM*.

18.2.1   UNAM

The *UNAM* network is run by Universidad Nacional Autonomidad de México (UNAM), the autonomous national university in Mexico City. It has 15 sites connected by leased lines and *TELEPAC* links and uses the **SECOBI** database access application. About 250,000 students could have access in principle [Trujillo 1987].

18.2.2   ITESM

ITESM is a network of the Instituto Tecnológico de Estudios Superiores de Monterrey (ITESM), or the Monterrey Technological Institute of Higher Education, a private university [Marti 1988]. The network was initiated from the Mexico City campus of ITESM and was operational in September 1987. It originally connected nine ITESM campuses and now connects 14. Eight more are expected to be online by November 1988, with all 26 connected by May 1989. Of these, one will be reached by a microwave connection, but the other 25 will be connected by satellite links, using *Morelos*.

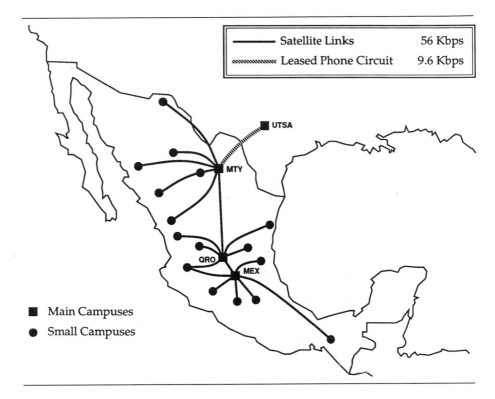

Figure 18.1. *ITESM map (November 1987) [Trujillo 1987]*

The network is arranged in two connected stars around the Mexico and Monterrey campuses, extending from Chiapas to Chihuahua, as shown in Figure 18.1 [Herrera and Guerra G. 1988]. There are 27,000 students in all of ITESM, including 11,000 at the Monterrey campus, where there are 250 faculty [Trujillo 1987].

The network is managed from the Mexico City campus. This campus has its own local area network using fiber optics and Ethernet [Herrera and Guerra G. 1988]. It connects machines ranging from an IBM 4381 to Apple Macintoshes and includes 16 minicomputers and 585 microcomputers in all. The users of these computers come mostly from computer systems engineering, but also from computer systems administration undergraduates and from electronic, industrial, and systems engineering, followed by electrical, mechanical, and administrative mechanical engineering. Not all engineering specializations use these machines or the network, and such use has not become popular in the social sciences or other areas [Marti 1988].

The satellite connections use Vitalink and Republic Telcom hardware to give the appearance of a single Ethernet. The **SECOBI** database software is used [Trujillo 1987]. There are experiments in progress involving digital image transmission [Marti 1988].

Interconnections with private networks are illegal in Mexico, but an interconnection between *ITESM* and *UNAM* is expected to occur eventually. There is a *BITNET* link through the University of Texas at San Antonio (UTSA). There are tentative plans for two connections to *NSFNET*, both through the National Center for Atmospheric Research (NCAR) in Boulder, Colorado: a 56Kbps link to Monterrey and a 1.544Mbps link to Mexico City [Herrera and Guerra G. 1988].

Access

Fernando Herrera
FHERRERA@VMTECMEX.BITNET
+52-871-10-11, ext. 1302, 1303
ITESM
Campus Estado de México
Direccion de Informatica
apdo. Postal 214
53100 Ciudad Satelite
Estado de México
Mexico

18.3   *Central America and the Caribbean*

This region is rather well organized in agricultural networking.

18.3.1   CATIENET

CATIENET is a network named after the Centro Agronómico Tropical de Investigación y Enseñanza (CATIE), or Tropical Agricultural Research and Training Center [Mata 1988a]. CATIE is a nonprofit regional organization headquartered in Turrialba, Costa Rica. It was created in 1973 by an agreement between the government of Costa Rica and the Inter-American Institute for Cooperation on Agriculture (IICA). More recently, CATIE has also acquired as members El Salvador, Guatemala, Honduras, Nicaragua, Panama, and the Dominican Republic. All of the CATIE member countries will participate in *CATIENET* when it becomes operational, which is expected in 1989 [Mata 1988b]. This is every Spanish-speaking Central American country, plus one in the Caribbean.

The purpose of *CATIENET* is to permit exchanging information about agriculture and forestry through electronic mail and database access and to share the computer resources of CATIE. The network is arranged in a star around the main CATIE computer, an IBM 9370. Currently there are a few microcomputers installed in the agricultural sectors of the member countries, and these serve as the other network nodes [Mata 1988b].

The initial services are electronic mail and file transfer, with access at every local CATIE office and at agricultural institutions (such as ministries, universities, and research centers) in the member countries. Distributed mailboxes and packet switching were considered important for cost reduction, leading CATIE to ask IBM for use of *VNET*, which has nodes in each of the member countries. But it was not possible to reach an agreement with IBM about this, primarily because of security concerns. A combination of dialup and packet switching technologies is being considered, using the telephone system and the Costa Rican PDN *RACSAPAC*, which is expanding into other countries [Mata 1988b].

There were some initial concerns about the quality of telephone service to Turrialba, which is 70 kilometers from San José, the capital of Costa Rica (this is a case of the *last mile* problem). UHF radio and microwave links were considered, but reliable communication between the two cities proved to be possible using leased and switched telephone lines [Mata 1988b]. The two main machines at CATIE in Costa Rica are connected by an Ethernet with TCP/IP protocols [Mata 1988a].

Planned future services in future stages of development of the network include batch remote job entry (second stage) and interactive database access (third stage). Connections are also wanted to U.S., Canadian, and European institutions that collaborate with CATIE. A connection to *BIT-NET* is being investigated for this purpose [Mata 1988b]. Video teleconferencing and distributed image processing are eventual goals [Mata 1988a].

Access
Francisco J. Mata
Computer Centre
Centro Agronómico Tropical de Investigación y Enseñanza (CATIE)
7170 Turrialba
Costa Rica

18.4   *Belize {BZ}*

There are no known networks in Belize.

18.5   *Costa Rica {CR}*

Costa Rica is the center of *CATIENET*. The conferencing system *UPGCN* is also located there.

18.5.1   UPGCN

This conferencing system was set up by the University for Peace (UPCR) in Costa Rica with the help of *PeaceNet* and the associated musicians' organization APC [Graham 1987]. It has UUCP connections with *PeaceNet* and *GreenNet* and, through them, with many networks and conferencing systems throughout the world.

UPGCN has the following purposes [Gutierrez 1987]:

- To compile a World Yellow Pages listing all documentation and organizations in peace-related fields
- International conferencing on peace-related subjects
- Access to databases and compilation of a local database
- Dissemination of peace information in coordination with INFORPAZ and *DIALOGUE,* a news service and newspaper run by UPCR

Access
University for Peace
Telex: 2331 Macaze
P.O. Box 199-1250
Escazu
Costa Rica

18.6   *Dominican Republic {DO}*

The Dominican Republic participates in *CATIENET*.

18.7   *El Salvador {SV}*

El Salvador participates in *CATIENET*.

18.8   *Guatemala {GT}*

Guatemala participates in *CATIENET*.

18.9   *Honduras {HN}*

Honduras participates in *CATIENET*.

18.10   *Nicaragua {NI}*

Nicaragua participates in *CATIENET*.

18.11   *Panama {PA}*

Panama participates in *CATIENET*.

18.12   *Puerto Rico {PR}*

Puerto Rico has an active local branch of *FidoNet* called *RED*.

18.12.1   **RED**

This is a *FidoNet* subnetwork (net 367 in zone 1, gateway *1:367/1*) in Puerto Rico [Davila 1988]. There were five nodes as of February 1988. The major echo (conference) on *RED* is called *LatinoNet*, and most discussions are held in Spanish and are about topics relating to Latin America — thus the inclusion of this section under Latin America even though Puerto Rico is a territory of the United States.

18.13   *Haiti {HT}*

The Center for Population and Family Health (CPFH) in the Faculty of Medicine of Columbia University (Columbia) in New York uses Kermit to reach Haiti and Africa. CPFH has been working in those places since 1982, with goals of improving family planning services and the health of children and mothers through both research and direct assistance. The previous method of data transfer was by card decks read into an IBM mainframe. In addition to switching to Kermit, CPFH has also switched to smaller machines, but they still use Columbia mainframes to access *BITNET*. However, some communications even in the States — e.g., with Johns Hopkins University — is with Kermit over direct links [Weatherby 1987].

18.14   *Cuba {CU}*

There is a connection to *IASnet* in Cuba.

18.15   *South America*
18.16   *Argentina {AR}*

There is a *BITNET* node in Argentina and a *UUNET* connection to the Department of Computer Science of the Facultad de Ciencias Exactas of the University of Buenos Aires with a gateway machine named *atina*, under the top level domain *AR*.

18.17   *Bolivia {BO}*

There are no known networks in Bolivia.

18.18   *Brazil {BR}*

There are no known networks in Brazil.

18.19   *Chile {CL}*

There is a *UUNET* connection to Chile and a *BITNET* host.

18.20   *Colombia {CO}*

There are no known networks in Colombia.

18.21   *Ecuador {EC}*

There are no known networks in Ecuador.

18.22   *French Guiana {GF}*

There are no known networks in French Guiana.

18.23   *Guyana {GY}*

There are no known networks in Guyana.

18.24   *Paraguay {PY}*

There are no known networks in Paraguay.

18.25   *Peru {PE}*

There are no known networks in Peru.

18.26   *Surinam {SR}*

There are no known networks in Surinam.

18.27   *Uruguay {UY}*

There are no known networks in Uruguay.

18.28   *Venezuela {VE}*

There are no known networks in Venezuela.

18.29   *References*

CARINET 1988.   CARINET, "CARINET Joins Forces with CGNET," *CARI-News*, vol. 1, no. 1, p. 1, CARINET, Inc., Washington, DC, August 1988.

Castañón 1988.   Castañón, Inés, "Sistema de Satélites Morelos," *Caminos del Aire*, pp. 41–43, 45, Internacional de Revistas, Mexico, D.F. 11560, September 1988. Organo Oficial de Mexicana de Aviación; Magazine of Mexicana Airlines, in Spanish and English.

Davila 1988.   Davila, Juan, "Como obtener un numero de Nodo en FidoNet 367 (RED de Puerto Rico)," *FidoNews: International FidoNet Association Newsletter*, vol. 5, no. 5, pp. 14–15, IFNA, St. Louis, MO, 1 February 1988.

Graham 1987.   Graham, Mark, "University for Peace Global Computer Network," *NetNews*, vol. 1, no. 5, p. 1, IGC, San Francisco, Winter 1987.

Gutierrez 1987.   Gutierrez, Claudio, "University for Peace Global Computer Network," *Proceedings of the International Academic Networkshop (Princeton, New Jersey, 9–11 November 1987)*, 1987.

Herrera and Guerra G. 1988.   Herrera, Fernando, and Guerra G., Antonio, Personal communications, 30 September 1988.

Hesser 1987.   Hesser, Phillip A., "CARINET: A Global Marketplace of Information," *Commercial News USA*, pp. 1, 2, 19, U.S. Department of Commerce, International Trade Administration, Washington, DC, September–October 1987.

Janus 1988.   Janus, Noreene, Personal communications, September 1988.

Marti 1988.   Marti, Beatriz, "El Instituto Tecnologico de Monterrey," *Caminos del Aire*, pp. 91–96, Internacional de Revistas, Mexico, D.F. 11560, September 1988. Organo Oficial de Mexicana de Aviación; Magazine of Mexicana Airlines, in Spanish and English.

Mata 1988a.   Mata, Francisco J., "CATIENET: Agricultural Computer Network," *Proceedings of the Special Conference of the International Council for Computer Communication (New Delhi, 17–30 October 1987)*, pp. 34–44, Elsevier, Amsterdam, November 1988.

Mata 1988b.   Mata, Francisco J., Personal communications, 23 November 1988.

Trujillo 1987.   Trujillo, Daniel, "Networks in Mexico," *Proceedings of the International Academic Networkshop (Princeton, New Jersey, 9–11 November 1987)*, 1987.

Weatherby 1987.   Weatherby, Norman, "Kermit at the Center for Population and Family Health," *Kermit News*, vol. 2, no. 1, pp. 5–6, November 1987.

19 *Middle East*

This chapter on the Middle East describes the states of the Persian Gulf (Kuwait, Bahrain, Qatar, United Arab Emirates, Oman, Iraq, and Iran), the Arabian peninsula (Saudi Arabia and the two Yemens), and the eastern Mediterranean and the Jordan Valley (Israel, Jordan, Lebanon, Syria, and Cyprus). This is everything east of the Mediterranean, north of the Red Sea, west of Pakistan, and south of Afghanistan, the Soviet Union, and Turkey.

19.1 *Persian Gulf and Arabian Peninsula*

19.1.1 GulfNet

GulfNet is a research network similar to *EARN* or *BITNET*. It has the same technology and services but is not yet interconnected with them.

GulfNet has nine nodes, seven in Saudi Arabia and two in Kuwait, as shown in Table 19.1. This network has existed since at least July 1986. Most systems apparently run IBM **VM**. There is a **NETSERV** program running at *SANCST00*.

19.2 *Kuwait {KW}*

See *GulfNet*.

Table 19.1. *GulfNet nodes*

Node	Organization
Saudi Arabia	
UQU00	Umm Al Qura University, Makkah
SAKAAU00	King Abdulaziz University, Jeddah
SAKSU00	King Saud University, Riyadh
SAKFU00	King Faisal University, Hufoof
SAUPM00	University of Petroleum and Minerals, Dhahran
SAIPA00	Institute of Public Administration, Riyadh
SANCST00	King Abdulaziz City for Science and Technology, Riyadh
Kuwait	
KUKISR00	Kuwait Institute of Scientific Research
KUIKSC00	IBM Kuwait Scientific Center

19.3   *Bahrain {BH}*

There is a PDN in Bahrain called *IDAS*.

19.4   *Qatar {QA}*

There is a PDN in Qatar called *IDAS*.

19.5   *United Arab Emirates {AE}*

There is a PDN in the United Arab Emirates called *TEDAS*.

19.6   *Oman {OM}*

There are no known networks in Oman.

19.7   *Iraq {IQ}*

There is a PDN in Iraq called *IDAS*.

19.8   *Iran {IR}*

There are no known networks in Iran.

19.9   *Saudi Arabia {SA}*

There is a PDN in Saudi Arabia called *IDAS*. See also *GulfNet*.

19.10   *Red Sea and Mediterranean*

There are no networks that cover this area.

19.11   *Yemen {YE}*

There are no known networks in Yemen.

19.12   *Democratic Yemen {YD}*

There are no known networks in Democratic Yemen.

19.13   *Israel {IL}*

The Israeli government supports a kibbutzim irrigation service network that is used to control water gates and monitor water flows. There is a PDN called *ISRANET* and a commercial network called *GOLDNET*, but the main general purpose network is the Israeli branch of *EARN*, called *ILAN*.

19.13.1   **ILAN**

The main high-level network in Israel is *ILAN*, or Israeli Academic Network (*IL* is the ISO3166 code for Israel), which is the Israeli branch of *EARN*.

There are 47 *ILAN* hosts [Nussbacher 1987; Nussbacher 1988a]. Their division by operating system is rather unusual for *BITNET* or *EARN* because there are so few IBM mainframes. Specifically, there are 17 **VMS**, 12 **UNIX**, 8 **VM**, 4 **NOS**, 3 **MVS**, and 3 **Primos**. Since the main advantage of the NJE protocols is their uniform implementation on **VM** systems as **RSCS**, and some of the operating systems on *ILAN* do not have complete NJE implementations (missing interactive messages or nonmail file transfer), the disadvantages of NJE (such as lack of remote login or general file transfer, detailed in the section on *BITNET* in Chapter 10) come to the fore.

To improve the general functionality of *ILAN*, the Israeli University Telecommunications Subcommittee (IUTS) considered converting the network to four other protocol suites: SNA, DECNET, ISO-OSI, and TCP/IP. To oversimplify the subcommittee's deliberations, SNA and DECNET were rejected because implementations of them are mostly proprietary to single companies and because each of them only has implementations for two of the six operating systems represented in *ILAN*. The ISO-OSI protocols seemed like a good idea, but implementations do not yet exist for all the necessary operating systems. On the other hand, TCP/IP implementations exist not only for all the current *ILAN* operating systems, but also for all of the ones that are likely to be desirable to connect to the network in the near future, such as **MS-DOS** or Cray's **UNICOS**. Most of the desired services (except accounting, authentication control, and interactive messages) and all of the desired underlying network technologies are supported. TCP/IP was already used by many Israeli university campus networks and is widely used in the United States in the *Internet*. A migration path from TCP/IP to ISO-OSI is already being developed by the U.S. Department of Defense (DoD), and some of the key software is already available.

The actual protocol migration path chosen involves installation of TCP/IP on all *ILAN* nodes by mid-1988, followed by a year or two of simultaneous use of TCP/IP and **RSCS**, followed by eventual retirement of **RSCS** and even more eventual migration to ISO-OSI (perhaps by 1992). Meanwhile, protocol conversion between NJE and TCP/IP must be done, not only between internal *ILAN* hosts, but also for communication with *EARN* and *BITNET* [Nussbacher 1987]. This stage was thought to present the toughest technical problems, but a solution was found: **RSCS** over TCP over IP. This makes **RSCS** a sibling protocol of FTP, TELNET, and other TCP/IP applications. *ILAN* benefits from work in that area done by the U.S. National Science Foundation (NSF) for *BITNET II*. This path was chosen because of the interactive messaging capability of NJE and the ability to send a file to another user without a password. While NSF uses **VM RSCS** over IP, *ILAN* uses **UNIX Urep** over IP. The most basic advantage is that users can still use the same software, but TCP/IP applications can also be used where supported [Nussbacher 1988b].

This path is in keeping with the *EARN* migration policy of permitting national networks to keep local protocols as long as they provide gatewaying facilities to the present NJE and the eventual ISO-OSI *EARN* network [Bryant 1987]. The responsibility for this protocol conversion is taken by Tel Aviv University, with the principal machine being *TAUNIVM*. Mail conversion is already in place, and an *Internet* DNS domain, AC.IL, is registered and in use, as in *VM1.TAU.AC.IL* (the domain name of *TAUNIVM*) or *HUJI.AC.IL*. In addition to the standard NJE services provided (mail, chat, LISTSERV, and NETSERV), Israel runs a PC Library server for users within Israel.

Access
Henry Nussbacher
Hank@VM1.TAU.AC.IL
Hank@TAUNIVM.BITNET
Hank@BITNIC.BITNET

19.14   *Jordan {JO}*

There are no known networks in Jordan.

19.15   *Lebanon {LB}*

There are no known networks in Lebanon.

19.16   *Syria {SY}*

There are no known networks in Syria.

19.17   *Cyprus {CY}*

Cyprus is an *EARN* member.

19.18   *References*

Bryant 1987.   Bryant, Paul, "EARN Migration Plans," European Academic Research Network, Rutherford Appleton Laboratory, Didcot, Oxfordshire, England, 20 April 1987.

Nussbacher 1987.   Nussbacher, Henry, "Conversion Plans from RSCS to Tcp/Ip for Israel Academic Network," *TCP-IP@SRI-NIC.ARPA*, Israeli University Telecommunications Subcommittee, Tel Aviv, 7 July 1987.

Nussbacher 1988a.   Nussbacher, Henry, Personal communications, 8 August 1988.

Nussbacher 1988b.   Nussbacher, Henry, "Conversion Plans from RSCS to Tcp/Ip for Israel Academic Network," Israeli University Telecommunications Subcommittee, Tel Aviv, 20 March 1988.

20 *Africa*

This chapter covers the continent of Africa. Its countries are groudescribed in two main groups: North Africa and sub-Saharan Africa.

20.1 *North Africa*

The countries of North Africa—that is, Egypt, Libya, and those of the Maghreb (Tunisia, Algeria, and Morocco)—tend to be more related to each other and to Europe than to sub-Saharan Africa. They are described here geographically from east to west.

20.2 *Egypt {EG}*

There is a PDN called *ARENTO* and a more general purpose network called *ENSTINET*. Egypt is an *EARN* member.

20.2.1 ENSTINET

ENSTINET has proposed a connection to *EARN*, and Egypt was accepted as a full *EARN* member in 1988. Meanwhile, *ENSTINET* is apparently reachable through Georgia Institute of Technology and, through *ENSTINET*, users can reach *GulfNet* [el-Shafei 1988].

20.3   *Libya {LY}*

There are no known networks in Libya.

20.4   *Tunisia {TN}*

The main network in Tunisia is *Afrimail*. Planning for electronic networks in Tunisia began in 1984 [Kamoun and sassi 1988], involving the Centre National de l'Informatique (CNI) and the Ministry of Communications. The major goals are decentralization and regionalization of data processing services and increased availability of resources through resource sharing. An X.21 circuit switching network became operational in the same year. A companion X.25 packet switching network that began in 1986 has three national switching centers (Tunis Kasbah, Tunis Hached, and Sfax), plus a node used for international connections to Paris and Rome. PADs are used to connect asynchronous terminals, but there are many synchronous terminals in the country that cannot be connected in this way. The experiment with parallel X.21 and X.25 networks led to the conclusion that the X.25 packet switching network is more appropriate for developing countries, largely because of its multiplexing property. There are plans for a videotext service modeled after France's *Minitel* and using a similar method of initially giving away terminals, but focusing on the professional environment rather than on home use.

20.4.1   Afrimail

Afrimail was initiated in Tunisia by the Centre National de l'Informatique (CNI) and the Inter-University Centre for Informatics and Automatics of Tunisia (CIRIA), in collaboration with the University of British Columbia (UBC) and the International Development Research Centre (IDRC), both in Canada [Kamoun et al. 1985]. Its purpose is to develop a bilingual electronic mail capability, using both French and Arabic. Any available infrastructure will be used, including X.25 services, leased lines, public telephone lines, and especially *Telex* links, since *Telex* is often the only reliable network in Africa and much of the Third World. The **Ean** software is being used. There are links to other countries through *UUCP* from the machine *tuniscni*, and UUCP is also used inside the country. There is a connection to *EARN* through Montpellier in France [Kamoun 1988]. The next phase of *Afrimail* is to install **Ean** in other African and Arab institutions and to interconnect them.

Access
farouk Kamoun
kamoun%tuniscni@inria.fr
+216-1-78-2996
Centre National de l'Informatique de Tunis
Tunis
Tunisia

20.5   *Algeria {DZ}*

There is an *EARN* connection to Algiers, Algeria.

20.6   *Morocco {MO}*

Morocco is an *EARN* member.

20.7   *Sub-Saharan Africa*

Packet radio finds wide application here due to the lack of land-based communication infrastructures, the great distances, and the already existing radio networks operated by various government agencies, companies, and outside groups such as the U.S. Peace Corps and Canadian University Service Overseas (CUSO). A usable system can be put together from, for example, a Toshiba 100 laptop computer, a Tyconics 150 packetizer, and a radio that is already used for other purposes. The whole assemblage may cost less than $500 and weigh less than 25 pounds.

There is also a great deal of use of Kermit and error correcting modems, for instance with *CGNET* [Lindsey 1987]. The idea of using computer mediated communications to link isolated villages in the developing world is not new [Price 1975], and several systems, such as *CARINET* and *CGNET*, currently practice something very similar to this.

20.7.1   **CGNET**

CGNET is a conferencing system specializing in agriculture that was founded in 1985 by the Consultative Group on International Agricultural Research (CGIAR), later joined by other organizations and individuals [CARINET 1988; Balson 1988]. The *CGNET* machine is a Digital **VMS** system located in Palo Alto, California. CGIAR is a group of 130 remote outposts in more than 70 countries, all involved in agricultural research. Their research is mostly sponsored by a consortium of 13 international agricultural research centers, which are themselves sponsored by the Food and Agriculture Organization (FAO) of the United Nations (UN), the World Bank, and the United Nations Development Program (UNDP). Their purpose is to improve food production in developing nations [Lindsey 1987].

There are about 200 mailboxes and an indirect community of about 10,000 people. Use of electronic mail has allowed marked reduction in CGIAR costs by reducing the use of more expensive services, such as *Telex* and physical travel [Lindsey 1987].

CGNET serves the same countries as *CARINET*, with which it has a cooperative agreement, plus 11 others, including Bangladesh, India, Sri Lanka, the Ivory Coast, and Ethiopia [CARINET 1988]. PDNs are mostly used, but there are also subscribers in places where such services are not available, such as Nepal, Kenya, Zimbabwe, Niger, and Mali. These are connected by international telephone direct dialing to a service in London. Still others cannot initiate international calls and are instead connected by Kermit links from Palo Alto. Examples include the International Crop Research Institute for the Semi-Arid Tropics (ICRISAT) in Hyderabad, India, and stations in Niamey, Niger; Ouagadougou, Burkina Faso; and Bamako, Mali [Lindsey 1987]. Although *CARINET* is based on *EIES* and *CGNET* is based on *Dialcom*, both use *Telenet*, which makes using the services of either easy for their users. *CGNET* also has an interface to *Telex* [CARINET 1988].

Access
Georg Lindsey
157:CGI100
+1-415-325-3061
Fax: 415-325-2313
Telex: 490 000 5788 (CGN UI)
CGNET Services
635 High Street
Palo Alto, CA 94301
U.S.A.

20.8   *Senegal {SN}*

The packet radio network *Alternet* operates in Senegal.

20.9   *Mali {ML}*

CGNET has subscribers in Mali.

20.10   *Ivory Coast {CI}*

There is an *EARN* connection to Abidjan in the Ivory Coast.

20.11   *Burkina Faso {HV}*

CGNET (The country was formerly known as Upper Volta, thus the ISO3166 code of *HV*, for Haute Volta.)

20.12   *Niger {NE}*

CGNET has subscribers in Niger.

20.13   *Nigeria {NG}*

There are no known networks in Nigeria.

20.14   *Cameroon {CM}*

There are no known networks in Cameroon.

20.15   *Ethiopia {ET}*

CGNET has subscribers in Ethiopia.

20.16   *Kenya {KE}*

The Institute for Global Communications (IGC), parent of *PeaceNet*, is setting up a similar system in Nairobi, Kenya.

20.17   *Zimbabwe {ZB}*

CGNET has subscribers in Zimbabwe.

20.18   *South Africa {ZA}*

Apparently there are internal networks in South Africa, but external connections are few. Sanctions proposed by the U.S. government are one specific example of reactions by foreign governments to the institution of *apartheid* in South Africa [Dyson et al. 1988; Congress 1988].

Connection requests in 1987 and 1988 from South African universities were turned down by *EARN*, by *BITNET*, by EUUG on behalf of *EUnet*, by USENIX on behalf of *UUNET*, and by *CSNET*. The PDN *SAPONET* connects to the rest of the world (as do the South African telephone and postal systems), and there are apparently *FidoNet* nodes in that country.

20.19   *References*

Balson 1988.   Balson, David, Personal communications, 16 December 1988.

CARINET 1988.   CARINET, "CARINET Joins Forces with CGNET," *CARI-News*, vol. 1, no. 1, p. 1, CARINET, Inc., Washington, DC, August 1988.

Congress 1988.   Congress, "H.R. 1580: The Anti-Apartheid Act Amendments of 1988, As Amended by the Committee on Foreign Affairs on May 3 1988," U.S. House of Representatives, Washington, DC, 4 April 1988. A House of Representatives Bill; not yet enacted as law.

Dyson et al. 1988.   Dyson, Edward E., Coward, Nicholas F., Cimadevilla, Francisco J., and Josman, Gerald, "Proposed Legislation Imposing Further Restrictions on Trade with South Africa," Baker & McKenzie, Menlo Park, CA, CA, 18 May 1988. Memorandum prepared for the USENIX Association.

el-Shafei 1988.   el-Shafei, Nayel, "Reaching GULFNET," *info-nets@think.com*, Internet, 20 September 1988.

Kamoun 1988.   Kamoun, farouk, Personal communications, August–September 1988.

Kamoun and sassi 1988.   Kamoun, farouk, and sassi, Mohamed ben, "Tunisia's Experience in the Promotion of Teleprocessing," *Proceedings of the Special Conference of the International Council for Computer Communication (New Delhi, 17–30 October 1987)*, pp. 1–10, Elsevier, Amsterdam, November 1988.

Kamoun et al. 1985.   Kamoun, farouk, sassi, Mohamed ben, and ayed, hella ben, "Afrimail Project," *Proceedings of the Second International Symposium on Computer Systems (Washington, D.C., September 1985)*, 1985.

Lindsey 1987.   Lindsey, Georg, "The Green Revolution," *Kermit News*, vol. 2, no. 1, pp. 4–5, November 1987.

Price 1975.   Price, Charlton R., "Conferencing via Computer: Cost Effective Communication for the Era of Forced Choice," in *The Delphi Method*, ed. Murray Turoff, Addison-Wesley, Reading, MA, 1975.

21   *Commercial Systems*

Many commercial networks and conferencing systems have already been described in the geographically organized chapters, but some of them are discussed in this chapter for several reasons:

- There are some common features, mostly having to do with the effects of charging fees.
- There are some common conferencing system implementations that are used on more than one actual system.
- Many of the major systems are located in the United States, and including them all in that section would have made it impractically large.

The commercial systems described in this chapter or this book are not all of the ones that exist. Selection has been essentially arbitrary, and inclusion or lack of inclusion of a system indicates nothing about the importance or commercial viability of the system.

21.1   *Charging and Access*

Commercial networks sell services to outside users for profit and without the limitations of access required by research, academic, military, or company networks, or even some cooperative networks. Administration is always centralized, though execution may be delegated. Fees are usually charged to individual persons or organizations on the basis of connect or CPU time used.

Some noncommercial networks charge fees, too. RARE wants its proposed continental research network to have volume fees charged directly to the users by the PTTs. *CSNET* charges the user. *BITNET*, *EARN*, and *Net-North* charge fees to participating institutions. These are all limited access academic or research systems. *UUNET* charges the user system, but not the individual user, and is nonprofit, but unlike *CSNET*, it does not have restrictions on who can subscribe. *DASnet* charges the user system, with itemization for each user, and is for-profit.

On a commercial service, more traffic is an advantage because it brings in more revenue, while on an anarchic network such as *USENET*, more traffic just means more expense. Users of either have to deal with information overload, although the administrations of some commercial systems claim that the availability of money and administration in the centralized services allows the development of sophisticated filtering mechanisms to limit the problem.

CompuServe, *The Source*, and many other such services aren't really networks. They consist of a few large computers closely coupled into a large distributed system and are accessed just like home personal computer bulletin board systems except that users get bills. This kind of centralization produces its own problems: during popular hours most of the dialup ports and PDNs used to reach them are saturated and the mainframes themselves are loaded. Many of them do support error correcting protocols such as Kermit, Xmodem, or CompuServe-B, however [da Cruz 1988].

21.2   *Directories*

21.2.1   NEMR

There is a business that gathers electronic mail addresses and makes them available to subscribers.

> **Access**
>
> National E-Mail Registry
> +1-215-245-4018
> DASnet: [DCMMCI]310-1760
> MCI: 310-1760 or 349-6145
> Easylink: 62023102
> Two Neshaminy Interplex, Suite 110
> Trevose, PA 19047-9905
> U.S.A.

21.3   *Forwarders*

21.3.1   **UUNET**

UUNET is described in detail in Chapter 12 on North America because it is particularly associated with *UUCP* and the *Internet*.

21.3.2   **DASnet**

DASnet was described in Chapter 12.

21.3.3   **COMPMAIL**

COMPMAIL is a service of *Dialcom*, which is described later in this chapter.

21.4   *Small Conferencing Systems*

These are smaller systems with clienteles specialized according to geography, employment, or activity.

21.4.1   **THE META NETWORK**

THE META NETWORK is a conferencing service owned and managed by Metasystems Design Group (MDG) for its clients, which include government agencies, Fortune 500 companies, small businesses, nonprofit associations, and city governments [Carlson 1988]. Examples include the American Bar Association (ABA), the City of Santa Monica, California, and the Defense and Space Systems Integration Group of Boeing Computer Services (BCS) [Opper 1988]. Many organizational development consultants also use this system.

The name *THE META NETWORK* was originally used by MDG and its clients when they were using the Confer system at Wayne State University (Wayne State), starting in March 1983. The offices of MDG are in the Washington, D.C., area, and in 1983 MDG started its own system, calling it *DCMETA*. It was an IBM PC/AT with four dialup ports, **XENIX**, several hundred participants, and the **Caucus** software. The old name of *THE META NETWORK* was used again starting in May 1988 when the PC/AT was replaced by a Compaq Intel 386 machine also running **XENIX** and with 16 lines, half direct dial and half connected to *CompuServe*.

Users can send mail through *DASnet* at a group rate [EMMS 1987]. There are close associations with the Institute for Networking Design (*IND*) in Tokyo [Aizu et al. 1988]. Partners in MDG, which was founded in

December 1982, include early proponents of interconnecting conferencing systems [Carlson 1988]. Frank Burns was apparently the original main proponent, starting in 1978. Lisa Carlson is apparently the inventor of the term *porting* (manually carrying conference articles from one machine to another). Both are founders of the Electronic Networking Association (ENA).

MDG is also the exclusive distributor of the **Caucus** software [Burns 1988]. One of the places they have started using this software is the City of Santa Monica, California, which has a system called *PEN* (Public Electronic Network) offering free accounts to all city residents [Carlson 1988].

Access

Metasystems Design Group, Inc.
+1-703-243-6622
2000 North 15th Street, Suite 103
Arlington, VA 22201
U.S.A.

21.4.2   NWI

NWI is a conferencing system for group clients such as churches and the World Future Society. It connects to *DASnet* [EMMS 1987].

Access

Networking and World Information, Inc.
800-624-6916
333 E River Drive
East Hartford, CT 06108
U.S.A.

21.4.3   Portal

Portal is a conferencing system used by group clients such as the Sierra Club. It connects to *DASnet* [EMMS 1987] and also to *USENET, UUCP,* and the *Internet*.

Access

Portal Communications Service
+1-408-973-9111
Customer Service
cs@cup.portal.com
10385 Cherrytree Lane
Cupertino, CA 95014
U.S.A.

21.4.4 WELL

The Whole Earth 'Lectronic Link (*WELL*) began in 1985 as an offshoot of the Point Foundation in cooperation with Network Technologies, Inc. (NETI) [Brand 1985]. The Point Foundation is the parent of the Whole Earth Catalog (*WEC*) and *Coevolution Quarterly (CQ)*, which is now *Whole Earth Review (WER)*. The *WELL* is a small conferencing system with a geographically localized clientele: most of them live or work within 100 miles of San Francisco.

There are more than 90 public conferences, each with a moderator. The moderators enforce nonsexist policies, and, except for private business conferences, noncommercial ones. There are no anonymous accounts because the administration wishes to cultivate responsible posters. Participants of most groups have met face to face. This is usually easy because of geographic location, and there are monthly parties at the *WELL* office. Online conferences are not just technical and businesslike, but also include hobbyist and social groups. There are even what amount to psychiatric encounter groups; these have an unusual feature, however, in that some of them have been meeting regularly almost daily for years. The community nature of the system, and especially of some of its conferences, has led to a noticeable tendency on the part of some users to find excuses to stay logged on even when there is nothing in particular going on (these are sometimes known as *WELL addicts*). This is rather like loitering at one's favorite coffee shop in Greenwich Village.

Services include mail and conferencing, both interactive and batch. A local magazine is published online, as are parts of other magazines and books [Brand 1985]. There is a paper newsletter called *Offline*. Users also have direct access to the underlying **4.3BSD UNIX** operating system, which runs on a VAX-11/750 with two Fujitsu Eagle disk drives. The system may be reached by direct dialup telephone or by *TYMNET*. In addition, the *WELL* is on *USENET* and *UUCP* and serves as one of the few public access entry points to those networks. While most *USENET* users are employees of organizations that have machines connected to *USENET*, *WELL* users can be (in principle) anyone who can dial up and submit a valid credit card number. The *WELL* also has a group subscription to *DASnet*, and users can thus reach many other networks by electronic mail.

Access
Cliff Figallo
+1-415-332-4335

WELL
27 Gate Five Road
Sausalito, CA 94965
U.S.A.

21.5   *Large Commercial Systems*

These support a variety of services, including ones primarily for entertainment.

21.5.1   **BIX**

BIX, or BYTE Information Exchange, uses the **CoSy** conferencing software and has been run by *BYTE* magazine since 1985 [Meeks 1985]. There were about 22,000 subscribers in November 1988 [Ellis 1988].

> **Access**
> BIX
> +1-603-924-7681
> 800-227-2983
> One Phoenix Mill Lane
> Peterborough, NH 03458
> U.S.A.

21.5.2   **CompuServe**

CompuServe provides many database services as well as CMC. Its electronic mail system is called *EasyPlex*. *EasyPlex* interconnects to *MCI Mail*, *InfoPlex*, *Telex*, and *TWX* and is limited to messages shorter than 100,000 characters.

> **Access**
> CompuServe Information System
> +1-614-457-8650
> 800-848-8990
> 5000 Arlington Center Blvd.
> P.O. Box 20212
> Columbus, OH 43220
> U.S.A.

21.5.3   **Comserve**

Comserve is actually not a commercial system, but it is listed here because its services are similar to those of the other systems described in this chapter.

Comserve is an information retrieval service for students and scholars of communications. There are about 3,700 users from 17 countries.

Comserve is accessible from *BITNET* at no charge. Funding comes from the Eastern Communication Association, the International Communication Association, and Rensselaer Polytechnic Institute.

Access

Comserve
SUPPORT@RPICICGE.BITNET
Dept. of Language, Literature, and Communication
Sage Labs
Rensselaer Polytechnic Institute
Troy, NY 12180
U.S.A.

21.5.4   Dialcom

Dialcom is a commercial mail service originally based in the United States. It uses X.400 [Licalzi 1987]. There are many specialized groups on this system, such as *ALAnet*, for the American Library Association (ALA); *NSF-MAIL*, for the National Science Foundation (NSF); and *ONR-MAIL*, for the Office of Naval Research (ONR).

Participate was used on *Dialcom* beginning in 1982. At the request of the American Bar Association (ABA), *Dialcom* added Caucus to its menu of services in May 1987 [Cook 1987], replacing Participate [Cook 1988].

One of the earliest commercial to noncommercial mail gateways, *COMPMAIL*, is implemented on *Dialcom*; it connects to the *Internet Intermail* gateway.

Interconnections

Dialcom subscribers use human names to refer to each other, at least on the same computer. But to reach people on other systems, an address consisting of a mailbox number and a system number is used, as in

    33:IXIZ135

The colon is equivalent in function to the at sign of many other systems. The at sign itself is the default *Dialcom* line deleting character, so subscribers who wish to send mail to systems that use it in network addresses must change their line delete character. This can be changed to something else, such as control U, by doing, e.g.,

    TERM NONE -KILL ^U

in the PARAM.INI file.

The relaying service between *Dialcom* and the *Internet* is *COMPMAIL*. It is implemented on *Dialcom* system 64. From *Dialcom*, mail should be sent to 64:CMP0817, with the actual destination address in the text as follows:

```
FORWARD: ARPA
TO: user@{DNS}
(blank line)
(text of message)
```

There is no provision for a *Subject:* line or for any other RFC822 headers.

For the other direction, an *Internet* user must send mail to intermail@isi.edu with text

```
Forward: COMPMAIL
To: user:host
(blank line)
(text of message)
```

Since this forwarding technique uses DNS addresses, it is actually not limited to the *Internet*, although the *Internet* side of the gateway, called *Intermail*, prefers that use be limited to appropriate researchers (see the *Internet* section in Chapter 11).

> **Access**
> Dialcom
> 800-435-7342
> 6120 Executive Blvd.
> Rockville, MD 20852
> U.S.A.

21.5.5   Dialog

Dialog is an information retrieval service with access to numerous large databases. It is reached by direct login over PDNs such as *DIALNET*, *TYMNET*, or *Telenet*. *Dialog* also sells CD ROM versions of some databases for use on personal computers.

> **Access**
> Dialog Information Services, Inc.
> +1-415-858-3785
> 800-334-2564
> Telex: 334499 (DIALOG)
> 3460 Hillview Avenue
> Palo Alto, CA 94304
> U.S.A.

21.5.6   GEnie

GEnie, or General Electric Network for Information Exchange, is a U.S. conferencing service; there are no overseas subscribers. *GEnie* provides access to numerous online databases and other information services. It is apparently not connected to any other systems for electronic mail.

> **Access**
> GEnie
> 800-638-9636
> 401 North Washington Street
> Rockville, MD 20850
> U.S.A.

21.5.7   OMNET

OMNET is a commercial conferencing system with extensive mail service and mailing lists that is primarily accessed by X.25 and that has a worldwide international scientific and engineering clientele. It is also known as *SCIENCEnet*. It has an online user directory and help facilities, printed manuals, and extensive customer support and training. Examples of conferences include the following [OMNET 1988]:

> AIR   Atmospheric Sciences
> EARTH   Solid Earth Sciences
> LIFE   Life Sciences
> OCEAN   Ocean Sciences
> POLAR   Interdisciplinary Polar Studies
> SPACE   Space Science and Remote Sensing

Limited mail can be sent to an *OMNET* user from academic and research networks through the *Internet Intermail* gateway by sending it to

> intermail@isi.edu

with text lines

> Forward: TELEMAIL
> To: [*user*/OMNET] MAIL/USA
> (blank line)
> (text of message)

Replies may be sent back to *Telemail* address

> [INTERMAIL/USCISI] TELEMAIL/USA

with body

> FORWARD: ARPA
> TO: *user@domain*
> (blank line)
> (text of message)

> **Access**
> OMNET
> +1-617-265-9230
> 137 Tonawanda Street
> Boston, MA 02124
> U.S.A.

21.5.8   The Source

The Source has 60,000 to 70,000 subscribers [Data Channels 1987]. This was the system that first made the **Participate** conferencing software available to the general public after its development on *EIES* [Meeks 1985].

> **Access**
> The Source
> 800-336-3366
> P.O. Box 1305
> McLean, VA 22102
> U.S.A.

21.5.9   Telebase

Telebase, founded in 1984, provides information retrieval services and specializes in sophisticated user interfaces to diverse databases. It sells its basic service to other companies, which then resell it under their names. This service is called EasyNet on *Telebase* (not to be confused with *EASYnet*, Digital's internal company network). Western Union calls it InfoMaster. *CompuServe* calls it IQuest. It is called SearchMaestro by the U.S. Department of Defense (DoD), EasySearch by Telecom Canada, SearchLink by IDG Communications, and Einstein by Addison-Wesley.

> **Access**
> Telebase Systems, Inc.
> +1-215-526-2800
> 763 West Lancaster Avenue
> Bryn Mawr, PA 19010
> U.S.A.

21.5.10   UNISON

UNISON is a conferencing system owned by Patelcomp, Inc. It uses **Participate** conferencing software [Cook 1987] and has a varied clientele, including Anglican churches worldwide. *UNISON*'s mail system is interconnected with many other systems, such as *DASnet, AT&T Mail, Dialcom, Deutsche Mailbox, EasyLink, EIES, Envoy 100, GeoMail, GeoNet, GOLDNET, MCI Mail, NWI, PeaceNet, Portal, The Source, Telecom Gold, Telebox, Telemail, Telex, TWICS, UUCP,* and the *WELL*.

> **Access**
> UNISON Telecommunications Service
> +1-513-731-2800
> 800-334-6122
> 2174 Seymour Avenue
> Cincinnati, OH 45237
> U.S.A.

21.6   *Mail Services*

These support one primary service—electronic mail—and have a high volume of business users.

21.6.1   AT&T Mail

AT&T Mail is a mail service that connects subscribers to each other and to the *UUCP* network with the UUCP protocol. It is owned and operated by AT&T [DeJager 1986].

> AT&T Mail Customer Assistance Center
> +1-908-668-6548
> 800-624-5672
> room 46A 10B150
> 5000 Hadley Road
> South Plainfield, NJ 07080
> U.S.A.

21.6.2   MCI Mail

MCI Mail is a commercial mail system. It is interconnected with *CompuServe* and *Telex* [Smith 1988]. The *Intermail* gateway at *a.isi.edu* provides experimental research mail exchange with the *Internet*.

Access
MCI Mail
+1-202-293-4255
2000 M Street N.W.
Washington, DC 20036
U.S.A.

21.6.3   Telemail

Telemail is a mail service operating on the *Telenet* PDN, both of which are owned by U.S. Sprint (Sprint). *Telemail* has gateways to *Telex*, *USPS*, and various other networks [Telenet 1987]. *Telemail* is connected to *DASnet*. There is also a research use gateway with the *Internet* (see Chapter 11 and also *Dialcom* in this chapter).

Access
See *Telenet* in Appendix A.

21.7   *Old Reliables*

21.7.1   Telex

Telex is a very widespread but slow data communication service. It is optimized for use with printers. In less industrialized parts of the world, *Telex* may be the only form of text electronic communication that is generally available and that connects to other countries.

21.7.2   TWX

TWX is a very slow communication service meant for short text messages to be printed. It is quite widespread.

21.8   *References*

Aizu et al. 1988.   Aizu, Izumi, Nakamura, Hiroyuki, Kitaya, Yukio, and Carlson, Lisa, "The Business of Networking in Japan: Past, Present and the Future," *Proceedings of ENA Conference (Philadelphia, 13 May 1988)*, Electronic Networking Association, 1988.

Brand 1985.   Brand, Stewart, "Gate Five Road," *Whole Earth Review*, no. 47, pp. 103–104, July 1985.

Burns 1988.   Burns, Frank, "How We Use Caucus in Developing and Managing Our Business," Metasystems Design Group, Inc., Arlington, VA, 23 August 1988.

Carlson 1988.   Carlson, Lisa, Personal communications, 30 November 1988.

Cook 1987.   Cook, Gordon, "A Survey of Computer Mediated Communications: Computer Conferencing Comes of Age," Gartner Group, Inc., Stamford, CT, 9 November 1987. This paper was published in a series available only to subscribers who paid a substantial fee.

Cook 1988.   Cook, Gordon, Personal communications, November 1988.

da Cruz 1988.   da Cruz, Frank, Personal communications, October–November 1988.

Data Channels 1987.   Data Channels, "Gateway Service Provides Connectivity Between Public, Private E-Mail Systems," *Data Channels*, p. 6, 15 July 1987.

DeJager 1986.   DeJager, Dale S., "AT&T Mail," *Proceedings of the 1986 Summer USENIX Conference (Atlanta, 9–13 June 1986)*, pp. 377–390, USENIX Association, Berkeley, CA, 1986.

Ellis 1988.   Ellis, Marg, Personal communications, 28 November 1988.

EMMS 1987.   EMMS, "E-Mail Refiler Connects 18 Systems," *EMMS*, vol. 11, no. 14, pp. 5–9, 15 July 1987.

Licalzi 1987.   Licalzi, Pamela, "DA Systems Adds Message Transfer," *Computer Systems News*, pp. 32, 35, 2 July 1987.

Meeks 1985.   Meeks, Brock N., "An Overview of Conferencing Systems," *BYTE*, vol. 10, no. 13, pp. 169–184, December 1985.

OMNET 1988.   OMNET, "OMNET Electronic Mail," OMNET, 1988.

Opper 1988.   Opper, Susanna, "A Groupware Toolbox," *BYTE*, vol. 13, no. 13, pp. 275–276, 278, 280, 282, December 1988.

Smith 1988.   Smith, Ken, "E-Mail to Anywhere," *PC World*, pp. 220–223, March 1988.

Telenet 1987.   Telenet, "Telenet's Public Data Network," U.S. Sprint, Reston, Virginia, 1987.

Appendixes

A   *Public Data Networks*

A public data network (PDN) is a network that is publicly accessible for a fee and that provides network layer services (and possibly also remote login). Many of these are based on X.25. They are frequently used as the infrastructure for other networks, and they are being connected worldwide. In Europe, such services are usually run by the government telephone service, or Poste, Téléphone, et Télégraphe (PTT). This is often the same government agency that runs the paper post and telephone services. The preferred European term for PDN is public switched data network (PSDN) or public packet switched data network (PPSDN). A term sometimes used for the common analog circuit switched telephone system is public switched telephone network (PSTN).

The first few pages of this chapter contain some brief notes on particular PDNs, organized geographically in the same categories as used in the previous chapters. Much of this information was taken from vendor literature, and its accuracy is not guaranteed, nor is this information exhaustive in either its coverage of individual networks or its inclusion of networks. The intention is merely to mention some interesting features of some PDNs.

The second set of information in this chapter is an exhaustive list of some basic attributes of every known functioning PDN throughout the world. This material was compiled by Jeffrey Shapard of *TWICS*.

Finally, there are tables comparing costs of various national and international communications services. These were prepared by Henry Nussbacher of *ILAN* and *BITNET*.

A.1   *North America*

A.1.1   Canada

A.1.1.1   *Datapac*

Datapac was the first public data network in the world [Prindeville 1988], beginning in 1976 [Schwartz 1987, 6].

A.1.2   United States

There is a plethora of PDN services in the United States, only a few of which are described here. Lack of inclusion of information on any PDN does not indicate any judgment as to the quality, availability, cost, or any other characteristic of any PDN.

A.1.2.1   *Telenet*

Telenet claims to be the world's largest PDN [Telenet 1987]. It is possible to get to many commercial services through *Telenet*, such as *The Source*, Dow Jones News/Retrieval, and the electronic edition of the Offical Airline Guides (OAG). *Telenet* has an INFORMATION login. Protocols supported for customers include asynchronous dialup, X.25, SDLC, 3270, and 2780/3780. Speeds range up to 56Kbps [Telenet 1987].

The *Telenet* network was developed by BBN as a copy of early *ARPANET* technology and was the first public packet switched network in the United States, beginning about 1974 [Roberts 1974]. BBN sold it to General Telephone and Electronic (GTE), which converted it to virtual circuit technology. GTE sold it to U.S. Sprint (Sprint), which is also known for its voice telephone network, and which announced in 1988 an international X.400 capability for its associated mail service, *Telemail* [Scott 1988].

> **Access**
> Telenet
> A U.S. Sprint Company
> +1-703-689-7500
> 800-TELENET
> 800-835-3638
> Telex: 7400057
> Telex: 248419
> 12490 Sunrise Valley Drive
> Reston, VA 22096
> U.S.A.

A.1.2.2   *TYMNET*

TYMNET claims to be the world's most ubiquitous network, with 750 U.S. locations and connections to 68 countries. Some services accessible through *TYMNET* include *Delphi*, TRW Information Services, Dow Jones News/ Retrieval [TYMNET 1988], and *UUNET* (which has a 56Kbps connection). *TYMNET* has an INFORMATION login that provides contact names and addresses for various international packet networks. Protocols supported include asynchronous dialup, X.25 and X.75, BSC, HASP RJE, X.PC, and MNP. Speeds range up to 56Kbps, and *TYMNET* claims to have been the first PDN to introduce a 9600bps asynchronous public dialup service in 1987, after being the first to feature 2400bps access in 1984 [TYMNET 1988].

The company was founded in 1969, became a common carrier in 1977, and was bought by McDonnell Douglas in 1983 [TYMNET 1988].

Access
TYMNET
800-872-7654
McDonnell Douglas Network Systems Company
2560 North First Street
San Jose, CA 95161-9019
U.S.A.

A.1.2.3   *Accunet*

Accunet is owned and operated by AT&T.

A.2   *Europe*

A.2.1   **European Community**

A.2.1.1   *EURONET*

EURONET was a network run by the European Community (EC). All European PDN traffic is now carried on the various national X.25 networks, such as *PSS* in the United Kingdom, *TRANSPAC* in France, and *Datex-P* in Germany [Dallas 1988].

A.2.2   **Denmark**

There are two competing PDNs in Denmark, *PAXNET* and *DATAPAK*.

A.2.3   France

A.2.3.1   *TRANSPAC*

TRANSPAC is very widely used by other services, such as *Minitel* and *ARISTOTE*. It is run by France Telecom (FT).

A.2.4   Ireland

A.2.4.1   *EIRPAC*

EIRPAC is the national X.25 packet switching network provided by Telecom Eireann (TE).

A.2.5   British Telecommunications

The Office of Telecommunications (OFTEL) is the regulatory body for telecommunications in the United Kingdom [Dallas 1988].

> **Access**
> Office of Telecommunications
> +44 1 822 1650
> Atlantic House
> Holborn Viaduct
> London EC1N 2HQ
> U.K.

A.2.5.1   *PSS*

British Telecom (BT) runs the domestic British PDN *PSS*. Trunk lines were at 48Kbps, being upgraded in 1988 to 2Mbps. International trunk lines are at 9600bps, and local leased lines are at 2400bps, 9600bps, and 48Kbps [Dallas 1988].

A.2.5.2   *IPSS*

IPSS, the International Packet Switching Service, is run by British Telecom International (PTI), which is a subsidiary of BT. *IPSS* acts as a gateway between *PSS* and all international X.25 networks. Even though *IPSS* has its own DNIC, foreign customers just specify the *PSS* DNIC, and U.K. customers just specify the DNIC of the foreign network; neither uses the *IPSS* DNIC [Dallas 1988].

A.2.5.3   *MERCURY 5000*

MERCURY 5000 is a domestic British PDN run by Mercury Data Network Services Ltd. (Mercury), a subsidiary of Mercury Communications Ltd., which is in turn a member of the Cable and Wireless Worldwide Communications Group (C&W) [Dallas 1988], which is mentioned again later in this appendix under Japan.

A.2.5.4   *MERCURY 5100*

MERCURY 5100 is an international gateway to *MERCURY 5000* and is also run by Mercury [Dallas 1988].

A.3   *Australasia*

A.3.1   **Australia**

There is an Australian PDN, *AUSTPAC*, and a videotext system, *VIATEL*, as well as two PDNs, *Keylink T* and *Keylink 7*. Also popular are *Fax* and *Telex* [Carss 1988].

A.3.2   **New Zealand**

There is at least one PDN in New Zealand, *PACNET*.

A.4   *Far East*

A.4.1   **Japanese Telecommunications**

There have been so many recent changes in the Japanese telecommunications industry that a bit of history may help the reader understand the many Japanese telecommunications companies. For many years, Nippon Telegraph and Telephone (NTT), owned completely by the government, was the sole domestic carrier, and Kokusai Denshin Denwa (KDD) was the sole international carrier. This led to a great emphasis on buying and developing everything in Japan, but it also caused KDD to have a rather international outlook. The two companies were so rigorously separated that KDD could not even operate its own domestic lines, having to use NTT facilities instead. Thus, all access to KDD services, which is to say all international access, had to go through NTT. Since NTT rates were rather high, due to no competition, those of KDD had to be, too [Shapard 1988].

This situation of twin monopolies began to change in 1985. The Japanese Diet (parliament) decided to deregulate the industry in order to introduce competition, liberalize use of existing circuits, and privatize NTT. The latter step was taken in April 1985. Responsibility for introducing competition was given to the Ministry of Posts and Telecommunications (MPT). MPT decides which companies can offer certain types of services, such as long distance or leased lines, and which ones can handle international connections. Up to 30 percent of an international carrier is permitted to be foreign owned, but none of a domestic carrier is permitted to be so. Foreign management of even the Japanese part of an international carrier is not permitted, both for national security reasons and because MPT can find no precedent in the developed world. For example, MPT explicitly refused permission (in November 1986) for the British firm C&W to assist in management of a new international Japanese carrier. Although C&W was not refused permission to invest, there seems to be some trepidation about that, too, and such investment was ordered reduced from a potential 20 percent to 5 percent. In the end, the group granted permission to run a new international carrier was not the one that included C&W [Agoston 1987].

There are now 11 new domestic common carriers in addition to NTT. Their efforts are most noticeable in long-distance carriers servicing the Tokyo–Osaka corridor. NTT itself is still mostly owned by the government, but shares are being sold to Japanese citizens. Many operations and divisions, including the domestic packet network *DDX-P*, are being made into subsidiary firms [Shapard 1988].

MPT is expected to approve only one competitor to KDD, to be the so-called *Daini KDD* ("second KDD"), because, although KDD has a billion dollar market, MPT does not want to divide it into too small pieces. KDD, meanwhile, has cut its costs and prices and is introducing new services and preparing for ISDN [Agoston 1987].

Some additional domestic packet switched networks include the following [Shapard 1988]:

NEC C&C/PC-VAN	Related to *GE Mark III*
Intech Tri-P	Related to *Telenet*
Fenix	Related to *CompuServe*
MasterNet	
KinoCosmonet	Private *TYMNET* system for databases
MaruNet	Another of the above

A.4.1.1   *DDX-P*

DDX-P stands for Digital Data eXchange, Packet-switching network, and refers to an internal Japanese network run by Nippon Telegraph and Telephone (NTT) [Quarterman and Hoskins 1986]. There is also a circuit switching network, like Canada's *Infoswitch*.

A.4.1.2   *VENUS-P*

VENUS-P is operated by Kokusai Denshin Denwa (KDD), a major Japanese international carrier and a former public corporation. KDD offers both dialup and tie-line access to *VENUS-P*. There is a gateway between *VENUS-P* and NTT's domestic *DDX-P* packet network. KDD also maintains leased line connections to other networks in the United States, the

United Kingdom, France, West Germany, and Singapore, and it has access agreements with most public international packet networks elsewhere [Shapard 1988; KDD 1985].

A.4.1.3   *NIS/TYMNET*

NIS/TYMNET, or Network Information Service, a joint venture between the Japanese trading company Marubeni and the McDonnell Douglas Information Services Group (formerly TYMNET), was the first organization after KDD to obtain MPT permission to operate an international Value-Added Network (VAN) service, including the assignment of a DNIC for use from other international services. *NIS/TYMNET* had been operating a domestic *TYMNET*-based service since mid-1987 and received authorization in December 1987 to begin international service, which it did shortly afterward. At present, *NIS/TYMNET* operates as a partner of *TYMNET* in the United States, using lines leased from KDD to handle the international traffic. If a *Daini KDD* were approved, lines might be leased from it instead. *NIS/TYMNET* is negotiating with International Record Carriers (IRCs) and packet networks elsewhere in order to increase their access [Shapard 1988].

A.4.2   Chinese Telecommunications

The appropriate agency to run a national PDN in China would be the Ministry of Posts and Telecommunications (MPT). Unfortunately, there is no such network, although MPT owns some point to point microwave links between major cities, as well as two experimental geosynchronous satellites. But the most basic infrastructure of local circuits is mostly missing, leading to a serious "last kilometer" problem [Maier 1988].

A.5   *Southeast Asia*

A.5.1   Malaysia

A.5.1.1   *MAYPAC*

The Malaysian Packet Switched Data Network, *MAYPAC* [Awang-Lah 1987], is provided by Malaysian Telecom Company (STM). Both X.25 (on leased lines) and X.28 (leased or dialup) interfaces are provided.

A.5.1.2   *MAYCIS*

The Malaysian Circuit Switched Data Network, *MAYCIS*, was expected to start in 1988, but its tariff structure was still undetermined [Awang-Lah 1987].

A.6   *South Asia*

A.6.1   India

A.6.1.1   *VIKRAM*

VIKRAM is run by the Indian Department of Telecommunications (DOT) and initially will have switches in eight cities and PADs in 12 cities, plus gateways to international networks [Garg and Ramani 1987]. Most of the links will be 9600bps or 19.2Kbps, with 64Kbps links between Delhi, Calcutta, Madras, and Bombay in a completely connected graph. It was expected to be operational by late 1988 [Gupta 1988].

A.7   *Latin America*

A.7.1   Mexico

A.7.1.1   *TELEPAC*

The Mexican X.25 network *TELEPAC* uses mostly 9600bps leased lines with 1200bps terminal PAD X.3 interfaces. It is completely saturated, to the point that bits are lost through the PADs, and no growth is planned until 1990. It is used, among other things, for **SECOBI**, which is a remote database access application. There are connections to *Telenet* and *TYMNET*.

A.7.1.2   *Morelos*

Morelos is a Mexican satellite network using the C and Ku bands [Trujillo 1987]. It has been operational since September 1985. The first users were Teléfonos de México (Telmex) and Petróleos Mexicanos (PEMEX). There are two satellites, Morelos I and Morelos II, each with 32 television channels and 32,000 telephone channels. There were 288 ground stations in September 1988, two of which are used for transmissions to the Far East and North America. Another 500 ground stations were expected to be installed in 1988.

Usage was to be divided into 28 percent television, 22 percent telephone between cities, 2 percent rural telephone, and 15 percent data, amounting to 80 percent of total capacity, with an expectation of 96 percent usage by 1991. Other uses include air traffic control in several airports, banks, insurance companies, and navigational services, as well as the educational network *ITESM* [Castañón 1988]. Many of the ground stations are provided by NEC, which also provides microwave communications in Mexico.

A.7.2   **Costa Rica**

A.7.2.1   *RACSAPAC*

RACSAPAC (Radiográfica Costarricense, S.A.) is owned and operated by Instituto Costarricense de Electricidad (ICE), the Costa Rican PTT. In addition to basic X.25 service, *RACSAPAC* provides electronic mail, teletext, videotext, EFT, and various other services [Gutierrez 1987]. *RACSAPAC* is also installing nodes in other Central American countries and has connections with other international PDNs [Mata 1988].

A.8   *Middle East*

Most of the countries in this region have PDNs.

A.9   *Africa*

There are few PDNs in Africa, but some do exist, such as *SYTRANPAK* in the Ivory Coast, *GABONPAC* in Gabon, and *SAPONET* in South Africa. Other African systems include *CGNET*, *CARINET*, and *Afrimail*.

A.10   *PDN Access*

This section contains a list of identification codes for every known PDN in the world, as well as a list of some hosts that provide information about some such networks.

The information included here was current as of 5 May 1988. It was supplied by Jeffrey Shapard of *TWICS*. He maintains an up-to-date version of it. He acknowledges the following sources:

KDD Data Comm. Dept. 4/1983
VENUS-P Manual (English) 9/1985
VENUS-P Manual (Japanese)
British Telecom (BT); 5/1988; hostess information service
Telenet 5/1988; online information service
TYMNET 5/1988; online information service

A.10.1   DNICs

Every PDN has a Data Network Identification Code (DNIC) that is used to locate it from another PDN in X.121 addressing. This subsection lists every known PDN in the world by country, its DNIC, its name, and the organizing company (carrier).

Country		DNIC	Network	Carrier
AN	Antigua	3443	AGANET	C&W (West Indies)
AR	Argentina	7220	ENTEL	Empresa Nac. de Telecom
AU	Australia	5052	AUSTPAC	Telecom Australia
AU	Australia	5053	MIDAS	OTC
AT	Austria	2320	—	Radio Austria
AT	Austria	2329	RADAUS	Radio Austria
BS	Bahamas	3640	BATELCO	Bahamas Telecom Corp.
BH	Bahrain	4263	IDAS (BAHNET)	Bahrain Telecom Co. (BTC)
BB	Barbados	3423	IDAS	Barbados Ext'l Telecom Ltd.
BE	Belgium	2062	DCS	RTT
BE	Belgium	2063	EURONET	—
BE	Belgium	2064	DCS	RTT
BM	Bermuda	3503	C&W	C&W (West Indies)
BR	Brazil	7240	INTERDATA	EMBRATEL
CA	Canada	3020	Datapac	TCTS
CA	Canada	3024	GLOBDAT	Teleglobe Ca.
CA	Canada	3025	GLOBDAT	Teleglobe Ca.
CA	Canada	3029	INFOSWITCH	CNCP
KY	Cayman Islands	3463	C&W CAYMAN	C&W Cayman
CN	China	4600	PKTELCOM	Beijing Telecom Adm.
CO	Colombia	7320	DAPAQ	Empresa Nac. de Telecom
CR	Costa Rica	7120	RACSAPAC	Radiográfica Costarricense
DK	Denmark	2381	Datex	—
DK	Denmark	2382	DATAPAK	PTT
DO	Dominican Republic	3700	UDTS	ITT
EG	Egypt	6020	ARENTO	Telecom Org. of Egypt
FI	Finland	2441	Datex	—
FI	Finland	2442	Datapak	PTT
FI	Finland	2443	Digipak	—
FR	France	2080	TRANSPAC	PTT
FR	France	2081	NTI	PTT

Country		DNIC	Network	Carrier
FR	France	2083	EURONET	PTT
GP	Fr. Antilles	3400	TRANSPAC	French PTT
GP	Fr. Guadeloupe	3400	DOMPAC	Ag. Comm. des Telecom
GF	Fr. Guyana	7420	—	—
MQ	Fr. Martinique	3400	DOMPAC	Ag. Comm. des Telecom
RE	Fr. Reunion	6470	DOMPAC	Ag. Comm. des Telecom
GA	Gabon	6282	GABONPAC	Telecom Int'l
DE	Germany, W. (FRG)	2623	EURONET	—
DE	Germany, W. (FRG)	2624	DATEX-P	DBP
GR	Greece	2022	HELPAK	Hellenic Telecom Org.
HN	Honduras	7080	HONDUTEL	Empresa Hondurena de Telecom
HK	Hong Kong	4542	IDAS/ITS	C&W
HK	Hong Kong	4542	INTELPAK	C&W
HK	Hong Kong	4544	DAS	C&W
HK	Hong Kong	4545	DATAPAK	—
HU	Hungary	2160	PCTO	PTT
IS	Iceland	2740	ICEP	PTT
ID	Indonesia	5101	SKDP	PTT
IQ	Iraq	4180	IDAS	BTC
IE	Ireland	2721	IPSS	—
IE	Ireland	2723	EURONET	—
IE	Ireland	2724	EIRPAC	Telecom Eireann
IL	Israel	4251	ISRANET	PTT
IT	Italy	2220	—	Italcable
IT	Italy	2222	DARDO	Italcable
IT	Italy	2223	EURONET	—
CI	Ivory Coast	6122	SYTRANPAK	Intelci
JM	Jamaica	3380	JAMANTEL	Jamaica Int'l Telecom Ltd.
JP	Japan	4401	DDX-P	NTT
JP	Japan	4406	NIS/TYMNET	Network Information Service
JP	Japan	4408	VENUS-P	KDD
KR	Korea, S. (ROK)	4501	DACOMNET	Data Comm. Corp.
KR	Korea, S. (ROK)	4503	DACOM	—
LU	Luxembourg	2703	EURONET	—
LU	Luxembourg	2704	LUXPAC	PTT
MX	Mexico	3340	TELEPAC	PTT
NL	Netherlands	2041	DATANETI	—
NL	Netherlands	2042	EURONET	—
NL	Netherlands	2044	DABAS	PTT

Country		DNIC	Network	Carrier
NZ	New Zealand	5301	IPSS	PTT
NO	Norway	2421	Datex	PTT
NO	Norway	2422	DATAPAK	PTT
PA	Panama	7141	INTEL	Instituto Nac. de Telecom
PE	Peru	7160	ENTEL	Empresa Nac. de Telecom
PH	Philippines	5150	ETPI	Eastern Telecom
PH	Philippines	5150	UDTS	Globe Macay C&R
PH	Philippines	5150	PGC	Phil. Global Comm., Inc.
PT	Portugal	2682	SABD	CPRM Telecom Int'l
QA	Qatar	4270	IDAS	BTC
SA	Saudi Arabia	4200	IDAS	BTC
SG	Singapore	5252	TELEPAC	Telecoms Singapore
ZA	South Africa	6550	SAPONET	SAPO
ES	Spain	2141	IBERPAC	CTNE
ES	Spain	2145	IBERPAC	CTNE
SE	Sweden	2401	TELEPAK	government
SE	Sweden	2402	DATAPAK	Swedish Telecom
SE	Sweden	2405	TELEPAK	government
CH	Switzerland	2284	TELEPAC	Suisse PTT
CH	Switzerland	2289	DATALINK	Radio Suisse
TW	Taiwan	4872	Pacnet	—
TW	Taiwan	4877	UDAS	ITA
TH	Thailand	3104	IDAR	—
TH	Thailand	5200	CAT	CAT
TT	Trinidad & Tobago	3740	TEXTEL	T&T External
AE	United Arab Emirates	4310	TEDAS	Emirates Telcom Corp.
GB	United Kingdom	2341	IPSS	BTI
GB	United Kingdom	2342	PSS	BT
GB	United Kingdom	2343	EURONET	—
GB	United Kingdom	2350	MERCURY	Mercury Comm. Ltd.
US	United States	3101	WUT	Western Union Digital Data
US	United States	3102	WUI	WUI Digital Datel
US	United States	3103	UDTS II	ITT
US	United States	3104	WUI	WUI Database Access
US	United States	3105	WUI	WUI Leased Channel
US	United States	3106	TYMNET	Tymnet
US	United States	3107	UDTS I	ITT Datel
US	United States	3108	ITT	ITT Short Term Voice/Data
US	United States	3109	DATEL I	RCA

Country		DNIC	Network	Carrier
US	United States	3110	Telenet	Telenet
US	United States	3111	DATEL II	RCA
US	United States	3112	WUT	Western Union Broadband
US	United States	3113	LSDS	RCA
US	United States	3114	INFOMASTER	Western Union
US	United States	3115	GRAPHNET	Graphnet Interactive
US	United States	3116	GRAPHNET	Graphnet Store & Forward
US	United States	3117	WUI Telex	WUI
US	United States	3118	GRAPHNET	Graphnet Facsimile
US	United States	3119	TRT	TRT Packet Switching
US	United States	3120	ITT	ITT Low Speed
US	United States	3121	FTCC	FTCC Datel
US	United States	3122	FTCC	FTCC Telex
US	United States	3123	FTCC	FTCC Leased Channel
US	United States	3124	FTCC	FTCC Packet Switching
US	United States	3125	UNINET	ITT Uninet
US	United States	3126	Autonet ADP Autonet	
US	United States	3127	GTE Telenet	GTE Telenet
US	United States	3128	TRT	TRT Telex
US	United States	3129	TRT	TRT Leased Channel
US	United States	3130	TRT	TRT Digital Data
US	United States	3131	RCA	RCAG Telex
US	United States	3132	CompuServe	CompuServe
US	Alaska, U.S.A.	3135	ALASKANET	Alascom
GU	Guam, U.S.A.	5350	RCA	RCA
PR	Puerto Rico, U.S.A.	3300	UDTS	ITT
PR	Puerto Rico, U.S.A.	3300	RCA/PR	RCA
PR	Puerto Rico, U.S.A.	3301	PRTC	Puerto Rico TelCo
VI	Virgin Is., U.S.A.	3320	UDTS	ITT

A.10.2   Hosts

Many PDNs operate hosts that provide information services for the PDNs. This is a brief directory of some of them. The information in it was current as of 8 May 1988.

The markers prepended to the DNIC field in Table A.1 mean:

>	Tried as of May 1988 and found to work
?	Tried as of May 1988, connected, but failed for some reason
No mark	Not yet tried

Table A.1. *PDN information hosts*

Host system	Country	Network	DNIC
ADP Autonet	United States	Autonet	> 3126 8801
ADP Autonet	United States	TYMNET	> 3106 (ADP)
ADP Autonet	United States	TYMNET	> 3106 002709
ADP Autonet	United Kingdom	PSS	> 2342 19200118
DataPac info	Hong Kong	DATAPAC	> 4545 500104
DATAPAK info	Norway	DATAPAK	? 2422 1100001018
Datex-P info	West Germany	Datex-P	> 2624 5621040000
Dutch PTT info	Netherlands	DATANETI	> 2041 2900090
Hostess info	United Kingdom	PSS	> 2342 1920100515
Hostess info	United Kingdom	PSS	> 2342 1920100620
ITALPAC bbs	Italy	ITALPAC	? 2222 632004
KDD VENUS-P info	Japan	VENUS-P	4408 2006001
KDD V-Pet bbs	Japan	VENUS-P	4408 20020
KDD V-Pet bbs	Japan	DDX-P	4401 3612971
Paris packets	France	NTI	> 2081 01
PSS clock	United Kingdom	PSS	> 2342 1920100605
Telenet info	United States	Telenet	> 3110 21200141
Telenet info	United States	Telenet	> 3110 513230
TELEPAC info	Singapore	TELEPAC	> 5252 116688
TYMNET info	United States	TYMNET	> 3106 (INFORMATION)
TYMNET outdial	United States	TYMNET	> 3106 900

A.11   *PDN Costs*

In other chapters, particularly those with information on RARE, *ILAN*, and *DFN*, remarks have been made about widely differing costs of data communications within and between various countries. This appendix graphically illustrates the problem with comparisons of costs of 64Kbps digital service in some countries.

This information was prepared by Henry Nussbacher of the Israeli Academic Network (*ILAN*) Information Center at Tel Aviv University [Nussbacher 1988]. The rates given are believed to have been accurate as of 15 May 1988, but many have no doubt changed since then.

Price figures are given in Table A.1 for links of various lengths for several countries. Separate sources were used for Israeli prices [Laurens 1987], 50km prices [Bezek 1987], and other European numbers [Eurodata 1988].

Rates for connecting to the United States are given in Table A.2 [Eurodata 1988 (Revision of Tariffs, October 1987)]. These are for connecting to the U.S. East Coast. They reflect only half of the cost, the other half being the rate for the link from the United States to the stated country.

Table A.2. *Rates for high speed links to the United States*

Country	56/64Kbps	1.544Mbps	Comment
United Kingdom: MCI	4,654	40,540	Satellite
United Kingdom: BTI	5,250	n/a	TAT8 fiber cable
France	6,017	49,557	Satellite
Netherlands	6,400	63,315	Terrestrial*
United Kingdom: BTI	7,200	49,500	Satellite
Netherlands	8,370	82,215	Satellite*
Switzerland	8,823	n/a	Satellite
Ireland	9,600	n/a	Satellite
Germany	9,939	90,361	Satellite
Belgium	10,350	57,504	Satellite
Japan	11,102	74,724	Satellite
Sweden	12,956	102,823	Satellite*
Italy	20,965	139,770	Satellite*
Israel	21,000	125,000	Satellite*

*No 1.544Mbps service available: this denotes 2Mbps service costs.
Source: Courtesy Henry Nussbacher
Note: Rates are in U.S. dollars per month.

Table A.3. *Rates from the United States and Canada to Europe*

Country	56/64Kbps	1.544Mbps	Comment
Canada	4,000	29,761	Only to UK, US, NL, CH, FR
United States: ITT	3,950	27,000	Satellite
United States: TRT	3,800	28,000	Satellite
United States: FTC	3,895	29,925	Satellite
United States: AT&T	4,500	40,000	Satellite
United States: TRT	4,000	40,000	TAT8 fiber cable (8/88)
United States: ITT	4,000	40,000	TAT8 fiber cable (8/88)

Source: Courtesy Henry Nussbacher
Note: Rates are in U.S. dollars per month.

Table A.3 lists costs from Canada and the United States to European destinations [Eurodata 1988 (Revision of Tariffs, October 1987)].

Table A.4 gives rates for prime-time daytime usage of the X.25 packet switching network in each country [Eurodata 1988 Revision of Tariffs, October 1987]. These rates do not reflect local usage and do not reflect international rates, nor do they include installation costs or monthly rental fees. The second part of each column is the rate in dollars based on the exchange rate of 5 February 1988 of the Foreign Commerce Bank, Zürich.

Table A.4. *Country rates for X.25 9600bps links*

Country	Network	Per hour		Per kilosegment		Currency
		Rates				
Sweden	Datex	21.00	/ 3.50	5.00	/ .83	crown
Netherlands	Datanet	1.50	/ .80	2.50	/ 1.33	guilder
Israel	Isranet	1.24	/ .80	1.24	/ .80	shekel
Austria	Datex	8.40	/ .71	14.00	/ 1.19	shilling
France	Transpac	3.12	/ .55	5.59	/ .99	franc
United Kingdom	PSS	.30	/ .53	.30	/ .53	sterling
Portugal	Telepac	66.00	/ .49	82.50	/ .61	escudo
Ireland	Eirpac	.30	/ .48	.30	/ .48	pound
Switzerland	Telepac	.60	/ .44	2.50	/ 1.82	franc
Luxembourg	Luxpac	15.00	/ .43	25.00	/ .71	franc
Belgium	DCS	12.15	/ .35	20.00	/ .57	franc
Germany	Datex-P	0.60	/ .35	3.30	/ 1.94	mark
Italy	Itapac	408.00	/ .33	1,780.00	/ 1.45	lira
Finland	Datapak	1.20	/ .30	2.50	/ .62	markka
Denmark	Datex	1.60	/ .25	None	/ .00	krone
Finland	Datex	.80	/ .20	None	/ .00	markka
Norway	Datapak	1.20	/ .19	6.25	/ .99	krone
Spain	Iberpac	15.75	/ .14	420.00	/ 3.75	peseta
Denmark	Datapak	.60	/ .09	6.00	/ .93	krone
Iceland	Icepak	3.60	/ —	11.00	/ —	krona

Note: Rates listed are high/low.

A.12   *References*

Agoston 1987.   Agoston, Thomas C., "New Developments in Japan's International Telecommunication Services Industry," *ENA NETWEAVER*, vol. 3, no. 5, pp. 4–5, May 1987.

Awang-Lah 1987.   Awang-Lah, Mohamed b., "RangKoM—The Malaysian Computer Network," *Proceedings of the International Academic Networkshop (Princeton, New Jersey, 9–11 November 1987)*, 1987.

Bezek 1987.   Bezek, "Sifranet and leased line price sheets," Bezek, Tel Aviv, 15 August 1987.

Carss 1988.   Carss, Brian, "Report of the AVCC/ACDP Joint Working Party on Networking: Executive Summary," AVCC/ACDP, Canberra, July 1988.

Castañón 1988.   Castañón, Inés, "Sistema de Satélites Morelos," *Caminos del Aire*, pp. 41–43, 45, Internacional de Revistas, Mexico, D.F. 11560, September 1988. Organo Oficial de Mexicana de Aviación; Magazine of Mexicana Airlines, in Spanish and English.

Dallas 1988.   Dallas, Ian, Personal communications, September 1988.

Eurodata 1988.   Eurodata, *Eurodata Foundation Yearbook (1987–1988)*, Eurodata Foundation, London, 1988.

Garg and Ramani 1987.   Garg, A., and Ramani, S., "Options for Networking Academic Centres in India," *Proceedings of the International Academic Networkshop (Princeton, New Jersey, 9–11 November 1987)*, pp. 3, 6, 8, 1987.

Gupta 1988.   Gupta, J. L., "Public Data Network," *2001*, pp. 76–77, 86, August 1988. *2001* is an Indian popular science magazine, formerly known as *Science Today*.

Gutierrez 1987.   Gutierrez, Claudio, "University for Peace Global Computer Network," *Proceedings of the International Academic Networkshop (Princeton, New Jersey, 9–11 November 1987)*, 1987.

KDD 1985.   KDD, "VENUS-P: International Packet-Switched Data Transfer Service," KDD, Tokyo, 1985.

Laurens 1987.   Laurens, Claude, "Tariff Analysis—National Digital Services at 64kb and 2Mb," La Gaude, France, 14 December 1987.

Maier 1988.   Maier, John H., "A Solution for Higher Education and Scientific Research Data Communication in the People's Republic of China," *CHINANET@TAMVM1.BITNET*, BITNIC.BITNET, College Station, TX, 28 February 1988.

Mata 1988.   Mata, Francisco J., Personal communications, 23 November 1988.

Nussbacher 1988.   Nussbacher, Henry, "Cost comparison of 64kb digital service in various countries," Israeli Academic Network Information Center, Tel Aviv, 15 May 1988.

Prindeville 1988.   Prindeville, Philip A., "Pleins feux sur les réseaux canadiens (Networking in Canada)," *ConneXions—The Interoperability Report*, vol. 2, no. 11, pp. 2–6, Advanced Computing Environments, Mountain View, CA, November, 1988.

Quarterman and Hoskins 1986.   Quarterman, John S., and Hoskins, Josiah C., "Notable Computer Networks," *Communications of the ACM*, vol. 29, no. 10, pp. 932–971, October 1986.

Roberts 1974.   Roberts, Lawrence G., "Data by the Packet," *IEEE Spectrum*, vol. 11, no. 2, pp. 46–51, February 1974.

Schwartz 1987.   Schwartz, Mischa, *Telecommunication Networks*, Addison-Wesley, Reading, MA, 1987.

Scott 1988.   Scott, Karyl, "Telenet Signs X.400 E-Mail Pacts," *PC Week/Connectivity*, vol. 5, no. 45, p. C/13, 7 November 1988.

Shapard 1988.   Shapard, Jeffrey, Personal communications, September 1988.

Telenet 1987.   Telenet, "Telenet's Public Data Network," U.S. Sprint, Reston, Virginia, 1987.

Trujillo 1987.   Trujillo, Daniel, "Networks in Mexico," *Proceedings of the International Academic Networkshop (Princeton, New Jersey, 9–11 November 1987)*, 1987.

TYMNET 1988.   TYMNET, "TYMNET at a Glance," McDonnell Douglas, San Jose, February 1988.

Computer Mediated Communication and the Law

B

By Benjamin Wright, J.D.

The advent of computer mediated communication (CMC) has a legal dimension. It is causing society to rethink the theory and letter of law conceived before the Information Age. This appendix highlights a handful of the especially interesting applications of law to CMC. This is not a complete discussion of the large and complex topics covered.

B.1   Electronic Crime

As a rule one cannot be criminally convicted for an act unless there is a law in place at the time of commission clearly making it a crime. In the field of computer related abuses, this concept has been the springboard for debate and legislative activity.

This appendix is designed to provide accurate and authoritative information in regard to the subject matter covered. It is included as a part of this book with the understanding that the publisher is not engaged in rendering legal, accounting, or other professional services. If legal advice or other expert assistance is required, the services of a competent professional person should be sought. – From a Declaration of Principles jointly adopted by a Committee of the American Bar Association and a Committee of Publishers.

Except as otherwise indicated, the law discussed here is that generally appertaining in the United States of America and the states thereof.

Benjamin Wright gratefully acknowledges the assistance of the reviewers of a prior draft of this appendix: Daniel L. Appelman, Esq., of Heller, Ehrman, White & McAuliffe in Palo Alto, California; John E. Draper, Principal Consultant, STC – International Computers Limited in Sheffield, England; M. Blake Greenlee, President, M. Blake Greenlee Associates, Ltd., in Wilton, Connecticut; and Joel Reidenberg, Esq., of Debevoise & Plimpton in Washington, D.C.

It has been argued that the use of computers is not so different from prior human endeavors as to necessitate special laws criminalizing computer abuses. The argument is that computer related crimes boil down to fraud, damage to, or theft of property, or other offenses for which there are adequate criminal laws. The computer is just an inanimate instrument that can facilitate or be the object of a misdeed. We have no special laws defining *file-cabinet crime*. Why do we need special laws defining *computer crime*?

Nevertheless, because criminal law is a device for depriving individual liberty, courts require it to define an offense with certainty before permitting conviction. Some courts have struggled under existing laws to convict defendants for the wrongful gaining of access to computers and other computer related misdeeds.

A classic example comes from a British case, *R. vs. Gold; R. vs. Schifreen*, (1988) 87 Cr. App. R. 257, [1988] 2 WLR 984. Two *hackers* dishonestly used the access numbers and passwords of others to log onto British Telecom's *Prestel* network. They read confidential information (which reportedly included the contents of the mailbox of the Duke of Edinburgh, Queen Elizabeth II's husband), altered data, and caused some users to be charged for things they had not purchased.

The mischief was analogous to tampering with postal mail, which may well have been a crime in the United Kingdom (as it generally is in the United States). But the postal mail was not involved. Nor did the United Kingdom have an applicable computer crime statute. So the authorities, grasping for straws, tried to convict the rascals under a forgery statute (the Forgery and Counterfeiting Act 1981), arguing that the introduction of false identification into the network amounted to forgery. The House of Lords was not persuaded. The words of the statute required the recording and storage of false identification. The House of Lords concluded that the false access numbers and passwords — which were retained in the *Prestel* system only momentarily — were not recorded and stored for a sufficient duration to permit prosecution under the statute. The case was dismissed.

A number of legislatures have responded to this type of problem, although the responses have not been uniform. Many U.S. states have criminalized various malicious acts involving computers, including fraud, unauthorized access, unauthorized alteration of programs, and destruction or theft of data or equipment.

The U.S. Congress has enacted relevant laws. It passed the Counterfeit Access Device and Computer Fraud Act of 1984, which it amended with the Computer Fraud and Abuse Act of 1986. This law generally prohibits (among other things) unauthorized access into a "Federal interest computer" (which includes certain computers used by the federal government or by financial institutions or connected to interstate networks), which access affects the data therein or the access of others thereto. It also penalizes unauthorized access into any computer that leads to the obtaining of certain information related to national security or financial records. In addition, it establishes penalties for trafficking in stolen computer access codes.

Further, the Electronic Communications Privacy Act of 1986 (ECPA) generally makes it a crime intentionally to intercept or disclose certain private electronic communications without authority. It also makes it an offense intentionally to access without authority (or exceed access authority in) a facility through which an electronic communication service is provided and thereby obtain, alter, or prevent authorized access to a stored communication.

On 2–3 November 1988, a computer worm infected the *Internet* network. Although the worm was benign in that it destroyed little if any data, it reproduced itself wildly and slowed the operation of parts of the network dramatically.

As this book went to press, federal authorities were investigating whether the person responsible for the worm had broken any laws, including the Computer Fraud and Abuse Act and the ECPA. Reportedly, the worm caused more trouble and spread more widely than the individual had intended, so there were questions of whether he had intent to do anything wrong or to invade protected computers. Also, as is commonly the case in computer related crime cases, it was uncertain whether there was sufficient solid evidence of who perpetrated the incident to secure a conviction.

There was also a question of whether a worm or virus attack violates current laws, as strictly interpreted. Earlier in 1988 proposed legislation, called the Computer Virus Eradication Act of 1988, had been introduced in the U.S. Congress, but it had not been enacted. This legislation would incorporate language specifically aimed at the intentional release of rogue programs and thus make prosecution easier.

B.2   *Network Service Provider Liability*

As are so many enterprises, the providers of CMC services are subject to potential liability under numerous headings. The law here is unsettled because wide use of the technology is new, the applications of the technology are varied, and there are few direct judicial or statutory pronouncements on the law. Drawing analogies from the law applying to other, older communications media furnishes some guidance, but it is imperfect.

B.2.1   Vicarious Liability

An interesting question is whether the administrator of a CMC system can be liable for the wrongful acts of the user—such as criminal activity or defamation.

B.2.1.1   *Criminal activities*

The case of Tom Tcimpidis illustrates the potential for liability for criminal activities conducted through a network. Tcimpidis ran a computer bulletin board from his home. Three stolen telephone access codes were anonymously posted on the board for the benefit of other users. The local telephone company traced the stolen codes to Tcimpidis's board.

Criminal charges were filed against him under a statute prohibiting the publication of telephone access codes. The prosecutor ultimately dropped the case for lack of sufficient evidence.

Whether Tcimpidis had the necessary knowledge of the illicit information on his board and intent to promote the illegal use of the board is debatable. It is also unsettled what First Amendment protections for freedom of speech and press should apply to someone like Tcimpidis. Still, it seems possible, given a sufficient showing of intent to promote a criminal activity and a sufficiently broad criminal statute, that a network administrator could be held liable in connection with user abuses.

B.2.1.2   *Defamation*

The exposure of a communications entity to liability for defamation originated by a separate party is related to the degree of control the entity exercises over the messages it handles. A broadcaster or newspaper, for example, is expected to screen material more carefully than a telephone or telegraph company does. By design broadcasters and newspapers can review and package the material they furnish to the public.

Telephone and telegraph systems, however, are intended to serve as fast conduits of relatively private information. Their duty to curb defamatory material is less.

But where does a CMC service fit into this scheme? It is not certain. The function of CMC systems vary widely, and seldom is any given one perfectly analogous to any traditional communications medium.

Consider the case *Hellar vs. Bianco*, 244 P.2d 757 (Cal. Dist. Ct. of App. 1952), which involved defamation through a nonconventional medium. An anonymous author scrawled a false remark about the chastity character of the plaintiff on the wall of the men's toilet room in the defendants' tavern. When the plaintiff learned of it, her husband telephoned the bartender at the tavern to demand its removal. The bartender replied that he was busy and would erase the writing when he got around to it.

Later that evening the husband appeared at the tavern and found the scurrilous matter still on the wall. The plaintiff subsequently sued the defendants to recover money damages. The appeals court in the case held that it was possible for the plaintiff to be awarded damages. Although the defendants had little ability to restrain the literary urges of their patrons, they were able to paint over compositions on their walls that infringed on the rights of others. The case was sent to a jury to determine whether the defendants, by failing to erase the message after learning about it (through their agent, the bartender), negligently allowed it to remain long enough to be charged with its "republication."

Analogy to cases such as *Hellar* suggests that the potential for network liability does exist, especially for bulletin board – type systems where messages are on public display for an extended duration. But it fails to show precisely what standards should apply. There are, for instance, questions of whether bulletin board operators have a proactive duty to review messages to weed out the libelous ones and what First Amendment protections apply to the operators.

B.2.2   Mishandling of Messages

The messages handled by a service provider can be very important to the users, especially if they are businesses that rely upon the timeliness and integrity of the information. If a provider, particularly a commercial one, undertook to deliver a communication and failed to do so satisfactorily, the law may provide a remedy for any injury that ensues. Unless there was a good message audit trail, however, the problem of proving precisely who was at fault could become quite thorny, especially if multiple service providers were involved.

The theory of recovery might spring from either contract law — for breach of an agreed obligation or standard of performance — or tort law — for negligence or misrepresentation of the capabilities or failings of a system. The recoverable damages in a commercial setting might include, in addition to the fee paid by the user to have the data conveyed, the damages that befell the user as a consequence of the mistake.

An example of how the law might work comes from a case involving a faulty telegram, *Postal Telegraph Cable Co. vs. Lathrop*, 23 N.E. 583 (Ill. 1890). Lathrop and Marley regularly used a local telegraph office to send messages for purchasing coffee beans. In one instance they tried to send a telegram to their broker to buy 1,000 bags of beans. The telegraph company inadvertently changed the amount to 2,000, so Lathrop and Marley ended up owning 2,000 bags. The price of coffee then dropped, and Lathrop and Marley were stuck holding the bags, 1,000 more than they had intended.

They sued, and the court awarded them both their direct damages, the fee they paid for sending the telegram, and their consequential damages, the difference between the price of 1,000 bags at the time of purchase and the price of 1,000 bags after the price dropped. An important factor in this case was that, according to the court, the telegraph company knew a good deal about the activities Lathrop and Marley were engaged in. When the company agreed to send the telegram, it could reasonably have foreseen that if it altered the message the plaintiffs would suffer the consequential damages that came to them.

One legal precaution a provider can take to help control but not necessarily eliminate this exposure to liability (in addition to the business precautions of competently operating its network and refraining from making inflated claims about it) is to enter agreements with users (or, if regulated, to file tariffs) that disclaim or limit liability.

B.3   *Electronic Contracts*

A commercial challenge is to use CMC for contracting purposes. Contracts are traditionally agreements written on paper that are signed with autographs, but in concept they need not take that form.

Some corporations are today contracting electronically. These companies (which include Texas Instruments, Westinghouse, and N.V. Philips) use a method known as electronic data interchange (EDI) to agree to routine contracts such as purchase orders and transportation orders. EDI is computer to computer communication using standardized electronic versions of common business documents.

Other procedures for contracting electronically are emerging. For example, securities exchanges are automating securities purchase and sale transactions. The Chicago Mercantile Exchange plans in 1989 to initiate an electronic exchange for trading of futures contracts and options.

The legal issues involved in electronic contracting are only beginning to be explored. The law is murky here. As of yet, no court decision holds that CMC contracts are or are not enforceable, but that does not preclude informed speculation on the subject.

What is needed to make a contract? A contract can be born anytime two parties exchange promises, irrespective of the medium of communication. Written exchanges, however, have traditionally been favored over oral ones because oral promises are often imprecise and hard to remember and prove.

In the United States, certain oral contracts are also unenforceable due to a law called the Statute of Frauds. It generally provides that to be enforceable many contracts must be supported by *written* and *signed* evidence.

Thus, the threshold questions to ask about CMC contracts are these: Will there be sufficient evidence to prove the relevant electronic messages? Will they be deemed *written*? Will they be deemed *signed*? The answers may vary from one application to another. It is worth noting that similar questions were asked about telegrams and telexes when they first appeared, and they were generally accepted as media for contractual communication.

B.3.1 Proof

Examples of potential sources of evidence for electronic contracts are these:

1. CMC service providers could keep message records. If kept in a reliable fashion, such records could be fairly credible because the record keeper is presumably neutral and trustworthy.
2. A neutral network user could keep a record. One entrepreneur has approached *ABA/net* with this idea: A sender would transmit his message to the neutral record keeper, who would record it and then forward it on to the recipient, asking the delivering network for an acknowledgment of receipt. The record keeper would be prepared to take his evidence of the message and the acknowledgment to court if the communication were ever challenged.
3. Each party could keep a complete, secure log of all messages it sends and receives. The credibility of a log could be relatively high if there were substantial barriers to its forgery or alteration. For instance, the log could be made, and kept under the control of, trustworthy employees who were insulated from any incentive to falsify the log.

B.3.2 Writing

The apparent purposes of the writing requirement are to coax the parties into thinking deliberately about their contract and to ensure that they keep a reliable record of it. Arguably, an accurately and securely recorded electronic message, which one can call up as characters on a screen or print on hard copy, serves those purposes and therefore is *written*. The court in *Ellis Canning Co. vs. Bernstein*, 348 F. Supp. 1212 (D. Colo. 1972), held that even a tape recording of an oral contract satisfies the writing requirement of the Statute of Frauds (though there is some authority to the contrary). It would nonetheless be useful for the statute to be updated to dispel doubt about whether electronic messages are *written*.

B.3.3   Signing

The subject of signing has two parts. First, which symbols or methods must be used to identify the party responsible for a message and to indicate her approval of it? Second, how does one prove that the data in a message are authentic?

B.3.3.1   *Identity*

Generally speaking, a legal signature is any symbol, be it an autograph, an X, a printed word, or some other mark, adopted by a party with the intention to authenticate a writing. The signature indicates who is responsible for a writing and that the party manifested an intention to be bound to it.

To assess the electronic techniques that might serve these purposes, one needs a healthy appreciation for the flaws of the traditional autograph. Autographs can be forged, they are often illegible, and their genuineness can be hard to prove.

Lawyers are aware of these warts. So when the situation justifies the effort, they bolster the ink autograph. They ask for dual signatures (one from each of two authorized signers) or attestations from witnesses or notaries. If the officer of a corporation is signing, lawyers might require that the corporate seal be impressed on the contract, too. Sometimes they even have a trusted third party, such as a bank, that knows the signatory guarantee that the autograph is true.

The simple text on a CMC message *signed: John Doe* is itself a signature. It is a symbol adopted by someone purporting to be John Doe for the purpose of authenticating a message. By itself, however, this signature is not very believable because it is easy to forge.

To a degree, network access codes and passwords, callback techniques, third party archives and audit trails, and network stamps that mark message time and origin identify the sender of a message. They can help make symbolic signatures more reliable. Granted, some network security features can be defeated; they do nevertheless pose a barrier to forgery and mistake. The greater the barrier, of course, the greater the certainty of identification.

The credibility of a signature can be increased by another order of magnitude if the parties build secret codes (such as personal identification numbers) into messages. Moreover, sophisticated cryptographic authentication techniques can to a high degree of certainty verify the source of a message. Circumstantial evidence, such as the return of an acknowledgment to the purported originator, might augment signatures too.

No manual or electronic symbol is guaranteed to be accepted, or guaranteed to be rejected, as a legal signature in court. So, in practice, the question of how secure a signature should be boils down to a cost – benefit trade-off in both the paper and electronic worlds. The issue is what level of controls and accompanying hassle are necessary to create the required degree of assurance that the symbol serving as signature is genuine. The answer will differ from transaction to transaction, depending on the importance of the transaction and the risk of repudiation.

B.3.3.2   *Authentication of data*

Electronic data are evanescent things. They can be lost, altered, or rearranged and leave little trace. Proving the authenticity of a "signed" electronic message would require showing that the "signature" is linked to the message contents and that the contents have not changed since origination.

Again, to properly understand the problem of authenticating electronic data one must appreciate the problem of authenticating words on paper. The difficulty is proving that the ink signature on the last page of a 36 page document adopts and approves all of the information on pages 1 – 35.

Lawyers work various schemes to tie words on paper together. They sequentially number the sheets of paper containing words and signatures. They staple the sheets. Sometimes they have signatories specially initial individual pages and even specific paragraphs. Occasionally they bind contracts into hardback books. Lawyers take these precautions because pages in stacks of paper can be switched or lost, either intentionally or inadvertently.

In the same vein, practical strategies can be devised for a CMC environment. First, we know that a secure, competent CMC system links together the many parts of a message and any "signature" or other identifying information as an intelligible unit. (If it did not, no one would use CMC. The technology would be a failure.) Second, the retention of a trustworthy record of the message, signature, and audit trail can preserve that unit and the interrelationship of its parts.

Loss, garbling, misdirection, or vandalism between creation and final disposition can be counteracted with combinations of hash totals, parity checks, encryption routines, network security features, cyclic redundancy checks, character and line counts, and so on. In addition, the return of an acknowledgment can tend to verify data.

The reliability of networks, and communications between networks, varies. Use of an untrustworthy network or an undependable gateway will make authentication more difficult.

B.3.4   Advance Agreements and Industry Standards

It is often prudent for parties contracting electronically to reach agreements in advance on issues such as signature, acknowledgment, timing, message format, routes of communication, and the Statute of Frauds. Industry-wide standards can deal with some of these issues, too. In EDI, for example, the International Chamber of Commerce in 1987 adopted *Uniform Rules of Conduct for Interchange of Trade Data by Teletransmission.*

B.4   *Copyright*

Copyright law fosters the wide broadcasting of ideas. Ironically, computer network technology, which performs so fabulously at disseminating information, is incompatible with some of the fundamental assumptions of copyright law.

In the United States the Copyright Act of 1976 protects "original works of authorship" (including literature, music, databases, software, and others) from unauthorized reproduction or adaptation or unauthorized public distribution, performance, or display once they are "fixed in a tangible medium of expression" (which can include recording on magnetic media such as tapes and disks). The protection is limited to original expressions of ideas or facts. The ideas or facts themselves are open to anyone to exploit in subsequent works.

A tenet of copyright law is that if someone copies a protected work without authority, he may be civilly or criminally liable. The ability to detect, and bring an enforcement action on the basis of, an infringement deters bootleg copying. Still, the strictness of the law is softened slightly by a doctrine known as the right of *fair use*, which permits limited copying for "fair" purposes, such as the making of copies for the classroom or for research.

Copyright laws are rooted in the concepts of print media. Although they have evolved with new technologies through the centuries, their effectiveness still rises from the assumption that it requires considerable effort and expense to wholesale manipulate, copy, or distribute a work. Digital technology renders that assumption obsolete.

Consider these ways in which computer technology clouds the application of copyright law:

1. A digital copy is identical to a digital original. Learning and proving that any particular copy was pirated, therefore, requires more effort.

2. The rapid, wildfire spreading of data is the hallmark of open computer networks. It is difficult to control or monitor the use of a digitized work on a network.

3. Computers can so quickly and cheaply manipulate data that it is hard to know how much manipulation of one copyrighted expression of facts and ideas transforms it into a new expression copyrightable by the manipulator.

4. The ease with which users can copy, reformat, or transmit a digitized work engenders the notion, whether right or wrong, that they should not have to pay a royalty every time they transfer it from one medium to another or share it with another user. While users may have an intuitive sense that such copying is authorized and within the *fair use* of the product they purchase, it can substantially erode the market for a work.

Hence debate simmers over how to formulate new, practical rules of property law for digitized expressions. Suggested solutions include technological controls, contract arrangements, and government regulation.

Technological controls might include embedded copy or transmit disabling signals, encryption/decryption systems, and network surveillance and billing techniques. These, however, appear expensive, authoritarian, and threatening to privacy interests.

Contract arrangements essentially work on the concept that a user would be given access to protected data only on the condition that she agree not to copy, alter, or redistribute the data without authority. The contract could fix precisely the extent to which rights are protected. This solution is relatively simple and flexible and certainly will be (and is being) employed, but the enforcement of it is difficult.

Finally, it has been suggested that a government agency tax users for the purchase of blank recording media (tapes and disks) and distribute the proceeds to copyright holders based on estimates of usage. This idea appears hard to implement fairly. The research necessary to determine, for example, how much disk capacity is being used nationwide to store personal letters to Mom and not *Encyclopedia Britannica* would be overwhelming.

B.5   *Telecommunications Service Regulation*

The provision of telecommunications services is subject to a vast web of local and national regulations and international treaties. Today these laws are in a dynamic state of flux.

Broadly, changes occurring in the United States and the European Community (EC) have some common themes, in part because in each case regulators are grappling with similar problems. The technology behind telecommunications service, which was historically provided by monopolies subject to differing degrees of regulation or state control, has merged with the technology for data processing (computers), which was historically provided in a competitive market. Authorities are searching for a new balance of regulation, monopoly, and competition that best serves their respective economies.

B.5.1   Regulation in the United States

In the United States telecommunications services are usually provided by private companies, and many aspects of service are regulated. Sources of regulation include the federal Communications Act of 1934 (Communications Act), which vests regulatory power in the Federal Communications Commission (FCC); the telecommunications laws of the many states, which are generally limited to intrastate communication; and the federal antitrust laws, as interpreted and enforced by the federal courts. The FCC's mission includes the regulation of interstate and foreign wire and radio communications so as to make available to the public adequate communications service at reasonable rates. The purpose of the antitrust laws is to foster commercial competition.

B.5.1.1   *Regulation under the Communications Act*

Originally under the Communications Act, interstate telephone service was a federally regulated monopoly. Telephone companies were deemed regulated communications *common carriers*, which provide services under tariffs that describe the services and applicable rates and are reviewed and approved by the FCC.

Data processing service providers were traditionally not deemed common carriers. With the gradual convergence of telecommunications and data processing technology, however, the distinction between regulated and unregulated service blurred. So, in its 1980 "Computer Inquiry II" decision, the FCC defined two categories of network service: *basic* and *enhanced*. The FCC stated:

> [B]asic service is limited to the common carrier offering of transmission capacity for the movement of information, whereas enhanced service combines basic service with computer processing applications that act on the format, content, code, protocol or similar aspects of the subscriber's transmitted information, or provide the subscriber additional, different, or restructured information, or involve subscriber interaction with stored information. 77 F.C.C.2d 384, 387 (1980) (Final Decision).

Today, essentially, basic service carriers must file tariffs and enhanced service providers need not.

The ability of basic service carriers to offer enhanced services is often restricted. The FCC has permitted the larger of such carriers, American Telephone & Telegraph Company (AT&T) and the Regional Bell Operating Companies (BOCs), to furnish enhanced services on the condition that they institute safeguards to prevent them from enjoying, by virtue of their huge resources and market position, unfair advantages over competitors in the enhanced services market. Under the FCC's 1986 "Computer Inquiry III" decision, these safeguards provide enhanced service competitors access to basic transmission networks (under concepts such as *comparably efficient interconnection* and *open network architecture*) that is essentially equivalent to the carrier's.

B.5.1.2 *AT&T breakup under the antitrust laws*

At one time AT&T provided both long-distance and local telecommunications service throughout much of the country, often as a monopoly. The U.S. Department of Justice brought an antitrust suit against the company in 1974. Under a court decree issued by federal judge Harold H. Greene in 1982, AT&T divested itself of its local operating companies (which now constitute the independent BOCs). Initially under the decree, AT&Tand long-distance telephone could offer long-distance telephone and many data communications services. The operating companies were limited essentially to providing local telephone service and access to long-distance services.

Since then Judge Greene has modified the restrictions on the operating companies, so they may offer limited additional services, such as voice messaging and so-called gateway services under which a company would tie together a number of information (videotext) services generated by independent vendors.

B.5.2 **Regulation in the EC**

It is common in countries other than the United States for a government owned monopoly, or an administration operating under a government franchise (commonly referred to as a PTT), to formulate and implement telecommunications regulations and provide telecommunications networks and services (together with postal services). Often independent networks operate only with the consent, and under the regulation of, the PTT (or a similar regulatory agency) and are tightly restricted in the services they can provide.

In the EC, liberalization is afoot, however. This is in part because it is mandated by the Treaty of Rome, the treaty that instituted the EC and is the legal basis for achieving a single European market in 1992.

The Commission of the European Community issued *Towards a Dynamic European Economy: Green Paper on the Development of the Common Market for Telecommunications Services and Equipment* in 1987 and other proposals on telecommunications policy since then. Generally, the commission proposes that the regulatory and operations functions be separated within the PTTs. It further proposes permitting the PTTs to provide network infrastructure and certain reserved services (covering at least voice telephony) exclusively, while other services (including perhaps data processing, electronic mail, and videotext) would be open to both the PTTs and other service providers on a competitive basis. The commission intends to promote (under a concept known as *open network provision*) open telecommunications networks so service providers may offer pan-European, value-added services.

As under the antitrust laws in the United States, there are provisions under the Treaty of Rome that can constrain the PTTs from exercising their regulatory and market power to stifle competition in the competitive services.

B.6   *Privacy, Fundamental Rights, Transborder Data Flows*

Information technology provides marvelous tools for the collection, review, sorting, and communication of information. Yet some fear the placement of these tools into service for the wrong ends. They foresee the massing of otherwise widely scattered bits of personal information into central databases. Big Brother of George Orwell's *Nineteen Eighty-Four* could then monitor our private lives. Others anticipate the breach of the confidentiality of our private messages or infringements on our freedom to communicate. Some legal safeguards have been adopted to counter these fears, but the area is subject to considerable controversy.

B.6.1   Privacy Law in the United States

The Fourth Amendment to the U.S. Constitution usually requires law enforcement agencies to obtain a search warrant before intercepting messages that enjoy a reasonable expectation of privacy. Unfortunately, it is not clear whether the contents of private CMC messages are be protected. Although users may believe their messages will be kept private, the expectation may not be reasonable in light of the control of network administrators over the messages.

In response to this uncertainty and other concerns, the U.S. Congress passed the Electronic Communications Privacy Act of 1986 (ECPA) to update the federal law against eavesdropping and restrict the interception or disclosure of private electronic communications. The law regulates the surveillance of electronic communications by law enforcement officials. It bars service providers from divulging certain messages without authority (as does section 705 of the Communications Act of 1934, as amended). The ECPA also restricts the manufacture, advertising, sale, and possession of devices intended to intercept electronic messages surreptitiously.

The Privacy Act of 1974 restricts the ability of the federal government to disclose information it has on individuals and provides them the right to review the information and have it corrected if inaccurate. Additional federal laws and a patchwork of state laws cover the collection and dissemination of personal information as well.

B.6.2   Privacy, National Security, and Transborder Data Flow

Other, particularly Western European, countries have enacted even more sweeping data privacy laws. They aim to safeguard individuals (and sometimes corporations) from the inappropriate accumulation and use of data pertaining to them. Frequently the laws place notice requirements and scope and time limits on the ability of public and private data collectors (the classic example being a credit bureau) to gather, store, and use personal data. They commonly grant data subjects rights to review data and to make corrections if the data is inaccurate.

The laws can be quite broad, covering any collection of electronic data organized on the basis of the identity of protected subjects. One British commentator noted that the United Kingdom's law is written so broadly that it could be read to require "Little Johnny at school" to register and pay a fee before using the school magazine's computer to log the number of goals each player on the school soccer team scored.

Often these laws restrict the right of the holders of data to transmit it across national boundaries. Sometimes licenses are required. The concern is that databases of personal information will gravitate toward countries with lenient privacy laws the way money gravitates toward tax havens (countries with favorable tax laws). Other reasons given for the restrictions include the need to control the power and influence of multinational corporations. Sometimes the regulations cover more than just data related to privacy.

Some observe that these restrictions on transborder data flows all too conveniently serve as trade barriers. They favor domestic over foreign data processing facilities.

Two international instruments set guidelines for permissible legal protections of personal data: the Organization for Economic Cooperation and Development Guidelines Governing the Protection of Privacy and Transborder Flows of Personal Data, 1980; and the Council of Europe Convention for the Protection of Individuals with Regard to Automatic Processing of Personal Data, 1981. They attempt to balance the competing interests of privacy and control on the one hand and the free exchange of information on the other.

The United States, while frowning on privacy- or protectionist-based data flow laws, is itself noted for impeding the flow of information (as electronic data or otherwise) across its borders to achieve national security and foreign policy goals. Among the relevant laws are the Export Administration Act and the Arms Export Control Act, which are implemented by regulations restricting the export of a vast array of "technical data." Some other countries have similar laws.

B.6.3   International Right to Communicate

Despite the foregoing, the libertarians can take heart. It has been asserted that, subject to legitimate regulation, there exists in international law support for a basic human right to communicate. The assertion is founded on Article 19 of the Universal Declaration of Human Rights, adopted unanimously by the General Assembly of the United Nations on 10 December 1948:

> Everyone has the right to freedom of opinion and expression; this right includes the freedom to hold opinions without interference and to seek, receive and impart information and ideas through any media and regardless of frontiers.

B.7   *Benjamin Wright*

Benjamin Wright is an electronic communications law attorney whose clients include companies implementing, or providing support services for, electronic data interchange (EDI). He regularly serves as a lecturer on legal issues at EDI training seminars held by TDCC: The Electronic Data Interchange Association (TDCC/EDIA) in Alexandria, Virginia. Under the sponsorship of TDCC/EDIA, he has written a monograph on EDI trading partner agreements and is now writing a complete book on EDI and the law, the publication of which he anticipates in 1989.

Mr. Wright is a Phi Beta Kappa graduate of Trinity University. He holds a law degree from Georgetown University, where he served as a senior editor for the law review *Law and Policy in International Business*.

Mr. Wright is licensed to practice law in Texas and is a member of the State Bar of Texas. He is not certified by the Texas Board of Legal Specialization in the area of electronic communications law, for that Board has not designated a certificate of special competence in that area.

Access
Benjamin Wright
Attorney and Counselor
+1-214-526-5254
CompuServe: 73457,2362
Dialcom: 144:ESQl7874
Telex: 4909942077
3420 Granada Avenue, Suite 400
Dallas, TX 75205
U.S.A.

B.8   *References**

B.8.1   Crime

Arnheim, Michael, "Head Note," *Solicitor's Journal*, vol. 132, no. 40, p. 1400, 7 October 1988.

Betts, Mitch, "'Virus' 'Benign' Nature Will Make It Difficult to Prosecute," *ComputerWorld*, p. 16, 14 November 1988.

Commentary, "Computer Crime," *Idea: The Journal of Law and Technology*, vol. 26, no. 4, pp. 163–171, 1986.

Gerth, Jeff, "Intruders into Computer Systems Still Hard to Prosecute," *New York Times*, p. 10, 5 November 1988.

Soma, John T., Smith, Paula J., and Sprague, Robert D., "Legal Analysis of Electronic Bulletin Board Activities," *Western New England Law Review*, vol. 7, pp. 571–626, 1985.

Taber, John K., "On Computer Crime," *Computer Law Journal*, vol. 1, no. 3, pp. 517–543, Winter 1979.

Wines, Michael, "'Virus' Eliminated, Defense Aides Say," *New York Times*, p. 1, 5 November 1988.

B.8.2   Liability

Comment, "An Electronic Soapbox: Computer Bulletin Boards and the First Amendment," *Federal Communications Law Journal*, vol. 39, no. 3, pp. 217–257, October 1987.

---

* References for this appendix are grouped in sections, with the numbers corresponding to the appendix section numbers to which the references apply (e.g., B.8.1 corresponds to Section B.1 of the text). There are no text citations for these references.

Gordon, Mark L., and Gilbert, Françoise, "Gateway Transactions: Electronic Data Interchange Systems," *The Computer Lawyer*, vol. 3, no. 11, pp. 14–21, November 1986.

Note, "Computer Bulletin Board Operator Liability for User Misuse," *Fordham Law Review*, vol. 54, no. 3, pp. 439–454, December 1985.

Note, "Computer Bulletin Boards and Defamation: Who Should Be Liable? Under What Standard?," *The Journal of Law & Technology*, vol. 2, no. 1, pp. 121–150, Winter 1987.

Shulman, Gail H., "Legal Research on USENET Liability Issues," *;login: The USENIX Association Newsletter*, vol. 9, no. 6, pp. 11–17, December 1984.

Soma, John T., Smith, Paula J., and Sprague, Robert D., "Legal Analysis of Electronic Bulletin Board Activities," *Western New England Law Review*, vol. 7, pp. 571–626, 1985.

Uyehara, Kim, "Let the Operator Beware," *Student Lawyer*, vol. 14, no. 8, pp. 28–33, April 1986.

B.8.3   Contract

ABA, "Electronic Messaging: A Report of the Ad Hoc Subcommittee on Scope of the U.C.C.," *ABA Pub. No. 507-0210*, American Bar Association, Chicago, 1988.

Chicago Mercantile Exchange, *Globex: The Global Electronic Exchange*, Chicago Mercantile Exchange, Chicago, 1988.

Draper, John E., "Security, Integrity & Legality: Barriers to EDI Progress in Europe," *Proceedings of Computer Aided Trade COMPAT '88 (The Hague, 29 February – 2 March 1988)*, Euromatica, S.A., Brussels, 1988.

Office of Technology Assessment, U.S. Congress, *Defending Secrets, Sharing Data: New Locks and Keys for Electronic Information*, U.S. Government Printing Office, Washington, DC, October 1987.

UN, "Legal Aspects of Automatic Trade Data Interchange," United Nations, Economic Commission for Europe, Committee on the Development of Trade, Working Party on Facilitation of International Trade Procedures, Geneva, 21 October 1982.

UN, "Legal Aspects of Trade Data Interchange," United Nations, Economic Commission for Europe, 25 February 1985.

UN, "Legal Value of Computer Records," *Commission on International Trade Law, Eighteenth Session (Vienna, Austria, 3–21 June 1985)*, no. Doc. A/CN.9/265, United Nations, New York, 21 February 1985.

Wright, Benjamin, *Legal Issues Impacting EDI: Electronic Data Interchange Trading Partner Agreements*, TDCC: The Electronic Data Interchange Association, Alexandria, VA, 1988.

B.8.4   Copyright

Fleishmann, Eric, "The Impact of Digital Technology on Copyright Law," *Computer/Law Journal*, vol. 8, no. 1, pp. 1–22, Winter 1987.

Kost, Robert, "Copyrights in the Information Age, Parts 1 and 2," *Netweaver*, vol. 3, no. 6–7, June and July 1987.

Miller, Nicholas P., and Blumenthal, Carol S., "Intellectual Property Issues," in *Toward a Law of Global Communications Networks*, ed. Anne W. Branscomb, pp. 227–237, Longman, New York, 1986.

Office of Technology Assessment, U.S. Congress, *Intellectual Property Rights in an Age of Electronics and Information*, U.S. Government Printing Office, Washington, D.C., April 1986.

Pool, Ithiel de Sola, and Solomon, Richard Jay, "Intellectual Property and Transborder Data Flows," *Stanford Journal of International Law*, vol. 16, pp. 113–139, Summer 1980.

B.8.5   Regulation

Barger, Robert W., "An Overview of the U.S.A. Regulatory Environment," *Proceedings of Distribution, Access & Communications (Amsterdam, 1–3 June 1988)*, Computer Law Association, Inc., Fairfax, VA, 1988.

Dougan, Diana Lady, "An International Policy Perspective on the Information Age," *IEEE Communications Magazine*, vol. 25, no. 1, pp. 18–23, January 1987.

Narjes, Karl-Heinz, "Toward a European Telecommunications Community: Implementing the Green Paper," *Telecommunications Policy*, pp. 106–108, June 1988.

Note, "The Computer Inquiries: Mapping the Communications/Information Processing Terrain," *Federal Communications Law Journal*, vol. 33, no. 1, pp. 55–115, Winter 1981.

Rich, Cynthia J., "European Telecommunications Policy: A US View," *Telecommunications Policy*, pp. 2–6, March 1988.

Scherer, Joachim, "European Telecommunications Law: The Framework of the Treaty," *European Law Review*, vol. 12, no. 5, pp. 354–372, October 1987.

Scherer, Joachim, "Telecommunications: Regulatory Environment in Europe," *Proceedings of Distribution, Access & Communications (Amsterdam, 1–3 June 1988)*, Computer Law Association, Inc., Fairfax, VA, 1988.

Soma, John T., "The Communications Regulatory Environment," *Computer Technology and the Law*, pp. 163–212, Shepard's/McGraw-Hill, Inc., Colorado Springs, CO, 1983, (Supp. 1988: 79–98).

Wolfson, Joel R., "Computer III: The Beginning or the Beginning of the End for Enhanced Services Competition," *IEEE Communications Magazine*, vol. 25, no. 8, pp. 35–40, August 1987.

B.8.6   Privacy

Feldman, Mark B., "The Right to Communicate Under International Law," in *Toward a Law of Global Communications Networks*, ed. Anne W. Branscomb, pp. 343–347, Longman, New York, 1986.

Millard, Christopher J., and Chance, Clifford, "Transborder Data Flows: The European Perspective," *Proceedings of Distribution, Access & Communications (Amsterdam, 1–3 June 1988)*, Computer Law Association, Inc., Fairfax, VA, 1988.

Moakes, Jonathan, "Data Protection in Europe, Part 1," *Journal of International Banking Law*, vol. 1, no. 2, pp. 77–85, 1986.

Rumbelow, Clive, "Privacy and Transborder Data Flow in the UK and Europe," *International Business Lawyer*, pp. 153–157, April 1984.

UN, "Legal Aspects of Automatic Trade Data Interchange," United Nations Economic Commission for Europe, Geneva, 21 October 1982.

List of Trademarks

Many commercial products are mentioned in this book. In no case does such identification imply recommendation or endorsement by the author or the publisher, nor does it imply that the products identified are better or worse than other similar products.

Interop and ConneXions—The Interoperability Report are trademarks of **Advanced Computing Environments (ACE)**

Confer II is a registered trademark of **Advertel Communication Systems, Inc.**

RFS and TLI are trademarks of **American Telephone & Telegraph (AT&T)**.

APOLLO, DOMAIN, Network Computing System, NCS, and DOMAIN/IX are trademarks of **Apollo Computer, Inc.**

Macintosh is a trademark of **Apple Computer**.

UNIX is a registered trademark of **AT&T Bell Laboratories**.

SPEARNET is a business name registered in all Australian states for all future networks in higher education on behalf of the **Australian Vice Chancellor's Committee** and **ACDP**.

Caucus is a trademark of **Camber-Roth**.

Cray X-MP/48 is a trademark of **Cray Research, Inc.**

DASnet is a registered trademark of **DA Systems, Inc.**

DEC, DECNET, TOPS-20, VMS, Ultrix, VAX, and PDP are registered trademarks of **Digital Equipment Corporation (Digital)**.

Dow Jones News/Retrieval is a registered trademark of **Dow Jones and Company, Inc.**

Official Airline Guides and OAG are trademarks of **Dun and Bradstreet Corporation**.

IEEE is a trademark of the **Institute of Electrical and Electronics Engineers, Inc**.

Netview and Netview-PC are trademarks of **International Business Machines Corporation**.

IBM, OS/2, System/36, System/38, and OS/400 are trademarks of **International Business Machines (IBM)**.

MNP and Microcom Networking Protocol are trademarks and a proprietary product of **Microcom, Inc**.

MS-DOS is a trademark of **Microsoft Corporation**.

HYPERchannel is a trademark of **Network Systems Corporation**.

No is in the **public domain**.

The Source is a registered service mark of **Source Telecomputing Corporation**.

NFS is a trademark of **Sun Microsystems, Inc**.

Telenet and Telemail are trademarks of **Telenet Communications Corporation**.

Fido and FidoNet are trademarks of **Tom Jennings**.

TYMNET is a registered trademark of **Tymnet, McDonnell Douglas Network Systems Company**.

Ethernet is a registered trademark of **Xerox Corporation**.

XNS is a trademark of **Xerox Corporation**.

Index

DECNET *(continued)*
    and *SPAN*, 373–375; and *Starlink*, 477–478;
    and *SUNET*, 498; and *SURFnet*, 465; and Syn-
    tax, 217; and *THEnet*, 333, 335; and *UNA*,
    504–505; and *UNINETT*, 495–496; and *USAN*,
    336; and *WESTNET*, 337–338
DECUS, 205
decwrl (host, *USENET*), 242, 369
Defence Research Establishment (DRE), **398**
Defense Advanced Research Projects Agency, *See*
    DARPA.
Defense Communications Agency (DCA), **144**,
    282, 284, 289–290
Defense Data Network Program Management
    Office (DDN/PMO), **144**, 289–290
Delaware (University of Delaware), **185**
Delegation à l'Informatique (DaI), **148**
Delphi (Delphi Method; conferencing system,
    United States), **153**; and Conferencing, Early,
    153–154; and Conferencing, Prehistory, 153;
    and *EIES*, 377; and *EMISARI*, 157; and
    PLANET, 158; and *TYMNET*, 621
Demco, John, 388, **395**
Democratic Yemen (country, with domain YD),
    593
DENet (Danish Ethernet Network; academic net-
    work, Denmark), 483, **486–487**
Denmark (country, with domain DK), 439, **486**,
    621; and COSINE, 194; and *DKnet*, 488; and
    DNIC of, 628; and *Ean Europe*, 436; and *EUnet*,
    427; and *NORDUnet*, 483–484; and *QZCOM*,
    500; see also *Centernet*, *DENet*, and *DKnet*; also
    mentioned *EARN*, *EUnet*, *NORDUnet*, and
    PAXNET.
Departamento Ingeniería Telemática, *See* DIT.
Department of Army (DoA), **381**
Department of Commerce (DoC), **183**, 283
Department of Defense, *See* DoD.
Department of Education and Science (DES), **142**,
    143, 476–477
Department of Electronics (DOE), **571**, 575
Department of Energy, *See* DoE.
Department of National Defence (DND), **398**
Department of Scientific and Industrial Research
    (DSIR), **525**, 527–528
Department of Telecommunications (DOT), **626**
DES (Department of Education and Science), **142**,
    143, 476–477
Deshpande, G. M., **574**
DESY (Deutsches Elektronen SYnchrotron), **434**
Deutsche Bundespost (DBP), **453**
Deutsche Mailbox (network), 613
Deutsches Elektronen SYnchrotron (DESY), **434**
Deutsches Institut für Normung (DIN), **177**
development, 129
Devillers, Yves, **440**
Devres (Devres, Inc.), **580**
Dewan Bahasa dan Pustaka (DBdP), **561**
dfn, 259
DFN (Deutsches Forschungsnetz; research net-
    work, Germany, Federal Republic of),

456–458; and *BELWÜ*, 460; and *BERNET*, 147;
    and *Dnet*, 455; and *Ean*, 259; and *Ean Europe*,
    436; and *ERNET*, 575; and *EUnet*, 426; and
    European Networking Concerns, 418; and
    German research community, 453; govern-
    ment funding of, 453; and *HMI-NET*, 147; and
    "keyword=value;" O/R form, 394; and
    Names, 128; and National Networks, 131; and
    NSFNET, 308; and PDN Costs, 632; predeces-
    sors of, 141, 452; and Protocol Conversion, 114;
    and RARE, 189–192; and *TWICS*, 550; and
    UNA, 504–505; and X.400, 78
DFO, 401
DG (Data General), **392**, 470, 574
DGT (Direction Générale Télécommunications),
    451
Dialcom (commercial mail network, U.S./World),
    609–610; and Caucus, 85; and *CGNET*, 600;
    and COMPMAIL, 605; and *DASnet*, 386; and
    Internet, 280–281; and *Keylink 7*, 524; and Par-
    ticipate, 84; and *PeaceNet*, 383; and *Telemail*,
    614; and UNISON, 613
Dialcom (program), 155
DIALNET (network), 610
Dialog (conferencing system, United States),
    610–611
Dial-up IP (CSNET Dial-up IP; research network,
    United States), 298–300, **299**
Dialup SLIP, 61
Diamond (application protocol), **79**
Dienste vom Datenvermittlungssystem
    Nordrhein-Westfalen (DVS-NW), **503**
Diet (Japanese Diet; standards, Japan), **197**
digest (application protocol), 79, 154
Digipak (PDN, Finland), **628**
Digital Access and Cross-connect System (DACS),
    315
digital audio tape (DAT), **167**
Digital Data Communications Message Protocol,
    See DDCMP.
Digital (Digital Equipment Corporation), **53, 140**;
    and Antarctic research stations {AQ}, 227–228;
    and *ARISTOTE*, 446; and Austria {AT}, 502;
    and *BCnet*, 404; and *BERNET*, 147; and
    CDNnet, 392; and *CGNET*, 599; and *Chinese
    OSI*, 555; and Company Networks, 126; and
    CoSy, 411; and *CRIM*, 405; and *CSIRONET*,
    523; and DECNET, 110; and Digital Network
    Architecture (DNA), 53; and *Dnet*, 455; and
    DSIRnet, 527; and *Ean in Spain*, 469; and
    EARN, 430; and *EASYnet*, 262; and *ERNET*,
    576; and *FNET*, 442; and *HARNET*, 552; and
    HEPnet, 229; and *HEPnet Europe*, 435; and
    Hosts, Sites, Users, and Mailboxes, 132; and
    INFOPSI, 519; and Japanese, 541; and *Mel-
    bourne*, 521; and *MFEnet*, 366; and NNTP, 83;
    and *NORDUnet*, 483; and *NSFNET*, 304, 307;
    and *NSI*, 369–370; and Operating Systems, 22;
    and Participate, 84; and *Queensland*, 521; and
    RARE, 192; and *SIS*, 506; and *SPAN*, 375; and

John S. Quarterman is a founder, with Smoot Carl-Mitchell, of Texas Internet Consulting of Austin, a firm specializing in networking and in UNIX standards and programming. After graduating from Harvard in 1977, he started his career as a computer scientist working on the ARPANET at Bolt Beranek and Newman.

Work on what would become The Matrix began in 1984, when Quarterman attempted to answer questions from graduate students at the University of Texas with a ten-page description of a few major networks and their interconnections. This was followed in 1986 by an article in Communications of the ACM that became the basic reference on the subject. This book is the successor to that article.

Quarterman has served on the USENIX Board of Directors since 1986. With Abraham Silberschatz and James L. Peterson he wrote the first comprehensive description of the 4.2BSD version of the UNIX operating system (1985). In 1988 he coauthored the authoritative book on 4.3BSD with the developers of that system.

John Quarterman is from Georgia and now lives in central Texas, but is often found in California. He was last seen heading west from Boston to Malaysia on his way to Austria.

The Matrix: An Electronic Version

Paper is not the most natural medium for network information that changes continuously. A book also imposes length limitations, and no index can provide the flexibility of a relational database.

We have started an ongoing interactive relational database of information related to the Matrix. This must be a collaborative project, and we expect to draw on information from a variety of sources even more extensive than those included in this book. Your suggestions could be very useful in developing a service you would want to use. Please fill out this questionnaire and send it to the address below. Feel free to photocopy this page (and only this page) to fill out yourself or to distribute to others.

Name _____ Address _____

Company _____ Electronic mail address _____

Occupation _____ Networks you use for work _____

Material: In addition to the material in the Matrix, there is far more material available from other sources. What kind of information would you like to have easy access to?

__Tutorial information about basic services such as mail__Descriptions of networks and conferencing systems__System interconnections and gateways__Network maps__Host lists__User directories__Lists of mailing lists, newgroups, and other online fora__Program descriptions__Programs__Protocol Descriptions Protocol specifications__Related documents, such as RFC's__Bibliography of other online material about networks__Actual online tutorial material by others about networks and protocols__Contents of related print journals__Catalog of videotapes__Schedules of conferences, workshops, and tutorials __Other _____

Access Methods: There are several popular methods of accessing material like that in the book; please indicate your preference.

__Hypertext. This is popular for catalogs__Menu and mouse. Probably the most common programmatic interface__Geographical maps and mouse. Maps as menus, as in an atlas__SQL database queries. For complicated inquiries__Other (please specify) _____

Platform: The underlying hardware and operating system affect development effort. Please indicate how many of each kind of platform you or your group would like to use with this service.

__MS/DOS__Macintosh__UNIX and X-Windows__VMS and X-Windows__Other and X-Windows __Other _____

Media: The source text for the Matrix occupies about 2 Megabytes online. Related background material already collected takes up about 50 Megabytes. Maps and other known material could easily occupy 100–200 Megabytes. All this data must be kept on some medium, such as a disk. Bigger is often better, but usually more expensive, and sometimes more static. Please indicate how much you would pay for access to the service via each medium of interest to you.

$_____CD-ROM. 600Mbytes $_____MS/DOS floppy. 1.4Mbytes $_____Macintosh floppy. 400K single, 800K double, 1.4Mbytes. $_____Tapes or floppies to read onto hard disk

Update Method: What method would you prefer to use to get updates? Please indicate the amount you would be willing to pay for each method of interest to you.

One year of quarterly disks: $_____CD-ROM $_____MS/DOS floppy $_____Macintosh floppy

Quarterly disks *plus* daily online updates: $_____Dialup Kermit $_____Dialup X-Modem
$_____Dialup UUCP $_____Dialup SLIP $_____Dedicated TCP/IP
$_____Other (please specify) _____

Prototype: A prototype of this service is already being developed. If you are interested in participating in initial tests, please contact us.

Thanks.

The Matrix
P.O. Box 14621
Austin, TX 78761
U.S.A.
matrix@tic.com
fax: +1-512-327-1274